TEE OFF FOR THE JIMMY FUND

Since 1983, Jimmy Fund Golf tournaments have raised funds for cancer research and treatment at Dana-Farber Cancer Institute. Become a Jimmy Fund Golf tournament director, and you can join the thousands of golfers doing their part to chip in and fight cancer.

"Running my tournament has been a way to realize something good out of a personal tragedy, and is my way of giving back to the dedicated physicians, nurses, and researchers at Dana-Farber who treated my son."

— BOB SARKISIAN
Director, Andrew Sarkisian Memorial Golf Tournament

1 in 31,000 golfers
will make a hole-in-one.

1 in 3 people will be
diagnosed with cancer.

———

YOU CAN CHANGE
THE ODDS.

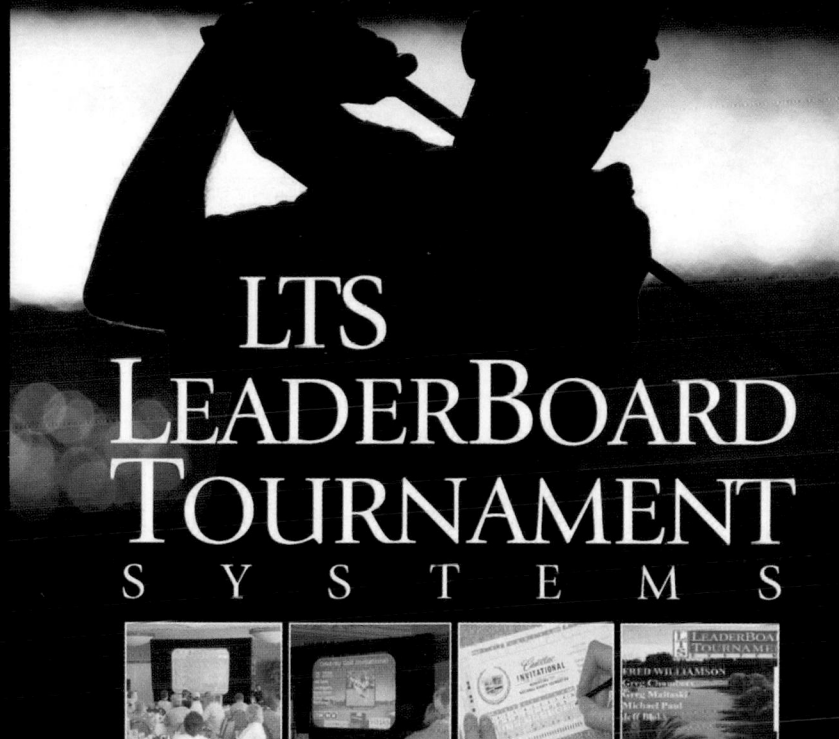

Good for a **FREE Electronic Raffle**
Presentation and 500 Custom Printed
Raffle Tickets At Your Next
LTS LeaderBoard of Boston Tournament

Expires 12/31/09

www.leaderboardboston.com

Good for a **10% Discount** on the
Service Fee for your next
LTS LeaderBoard of Boston Tournament

Expires 12/31/09

www.leaderboardboston.com

Good for a **Interactive Golf Trivia Contest**
At Your Next LTS LeaderBoard of
Boston Tournament

Expires 12/31/09

www.leaderboardboston.com

We do one thing well.
We just happen to do it four ways.

Dreams take shape in many ways. Gut-wrenching power cat-like response and
next generation technology comes standard in all of them. From the pure top-down
roadster experience to the sports-car agility of the Cayenne. Every Porsche is
engineered with a no-compromise approach to performance.
Visit us today at Rietzl Porsche, offering personalized sales and service excellence since 1970.

Cayenne, Cayman, Boxster, 911 Carrera

Rietzl Porsche
781-261-5000
59 Pond Street
Norwell, MA 02061
rietzl.porschedealer.com

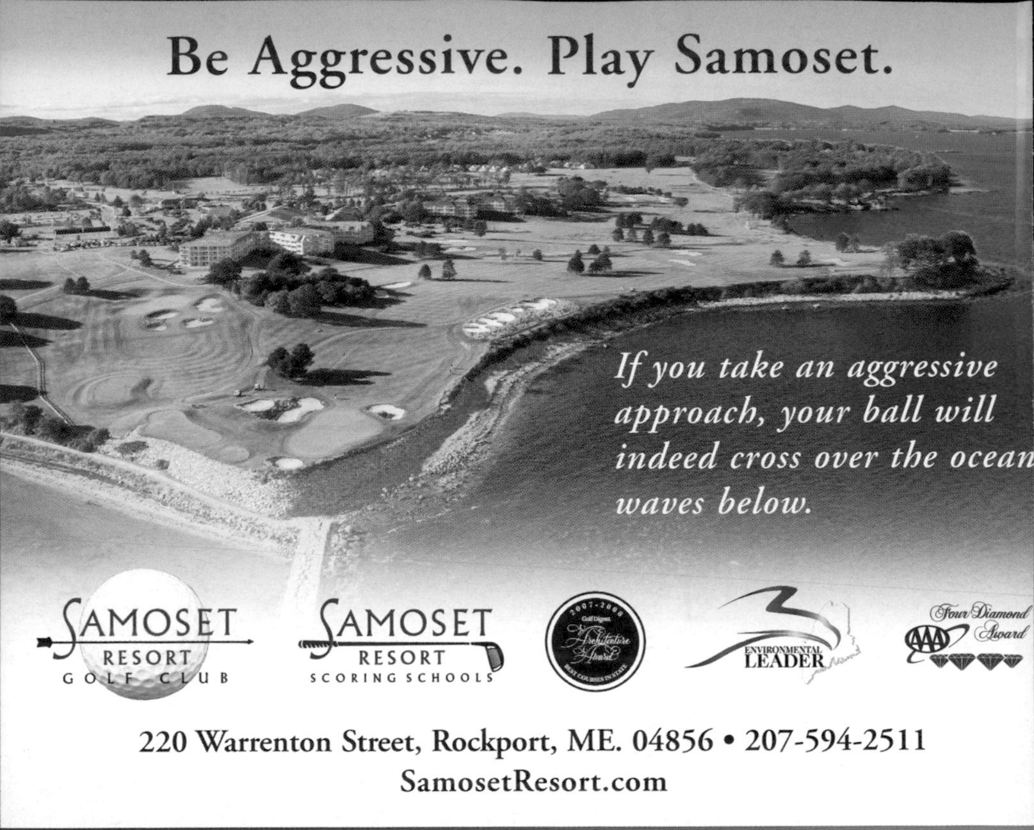

Raise your game.
Come up to the mountain.

Green Mountain National Golf Course

Vermont's Championship Golf Course

NEW ENGLAND GOLFGUIDE®

THE DIRECTORY FOR PUBLIC PLAY™

2009

Six States. 650 Courses. One Book.™

The Balsams, Dixville Notch, NH

Welcome to our **20th year** of providing New England's most complete listing of information on public courses in Connecticut, Maine, Massachusetts, New Hampshire, Rhode Island, and Vermont. Reader comments welcome and encouraged. Visit us online.

BallMarker Press, LLC.
464 Common Street Suite 358
Belmont, MA 02478
www.newenglandgolfguide.com
617-417-9780

NEW ENGLAND GOLFGUIDE® 2009
THE DIRECTORY FOR PUBLIC PLAY™

Publisher/Editor:	John DiCocco
Sales Team:	Lee Barber, Director; Paul Bellacqua, Neal Fay, Brian Lane
Book and Web Designer:	Adam Katz, www.akatzdesign.com
Ad Design:	Dave Linde, Lindesign
Web Tech Development:	Mike Regan, Empire Software
Contributors:	Stephen Dailey, Eric Siegel
Publisher's Assistant:	Erin Brenengen
Data Lieutenants:	Rachel Coburn, Shay DiCocco, Abbi Neel

Course Ratings by Bill Anderson, Don Aronson, Stephen Dailey, Gerry Dickhaut, Gene Goldstein, Glen Guillemette, Mike Landry, John Scotto, Eric Siegel, and Rick Walsh.

Special thanks to Mike Braddon, Larry DiGiammarino, Don McCauley, Adam Naylor, the UPS Team, and the amazingly patient Connie DiCocco.

The New England GolfGuide is an annual, printed in the autumn of each year.

New England GolfGuide, its advertisers, and contributors do not assume liability for any inaccuracies within these pages. **Every effort has been made to contact each course listed by mail and phone to verify and update the latest information. All prices, scorecards and distances, slopes and ratings, and coupon offers are subject to change or revocation by the course at any time.** We go to print in late October, and many courses do not announce 2009 rates or other changes until just before opening in the Spring. We apologize for any errors that may appear and appreciate hearing any corrections for the next edition. You may also send corrections to editor@newenglandgolfguide.com.

For continual updates throughout the year, new coupons and offers, and a listing of corrections, please visit Newenglandgolfguide.com frequently.

Welcome to 2009

It's our **20th Anniversary Edition**. Wow. What began as a project of two Boston University MBA students has grown into a regional staple. To celebrate our anniversary, we'll be having special promotions and giveaways all year long.

To get in on the fun, join the Golf Guide Community—at no cost—on our website. Read more on page 23.

We've assembled a bigger and more wide-spread Rating Team this year, and you'll note that from their 2008 visits we have changed ratings at quite a number of clubs, mostly upward.

We hope 2009 will be the year you break 100, 90, 80, 70—whatever your goal. To help you get there, we'll be offering free tips, free golf, and a few surprises you won't want to miss. Visit **newenglandgolfguide.com** today.

Only one new course joins the Golf Guide this year: **Old Marsh** in Wells, Maine. A sister course to stunning **Sunday River**, it opens with an impressive 3.5 star rating. Two Massachusetts courses changed names: **Carriage Pines** is the former Rowley CC, and **The Back Nine Club** is the former Heritage Hill.

Again, watch the website for updates.

What's new in the 2009 Edition?

- We're bigger and better than ever. **592 pages** packed with the info you've requested.
- A brand new **Featured Courses** section.
- A brand new listing of **New England Driving Ranges**.
- New **2009 Coupons** to once again save you thousands of dollars.
- The **2009 Top 100 Courses in New England**.
- The **2009 Top 50 Values in New England**.
- Updated info on each course.
- Further refinements to our maps.
- A new look and feel to our website: **newenglandgolfguide.com**.

Thanks once again to the hundreds of readers who have sent comments, corrections, and suggestions. Keep in touch—we're here for you.

John

Contents

YOUR GUIDE TO THE GOLFGUIDE

Finding the Courses

Features

Featured Courses For 2009

The Extras: Coupons & Offers

The Course Listings

GB RTE 495

SE MA/ CAPE

CTRL/ WEST MA

RI

NH

VT

N ME

S ME

NE CT

SW CT

Index to Golf Courses

ALPHABETICALLY BY STATE & COURSE

Connecticut

Maine

Massachusetts

Massachusetts cont'd.

Massachusetts cont'd.

New Hampshire

Vermont cont'd.

Index to Golf Courses

ALPHABETICALLY BY STATE & CITY/TOWN

Connecticut

Maine

Massachusetts

Massachusetts cont'd.

Vermont

The Ultimate New England Golf Road Trip

By John DiCocco

Want to play the very best courses in New England? Here's my recommendation for a loop you can jump into at any point.

Say you start in the southwest corner of New England. Call for a tee time at **Richter Park** (✪✪✪✪) in Danbury, CT. This course has a slightly "muni" feel because so many locals love it and wish we'd stop sharing their secret. But the conditions say "private." It's a marvelous track built for those who love their drivers, and those who know how to putt. Lots of hills, gorgeous rolling fairways, and sculptured greens make it one of the region's very best.

Your backup is nearby **Oxford Greens** (✪✪✪½) in Oxford, off Route 84 (exit 15 to Route 67). Wonderful holes, with plenty of challenge provided by water and surrounding woods. If you can handle the back tees, Oxford offers 7186 yards at a slope of 135.

That night, drive east and find a B&B in quaint Newport, Rhode Island. Your Day Two challenge is the sprawling **Newport National** (✪✪✪✪), located in Middletown. Newport National is a links-style Arthur Hills design with marvelous mounding and the strategic use of grasses to deceive the golfer and define the line of play. With few trees in the center of the course, the impression is a huge expanse of land dotted by distant flags. You'll find long daunting par 5s, a drivable(?) par 4 under 300 yards, and greens that actually welcome run-up shots. Don't be put off by the trailer-as-clubhouse. Come for the golf; it's as good as it gets.

Can't book Newport? Try **Montaup Country Club** (✪✪✪½) in Portsmouth, RI. It's a less taxing design, opened in 1929, but beautifully manicured and perhaps a good breather for what's next. That night head up to Plymouth, MA and find a hotel.

The choices are abundant in the Plymouth, MA area, but we're recommending **Pinehills Jones** (✪✪✪✪✪), right in Plymouth. Set over and through the "kettles" (deep channels carved by passing glaciers), the golfer will find variety galore and challenge a-plenty. From the opening hole that calls for a perfect draw, to a 219-yard par 3 that plays longer(!), to an easy-looking but vexing 4-3-4 finish, this is a delight. If Jones is booked, try its sister, Pinehills Nicklaus. Or consider Waverley Oaks—it's just across Route 3, and 2009 will be its curtain call before it becomes the site of "Hollywood East," a set of movie studios. Really.

Pinehills Jones, Plymouth, MA

That evening head up Route 3 to Route 95 to Route 2 and find a room in Concord, MA or thereabouts.

Next up is the Brian Silva gem, **RedTail** (✪✪✪✪½), in Devens, MA, site of the 2009 US Women's Public Links Championship. Bring every club, keep your nerves in check, and be sure to notice the unusual surroundings. This fantastic track was built on a former military training ground (where you can still see a few bunkers that don't have sand). One hole after another is visually stunning—don't be too distracted or your score will balloon in a hurry. Got time for another 18? Go play **Butter Brook** (✪✪✪✪) in Westford, MA, the 2006 Mark Mungeam design that is rapidly climbing the popularity polls.

Next head north, but not too far.

Your next stop is **Atkinson Resort** (✪✪✪✪) in Atkinson, NH, where you can book a room on the spacious grounds. Atkinson demands your attention for a full 18 holes. Even the middle tees, at just 6088 yards, play to a slope of 133. So bring a few extra balls, just in case. Many holes are accentuated by huge granite outcroppings, and a pond here or there is just perfectly placed to catch an errant shot. Even so, you'll love your day here.

Head over toward the New Hampshire shore to Somersworth, NH, and find **The Oaks** (✪✪✪½), a Brad Booth 2005 track. There's plenty of length and challenge for all abilities, and the parkland setting is accentuated by subtle placements of water and sand. Add in frequent elevation changes and you have a typical New England style course, with atypical style and charm.

That night, drive just a few more miles up the coast to York, Maine.

Samoset Resort, Rockport, ME

In York you'll find **The Ledges** (✪✪✪½), another visually dazzling layout that takes advantage of the regional topography that is dotted with guess what—ledges. Lots of uphills, downhills, and shots from elevated tees and approaches to elevated greens, all influenced by the exposed faces of the ubiquitous rocky slabs.

Now you have a decision to make: the Downeaster way or the Just Due North. Each offers rewards.

You can continue way up the coast (another three hours or so) (stop at L.L. Bean on the way) to **Samoset Resort** (✪✪✪✪) in Rockport, ME. Recent renovations to the course and the hotel have brought many new fans to add to the annual regulars. Known for its ocean views, lush fairways, impeccable greens, and fairness for all abilities, it still has a lot of teeth from the back tees (6617 yards, 130 slope). It's a place to feel pampered. Plus the rates go down after 2pm.

The second leg of the Downeaster swings back inland toward Waterville, where your prize is **Belgrade Lakes**(✪✪✪✪), in Belgrade Lakes, ME. With caddies available, and one amazing hole after another with mountainside and valley views, it's easy to see why this lands on so many New Englander's annual must-play list. Architect Clive Clark hit a homerun here. (By the way, if you visit the website, you will go—it's *that* enticing.)

Can we keep the thrills coming? You bet.

Head westward again, and bed down in Carrabassett Valley, home to **Sugarloaf Golf Club** (✪✪✪½), long the reigning queen of the North Country. Her majestic views exude the best combination of Robert Trent Jones design and the Maine wilderness. This is a mountain course. Even the middle tees at just 5946 yards create an immense challenge, with a 138 slope. From the backs at 6457 yards, fuhgeddaboudit—that 143 slope will wipe you off the mountain. You go to Sugarloaf not for the low round of your life, but maybe for the best golf high.

The second choice is the Just Due North trek. From either The Oaks in NH or The Ledges in Southern Maine, follow Route 95 and go north to Route 26. Spend the night at the Gideon Hastings House in Bethel. Call early—it's small but has a terrific Italian restaurant.

And for coffee that morning in Bethel, how can you beat a place named DiCocca's?

But ah, the golf that awaits you is way up the mountain. **Sunday River** (✪✪✪✪½) in Bethel is the kind of awe-inspiring place God and the Devil might decide to have their own Ryder Cup. There are so many opportunities for heroic—and tragic—shots, so many hold-your-breath-and-swing holes, you can just see the two of them (God hitting miracle after miracle "Bet even Tiger couldn't hit that sweet fade," he'd snicker, and the Devil putting curses and spells on every ball, his own and God's,) but the course would still awe them both.

What I love best about Sunday River are the green complexes, many with depressions just off the putting surface to save wayward approach shots. Of course from there, you still have to navigate the short grass, which is usually armed with more subtle undulations than a belly dancer. The conditions? Excellent? The people? Superb. The golf? Heavenly.

(Oh that match? Naturally, God won. The Devil was DQ'd back on the seventeenth hole for hitting God's ball into a small pond, and even though it wouldn't sink, the officials called it unsportsmanlike. And then their hats caught fire).

Next up, take Route 2 across the border to Vermont and dial in Ludlow on the GPS.

Your treat this day is **Okemo Valley Golf Club** (✪✪✪✪), a course that slightly defies convention, but succeeds in the process. In this mountain valley, there is plenty of wonderful topography around. But designer Steve Durkee doubled or tripled the available palette with grasses of amazing reds, golds, and greens. He allowed some of the grass to become deep and hay-like, a certain club-grabber, and others to present a visual menace but actually being so thin as to offer almost no trouble at all. To play some holes at Okemo is to feel almost like canoeing down a river, as the wind-combed hillocks bob around you.

Got another day in Vermont? Head straight to **Green Mountain National** (✪✪✪✪) in Killington. The first hole is a roomy par 5. Then the second gets your heart pumping with a blind drive followed by a 150-yard downhill carry over a pond to a crescent landing area where you can't go left, right, or long. GMNC has a rustic clubhouse, a welcoming staff, and offers a pure golf experience for any level player.

Any gas left? Any money? On the way south through MA, hit one of these three classics. Right down Route I-91 is **Crumpin Fox** (✪✪✪✪½) in Bernardston, MA, a Roger Rulewich design with amazing variety, brilliant challenges, and serene vistas. **Taconic Golf Club** (✪✪✪✪½), a Stiles and Van Kleek 1896 design in Williamstown, MA, is the home course for Williams College, and many think it is the finest course in the six-state region. For those who like newer, more grandiose designs, consider **The Ranch** (✪✪✪✪), in Southwick, MA which uses a mountain and valley to absolute maximum advantage. There's a wow factor on almost every hole.

This gives you a good start on your New England must-play list. On the web this year, we'll list several lower mileage tours with smaller radii, where we'll add a few of the other special tracks we just couldn't fit here. Enjoy.

New England GolfGuide Online

What's In It For You?

For several years we had the world's only one-page website. Yes, today, we too find that amazing.

Then we built one that was all about what we were all about. Rookie error—except we weren't rookies.

So now we have something that we hope you'll like: a website that actually serves *you*.

We'll have more timely information, including corrections to the book as soon as we learn about them. And news about new courses opening, old ones closing, or specials of the week.

We'll have discussion boards where you, the New England golfer, will pick the topics, ask the questions, provide the answers, and share what you know. Cool course design? Best teachers? Crazy betting games? Great trips? Worthwhile charity tournaments? You name it, we'll run it.

One feature we're really excited about is our unique Rate-A-Course page, where you'll be able to tell us your thoughts on any New England course. Judge your ratings versus the official Golf Guide raters. The reputations of courses may rise and fall with your words; we'll see.

We'll have exclusive limited-time coupons to New England's best courses.

We're even talking about partnering with an online golf retailer to offer NEGG specials on clothing and equipment, exclusive to New England Golf Guide members. Stay tuned.

Join up. Membership is free.

Plus we have all the featured courses, book reviews, notices of tournaments, and a few surprises that are still in the works.

Visit newenglandgolfguide.com

You'll like it. We've figured it out this time. We did. Really.

The EgoBagger: Golf's Biggest Loser?

By Eric Siegel

In golf, where integrity is expected, penalties are often assessed on oneself, and cheating has long been considered an activity believed to be for "other" sports, there is something going on that is inconsistent with these virtues. At least on the surface it appears inconsistent. We refer to the egobagger.

The egobagger is the opposite of a sandbagger.

You know the sandbagger: his best scores somehow never get posted to his scoring record, allowing for an inflated handicap index, perfect for the club championship or a high stakes match. The sandbagger cannot survive too long at the same club without discovery, or becoming a social outcast. A couple of losses in a Nassau by scores of 6 & 5 and 5 & 4 alert the sandbagger's competitor that there is no sense in chasing good money after bad. The sandbagger will quickly run out of pigeons. And friends.

The egobagger may be more prevalent, more difficult to detect, and quite frankly, usually welcome at the net flights of the club championship.

This golfer usually isn't picking the pockets of his Saturday morning Nassau group. He's the one buying the drinks. No one questions his index at the 19th hole behind his back. Whenever the egobagger wants a game, he can find one, and he usually is as well-liked as anybody in your group or club.

His judgment and vanity may be the source of gossip, because it seems rather obvious to those around him what is going on. But his integrity is rarely questioned. But maybe we need to look a little deeper. Why doesn't anyone really want to be his four-ball partner? Club tournament after tournament he underachieves in his flight, and he is often heard right around the 16th tee, mentioning that he hasn't played this bad all year. Who does he think he's fooling?

Who is this egobagger? What motivates him? Is he in your group? Are *you* an egobagger?

It seems to start with some success.

Say he has been a 16 handicap for awhile. But he hits a hot streak, and plays some better rounds on good courses and shoots an 84, another 84, an 82, and suddenly he finds himself dropping to that handicap level he always thought was his to claim. He hits, say, 12.2. But golf is a hard game and without lots of practice and many rounds of play, poor rounds will always follow.

Suddenly there is a dilemma. The golfer has been so proud of his 12 handicap index that he has told everyone of his success. He can't help himself. So he shoots 98 on a windy, rainy day, and thinks, "Well, that wasn't my real game today," and he doesn't turn in the score. After a business trip, a 93 was not indicative of "the score I could have shot with more sleep and less work preceding the round." A steamy hot and humid day was too much of a contributor to the 101 he deems not necessary to include in the handicap record.

Is the egobagger a cheater? Is he compromising the integrity of the game? [Let's be clear, the USGA handicap systems says you must post every round played, with very few exceptions.] So, the egobagger, aware of this, assuages his guilt by adding up his score 49 + 48 = 97 (- special allowances for heat, bad lies, ball mark, lipout, and bird-chirp-in-the middle-of-backswing). Hm, a smooth 85.

Is anyone being hurt by the egobagger? For starters, he takes the place in the A or B flight of a championship that should go to a real 12 handicap. But the crime does carry its own punishment.

As the poor scores reflecting his back-to-normal play are not posted, the egobagger is having trouble winning matches. The truth is, his handicap would be back to the appropriate 15 or 16, and he would be winning his share if he were posting all his scores. But his vanity depresses his index. The egobagger is in a losing cycle that he can't get escape because he is not really a 12. As the season rolls on, 30 to 40 percent of his scores are not being posted, but he is able to maintain that handicap index. His pals can't wait till Saturday's Nassau.

In our society, ego has its place, and many accomplishments follow cockiness, especially in sports. One of two things will happen to the egobagger as it is difficult to maintain the status and be a golfaholic. Either lessons and practice will become his focus so he will really become a better player. Or he will become less interested in the game, and slowly become a 10-times-a-year player. Then he has his built-in excuse why he can't shoot his "handicap." You'll find people responding both of these ways, at all skill levels.

It's understandable how it happens, and who knows how many players who have really improved their game were then pressured into practice and dedication brought about by their own ego? Is this a bad thing?

A season or two of a deflated handicap index has motivated many single digit golfers to enjoy the game more than they thought possible. This is a cycle that takes place at private clubs, the Thursday night nine-hole leagues, and probably every club listed in this book. Certainly you know one, or several, of his kind.

So we suggest leaving him alone, as nature will take its course. Incidentally, we have an opening in our Saturday morning foursome. If you know an egobagger, give him my number, I would love to play a match against him.

THE TOP 100
New England Public Golf Courses

The following is the 2009 list of the very best golf courses in New England. To make this cut, a course has to earn a *New England GolfGuide*™ three star rating or greater. Of the 650 public courses covered in this book, only 15 percent make it on this list.

We determine ratings using a uniform set of criteria and compiled by our experienced multi-state rating team. We also take reader feedback seriously and incorporate your comments when appropriate. It is our view that providing you with current and accurate course rating information will only add to your golfing pleasure. In the spirit of constant improvement, we continue to enhance our Course Rating Methodology as well as expand the use of our popular Value Rating™.

Course Rating—The course ratings are based on a 1 to 5 star scale. For example, we reserve the 5-star (✪✪✪✪✪) rating for only a handful of the clearly outstanding courses followed by ✪✪✪✪ for excellent, ✪✪✪ for very good, ✪✪ for good and ✪ for average and below. As an added enhancement, we also include ½ star ratings to help distinguish the unique characteristics of one course from another.

The New England GolfGuide rating uses criteria which include:

1. **Course layout.** Is it interesting and varied? How many of the holes are memorable? Is the course challenging but also fair? Would this course present an interesting and different challenge every time you played it?
2. **Course Condition.** What are the average conditions of the tees, fairways, rough, hazards, and greens? What is the overall level of maintenance and attention to detail? How mature is the course?
3. **Course Staff, Facilities, and Restrictions.** How helpful and courteous is the staff? Are there adequate amenities? Are there any restrictions that would detract from the golfing experience and are walkers allowed?
4. **Golfer Feedback.** We view this as an important means of gaining insight into the courses of New England. As in years past we strongly encourage you to provide us with your assessment of the courses you have played. Your feedback provides additional support for our ratings.

NEGG Top 100
2009 Rated Courses

(18-hole, non-par 3 courses, based on star ratings and rater feedback).

5 Star Courses ✪✪✪✪✪

Massachusetts

Pinehills GC (Nicklaus)	Plymouth, MA
Pinehills GC (Jones)	Plymouth, MA

4½ Star Courses ✪✪✪✪½

Maine

Sunday River GC	Bethel, ME

Massachusetts

Blackstone National GC	Sutton, MA
Crumpin-Fox	Bernardston, MA
Farm Neck Golf Club	Oak Bluffs, MA
Granite Links Golf Club	Quincy, MA
Red Tail Golf Club	Devens, MA
Taconic GC	Williamstown, MA

4 Star Courses ✪✪✪✪

Connecticut

Fox Hopyard CC	East Haddam, CT
Great River GC	Milford, CT
Richter Park GC	Danbury, CT
Wintonbury Hills GC	Bloomfield, CT

Maine

Belgrade Lakes GC	Belgrade Lakes, ME
Samoset Resort	Rockport, ME
Sugarloaf GC	Carrabassett, ME

Massachusetts

Butter Brook	Westford, MA
Cyprian Keyes	Boylston, MA
The Ranch GC	Southwick, MA
Shaker Hills Golf Club	Harvard, MA
Waverly Oaks Golf Club	Plymouth, MA

New Hampshire

Atkinson Resort	Atkinson, NH

Rhode Island

Newport National GC	Middletown, RI

Vermont

Green Mountain National	Killington, VT
Okemo Valley GC	Ludlow, VT

3½ Star Courses ✪✪✪½

Connecticut

Gillette Ridge	Bloomfield, CT
Lake of Isles GC & Resort	N. Stonington, CT
Oxford Green GC	Oxford, CT
Quarry Ridge GC	Portland, CT
Sterling Farms	Stamford CT

Maine

Dunegrass GC	Old Orch. Beach, ME
Kebo Valley	Bar Harbor, ME
The Ledges GC	York, ME
Northport GC	Belfast, ME
Old Marsh	Wells, ME
Sable Oaks Golf Club	S. Portland, ME
Sugarloaf Golf Club	Carrabassett Vly, ME

Massachusetts

Acushnet River Valley GC	Acushnet, MA
Blissful Meadows	Uxbridge, MA
Captains GC	Brewster, MA
Cranwell Resort	Lenox, MA
Crosswinds GC	Plymouth, MA
Dennis Pines	Dennis, MA
Juniper Hills GC	Northborough, MA
New England CC	Bellingham, MA
Poquoy Brook GC	Lakeville, MA
Southers Marsh GC	Plymouth, MA
Wachusett CC	W. Boylston, MA

New Hampshire

Baloams Panorama GC	Dixville Notch, NH
Breakfast Hill GC	Greenland, NH
Bretwood GC (North)	Keene, NH
Campbell's Scot. Highlds	Salem NH
Hanover CC	Hanover, NH
Laconia CC	Lakeport, NH
Lochmere GC	Tilton, NH
Mt. Washington Hotel	Bretton Woods, NH
Oaks Golf Links	Somersworth, NH
Owl's Nest GC	Campton, NH
Passaconaway CC	Litchfield, NH
Portsmouth CC	Greenland, NH
Stonebridge GC	Goffstown, NH

Rhode Island

Montaup CC	Portsmouth, RI

Vermont

Haystack GC	Wilmington, VT
Woodstock Inn & Resort	Woodstock, VT

3 Star Courses ✪✪✪

Connecticut

Lyman Orchards GC	Middlefield, CT
Shennecossct GC	Groton, CT
Sterling Farms	Stamford
Tashua Knolls CC	Trumbull, CT
Tunxis Plantation (White)	Farmington, CT

Maine

Cape Neddick	Ogunquit
Fox Ridge Golf Club	Auburn, ME
Links at Outlook, The	South Berwick, ME
Nonesuch River GC	Carborough, ME
Point Sebago GC	Casco, ME
Spring Meadows GC	Gray, ME
Toddy Brook GC	North Yarmouth, ME

Massachusetts

Atlantic Country Club	Plymouth, MA
Bass River GC	South Yarmouth, MA
Bayberry Hills	Yarmouth, MA
Braintree Muni. GC	Braintree, MA
Cranberry Valley GC	Harwich, MA
Dennis Pines GC	S. Dennis, MA
Far Corner Golf Course	W. Boxford, MA
Foxboro CC	Foxborough, MA
Highfields Golf & CC	Grafton, MA
Meadow Creek	Dracut, MA
Trull Brook	N. Tewksbury, MA
Wahconah	Dalton, MA

New Hampshire

Bretwood GC (South)	Keene, NH
Canterbury Woods	Canterbury, NH
Eastman Golf Links	Grantham, NH
Overlook GC	Hollis, NH
Windham CC	Windham

Rhode Island

North Kingstown Muni.	N. Kingstown, RI
Richmond Country Club	Richmond, RI

Vermont

Equinox CC	Manchester, VT
Killington Golf Resort	Killington, VT
Mount Snow Golf Club	Mount Snow, VT
Neshobe Golf Club	Brandon, VT
Rutland CC	Rutland, VT

---

*The *New England GolfGuide* uses a five star rating system when evaluating golf courses. This rating takes into account course layout, condition, variety, challenge, amenities, and professionalism of the staff. A course that has earned a rating of 1 Star is average, 2 Star represents a good course, 3 Star is considered very good. A 4 Star course offers an superior experience and a 5 Star rating is reserved for only the most exceptional courses.

Top 50 Golfing Values in New England 2009

The New England GolfGuide Value Rating™ is provided to help our reader's identify the courses that deliver the best value for golfing dollar ($$$). The Value Rating™ compares only the top courses, the ones that have earned the New England GolfGuide three star rating (❋❋❋) or above*, *with an 18-hole weekend green and cart fee of $90 or less. This rating balances price, NEGG star rating, reader feedback, and the reports from our NEGG Course Rater team.*

Of the 650 public golf courses listed in this book, there are only a select group of courses, approximately 8 percent, which earn this Value Rating™.

Note: a course can have a high stand-alone star rating but if the cost of golfing is above the $90 cutoff, it will not earn the right to be a New England GolfGuide Value Course.

Of course, only you can judge the value of a day on Course A versus Course B. But we've compiled the data on the most objective basis we can and we'll stand by our list. This is just another opportunity for you to send us feedback. Did we miss any great values? Did we rate some course too high or too low? If enough readers tell us something they can move the needle.

Each year, the biggest task of our editorial staff is to update the listed information for 650 courses. In a period of uncertain economics, most courses have told us they are holding their rates steady for a year. As it turns out, the average weekend cost of playing 18 holes of golf, with a cart, across all New England public courses has remained relatively flat, $64.39, only a $.39 increase from last season.

In addition to courses with the New England GolfGuide Value Rating™, golfers who like to play into fall or start in early spring can also find a wide variety of wonderful off-season specials. Many of the courses listed in our book have substantial off-season discounts from the standard green fee which can be accessed by going directly to their websites.

Also, several resort courses such as the **Woodstock Inn & Resort** in Vermont, **Atkinson Resort & Country Club,** and **The Balsams Resort** in New Hampshire, **Poland Spring Resort, Sunday River,** and **Sugarloaf Golf Club** in Maine, and **Cranwell Resort** and **Crumpin Fox** in Massachusetts all offer golf and stay packages which can be a great way to enjoy golf and the other relaxing aspects of the game. Try **Farm Neck** on Martha's Vineyard in April or October and that may be the best deal of all.

Lastly, don't forget the Fall golf bonus; many courses in the southern areas of New England including Cape Cod provide fine playing conditions and discounts starting in October (and a few stay open year-round).

With the Value Rating™, the New England GolfGuide has given you yet another good reason to get out there and swing.

Top 50 Value Ratings
New England GolfGuide
2009 Season

The New England Golf Guide takes the top-rated courses in our listings, and using a formula that balances price, star ratings, reader comments, and rater evaluations. The resulting list below is a ranking of the Top 50 Best Golfing Values in New England for prices as predicted for 2009.

RANK	RATING	COURSE	STATE	GOLF	CART	$ TOTAL
1.	●●●½	Southers Marsh	MA	37	12	49
2.	●●●½	Bretwood	NH	42	13	55
3.	●●●½	Quarry Ridge	CT	55	inc.	55
4.	●●●	Stanley	CT	33	15	48
5.	●●●½	Acushnet	MA	45	15	60
6.	●●●½	Lochmere	NH	60	inc.	60
7.	●●●½	Sable Oaks	ME	45	15	60
8.	●●●½	Juniper Hills	MA	44	17	61
9.	●●●	Topstone	CT	41	12	53
10.	●●●½	Montaup	RI	45	18	63
11.	●●●	N. Kingston	RI	39	15	54
12.	●●●½	Campbell's Scottish	NH	49	15	64
13.	●●●	Exeter	RI	55	inc.	55
14.	●●●	Nonesuch River	ME	40	15	55
15.	●●●½	Poquoy Brook	MA	49	16	65
16.	●●●½	Gillette Ridge	CT	65	inc.	65
17.	●●●	Neshobe	VT	40	16	56
18.	●●●	Nippo Lake	NH	42	15	57
19.	●●●	Tradition at Wallingford	CT	57	inc.	57
20.	●●●●	Richter Park	CT	64	13	77
21.	●●●	Canterbury Woods	NH	58	inc.	58
22.	●●●	Shennecosset	CT	42	16	58
23.	●●●	Tunxis White	CT	43	15	58
24.	●●●½	Blissful Meadows	MA	51	17	68
25.	●●●●	Butter Brook	MA	78	inc.	78
26.	●●●½	Passaconaway	NH	54	15	69
27.	●●●●	Okemo Valley	VT	79	inc.	79
28.	●●●●	Wintonbury Hills	CT	79	inc.	79
29.	●●●●	Atkinson	NH	62	18	80
30.	●●●	Braintree	MA	45	15	60
31.	●●●	Glen Ellen	MA	50	10	60
32.	●●●	Kettle Brook	MA	60	inc.	60

INC. = INCLUDED IN WEEKEND GREEN FEE
(*Prices reflect anticipated 2009 fees but are subject to change without notice. Please call ahead.)

RANK	RATING	COURSE	STATE	GOLF	CART	$ TOTAL
33.	✪✪✪	Fox Ridge	ME	44	16	60
34.	✪✪✪	Far Corner	MA	46	15	61
35.	✪✪✪	Highfields	MA	61	inc.	61
36.	✪✪✪½	Breakfast Hill	NH	57	15	72
37.	✪✪✪	Trull Brook	MA	47.5	14.5	62
38.	✪✪✪	Aroostook Valley	ME	45	17	62
39.	✪✪✪✪	Cyprian Keyes	MA	66	18	84
40.	✪✪✪✪	Shaker Hills	MA	85	inc.	85
41.	✪✪✪½	Sterling Farms	CT	50	25	75
42.	✪✪✪½	Hanover	NH	59	16	75
43.	✪✪✪	Meadow Creek	MA	49	16	65
44.	✪✪✪	Links, The	ME	50	15	65
45.	✪✪✪	Lyman Orchards	CT	65	inc.	65
46.	✪✪✪½	Dennis Pines	MA	60	16	76
47.	✪✪✪	Windham	NH	50	16	66
48.	✪✪✪½	Oaks, The	NH	60	18	78
49.	✪✪✪✪	Green Mountain	VT	90	inc.	90
50.	✪✪✪½	Haystack	VT	79	inc.	79

INC. = INCLUDED IN WEEKEND GREEN FEE

In addition, there are numerous great courses that offer reduced rates during off-peak times and off-peak months.

The New England GolfGuide uses a five star rating system when evaluating golf courses. This rating takes into account both course layout and condition. A course that has earned a rating of 1 Star is average, 2 Star represents a good course, 3 Star is considered very good where as a course that has earned a 4 Star is excellent and a 5 Star rating is reserved for only the most exceptional courses.

Caution, the Value Rating does not take into account the cost associated with activities at the 19th hole, which we recommend only after play has finished. Please golf responsibly.

Driving Range Directory

Connecticut Driving Ranges by Town

Mountain-View Golf Driving Range	2061 Berlin Turnpike, Berlin 06037	(860) 828-5358
Woodhaven Country Club	275 Miller Road, Bethany 06524	(203) 393-3230
Stony Hill Long Drive	46 Stony Hill Road, Bethel 06801	(203) 778-2777
Mar-Lea Miniature Golf Range	244 Boston Turnpike, Bolton 06043	(860) 649-7023
Golf Quest Family Sports Center	1 Sandout Road, Brookfield 06804	(203) 775-3556
Burlington Golf Center & Practice	Rural Route 4, Burlington 06013	(860) 675-7320
Chesire Academy Of Golf	1550 Highland Avenue, Cheshire 06410	(203) 271-1403
Colchester Driving Range	160 Old Hebron Road, Colchester 06415	(860) 537-4653
Rockpile Driving Range	113 Rock Hall Road, Colebrook 06021	(860) 379-5161
Torza's Professional Golf Center	98 Sebethe Drive, Cromwell 06416	(860) 632-1132
Meadowridge Golf Center	20 North Road, East Windsor 06088	(860) 623-9500
Pleasant View Golf Park	110 North Street, Enfield 06082	(860) 763-4202
Tunxis Fore	1024 Farmington Ave., Farmington 06032	(860) 674-8924
Great Brook Golf Center	850 Route 84, Groton 06340	(860) 448-0938
East Hartford Golf Center	55 Hillside Avenue, Hartford 06106	(860) 282-7809
Goodwin Golf Course	1130 Maple Avenue, Hartford 06114	(860) 956-3601
Toll Gate Golf Range	590 Torrington Road, Litchfield 06759	(860) 496-4653
Klein's Golf Range	391 Durham Road, Madison 06443	(203) 245-1139
Golf Center Of Manchester	60 Progress Drive, Manchester 06040	(860) 646-6479
Club Golf	109 Adams Street, Manchester 06040	(860) 645-6363
Highland Ridge Golf Range	87 Highland Road, Mansfield Center 06250	(860) 423-9494
Indian Springs Golf Club	132 Mack Road, Middlefield 06455	(860) 349-8109
Newfield Golf Driving Range	500 Newfield Street, Middletown 06457	(860) 347-1750
Connecticut Golf Center	562 Danbury Road, New Milford 06776	(860) 354-0012
Only Game In Town	275 Valley Service Road, New Haven 06473	(203) 239-4653
Golf Training Center	145 Main Street, Norwalk 06851	(203) 847-8008
Malerba's Golf Driving Range	650 New London Turnpike, Norwich 06360	(860) 889-5770
CherryStones	218 Shore Road, Old Lyme 06371	(860) 434-1721
Prospect Golf Driving Range	144 Waterbury Road, Prospect 06712	(203) 758-4121
Belmont's Ridgefield Golf Range	824 Ethan Allen Highway, Ridgefield 06877	(203) 431-8989
Golf Center of Connecticut	784 River Road, Shelton 06484	(203) 929-6500
Pleasant View Golf Center	452 South Road, Somers 06071	(860) 749-5868
Golf Quest Family Sports Center	125 Jude Lane, Southington 06489	(860) 621-3663
Raceway Golf Club	252 E Thompson Road, Thompson 06277	(860) 923-9591
Rockledge Golf Shop & Driving	289 S Main Street, West Hartford 06107	(860) 521-3156
Brown's Driving Range	1847 Poquonock Avenue, Windsor 06095	(860) 688-1745

New Hampshire Ranges by Town

Souhegan Woods Golf Club	65 Thornton Ferry Road, Amherst 03031	(603) 673-0200
White Mountain Country Club	3 Country Club Lane, Ashland 03217	(603) 536-2227
Candia Woods Golf Links	313 South Road, Candia 03034	(603) 483-2307
Beaver Meadow Golf Course	1 Beaver Meadow Street, Concord 03301	(603) 224-2828
Twin Pines Driving Range	Route 125, Epping 03042	(603) 679-9911
Driving Range	Route 124, Greenville 03048	(603) 878-1324
Legends Golf & Family	18 Legends Drive, Hooksett 03106	(603) 627-0099
Green Meadow Golf Club	9 River Road, Hudson 03051	(603) 598-3838
Funspot	Rural Route 3, Laconia 03246	(603) 366-4377

Lisbon Village Country Club	Bishop Road, Lisbon 03585	(003) 838-6004
John Cain Golf Club	Unity Road, Newport 03773	(603) 863-7787
Sagamore Golf Club	North Road, North Hampton 03862	(603) 964-8393
Lochmere Golf & Country Club	Rural Route 3, Tilton 03276	(603) 528-4653
Fore-U Golf Center	298 Plainfield Road, West Lebanon 03784	(603) 298-9702

Rhode Island Driving Ranges by Town

Narragansett Driving Range	1141 Boston Neck Road, Narragansett 02882	(401) 284-0005
Smithfield Driving Range	661 Douglas Pike, Smithfield 02917	(401) 231-3726
Green Meadows Golf	117 Dunns Corner Road, Westerly 02891	(401) 322-9888

Vermont Driving Ranges by Town

Mt. Anthony Country Club	180 Country Club Drive, Bennington 05201	(802) 447-7079
Essex Country Club	332 Old Stage Road, Essex Junction 05451	(802) 879-3232
Practice Tee	Route 7A, Manchester 05254	(802) 362-3100
Arrowhead Golf Course	350 Muray Avenue, Milton 05468	(802) 893-0234
Mount Snow Golf Club	Country Club Road, Mount Snow 05356	(802) 464-4254
Proctor Pittsford Country Club	Corn Hill Road, Pittsford 05763	(802)483-9379
St. Johnsbury Country Club	Route, St. Johnsbury 05819	(802) 748-9894
Stratton Mountain Resort	Rural Route 1, Stratton Mountain 05155	(802) 297-4114
Basin Harbor Club	Basin Harbor Road, Vergennes 05491	(802) 475-2309
Blush Hill Country Club	Blush Hill Road, Waterbury 05676	(802) 244-8974

Maine Driving Ranges by Town

Roy's Golf Center	2514 Turner Road, Auburn 04210	(207) 782-2801
XL Indoor/Outdoor Golf	620 Hammond Street, Bangor 04401	(207) 848-5850
Long Shot Golf Center	305 Bath Road, Brunswick 04011	(207) 725-6377
Vokes' Mini-Strokes	Bar Harbor Road, Ellsworth 04605	(207) 667-9519
Tee 'Em Up Golf Center	Route 100, Gray 04039	(207) 657-4653
Sugarloaf Sports & Fitness Center	Sugarloaf Access Road, Kingfield 04947	(207) 237-2000
College Street Driving Range	601 College Road, Lewiston 04240	(207) 786-7818
T's Golf	Range Way & Route 202, Manchester 04351	(207) 621-8633
Fore Season Golf	1037 Forest Avenue, Portland 04103	(207) 797-8835
Riverside Municipal Golf Course	1158 Riverside St., Portland 04103	(207) 797-3524
Cascade Golf Range	Rural Route 1, Saco 04072	(207) 282-3524
Mountain View Golf Range	Route 109, Sanford 04073	(207) 324-0436
Nonesuch River Golf Club	304 Gorham Road, Scarborough 04074	(207) 883-0007
Pine Ridge Golf Center	Route. 15, Box 4660, Sedgwick 04676	(207) 359-6788
Tee Shots	1126 N Berwick Road, Wells 04090	(207) 646-2727
Tee 'N Tee Golf Land	27 Bridgton Road, Westbrook 04092	(207) 797-6753
Sonny's Driving Range	108 Cove Hill Road, Winterport 04496	(207) 223-5242

Massachussetts Driving Ranges by Town

Mushy's Driving Range	369 Main Street, Agawam 01001	(413) 786-6672
Sarkisian Driving Range	153 Chandler Road, Andover 01810	(978) 688-5522
Atlantic Golf Center	754 Newport Ave, Attleboro 02703	(508) 761-5484
McGolf Driving Range	541 Southbridge Street, Auburn 01501	(508) 832-0557
South Meadow Golf Range	317 South Street, Berlin 01503	(978) 838-2333
Sun 'n' Air Driving Range	210 Conant Street, Danvers 01923	(978) 774-8180
McGolf Limited	150 Bridge Street, Dedham 02026	(781) 326-9616

Ridder Golf Course	300 Oak Street, East Bridgewater 02333	(781) 447-6613
Falmouth Country Club	630 Carriage Shop Rd., East Falmouth 02536	(508) 548-3211
Fenway Golf Range & Pitch	112 Allen Street, East Longmeadow 01028	(413) 525-6495
EaSthampton Golf	103 Northampton St., Easthampton 01027	(413) 529-2300
Groton Country Club	94 Lovers Lane, Groton 01450	(978) 448-2564
Groveland Fairways	156 Main Street, Groveland 01834	(978) 373-2872
WeStern Mass Family Golf Center	294 Russell Street, Hadley 01035	(413) 586-2311
Garrison Par 3 Golf Center	660 Hilldale Avenue, Haverhill 01832	(978) 374-9380
Pine Crest Golf Club	212 Prentice Street, Holliston 01746	(508) 429-9871
Hyannis Golf Club	Route 132, Hyannis 02601	(508) 362-2606
Tee Time Driving Range	New Report Turnpike, Ipswich 01938	(978) 356-6599
Lancaster Golf Center	138 Old Union Turnpike, Lancaster 01523	(978) 537-8922
Bakers Driving Range & Golf	658 South Main Street, Lanesboro 01237	(413) 443-6102
Stone Meadow Golf	675 Waltham Street, Lexington 02173	(781) 863-0445
Lakeview Driving Range	449 Whalom Road, Lunenburg 01462	(978) 345-7070
Sagamore Spring Golf Club	1282 Main Street, Lynnfield 01940	(781) 334-3151
Mendon Driving Range	Route 16, Mendon 01756	(508) 478-6295
Whirlaway Sports Center	500 Merrimack Street, Methuen 01844	(978) 688-8356
Lakeville Golf Practice Range	10 Rock Street, Middleboro 02346	(508) 947-1865
Golf Country	160 S Main Street, Middleton 01949	(978) 774-4476
Paradise Springs Golf	25 Lonergan Road, Middleton 01949	(978) 750-4653
Quaboag Valley Mini-Golf	15 Hospital Road, Monson 01057	(413) 283-4388
Natick Golf Learning Center	218 Speen Street, Natick 01760	(508) 651-2406
Airport Golf Driving Range	582 Kelley Boulevard, N. Attleboro 02760	(508) 643-2229
Pappas Indoor Golf & Baseball	70 Princeton Street, N. Chelmsford 01863	(978) 251-3933
Caddy Shack	900 State Road, N. Dartmouth 02747	(508) 991-7976
East Coast Golf Academy	333 SW Cutoff, Northborough 01532	(508) 842-3311
Golf Learning Center	19 Leonard Street, Norton 02766	(508) 285-4500
Sandbaggers Practice Range	829 Washington St., Pembroke, 02339	(781) 826-1234
Holly Ridge Golf Club	121 Country Club Road, Sandwich 02563	(508) 428-5577
Seekonk Driving Range	1977 Fall River Avenue, Seekonk 02771	(508) 336-8074
Easton Country Club	265 Purchase Street, S. Easton 02375	(508) 238-2500
Coles River Family Fun Center	358 G.A.R. Highway, Swansea 02777	(508) 675-8767
Max's Country Golf	383 Middlesex Road, Tyngsboro 01879	(978) 649-2020
Golf Masters	2250 Providence Highway, Walpole 02081	(508) 668-8222
Bryant Farm Driving Range	123 Sandwich Road, Wareham 02571	(508) 295-8773
Rotary Driving Range	Route 9, Westborough 01581	(508) 366-5327
East Mountain Country Club	1458 E Mountain Road, Westfield 01085	(413) 568-1539
Golf Acres	319 Union St., Westfield 01085	(413) 568-1075

Featured Courses 2009

Put these on your must-play list.

This new section gives you a closer look at some of our region's most highly rated and enjoyed courses.

Whenever you visit, tell them you saw them in the Golf Guide.

And after you visit, go online and rate the course at newenglandgolfguide.com.

Every vote counts, and every voter has a chance to win free golf and other golf products all year long.

CONNECTICUT
Sterling Farms, Stamford
Tunxis Plantation, Farmington

MAINE
Belgrade Lakes, Belgrade Lakes
Cape Neddick, Ogunquit
Fox Ridge, Auburn
The Ledges, York
The Links at Outlook, South Berwick
Nonesuch River, Scarborough
Samoset, Rockport, & Sable Oaks, S. Portland
Spring Meadows, Gray

MASSACHUSETTS
Acushnet River, Acushnet
Bass River, S. Yarmouth
Blissful Meadows, Uxbridge
Butter Brook, Westford
Cyprian Keyes, Boylston
Far Corner, West Boxford
Hampden, Hampden
Highfields, Grafton
Juniper Hill, Northboro
Meadow Creek, Dracut
Pine Ridge, North Oxford
Pinehills, Plymouth
Red Tail, Devens
Shaker Hills, Harvard
Southers Marsh, Plymouth

NEW HAMPSHIRE
Atkinson, Atkinson
Breakfast Hill, Greenland
Lochmere, Tilton (in back)
Stonebridge, Goffstown
Windham, Windham

VERMONT
Green Mountain, Killington
Haystack, Wilmington
Mount Anthony, Bennington

Sterling Farms | Stamford, CT

Escape to the Quiet.

Nestled in a quiet park-like setting, just 40 minutes outside New York City in Stamford, Connecticut, Sterling Farms is an 18-hole public golf facility laid out over 144 acres of a once active dairy farm. Originally designed by Architect Geoffrey Cornish in 1969 and renovated by Architect Robert McNeill in 2005, the par 72 course opened in the spring of 1972.

Sterling Farms' rolling terrain guides you through the picturesque farm buildings and challenging holes, including its difficult par 3s, which demand distance, accuracy, and good putting to score well. With a variety of tees to play from, golfers of all skill levels are offered a fair and fun challenge.

At 6310 yards from the back tees, and slope of 127, Sterling Farms presents a fair and reasonable test. Move up one set of tees to 6082, and slope 123, and a bogey-level player should have a fine and fun day.

The front nine is hilly with several elevated tees or greens. The back nine is flatter. Overall, most of the fairways are wide and forgiving.

With five ponds on the property, water dictates the line of play on several holes, including the 14th, where two ponds dictate a thoughtful approach. The bunkering around the course is particularly well-planned for defending par. This course has well-maintained greens and fairways.

Noted for its meticulous condition, layout, heated driving range and amenities, the facility gets rated the #1 public golf course in Fairfield County year after year.

In 2005, Sterling Farms began an extensive renovation project to the tees and greens and a new practice facility with a sand trap, chipping green, and putting green behind the pro shop. The club plans to phase in future improvements over the next few years until the entire golf course is updated.

Even though it enjoys much popularity, there's always room for more friends at Sterling Farms. Try it out.

sterling farms

golf course

Play and Practice at Fairfield County's number #1 Public Golf Facility located just 40 minutes outside Manhattan!

Nestled in a quiet park like setting of Stamford, CT, Sterling Farms rolling terrain guides you through the picturesque farm building and challenging holes of a once active dairy farm. Golfers of all skill levels are offered a fair and fun test of the game.

Our Covered and HEATED Driving Range is open year round 7 days a week so you can groove your swing in the winter months for the spring.

Please call us to host your next Corporate or Charity Golf event, dates are available at great prices for the 2009 season.

For more information please call 203-461-9090.

sterlingfarmsgc.com

Tunxis Plantation

Farmington, CT

Tunxis Trio: A Treat To Play.

Tunxis Plantation in Farmington Valley offers 45 wonderful holes for your golfing pleasure.

Tunxis opened in 1962 with 18, and added 9 holes in 1964, 9 more in 1985, and a final 9 in 1995. All were designed by Al Zikorus.

The 300-acre complex features three courses, but each with its own character. The Green 18 is a links-style layout, with fairway mounds that dictate strategy. The Green offers longer, tougher par 3 holes, that stretch out the par 70 to feel like more.

The White 18 is a more parkland style, playing though the many old-growth trees. But it also has water. The 7th green seen in the ad (right) shows a typical White Course challenge. The lake on this course presents several demanding approach shots to island or peninsulas greens.

Despite the numerous rounds, the staff maintains a consistently high level of quality throughout. The *New England Golf Guide* wrote about the White: "Bring your driver—the fairways are so wide you could be approaching from anywhere across a 50-yard expanse at some places...The greens are medium to large, with enough slyness to challenge even A players."

The 9-hole Red Course is a par 35 with one par 5, and plays along the Farmington River. For a quick day at the course, this is just the ticket.

With multiple courses, Tunxis Plantataion is able to host tournaments and outings more easily than most. It also allows them to always keep at least one course open for public play every day. A grass tee range and multiple snack bars around the course add to the pleasure.

Head pro Lou Pandolfi, PGA, also extols the other offerings of Tunxis. "We host many weddings and other functions here, both in the clubhouse and the large pavilion. It's a great place for weddings, showers, business meetings, and family gatherings.

"An active family program after 1pm on weekends is also gaining momentum." Come try us," says Pandolfi.

Tunxis Plantation is right off Route I-84, Exit 39, in Farmington, CT.
860-677-1367

Belgrade Lakes

Belgrade Lakes, ME

Where Golf Really Rocks.

Now this is a golf course people will drive miles and miles to visit.

Belgrade Lakes in Belgrade, ME, opened in 1999, is simply breathtaking.

Literally carved out of the wilderness granite by British designer Clive Clark, this course offers one thrill after another, hole by hole by hole.

And it starts on the first hole, a 424-yard par 4 with an elevated tee that just begs for a long tee shot to a fairway 120 feet below. The par 71, 6723-yard course plays to a slope of 135 and USGA rating of 72.2 from the back tees. The player is treated to similar vistas all day long. Visit the website to experience the spectacle on your desktop.

Truly a mountain course, you'll find elevated tees, greens and sometimes, fairways. And boulders. Boulders left, boulders right, boulders behind greens, boulders running across the fairway. They're everywhere, and if you ever dreaded sand, you'll be terrified of what a boulder does to an offline shot. So try not to bring them into play.

Overall, the course is in excellent condition from tee to green, with plenty of water to feed the grass (without disturbing the players). For all the challenges here, the water hazards are rather easily avoided.

What you can't avoid are the tricky greens. From the very subtle to the not-at-all subtle, you'll find plenty of opportunities to read and re-read your putts.

Belgrade has earned the attention of many national publications, and deservedly so. Clark got it all right, the routing, the blending of scenery and strategy, the use of the land to define the course, not vice versa (even with a few thousand rocks moved).

The players who will do well here are those who can forgo the power game on certain holes and simply play for position. They'll let the course come to them, so to speak. Sure there are places to bomb away, but maneuvering into optimum position is what wins on the big tour, and usually provides better scores everywhere else as well. Especially at Belgrade Lakes.

A Gem in the Wilderness

Top 100 Courses You Can Play - Golf Magazine
America's 100 Greatest Golf Courses - Golf Digest
Best In State - DownEast Magazine
Number One Course In Maine - Golf Magazine

A Clive Clark Design

BELGRADELAKES

www.belgradelakesgolf.com
207 – 495 –4653

Cape Neddick | Ogunquit, ME

New Practice Area Awaits Cape Neddick Golfers

The last ten years have seen Cape Neddick Country Club transformed from a 9-hole course with no bunkers to a beautifully maintained, well-bunkered, 18-hole semi-private facility.

The original Donald Ross design was an 18-hole course from its construction until the beginning of World War II when the back nine was closed. It remained a 9-hole course until 1998 when Brian Silva's redesign was opened to again bring 18-holes to CNCC. The old holes were creatively integrated with the new holes (16, 17, & 18 are the former 7, 8, & 9) to bring a seamless transition when making the turn. The club now boasts a membership of 350 with public tee-times available up to 5 days in advance. (Members have 7 day privileges.) Situated on Shore Road between York and Ogunquit, the course is in the perfect spot for vacationing guests as well as locals who don't have to travel too far off the path to enjoy a great round of golf.

The addition of the practice facility has been a great benefit to the club. The Club also hosts group outings and tournaments. Try Cape Neddick soon.

CAPE NEDDICK
COUNTRY CLUB

18 hole, semi-private golf course
public tee-times available

Fabulous Fairways,
Food & Friends

Just an hour north of Boston
Located on scenic Shore Road in Cape Neddick, ME
207-361-2011
www.capeneddickgolf.com

Fox Ridge | Auburn, ME

Is This Your New Must-Play Course?

With so many courses in New England, it's easy to overlook a number of great ones. This one deserves more notice. Readers, please put Fox Ridge on your must-play list.

This delightful track, in the words of a *New England Golf Guide* course rater, is "a blend of St. Andrews and the Maine seacoast: stone walls, stone bridges, and island greens." The course features a gentle blend of rolling hills, lined with native fescue, babbling brooks, and century-old stone walls, the traditional property lines of New England farmers.

The mostly links-style course is situated on over 200 acres of rolling countryside in south Auburn, Maine and is designed to take advantage of the natural lay of the land. This is truly a design that will demand every shot in your bag.

Superbly maintained and stretching a bold 6814 yards, the par 72 Fox Ridge is a 132 slope from the back, and a bit tamer 126 from the 6297 middle tees.

Part of the higher slope comes from the subtle greens. Putt well—or putt often. Give yourself a treat; come to Fox Ridge for a change of pace soon.

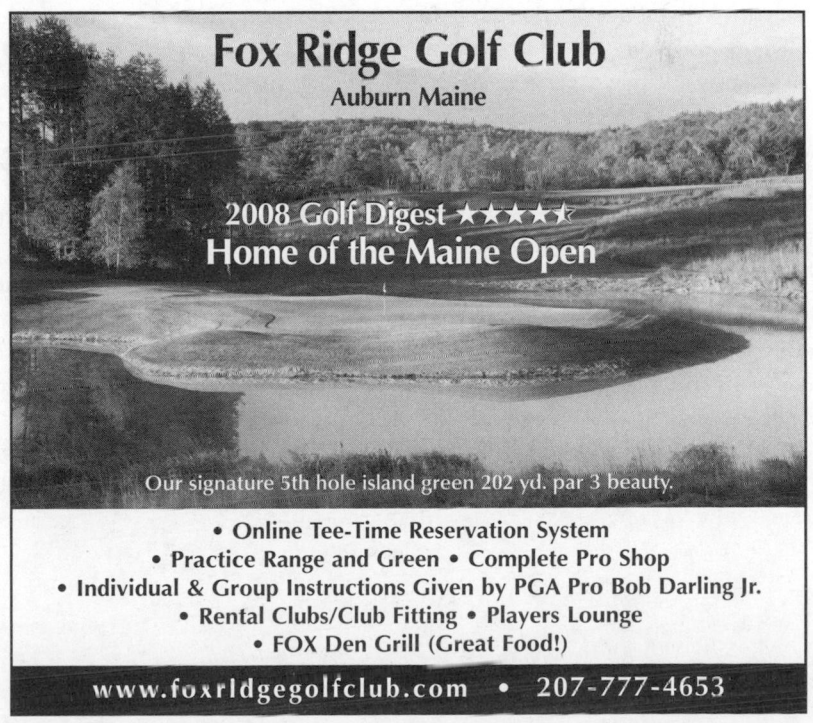

Fox Ridge Golf Club
Auburn Maine

2008 Golf Digest ★★★★½
Home of the Maine Open

Our signature 5th hole island green 202 yd. par 3 beauty.

• Online Tee-Time Reservation System
• Practice Range and Green • Complete Pro Shop
• Individual & Group Instructions Given by PGA Pro Bob Darling Jr.
• Rental Clubs/Club Fitting • Players Lounge
• FOX Den Grill (Great Food!)

www.foxridgegolfclub.com • 207-777-4653

The Ledges | York, ME

An Excellent Course, And Getting Better.

The Ledges Golf Club (York, ME) is clearly the gateway to any memorable Maine golf trip. Conveniently located minutes from I-95 and the Maine/NH border, it's an easy ride from both Boston and Portland. Breathtaking views of the rugged Maine landscape make The Ledges a true escape from your daily routine. The golf course sits on protected land that will prevent you from seeing a house or condo the entire round. Your only distraction from the great golf will be scenic vistas and the native wildlife of southern Maine.

The Ledges has four sets of tees ranging from 6,981 to 5,000 yards and widely known as the finest public golf experience on the seacoast. Course architect Brad Booth has designed a fair and challenging layout that gives players of all abilities the opportunity to hit every club in the bag. Those who frequent The Ledges know their work isn't done once they reach the green. The Ledges consistently has first rate putting surfaces that have challenged tour players and weekend warriors alike.

The Ledges will feature some welcome additions in 2009 with three major projects completed by the end of the '08 season. The driving range has a fresh look with a brand new 2,200 square foot Tee-Line synthetic turf practice tee as well as 8,000 additional square feet of natural turf. The Ledges is now a great place to play and practice.

Out on the course, players will find a brand new comfort station between #7 and #17. The clubhouse has undergone a major addition, expanded seating in the dining room and a new kitchen, making the 19th hole a great place to enjoy a burger and a beverage to talk about your round. Take advantage of the meeting facility for your next corporate meeting/golf outing.

The Ledges is a unique public facility designed to be your private club for the day. Nine-minute tee-times keep rounds moving at a good pace. Friendly familiar service makes you feel right at home without any pretension. Exceptional course conditions that rival some of the finest private clubs around. Come play golf in Maine and find out what people are talking about after they play The Ledges.

Check out The Ledges Golf Club on-line at www.ledgesgolf.com. Book tee-times, see the various "Play and Stay" packages, the latest Ledges news, and much more.

Links at Outlook

South Berwick, ME

18 Holes, Two Experiences.

If you're seeking a different golf experience, consider the Links at Outlook. You can play two styles of courses, but all in one scenic setting. It's just 45 minutes from Portland or 75 minutes from Boston.

The Links at Outlook start you off with a links-style nine, but without the ocean. The front nine (a former farm) is mostly treeless, with high grasses and gentle mounding defining the fairways. Here you'll find challenging, undulating greens, where you can run a ball up along the ground (a seemingly forgotten art). Open land usually means breezes, and often there are plenty enough to keep you alert on this lovely track.

The back nine has a distinctly different character. Fir trees line the fairways as the course climbs over and around a hill that eventually places you nearly 200 feet over the flatter front nine. From several spots up here, you can see the front nine holes, as well as some of the mountains many miles distant.

It's the front-to-back difference that makes for the appeal of the links at Outlook. On the front nine, you can hit lots of drivers and play the big game. On the back, you have to play more strategically through the narrower fairways.

To really have a different look at the course, play different tees on successive visits. There's a difference of about 1000 yards between the blacks and the whites, and the former makes for a very tough course. Says head pro Dave Paskowski, PGA, "We hosted the Seacoast Amateur last year, the area's most prestigious event, and they found it all they could handle from the back. Many had played a scramble here from the blues earlier in the year, and thought they knew the course. Well, only about 20 players even broke 80. It was definitely a surprise for them." Most players will have a fine time from the whites or blues, he says.

Paskowski says the staff is happy to host outings, tournaments, weddings, and personal and business meetings of all kinds. The restaurant stays open and even offers Sunday brunch through the winter. Make the trip.

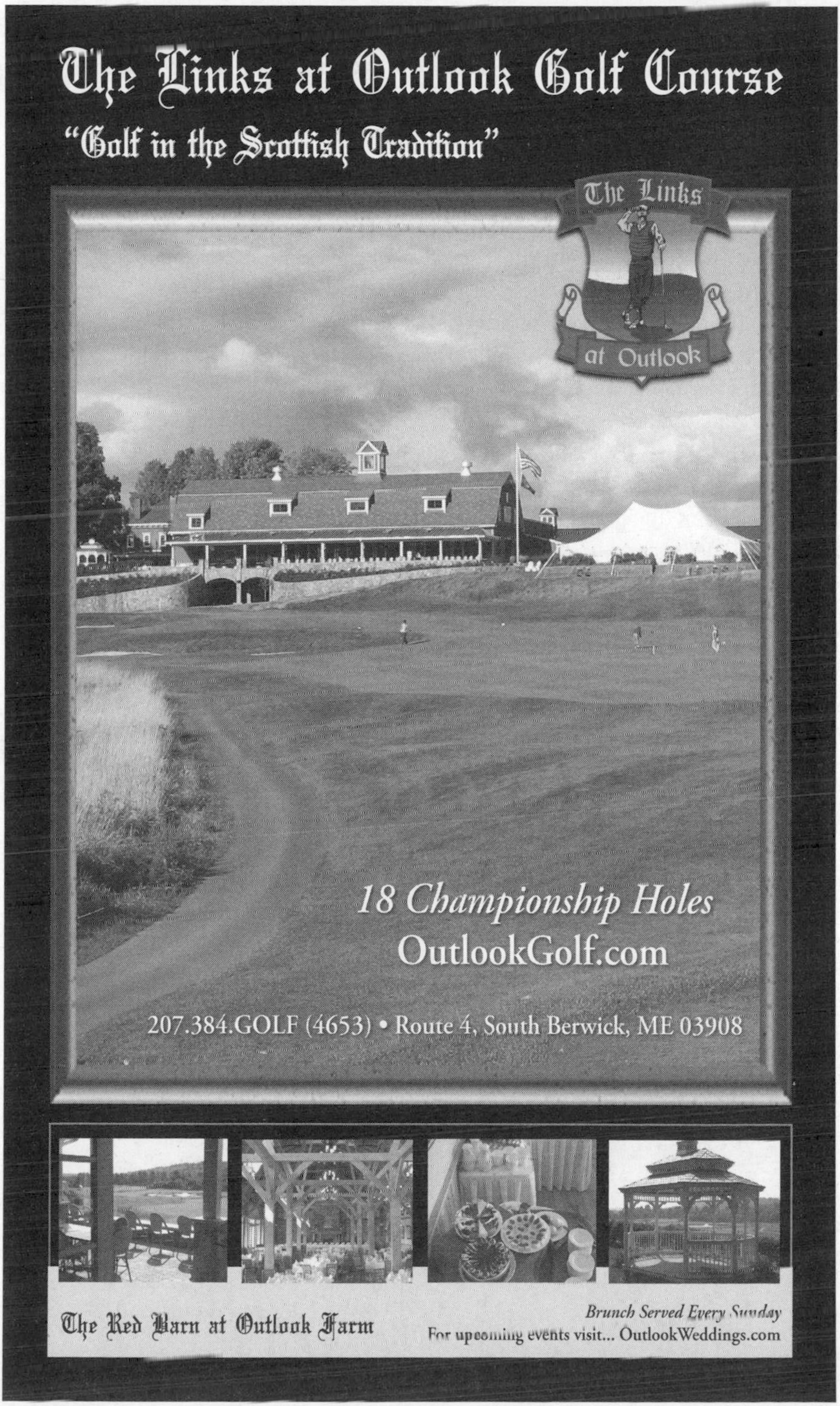

The Links at Outlook Golf Course
"Golf in the Scottish Tradition"

18 Championship Holes
OutlookGolf.com

207.384.GOLF (4653) • Route 4, South Berwick, ME 03908

The Red Barn at Outlook Farm

Brunch Served Every Sunday
For upcoming events visit... OutlookWeddings.com

Nonesuch | Scarborough, ME

Are You Coming to Scarborough Golf?

Just a bit south of Portland, Maine sits Scarborough, a charming town with four-season appeal. And within the boundaries of that town lies Nonesuch River Golf Club, just heading into its 12th year of providing exceptional golf season memories.

The 18-hole par 70 course attracts players from all over New England and points beyond. Known for a professional, first class operation, Nonesuch provides an affordable, and memorable experience.

As a rule, the greens putt true, and medium fast. Rolling hills add visual interest and they help guide well-hit shots further down the fairways.

With bent grass fairways and greens, and loads of variety it's easy to see why it's so popular. The practice facility, perhaps the most extensive in Greater Portland, includes grass tees on the range, a practice bunker, and two putting greens, and a full golf academy for individual and group lessons.

The golf is great, the scenery is wonderful, the clubhouse is inviting, and the staff is eager to make your round a pleasure. That's makes for an easy decision.

Samoset | Rockport, ME
Sable Oaks | South Portland, ME

Two Gorgeous Sisters.

The great just keep getting better. Samoset Resort, already lauded nationally as a true destination course and resort, is upping the ante. The resort celebrates its 125th anniversary this year, and will celebrate along the way with newly renovated guest rooms, and a new spa, restaurant, and pool in 2009.

The course itself, built in 1902, is always magnificent, benefiting from the ocean mists and the loving care of a devoted staff. Some call it a Pebble Beach of the East, with a full seven holes playing alongside or across a piece of the ocean.

The course design uses elevation changes along the rocky coast to dare shots over crashing waves, or to persuade others to hug the well-grassed "inland" route to the hole. But anywhere on the course, you can feel the ocean's presence.

The Samoset went through several renovations from 1999 – 2001, including the 4th, 5th, 12th, and 14th holes. These, along with the brand new 18th hole (now regarded as one of the toughest finishing holes in New England) were all designed by New England architect Bradley Booth. Samoset recently won the State of Maine Environmental Leader award.

Further down the coast in South Portland is Samoset's sister course, Sable oaks Golf Club, a Cornish and Silva 1989 design.

Once again you find elegant golf holes, this time arrayed around a high piece of land off the water. You'll be treated to some challenging but enjoyable golf, surrounded by woods and ponds, with soft fairways and gently rolling, manicured greens.

Enjoy wide, inviting fairways on a par 70, 6359-yard track. It sounds short, but the challenge lies in the playing to optimal positions. Water is in play on perhaps three holes, but wetlands everywhere require several carries for a drive or an approach. Relatively easy to walk, Sable has a private club feel but is eminently approachable, and most affordable. Just minutes from the Maine Turnpike and the Portland Airport, it's easy to reach from anywhere.

Call about the club's stay and play packages and visit the website to 'tour" the course.

Please see the Samoset and Sable Oaks full color ads inside the front cover.

Spring Meadows | Gray, ME

Green Fees? Affordable. Fun? Priceless.

Spring Meadows Golf Club, an 18 hole championship course located in Gray, Maine has a naturally beautiful and challenging layout offering plush fairways and superb greens. The par 71 course offers a challenge for golfers of all abilities with 4 sets of tees ranging from 4,706 yards to 6,656 yards.

On land that was once a dairy farm, each hole adds to the overall beauty of the course with defined tree lines, ponds, bunkers, brooks, and unique designs crafted by noted Maine architect Brad Booth.

As you approach the greens, you'll find them to be consistent from your first to your finishing putt. And the fairways are so plush at Spring Meadows that you your ball just sits up as if you placed it on a tee.

As you play this lovely layout, you'll find opportunities to test each club in your bag as you decide which pins to attack—or not. Spring Meadows Golf Club has earned the reputation for having excellent course conditions at an affordable cost. Only two hours from Boston's North Shore, it's certainly worth the drive. Add it to your play list today.

'Must-Play' Golf

Spring Meadows Golf Club at Cole Farms

"100 Must-Play Courses of New England"

GolfStyles Boston

Spring Meadows
GOLF CLUB AT COLE FARMS
Gray, Maine
(207) 657-2586

Naturally beautiful, challenging layout
- Designed by Brad Booth of Faxon & Booth
- Plush fairways, superb greens, four sets of tees
- A great experience for golfers of all abilities

20 minutes from Portland. 1 mile from Turnpike Exit 63. Route 100 North.

VISIT www.springmeadowsgolf.com **AND THEN COME PLAY THE COURSE**

Juniper Hill Golf Course

Northboro, MA

Two Challenging and Fun Courses.

With two different styles of courses, Juniper Hill Golf Course is a great place to meet people for a friendly round of golf, any day of the week. The Riverside Course, which opened over 75 years ago, is best described as sporty, interesting and picturesque. The Assabet River winds through this New England style course providing a beautiful setting amid the rolling hills and century old stone walls. The Lakeside Course provides more of a challenge with a Carolina-style that takes full advantage of the New England terrain. As you play the course more, you will become more comfortable with its challenge. All in all, it is a great place to visit and enjoy.

The friendly staff and recently expanded facilities make round of golf, or a small or large outing a pleasant event. The staff and facilities accommodate non-golf events as well. The Golf Teaching Center, adjacent to the golf course, provides a place to warm up before the round or work on ones' skills with the PGA staff.

Juniper Hill is located a short distance from several major highways in central Massachusetts, so it is convenient for golfers from all areas of New England.

Juniper Hill Golf Course
202 Brigham Street
Northboro, MA
508 393-2444
www.juniperhillgc.com

Juniper Hill is a 36 Hole Golf Course. Plan your next outing or function with us! We can accommodate from 3 to 300 guests in a variety of settings

Golf builds lasting friendships

Golf Teaching Center
508 351-9500

Acushnet River | Acushnet, MA

Acushnet, Where Silva Created Gold.

Acushnet River Valley Golf Course, in Acushnet, MA, was designed by nationally renowned golf course architect Brian Silva. He has created a premiere golfing experience.

Acushnet River Valley offers two diverse layouts in one 18-hole championship course. On the front nine, you stroll through tall white pines, each hole its own cathedral. The back nine are sculpted over a Scottish links layout, with mounding and grasses reminiscent of the original traditions of course design and layout. The two sides compliment one another in perfect balance.

You'll need to play Acushnet only once to realize the reason why people thoroughly enjoy a day here. But the more you return, perhaps the more you'll unravel the secrets to scoring well against this proud layout. It's the kind of place that definitely grows on you.

Everyone is welcome, and all skill levels are offered a challenging and fun experience when they visit.

Brian Silva has found the secret to GOLF COURSE DESIGN ..... Boston Globe / Four Stars Golf Digest 2004 *"Best Places to Play"*

Front 9 - Pine Alley Fairways   Back 9 - Scottish Links

ACUSHNET RIVER VALLEY
GOLF COURSE

www.GolfAcushnet.com
685 Main Street / Acushnet, MA 02743 / 508-998-7777 / 7 Day advance Tee Times

Bass River | Yarmouth, MA

Ross Design, Ocean Breezes. Ahhhhhhh.

Bass River is a quintessential Cape Cod course, and a wonderful manifestation of the genius of Donald Ross. Ross knew how to add visual cues for the golfer to get to the green, while also adding visual miscues when he or she arrived on the greens.

It's because of the greens you want to play Bass River. Most are quite small, but full of subtlety and intrigue for the first time player. The course sits on the water and because of that ocean breezes come into play on many holes. And depending on the day, they can come from any direction.

While Bass River is not a long course, the challenge comes from having to hit good to great approach shots. Most golfers love to have a wedge or nine-iron into the green. Bass River allows such opportunities. The caveat of course, is to stay on the correct side of the hole, and most usually the front of the green.

Come enjoy the pine-lined fairways, the very lush greens, and the smells of the sea. Bass River offers multiple rewards.

Afterwards in the clubhouse, hoist a frosty one to Donald Ross, and to yourself for finding Bass River.

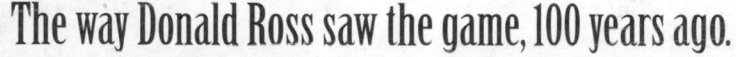

Blissful Meadows

Uxbridge, MA

Two Courses In One.

Blissful Meadows Golf Club is an exceptional walk in the park. (Though you may want a cart on the back nine.)

This wonderful layout was designed by Brian Silva, named *Golf World* magazine's "2000 Architect of the Year." The course measures 6,588 yards with a slope of 128 and a rating of 71.3. Both high and low handicappers will enjoy it here.

Blissful has two characters. The front side ambles across and around gentle hills and a bit of strategically placed water. After the opening hole, which requires a rather tight shot through trees on both sides of the fairway, the course opens up and encourages aggressive play to its greens.

The front is where you want to score, because on the back, you just have to hang on for the adventures. From the par 5 tenth, which climbs a long dogleg left up a hill, followed by a way down and way up 11th, you'll know you're on a different and fun nine. Along the way you'll encounter the remnants of an old silver mine, a couple of daunting carries, and more. You'll  end with three of the finest finishing holes anywhere, especially 18, which calls for an approach over water.

This is a very well-conditioned golf course, and the greens can be medium-fast to fast, and further complicated by their many undulations.

With the round is done, come relax in the Meadowview Tavern, an inviting spot to total your scorecard.

Blissful Meadows Golf Club, owned by the Bliss family, features a fully-stocked pro shop with the latest selection of golf equipment. The practice facilities are also first rate, and include a putting green, grass driving range, target greens, and a practice sand trap. PGA professional Matt Griffith has put together a variety of instructional programs ranging from private lessons to clinics of twenty students.

Blissful can bring out the best in your game. Come out and try this wonderful course set in the placid farming region of south-central Massachusetts.

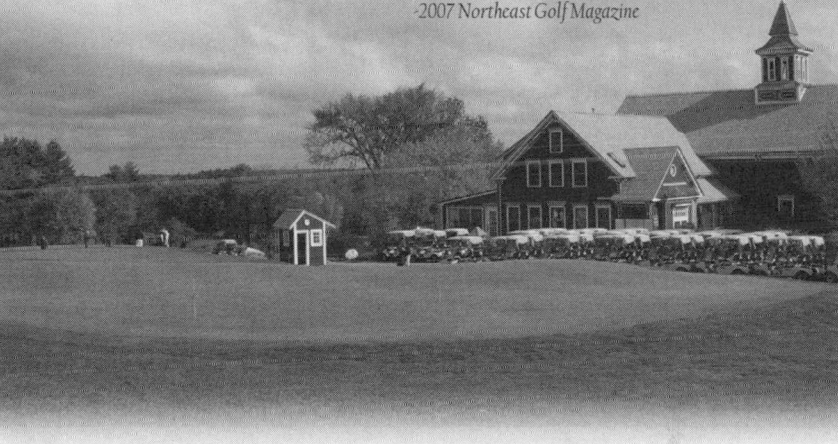

Butter Brook | Westford, MA

Ever since Butter Brook Golf Club in Westford burst on the scene with nine holes in 2004, and added nine more in 2006, it has gained popularity year after year.

The striking Mark Mungeam design (which rates a *New England Golf Guide* 4 stars) combines several elements of the land that was there with artistic touches that seem the more natural the more often one plays there.

The round opens with a fine tester. The par 5 first tee requires a slight uphill carry to a slightly blind lie, a second shot down a tree-lined corridor, and then an approach to a green guarded by a deep swale in front. Next up is a go-for-broke driver or two-layup 316-yard par 4, and at that point you begin to see you'll be thinking course management all day long (which is never a bad thing anyway).

Perhaps the best four in the course is number six. Standing on the tee, players may feel indecisive as to how to play the longest of three par 4's on the front nine. The best tee shot is a slight fade over the left fairway bunkers that use the back slope to kick shots forward. Other players may try to blast it down the right side, flirting with the pond. The green is guarded by a front right bunker and chipping areas to left and rear.

Water is a central element to Butter Brook, with several ponds sitting right where you wish they weren't. Unless you hit the ball where you're supposed to hit it. As you come around to the newer back nine, you find that Mr. Mungeam had time to develop new ideas. Huge waste bunkers and tall fescue appear on this side, and introduce visual variety as well as tee shot indecision. There's even a hole like St. Andrew's famed road hole. The owners and Mungeam decided to leave the barn intact (despite its rather "rustic" condition), and keep it in play.

Add to these thrills a couple of peninsula greens, a long stream that sits just in range between two adjoining fairways, great 9th and 18th holes and you have a masterful course that will bring you back for plenty more.

Back tee yardage for this par 72 track is 6702 yards and 133 slope, but the middle at 6174 and 128 is plenty for almost anyone.

This is a course you'll want to visit time and again.

Cyprian Keyes | Boylston, MA

Try the Cyprian Experience.

Opened in 1997, Cyprian Keyes Golf Club is named after Cyprian Keyes, who built the home on the property in 1734. Cyprian Keyes Golf Club offers 27 holes of golf — an award winning 18-hole championship course and perhaps the best par-3 course in the state.

More than just a golf course, it also includes a golf school, golf shop, driving range and New England's only Callaway Performance Center. The colonial-style clubhouse features four function rooms and a restaurant. All rooms, including Cyprian's Restaurant, have outdoor access via a patio or deck, as well as breathtaking views of the course and surrounding countryside.

While Cyprian Keyes Golf Club offers some membership options, it is always open to the public. The championship course includes five sets of tees and plays from 5,029 to 6,871, yards so golfers of every skill level enjoy their golfing experience. The par-3 course — nine holes between 85 and 165 yards, impeccably manicured and with large greens — is a favorite for families and for kids and a tremendous place for low handicappers to practice their irons and short game.

In May 2008, about 1,000 people attended the Grand Opening of the Callaway Performance Center at Cyprian Keyes with LPGA legend Annika Sorenstam as the celebrity host. One of just 10 in the country, the center offers cutting edge technology previously available only to professionals. Golfers can have their swings analyzed and their clubs precision fitted. "Golfers of every skill level can benefit greatly from the data gathered in just one hour and a half session at the Callaway Performance Center," Frem says. Frem reminds golfers that reservations are required for the private sessions in the Performance Center.

Cyprian Keyes Golf Club is a great destination for everything from golf to wedding receptions, precision club fittings to business meetings, dinner to golf lessons and everything in between. At Cyprian Keyes you can experience it all and as they say "enjoy the experience."

Far Corner | West Boxford, MA

For the Peace, and For the Challenge.

If you want a course that offers peace and quiet with your challenge, consider Far Corner in West Boxford, MA. It's 27 holes, a New England rarity, which means they can handle more golfers and move them around the course with less delay. Add to that the beauty of old growth trees, several ponds and dramatic elevation changes and you get: a decent pace at a lovely quiet place. Marvelous.

Far Corner, designed by venerable Geoffrey Cornish in 1967 is run by one of the region's most respected families, the Flynns, who also manage several other courses. At a Flynn course you can expect at least three things: a friendly staff, lovingly attended greens, and a casual, relaxed atmosphere, where the most important thing on anyone's mind is the golf.

Far Corner has hosted uncounted Massachusetts and New England championships, and the reason is that it has it all. It makes for a terrific tournament setting, and the club hosts numerous annual outings. From long, wide-open fairways, to an "inland" island green, to blind shots that must curve over a mountain top, to snap-your-neck doglegs, you'll use every club and probably hit shots you've never tried before. There is possibly more variety here hole-by-hole than anywhere else in the state.

The course has three nines spread over 250 acres, the Heron, the Fox, and the Hawk 9s, and players are able to play any one, two, or three for various rates, depending on the day and the time they tee off.

The staff, ably led by John O'Connor, NEPGA Teacher of the Year 2006, welcomes all inquiries about group and private lessons, group clinics, and golf outings from 16 to 214 players.

Come try Far Corner, it's really not that far.

Hampden Country Club | Hampden, MA

For Golf, For Special Events.

At Hampden Country Club, dramatic elevation changes produce a challenging golf course with spectacular vistas. Seven holes wander along the base of Goat Hill with gorgeous sunsets and views to the west. The other 11 holes meander through open meadows crossing brooks and ponds to create an interesting variety of approaches. The views, the natural wetlands, and the landscape offer a wonderful setting for a championship golf course. Players of all skill levels will enjoy this course and it is always open to the public.

At 6833 yards from the back tees, the slope is a daunting 134 for this par 72 design. Move up to the middle tees at 6349 though, and you'll have a 129 slope and perhaps a better chance to get home on the longer holes.

This is a moderately hilly layout, but walkable, and the various water hazards dictate the line of play and the degree of bravado or discretion you apply hole by hole. (We suggest discretion.)

It's a most enjoyable course, noted for fine conditions and a friendly welcoming staff that has obvious pride in its course.

For outings, banquets, business meetings, and weddings, Hampden provides an elegant yet relaxed setting. The club features panoramic views unmatched by any other banquet hall in the area.

The clubhouse has every service you need and expect from a first class private country club.

Menus for all events are prepared by the club's own chef and experienced staff. You can also create the menu that works for you and your event, and the staff at Hampden will make sure that your banquet is a wonderful success.

The ballroom (seating up to 300) has two separate bars, a parquet dance floor, ample space, and wondrous views. Whether your event is a wedding or a corporate outing, the setting is ideal.

Highfields | Grafton, MA

The first thought after a round at Highfields is "Now that was a challenge!"

This strategic Mark Mungeam design demands your full attention the entire round. Pars are meant to be earned, and the rewards for a well-played hole are well worth the effort.

From the back tees of 7021, the slope is 140. For those with stronger feelings of self-preservation, the middle tees at 6024 still offer a 131 slope and plenty of course to maneuver around.

From where does the challenge emanate? Several doglegs force well-positioned tee shots, and although you can hit driver frequently, it may not always be the wisest play.

Several water hazards add shape and decision-making, and a few blind shots also test your risk threshold.

The course is well maintained, with fairways the condition of much older courses.

Opened in 2002, it has matured quite nicely, with more improvements both on and off the course each year.

The Highfields at Grafton is another part of the story. This new planned community is set on several hundred acres of remarkably scenic, prime land boasting panoramic vistas and added privacy for homeowners.

The homes have course views, and vice versa, but the homes are set comfortably back from the lines of play. As a planned golf and residential community, the developers have taken care to respect both. Additional green spaces and tree-lined buffer areas add visual beauty and community integrity.

Woven throughout are the eighteen scenic and testing championship golf holes.

Homesites are now available. To learn more about Highfields homes and see the community plans and amenities, visit soon. And don't forget your golf clubs.

Meadow Creek | Dracut, MA

Take the Strategic Approach.

Strategy can be defined as a systematic plan of action. At Meadow Creek, a new 18-hole, 6501 yard championship golf course in Dracut, MA, bring all your strategy and get ready to have a fun and challenging round of golf. With views of Boston to the south and rolling hills throughout the golf course, spending a day at Meadow Creek will be unique, picturesque, and enjoyable.

With four tee boxes for every player level, and large, receptive greens, golfers of all abilities can experience the full pleasure of golfing at this gem.

Each hole is a new experience. Jeffrey Brem, a new course designer, utilized all the varied terrain that nature provided to present every hole as a unique challenge. The variety is wonderful and the routing is entertaining to those who appreciate such nuances. The course sits comfortably on the shoulders of the land, as Brem was careful to avoid any forced-looking holes. The tempo and flow seem completely natural.

The front nine holes are fairly open, as they sweep down and back through meadows. Gently swaying grasses define some fairways while others are lined with old farming stone walls bringing forth a historic New England charm.

Generally you'll get to hit driver on the wide front 9. But the course switches gears on the back, with tighter fairways, and a greater variation in elevation. Part of the benefit of that, however, are the spectacular views.

You'll find water hazards, too, on both the front and the back, but not if you use your strategic playing mind.

While Meadow Creek requires a few carries, none is unreasonable, and it's clear that the course is well thought out for those who prefer to concentrate on direction over distance.

Meadow Creek opened for full play in 2007. Better hustle out there and get in your first round before the word really gets out. No doubt, you will enjoy golfing here.

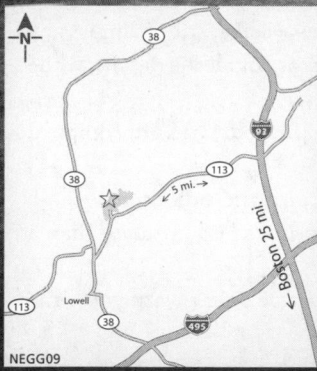

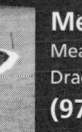

Pine Ridge | North Oxford, MA

What's your Pleasure?

What are you looking for in a course? Scenic views? That's Pine Ridge, in North Oxford, MA.

Want exceptionally manicured greens, where the ball rolls true and the well-read putt drops in? That's Pine Ridge.

Want to get out of the city without having to drive far at all? That's correct again, Pine Ridge.

Pine Ridge Country Club is an 18-hole, par 71, public course, situated 10 minutes south of Worcester, MA, and located close to the major highways of Central Massachusetts. The course is easily accessed off Route 56, and convenient to Routes 290, 495, and the Mass. Turnpike. For over 35 years, Pine Ridge has been one of Worcester County's favorite places to play.

With relatively few bunkers on the course and a picturesque layout, this is an excellent course for players of all skill levels.

The club facilities include a comfortable clubhouse with a full bar and lounge, function room and kitchen. Or enjoy the outside deck overlooking the first and third tees.

Pine Ridge now has a large selection of pro shop merchandise, with top brand names added.

A specialty of Pine Ridge is its golf outing program. If you've been looking for a professional, full service staff to help you organize a special event of almost any size, look no further. The warm, welcoming staff take care of all the details, while you and your guests enjoy the day.

In addition, carts are provided for your comfort. The golf carts are equipped with roofs, ball washers, and course yardage guides.

In addition, many area businesses schedule meetings and office parties in a setting that's more comfortable, more scenic, more private and intimate than a restaurant or hotel ballroom.

If this becomes your favorite course—and don't say we didn't warn you—the club offers affordable membership options as well.

To learn more, visit the website pineridgegolf.net. It's one of the better course websites around, and includes a yardage guide, outing details, and menus.

Pinehills Jones & Nicklaus | Plymouth, MA

Five Star Choices. Times Two.

At Pinehills, it's all about the golf. From the attended bag drop to the extensive practice facilities, Pinehills leaves no doubt about its purpose.

Two 18-hole designs await your pleasure: Jones and Nicklaus. The Rees Jones, as the website says, "is characterized by his signature style, challenging to play, enjoyable for both experts and novices alike, and respectful of the land, with built-in subtleties that offer a new playing experience every time."

Of the two, the Jones course requires more precise tee shots and approaches, and rewards you with easier putts. From the first tee, you're off to work, negotiating an uphill dogleg left to a well-guarded green. The ninth is an eye-opening par 5 that requires a carry over a hillside, a medium-length second shot, and an approach to a thin but wide green, fronted by a pond. The par 5 15th hole requires a carry over an abyss of brush to a rising fairway and a distant elevated green.

The Nicklaus 18, designed by Jack Nicklaus II, has a different character, with much of the same appeal. Also cut around and through the kettles (carved by glaciers), the Nicklaus design offers somewhat broader landing areas, but more challenging putts once you reach the green. Favorites include the daunting third hole, a long par 3 that requires a carry over a fronting trap, and the wonderful eighteenth, which requires a semi-blind tee shot that must find the fairway rather than the long-stretching pond which guards the green.

There is great variety, beauty, and challenge all around. The marvelous practice facilities and cart are included in your fee. Arrive early enough to take advantage. After your round, enjoy the inviting grill and lounge.

Pinehills is the only five-star rated golf club in the *New England Golf Guide 2009 Edition*. Come play once and you'll return again and again.

Please see the Pinehills full color ad inside the back cover.

Shaker Hills | Harvard, MA

Try the Shaker Hills Experience.

Ever since opening to national acclaim in 1991, Shaker Hills has been raising expectations about what upscale public golf can be.

From your first drive up the winding picturesque entrance to your final drive on our spectacular 18th fairway, everything about Shaker Hills says quality. Take a look at the new online photo tour to truly sense the pristine beauty of Shaker Hills.

The 6,850 yard 18-Hole par 71 layout, nestled among pines, stone outcroppings, and rolling landscape, features bentgrass throughout the course. Multiple tee positions on every hole provide an endless variety of attack angles and landing areas, making the course ideal for both experienced and beginner golfers.

Noted golf architects Brian Silva and Mark Mungeam (with considerable cooperation from the Creator) have fashioned a beautiful and unique golf course that's challenging yet fair.

Here are two examples of the Shaker Hills golf experience. One of the most beautiful and demanding holes in New England, No. 3 is one of the signature holes here. A wide, shallow green offers an inviting target from an elevated, five-tier tee. Sand awaits long shots, and a small pond lurks to the left to snare off-line birdie-bids. Club selection can range from lofted woods to mid-irons.

And consider the unusual 18th. Your first chore is to carry your drive over a large waste area. Then you need to plan your next shot around an outcropping of ledge which splits the fairway. If you haven't found the right landing spot, your might have a blind approach to downhill green.

But what really sets Shaker Hills apart from other public courses is its "private club" atmosphere and amenities. The club specializes in hosting tournaments and fundraisers and providing the extra touches.

An ample pro shop can provide all the prizes you need, as well as expert club-fitting. Says PGA head pro Mike Herrick, "If every golfer were the same size and had the same swing, every golfer could use the same set of clubs. But studies show as many as 9 of 10 golfers are playing with clubs not perfectly matched to their needs. We can help them out."

Put Shaker Hills on your list of the courses you really must see—or get back to—in 2009.

Please see the Shaker Hills full color ad inside the front cover.

Red Tail | Devens, MA

Red Tail to Host U.S. Women's Amateur Public Links June 22-27, 2009

This is a big one.

Red Tail Golf Club, the magnificent Brian Silva design in Devens, MA will host the 2009 U.S. Golf Association Women's Amateur Public Links Championship, June 22-27. The tournament was devised as a championship for female amateurs who play on public courses. Members of private clubs are barred from entry.

Often referred to as the Publinx, eligibility is similar to that for the United States Women's Amateur Golf Championship. Golfers must follow the USGA's guidelines for amateur status, and there are no age restrictions. Entries are accepted from golfers with a USGA handicap index of 18.4 or lower, as opposed to 5.4 for the U.S. Women's Amateur.

Jim Pavlik has been the general manager and head pro since Red Tail opened. "From the moment I saw the design, before it was even grassed in," says Pavlik, "I knew this was a championship caliber course."

In 2002, he invited the USGA to come take a look, and over the course of several visits, they agreed Red Tail should host an event. Only two changes were requested by the officials: grow the rough to two inches and change the 10th tee to a putting green.

From the first tee, which calls for an uphill carry, to the last green (pictured in the ad right), which is guarded by a pond and bunkers, and must be approached (often) from a downhill lie. Note how close the water is to the putting surface. Red Tail demands the best from a golfer.

The course features exceptional variety, laid out through the former military base of Fort Devens.

Some believe this is Silva's finest design. It employs many of his signature angled fairways and angled greens. He had an amazing canvas, granted, but he seems to have taken more chances at Red Tail, innovating in bunker design, and even allowing several of the greens to aid, rather than defend against, slightly offline putts.

Perhaps the most famous hole is 17, a dogleg right par 4 with a desert-size waste bunker which forces a player to consider how much carry will result in a safe landing. The Pub Links women will have their hands full all week.

Pavlik and his staff are actively recruiting 600 volunteers to work in all of the facilities during the tournament. E-mail to rjobinrtgc@yahoo.com to contact the volunteer committee chairperson.

Admission is free and highly encouraged.

THE
Ultimate *Golf*
EXPERIENCE

2009
U.S. Women's Amateur
Public Links Championship
June 22-27

Photo by George N. Peet · 3rd Hole

Tee times 7 days in advance
978-772-3273

AUDUBON
INTERNATIONAL
Certified Signature Sanctuary

35 Miles West of Boston Route 2 Exit 37B Jackson Rd · Patton Road Devens, MA 01432
www.redtailgolf.net

Southers Marsh | Plymouth, MA

What's Red and Green and Fun All Over?

New England Golf Guide editor John DiCocco calls Southers Marsh in Plymouth "One of my ten favorite courses in Massachusetts. It has 18 wonderful holes, and the nicest, most sincere group of owner managers you'll find anywhere, the Stearns family. They care about their golfers, and they care about their course."

Maybe they're always in such a good mood because of their surroundings. The course was designed around and through a working cranberry bog. That means from the clubhouse, or anywhere around the course itself, there is a visual feast of pink and lime, or red and green, for much of the year.

Southers Marsh is a par 31-30-60 with seven par 4s and eleven par 3s. Total yardage from the back tees is 4111, perfect for a quicker-than-usual 18, but stop right there if you're thinking "pitch-and-putt." No way. There are carries a-plenty over the bogs, strategically placed bunkers, and long grasses designed to force certain shots. And contoured greens to keep par a challenge. The shortest hole on the course, the 12th, a mere 97 yards, is actually one of the toughest because it's an island green which looks like a sliver from the tee. There's no bailout either—it's hit-the-green or surrender to the bog.

That's followed by the 13th, a dogleg right par 4 of 304 yards that plays like 395 because it's all uphill, with a well-defended green. The finishing holes of 4-3-3-4 can crunch many a good scorecard.

Even the most accomplished golfers will be challenged, but four sets of tees ensure that golfers of all abilities will be able to enjoy themselves. The club has a 300-yard driving range and a full service restaurant with a beautiful mahogany deck overlooking the course. The restaurant is well known locally for the good food and good cheer well after the last golfer has come in and the Stearns are happy to host a party or wedding in a most inviting setting.

Southers Marsh Golf Club

Voted Plymouth's Best Golf Course
2003, 2004, 2005 & 2006
www.southersmarsh.com ◊ 508-830-3535

Atkinson Resort & Country Club | Atkinson, NH

LEFT: *An aerial view of the Atkinson Resort & Country Club featuring the beautiful putting greens, picturesque Trellis Area, and outdoor patio dining. Photo by Intrepid Photography.*

RIGHT: *Golfers putting on the Par 4, 333-yard 13th green which is surrounded by sloping fairways and stunning granite rocks.*

The Atkinson Resort & Country Club, located in scenic Atkinson, New Hampshire, is a state-of-the-art facility that provides the public with many offerings typically only found at the finest private country clubs. Whether you are looking for a top-notch golf course or a superb dining experience, you'll find it at the Atkinson Resort & Country Club.

As a guest, you'll easily see why the unique restaurant, lively tavern, comfortable overnight accommodations, and social and conference facilities are second-to-none.

The club's breathtaking 18-hole championship golf course, rated four stars by *New England Golf Guide*, with its manicured greens and stunning fairways allows golfers to enjoy the picturesque surroundings New Hampshire is so well known for, while still being in a public setting. Some of the amenities Atkinson Resort & Country Club offers to enhance your golfing experience include:

- GPS equipped golf carts
- Locker rooms
- Private golf lessons and group clinics from our golf professionals
- Corporate meetings and golf packages
- Fieldstone Suites rooms for overnight or extended stays
- Four year-round indoor golf simulators featuring over 25 golf courses
- The Willowcreek Golf Academy—a state of the art, year-round practice facility featuring twelve heated hitting bays, two indoor bays equipped with V1 software for the best instruction, and an indoor putting surface.

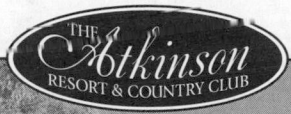

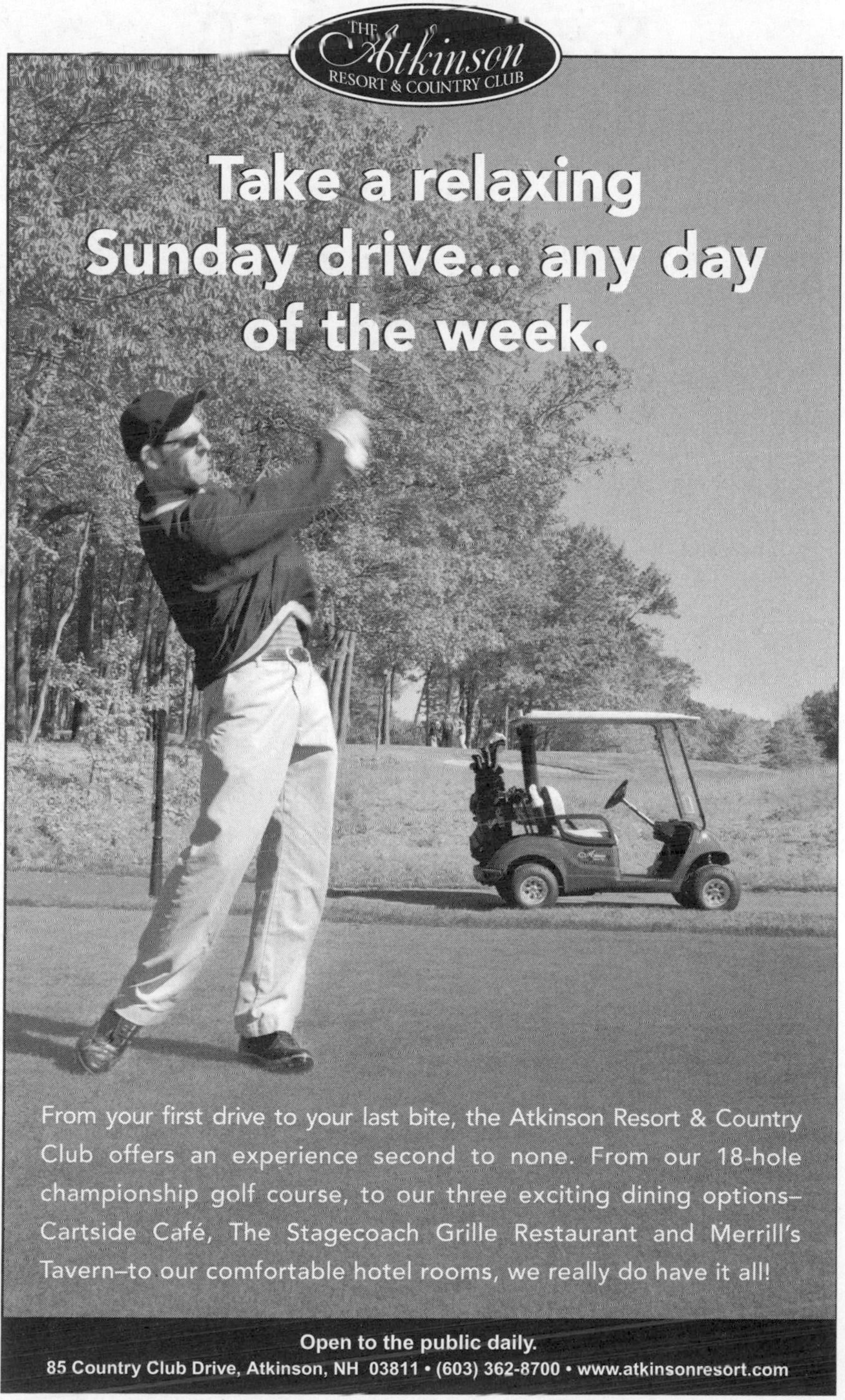
THE Atkinson
RESORT & COUNTRY CLUB
Take a relaxing Sunday drive... any day of the week.
From your first drive to your last bite, the Atkinson Resort & Country Club offers an experience second to none. From our 18-hole championship golf course, to our three exciting dining options–Cartside Café, The Stagecoach Grille Restaurant and Merrill's Tavern–to our comfortable hotel rooms, we really do have it all!
Open to the public daily.
85 Country Club Drive, Atkinson, NH 03811 • (603) 362-8700 • www.atkinsonresort.com

Breakfast Hill Golf Club | Greenland, NH

Try It, Just Once...

Serving as working New Hampshire farmland until 1956, a long-lived dream became a reality in 2000 when a championship 18-hole layout was completed. Quaintly nestled under trademark soaring pines sits an upscale public golf course still premature in age yet in its prime amongst the area's best layouts.

Breakfast Hill Golf Club, designed by renowned golf course architect Brian Silva, sits on 170 acres of family-owned land dating back more than 250 years.

The championship par 71 layout has consistently been ranked among New Hampshire's very best by multiple golf publications.

The practice facility is one of the most all-inclusive in the area. Every aspect of one's precision can be tested and enhanced. The driving range includes four target greens with varying distances. A practice bunker sits on a hilltop with a sprawling view of the practice facility and the club's closing holes, and the 10,000 square foot putting green can be a perfect boost to one's short game improvement.

The 18-hole track is second to none but experiencing the Hill is not limited to your on-course endeavors. A state-of-the-art clubhouse flanked with cedar shingles and beaming white trim has become home to golf receptions, private business excursions, and jovial celebrations for family and friends, all while overlooking the picturesque patio and finishing holes. Don't forget to visit the expansive golf shop which carries only the best lines in golf equipment and apparel.

In the club's short but storied tenure, the best in state and locally sanctioned golf tournaments, professionals from all walks of life, and average weekend warriors have flocked to the club's rolling fairways, contoured greens, picturesque woodlands, and exposed granite boulders just to say that they experienced "The Hill." As Breakfast Hill quickly approaches its first decade of excellence, come enjoy a hospitable day on the links while situated on a piece of land that supports the conservation of all its natural resources.

The course is just minutes from I-95 and only an hour from Boston, Manchester, and Portland. Come judge for yourself what Breakfast Hill has to offer. You'll be back.......

Stonebridge Country Club | Goffstown, NH

The Rebirth of Stonebridge CC in Goffstown

Stonebridge Country Club, an award-winning semi-private golf club located just 10 minutes from Manchester and one of the most picturesque courses in New Hampshire, was acquired in July of 2008 by two local families who have already made major investments in the facility.

Most noteworthy are the newly paved cart paths, plus clubhouse renovations and landscaping. Opened in 1997 on a scenic hilltop with commanding views of the surrounding countryside, Stonebridge is home to the #1 golf hole in New Hampshire (according to WMUR television), the breathtaking par 3 sixth, visible as you enter the property.

But don't let the beautiful surroundings and opening holes lull you into complacency — this course demands your full attention. The Phil Wogan design is a championship 6,808 yards long, and is rated 73.3 with a slope of 138. Many holes are tight and hilly, the greens are fast and undulating, while water and bunkers await errant shots. The first 3 holes are fairly open and forgiving. Number four is a pretty par 3 with bunkers protecting the front, and woods behind for those who misjudge the distance on this downhill hole.

After finishing the straightaway par 4 fifth, the fun really begins at number six, the signature hole that reminds many of Augusta's twelfth. From the tips it is 182 yards of carry over a stonewall-framed pond to a side-facing green adjacent to the namesake stone bridge.

So many great holes. There is no relaxing after the turn. The tenth is a long par 5, starting with a serious risk/reward tee shot over trees on the right. Fourteen is the #1 handicap hole and for good reason. It's an intimidating 560 yards from the back, starting with a tight downhill drive and no place to miss right or left. Put your ego and your driver away to escape with a respectable score. Eighteen is a great finishing hole, with an open tee shot followed by a precision second that must navigate two ponds, a bunker and the hill behind its small green.

After your round, Stonebridge offers a full-service restaurant and bar, featuring fireside or outdoor dining. Linger long enough to enjoy the spectacular views and sunsets from the clubhouse deck.

Please see the Stonebridge full color ad inside the back cover.

Windham Country Club | Windham, NH

A Club That Scores and Cares.

Windham Country Club looks like a mighty challenge from many tees. And it is. But if you play smart (maybe the toughest challenge in golf!), you can make pars. Elevated tees and greens, some water here and there, and a few massive boulders make this a memorable course to play.

Local knowledge is a wonderful thing, so repeat visits are highly encouraged to learn the dos and don'ts of where to aim at Windham.

Opened in 1995, this delightful daily fee layout places a real emphasis on golf outings. From the great clubhouse to the attentive pro staff, Windham takes care of a group's whole day. Says Windham head pro Joanne Flynn, "We do literally everything for outing organizers, from setting up their brochures, to signage, hole in one insurance, scoring, on-course contests, pre-event planning, prizes, all day-of-event services, and anything they may need. We can handle any scoring format and of course, all meals. A huge majority of groups who try us end up as repeat customers year after year."

The club also has another specialty: its affiliation with Northeast Passage. Northeast Passage is a nationally recognized leader in the provision of innovative therapeutic recreation services. Northeast Passage delivers disability-related health promotion and adapted sports programs throughout New England, and is a program of the University of New Hampshire's College of Health and Human Services and is an affiliate of Disabled Sports USA.

Windham, in conjunction with Northeast Passage, runs an adaptive golf program to introduce individuals with disabilities to the game through instruction and on-course play.

"We provide specialized clubs, grip aids, as well as solo rider adaptive golf carts," says Flynn, "to make accessing the course easier for wheelchair users and others with mobility impairments." The program helps individuals learn the best way to get back on the course after an injury or experience golf for the first time in a safe and supportive atmosphere. The course provides carts free to those who require them.

Come visit Windham soon.

WINDHAM
W
COUNTRY CLUB

★★★★

Golf Digest

Public Golf Facility with Private Club Atmosphere
Championship 18 hole layout
All Grass Multi-tiered Golf Range
Corporate & Charity Golf Outings Availability
Largest Junior Program in Southern New Hampshire
Handicap Accessible Golf Carts

(603) 434-2093   windhamcc.com

Green Mountain National

Killington, VT

Green Mountain: Accessible & Exceptional

While Vermont has some of the finest golf courses in Northeast, the beauty and design of Green Mountain National Golf Course ranks among the entire region's finest. *New England Golf Guide* ranks GMNGC a four-star for the first time in 2009, and it was admittedly overdue.

With an exceptionally varied, and some might say robust, layout, the course exudes a championship feel, from the pro shop to the lounge, from the mountain setting to the last putt on 18.

It's a great experience for golfers of all ability levels. Multiple tees allow you to take on the course at the appropriate level for your game. In fact, it's not a bad idea at all to play your first round from the

middle tees before hiking to the back tees. A little local knowledge might save a few balls and a few surprises, and give you more confidence for the second round.

Located in the heart of Central Vermont, just off Route 100, the Vermont Golf Trail, just minutes away from the Killington Resort, there are many exceptional lodging choices available within minutes of the course and multiple activities for you and your family to enjoy during your visit.

Green Mountain National is also perfect for outings or tournaments. The course specializes in golf instruction as well as activities designed specifically for women golfers.

What separates this course from others is its unique and challenging design features. Generously carved out of the Green Mountains, the course offers solitude and a private golf experience that delights players and changes from hole to hole.

Although you'll know you're in the mountains, you needn't be a Sherpa to play. Gently sloping fairways that feature generous landing areas, distinctive changes in elevation, and undulating greens provide natural beauty. View the centuries-old rock formations carved by the glaciers, and be sure to stop a moment on the #16 Tee, as you enjoy the panoramic views in a spectacular setting.

Take a moment to explore the website gmngc.com and see what Green Mountain National Golf Course has to offer.

Please see the Green Mountain National full color ad in the front of the book.

PICTURED: *One of the many picturesque greens at Green Mountain National.*

Haystack | Wilmington, VT

At the southern end of Vermont lies a wonderful Desmond Muirhead design: Haystack Golf Club in Wilmington. Though the course has undergone many changes since Muirhead's original work in 1972, most are in the area of conditioning, new grasses, and refinement.

Today a first-time player is struck by the beauty of the course, as it wraps around the hillsides and ridges of this ski-region landscape. Such placement means elevated tees and greens, and occasional sidehill lies if one isn't driving right down the middle.

Though hilly, many find it eminently walkable.

Granite outcroppings frame some greens and fairways, as do long wooded lanes. What players comment upon most are the greens: "Slippery, sweet, and true," says Jim Baxter, a vacationer from Michigan. Several greens have sizable breaks, influenced by the surrounding hillsides, but one must be alert and sometimes step back to get perspective. "I read putts on two holes in a row that broke the totally opposite direction from what I saw!" says Baxter. "That was worth $5," laughs his partner Allen Durell.

That's one of the quirks of mountain golf, and one of the delights of a little local knowledge going a long way.

For those who love drivers, come on down. Several generous fairways await the "big dog," including the spectacular par 5 eleventh hole, which features a 250-foot drop-off from the tee. Whale away and you might have just a short iron to the green. From there, you face long and short, up and down holes that will delight just about any player.

With a slope of 128 from the blues at 6549 yards, and slope 125/6164 yards from the whites, Haystack presents an opportunity to score well or card a few double bogeys—that part is up to you.

The clubhouse sports a fine grill and bar overlooking the course, the 19th Hole Lounge, complete with a billiards table if you still have that urge to sink a few.

Come try Haystack, and call about the stay-and-play packages.

Mt. Anthony Country Club | Bennington, VT

For the past 18 months a major restoration has been underway to transform Mt. Anthony Country Club's scenic 18-hole course into one of Vermont's premier golf destinations. With spectacular Green Mountain vistas, the renovated tee boxes, bunkers, cart paths, fairways, and greens promise an exciting challenge for golfers of all skill levels.

Mount Anthony's design might be described as "short and sneaky," according to one local player. There are lots of hills and sidehill lies, complicated by approach shots to smallish, old style greens. (The club moved its course location to its present site in 1927.)

While the club is slowly enlarging some of the greens (maybe one or two a year), the course will retain its classic look and feel. The greens have a reputation for speed—it's definitely possible to putt off the green during drier days. Because of the hills, a player gets spectacular vistas from certain tee boxes or greens, and it's an absolute rainbow during the fall foliage season. The old growth pines, maples, and birches line and define the direction of play.

The club has added a new locker room, and a four-star restaurant serves ready to serve the public seven days a week. Although Mount Anthony has memberships, the club is open to the public.

But Mt. Anthony has even more to offer. Take advantage of the luxurious locker rooms before a delicious lunch, dinner, or cocktails in the newly-renovated clubhouse and restaurant. The grille offers refined American cuisine in a warm and casual ambiance. The banquet rooms and catering service are available year round for events with up to 225 guests. While visiting us, be sure to stop by the fully stocked golf shop.

Come see what's new at one of Vermont's oldest and most beloved country clubs. You'll fall in love with Mt. Anthony all over again.

MT. ANTHONY
COUNTRY CLUB
——— 1897 ———

Experience the new Mt. Anthony
Open to the public seven days a week

- Redesigned 18 Hole, par 71 course, nestled in the Green Mountains
- Newly renovated Clubhouse, Locker Rooms, Golf Shop
- Fine dining at The GRILLE serving lunch and dinner daily
- Elegant banquet facilities available for 10 - 225 guests year round
- Golf Rates Weekdays (Mon - Thurs)   18 Holes $45
  Weekends (Fri, Sat, Sun and Holidays) 18 Holes $55
  Cart Fees (optional) $18 per person. New fleet of carts.
- 2009 Memberships available. Call Clubhouse at 802-442-2617

Located a few blocks from Historic Old Bennington; one hour east of Albany; 25 minutes from Williamstown, MA and 25 minutes from Manchester, VT. Only 3.5 hours from NYC and Boston.

180 Country Club Dr. Bennington VT 05201 802-447-7079 www.mtanthonycc.com

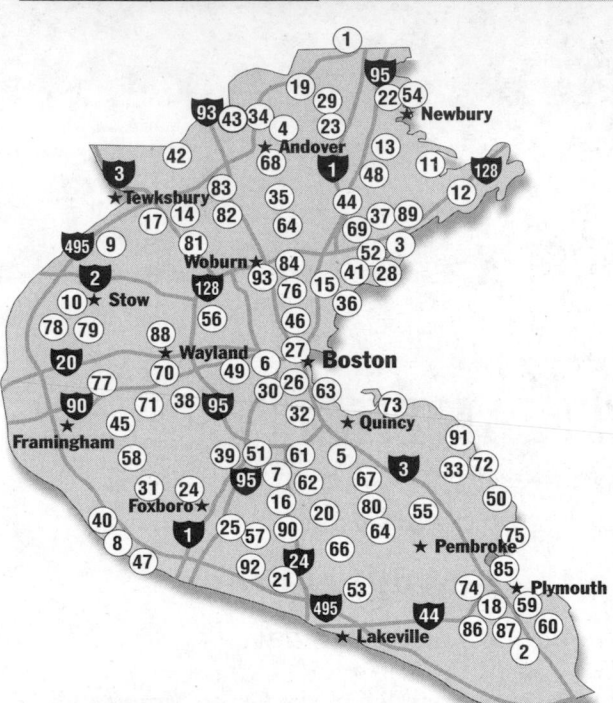
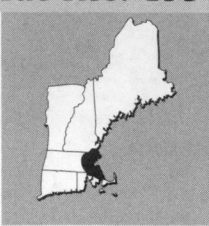

Olde Salem Greens	52
Olde Scotland Links	53
Ould Newbury GC	54
Pembroke Country Club	55
Pine Meadows GC	56
Pine Oaks GC	57
Pinecrest Golf Club	58
Pinehills Golf Club (Jones)	59
Pinehills Golf Club (Nicklaus)	60
Ponkapoag GC (#1)	61
Ponkapoag GC (#2)	62
Presidents Golf Course	63
Reedy Meadow GC at Lynnfield	64
Ridder Golf Club	65
River Bend CC	66
Rockland Country Club	67
Rolling Green GC	68
Sagamore Spring GC	69
Sandy Burr CC	70
Sassamon Trace Golf Course	71
Scituate Country Club	72
South Shore CC	73
Southers Marsh Golf Club	74
Squirrel Run CC	75
Stoneham Oaks	76
Stony Brook Golf Course	77
Stow Acres CC (North)	78
Stow Acres CC (South)	79
Strawberry Valley GC	80
Swanson Meadows	81
Tewksbury CC	82
Trull Brook Golf Course	83
Unicorn Golf Course	84
Village Links	85
Waverly Oaks Golf Club	86
Waverly Oaks–Challenger 9	87
Wayland Country Club	88
Wenham Country Club	89
White Pines Golf Course	90
Widow's Walk Golf Course	91
Willowdale Golf Course	92
Woburn Country Club	93

Amesbury Golf & CC	1	Franklin Park	26
Atlantic Country Club	2	Fresh Pond Golf Club	27
Beverly Golf & Tennis	3	Gannon Muni. GC	28
Bradford Country Club	4	Garrison Golf Center	29
Braintree Muni. GC	5	George Wright GC	30
Brookline GC at Putterham	6	Glen Ellen CC	31
Brookmeadow CC	7	Granite Links Golf Club	32
Bungay Brook Golf Club	8	Green Harbor Golf Club	33
Butter Brook Golf Club	9	Hickory Hill GC	34
Butternut Farm GC	10	Hillview Golf Course	35
Candlewood Golf Club	11	Kelley Greens By The Sea	36
Cape Ann Golf Club	12	Lakeview Golf Club	37
Carriage Pines	13	Leo J. Martin GC	38
CC of Billerica	14	Lost Brook Golf Club	39
Cedar Glen Golf Club	15	Maplegate Country Club	40
Cedar Hill Golf Club	16	Meadow at Peabody, The	41
Chelmsford Country Club	17	Meadow Creek	42
Crosswinds Golf Club	18	Merrimack Valley GC	43
Crystal Springs CC	19	Middleton Golf Course	44
D.W. Fields Golf Course	20	Millwood Farm Golf Course	45
Easton Country Club	21	Mt. Hood Golf Course	46
Evergreen Valley GC	22	New England CC	47
Far Corner Golf Course	23	New Meadows GC	48
Fore Kicks GC & Sports Complex	24	Newton Commonwealth GC	49
		North Hill CC	50
Foxborough Country Club	25	Norwood Country Club	51

Amesbury Golf & Country Club   NR   1

Monroe Street
Amesbury, MA (978) 388-5153
www.amesburygolf.com

Tees	Holes	Yards	Par	USGA	Slope
BACK					
MIDDLE	9	3048	35	70.5	125
FRONT	9	2691	35	71.9	126

Club Pro: Butch Mellon
Payment: Cash, Personal Checks
Tee Times: 5 days adv.
Fee 9 Holes: Weekday: $18   **Weekend:** $20
Fee 18 Holes: Weekday: $28   **Weekend:** $32
Twilight Rates: No   **Discounts:** None
Cart Rental: $15pp/18, $7.50pp/9   **Driving Range:** No
Lessons: No **Schools:** No   **Junior Golf:** Yes
Membership: Yes   **Architect/Yr Open:** Wayne Stiles/1923
Other: Clubhouse / Lockers / Showers / Snack Bar / Bar-Lounge

Great 1st tee panorama. Featured in *Yankee Magazine*. Beaches nearby. Fairways are better!

	1	2	3	4	5	6	7	8	9
PAR	4	3	4	4	5	4	4	3	4
YARDS	381	170	349	309	524	299	365	162	380
PAR									
YARDS									

Directions: Take I-95 North to Route 110 West; then take right at lights near Burger King; take right onto Monroe Street. Course is 1/3 mile on left.

Atlantic Country Club   ✪✪✪   2

450 Little Sandy Pond Road
Plymouth, MA (508) 759-6644
www.atlanticcountryclub.com

Tees	Holes	Yards	Par	USGA	Slope
BACK	18	6262	72	70.8	127
MIDDLE	18	5840	72	69.0	119
FRONT	18	4918	72	68.3	116

Club Pro: Don Daley, PGA
Payment: Cash, Visa, MC
Tee Times: 7 days adv.
Fee 9 Holes: Weekday: $28 M-Th   **Weekend:** $33 F/S/S/H
Fee 18 Holes: Weekday: $48 M-Th   **Weekend:** $58 F/S/S/H
Twilight Rates: After 3pm   **Discounts:** None
Cart Rental: $18pp/18, $9pp/9   **Driving Range:** Yes
Lessons: $30/half hour **Schools:** No   **Junior Golf:** No
Membership: Yes   **Architect/Yr:** Cornish, Silva, & Mungeam/1994
Other: Soft Drinks / Snack Bar / Banquet Facilities

COUPON

Players Comments: "Great track at a reasonable price. Many fine holes with challenging tee box selection. Compares with the best in state." "Great putting greens." Mon-Thurs, 12:30 - 2:30pm special.

	1	2	3	4	5	6	7	8	9
PAR	4	3	4	5	4	5	3	4	4
YARDS	302	144	410	475	343	467	134	387	345
	10	11	12	13	14	15	16	17	18
PAR	4	3	4	4	5	4	5	3	4
YARDS	336	156	310	281	460	330	491	105	364

Directions: Route 3 to Exit 2. Take left at bottom of Exit ramp. Take first right onto Herring Pond Road. Right onto Long Pond Road. Left onto Carter's Bridge Road. Right onto Upland Road to Little Sandy Pond Road. Course is 1 mile on left.

Beverly Golf & Tennis

★★½ **3**

134 McKay Street
Beverly, MA (978) 922-9072
www.beverlygolfandtennisclub.net

Tees	Holes	Yards	Par	USGA	Slope
BACK	18	6237	70	70.1	123
MIDDLE	18	5966	70	69.2	121
FRONT	18	5429	73	70.3	113

Club Pro: Rich Nagel
Payment: All Major
Tee Times: 7 days adv.
Fee 9 Holes: Weekday: $22   **Weekend:** $24
Fee 18 Holes: Weekday: $40   **Weekend:** $45
Twilight Rates: S/S after 2pm $39 w/cart   **Discounts:** Senior & Junior
Cart Rental: $15pp/18, $16/9 per cart   **Driving Range:** Practice area
Lessons: By appointment   **Schools:** Yes   **Junior Golf:** Yes
Membership: Yes   **Architect/Yr Open:** 1910
Other: Clubhouse / Lockers / Showers / Snack Bar / Restaurant / Bar-Lounge

Player Comments: "Several long par 4s. Good challenge." Members weekends until 1:30. Resident discount.

	1	2	3	4	5	6	7	8	9
PAR	4	4	3	4	4	3	4	5	4
YARDS	431	413	147	390	271	159	372	571	300
	10	11	12	13	14	15	16	17	18
PAR	4	3	3	5	4	3	4	5	4
YARDS	266	235	193	462	347	143	382	500	384

Directions: I-95/Route 128 to Exit 20B, right off ramp. Go through fork keeping Henry's Market on your right. Next fork go left, 1/2 mile on right.

Bradford Country Club

★★ **4**

201 Chadwick Road
Bradford, MA (978) 372-8587
www.bradfordcc.com

Tees	Holes	Yards	Par	USGA	Slope
BACK	18	6311	70	72.4	132
MIDDLE	18	5697	70	69.6	127
FRONT	18	4614	70	67.6	123

Club Pro: Peter Vlahos, PGA
Payment: Visa, MC, Amex, Disc
Tee Times: 5 days adv.
Fee 9 Holes: Weekday: $19   **Weekend:** $22
Fee 18 Holes: Weekday: $37   **Weekend:** $42
Twilight Rates: No   **Discounts:** Senior & Junior
Cart Rental: $18pp/18, $10pp/9   **Driving Range:** No
Lessons: $35/half hour, $60/hour   **Schools:** No   **Junior Golf:** Yes
Membership: Yes   **Architect/Yr Open:** Cornish & Silva/1989
Other: Clubhouse / Bar-Lounge / Restaurant / Lockers / Outings / Leagues
GPS: Yes

Clubhouse and 8 holes newly remodeled. All carts have GPS. Open March - November.

	1	2	3	4	5	6	7	8	9
PAR	4	4	3	4	4	3	4	5	4
YARDS	368	346	156	375	382	146	353	491	479
	10	11	12	13	14	15	16	17	18
PAR	4	3	5	4	4	4	4	3	4
YARDS	427	195	510	413	418	401	410	171	428

Directions: I-495 to Exit 48. North on Route 125 to Salem Street. Turn right. Right onto Boxford Road (1st street after Bradford House Restaurant). Take first right on Chadwick Road to Clubhouse.

Braintree Muni Golf Course ✪✪✪ 5

101 Jefferson Street
Braintree, MA (781) 843-6513
www.braintreegolf.com

Tees	Holes	Yards	Par	USGA	Slope
BACK	18	6554	72	71.6	129
MIDDLE	18	6212	72	70.5	127
FRONT	18	5386	72	71.0	117

Club Pro: Bob Beach
Payment: Cash, Visa, MC
Tee Times: 6 days adv.
Fee 9 Holes: Weekday: None **Weekend:** None
Fee 18 Holes: Weekday: $36 **Weekend:** $45
Twilight Rates: After 4pm **Discounts:** Residents, Seniors, Juniors
Cart Rental: $15/18, $7.50/9 per cart **Driving Range:** Limited
Lessons: $50/half hour **Schools:** **Junior Golf:**
Membership: **Architect/Yr Open:**
Other: Restaurant / Clubhouse / Snack Bar **GPS:**

2005 NE PGA Teacher of the Year, specializing in disabled players. "An overlooked gem. Generous fairways combine with great sloping greens and excellent conditions. Best value in Greater Boston." –JD

	1	2	3	4	5	6	7	8	9
PAR	4	4	3	4	3	5	4	5	4
YARDS	335	335	171	302	165	494	383	500	364
	10	**11**	**12**	**13**	**14**	**15**	**16**	**17**	**18**
PAR	5	4	3	5	4	4	3	4	4
YARDS	481	408	172	465	411	391	174	347	314

Directions: I-93 to Route 3 South to Exit 6. Take Route 37 South for 2 miles. Right on Jefferson Street. Club is on the right.

Brookline GC at Putterham ✪✪ 6

1281 West Roxbury Parkway
Brookline, MA (617) 730-2078
www.brooklinegolfclub.com

Tees	Holes	Yards	Par	USGA	Slope
BACK	18	6317	71	70.4	124
MIDDLE	18	5958	71	68.4	117
FRONT	18	5596	72	72.5	119

Club Pro: B. Bain, PGA, J. Neville, Dir.
Payment: Visa, MC, Amex, Cash
Tee Times: 3 days adv.
Fee 9 Holes: Weekday: $23 M-Th till 7:30am **Weekend:** $27 6am-7am
Fee 18 Holes: Weekday: $36 M-Th **Weekend:** $49 F/S/S/H
Twilight Rates: After 4pm **Discounts:** Residents, Juniors
Cart Rental: $18pp/18, $13pp/9 **Driving Range:** No
Lessons: $45/half hour **Schools:** Junior **Junior Golf:** Yes
Membership: No **Architect/Yr Open:** Stiles & Van Kleek/1931
Other: Restaurant / Clubhouse / Bar-Lounge **GPS:**

Tight fairways, elevated greens, low terrain, small hills, and lots of brooks. Dress code: collared shirts.

	1	2	3	4	5	6	7	8	9
PAR	5	4	3	4	3	5	4	4	4
YARDS	460	335	148	317	177	506	340	390	365
	10	**11**	**12**	**13**	**14**	**15**	**16**	**17**	**18**
PAR	4	4	3	4	4	5	4	3	4
YARDS	330	290	119	380	400	520	330	160	391

Directions: I-95 to Route 9 East, 4 miles to Chestnut Hill Mall on left. Exit onto Hammond Street. Go to rotary; 4th right to Newton Street. 100 yrds on left. From Boston: Route 9 to Hammond Street. Turn left. 1 mile to rotary — 4th right to Newton Street. 100 yards on left.

Brookmeadow Country Club

NR   ▶ 7

100 Everendon Road
Canton, MA (781) 828-4444
www.brookmeadowgolf.com

Tees	Holes	Yards	Par	USGA	Slope
BACK	18	6659	72	71.7	123
MIDDLE	18	6239	72	70.1	118
FRONT	18	5606	72	71.2	114

Club Pro: Steve Landi, PGA
Payment: Cash, Visa, MC
Tee Times: 7 days adv.
Fee 9 Holes: Weekday: $25 M-Th after 1pm **Weekend:**
Fee 18 Holes: Weekday: $40 M-Th   **Weekend:** $56 F/S/S/H
Twilight Rates: After 4pm   **Discounts:**
Cart Rental: $9pp/9, $16pp/18   **Driving Range:**
Lessons: Call for rates **Schools:** No   **Junior Golf:** Yes
Membership: Yes   **Architect/Yr Open:** Frank Simoni/1967
Other: Clubhouse / Lockers / Showers / Snack Bar / Bar-Lounge / Function Room

Relatively flat, easy to walk, but fun and challenging for all levels. "Many improvements. If you haven't been in 5 years, it's definitely worth a new visit." –RJ

	1	2	3	4	5	6	7	8	9
PAR	4	4	4	3	4	3	4	5	5
YARDS	376	387	308	163	346	151	385	434	522
	10	**11**	**12**	**13**	**14**	**15**	**16**	**17**	**18**
PAR	4	3	5	4	4	3	5	4	4
YARDS	348	179	454	351	358	192	530	351	404

Directions: I-95 to exit 11A (Neponset Street in Canton). Go 1 mile and take a right before the viaduct (stone bridge) onto Walpole Street. Club is 1 mile on right.

Bungay Brook Golf Club

✪✪½   ▶ 8

30 Locust Street
Bellingham, MA (508) 883-1600
www.bungaybrook.com

Tees	Holes	Yards	Par	USGA	Slope
BACK	9	3136	36	70.2	120
MIDDLE	9	2885	36	69.2	113
FRONT	9	2314	36	66.8	110

Club Pro: Jim Cook, PGA, Teaching Pro
Payment: Visa, MC, Amex
Tee Times: 2 weeks in adv.
Fee 9 Holes: Weekday: $21 before noon/$27 after noon
         Weekend: $28 F/S/S
Fee 18 Holes: Weekday: $42 before noon/$46 after noon
         Weekend: $52 F/S/S

COUPON

Twilight Rates: No   **Discounts:** Senior & Junior
Cart Rental: $6pp/9   **Driving Range:** Yes
Lessons: Yes **Schools:**   **Junior Golf:**
Membership: No   **Architect/Yr Open:** Howard Maurer/2002
Other: Restaurant / Bar-Lounge   **GPS:**

Fine conditions, fast greens, fast pace. All-grass driving range. Worth a visit.

	1	2	3	4	5	6	7	8	9
PAR	4	3	4	5	3	4	5	4	4
YARDS	278	153	313	450	107	421	434	393	336
PAR									
YARDS									

Directions: I-495 to Exit 16. 4 miles to Bellingham town line. First left Locust Street; 1/2 mile to course.

Butter Brook Golf Club ✪✪✪✪ ▶9

157 Carlisle Road
Westford, MA (978) 692-6560
www.butterbrookgc.com

Tees	Holes	Yards	Par	USGA	Slope
BACK	18	6702	72	72.6	133
MIDDLE	18	6174	72	70.4	128
FRONT	18	4849	72	69.4	120

Club Pro: Matt Hibbert, PGA
Payment: Visa, MC, Amex, Disc
Tee Times: 7 days adv.
Fee 9 Holes: Weekday: $35   **Weekend:** After 3pm
Fee 18 Holes: Weekday: $50   **Weekend:** $78 w/cart
Twilight Rates: After 3pm, $45 wkd/9, $65 wkd/18
Discounts: Senior & Junior - $5 off weekday
Cart Rental: $9pp/9, $18pp/18   **Driving Range:** Yes
Lessons: Yes **Schools:** Yes   **Junior Golf:** Yes
Membership: Yes   **Architect/Yr Open:** Mark Mungeam/2002
Other: Bar-Lounge   **GPS:**

COUPON

"Family-owned and operated with great pride. Challenging track with wonderful variety." –JD
180 acres of serene rolling hills, tall pine trees, beautiful ponds, and a babbling brook. Now 18 holes.
Voted one of the 100 Must Play Courses in New England.

	1	2	3	4	5	6	7	8	9
PAR	5	4	3	4	3	4	5	3	5
YARDS	517	316	136	403	136	436	554	171	618
	10	11	12	13	14	15	16	17	18
PAR	4	3	5	4	3	4	5	4	4
YARDS	383	249	521	321	199	447	524	416	355

Directions: I-495 Exit 32 Boston Road toward Route 225/Westford. Proceed toward Route 110
(.3 miles). Cross over Route 110. Follow for 1.2 miles to end of road. Left onto Route 225 East for
1.2 miles. Entrance on right.

Butternut Farm Golf Club ✪✪✪ ▶10

115 Wheeler Road
Stow, MA (978) 897-3400
www.butternutfarm.com

Tees	Holes	Yards	Par	USGA	Slope
BACK	18	6302	70	71.2	130
MIDDLE	18	5755	70	69.3	126
FRONT	18	4778	70	67.6	117

Club Pro: Trevor Page
Payment: Most Major
Tee Times: 5 days adv.
Fee 9 Holes: Weekday: $26   **Weekend:**
Fee 18 Holes: Weekday: $37 M-Th, $42 F   **Weekend:** $49
Twilight Rates: After 2pm $38, after 3pm $29   **Discounts:** Senior
Cart Rental: $16pp/18   **Driving Range:** No
Lessons: No **Schools:** No   **Junior Golf:** No
Membership: Yes   **Architect/Yr Open:** Robert Page III/1993
Other: Clubhouse / Restaurant / Bar-Lounge / Snack Bar / Lockers / Function Rooms

Brand new clubhouse. Carolina-type fairways, real tight, bent grass on fairways and tees, tall trees. "Great
shape. Greens are lush. Challenging, fair—but choose the right tees—or else." Four function rooms.

	1	2	3	4	5	6	7	8	9
PAR	4	3	4	3	4	4	5	4	5
YARDS	314	155	375	150	403	383	434	268	452
	10	11	12	13	14	15	16	17	18
PAR	5	3	4	3	4	4	3	4	4
YARDS	600	128	351	190	364	325	173	340	350

Directions: I-495 to Exit 27. Take Route 117 East for approximately 4 miles. Take right onto Wheeler
Road. Or, Route 2 West to Route 62 West. Follow through Stow center to 1st set of lights. Take left.
2nd right is Wheeler Road.

Candlewood Golf Course   NR 11

75 Essex Road (Route 133)
Ipswich, MA (978) 356-5377

Club Pro:
Payment: Cash only
Tee Times: No
Fee 9 Holes: Weekday: $14
Fee 18 Holes: Weekday: $19
Twilight Rates: After 5pm $11
Cart Rental: $20pp/18, $12pp/9
Lessons: Schools: No
Membership: Yes
Other: Snack Bar

Tees	Holes	Yards	Par	USGA	Slope
BACK					
MIDDLE	9	2108	32		
FRONT					

Weekend: $15
Weekend: $20
Discounts: Senior
Driving Range: No
Junior Golf: No
Architect/Yr Open:
GPS:

Course is easy to walk and good for senior citizens and beginners.
Monday-Friday Senior Citizens play for $10.

	1	2	3	4	5	6	7	8	9
PAR	4	4	3	3	3	4	4	4	3
YARDS	350	350	120	140	135	253	290	280	190
PAR									
YARDS									

Directions: I-95/Route 128 to Route 1A to Route 133 in Ipswich. Turn right at hospital on 133.

Cape Ann Golf Club   NR 12

99 John Wilse Avenue (Route 133)
Essex, MA (978) 768-7544
www.capeanngolf.com

Club Pro: No
Payment: Cash, Visa, MC
Tee Times: Yes
Fee 9 Holes: Weekday: $20
Fee 18 Holes: Weekday: $35
Twilight Rates: After 4pm
Cart Rental: $13pp/18, $8pp/9, $3/pull
Lessons: No **Schools:** No
Membership: Yes
Other: Bar-Lounge / Snack Bar

Tees	Holes	Yards	Par	USGA	Slope
BACK					
MIDDLE	9	5862	69	67.2	110
FRONT	9	4424	68	65.2	102

Weekend: $20
Weekend: $35
Discounts: Senior & Junior
Driving Range: No
Junior Golf: No
Architect/Yr Open: Donald Ross/1931
GPS:

Recent improvements include irrigation, putting green and new tee boxes.

	1	2	3	4	5	6	7	8	9
PAR	4	4	3	4	4	4	3	4	4
YARDS	342	364	169	414	336	278	197	385	341
	10	11	12	13	14	15	16	17	18
PAR	4	4	3	5	4	4	3	4	4
YARDS	357	379	181	462	346	289	258	410	354

Directions: I-95/Route 128 to Exit 15 (School Street); follow signs toward Essex. Go North on Route 133. Course is 2 miles up on the right.

Carriage Pines Golf Club

NR 13 ▶

235 Dodge Road
Rowley, MA (978) 948-2731
www.rowleygolf.com

Tees	Holes	Yards	Par	USGA	Slope
BACK					
MIDDLE	9	3325	36	70.7	127
FRONT	9	2470	70	67.5	109

Club Pro: Paul Nimblett, Tammy White
Payment: Visa, MC, Amex, Disc
Tee Times: 1 week in adv.
Fee 9 Holes: Weekday: $18 **Weekend:** $20
Fee 18 Holes: Weekday: $33 **Weekend:** $37
Twilight Rates: Before 8am & after 6pm **Discounts:** Senior & Junior
Cart Rental: $28pp/18, $14pp/9 **Driving Range:** $10/lg, $6/med, $4/sm
Lessons: Yes **Schools:** Yes **Junior Golf:** Yes
Membership: Yes **Architect/Yr Open:**
Other: Clubhouse / Restaurant / Bar-Lounge / Short Game School / Parent-Child Lessons

COUPON

Formerly Rowley Country Club. "Voted best 9-hole course on the North Shore." –JF (PGA) Nike golf camps. Condition is best ever. Come try us. Yardage below from back tees.

	1	2	3	4	5	6	7	8	9
PAR	4	3	4	5	4	4	3	5	4
YARDS	390	210	435	480	360	360	225	500	365
PAR									
YARDS									

Directions: I-95 to Exit 54A (Rowley/Georgetown). 2 miles to Carriage Pines Golf Club sign and make left. Follow for 1 mile, club is on right.

Cedar Glen Golf Club

NR 14 ▶

60 Water Street
Saugus, MA
(781) 233-3609

Tees	Holes	Yards	Par	USGA	Slope
BACK	9	3014	35		
MIDDLE	9	2945	35	67.0	107
FRONT	9	1500	35	67	107

Club Pro:
Payment: Cash Only (ATM on premises)
Tee Times: No
Fee 9 Holes: Weekday: $20 **Weekend:** $29
Fee 18 Holes: Weekday: **Weekend:**
Twilight Rates: No **Discounts:** Senior & Junior $14 wkdays
Cart Rental: $13pp/9 **Driving Range:** No
Lessons: No **Schools:** **Junior Golf:** No
Membership: No **Architect/Yr Open:**
Other: Clubhouse / Snack Bar **GPS:**

New watering system. New tees. Friendly fun course; lots of regulars.

	1	2	3	4	5	6	7	8	9
PAR	4	5	3	4	4	3	4	4	4
YARDS	350	475	220	335	380	135	310	340	400
PAR									
YARDS									

Directions: Take I-95 to Walnut Street. Follow Walnut Street east to Water Street. Take right, course is on left.

Cedar Hill Golf Club

NR ▶ 15

1137 Park Street
Stoughton, MA (781) 344-8913
www.stoughton.org

Tees	Holes	Yards	Par	USGA	Slope
BACK	9	2208	33	61.2	105
MIDDLE	9	2155	33	61.2	105
FRONT					

Club Pro: No
Payment: Cash Only
Tee Times: No
Fee 9 Holes: Weekday: $18
Fee 18 Holes: Weekday: $22
Twilight Rates: After 4pm
Cart Rental: $25pp/18, $15pp/9 $3/pull
Lessons: No Schools: No
Membership: Yes
Other: Snack Bar / Bar-Lounge / Clubhouse

Weekend: $21
Weekend: $25
Discounts: Senior & Junior
Driving Range: No
Junior Golf: No
Architect/Yr Open:
GPS:

A place to come play a quick enjoyable round especially for ladies and seniors. Get a frequent player card, play 9 rounds and get the 10th free.

	1	2	3	4	5	6	7	8	9
PAR	4	4	4	4	3	4	3	3	4
YARDS	258	302	286	268	120	324	140	176	281
PAR									
YARDS									

Directions: Route 24, Exit 18B, turn onto Route 27. Course is on left.

Chelmsford Country Club

NR ▶ 16

66 Park Road
Chelmsford, MA (978) 256-1818
www.sterlinggolf.com

Tees	Holes	Yards	Par	USGA	Slope
BACK					
MIDDLE	9	2427	33	64.2	108
FRONT	9	2202	34	66.1	109

Club Pro: Brad Durrin, PGA
Payment: Visa, MC, Amex, Discover, Cash
Tee Times: 4 days adv.
Fee 9 Holes: Weekday: $18
Fee 18 Holes: Weekday: $24
Twilight Rates: Weekends only
Cart Rental: $14pp/18, $8pp/9
Lessons: Yes Schools: Yes
Membership: Yes
Other: Snack Bar / Bar-Lounge / Function Hall

Weekend: $20
Weekend: $27
Discounts: Senior & Junior
Driving Range: Yes
Junior Golf: Yes
Architect/Yr Open: 1954; C. Fitzgerald/1962
GPS:

COUPON

A fun golf course for all playing levels. Overall enhanced conditions. Managed by Sterling Golf Management, Inc. Beginner-friendly course. Bar and lounge.

	1	2	3	4	5	6	7	8	9
PAR	4	3	3	5	4	3	4	4	3
YARDS	237	196	140	453	352	120	318	415	196
PAR									
YARDS									

Directions: I-495 to Route 110 to Chelmsford Center. Then take Route 27 South. Take left onto Park Road. Course is 200 yards on left.

Country Club of Billerica

NR 17

Baldwin Road
Billerica, MA
(978) 667-9121 ext. 22
www.countryclubofbillerica.com

Tees	Holes	Yards	Par	USGA	Slope
BACK	18	5847	69	67.9	123
MIDDLE	18	5598	69	66.4	119
FRONT	18	4791	69	66.5	115

Club Pro: Steve Miller
Payment: Cash or Credit Card
Tee Times: Call 12pm Tues for S/S/H
Fee 9 Holes: Weekday: $21   **Weekend:** $23
Fee 18 Holes: Weekday: $31   **Weekend:** $35
Twilight Rates: After 6pm   **Discounts:** None
Cart Rental: $28/18, $18/9 per cart   **Driving Range:** $8 large, $6 small
Lessons: $45/half hour **Schools:** Yes   **Junior Golf:** Yes
Membership: Yes   **Architect/Yr Open:** Phil Wogan/1971
Other: Restaurant / Bar-Lounge / Clubhouse   **GPS:**

COUPON

Challenging and affordable for all. Picturesque layout between tall trees. Easy walk. New green on #5 in 2006. Great 19th hole.

	1	2	3	4	5	6	7	8	9
PAR	5	3	4	5	3	4	3	3	4
YARDS	465	160	371	490	115	376	147	138	392
	10	**11**	**12**	**13**	**14**	**15**	**16**	**17**	**18**
PAR	4	4	4	3	4	4	3	5	4
YARDS	296	360	234	153	396	294	190	552	382

Directions: I-95/Route 128 to Route 3A North. Take Route 3A North into Billerica Center. Take right before Friendly's restaurant and at the end of the road, take a right and then the third left onto Baldwin Street. Course is on right.

Crosswinds Golf Club

✪✪✪½ 18

424 Long Pond Road
Plymouth, MA (508) 830-1199
www.golfcrosswinds.com

Tees	Holes	Yards	Par	USGA	Slope
BACK	27/18	6523	72	72.1	133
MIDDLE	27/18	7102	72	70.2	129
FRONT	27/18	5371	72	71.7	126

Club Pro: Dan Neary
Payment: Visa, MC, Amex
Tee Times: 7 days adv.
Fee 9 Holes: Weekday: $30 M-Th   **Weekend:** $40 F/S/S/H
Fee 18 Holes: Weekday: $47 M-Th   **Weekend:** $66 F/S/S/H
Twilight Rates: No   **Discounts:**
Cart Rental: $15pp/9, $30pp/18   **Driving Range:** $9 large, $3 small
Lessons: Yes **Schools:** Yes   **Junior Golf:** Yes
Membership: No   **Architect/Yr Open:** Hurdzan/Fry/2002
Other: Bar / Grille / Outdoor Function Area Tented   **GPS:**

COUPON

Player Comments: "Maturing nicely. New superintendent has brought quality way up. "Definitely an upgrade from its first seasons." –JD

	1	2	3	4	5	6	7	8	9
PAR	5	4	4	4	5	3	4	3	4
YARDS	490	355	317	326	491	141	340	162	360
	10	**11**	**12**	**13**	**14**	**15**	**16**	**17**	**18**
PAR	4	3	4	5	5	4	4	3	4
YARDS	370	138	376	475	471	398	296	164	366

Directions: Route 3 to Exit 5. Right off exit onto Long Pond Road. Follow Long Pond Road 4 miles. Crosswinds Golf Club entrance on left.

Crystal Springs Country Club NR 19

940 North Broadway
Haverhill, MA (978) 374-9621

Tees	Holes	Yards	Par	USGA	Slope
BACK	18	6706	72	72.0	114
MIDDLE	18	6436	72	70.8	112
FRONT	18	5596	72	71.1	116

Club Pro: Ed Tompkins, PGA
Payment: Cash Only
Tee Times: Wkends 7 days
Fee 9 Holes: Weekday: $15
Fee 18 Holes: Weekday: $30
Twilight Rates: No
Cart Rental: $30/18, $15/9 per cart
Lessons: $35/half hour **Schools:** No
Membership: Yes
Other: Snack Bar / Restaurant / Bar-Lounge

Weekend: $15 before 8am, after 3pm
Weekend: $40
Discounts: None
Driving Range: Yes
Junior Golf: No
Architect/Yr Open: Geoffrey Cornish/1961
GPS:

Under new management. Golfers who hit for distance will enjoy Crystal Springs.

	1	2	3	4	5	6	7	8	9
PAR	4	3	4	4	5	3	4	5	4
YARDS	367	213	351	395	472	207	387	475	415
	10	**11**	**12**	**13**	**14**	**15**	**16**	**17**	**18**
PAR	4	5	4	3	4	4	3	4	5
YARDS	389	491	394	210	332	316	135	415	472

Directions: I-495 to Exit 50 (Route 97). At end of ramp, go across Route 97 to monument, and turn left at the blinking red light. Course is 2.5 miles on left.

D.W. Fields Golf Course NR 20

331 Oak Street
Brockton, MA (508) 580-7855

Tees	Holes	Yards	Par	USGA	Slope
BACK	18	5972	70	68.4	120
MIDDLE	18	5630	70	66.9	116
FRONT	18	5370	70	70.1	111

Club Pro: Brian Mattos, PGA
Payment: Visa, MC
Tee Times: 1 day adv.
Fee 9 Holes: Weekday: None
Fee 18 Holes: Weekday: $25 (M-Th)
Twilight Rates: After 4pm
Cart Rental: $15pp
Lessons: $30 **Schools:** No
Membership: $300/resident, $1150/non-resident
Architect/Yr Open: Stiles & Van Kleek/1926
Other: Snack Bar

Weekend: None
Weekend: $30
Discounts: Junior
Driving Range: No
Junior Golf: Yes

COUPON

Considered an easy walker. Open year round. Rates could change. New dress code.

	1	2	3	4	5	6	7	8	9
PAR	4	5	5	4	3	4	4	3	4
YARDS	305	485	485	300	165	340	335	135	355
	10	**11**	**12**	**13**	**14**	**15**	**16**	**17**	**18**
PAR	4	4	4	4	3	4	4	3	4
YARDS	315	340	360	405	125	300	345	175	360

Directions: Route 24 to Exit 18B, 3 sets of lights and take a right onto Oak Street. Course is 1.5 miles on the left.

Easton Country Club ◎◎ 21 ▶

265 Purchase Street
South Easton, MA (508) 238-2500
www.eastoncountryclub.com

Club Pro: Tom Green
Payment: Visa, MC, Amex, Disc
Tee Times: 3 days adv.

Tees	Holes	Yards	Par	USGA	Slope
BACK	18	6328	71	68.9	119
MIDDLE	18	6050	71	67.5	114
FRONT	18	5271	71	70.2	112

Fee 9 Holes: Weekday: $24 after 12   **Weekend:** No
Fee 18 Holes: Weekday: $35 (M-Th)   **Weekend:** $40
Twilight Rates: After 4pm   **Discounts:** Senior & Junior
Cart Rental: $13pp/18   **Driving Range:** $6/bucket
Lessons: $40/45 **Schools:** Yes   **Junior Golf:** No
Membership: Full, Weekday, Junior   **Architect/Yr Open:** Sam Mitchell/1961
Other: Clubhouse / Lockers / Showers / Snack Bar / Bar-Lounge / Function Room

New drainage on greens. Wide fairways and large greens make enjoyable round, but look out for the last 4 holes: A par 4 over water, a par 3 over a creek, and 2 long par 4s.

	1	2	3	4	5	6	7	8	9
PAR	4	5	4	3	4	3	4	4	5
YARDS	390	486	269	136	382	159	411	304	488
	10	11	12	13	14	15	16	17	18
PAR	4	4	4	5	3	4	3	4	4
YARDS	331	353	330	519	140	361	162	410	419

Directions: Take Route 24 South to Exit 17B. Take Route 123 West to Route 138 South to Purchase Street on right (approx. 2 miles). Take a right onto Purchase Street; course is 7/10 mile on left.

Evergreen Valley Golf Course NR 22 ▶

18 Boyd Drive
Newburyport, MA (978) 463-8600
www.evergreenvalleygolf.com

Club Pro: Donna Koen
Payment: Cash or Check
Tee Times: No

Tees	Holes	Yards	Par	USGA	Slope
BACK	9	2997	35	67.4	108
MIDDLE	9	2902	35	67.4	108
FRONT	9	2631	35	67.4	108

Fee 9 Holes: Weekday: $10   **Weekend:** $10-$14
Fee 18 Holes: Weekday: $20   **Weekend:** $20-$25
Twilight Rates: No
Discounts: Senior $9 greens fee Tuesdays, $10 greens fee Saturdays
Cart Rental: $25/18, $14/9 per cart, $3/pull   **Driving Range:** No
Lessons: Yes **Schools:** No   **Junior Golf:** No
Membership: Yes   **Architect/Yr Open:** Francis Vitale Sr.
Other: Snack Bar and Deck   **GPS:**

Located in historic Newburyport, MA. 9 holes, 2 sets of tees. Open April - November. Drainage improvements. Fees subject to change.

	1	2	3	4	5	6	7	8	9
PAR	4	4	4	5	3	4	4	3	4
YARDS	370	300	420	460	155	390	305	165	215
PAR									
YARDS									

Directions: I-95 to Exit 57. Go East. Take left on Noble Road (across from Papa Gino's), then left at stop sign. 300 feet on left is entrance to club.

GB
RTE
495

Far Corner Golf Course ✪✪✪ ▶ 23

5 Barker Road
West Boxford, MA (978) 352-8300
www.farcornergolf.com

Tees	Holes	Yards	Par	USGA	Slope
BACK	27/18	6719	72	72.9	130
MIDDLE	27/18	6189	72	70.9	126
FRONT	27/18	5655	73	71.4	115

Club Pro: Bob Flynn, PGA
Payment: Cash, MC, Visa
Tee Times: 7 days adv.
Fee 9 Holes: Weekday: $20.50 **Weekend:** $23
Fee 18 Holes: Weekday: $41 **Weekend:** $46
Twilight Rates: After 4pm weekends **Discounts:** Senior & Junior
Cart Rental: $18pp/18, $9pp/9 **Driving Range:** All grass
Lessons: $45/half hour, 6 lessons for $240 **Junior Golf:** Yes
Membership: No **Schools:** Yes **Architect/Yr Open:** Geoffrey Cornish/1967
Other: Snack Bar / Restaurant / Bar-Lounge / Clubhouse / Showers

A classic on the North Shore. Terrific, friendly staff. 27 holes - 3rd nine: Yardage: 3092, Championship Par: 36, Slope: 131. Enlarged driving range. Open year round.

	1	2	3	4	5	6	7	8	9
PAR	5	4	4	3	4	4	3	4	5
YARDS	510	350	310	190	460	330	170	390	450
	10	11	12	13	14	15	16	17	18
PAR	4	5	4	5	4	3	4	3	4
YARDS	270	470	360	530	380	170	320	135	390

Directions: I-95 North, to Exit 53B to Route 97 Georgetown. Follow to Route 133 West, to West Boxford Village. Go right onto Main Street. Course is 2 miles on left.

Fore Kicks GC & Sports Complex NR ▶ 24

10 Pine Street
Norfolk, MA (508) 384-4433
www.forekicks.com

Tees	Holes	Yards	Par	USGA	Slope
BACK					
MIDDLE	9	1003	27		
FRONT					

Club Pro: C. Estes, J. Marston
Payment: Cash & Credit
Tee Times: Yes
Fee 9 Holes: Weekday: $12/day, $15/night **Weekend:** $15 S/S
Fee 18 Holes: Weekday: $17/day, $20/night **Weekend:** $20 S/S
Twilight Rates: No **Discounts:** Senior & Junior
Cart Rental: $3pp/pull **Driving Range:** Indoors
Lessons: Yes **Schools:** Yes **Junior Golf:** Yes
Membership: Yes **Architect/Yr Open:** Brian Silva/2002
Other: Lounge / Indoor Soccer / Basketball Courts / Pro Shop / Putting Course / Fully Lighted Golf Course to 10pm

COUPON

Links-style. "Impressive multi-sport complex." –AP Lighted for night play. Features an indoor air-conditioned driving range.

	1	2	3	4	5	6	7	8	9
PAR	3	3	3	3	3	3	3	3	3
YARDS	115	112	81	78	118	93	122	127	157
PAR									
YARDS									

Directions: I-495 to Route 1 North to Pine Street Exit in Foxboro. Right-hand turn after exiting Route 1 onto Pine Street. Course is 2 miles down on left.

Foxborough Country Club ✪✪✪ ▶ 25

33 Walnut Street
Foxborough, MA (508) 543-4661
www.foxboroughcc.com

Club Pro: Louis Rivers, PGA
Payment: Visa, MC, Amex, Disc
Tee Times: Call ahead for availability
Fee 9 Holes: Weekday:
Fee 18 Holes: Weekday: $50 M-Th
Twilight Rates: No
Cart Rental: $15pp/18
Lessons: $40/half hour **Schools:** No
Membership: Yes
Other: Restaurant / Bar- Lounge

Weekend:
Weekend: $50 F/S/S/H
Discounts: Junior (up to 18yrs) $15pp/18
Driving Range: Yes
Junior Golf: No
Architect/Yr Open: Geoffrey Cornish/1955
GPS:

Tees	Holes	Yards	Par	USGA	Slope
BACK	18	6850	72	72.2	126
MIDDLE	18	6607	72	70.9	123
FRONT	18	5627	72	73.4	122

Player Comments: "Excellent golf course, tough but fair. Great greens." Be sure to call for tee times. Improved drainage systems. Dress code. Semi-private.

	1	2	3	4	5	6	7	8	9
PAR	4	4	3	5	4	3	4	4	5
YARDS	385	390	190	500	325	185	318	425	531
	10	11	12	13	14	15	16	17	18
PAR	4	5	3	4	4	4	4	3	5
YARDS	385	551	165	325	320	410	425	157	475

Directions: I-95 to Exit 7B (140 North) towards Foxborough. Take first left onto Walnut Street. Club will be on left after stop sign.

Franklin Park (William J. Devine GC) NR ▶ 26

1 Circuit Drive
Dorchester, MA (617) 265-4084

Club Pro: George Lyons
Payment: Visa, MC
Tee Times: Weekends & Holidays
Fee 9 Holes: Weekday: $21.50
Fee 18 Holes: Weekday: $36
Twilight Rates: No
Cart Rental: $20pp/18, $11pp/9
Lessons: $50/half hour **Schools:** No
Membership: Yes, waiting list
Other: Clubhouse / Snack Bar / Lockers / Function Facility

Weekend: $25.50
Weekend: $42
Discounts: Senior & Junior
Driving Range: No
Junior Golf: Yes
Architect/Yr Open: Donald Ross/1896

Tees	Holes	Yards	Par	USGA	Slope
BACK	18	5966	70	69.8	127
MIDDLE	18	5622	70	68.1	121
FRONT	18	5031	7270	64.7	115

Second oldest public course in the US, a Donald Ross design. Some terrific holes, some wet ones. A little money from the state would go a long way to restoring this terrific layout. Across from Franklin Park Zoo.

	1	2	3	4	5	6	7	8	9
PAR	4	4	4	3	4	4	4	3	4
YARDS	378	302	404	163	344	334	370	149	331
	10	11	12	13	14	15	16	17	18
PAR	4	5	4	3	4	3	4	4	5
YARDS	299	502	382	118	338	152	327	267	462

Directions: Follow signs to Franklin Park Zoo. Take 93 North/South. Take Columbia Road exit. Follow Columbia Road to Franklin Park.

Fresh Pond Golf Club ✪✪½ 27

691 Huron Avenue
Cambridge, MA (617) 349-6282
www.freshpondgolf.com
Club Pro: R. Carey, dir. of golf
Payment: Cash, Check, Visa, MC
Tee Times: Weekends only
Fee 9 Holes: Weekday: $22
Fee 18 Holes: Weekday: $32
Twilight Rates: No
Cart Rental: $14pp/18, $9pp/9
Lessons: 50/half hour **Schools:** No
Membership: Yes
Other: Snack Bar, Vending Machines

Tees	Holes	Yards	Par	USGA	Slope
BACK	9	2931	35	70.0	120
MIDDLE	9	2732	35	66.9	111
FRONT	9	2306	35	66.5	114

Weekend: $26
Weekend: $38
Discounts: Sr & Jr $14, residents only
Driving Range: No
Junior Golf: Yes
Architect/Yr Open: Donald Ross
GPS:

Great course for all levels. Season tickets available. Off-season rates. Conditions better than ever. Great pro shop. Open Apr. - Dec.

	1	2	3	4	5	6	7	8	9
PAR	4	4	3	4	5	3	4	3	5
YARDS	417	312	169	401	476	221	370	147	465
PAR									
YARDS									

Directions: I-95 to Route 2 East to Cambridge. Go west on Huron Avenue to course.

Gannon Municipal Golf Course ✪✪½ 28

60 Great Woods Road
Lynn, MA (781) 592-8238
www.gannongolfclub.com
Club Pro: Mike Foster, PGA
Payment: Visa, MC
Tee Times: 2 days adv.
Fee 9 Holes: Weekday: $19
Fee 18 Holes: Weekday: $34
Twilight Rates: After 3:30pm
Cart Rental: $15pp/18, $7.50pp/9
Lessons: No **Schools:** No
Membership: Residents only
Other: Snack Bar / Grille

Tees	Holes	Yards	Par	USGA	Slope
BACK	18	6106	70	69.9	118
MIDDLE	18	6036	70	67.9	113
FRONT	18	5215	71	68.8	115

Weekend: $21 after 3:30pm
Weekend: $42 Spring/Fall only
Discounts: Resident
Driving Range: No
Junior Golf: Yes
Architect/Yr Open: Wayne Stiles
GPS:

Player Comments: "Beautiful well-maintained course. Very busy." Open to public after 3:30pm weekends. Outstanding condition, fabulous layout. Hills galore. Resident rates. Strong junior golf program. 11th hole rebuilt.

	1	2	3	4	5	6	7	8	9
PAR	4	4	4	4	4	3	4	4	3
YARDS	346	309	357	404	333	187	318	414	216
	10	**11**	**12**	**13**	**14**	**15**	**16**	**17**	**18**
PAR	4	4	4	4	3	5	3	4	5
YARDS	309	335	401	383	158	486	228	319	588

Directions: I-95/Route 128 to Exit 44B, Route 129 Lynn, bear right. Take second exit at rotary marked Route 129 Lynn. Go 1.9 miles. Take immediate right after church to Great Woods Road. Go 2 blocks, through 2 stone pillars, turn left. Golf course is up the hill.

Garrison Golf Center

654 Hilldale Avenue
Haverhill, MA (978) 374-9380
www.garrisongolf.com

Club Pro: Ted Murphy
Payment: Cash, Visa, MC
Tee Times: No
Fee 9 Holes: Weekday: $9
Fee 18 Holes: Weekday: $17
Twilight Rates: No
Cart Rental: $1/pull
Lessons: $45/session **Schools:** Yes
Membership: No
Other: 10 play tickets $70

Tees	Holes	Yards	Par	USGA	Slope
BACK					
MIDDLE	9	1005	27		
FRONT					

Weekend: $10
Weekend: $19
Discounts: Senior & Junior
Driving Range: $5/bucket
Junior Golf: Yes
Architect/Yr Open: Manuel Francis
GPS:

COUPON

A short testing 9-hole par 3 with beautiful Vesper Velvet greens. Designed in 1966 by legendary Manuel Francis. Great course for women and juniors.

	1	2	3	4	5	6	7	8	9
PAR	3	3	3	3	3	3	3	3	3
YARDS	105	100	130	75	100	130	130	135	100
PAR									
YARDS									

Directions: I-495 toward Haverhill at Exit 50. Straight across to stop sign. Straight across to next stop, take a left on Hilldale Avenue. Course is 1/4 mile on left.

George Wright Golf Club

420 West Street
Hyde Park, MA (617) 364-2300
www.georgewrightgolfcourse.com

Club Pro: Scott Allen, PGA
Payment: Visa, MC
Tee Times: S/S 2 days adv
Fee 9 Holes: Weekday: $21 M-F
Fee 18 Holes: Weekday: $35 M-F
Twilight Rates: No
Cart Rental: $18pp/18, $10pp/9
Lessons: $40/half hour **Schools:** No
Membership: Yes
Other: Snack Bar / Bar-Lounge

Tees	Holes	Yards	Par	USGA	Slope
BACK	18	6367	70	69.5	126
MIDDLE	18	6166	70	68.6	123
FRONT	18	5054	70	70.3	115

Weekend: $25 S/S/H
Weekend: $41 S/S/H
Discounts: Junior rate, inquire
Driving Range: No
Junior Golf: Yes
Architect/Yr Open: Donald Ross/1938
GPS:

Boston resident rates. When conditions are good, it's a great track. 2008 was a banner year for conditions. Let's hope for a similar 2009. After an easy 2 holes to get you warmed up, it kicks into gear and keeps you working hard the rest of the day.

	1	2	3	4	5	6	7	8	9
PAR	4	4	5	3	4	4	4	3	4
YARDS	367	313	480	150	400	380	387	162	440
	10	11	12	13	14	15	16	17	18
PAR	4	4	4	4	3	5	4	3	4
YARDS	449	347	399	360	182	493	318	158	372

Directions: I-95/Route 128 to Route 1 North to Washington Street (left) in Hyde Park. Take a right onto Beach Street. Follow signs to course.

Glen Ellen Country Club   ✪✪✪   ▶ 31

84 Orchard Street, Route 115
Millis, MA (508) 376-2775
www.glenellencc.com

Tees	Holes	Yards	Par	USGA	Slope
BACK	18	6634	72	72.0	125
MIDDLE	18	6112	72	70.1	123
FRONT	18	5148	72	69.4	122

Club Pro: Andy Ingham, PGA
Payment: Most Major Credit Cards
Tee Times: 7 days adv.
Fee 9 Holes: Weekday: $22
Fee 18 Holes: Weekday: $38
Twilight Rates: 3pm-5pm
Cart Rental: $10pp/18
Lessons: Yes **Schools:** Yes
Membership: Yes
Other: Snack Bar / Showers / Bar-Lounge

Weekend:
Weekend: $50
Discounts: Senior & Junior
Driving Range: $7/bucket
Junior Golf: Yes
Architect/Yr Open: Ron Pritchard/1963
GPS:

COUPON

Classical golf architecture, nicely laid into the existing land. Many wide-open fairways allow plenty of drivers, and ability to recover from errant shots.

	1	2	3	4	5	6	7	8	9
PAR	4	3	4	4	4	5	4	3	5
YARDS	428	155	375	315	346	506	335	119	445
	10	11	12	13	14	15	16	17	18
PAR	5	4	3	4	4	4	4	5	3
YARDS	500	407	178	382	353	332	363	428	145

Directions: I-495 to Route 109 East (Exit 19). Left at 3rd light (4 miles) onto Holliston. Right after 2 miles onto Goulding Street. Course is 1 mile on left.

Granite Links Golf Club   ✪✪✪✪½   ▶ 32

100 Quarry Hills Drive
Quincy, MA (617) 689-1900
www.granitelinksgolfclub.com

Tees	Holes	Yards	Par	USGA	Slope
BACK	18	6858	72	73.4	141
MIDDLE	18	6497	72	71.6	134
FRONT	18	5001	72	70.6	124

Club Pro: Stephen Clancy, PGA
Payment: Visa, MC, Amex, Disc
Tee Times: 4 days in advance
Fee 9 Holes: Weekday: $60 w/cart M-W
Fee 18 Holes: Weekday: $100 w/cart M-W
Twilight Rates: After 4pm
Cart Rental: Included
Lessons: $50/half hour, $95/hr, 5 lessons $225
Membership: Yes
Other: Restaurant / Clubhouse / Lockers (members only) / Showers / Bar-Lounge
GPS: Yes

Weekend: $70 w/cart Th/F/S/S
Weekend: $125 w/cart Th/F/S/S
Discounts: Milton/Quincy residents
Driving Range: $10/bucket
Junior Golf: Yes
Architect/Yr Open: John Sanford/2002

Semi-private 27-hole golf course with dramatic views of Boston skyline, Harbor, and Blue Hills. "Links-style definition of holes with varied grasses, yet dramatic elevation changes as well. Course in exceptional condition." "Truest putting greens in the state."

	1	2	3	4	5	6	7	8	9
PAR	5	4	4	3	4	4	3	5	4
YARDS	570	409	436	205	385	359	185	487	367
	10	11	12	13	14	15	16	17	18
PAR	4	3	4	5	4	3	4	4	5
YARDS	480	179	452	516	383	223	364	349	509

Directions: I-93 to Exit 8 (Furnace Brook Parkway). Follow signs to Ricciuti Drive. Follow signs to Quarry Hills Entrance. Just 7 miles south of Boston.

Green Harbor Golf Club

624 Webster Street
Marshfield, MA (781) 834-7303
www.greenharborgolfclub.com

Club Pro: Charles Lanzetta, dir. of golf
Payment: Cash, Visa, MC
Tee Times: 7 days adv.

Tees	Holes	Yards	Par	USGA	Slope
BACK	18	6245	71	69.6	122
MIDDLE	18	5757	71	67.8	115
FRONT	18	4967	71	68.5	114

Fee 9 Holes: Weekday: $22   **Weekend:** $25
Fee 18 Holes: Weekday: $35   **Weekend:** $45
Twilight Rates: After 5:30pm
Discounts: Srs. Tues 6am-12pm $16/9, $26/18; Jrs. M-Th 12pm $16/9, $26/18
Cart Rental: $4/pull   **Driving Range:** No
Lessons: Yes **Schools:** No   **Junior Golf:** Yes
Membership: No   **Architect/Yr Open:** Manuel Francis/1971
Other: Clubhouse / Snack Bar / Lounge   **GPS:**

Flat, open course. Water on 5 holes. Features velvet bent grass. Open March 15 - December 15.

	1	2	3	4	5	6	7	8	9
PAR	4	4	4	4	3	4	5	3	4
YARDS	406	353	347	300	155	310	507	155	318
	10	11	12	13	14	15	16	17	18
PAR	4	5	5	4	4	3	4	3	4
YARDS	349	505	462	345	280	185	364	158	316

Directions: I-93 to Route 3 South to Exit 12 (Route 139). 139 East 4.5 miles. Right on Webster Street, 1 mile on left.

Hickory Hill Golf Course

200 North Lowell Street
Methuen, MA (978) 686-0822

Tees	Holes	Yards	Par	USGA	Slope
BACK	18	6287	71	70.8	123
MIDDLE	18	6017	71	69.6	119
FRONT	18	5397	71	70.7	121

Club Pro:
Payment: Visa, MC, Cash
Tee Times: 7 days in advance
Fee 9 Holes: Weekday: $23 M-F   **Weekend:** $28
Fee 18 Holes: Weekday: $40 M-Th $45 F   **Weekend:** $49
Twilight Rates: After 3pm   **Discounts:** Senior & Junior (Senior T-Th am)
Cart Rental: $16pp/18, $11pp/9   **Driving Range:** Yes
Lessons: **Schools:** No   **Junior Golf:** No
Membership: No   **Architect/Yr Open:** Manuel Francis/1968
Other: Clubhouse / Showers / Bar-Lounge   **GPS:**

We offer a senior discount Tuesday, Wednesday, and Thursday 7am - 12pm, $35 walk, $45 ride. Have clubhouse/bar & grill/showers. Good variety of holes, tougher back nine.

	1	2	3	4	5	6	7	8	9
PAR	4	3	5	4	4	5	4	3	4
YARDS	349	173	511	382	379	513	367	155	348
	10	11	12	13	14	15	16	17	18
PAR	5	4	4	3	4	4	4	3	4
YARDS	489	390	340	141	326	357	304	114	379

Directions: I-93 to Exit 46. Take Route 113 West, follow 1.5 miles, course is on left.

Hillview Golf Course

149 North Street
No. Reading, MA (978) 664-4435
www.hillviewgc.com

Tees	Holes	Yards	Par	USGA	Slope
BACK	18	5802	69	67.4	120
MIDDLE	18	5251	69	65.2	118
FRONT	18	4500	69	66	110

Club Pro: Chris Carter, PGA
Payment: Cash or Credit
Tee Times: Yes
Fee 9 Holes: Weekday: $19   **Weekend:** $22
Fee 18 Holes: Weekday: $36   **Weekend:** $39
Twilight Rates: No   **Discounts:** Sr. & Jr. (M-Th) before noon
Cart Rental: $26/18, $13/9 per cart   **Driving Range:** $6/lg, $3/sm
Lessons: $50/half hour **Schools:** No   **Junior Golf:**
Membership: No   **Architect/Yr Open:** 1950s
Other: Snack Bar / Restaurant / Bar-Lounge / Clubhouse

A popular course in a good location. Interesting layout. Greens renovations new for 2009.

	1	2	3	4	5	6	7	8	9
PAR	5	3	4	4	4	4	4	5	3
YARDS	484	170	410	325	357	323	394	539	191
	10	11	12	13	14	15	16	17	18
PAR	4	4	4	4	3	4	3	4	3
YARDS	372	310	346	355	180	324	236	239	173

Directions: I-93 to Exit 40 and follow Route 62 East 1-1/2 miles. Turn left on North Street. Course is 1/2 mile up on left.

Kelley Greens By The Sea

1 Willow Road
Nahant, MA
(781) 581-0840 ext. 101
www.kelleygreens.com

Tees	Holes	Yards	Par	USGA	Slope
BACK	9	1940	60	60.0	103
MIDDLE	9	1865	30	57	87
FRONT	9	1671	60	60.0	103

Club Pro: John Fennell, Teaching Pro
Payment: Cash, Credit Cards
Tee Times: 3 days adv.
Fee 9 Holes: Weekday: $15 M-F   **Weekend:** $18
Fee 18 Holes: Weekday: $25   **Weekend:** $28
Twilight Rates: No   **Discounts:** None
Cart Rental: $20/18, $12/9 per cart   **Driving Range:** No
Lessons: $35/half hour **Schools:** No   **Junior Golf:** Yes
Membership: Yes   **Architect/Yr Open:**
Other: Snack Bar / Restaurant / Lounge   **GPS:**

Newly renovated clubhouse w/5 star chef (open year round). Improvements have made course more user- friendly. An average golfer can usually cover 9 holes in under 2 hours. Residents' discount.

	1	2	3	4	5	6	7	8	9
PAR	3	3	3	3	3	4	4	4	3
YARDS	137	179	186	142	213	325	260	249	174
PAR									
YARDS									

Directions: Route 1A to Lynn Center. Go toward Nahant over causeway (Nahant Road). Follow signs to course.

Lakeview Golf Course

NR 37

Route 1A
Wenham, MA (978) 468-6676
www.lakeviewgc.com
Club Pro: Bill Flynn, PGA
Payment: Cash, MC, Visa
Tee Times: Yes
Fee 9 Holes: Weekday: $16
Fee 18 Holes: Weekday: $24
Twilight Rates: No
Cart Rental: $7pp/9, $14pp/18
Lessons: Private and group **Schools:** No
Membership: No
Other: Snack Bar

Tees	Holes	Yards	Par	USGA	Slope
BACK	9	2001	31		
MIDDLE	9	1836	31	59.3	91
FRONT	9	1550	31		

Weekend: $18
Weekend: $28
Discounts: Senior & Junior $12
Driving Range: No
Junior Golf: Yes
Architect/Yr Open: 1918
GPS:

COUPON

Executive-style golf course. Senior rate $12 for 9 holes, M-W, before noon. Junior rate Saturday after 2pm is $12 for 9 holes.

	1	2	3	4	5	6	7	8	9
PAR	4	3	3	4	3	4	3	3	4
YARDS	325	215	165	320	125	255	150	160	325
PAR									
YARDS									

Directions: I-95/Route 128 to Exit 20 North (Route 1A). The course is 2 miles on the right.

Leo J. Martin Golf Club

NR 38

85 Park Road
Weston, MA (781) 894-4903

Club Pro: Mike Wortis, PGA
Payment: Visa, MC
Tee Times: Weekends
Fee 9 Holes: Weekday: $17 M-Th
Fee 18 Holes: Weekday: $22 M-Th
Twilight Rates: No
Cart Rental: $28/18, $16/9 per cart
Lessons: $45/half hour **Schools:** Jr.
Membership: No
Other: Snack Bar

Tees	Holes	Yards	Par	USGA	Slope
BACK	18	6320	72	70.7	126
MIDDLE	18	6140	72	67.6	118
FRONT	18	6140	75	70.9	116

Weekend: $19 F/S/S/H
Weekend: $25 F/S/S/H
Discounts: Sr. & Jr. weekdays M-Th
Driving Range: $12/lg, $7/sm
Junior Golf: Yes
Architect/Yr Open: Donald Ross
GPS:

Considered an easy walker. Seniors seem to enjoy it. Tee times first come, first serve M-F. "Friendly beginners course."

	1	2	3	4	5	6	7	8	9
PAR	4	5	3	5	3	4	4	4	4
YARDS	315	500	155	525	140	360	325	355	265
	10	11	12	13	14	15	16	17	18
PAR	3	4	3	4	4	4	5	4	5
YARDS	140	290	240	400	420	360	530	260	560

Directions: Where I-95/Route 128 meets I-90 (Mass Pike). From Mass Pike Weston exit (Route 30), take first left onto Park Road to course on left.

Lost Brook Golf Club

NR ▶ 39

750 University Avenue
Westwood, MA (781) 769-2550
www.lostbrookgolfclub.com

Tees	Holes	Yards	Par	USGA	Slope
BACK					
MIDDLE	18	3002	54		
FRONT	18	2468	58		

Club Pro: No
Payment: Cash, Credit Cards
Tee Times: Weekends
Fee 9 Holes: Weekday: $16
Fee 18 Holes: Weekday: $25
Twilight Rates: Yes
Cart Rental: $3/pull
Lessons: Yes **Schools:** No
Membership: No
Other: Clubhouse / Snack Bar

Weekend: $18
Weekend: $2
Discounts: Senior & Junior
Driving Range: No
Junior Golf: No
Architect/Yr Open: Sam Mitchell/1967
GPS:

COUPON

Expertly maintained par 3 golf course. Tree-lined fairways surround the elevated greens.

	1	2	3	4	5	6	7	8	9
PAR	3	3	3	3	3	3	3	3	3
YARDS	93	198	212	202	141	158	176	190	111
	10	11	12	13	14	15	16	17	18
PAR	3	3	3	3	3	3	3	3	3
YARDS	170	171	168	162	126	148	202	190	185

Directions: I-95/Route 128 to Exit 13. Follow University Avenue approximately 1.5 miles to course located at Meditech. Course is on the left.

Maplegate Country Club

◐◐ ▶ 40

160 Maple Street
Bellingham, MA (508) 966-4040
www.maplegate.com

Tees	Holes	Yards	Par	USGA	Slope
BACK	18	6815	72	74.2	133
MIDDLE	18	5837	72	69.5	122
FRONT	18	4852	72	70.2	124

Club Pro: Greg Dowdell
Payment: Visa, MC, Amex, Disc
Tee Times: 7 days adv.
Fee 9 Holes: Weekday: $27, $33 w/cart M-Th
Fee 18 Holes: Weekday: $53, $71 w/cart M-Th
Twilight Rates: After 1pm
Cart Rental: $17pp/18
Lessons: Yes **Schools:** Jr. & Sr.
Membership: Yes
Other: Snack Bar

Weekend: $41 w/cart F/S/S
Weekend: $63, $81 w/cart F/S/S
Discounts: Senior & Junior
Driving Range: Yes
Junior Golf: Yes
Architect/Yr: Leonard French & Phil Wogan/1991
GPS: Yes

COUPON

Must be straight shooter, but interesting layout for all abilities. Carts required weekends, holidays before noon.

	1	2	3	4	5	6	7	8	9
PAR	5	4	3	5	4	4	4	3	4
YARDS	515	335	173	522	431	435	417	145	434
	10	11	12	13	14	15	16	17	18
PAR	4	4	3	4	5	3	5	4	4
YARDS	376	382	191	388	510	227	530	357	447

Directions: I-495 to Exit 18 bear right. Take 126 North. Right at first light to Maple Street. Course is 1 mile on left.

Meadow at Peabody, The ⊗⊗ ▶ 41

80 Granite Street
Peabody, MA (978) 532-9390
www.peabodymeadowgolf.com

Tees	Holes	Yards	Par	USGA	Slope
BACK	18	6708	71	72.4	128
MIDDLE	18	5869	71	69.4	121
FRONT	18	5136	71	70.8	123

Club Pro:
Payment: Visa, MC, Amex
Tee Times: 3 days adv.
Fee 9 Holes: Weekday: $21 ($18/resident) **Weekend:** $22 ($19/resident)
Fee 18 Holes: Weekday: $40 ($34/resident) **Weekend:** $42 ($36/resident)
Twilight Rates: No **Discounts:** Sr. & Jr. before noon M-F
Cart Rental: $8pp/9, $15pp/18 **Driving Range:** No
Lessons: $40/45 min. **Schools:** No **Junior Golf:** Yes
Membership: No **Architect/Yr Open:** Silva & Cornish/2001
Other: Restaurant / Showers **GPS:**

Player Comments: "A real workout for the first visit, a ton of fun your next few times around." "Fun layout, hilly, but fair course." "Careful—several blind shots." Dress code. Lodging available at nearby Marriott.

	1	2	3	4	5	6	7	8	9
PAR	5	4	4	4	4	3	5	3	4
YARDS	526	343	312	324	388	110	437	146	372
	10	11	12	13	14	15	16	17	18
PAR	4	5	3	4	4	4	3	4	4
YARDS	360	457	153	389	319	329	143	341	420

Directions: I-95/Route 128 to Exit 28 (Forest Street/Centennial Drive). Bear right at end of ramp. Go through lights at bottom of hill to Summit. Left onto Lynnfield Street, Left onto Washington Street. Immediate right onto Granite Street. Street dead-ends to course.

Meadow Creek Golf Club ⊗⊗⊗ ▶ 42

Five Clubhouse Lane
Dracut, MA (978 459-5129
www.meadowcreekgolfclub.com

Tees	Holes	Yards	Par	USGA	Slope
BACK	18	6501	71	72.7	134
MIDDLE	18	6009	70	70.1	131
FRONT	18	5549	71	68.1	125

Club Pro:
Payment: Cash, Visa, MC
Tee Times: 7 days adv.
Fee 9 Holes: Weekday: $23 **Weekend:** $28
Fee 18 Holes: Weekday: $39 **Weekend:** $49
Twilight Rates: After 4pm **Discounts:**
Cart Rental: $10pp/9, $16pp/18 **Driving Range:** No
Lessons: No **Schools:** No **Junior Golf:** Yes
Membership: Yes **Architect/Yr Open:** Jeffrey Brem/2007
Other: **GPS:**

COUPON

"Consistently challenging hole-by-hole. Several huge greens with lots of undulation make approach shots critical. Front 9 is wide open, back 9 gets tighter. A great day of golf for any level of player." –JD "Can't wait for this place to mature--alraedy it's great fun!." -EG

	1	2	3	4	5	6	7	8	9
PAR	4	4	4	3	5	4	4	4	3
YARDS	370	496	367	140	505	367	403	392	186
	10	11	12	13	14	15	16	17	18
PAR	4	4	3	4	4	3	5	4	4
YARDS	453	384	197	328	398	141	573	365	436

Directions: I-93 to Route 113 West. Go Right onto Meadow Creek Drive.

Merrimack Valley Golf Course   NR ▶ 43

210 Howe Street
Methuen, MA (978) 685-9717

Tees	Holes	Yards	Par	USGA	Slope
BACK	18	6220	71	69.3	120
MIDDLE	18	5871	71	67.7	117
FRONT	18	5151	72	72.3	116

Club Pro: Stephen Kattar
Payment: Cash, Check
Tee Times: Weekends and holidays
Fee 9 Holes: Weekday: $14
Fee 18 Holes: Weekday: $20
Twilight Rates: After 3pm wkds/6pm wkdys $10
Cart Rental: $14pp/18, $7pp/9
Lessons: Yes **Schools:** No
Membership: Yes
Other: Restaurant / Bar-Lounge

Weekend: $16 before 7
Weekend: $25
Discounts: None
Driving Range: No
Junior Golf: Yes
Architect/Yr Open: Donald Ross/1906
GPS:

Improvements include better drainage. Noted for plush greens. In the process of a complete tee-to-green renovation on 18 holes, all new tees, all new irrigation, fairways, greens, drainage. Should be completed in early summer '09.

	1	2	3	4	5	6	7	8	9
PAR	5	4	4	3	4	4	3	4	4
YARDS	454	342	312	158	386	404	187	354	301
	10	11	12	13	14	15	16	17	18
PAR	4	3	5	4	4	5	3	4	4
YARDS	356	158	441	418	310	482	138	405	265

Directions: I-495 to Exit 47, Route 213. Take Exit 3 off Route 213. At lights at end of exit ramp, go left. Club is 3/4 mile on left.

Middleton Golf Course   ✪✪✪ ▶ 44

105 South Main Street
Middleton, MA (978) 774-4075
www.middletongolf.com

Tees	Holes	Yards	Par	USGA	Slope
BACK	18	3215	54	57.0	83
MIDDLE	18	3000	54	53.9	75
FRONT	18	2280	54	52.1	71

Club Pro: Chris Costa
Payment: Major Credit Cards, Cash
Tee Times: On our website
Fee 9 Holes: Weekday: $22
Fee 18 Holes: Weekday: $35
Twilight Rates: Monday & Friday only
Cart Rental: $15pp/18, $10pp/9
Lessons: Yes **Schools:** Yes
Membership: No
Other: Clubhouse / Bar (beer & wine only) / Greenside Cafe / Club Fitting Center

Weekend: $22
Weekend: $35
Discounts: Senior & Junior
Driving Range: Lessons only
Junior Golf: Yes
Architect/Yr Open: Geoffrey Cornish/1966

COUPON

Player Comments: "Extremely well maintained, friendly staff, and excellent pro shop." "Very good greens." Open year round. One of the nation's top par 3 courses.

	1	2	3	4	5	6	7	8	9
PAR	3	3	3	3	3	3	3	3	3
YARDS	170	160	185	170	150	170	145	215	190
	10	11	12	13	14	15	16	17	18
PAR	3	3	3	3	3	3	3	3	3
YARDS	135	110	195	160	155	240	215	225	225

Directions: I-95 to Route 114 West about 2.5 miles. Parking lot entrance on the left.

Millwood Farm Golf Course

175 Millwood Street
Framingham, MA (508) 877-1221
www.milwoodgc.com

Tees	Holes	Yards	Par	USGA	Slope
BACK					
MIDDLE	14	3798	53	31.4	102
FRONT					

Club Pro: No
Payment: Visa, MC
Tee Times: 7 days adv.
Fee 9 Holes: Weekday: $27   **Weekend:** $30
Fee 18 Holes: Weekday: **Weekend:**
Twilight Rates: After 5pm   **Discounts:** Senior ($21 M-F)
Cart Rental: $10pp   **Driving Range:** No
Lessons: No   **Schools:** No   **Junior Golf:** No
Membership: No   **Architect/Yr Open:** William Drake/1967
Other: Snack Bar   **GPS:**

A friendly family-owned course, with 14 holes. Added traps on 7th hole. New tee on 9th. Open April to November.

	1	2	3	4	5	6	7	8	9
PAR	4	3	4	4	4	3	4	4	5
YARDS	338	112	306	230	363	156	281	312	438
	10	11	12	13	14	15	16	17	18
PAR	4	3	4	3	4				
YARDS	362	160	295	138	307				

Directions: Route 9 to Edgell Road. At light, make right onto Edgell Road for 1 mile. Turn left onto Belknap Road, then third right onto Millwood Street.

Mt. Hood Golf Course

100 Slayton Road
Melrose, MA (781) 665-6656
www.playgolfne.com

Tees	Holes	Yards	Par	USGA	Slope
BACK					
MIDDLE	18	5540	69	65.7	107
FRONT	18	5318	74	NA	NA

Club Pro: Mike Farrell, PGA
Payment: Visa, MC, Amex, Disc
Tee Times: Weekends, 5 days adv.
Fee 9 Holes: Weekday: $24   **Weekend:** $28
Fee 18 Holes: Weekday: $41   **Weekend:** $47
Twilight Rates: No   **Discounts:** Senior & Junior
Cart Rental: $16pp/18, $8.50pp/9   **Driving Range:** No
Lessons: $30/half hour   **Schools:**   **Junior Golf:** No
Membership: Yes   **Architect/Yr Open:**
Other: Clubhouse / Showers / Snack Bar / Restaurant / Bar-Lounge

Hole #12 redone, overlooks Boston skyline. Now under Friel Management. "If you haven't been here in a few seasons, you'll like all the changes."

	1	2	3	4	5	6	7	8	9
PAR	5	4	3	5	4	4	3	4	3
YARDS	477	340	202	532	303	338	215	362	180
	10	11	12	13	14	15	16	17	18
PAR	3	4	4	4	5	3	4	4	3
YARDS	140	282	386	332	450	210	321	304	166

Directions: Route 1, Take left onto Essex Street then left onto Waverly Avenue. Take left onto Slayton Road.

New England Country Club

180 Paine Street
Bellingham, MA (508) 883-2300
www.newenglandcountryclub.com

Tees	Holes	Yards	Par	USGA	Slope
BACK	18	6430	71	70.8	130
MIDDLE	18	5867	71	67.2	122
FRONT	18	4908	71	68.7	121

Club Pro: Mark Copithorne
Payment: Visa, MC
Tee Times: 5 days/weekday
Fee 9 Holes: Weekday: $39 w/cart M-Th **Weekend:** $46 w/cart F/S/S
Fee 18 Holes: Weekday: $67 w/cart M-Th **Weekend:** $81 w/cart F/S/S
Twilight Rates: After 1pm $53 M-Th, $63 F/S/S **Discounts:** None
Cart Rental: Included **Driving Range:** All grass
Lessons: $45/45 min **Schools:** Clinics **Junior Golf:** No
Membership: Yes, full and partial **Architect/Yr Open:** Hale Irwin/1990
Other: Clubhouse / Restaurant / Pub / Outdoor Deck / Tent / GPS Carts
GPS: Yes

It only looks short on the card; great course from the whites—absolute killer from the blues. Great variety of holes. GPS in carts and multiple sets of tees.

	1	2	3	4	5	6	7	8	9
PAR	5	4	4	3	5	3	4	4	4
YARDS	497	357	314	145	490	122	386	320	352
	10	11	12	13	14	15	16	17	18
PAR	4	5	3	4	4	4	3	4	4
YARDS	355	501	145	382	327	297	140	340	397

Directions: I-495 North to Exit 16 (King Street). Continue West on King Street for 6 miles. At light make a left onto Wrentham Street. Bear right at the fire station onto Paine Street. Course is .25 miles up hill on left.

New Meadows Golf Club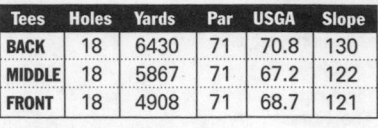

32 Wildes Road
Topsfield, MA (978) 887-9307
www.newmeadowsgolf.com

Tees	Holes	Yards	Par	USGA	Slope
BACK					
MIDDLE	9	2883	35	64.8	117
FRONT					

Club Pro: Victor Skop, PGA
Payment: Cash, Check
Tee Times: Call ahead
Fee 9 Holes: Weekday: $17 **Weekend:** $19
Fee 18 Holes: Weekday: $32 **Weekend:** $36
Twilight Rates: No **Discounts:** None
Cart Rental: $24pp/18, $12pp/9 **Driving Range:** No
Lessons: No **Schools:** No **Junior Golf:** No
Membership: No **Architect/Yr Open:** Phil Wogan/1964
Other: Clubhouse / Snack Bar **GPS:**

New Meadows is a Phil Wogan-designed course (1964) which offers a relaxed atmosphere for golfers of all ages and handicap ranges. It is especially enjoyable for seniors, women, juniors, and mid- to high- handicap golfers. Please call for tee times. Fees subject to change.

	1	2	3	4	5	6	7	8	9
PAR	4	4	3	4	4	4	5	3	4
YARDS	352	365	160	348	345	368	459	128	358
PAR									
YARDS									

Directions: New Meadows is 1.9 miles North of the US Route 1 and Route 97 intersection. It is also 3.2 miles South of the US Route 1 and Route 133 intersection.

Newton Commonwealth GC   ✪◑ 49 ▶

212 Kenrick Street
Newton, MA (617) 630-1971
www.sterlinggolf.com

Tees	Holes	Yards	Par	USGA	Slope
BACK	18	5354	70	65.8	122
MIDDLE	18	4992	70	64.5	117
FRONT	18	4329	70	65.8	118

Club Pro: Bob Travers, PGA
Payment: Cash, Most Credit Cards
Tee Times: 4 days adv.
Fee 9 Holes: Weekday: $24 M-Th
Fee 18 Holes: Weekday: $30 M-Th
Twilight Rates: After 5pm
Cart Rental: $15pp/18, $9pp/9
Lessons: $55 **Schools:** No
Membership: Yes
Weekend:
Weekend: $37 F-Sun
Discounts: Sr./Jr. $18 M-Th before 8am
Driving Range: No
Junior Golf: No
Architect/Yr Open: Donald Ross/1897
Other: Snack Bar / Twilight Golf After League Play, $18 Every Day

New routing makes this a "new course" for anyone who hasn't been here recently. Resident discounts. Well-stocked pro shop. Friendly staff. Open year round. Donald Ross greens make par a challenge. New irrigation relieves formerly wet holes.

	1	2	3	4	5	6	7	8	9
PAR	4	5	3	3	5	4	3	5	3
YARDS	252	476	179	110	435	255	162	473	180
	10	11	12	13	14	15	16	17	18
PAR	4	4	3	4	4	5	3	4	4
YARDS	259	295	148	263	231	422	130	376	355

Directions: I-95/Route 128 to Route 30 East exit. Follow 4.8 miles to Grant Avenue. Go left and follow the golfer logo signs.

North Hill Country Club   ✪✪ 50 ▶

29 Merry Avenue
Duxbury, MA (781) 934-3249
www.johnsongolfmanagement.com

Tees	Holes	Yards	Par	USGA	Slope
BACK	9	3456	36	74.6	131
MIDDLE	9	3324	36	71.2	121
FRONT	9	2887	736	68.2	117

Club Pro: Bill Allen, PGA
Payment: Most Major Credit Cards
Tee Times: 7 days adv.
Fee 9 Holes: Weekday: $18
Fee 18 Holes: Weekday: $30
Twilight Rates: No
Cart Rental: $15pp/18, $8pp/9
Lessons: Private and Group **Schools:** No
Membership: Yes
Other: Snack Bar / Bar-Lounge / Clubhouse
Weekend: $20
Weekend: $33
Discounts:
Driving Range: Limited
Junior Golf: Yes
Architect/Yr Open: William Mitchell/1962
GPS:

"Nice layout. Fun track." From the tips, a real challenging course.

	1	2	3	4	5	6	7	8	9
PAR	5	4	4	3	4	5	4	3	4
YARDS	555	438	426	205	350	488	374	190	430
PAR									
YARDS									

Directions: Route 3 to Exit 11, get off Route 14 East, course is approximately 2 miles on right (Merry Avenue).

Norwood Country Club

NR **51**

400 Providence Highway
Norwood, MA (781) 769-5880
www.norwoodcc.com

Club Pro:
Payment: Most Major Credit Cards
Tee Times: 1 week adv.
Fee 9 Holes: Weekday: $19
Fee 18 Holes: Weekday: $28
Twilight Rates: $28 1pm on wkds, Sat and Sun
Cart Rental: $9pp/9, $15pp/18
Lessons: $50/half hour **Schools:** No
Membership: Inner Club and Junior
Other: Clubhouse / Lockers / Showers / Bar-Lounge

Tees	Holes	Yards	Par	USGA	Slope
BACK	18	6292	71	67.1	112
MIDDLE	18	6092	71	65.9	108
FRONT	18	5950	71	68.7	108

Weekend: $22 after 12pm
Weekend: $33 after 12pm
Discounts: Senior
Driving Range: $10/lg, $5/sm
Junior Golf: Yes
Architect/Yr Open: Sam Mitchell/1975

COUPON

A straightaway track. Excellent course for seniors and beginners. Easy to walk. Rates subject to change.
Under new management.

	1	2	3	4	5	6	7	8	9
PAR	4	4	4	4	5	4	3	3	5
YARDS	360	280	320	395	435	320	156	130	450
	10	11	12	13	14	15	16	17	18
PAR	4	4	5	3	4	3	4	4	4
YARDS	300	305	480	150	347	130	390	330	367

Directions: I-95/Route 128 to Route 1 South to Norwood. Note: course is on the Northbound side
of Route 1. To change direction, go to Norwood exit and then go around rotary and head North.

Olde Salem Greens

NR **52**

54 Mason Street
Salem, MA (978) 744-2149

Club Pro:
Payment: Cash Only
Tee Times: M-F 1 day adv. S/S 2 days
Fee 9 Holes: Weekday: $18
Fee 18 Holes: Weekday: $33
Twilight Rates: After 7pm
Cart Rental: $26/18, $13/9 per cart
Lessons: Residents only **Schools:**
Membership: Resident Passes
Other: Snack Bar / Bar-Lounge

Tees	Holes	Yards	Par	USGA	Slope
BACK	9	3646	35	68.4	116
MIDDLE	9	3028	35	68.5	116
FRONT	9	2483	35	68.4	112

Weekend: $19
Weekend:
Discounts: Sr. & Jr. (with restrictions)
Driving Range: No
Junior Golf: No
Architect/Yr Open:
GPS:

Residents' rate. New putting green.

	1	2	3	4	5	6	7	8	9
PAR	4	3	4	5	4	4	4	3	4
YARDS	374	253	367	545	345	398	291	153	304
	10	11	12	13	14	15	16	17	18
PAR	4	3	4	5	4	4	4	3	4
YARDS	374	253	367	545	345	398	291	153	304

Directions: I-95/Route 128 to Route 114 toward Salem. Take Essex Street to Highland Avenue.
Take a left on Wilson Street to course.

Olde Scotland Links ✪✪✪ 53 ▶

GB RTE 495

695 Pine Street
Bridgewater, MA (508) 279-3344
www.oldescotlandlinks.com

Club Pro:
Payment: Visa, MC, Amex, Disc
Tee Times: 7 days adv.
Fee 9 Holes: Weekday: $22
Fee 18 Holes: Weekday: $40
Twilight Rates: No
Cart Rental: $32/18, $18/9 per cart
Lessons: Yes **Schools:** Yes
Membership:
Other: Snack Bar

Tees	Holes	Yards	Par	USGA	Slope
BACK	18	6790	72	72.6	126
MIDDLE	18	6306	72	70.3	124
FRONT	18	5396	72	70.9	117

Weekend: $25
Weekend: $49
Discounts: Senior & Junior
Driving Range: Yes
Junior Golf: Yes
Architect/Yr: Cornish, Silva, Mungeam/1997
GPS:

COUPON

Player Comments: "Nice layout." "Beautiful design, affordable." Walkable and enjoyable for all abilities. Open year-round.

	1	2	3	4	5	6	7	8	9
PAR	4	4	3	4	4	5	4	3	5
YARDS	400	372	154	302	372	519	359	189	456
	10	11	12	13	14	15	16	17	18
PAR	4	4	5	3	4	4	3	4	5
YARDS	435	359	520	205	357	362	130	321	494

Directions: I-95 to Route 24 South to Exit 15. Follow Route 104 East for about 1/2 mile to first set of lights. Take right onto Old Pleasant Street and follow for 2 miles. Course is on the right.

Ould Newbury Golf Course ✪✪ 54 ▶

329 Newburyport Turnpike (Route 1)
Newbury, MA (978) 465-9888
www.ouldnewbury.com

Club Pro: James Hilton
Payment: Cash, Disc, MC, Visa
Tee Times: No
Fee 9 Holes: Weekday: $25
Fee 18 Holes: Weekday: $38
Twilight Rates: No
Cart Rental: $36pp/18, $23pp/9
Lessons: $50/45 min. **Schools:** No
Membership: Yes
Other: Clubhouse / Lockers / Showers / Snack Bar

Tees	Holes	Yards	Par	USGA	Slope
BACK	9	3115	35	71.8	129
MIDDLE	9	2943	35	69.4	120
FRONT	9	2723	38	71.3	126

Weekend:
Weekend:
Discounts: None
Driving Range: No
Junior Golf: No
Architect/Yr Open: 1916

Sig. Hole: #9 is a 207-yard uphill par 3 that requires a shot over a 50-foot hickory tree. Closed to public on weekends.

	1	2	3	4	5	6	7	8	9
PAR	4	5	4	4	4	3	4	4	3
YARDS	394	453	359	401	298	143	373	318	204
PAR									
YARDS									

Directions: I-95 to Exit 55 (Central Street/Byfield-Newbury). Turn East and follow signs to Governor Dummer Academy. At the intersection of Route 1, turn left. Club entrance is 600 yards on the right.

Pembroke Country Club

✪✪½

55

West Elm Street
Pembroke, MA (781) 826-5191
www.pembrokecc.com

Club Pro: Richard Fedor, PGA
Payment: Visa, MC, Cash, Check
Tee Times: Wed am for S/S
Fee 9 Holes: Weekday: $15 walk, $24 ride
Fee 18 Holes: Weekday: $30 walk, $42 ride
Twilight Rates: After 4pm
Cart Rental: Included
Lessons: $45/half hour **Schools:** Junior
Membership: Yes
Other: Clubhouse / Snack Bar / Restaurant / Bar-Lounge / Junior Memberships

Tees	Holes	Yards	Par	USGA	Slope
BACK					
MIDDLE	18	6532	71	71.1	124
FRONT	18	5887	75	73.4	120

Weekend: $25 walk, $31 ride
Weekend: $40 walk, $52 ride
Discounts: Sr/Jr $30/w/cart, $15 M-F Jr
Driving Range: $5/bucket
Junior Golf: No
Architect/Yr Open: Phil Wogan/1972

COUPON

Returning to former glory. "Very friendly staff. Nice course, lots of water and sand. Some great par 4s." –DL

	1	2	3	4	5	6	7	8	9
PAR	5	4	3	4	4	4	3	4	4
YARDS	531	341	221	434	421	349	143	436	344
	10	**11**	**12**	**13**	**14**	**15**	**16**	**17**	**18**
PAR	4	3	4	5	4	4	4	3	5
YARDS	415	168	431	564	341	370	345	188	490

Directions: Route 3 to Exit 13, right onto Route 53 South, take right at 5th light onto Broadway. Take left at island onto Elm Street. Course is 2 miles on right.

Pine Meadows Golf Club

NR

56

255 Cedar Street
Lexington, MA (781) 862-5516
www.pinemeadowsgolfclub.com

Club Pro:
Payment: Cash or Check
Tee Times: 7 days adv.
Fee 9 Holes: Weekday: $20
Fee 18 Holes: Weekday: No
Twilight Rates: No
Cart Rental: $7.50pp/9
Lessons: No **Schools:** No
Membership: No
Other: Snack Bar

Tees	Holes	Yards	Par	USGA	Slope
BACK					
MIDDLE	9	2759	35	64.5	110
FRONT	9	2405	35	69.2	117

Weekend: $22
Weekend: No
Discounts: Srs. & Jrs. (M-Th), Resident $16
Driving Range: No
Junior Golf: No
Architect/Yr Open:
GPS:

The course has open fairways and is excellent for beginners and intermediate players.

	1	2	3	4	5	6	7	8	9
PAR	5	5	4	3	4	3	4	4	3
YARDS	484	481	241	225	336	201	324	301	166
PAR									
YARDS									

Directions: I-95/Route 128 to Exit 31A. Go through 2 lights, take right onto Hill Street, take right onto Cedar Street.

Pine Oaks Golf Course

68 Prospect Street
S. Easton, MA (508) 238-2320
www.pineoaks.com

Club Pro: Leigh Bader, PGA
Payment: Visa, MC, Amex, Disc
Tee Times: No

Tees	Holes	Yards	Par	USGA	Slope
BACK	9	2973	34	67.0	115
MIDDLE	9	2912	34	67	111
FRONT	9	2500	34	67.0	111

Fee 9 Holes: Weekday: $21   **Weekend:** $23
Fee 18 Holes: Weekday: $28   **Weekend:** $33
Twilight Rates: After 5pm, $18/wkdy, $17/wknd   **Discounts:** Senior & Junior M-F
Cart Rental: $13pp/9, $23pp/18   **Driving Range:** No
Lessons: Yes **Schools:** Yes   **Junior Golf:** Yes
Membership: Yes   **Architect/Yr Open:** Geoffrey Cornish/1964
Other: Clubhouse / Lockers / Snack Bar / Bar-Lounge / Discount Golf Shop

COUPON

New short game practice area. Plenty of water for a 9-hole course. New bunkers with 5 new tee areas. *Golf Shop Operations* "Top 100 Pro Shop" for the last 10 years.

	1	2	3	4	5	6	7	8	9
PAR	4	5	4	3	4	3	3	4	4
YARDS	326	558	407	175	378	245	149	302	372
PAR									
YARDS									

Directions: Route 24 to Exit 16B, straight for 3.5 miles, right on Prospect Street.

Pinecrest Golf Club

212 Prentice Street
Holliston, MA (508) 429-9871
www.pinecrestgolfclub.org

Club Pro: Andy Ingham, PGA
Payment: Cash or Credit
Tee Times: Sat, Sun

Tees	Holes	Yards	Par	USGA	Slope
BACK					
MIDDLE	18	4906	66	63.2	103
FRONT	18	4260	66	63.2	103

Fee 9 Holes: Weekday: $17   **Weekend:** $21
Fee 18 Holes: Weekday: $28   **Weekend:** $32
Twilight Rates: After 5pm wkdys, 4pm wknds   **Discounts:** Senior & Junior
Cart Rental: $15pp/18, $8pp/9   **Driving Range:** Yes, grass
Lessons: Yes **Schools:** Yes   **Junior Golf:** Yes
Membership: Residents only   **Architect/Yr Open:** 1955
Other: Clubhouse / Snack Bar / Bar-Lounge / Restaurant

COUPON

The course is relatively level and easy to walk. Very tight greens that are a true test of one's iron shot accuracy. The par 3s are fairly long. Most golfers are able to play 18 holes in under 4 hours.

	1	2	3	4	5	6	7	8	9
PAR	4	3	4	3	4	3	4	4	4
YARDS	398	165	275	153	325	190	317	305	295
	10	11	12	13	14	15	16	17	18
PAR	3	4	3	5	4	4	4	3	3
YARDS	165	264	205	472	245	405	305	200	222

Directions: I-495 to Route 85 Exit 20 toward Holliston. Follow 3 miles to first flashing yellow light. Take right onto Chestnut Street, look for signs.

Pinehills Golf Club (Jones) ✪✪✪✪✪ 59 ▶

54 Clubhouse Drive
Plymouth, MA (508) 209-3000
www.pinehillsgolf.com

Tees	Holes	Yards	Par	USGA	Slope
BACK	18	7175	72	73.8	135
MIDDLE	18	6762	72	72.4	131
FRONT	18	6201	72	69.6	125

Club Pro: John Tuffin, PGA
Payment: Visa, MC, Amex, Checks
Tee Times: 7 days adv.
Fee 18 Holes: Weekday: $95 cart/range balls M-Th
    Weekend: $105 cart/range balls F/S/S/H
Twilight Rates: After 3pm M-Th $60, after 2pm $70 F/S/S
Discounts: None
Cart Rental: Included   **Driving Range:** Natural Grass
Lessons: Yes **Schools:** Yes   **Junior Golf:** Yes
Membership: Yes   **Architect/Yr Open:** Rees Jones/2001
Other: Clubhouse / Grill / Bar / Banquet Facilities / Lockers / Showers / Restaurant

"Excellent layout. Challenging but fair for men or women. Friendliest staff, best service ever encountered." –AP
"Greens slightly easier than Nicklaus, but tougher to get to them. Many dramatic holes." –JD

	1	2	3	4	5	6	7	8	9
PAR	4	4	5	3	4	4	3	4	5
YARDS	348	404	501	177	403	431	165	397	552
	10	11	12	13	14	15	16	17	18
PAR	4	5	4	4	3	5	4	3	4
YARDS	360	548	420	370	219	495	401	169	402

Directions: Route 3 South, Exit 3. Turn left and follow signs.

Pinehills GC (Nicklaus) ✪✪✪✪✪ 60 ▶

54 Clubhouse Drive
Plymouth, MA (508) 209-3000
www.pinehillsgolf.com

Tees	Holes	Yards	Par	USGA	Slope
BACK	18	6640	72	71.7	131
MIDDLE	18	6129	72	69.3	125
FRONT	18	5185	72	69.4	123

Club Pro: John Tuffin, PGA
Payment: Visa, MC, Amex, Checks
Tee Times: 7 days adv. (866) 855-4653
Fee 9 Holes: Weekday: **Weekend:**
Fee 18 Holes: Weekday: $95 cart/range balls M-Th
    Weekend: $105 cart/range balls F/S/S/H
Twilight Rates: After 3:30pm   **Discounts:** None
Cart Rental: Included   **Driving Range:** Natural grass/mats
Lessons: Yes **Schools:** Yes   **Junior Golf:** Yes
Membership: No   **Architect/Yr Open:** Jack Nicklaus II/2002
Other: Clubhouse / Grill / Bar / Banquet Facilites / Lockers / Showers / Restaurant / Caddy Program

Player Comments: "Broader fairways than Jones, trickier greens." Great and beautiful design, fine clubhouse, top-flight service. *New England Golf Guide's* first-ever 5-star course.

	1	2	3	4	5	6	7	8	9
PAR	4	5	3	4	4	5	3	4	4
YARDS	357	500	199	365	357	491	145	343	326
	10	11	12	13	14	15	16	17	18
PAR	4	5	4	3	4	3	5	4	4
YARDS	365	486	403	165	280	144	486	344	373

Directions: Route 3 South, Exit 3. Turn left and follow signs.

Ponkapoag Golf Club (#1)

NR 61

2167 Washington Street
Canton, MA (781) 828-4242
www.ponkapoaggolf.com

Club Pro: Michael Fleming, PGA
Payment: Visa, MC, Cash
Tee Times:

Tees	Holes	Yards	Par	USGA	Slope
BACK	18	6545	72	72.0	126
MIDDLE	18	6010	72	69.8	120
FRONT	18	5316	74	70.8	115

Fee 9 Holes: Weekday: $17 M-Th
Fee 18 Holes: Weekday: $22 M-Th
Twilight Rates: No
Cart Rental: $30/18, $18/9 per cart
Lessons: $40/half hour **Schools:** Junior
Membership: Limited, Juniors
Other: Restaurant / Clubhouse / Beer & Wine / Showers

Weekend: $17 F/S/S
Weekend: $25 F/S/S
Discounts: Sr. & Jr. weekdays
Driving Range: $6/bucket
Junior Golf: Yes
Architect/Yr Open: Donald Ross

A great design by Donald Ross suffering from neglect. "Rustic." April -December.

	1	2	3	4	5	6	7	8	9
PAR	4	3	5	4	4	4	4	3	5
YARDS	370	135	490	304	375	412	380	170	425
	10	11	12	13	14	15	16	17	18
PAR	4	5	3	5	4	4	3	4	4
YARDS	335	440	162	440	344	382	206	345	295

Directions: I-93 to Exit 2A. Go South on Route 138 (Washington Street) into Canton. Clubhouse is on left at first light.

Ponkapoag Golf Club (#2)

NR 62

2167 Washington Street
Canton, MA (781) 828-4242
www.ponkapoaggolf.com

Club Pro: Michael Fleming, PGA
Payment: Visa, MC, Cash
Tee Times:

Tees	Holes	Yards	Par	USGA	Slope
BACK	18	6195	71	70.3	116
MIDDLE	18	5712	71	67.5	112
FRONT	18	5028	72	68.5	113

Fee 9 Holes: Weekday: $17 M-Th
Fee 18 Holes: Weekday: $22 M-Th
Twilight Rates: No
Cart Rental: $30pp/18, $18pp/9
Lessons: $40/half hour **Schools:** Jr. Yes
Membership: Limited, Juniors
Other: Restaurant / Clubhouse / Beer & Wine / Showers

Weekend: $17 F/S/S
Weekend: $25 F/S/S
Discounts: Senior & Junior
Driving Range: $6/bucket
Junior Golf: Yes
Architect/Yr Open: Donald Ross

A great design suffering from neglect. "Playing here is 'roughing it.' Don't bring new clubs." –RM
Designed by Donald Ross.

	1	2	3	4	5	6	7	8	9
PAR	4	4	3	5	4	4	4	3	4
YARDS	364	407	188	456	249	389	312	150	377
	10	11	12	13	14	15	16	17	18
PAR	5	3	4	5	4	3	4	4	4
YARDS	450	125	315	448	320	160	340	300	362

Directions: I-93 South to Exit 2A. Go South on Route 138 (Washington Street) into Canton. Clubhouse is on left at first light.

Presidents Golf Course ✪✪

357 West Squantum Street
Quincy, MA (617) 328-3444
www.presidentsgc.com

Club Pro: Don Small, PGA
Payment: Cash, Visa, MC
Tee Times: 2 days adv. for Fri/Sat/Sun
Fee 9 Holes: Weekday:
Fee 18 Holes: Weekday: $37 M-Th
Twilight Rates: After 4pm
Cart Rental: $15pp/18
Lessons: $35/half hour **Schools:** No
Membership: Yes

Tees	Holes	Yards	Par	USGA	Slope
BACK	18	5645	70	66.8	125
MIDDLE	18	5055	70	66.4	118
FRONT	18	4425	71	65.0	112

Weekend:
Weekend: $46
Discounts: Senior & Junior (M-Th)
Driving Range: No
Junior Golf: Yes
Architect/Yr Open: Tom & George Fazio/1979

Other: Clubhouse / Lockers / Showers / Snack Bar / Restaurant / Putting Green

Player Comments: "Home of Norfolk County Classic. Championship tees are true test of your short game. Greens are sloping and fast. You have to have the short stick working well." Bunker renovations.

	1	2	3	4	5	6	7	8	9
PAR	4	3	4	3	5	4	3	4	4
YARDS	300	90	270	150	440	355	120	350	285
	10	11	12	13	14	15	16	17	18
PAR	3	4	5	3	4	5	5	4	3
YARDS	150	260	465	165	365	460	425	300	105

Directions: I-93 to Exit 11A. Take left at first light (approx. 1 mile). Take left at next light. From I-93 North, take Exit 9. Go straight approx. 1 mile. Right 1 mile at lights. Left at next light.

Reedy Meadow GC at Lynnfield NR

195 Summer Street
Lynnfield, MA (781) 334-9877
www.town.lynnfield.ma.us/golf

Club Pro: Don Lyons, PGA
Payment:
Tee Times: No
Fee 9 Holes: Weekday: $20
Fee 18 Holes: Weekday: $30
Twilight Rates: After 6pm
Cart Rental: $8pp/9, $13pp/13
Lessons: Yes **Schools:** No
Membership: Yes

Tees	Holes	Yards	Par	USGA	Slope
BACK	9	2560	34	63.8	
MIDDLE	9	2485	34	63.0	102
FRONT	9	2240	68	64.8	94

Weekend: $21
Weekend: $31
Discounts: Senior (weekday) & Junior
Driving Range: No
Junior Golf: Yes
Architect/Yr Open:
GPS:

Other: Clubhouse / Bar-Lounge / Snack Bar

Newly named in 2007. Player Comments: "Wide-open fields and an island par 3." Dress code. New carts and tee mats. New machinery to better cut and maintain the course.

	1	2	3	4	5	6	7	8	9
PAR	4	4	3	4	5	3	4	4	3
YARDS	350	355	225	260	476	139	270	340	145
PAR									
YARDS									

Directions: I-95/Route 128 to Exit 41; follow to Main Street in Lynnfield Center.

Ridder Golf Club

Route 14, Oak Street
Whitman, MA (781) 447-9003
www.ridderfarm.com

65

Tees	Holes	Yards	Par	USGA	Slope
BACK	18	5909	70	68.1	113
MIDDLE	18	5857	70	66.3	110
FRONT	18	4981	70	67.1	107

Club Pro: Tim Kilcoyne
Payment: Visa, MC
Tee Times: 7 days
Fee 9 Holes: Weekday: $20   **Weekend:** $25
Fee 18 Holes: Weekday: $37.50   **Weekend:** $47.50
Twilight Rates: No   **Discounts:** Junior
Cart Rental: $12.50pp/18, $6.25pp/9   **Driving Range:** Yes
Lessons: $45/half hour   **Schools:** Jr.   **Junior Golf:** Yes
Membership: Yes, annual fee   **Architect/Yr Open:** Hohman & Cornish/1961
Other: Restaurant / Snack Bar / Bar-Lounge   **GPS:**

Junior summer program. New 6th tee. Open March - December. Great walking course. Roomy fairways on front, tighter back 9.

	1	2	3	4	5	6	7	8	9
PAR	4	4	3	4	4	4	4	3	4
YARDS	334	368	154	289	384	299	257	197	387
	10	11	12	13	14	15	16	17	18
PAR	4	5	4	3	4	3	4	5	4
YARDS	312	468	370	166	427	225	385	476	359

Directions: Route 3 to Route 18 South for 9-10 miles. Then Route 14 East for 2.2 miles.

River Bend Country Club

250 East Center St
West Bridgewater, MA
(508) 580-3673
www.riverbendcc.com

  66

Tees	Holes	Yards	Par	USGA	Slope
BACK	18	6312	71	69.9	125
MIDDLE	18	5773	71	67.6	124
FRONT	18	4915	71	67.7	120

Club Pro: Lyman J. Doane II, PGA
Payment: Most Major Cards, No Checks
Tee Times: 7 days adv.
Fee 9 Holes: Weekday: $20   **Weekend:** $24 after 2pm F/S/S
Fee 18 Holes: Weekday: $37   **Weekend:** $44 F, $48 S/S
Twilight Rates: After 2pm weekends   **Discounts:** Sr.-Jr., M-F
Cart Rental: $14pp/18   **Driving Range:** No
Lessons: No   **Schools:**   **Junior Golf:** No
Membership: Yes, Inner Club   **Architect/Yr Open:** Phil Wogan/1997
Other: Bar-Lounge / Snack Bar   **GPS:**

Sig. Hole: #17, 162-yard par 3. "...manicured magnificently, very fair greens." –RW "Great conditions. The greens hold and putt wonderfully." –KR "Key to scoring here is smart course management. Use the driver less." –AG

	1	2	3	4	5	6	7	8	9
PAR	4	5	4	3	4	4	4	3	4
YARDS	330	436	286	113	333	345	337	166	361
	10	11	12	13	14	15	16	17	18
PAR	4	4	4	4	3	4	5	3	5
YARDS	358	326	363	317	171	340	501	162	516

Directions: I-95/Route 128 to Route 24 South. Take Exit 16A onto Route 106 East for 2.5 miles. Course is on the right.

Rockland Golf Course

276 Plain Street
Rockland, MA (781) 878-5836
www.rocklandgolfcourse.com

Club Pro: Charles Lanzetta, Dir. of Golf
Payment: Visa, MC, Disc
Tee Times: 3 days adv.

Tees	Holes	Yards	Par	USGA	Slope
BACK	18	3300	54	56.0	78
MIDDLE	18	3014	54	58.0	87
FRONT	18	2100	60	N/A	N/A

Fee 9 Holes: Weekday: $15 **Weekend:** $15
Fee 18 Holes: Weekday: $25 **Weekend:** $27.50, $19.95 after 2pm
Twilight Rates: After 6pm **Discounts:** Senior
Cart Rental: $8.50pp/9, $13.65pp/18 **Driving Range:** No
Lessons: $40/half hour **Schools:** Yes **Junior Golf:** Yes
Membership: Yes **Architect/Yr Open:** Skip & Phil Wogan/1964
Other: Clubhouse / Snack Bar / Restaurant / Bar-Lounge

Longest par 3 course in the nation. Tees and greens are in fine shape, but rough areas can balloon your scores. "Nice course, easy to play, easy to walk."

	1	2	3	4	5	6	7	8	9
PAR	3	3	3	3	3	3	3	3	3
YARDS	212	136	202	137	146	152	171	95	207
	10	11	12	13	14	15	16	17	18
PAR	3	3	3	3	3	3	3	3	3
YARDS	227	202	137	145	162	228	152	132	171

Directions: Route 3 to Exit 16B. Left onto Route 139 for 3 to 4 miles. Course is on right.

Rolling Green Golf Course

911 Lowell Street
Andover, MA (978) 475-4066
www.rollinggreengolf.biz

Club Pro:
Payment: Visa, MC
Tee Times: No

Tees	Holes	Yards	Par	USGA	Slope
BACK					
MIDDLE	9	1500	27		
FRONT					

Fee 9 Holes: Weekday: $16 **Weekend:** $17
Fee 18 Holes: Weekday: $23 **Weekend:** $24
Twilight Rates: No **Discounts:** Senior & Junior
Cart Rental: $3/9, $6/18 pull cart **Driving Range:** $6/sm, $8/lg bucket
Lessons: Yes **Schools:** No **Junior Golf:** No
Membership: No **Architect/Yr Open:**
Other: Snack Bar **GPS:**

Now an executive 9-hole course. Brand-new 12-stall driving range.

	1	2	3	4	5	6	7	8	9
PAR	3	3	3	3	3	3	3	3	3
YARDS	180	195	105	170	240	120	175	170	145
PAR									
YARDS									

Directions: I-93 to Exit 43. Right onto Route 133 East. Take your first left.

Sagamore Spring Golf Club

NR ▶ **69**

1287 Main Street
Lynnfield, MA (781) 334-3151
sagamoregolf.com

Tees	Holes	Yards	Par	USGA	Slope
BACK	18	5936	70	68.6	119
MIDDLE	18	5505	70	66.5	114
FRONT	18	4784	70	66.5	112

Club Pro: Steven Vaughn, PGA
Payment: Cash, Credit Cards
Tee Times: 4 days adv.
Fee 9 Holes: Weekday: $23, $33w/cart   **Weekend:** $25, $35 w/cart
Fee 18 Holes: Weekday: $40, $56w/cart   **Weekend:** $4, $62 w/cart
Twilight Rates: 3 hrs before sunset all you can play weekends/holidays only/$17
Discounts: Junior*

COUPON

Cart Rental: $10pp/9, $16pp/18   **Driving Range:** $8/xl, $5/lg bucket
Lessons: $50/half hour **Schools:** No   **Junior Golf:** Yes
Membership: No   **Architect/Yr Open:** Richard Luff/1929
Other: Clubhouse / Showers / Snack Bar

Good pro shop. "Number 9 is a devilish par 3." –NB Course was re-rated in 2007.
*New juniors 'Pay Their Age' every weekday and weekends after 1pm.

	1	2	3	4	5	6	7	8	9
PAR	5	4	5	4	4	3	4	3	3
YARDS	465	344	473	364	276	146	336	179	198
	10	11	12	13	14	15	16	17	18
PAR	4	5	5	4	3	4	4	3	3
YARDS	247	499	431	398	137	330	317	185	180

Directions: Exit 41 off I-95/Route 128. Turn right off exit ramp onto Main Street. 3 miles.

Sandy Burr Country Club

❂❂½ ▶ **70**

103 Cochituate Road
Wayland, MA (508) 358-7211
www.sandyburr.com

Tees	Holes	Yards	Par	USGA	Slope
BACK	18	6412	72	70.8	125
MIDDLE	18	6229	72	69.9	122
FRONT	18	4561	72	66.2	110

Club Pro: Charles Estes
Payment: Most Major
Tee Times: Monday for following week
Fee 9 Holes: Weekday: $30   **Weekend:** $30 twilight only
Fee 18 Holes: Weekday: $47   **Weekend:** $54
Twilight Rates: After 2:30pm   **Discounts:** Senior & Junior M-Th
Cart Rental: $19pp/18, $10.50pp/9   **Driving Range:** No
Lessons: $50/half hour **Schools:** No   **Junior Golf:** No
Membership: No   **Architect/Yr Open:** Donald Ross/1922
Other: Clubhouse / Snack Bar / Bar-Lounge / Showers

Player Comments: "A great Donald Ross course with a good mix of holes. Good to very good shape—depending on the month." Early bird and midday 9-hole rate. Twilight rates.

	1	2	3	4	5	6	7	8	9
PAR	5	5	3	4	3	4	4	4	4
YARDS	471	491	147	429	220	409	335	353	281
	10	11	12	13	14	15	16	17	18
PAR	3	5	4	3	4	4	4	5	4
YARDS	193	450	384	185	369	352	409	521	406

Directions: I-95/Route 128 to Route 20 West exit, at Wayland Center take left onto Route 27 South. Course is 1/4 mile on right.

Sassamon Trace Golf Course ✪✪  71

233 South Main Street
Natick, MA (508) 655-1330
www.sassamontrace.com

Club Pro: Pete Meagher, PGA
Payment: Visa, MC, Amex, Cash
Tee Times: 7 days adv.
Fee 9 Holes: Weekday: $22
Fee 18 Holes: Weekday: $44
Twilight Rates: After 6:30pm
Cart Rental: $16pp/18, $8pp/9
Lessons: $50/45 min **Schools:** No
Membership: Yes
Other: Restaurant / Clubhouse

Tees	Holes	Yards	Par	USGA	Slope
BACK	9	2383	32	31.7	111
MIDDLE	9	2167	32	30.9	107
FRONT	9	1744	32	29.8	96

Weekend: $24
Weekend: $48
Discounts: Sr. & Jr. (weekdays)
Driving Range: No
Junior Golf: Yes
Architect/Yr: Cornish, Silva, and Mungeam/2001
GPS:

COUPON

MetroWest's most unique 9-hole layout. Expansive greens place a premium on putting. A blend of links and traditonal styles.

	1	2	3	4	5	6	7	8	9
PAR	3	4	3	5	3	4	3	3	4
YARDS	158	326	180	529	162	341	177	143	367
PAR									
YARDS									

Directions: I-95/Route 128, to Exit 20 (Route 9 West) and follow for 6.5 miles to Route 27 South. Course is 3 miles South on Route 27 on right.

Scituate Country Club ✪✪½ 72

91 Driftway
Scituate, MA (781) 545-9768
www.scituatecc.com

Club Pro: Jim Dee, PGA
Payment: Cash Only
Tee Times: 2 days adv.
Fee 9 Holes: Weekday: $28 after 11am Mon
Fee 18 Holes: Weekday: $38 after 11am Mon
Twilight Rates: No
Cart Rental: $14pp/18, $9pp/9
Lessons: $50/half hour **Schools:** No
Membership: Yes
Other: Restaurant / Clubhouse / Bar-Lounge / Showers / Lockers / Snack Bar

Tees	Holes	Yards	Par	USGA	Slope
BACK	9	3077	35		
MIDDLE	9	2974	35	69.7	121
FRONT	9	2704	36	71.6	119

Weekend: No public play
Weekend: No public play
Discounts: None
Driving Range: No
Junior Golf: No
Architect/Yr Open:

Open to the public on Mondays only after 11 am. Beautifully maintained seaside golf links with rolling terrain. Great shape. New pro shop. Open April - December.

	1	2	3	4	5	6	7	8	9
PAR	4	3	5	4	4	4	4	3	4
YARDS	407	156	504	373	308	359	357	124	386
PAR									
YARDS									

Directions: Route 3 to Exit 13. Go left off exit. Go to first set of lights, take right onto Route 123. Go to end, go straight across Route 3A. Go onto Driftway Road. Course is 1 mile on right.

South Shore Country Club ✪✪½ ▸73

274 South Street
Hingham, MA (781) 749-8479
www.southshorecc.com

Tees	Holes	Yards	Par	USGA	Slope
BACK	18	6444	72	71.0	128
MIDDLE	18	6197	72	69.9	124
FRONT	18	5064	72	69.3	116

Club Pro:
Payment: Visa, MC, Cash, Check
Tee Times: 7 days adv.
Fee 9 Holes: Weekday: $30 M-Th $36 F   **Weekend:**
Fee 18 Holes: Weekday: $42 M-Th $47 F   **Weekend:** $47 after 11am
Twilight Rates: After 5pm   **Discounts:** Sr. & Jr. weekdays
Cart Rental: $16pp/18, $9pp/9   **Driving Range:** Yes
Lessons: Call for details **Schools:** Yes, Jr.   **Junior Golf:** Yes
Membership: Currently a waiting list   **Architect/Yr Open:** Stiles & Van Kleek/1922
Other: Snack Bar / Restaurant / Bar-Lounge / Clubhouse / Lockers / Showers

Gets more enjoyable with every replay. Classic design. Course in excellent condition.

	1	2	3	4	5	6	7	8	9
PAR	4	3	5	4	4	4	4	3	5
YARDS	277	156	521	319	371	410	360	197	502
	10	11	12	13	14	15	16	17	18
PAR	4	3	4	4	4	5	4	3	5
YARDS	295	179	372	401	327	530	380	148	452

Directions: Route 3 to Exit 14 onto Route 228 North. At 4-mile mark, exit Route 228 and continue straight onto Central Street. At 2nd 4-way stop, turn left onto South Street. Go 1/2 mile, club is on left.

Southers Marsh Golf Club ✪✪✪½ ▸74

30 Southers Marsh Lane
Plymouth, MA (508) 830-3535
www.southersmarsh.com

Tees	Holes	Yards	Par	USGA	Slope
BACK	18	4111	61.0	61.8	112
MIDDLE	18	3694	61	60.4	109
FRONT	18	2907	61	58.2	93

Club Pro: Ted Flynn
Payment: Visa, MC, Amex, Disc, No Checks
Tee Times: 7 days adv.
Fee 9 Holes: Weekday: **Weekend:**
Fee 18 Holes: Weekday: $30 M-Th   **Weekend:** $37 F/S/S
Twilight Rates: After 3pm   **Discounts:** Sr. (M-Th) & Jr. (7 Days)
Cart Rental: $12pp/18   **Driving Range:** Yes
Lessons: $30/half hour **Schools:** No   **Junior Golf:**
Membership: Yes   **Architect/Yr Open:** D. Tibbett/2001
Other: Restaurant / Clubhouse / Bar-Lounge   **GPS:**

COUPON

Wins accolades from all levels of players. Each par is well-earned. "Outstanding conditions, staff, and beauty (set among cranberry bogs). Should be on your must-play list." –JD

	1	2	3	4	5	6	7	8	9
PAR	4	3	3	4	3	4	3	4	3
YARDS	300	139	175	353	138	285	129	263	158
	10	11	12	13	14	15	16	17	18
PAR	3	3	3	4	3	4	3	3	4
YARDS	123	121	97	304	121	314	157	165	352

Directions: Route 3 to Exit 6B (or 6 and turn left at bottom of ramp from the South) toward Carver. At second light, turn left onto Pilgrim Hill Road. Turn right at light onto Federal Furnace Road. After 4 miles, SMGC on left. Also minutes from Exit 2 off Route 495.

Squirrel Run Country Club ✪✪ 75

32 Elderberry Drive
Plymouth, MA (508) 746-5001
www.golfatsquirrelrun.com

Tees	Holes	Yards	Par	USGA	Slope
BACK	18	2859	57	55.4	85
MIDDLE	18	2338	57	53.7	82
FRONT	18	1990	57	56.0	83

Club Pro: David Moore, PGA
Payment: Visa, MC
Tee Times: 7 days adv.
Fee 9 Holes: Weekday: No **Weekend:** No
Fee 18 Holes: Weekday: $27 **Weekend:** $30
Twilight Rates: After 4pm **Discounts:** Senior & Junior
Cart Rental: $22/18 per cart **Driving Range:** No
Lessons: Yes **Schools:** No **Junior Golf:** Yes
Membership: Yes **Architect/Yr Open:** Ray Richard/1991
Other: Restaurant / Clubhouse / Bar-Lounge / Snack Bar

Player Comments: "A challenge to anyone's short game." "Immaculate greens and tees." Sister course: Village Links. Winner of the 2006 Plymouth Golden Sprinkler Award for Service & Condition.

	1	2	3	4	5	6	7	8	9
PAR	4	3	3	3	4	3	3	3	4
YARDS	286	105	125	90	263	98	131	123	206
	10	11	12	13	14	15	16	17	18
PAR	3	3	3	3	3	3	3	3	3
YARDS	99	78	102	102	140	100	116	74	100

Directions: Route 3 to Exit 6. Go approximately 2 miles to course on left. Look for Squirrel Run sign.

Stoneham Oaks NR 76

101 R Montvale Avenue
Stoneham, MA (781) 438-7888

Tees	Holes	Yards	Par	USGA	Slope
BACK					
MIDDLE	9	1125	27	N/A	N/A
FRONT					

Club Pro: Kent Pratt, PGA
Payment: Cash Only
Tee Times: No
Fee 9 Holes: Weekday: $10 after 2pm **Weekend:** $16
Fee 18 Holes: Weekday: $20 after 2pm **Weekend:** $27
Twilight Rates: No **Discounts:** Senior & Junior
Cart Rental: $13/9 per cart, $2/pull **Driving Range:** No
Lessons: $40/half hour **Schools:** No **Junior Golf:** No
Membership: No **Architect/Yr Open:**
Other: **GPS:**

Very hilly, many trees. Very scenic. Various reduced weekday rates between 7am and 2pm.

	1	2	3	4	5	6	7	8	9
PAR	3	3	3	3	3	3	3	3	3
YARDS	89	147	179	128	95	113	153	139	82
PAR									
YARDS									

Directions: I-93 to Exit 36, Stoneham, Montvale Avenue, 1 block. Course is at rear of the Stoneham Ice Rink.

Stony Brook Golf Course

NR ▶ 77

70 Valley Road
Southboro, MA (508) 485-3151
www.stonybrook.com

Club Pro: Jack Hester, PGA
Payment: Visa, MC
Tee Times: Yes
Fee 9 Holes: Weekday: $13
Fee 18 Holes: Weekday: $18
Twilight Rates: After 6:30pm
Cart Rental: $2/pull
Lessons: Yes **Schools:** Kids Camps
Membership: No
Other: Snack Bar / Accessories / Kids' Camps

Tees	Holes	Yards	Par	USGA	Slope
BACK					
MIDDLE	9	1342	27		
FRONT					

Weekend: $13
Weekend:
Discounts: Senior & Junior
Driving Range: No
Junior Golf: No
Architect/Yr Open: Ernest Kallender/1970
GPS:

Player Comments: "No-frills course, but always improving. Plays fair. Greens are beautiful, honest but must be read right. Need accurate iron play." Good for beginners and experienced golfers.

	1	2	3	4	5	6	7	8	9
PAR	3	3	3	3	3	3	3	3	3
YARDS	145	138	210	125	132	165	169	107	151
PAR									
YARDS									

Directions: Accessible from Routes I-90, I-495, and Route 9. Located in Southboro off Route 30 on Valley Road.

Stow Acres CC (North)

✿✿✿ ▶ 78

58 Randall Road
Stow, MA (978) 568-1100
www.stowacres.com

Club Pro: Dave Carlson, PGA
Payment: Visa, MC, Amex
Tee Times: 10 days adv.
Fee 9 Holes: Wkdy: $29 M-Th (rates sub. to change)
Fee 18 Holes: Weekday: $49 M-Th
Twilight Rates: After 4pm
Cart Rental: $18pp/18
Lessons: $80/hour **Schools:** Yes
Membership: Gold Card membership
Other: Clubhouse / Snack Bar / Bar-Lounge

Tees	Holes	Yards	Par	USGA	Slope
BACK	18	6939	72	72.8	130
MIDDLE	18	6310	72	70.5	127
FRONT	18	6011	72	72.5	130

Weekend: $39 F/S/S
Weekend: $64 F/S/S
Discounts: Senior & Junior weekdays
Driving Range: $9/lg, $7/med, $5/sm bucket
Junior Golf: Yes
Architect/Yr Open: Geoffrey Cornish/1972
GPS:

PGA Tour Qualifier site. Championship layout. Black tees added. Open mid-March to mid-December.
*Play-before-work special: before 7:50am weekdays $39/18 holes.

	1	2	3	4	5	6	7	8	9
PAR	5	4	4	4	5	3	4	3	4
YARDS	503	374	354	387	472	180	318	165	426
	10	11	12	13	14	15	16	17	18
PAR	4	4	5	3	4	4	3	4	5
YARDS	359	392	424	169	340	369	166	376	536

Directions: I-95/Route 128 to Route 20/117 Exit. Go West on Route 117 approx. 15 miles; left in Stow Center onto Route 62 West, follow signs from Route 62 to course.

Stow Acres CC (South) ✪✪✪

58 Randall Road
Stow, MA (978) 568-1100
www.stowacres.com

Tees	Holes	Yards	Par	USGA	Slope
BACK	18	6520	72	71.8	120
MIDDLE	18	6105	72	70.5	118
FRONT	18	5642	72	72.5	120

Club Pro: Dave Carlson, PGA
Payment: Visa, MC, Amex
Tee Times: 10 days adv.
Fee   9 Holes: Wkdy: $26 (rates subject to change) **Weekend:** $33
Fee 18 Holes: Weekday: $39   **Weekend:** $54
Twilight Rates: After 4pm   **Discounts:** Senior & Junior weekdays
Cart Rental: $18pp/18   **Driving Range:** $9/lg, $7/med, $5/sm bucket
Lessons: $80/hour **Schools:** Yes   **Junior Golf:** Yes
Membership: Yes   **Architect/Yr Open:** Geoffrey Cornish/1965
Other: Clubhouse / Snack Bar / Bar-Lounge   **GPS:**

Variety of instructional packages. Variety of inner clubs. New cart paths. Course conditions improved.
Prices subject to change. *Play before work special - before 7:50am weekdays $33/18 holes.

	1	2	3	4	5	6	7	8	9
PAR	4	4	3	4	5	5	3	4	4
YARDS	375	416	123	301	476	487	212	346	368
	10	**11**	**12**	**13**	**14**	**15**	**16**	**17**	**18**
PAR	5	3	4	4	5	3	4	3	5
YARDS	543	127	366	292	441	151	407	167	507

Directions: Route I-95/128 to Route 20/117 Exit. Go West on Route 117 approx. 15 miles;
left in Stow Center onto Route 62 West, follow signs from Route 62 to course.

Strawberry Valley Golf Course

164 Washington Street
Abington, MA (781) 878-2845
www.johnsongolfmanagement.com

Tees	Holes	Yards	Par	USGA	Slope
BACK					
MIDDLE	9	2280	34	66.9	99
FRONT					

Club Pro: Bill Allen, PGA
Payment: Visa, MC, Amex, Disc
Tee Times: Daily 6am-8am
Fee   9 Holes: Weekday: $17 walk/$25 ride   **Weekend:** $19 walk/$27 ride
Fee 18 Holes: Weekday: $29 walk/$44 ride   **Weekend:** $33 walk/$48 ride
Twilight Rates: No   **Discounts:** Senior & Junior $15/9 holes weekday
                                                      $26 walking weekday resident/jr/sr
Cart Rental: $16/9, $30/18 per cart, $5/pull   **Driving Range:** No
Lessons: Call for details **Schools:** No   **Junior Golf:** Yes
Membership: Limited   **Architect/Yr Open:**
Other: Snack Bar   **GPS:**

Player-friendly. Features senior, junior and beginner play. New management. Open year round.

	1	2	3	4	5	6	7	8	9
PAR	4	4	4	4	4	3	3	4	4
YARDS	228	357	385	233	215	119	132	302	309
PAR									
YARDS									

Directions: Route 3 to Route 18 South. Course is approximately 7 miles on right.

Swanson Meadows   ✪✪ 81 ▶

216 Rangeway Road
North Billerica, MA (978) 670-7777
www.swansonmeadows.com

Club Pro:
Payment: Visa, MC
Tee Times: Yes, 7 days
Fee 9 Holes: Weekday: $19
Fee 18 Holes: Weekday: $38
Twilight Rates: No
Cart Rental: $14/9 per cart
Lessons: Schools:
Membership: Yes, Season Passes
Other: Restaurant / Lounge

Tees	Holes	Yards	Par	USGA	Slope
BACK					
MIDDLE	9	2180	32		
FRONT	9	1829	32		

Weekend: $23
Weekend: $46
Discounts: Senior
Driving Range: No
Junior Golf:
Architect/Yr: Cornish, Silva, Mungeam/2001
GPS:

"Layout squeezed onto a moderate space." –RW Player Comments: "Quick hike after work." New clubhouse, restaurant, and lounge.

	1	2	3	4	5	6	7	8	9
PAR	4	4	4	3	3	4	3	3	4
YARDS	360	286	345	163	119	296	121	146	344
PAR									
YARDS									

Directions: Route 3 to Exit 29. Take Route 129 East. Off ramp, go 1 mile, take right on to Rangeway Road. Course is 1 mile on left.

Tewksbury Country Club   ✪✪ 82 ▶

1880 Main Street
Tewksbury, MA (978) 640-0033
www.tewksburycc.com

Club Pro: Mike Rogers, PGA
Payment: Visa, MC, Amex, Disc
Tee Times: Friday/Saturday/Sunday
Fee 9 Holes: Weekday: $20
Fee 18 Holes: Weekday: $30
Twilight Rates: After 3pm
Cart Rental: $14pp/18, $8pp/9
Lessons: Yes **Schools:** Junior
Membership: Yes
Other: Clubhouse

Tees	Holes	Yards	Par	USGA	Slope
BACK	9	2701	33	33.3	114
MIDDLE	9	2529	33	32.2	112
FRONT	9	1971	33	31.4	107

Weekend: $24
Weekend: $40
Discounts: Senior & Junior
Driving Range: No
Junior Golf: Yes
Architect/Yr Open: Frank Stasio/1998
GPS:

Player Comments: "Nice 9 holes, great staff, and great pro. Seems you can always get a good tee time. Nice layout and the price is right." 4 sets of tees challenge all golfers.

	1	2	3	4	5	6	7	8	9
PAR	4	3	3	4	4	5	4	3	3
YARDS	350	179	148	397	336	475	330	161	136
PAR									
YARDS									

Directions: I-93 to Exit 42 (Dascomb Road) toward Tewksbury. Turn left onto Shawsheen Street. Follow Shawsheen to Route 38. Turn right onto Livingston Street. From Route 128, take Route 38 North to Livingston Street.

Trull Brook Golf Course ✪✪✪ ▶83

170 River Road
Tewksbury, MA (978) 851-6731
www.trullbrook.com

Tees	Holes	Yards	Par	USGA	Slope
BACK	18	6345	72	69.8	123
MIDDLE	18	6006	72	68.8	122
FRONT	18	5193	72	69.6	118

Club Pro: Al Santos, PGA
Payment: Visa, MC
Tee Times: 1 week adv.
Fee 9 Holes: Weekday: $22.50 M-F pm   **Weekend:** $24
Fee 18 Holes: Weekday: $42 M-Th   **Weekend:** $46 F $47.50S/S/H
Twilight Rates: After 5pm
Discounts: Sr. & Jr. (M-Th), Clergy: $16; Junior under 17 accompanied with adult: $31.50/18
Cart Rental: $29/18, $15/9 per cart   **Driving Range:** No
Lessons: Yes **Schools:** No   **Junior Golf:** No
Membership: No   **Architect/Yr Open:** Geoffrey Cornish/1962
Other: Clubhouse / Lockers / Showers / Snack Bar / Winter Tennis Center

Player Comments: "Very well kept. Nice greens." "Challenging course. Scenic." Geoffrey Cornish design. Dress code. Open dawn to dusk.

	1	2	3	4	5	6	7	8	9
PAR	4	5	4	3	4	3	5	4	4
YARDS	338	498	383	123	368	138	470	353	323
	10	11	12	13	14	15	16	17	18
PAR	4	3	5	4	4	3	4	5	4
YARDS	323	168	463	323	343	178	373	458	383

Directions: From I-495 or I-93, take Route 133 exit, follow West toward Lowell. At Mobil station, sharp right onto River Road. Course is 1/3 mile on left.

Unicorn Golf Course ✪✪ ▶84

460 William Street
Stoneham, MA (781) 438-9732

Tees	Holes	Yards	Par	USGA	Slope
BACK	9	3234	35	70.8	126
MIDDLE	9	3185	35	69.6	121
FRONT	9	2902	37	73.0	124

Club Pro: Carl Marchio
Payment: Cash Only
Tee Times: No
Fee 9 Holes: Weekday: $19   **Weekend:** $20
Fee 18 Holes: Weekday: No   **Weekend:** No
Twilight Rates: No   **Discounts:** Senior & Junior (M-F), Resident
Cart Rental: $13/9 per cart   **Driving Range:** No
Lessons: Yes **Schools:** No   **Junior Golf:** No
Membership: No   **Architect/Yr Open:** Stiles & Van Kleek/1928
Other: Snack Bar   **GPS:**

Stoneham resident rates. The course is relatively level; easy walk. Nice par 3s, and #7 and #9 are great holes.

	1	2	3	4	5	6	7	8	9
PAR	4	4	4	3	4	5	4	3	4
YARDS	389	326	335	168	395	499	448	178	447
PAR									
YARDS									

Directions: I-93 to Montvale Avenue. Follow to end. Take left onto Route 28, then left at next set of lights (Williams Street). Course is 1/4 mile on left.

Village Links

265 South Meadow Road
Plymouth, MA (508) 830-4653
www.golfatvillagelinks.com

Club Pro: David L. Moore, PGA
Payment: Visa, MC
Tee Times: 7 days adv.

Tees	Holes	Yards	Par	USGA	Slope
BACK	18	2407	54		
MIDDLE	18	1986	54	52.8	78
FRONT					

Fee 9 Holes: Weekday: **Weekend:**
Fee 18 Holes: Weekday: $25   **Weekend:** $27
Twilight Rates: Yes   **Discounts:** Senior & Junior
Cart Rental: $16pp/18   **Driving Range:**
Lessons: $40/half hour   **Schools:** Yes   **Junior Golf:** Yes
Membership: **Architect/Yr Open:** Ray Richard/2000
Other: Restaurant / Clubhouse / Bar-Lounge   **GPS:**

18-hole par 3, executive-style. Associated with Pinehurst Village. Sister course to Squirrel Run. "Excellent holes include #4, 5, 8, 11, 15, 17." –AP

	1	2	3	4	5	6	7	8	9
PAR	3	3	3	3	3	3	3	3	3
YARDS	134	141	159	57	114	124	113	60	76
	10	11	12	13	14	15	16	17	18
PAR	3	3	3	3	3	3	3	3	3
YARDS	133	112	130	84	79	96	136	74	164

Directions: Route 3 to Exit 6 West (Route 44). Turn left at the 3rd set of lights onto Seven Hills Road. Turn right at the 1st set of lights onto South Meadow Road. Village Links is 2.5 miles on the right.

Waverly Oaks - Challenger 9

444 Long Pond Road
Plymouth, MA (508) 224-6016
www.waverlyoaksgolfclub.com

Club Pro:
Payment: Most Major Credit Cards
Tee Times: Walk-up 7 days a week

Tees	Holes	Yards	Par	USGA	Slope
BACK	9	2268	33		
MIDDLE	9	2005	33		
FRONT	9	1659	33		

Fee 9 Holes: Weekday: $25 w/cart   **Weekend:** $32.50 w/cart F/S/S
Fee 18 Holes: Weekday: **Weekend:**
Twilight Rates: No   **Discounts:** Junior
Cart Rental: Included   **Driving Range:** $5/lg, $3/sm
Lessons: Yes   **Schools:** Yes   **Junior Golf:** Yes
Membership: No   **Architect/Yr Open:** Brian Silva/1998
Other: Play Pass Packs Available   **GPS:**

COUPON

Player Comments: "Pure fun! A great opening hole. Several par 4s reachable from tee." 3 sets of tees. First come, first serve. Executive course layout for golfers of all levels.

	1	2	3	4	5	6	7	8	9
PAR	4	4	4	3	4	4	4	3	3
YARDS	298	298	199	103	334	259	255	159	94
PAR									
YARDS									

Directions: Take Route 3 to Exit 3, follow signs.

Waverly Oaks Golf Club ✪✪✪✪

444 Long Pond Road
Plymouth, MA (508) 224-6016
www.waverlyoaksgolfclub.com
Club Pro:
Payment: Visa, MC, Amex, Disc
Tee Times: 7 days adv.
Fee 9 Holes: Weekday: $25 w/cart
Fee 18 Holes: Weekday: $75 w/cart
Twilight Rates: After 2pm
Cart Rental: Included
Lessons: $35/half hour **Schools:** No
Membership: Season Pass

Tees	Holes	Yards	Par	USGA	Slope
BACK	18	7114	72	73.5	130
MIDDLE	18	6682	72	71.3	126
FRONT	18	5587	72	71.4	127

Weekend: $35 w/cart
Weekend: $95 w/cart
Discounts: None
Driving Range: $5/lg., $3/sm.
Junior Golf: Yes
Architect/Yr Open: Brian Silva /1998

COUPON

Other: Full Restaurant / Clubhouse / Bar-Lounge / Showers / Corporate Outings / Small Group Outings

Player Comments: "Best course all round I've played. Not a blemish. Money well worth it." "A gem." –RW
Improvements at 17th hole. Tee times can be made online at www.waverlyoaksgolfclub.com.

	1	2	3	4	5	6	7	8	9
PAR	4	4	3	5	5	4	4	3	4
YARDS	325	394	191	502	515	432	410	184	353
	10	**11**	**12**	**13**	**14**	**15**	**16**	**17**	**18**
PAR	4	4	4	5	3	4	5	3	4
YARDS	386	372	311	512	163	449	606	221	356

Directions: Route 3 to Exit 3. Right off ramp. Right at first stop sign. Entrance 2 miles on right.

Wayland Country Club ✪✪½

121 Old Sudbury Road
Wayland, MA (508) 358-4775
www.waylandcc.com
Club Pro: John Gordon, PGA
Payment: Credit Cards, Cash
Tee Times: Call Monday for weekends
Fee 9 Holes: Weekday: $25
Fee 18 Holes: Weekday: $36
Twilight Rates: After 6pm
Cart Rental: $16pp/18, $10pp/9
Lessons: $40-$80/hour **Schools:** No
Membership: Yes
Other: Restaurant / Clubhouse / Snack Bar / Bar-Lounge
GPS: Yes

Tees	Holes	Yards	Par	USGA	Slope
BACK	18	5974	70	67.9	114
MIDDLE	9	5836	70	68.2	112
FRONT	18	4875	71	68.2	111

Weekend: $28
Weekend: $46
Discounts: Senior & Junior
Driving Range: No
Junior Golf: Yes
Architect/Yr Open: Mitchell/1920s

Course is fairly flat with small greens and alternating wide and narrow fairways. Easy to walk. Great staff.

	1	2	3	4	5	6	7	8	9
PAR	5	4	4	3	4	3	4	3	4
YARDS	443	412	384	139	353	188	260	153	405
	10	**11**	**12**	**13**	**14**	**15**	**16**	**17**	**18**
PAR	4	4	5	4	3	4	4	3	5
YARDS	320	326	500	346	174	378	400	198	457

Directions: I-95/Route 128 to Route 20 West; right onto Route 27 North; approximately 1 mile right.

Wenham Country Club   ✪✪   ▶ 89

Main Street
Wenham, MA (978) 468-4714
www.wenhamcountryclub.com

Club Pro: Darin Chin-Aleong, PGA
Payment: Cash, Credit Cards
Tee Times: Weekends
Fee 9 Holes: Weekday: $22
Fee 18 Holes: Weekday: $34
Twilight Rates: After 5pm
Cart Rental: $17pp/18, $10pp/9
Lessons: Yes **Schools:** No
Membership: Yes
Other: Snack Bar until 2pm Thursday - Sunday

Tees	Holes	Yards	Par	USGA	Slope
BACK					
MIDDLE	18	4554	65	62.8	109
FRONT	18	4321	67	65.2	108

Weekend: $22 (after 12pm)
Weekend: $40 (after 12pm)
Discounts: None
Driving Range: No
Junior Golf: Yes
Architect/Yr Open: 1899
GPS:

COUPON

Semi-private but open to public 7 days a week. Call for available times. In operation for over 100 years.

	1	2	3	4	5	6	7	8	9
PAR	4	3	3	4	3	4	3	4	3
YARDS	347	115	187	279	208	309	153	278	170
	10	11	12	13	14	15	16	17	18
PAR	3	5	3	3	4	4	4	4	4
YARDS	216	413	186	136	357	246	382	300	272

Directions: I-95/Route 128 to Exit 20A. Route 1A toward Hamilton. Club is approximately 2 miles ahead on the right.

White Pines Golf Course   NR   ▶ 90

549 Copeland Street
Brockton, MA
(508) 586-3260

Club Pro:
Payment: Cash only
Tee Times:
Fee 9 Holes: Weekday: $17
Fee 18 Holes: Weekday: $24
Twilight Rates: No
Cart Rental: $12pp/18, $8pp/9
Lessons: **Schools:** No
Membership: No
Other:

Tees	Holes	Yards	Par	USGA	Slope
BACK					
MIDDLE	9	2687	36		
FRONT					

Weekend: $18
Weekend: $25
Discounts: Senior & Junior
Driving Range: None
Junior Golf:
Architect/Yr Open: 1926
GPS:

Rolling terrain, friendly staff, greens in excellent condition this year.

	1	2	3	4	5	6	7	8	9
PAR	4	4	5	4	4	4	3	4	4
YARDS	235	389	467	267	246	334	127	282	340
PAR									
YARDS									

Directions: Route 24 to Exit 16A (Route 106). Take left onto Crescent Street. After 1.5 miles, go left onto North Elm. Club is 1.5 miles on left.

Widow's Walk Golf Course ❂❂½   91

250 The Driftway
Scituate, MA (781) 544-0032
www.widowswalkgolf.com

Club Pro: Bob Sanderson, PGA
Payment: Visa, MC, Amex, Disc
Tee Times: 4 days adv.

Tees	Holes	Yards	Par	USGA	Slope
BACK	18	6403	72	71.2	129
MIDDLE	18	6062	72	69.6	127
FRONT	18	4562	72	66.2	113

Fee 9 Holes: Weekday: $20 M-Th
Fee 18 Holes: Weekday: $34 M-Th
Twilight Rates: No
Cart Rental: $28pp/18, $16pp/9
Lessons: $50/45 minutes **Schools:** No
Membership: Weekday only
Other: Restaurant / Bar

Weekend: $24 F/S/S
Weekend: $42 F/S/S
Discounts: Senior & Junior M-Th
Driving Range: $3.50/bucket
Junior Golf: Yes
Architect/Yr Open: Michael Hurdzan/1997
GPS:

COUPON

Challenging course, very well groomed, great ocean views. Some of the best public greens anywhere.
Rated 4 stars *Golf Digest* 'Best Places to Play'

	1	2	3	4	5	6	7	8	9
PAR	5	3	4	4	4	5	3	4	5
YARDS	504	126	350	351	302	486	167	313	481
	10	**11**	**12**	**13**	**14**	**15**	**16**	**17**	**18**
PAR	4	3	4	4	3	5	4	3	5
YARDS	425	140	313	412	183	486	312	191	520

Directions: Route 3 to Exit 13, Route 53 North to Route 123 East. 6 miles on Route 123 East
to rotary. Second right on rotary. Course is 7/10 mile on left.

Willowdale Golf Course NR 92

54 Willow Street
Mansfield, MA (508) 339-3197

Club Pro: No
Payment: Cash Only
Tee Times: No

Tees	Holes	Yards	Par	USGA	Slope
BACK					
MIDDLE	9	1935	30		
FRONT					

Fee 9 Holes: Weekday: $15
Fee 18 Holes: Weekday: $18
Twilight Rates: No
Cart Rental: $2/pull
Lessons: No **Schools:** No
Membership: No
Other: Snack Bar / Bar-Lounge / Clubhouse

Weekend: $17
Weekend: $20
Discounts: Senior M-F $1 off
Driving Range: No
Junior Golf: Yes
Architect/Yr Open:
GPS:

Executive-style course, considered an easy walker. Open April 1 - December 1.

	1	2	3	4	5	6	7	8	9
PAR	4	3	3	4	4	3	3	3	3
YARDS	265	180	190	320	285	180	100	210	205
PAR									
YARDS									

Directions: I-95 to Mansfield exit. Route 140 to Mansfield Center, School Street exit. First right on
Willow Street.

Woburn Country Club

5 Country Club Road
Woburn, MA (781) 933-9880

Tees	Holes	Yards	Par	USGA	Slope
BACK					
MIDDLE	9	2996	34	68.9	121
FRONT	9	2565	35	68.0	104

Club Pro: Paul Barkhouse, PGA
Payment: Visa, MC
Tee Times: 2 days/weekends only
Fee 9 Holes: Weekday: $20   **Weekend:** $21
Fee 18 Holes: Weekday: $29   **Weekend:** $34
Twilight Rates: No   **Discounts:** Senior & Junior (weekdays only)
Cart Rental: $28/18, $16/9 per cart   **Driving Range:** No
Lessons: $40/half hour **Schools:** No   **Junior Golf:** Yes
Membership: Residents only   **Architect/Yr Open:**
Other: Restaurant / Snack Bar / Function Hall   **GPS:**

Small greens. Need a good short game to score well, every lie in the book. Dress code required. Resident rates available.

	1	2	3	4	5	6	7	8	9
PAR	4	4	4	4	4	4	3	4	3
YARDS	373	363	359	371	410	326	190	389	215
PAR									
YARDS									

Directions: I-93 to I-95/Route 128 South, Exit 33A (Winchester), straight through Woburn Four Corners, take left at first set of lights onto Country Club Road.

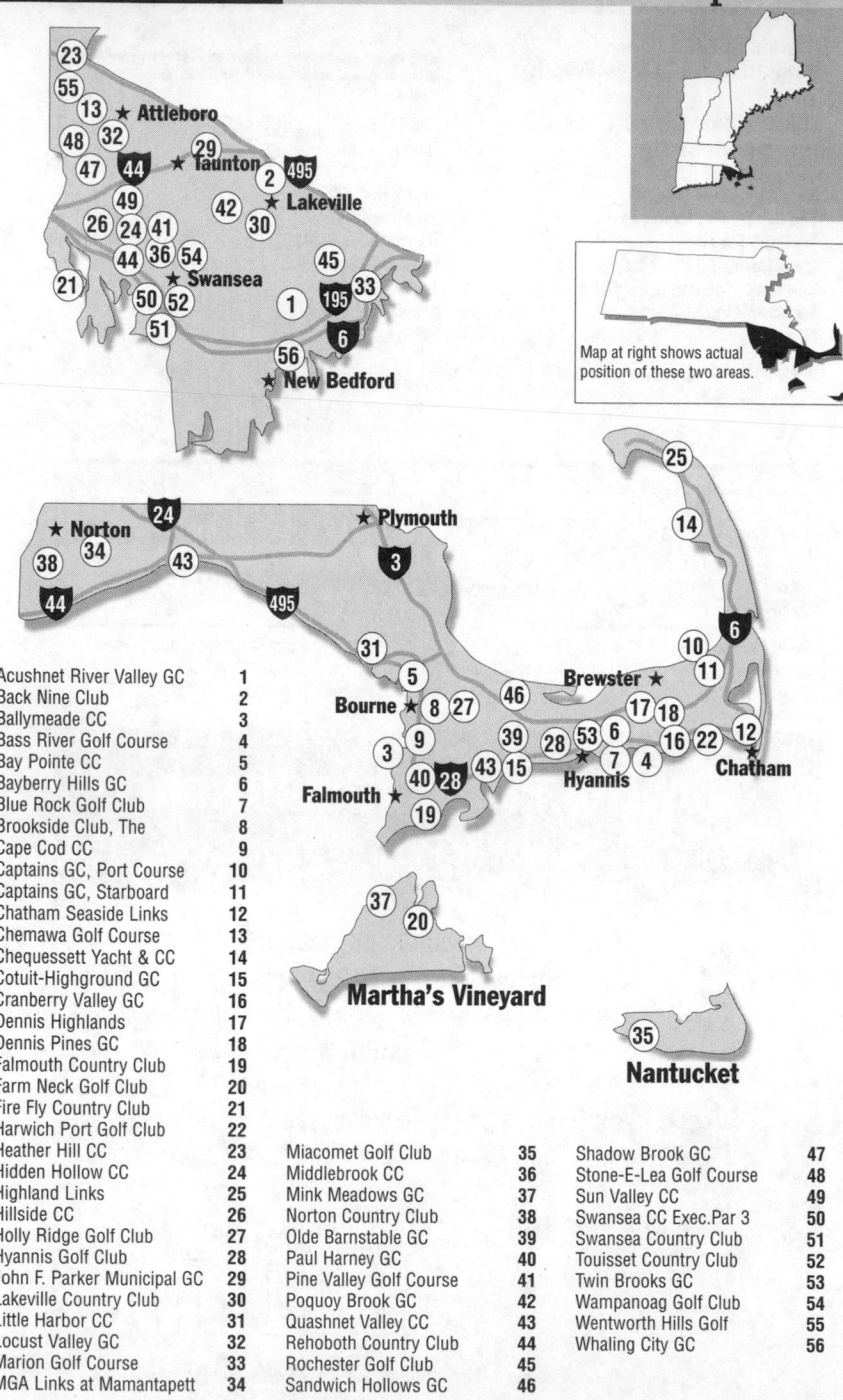

Map at right shows actual position of these two areas.

Martha's Vineyard

Nantucket

Acushnet River Valley GC	1
Back Nine Club	2
Ballymeade CC	3
Bass River Golf Course	4
Bay Pointe CC	5
Bayberry Hills GC	6
Blue Rock Golf Club	7
Brookside Club, The	8
Cape Cod CC	9
Captains GC, Port Course	10
Captains GC, Starboard	11
Chatham Seaside Links	12
Chemawa Golf Course	13
Chequessett Yacht & CC	14
Cotuit-Highground GC	15
Cranberry Valley GC	16
Dennis Highlands	17
Dennis Pines GC	18
Falmouth Country Club	19
Farm Neck Golf Club	20
Fire Fly Country Club	21
Harwich Port Golf Club	22
Heather Hill CC	23
Hidden Hollow CC	24
Highland Links	25
Hillside CC	26
Holly Ridge Golf Club	27
Hyannis Golf Club	28
John F. Parker Municipal GC	29
Lakeville Country Club	30
Little Harbor CC	31
Locust Valley GC	32
Marion Golf Course	33
MGA Links at Mamantapett	34

Miacomet Golf Club	35
Middlebrook CC	36
Mink Meadows GC	37
Norton Country Club	38
Olde Barnstable GC	39
Paul Harney GC	40
Pine Valley Golf Course	41
Poquoy Brook GC	42
Quashnet Valley CC	43
Rehoboth Country Club	44
Rochester Golf Club	45
Sandwich Hollows GC	46

Shadow Brook GC	47
Stone-E-Lea Golf Course	48
Sun Valley CC	49
Swansea CC Exec.Par 3	50
Swansea Country Club	51
Touisset Country Club	52
Twin Brooks GC	53
Wampanoag Golf Club	54
Wentworth Hills Golf	55
Whaling City GC	56

KEY TO THE STAR RATINGS:
5✪= Outstanding 4✪= Excellent 3✪= Very Good 2✪= Good 1✪= Average **NR** = Not Rated

Acushnet River Valley GC ⊕⊕⊕¹/₂ ▶ 1

685 Main Street
Acushnet, MA (508) 998-7777
www.golfacushnet.com

Club Pro: Daniel Beaulieu, PGA
Payment: All Types
Tee Times: 7 days adv.
Fee 9 Holes: Weekday: $20
Fee 18 Holes: Weekday: $38
Twilight Rates: After 3pm
Cart Rental: $15pp/18, $8pp/9
Lessons: $40 **Schools:** Yes
Membership: Season Passes
Other: Snack Bar / Clubhouse / Bar-Lounge

Tees	Holes	Yards	Par	USGA	Slope
BACK	18	6302	72	70.0	122
MIDDLE	18	5735	72	66.9	116
FRONT	18	5099	72	68.4	115

Weekend: $26
Weekend: $45
Discounts: Junior
Driving Range: $6/lg, $4/sm bucket
Junior Golf: Yes
Architect/Yr Open: Brian Silva/1998
GPS: Yes

COUPON

Dick LaGrasse School of Golf. "Region's best kept secret." Pine Alley front 9, Scottish Links back 9 — 2 golf courses in 1. "Our group comes down every year from NH. We love it." –RM

	1	2	3	4	5	6	7	8	9
PAR	4	4	4	5	4	3	4	3	5
YARDS	375	289	275	436	336	119	382	141	501
	10	11	12	13	14	15	16	17	18
PAR	4	3	5	4	5	4	4	3	4
YARDS	315	113	470	388	529	257	328	145	336

Directions: I-95/Route 128 to Route 24 South to Route 140 South. Take Exit 6 to Route 18 South. Stay on Route 18 South for 2 miles. At lights, turn left onto Tarkiln Hill Road, which becomes Main Street in Acushnet. Course will be on left about 2 miles after Acushnet Town Hall.

Back Nine Club, The ⊕⊕¹/₂ ▶ 2

17 Heritage Hill Drive
Lakeville, MA (508) 947-9991
www.thebacknineclub.com

Club Pro: Joe Klein
Payment: Visa, MC, Amex, Disc
Tee Times: Yes
Fee 9 Holes: Weekday: $15
Fee 18 Holes: Weekday: $27
Twilight Rates: After 3pm
Cart Rental: $20pp/18, $10pp/9, $3/pull
Lessons: Yes **Schools:** No
Membership: Yes
Other: Leagues / Outings

Tees	Holes	Yards	Par	USGA	Slope
BACK	18	3012	54	54.7	84
MIDDLE	18	2575	54	54.7	84
FRONT	18	2155	54	54.7	84

Weekend: $20
Weekend: $31
Discounts: Senior & Junior
Driving Range: No
Junior Golf: No
Architect/Yr Open: Geoffrey Cornish/1974
GPS:

COUPON

Previously Heritage Hill Country Club. Under new ownership. Completely renovated clubhouse now with full restaurant and bar. Renovated pro shop and new outside deck. Course renovations are ongoing. Sig. Hole: #16, 145-yard par 3. Beginner-friendly certified by NGCOA. Open all year round.

	1	2	3	4	5	6	7	8	9
PAR	3	3	3	3	3	3	3	3	3
YARDS	155	190	160	140	145	155	115	170	145
	10	11	12	13	14	15	16	17	18
PAR	3	3	3	3	3	3	3	3	3
YARDS	140	130	125	110	145	120	145	160	125

Directions: Take I-495 to Exit 5. Go South on Route 18. Go through intersection of Route 18 and Route 10 and take first right after mini-mart onto Highland Road. Take first right onto Heritage Hill Drive and course is 1/4 mile down road.

Ballymeade Country Club ✪✪½ 3

125 Falmouth Woods Road
North Falmouth, MA (508) 540-4005
www.ballymeade.com

Tees	Holes	Yards	Par	USGA	Slope
BACK	18	6928	72	74.3	139
MIDDLE	18	6358	72	71.7	134
FRONT	18	5001	72	69.9	119

Club Pro: Craig Garris, PGA
Payment: Cash, Credit Cards
Tee Times: 1 week adv.
Fee 9 Holes: Weekday: **Weekend:**
Fee 18 Holes: Weekday: am $71, 12pm $56, 3pm $37 all w/cart
Weekend: am $81, 12pm $66, 3pm $40 all w/cart
Twilight Rates: After 12pm and 3pm   **Discounts:** None
Cart Rental: Included   **Driving Range:** $8/lg bucket
Lessons: $50/half hour $75/hr **Schools:** No   **Junior Golf:** Yes
Membership: Yes   **Architect/Yr Open:** Jim Fazio/1988
Other: Restaurant / Clubhouse / Bar-Lounge / Lockers / Snack Bar / Showers
GPS: Yes

Player Comments: "Challenging. Scenic." Hole 11: Highest point on Cape; can see the Bay, New Bedford, over Marion to Fairhaven, all the boats in between. Off-season rates. Open year-round.

	1	2	3	4	5	6	7	8	9
PAR	4	3	5	4	3	4	4	5	4
YARDS	355	183	464	333	164	419	367	464	390
	10	11	12	13	14	15	16	17	18
PAR	5	3	4	4	3	4	4	4	5
YARDS	500	164	403	415	380	331	156	367	503

Directions: Over Bourne Bridge to Route 28 South. Exit at North Falmouth Route 151, 9 miles from the bridge. Turn right off the exit ramp. Course is less than 1 mile on the right.

Bass River Golf Course ✪✪✪ 4

62 Highbank Road
South Yarmouth, MA
(508) 398-9079
www.golfyarmouthcapecod.com

Tees	Holes	Yards	Par	USGA	Slope
BACK	18	6129	72	68.5	115
MIDDLE	18	5709	72	66.4	107
FRONT	18	5136	72	68.7	113

Club Pro: Fred Ghioto
Payment: Visa, MC, Disc
Tee Times: 7 days adv. (508) 398-4112
Fee 9 Holes: Weekday: No   **Weekend:** No
Fee 18 Holes: Weekday: $55   **Weekend:** $55
Twilight Rates: After 2pm   **Discounts:** None
Cart Rental: $18pp/18, $10.25pp/9   **Driving Range:** No
Lessons: Yes **Schools:** No   **Junior Golf:** No
Membership: No   **Architect/Yr Open:** Donald Ross/1900
Other: Clubhouse / Snack Bar / Bar-Lounge   **GPS:**

Proximity to river creates constant breezes. Excellent condition. Carts with GPS. "Ross design—smallish, tilted greens are exceptional." –JD

	1	2	3	4	5	6	7	8	9
PAR	3	4	4	4	4	4	3	5	3
YARDS	165	282	391	329	348	282	105	464	155
	10	11	12	13	14	15	16	17	18
PAR	4	4	5	5	3	4	5	4	4
YARDS	247	386	450	500	140	333	474	319	339

Directions: Route 6 to Exit 8. Right off ramp take 1st left after high school to course.

Bay Pointe Country Club ✪✪½ 5

19 Bay Pointe Drive
Onset, MA (508) 759-8802
www.baypointecc.net

Tees	Holes	Yards	Par	USGA	Slope
BACK					
MIDDLE	18	6201	70	71.6	125
FRONT	18	5380	72	71.3	125

Club Pro: Tom Tobey, PGA
Payment: Cash, Visa, MC, Amex
Tee Times: 3 weeks adv.
Fee 9 Holes: Weekday: $15
Fee 18 Holes: Weekday: $27
Twilight Rates: After 1:30pm
Cart Rental: $18pp/18, $9pp/9
Lessons: $50/half hour **Schools:** No
Membership: Yes
Weekend: $20
Weekend: $37
Discounts: Yes
Driving Range: Irons only
Junior Golf: No
Architect/Yr Open: Geoffrey Cornish/1963

COUPON

Other: Clubhouse / Lockers / Showers / Snack Bar / Restaurant / Bar-Lounge / Pool / Tennis

Lots of improvements made, under new ownership. Great staff. Located at western mouth of Cape, 5 minutes from Bourne Bridge. Typical Cape course, superbly manicured, excellent greens and fairways. Juniors, senior discounts. Open year round.

	1	2	3	4	5	6	7	8	9
PAR	5	4	4	3	4	4	3	3	5
YARDS	481	465	384	189	452	283	101	227	517
	10	11	12	13	14	15	16	17	18
PAR	3	4	3	4	3	5	4	5	4
YARDS	195	391	203	360	208	526	337	492	390

Directions: I-495 turns into Route 25. Take Exit 1 from Route 25. At 7th light go right, course 2/3 mile on right. From Route 3 South take Route 6 at Sagamore Rotary toward Wareham. Cross Buttermilk Bay into Wareham and go left at first light. Course 2/3 mile on right.

Bayberry Hills GC/Bayberry Links ✪✪✪ 6

West Yarmouth Road
South Yarmouth, MA
(508) 394-5597
www.golfyarmouthcapecod.com

Tees	Holes	Yards	Par	USGA	Slope
BACK	27/18	6523	72	71.7	125
MIDDLE	27/18	6067	72	69.6	119
FRONT	27/18	5323	72	69.4	111

Club Pro: Don Geay, golf dir.
Payment: Visa, MC, Disc
Tee Times: 7 days adv. (508) 398-4112
Fee 9 Holes: Weekday: $40.75 cart included **Weekend:** $40.75 cart included
Fee 18 Holes: Weekday: $81 cart included **Weekend:** $81 cart included
Twilight Rates: After 2pm $50/18 walking, 4pm $33/18 walking
Discounts: Junior
Cart Rental: Included
Lessons: By appointment **Schools:** No
Membership: Yes, non-resident/resident rates
Other: Clubhouse / Bar-Lounge / Restaurant
Driving Range: $10/lg., $7/md., $4/sm.
Junior Golf: No
Architect/Yr Open: Cornish/Silva/1988
GPS:

Immaculate condition; great layout. New irrigation system in 2006. Newer third 9, Bayberry Links is open, links-style.

	1	2	3	4	5	6	7	8	9
PAR	4	5	3	4	4	4	5	3	4
YARDS	375	485	140	336	335	350	505	146	350
	10	11	12	13	14	15	16	17	18
PAR	4	4	3	4	4	5	4	3	5
YARDS	372	384	130	320	352	503	349	160	475

Directions: Take Exit 8 off Route 6 East. Turn South onto Station Avenue. Take right at second traffic light, Old Townhouse Road to 4-way stop. Cross into Bayberry Hills.

Blue Rock Golf Club ✪✪✪

48 Todd Road,
South Yarmouth, MA (508) 398-9295
www.bluerockgolfcourse.com

Tees	Holes	Yards	Par	USGA	Slope
BACK	18	2890	54	56.4	83
MIDDLE	18	2563	54	56.4	83
FRONT	18	2170	54	55.8	80

Club Pro: Pat Fannon, PGA
Payment: Visa, MC, Cash, Check
Tee Times: 7 days adv.
Fee 9 Holes: Weekday: **Weekend:**
Fee 18 Holes: Weekday: $45   **Weekend:** $49
Twilight Rates: $40 after 12pm; $30 after 4pm
Discounts: Senior (before 8:30am $35) & Junior (17 and under $28)
Cart Rental: $24/18 per cart, $6 pull cart   **Driving Range:** Members only
Lessons: Please call **Schools:** Yes   **Junior Golf:** Yes
Membership: Yes   **Architect/Yr Open:** Geoffrey Cornish/1962
Other: Clubhouse / Snack Bar / Restaurant / Bar-Lounge / Hotel / Tennis / Pool / Golf School /
          Golf Clinic

"A great test for your short game; lots of wonderful carries and challenges. A better challenge than some regulation courses." –JD

	1	2	3	4	5	6	7	8	9
PAR	3	3	3	3	3	3	3	3	3
YARDS	103	127	118	125	247	145	170	165	165
	10	11	12	13	14	15	16	17	18
PAR	3	3	3	3	3	3	3	3	3
YARDS	150	117	190	147	185	185	144	129	173

Directions: Take Mid-Cape Highway East to Exit 8. Turn right off the ramp. First left White's Path, right to intersection, turn left on Great Western Road. Course is 1/4 mile on right.

Brookside Club, The ✪✪½ ▶ 8

11 Brigadoon Road (Route 28)
Bourne, MA (508) 743-4653
www.thebrooksideclub.com

Tees	Holes	Yards	Par	USGA	Slope
BACK	18	6400	70	71.1	126
MIDDLE	18	5814	70	68.1	124
FRONT	18	5130	70	69.6	118

Club Pro: Dwight Bartlett Jr.
Payment: Visa, MC, Amex, Disc
Tee Times: 7 days adv.
Fee 9 Holes: Weekday: **Weekend:**
Fee 18 Holes: Weekday: $60 M-Th w/cart   **Weekend:** $70 F/S/S w/cart
Twilight Rates: After 3pm   **Discounts:** Sr., Jr., Ladies-Th
Cart Rental: Included   **Driving Range:** $6/bucket
Lessons: $50/half hour **Schools:** No   **Junior Golf:** Yes
Membership: No   **Architect/Yr Open:** Michael Hurdzan, 1986
Other: Bar / Sunset Grille Restaurant   **GPS:**

Course noted for scenic ocean views and unique terrain. Carts are required on the weekends. Functions/ outings welcome!

	1	2	3	4	5	6	7	8	9
PAR	4	3	4	4	5	3	4	4	4
YARDS	379	156	359	365	503	96	361	421	332
	10	11	12	13	14	15	16	17	18
PAR	5	4	4	3	4	4	4	3	4
YARDS	576	336	330	155	354	306	313	130	342

Directions: Routes I-495/25 over Bourne Bridge to Route 28 South. Course is 1.4 miles on right.

Cape Cod Country Club

✪✪½ 9

Theater Road
North Falmouth, MA (508) 563-9842
www.capecodcountryclub.com

Club Pro: C. Holmes, golf dir., J. Munroe, PGA
Payment: Cash, MC, Visa
Tee Times: 7 days

Tees	Holes	Yards	Par	USGA	Slope
BACK	18	6404	71	71.7	129
MIDDLE	18	6018	71	69.6	125
FRONT	18	5348	72	71.0	120

Fee 9 Holes: Weekday: $27 after 2pm M-Th **Weekend:** $32 after 2pm
Fee 18 Holes: Weekday: $42 M-Th **Weekend:** $56 F/S/S
Twilight Rates: After 2pm **Discounts:** Tues/Ladies, Wed/Sr.
Cart Rental: $16pp/18 **Driving Range:** No
Lessons: Call for details **Schools:** No **Junior Golf:** No
Membership: No **Architect/Yr Open:** Emmet & Tull/1928
Other: Clubhouse / Snack Bar / Bar-Lounge **GPS:**

Sig. Hole: #14, The Volcano, is the most talked-about hole. Course plays longer than the scorecard statistics. The impeccable fairways are lined with pine trees.

	1	2	3	4	5	6	7	8	9
PAR	4	3	5	4	4	5	4	4	3
YARDS	307	175	460	419	360	509	300	407	156
	10	11	12	13	14	15	16	17	18
PAR	4	5	3	5	4	3	3	4	4
YARDS	405	515	220	461	351	180	183	300	310

Directions: Take Route 28 South of Bourne Bridge, take right onto Route 151. Course is approximately 3 miles on right.

Captains Golf Course (Port)

✪✪✪½ 10

1000 Freeman's Way
Brewster, MA (508) 896-1716
www.captainsgolfcourse.com

Club Pro: Mark O'Brien
Payment: Visa, MC
Tee Times: Up to 1 year adv.

Tees	Holes	Yards	Par	USGA	Slope
BACK	18	6724	72	73.5	130
MIDDLE	18	6164	72	70.7	128
FRONT	18	5345	72	71.1.	119

Fee 9 Holes: Weekday: **Weekend:**
Fee 18 Holes: Weekday: $64 **Weekend:** $64
Twilight Rates: After 4pm **Discounts:** Junior, $5 after 5pm
Cart Rental: $16pp/18, $8pp/9 **Driving Range:** $8/lg, $5/sm bucket
Lessons: Yes **Schools:** Yes **Junior Golf:** Yes
Membership: Yes **Architect/Yr Open:** Brian Silva 1985
Other: Bar and restaurant. **GPS:**

COUPON

Player Comments: "Holes 12 through 16 are a spectacular sequence." Reservations available online. New irrigation system. Lower Cape's best 2 layouts.

	1	2	3	4	5	6	7	8	9
PAR	4	4	3	4	3	5	4	5	4
YARDS	321	374	160	361	141	508	427	529	337
	10	11	12	13	14	15	16	17	18
PAR	4	3	5	5	4	3	4	3	5
YARDS	357	177	515	408	353	153	336	197	510

Directions: Route 6 to Exit 11. Right off exit ramp and travel 1.5 miles to Freeman's Way on right. Turn onto Freeman's and course is 1.5 miles on right.

Captains Golf Course (Starboard) ✪✪✪

11

1000 Freeman's Way
Brewster, MA (508) 896-1716
www.captainsgolfcourse.com

Club Pro: Mark T. O'Brien, Director of Ops.
Payment: Visa, MC
Tee Times: Up to 1 Year in adv.
Fee 9 Holes: Weekday:
Fee 18 Holes: Weekday: $64
Twilight Rates: After 4pm
Cart Rental: $16pp/18, $8pp/9
Lessons: Yes **Schools:** Yes
Membership: Yes
Other: Bar and restaurant.

Tees	Holes	Yards	Par	USGA	Slope
BACK	18	6776	72	72.6	130
MIDDLE	18	6198	72	69.4	123
FRONT	18	5359	72	71.2	116

Weekend:
Weekend: $64
Discounts: Junior, $5 after 5pm
Driving Range: $8/lg, $5/sm bucket
Junior Golf: Yes
Architect/Yr Open: Brian Silva/1985
GPS:

COUPON

Player Comments: "Excellent layout. Best-conditioned course I've played." Reservations avaliable online. New irrigation system. Come play both sides.

	1	2	3	4	5	6	7	8	9
PAR	4	3	5	4	3	4	5	4	4
YARDS	352	131	491	401	178	287	507	370	322
	10	**11**	**12**	**13**	**14**	**15**	**16**	**17**	**18**
PAR	4	3	4	5	4	4	4	3	5
YARDS	344	182	326	481	378	361	427	156	504

Directions: Route 6 to Exit 11. Right off exit ramp and travel 1.5 miles to Freeman's Way on right. Turn onto Freeman's and course is 1.5 miles on right.

Chatham Seaside Links

NR

209 Seaview Street
Chatham, MA (508) 945-4774
www.mychatham.com/chathamgolf.html

Club Pro: Dennis Donohoe
Payment: Cash, MC, Visa
Tee Times: No
Fee 9 Holes: Weekday: $19
Fee 18 Holes: Weekday: $30
Twilight Rates: No
Cart Rental: $12pp/18, $7.50pp/9
Lessons: **Schools:** No
Membership: Yes
Other: Snacks

Tees	Holes	Yards	Par	USGA	Slope
BACK					
MIDDLE	9	2465	34	65.6	107
FRONT	9	2400	34	65.6	109

Weekend: $19
Weekend: $30
Discounts: Senior & Junior
Driving Range: No
Junior Golf: No
Architect/Yr Open: 1895
GPS:

Links-style golf course with ocean views. Course irrigated. Open April 1 to October 31.

	1	2	3	4	5	6	7	8	9
PAR	4	4	3	3	4	4	4	4	4
YARDS	295	285	150	140	350	305	325	295	320
PAR									
YARDS									

Directions: Route 6 to Exit 11 (Route 137). Go left to Route 28 and left again to Main Street Chatham. Take Seaview off Main Street to course.

Chemawa Golf Course   ✪✪ ▶ 13

325 Cushman Road
North Attleboro, MA
(508) 399-7330

Tees	Holes	Yards	Par	USGA	Slope
BACK	18	5267	68	65.1	113
MIDDLE	18	4884	68	63.5	110
FRONT	18	4351	69	64.6	109

SE MA/ CAPE

Club Pro: Glen Bourgue
Payment: Most Major
Tee Times: Weekend only
Fee 9 Holes: Weekday: $19   **Weekend:** $22
Fee 18 Holes: Weekday: $28   **Weekend:** $34
Twilight Rates: No   **Discounts:** Senior, $24pp/18, $18pp/9
Cart Rental: $26pp/18, $13pp/9   **Driving Range:** No
Lessons: No **Schools:** No   **Junior Golf:** No
Membership: No   **Architect/Yr Open:** Steve Espisito/1956
Other: Snack Bar / Bar-Lounge / Enlarged Putting Green

Player Comments: "Parkland layout presents water and wetlands in play on 11 holes with generous driving zones. Early version of the island green on 16th." "Challenging, difficult."

	1	2	3	4	5	6	7	8	9
PAR	4	4	4	4	4	4	5	4	3
YARDS	334	286	324	321	312	236	427	265	136
	10	11	12	13	14	15	16	17	18
PAR	4	3	4	3	3	4	3	4	4
YARDS	348	126	309	146	198	332	109	265	410

Directions: I-95 South to I-295 toward Woonsocket, Route 1 South. Take right onto May Street, then take a right onto Cushman Road.

Chequessett Yacht & CC   ✪✪ ▶ 14

680 Chequesset Neck Road
Wellfleet, MA (508) 349-3704
www.cycc.net

Tees	Holes	Yards	Par	USGA	Slope
BACK					
MIDDLE	9	2621	35	66.1	107
FRONT	9	2387	35	67.9	110

Club Pro: Barbara Boone, PGA
Payment: Visa, MC
Tee Times: Unlimited w/CC
Fee 9 Holes: Weekday: $32   **Weekend:** $32
Fee 18 Holes: Weekday: $46   **Weekend:** $46
Twilight Rates: After 5pm   **Discounts:** Juniors after 12pm $15pp/9
Cart Rental: $16pp/18, $10pp/9   **Driving Range:** No
Lessons: $45/hour **Schools:** No   **Junior Golf:** Yes
Membership: Yes   **Architect/Yr Open:** 1929
Other: Snack Bar (Seasonal) / Tennis / Sailing   **GPS:**

Gorgeous view of bay. Well bunkered. Numerous water hazards. Junior lesson series.

	1	2	3	4	5	6	7	8	9
PAR	4	3	4	5	3	4	4	4	4
YARDS	234	127	368	435	109	314	373	380	281
PAR									
YARDS									

Directions: From Orleans rotary take Route 6 to Wellfleet. At Wellfleet Center go left at light onto Main Street. Take left on Commercial Street toward harbor. Go 1.5 miles past the harbor to the course on the right.

Cotuit-Highground Golf Course NR 15 ▶

31 Crockers Neck Road
Cotuit, MA (508) 428-9863

Tees	Holes	Yards	Par	USGA	Slope
BACK					
MIDDLE	9	1290	28		
FRONT	9	1059	28		

Club Pro: Steve Heher, PGA
Payment: Cash only
Tee Times: No
Fee 9 Holes: Weekday: $15
Fee 18 Holes: Weekday: $20
Twilight Rates: After 4pm
Cart Rental: Some available
Lessons: Yes **Schools:** N/R
Membership: Yes
Other: Bar-Lounge / Snack Bar

Weekend: $15
Weekend: $20
Discounts: Senior & Junior
Driving Range: No
Junior Golf: Yes
Architect/Yr Open: 1927
GPS:

Player comment: "Good value." Family fun. Links-style course, very tight greens. Accuracy is very important. Open year-round.

	1	2	3	4	5	6	7	8	9
PAR	3	3	4	3	3	3	3	3	3
YARDS	115	180	290	130	140	110	100	180	115
PAR									
YARDS									

Directions: Take Route 6 to Exit 2 (Route 130 South), left onto Route 28, right onto Main Street in Cotuit Center. Take right onto School Street then second left onto Crocker Neck Road.

Cranberry Valley Golf Course ✪✪✪ 16 ▶

183 Oak Street
Harwich, MA (508) 430-5234
www.cranberrygolfcourse.com

Tees	Holes	Yards	Par	USGA	Slope
BACK	18	6745	72	71.9	129
MIDDLE	18	6296	72	70.4	125
FRONT	18	5518	72	71.5	115

Club Pro: Dennis Hoye, PGA
Payment: Cash, Visa, MC
Tee Times: 2 days adv.
Fee 9 Holes: Weekday: No
Fee 18 Holes: Weekday: $62
Twilight Rates: After 2:30pm
Cart Rental: $16pp/18
Lessons: $45/half hour **Schools:** Jr.
Membership: Yes, residents
Other: Restaurant/Bar

Weekend: No
Weekend: $62
Discounts: None
Driving Range: $4/sm, $6/lg bucket
Junior Golf: Yes
Architect/Yr Open: Cornish & Robinson/1974
GPS:

Player Comments: "Very fine play, great condition." Large teeing areas and 53 sand bunkers. Open March - Dec. Seasonal rates. Hosted 2006 Mass Women's State Open. All traps recently renovated. New range expanded.

	1	2	3	4	5	6	7	8	9
PAR	4	5	4	3	4	4	3	5	4
YARDS	365	505	390	197	435	340	176	510	383
	10	11	12	13	14	15	16	17	18
PAR	4	4	4	3	5	4	4	3	5
YARDS	361	352	372	174	445	308	443	205	521

Directions: Take Exit 10 off Route 6 East. Take a right off the ramp and take first left at 4-way stop onto Queen Anne Road. Take third right (Oak Street). 1/2 mile on left.

Dennis Highlands Golf Course ✪✪½   17

825 Old Bass River Road
Dennis, MA (508) 385-8347
www.dennisgolf.com

Club Pro:
Payment: MC, Visa, Discover, Cash
Tee Times: 4 days adv. up to 7 for non-members

Tees	Holes	Yards	Par	USGA	Slope
BACK	18	6464	71	70.9	120
MIDDLE	18	6076	71	68.5	117
FRONT	18	4927	71	67.8	112

Fee 9 Holes: Weekday: $35, 5:30am-7am/after 1pm only
Fee 18 Holes: Weekday: $60   **Weekend:** $60
Twilight Rates: After 1pm $35, after 5pm $20   **Discounts:** None
Cart Rental: $16pp/18, $11pp/9   **Driving Range:** $7/lg., $4/sm.
Lessons: Call for appt. **Schools:** Yes   **Junior Golf:** Yes
Membership: Residents
Architect/Yr Open: Jack Kidwell/ Michael Hurdzan/1983
Other: Clubhouse / Restaurant / Bar-Lounge

Putting is key to good round. Seasonal rates. Enlarged some tees and rebuilt 7th green. Open year round. Family friendly venue.

	1	2	3	4	5	6	7	8	9
PAR	4	5	3	4	4	4	3	5	3
YARDS	309	494	151	331	347	409	160	472	141
	10	11	12	13	14	15	16	17	18
PAR	4	3	4	4	4	5	3	4	5
YARDS	371	151	365	392	383	529	170	377	519

Directions: Take Route 6 to Exit 9B, follow 1/2 mile. Take left onto Bob Crowell Road. At end take right onto Old Bass River Road, course is 2.4 miles up on left.

Dennis Pines Golf Course   ✪✪✪½   18

50 Golf Course Road
South Dennis, MA (508) 385-8347
www.dennisgolf.com

Club Pro:
Payment: Visa, MC, Disc, Cash
Tee Times: Up to 7 days adv.

Tees	Holes	Yards	Par	USGA	Slope
BACK	18	7029	72	74.2	133
MIDDLE	18	6525	72	72.1	131
FRONT	18	5845	72	73.6	126

Fee 9 Holes: Weekday: $35, 5:30am-7am/after 1pm only
Fee 18 Holes: Weekday: $60   **Weekend:** $60
Twilight Rates: After 1pm $35, After 5pm $20   **Discounts:** None
Cart Rental: $16pp/18, $11pp/9   **Driving Range:** $7/lg., $4/sm.
Lessons: Yes **Schools:** Yes   **Junior Golf:** Yes
Membership: Yes   **Architect/Yr Open:** Henry Mitchell/1964
Other: Snack Bar / Restaurant / Bar-Lounge   **GPS:**

One of Cape's busiest courses. Wonderful layout with dramatic holes set among tall pines.
*Early morning and twilight rates.

	1	2	3	4	5	6	7	8	9
PAR	4	4	5	3	5	4	3	4	4
YARDS	373	369	471	188	476	423	187	442	389
	10	11	12	13	14	15	16	17	18
PAR	4	4	5	3	4	5	4	3	4
YARDS	351	357	518	172	405	472	344	183	405

Directions: Take Exit 9B off of Route 6, proceed North on Route 134, take a right approximately 2.5 miles to Golf Course Road, Dennis Pines Golf Course is located at the end of Golf Course Road.

Falmouth Country Club

NR 19

630 Carriage Shop Road
Falmouth, MA (508) 548-3211
www.falmouthcountryclub.com

Club Pro: Ryan Phelps, PGA
Payment: Visa, MC
Tee Times: 14 days adv.

Tees	Holes	Yards	Par	USGA	Slope
BACK	18	6665	72	70.0	118
MIDDLE	18	6234	72	68.8	114
FRONT	18	5551	72	74	125

Fee 9 Holes: Weekday: $25/walk
Fee 18 Holes: Weekday: $45/non-res, $35/res
Twilight Rates: After 2pm
Cart Rental: $13pp18, $10pp/9
Lessons: Yes **Schools:** Yes
Membership: No
Other: Clubhouse / Snack Bar / Bar-Lounge

Weekend: $25/walk, $33/ride
Weekend: $60/non-res, $50/res
Discounts: None
Driving Range: $5/bucket
Junior Golf: No
Architect/Yr Open: Vinnie Bartlett/1969
GPS:

COUPON

27 holes—an 18-hole course and a 9-hole, now managed by Billy Casper Golf Management.

	1	2	3	4	5	6	7	8	9
PAR	4	3	4	4	4	3	4	5	4
YARDS	400	175	370	384	403	174	318	531	426
	10	11	12	13	14	15	16	17	18
PAR	5	4	3	4	5	5	4	3	4
YARDS	516	385	151	427	545	500	380	190	390

Directions: Take Route 28 South into Falmouth. Take right onto Route 151 East, follow 3.5 miles to Sandwich Road on right. Look for signs, left onto Carriage Shop Road.

Farm Neck Golf Club

✪✪✪✪½ 20

1 Farm Neck Road
Oak Bluffs, MA (508) 693-3057

Club Pro: Mike Zoll, PGA
Payment: Visa, MC, Amex, Cash
Tee Times: 2 days adv.

Tees	Holes	Yards	Par	USGA	Slope
BACK	18	6815	72	72.8	135
MIDDLE	18	6301	72	70.5	133
FRONT	18	4987	72	64.3	118

Fee 9 Holes: Weekday: $85 (in season)
Fee 18 Holes: Weekday: $145 (in season)
Twilight Rates: After 4pm
Cart Rental: $15pp/18, $7.50pp/9
Lessons: $50/half hour **Schools:** No
Membership: Waiting list
Other: Restaurant / Bar-Lounge / Snack Bar / Lockers / Showers

Weekend: $85 (in season)
Weekend: $145 (in season)
Discounts: None
Driving Range: $10/lg, $7/med, $5/sm bucket
Junior Golf: Yes
Architect/Yr Open: Cornish/1979; Robinson/1996

Scenic, splendid, and challenging with ocean breezes and views, meadows and interior woodlands. "A treasure." "Pure golf experience." –JD Off-season rates a great value: call ahead.

	1	2	3	4	5	6	7	8	9
PAR	4	5	4	3	4	3	4	5	3
YARDS	378	490	340	157	325	189	371	486	175
	10	11	12	13	14	15	16	17	18
PAR	4	5	4	4	4	3	4	4	5
YARDS	376	519	379	343	331	163	388	368	523

Directions: On Country Road in Oak Bluffs, Martha's Vineyard.

Fire Fly Country Club

320 Fall River Avenue
Seekonk, MA (508) 336-6622

Tees	Holes	Yards	Par	USGA	Slope
BACK	18	3644	59	58.0	87
MIDDLE	18	3083	59	55.4	81
FRONT	18	2786	59	58.0	86

Club Pro: Keith Allcock, PGA
Payment: Visa, MC
Tee Times: Yes, for weekends
Fee 9 Holes: Weekday: $16 **Weekend:** $17
Fee 18 Holes: Weekday: $20 **Weekend:** $23
Twilight Rates: After 7pm

COUPON

Discounts: Sr & Jr (M-F) $17/18 M-F, $18/18 weekend
Cart Rental: $13pp/18, $7.50pp/9, $10/senior **Driving Range:** $6/bucket
Lessons: $40/half hour, $25/Jr. **Schools:** No **Junior Golf:** Yes
Membership: Yes **Architect/Yr:** Joanne Carner & Don Hoenig/1962
Other: Snack Bar / Restaurant / Bar-Lounge

Executive course, great for beginners and seasoned golfers who like to practice their short game. Junior clinics available at the Golf Learning Center.

	1	2	3	4	5	6	7	8	9
PAR	3	3	3	3	4	3	4	4	3
YARDS	145	150	148	147	441	122	286	251	123
	10	11	12	13	14	15	16	17	18
PAR	4	3	3	3	3	3	3	4	3
YARDS	240	146	126	87	139	155	182	240	134

Directions: From Providence I-95 to I-195 East to Exit 1 MA (Seekonk/Barrington). (From Fall River 195 West to Exit 1 MA.) Go North on Route 114. At fork, bear left. Take right at Fire Fly.

Harwich Port Golf Club

South Street
Harwich Port, MA (508) 432-0250
www.harwichport.com

Tees	Holes	Yards	Par	USGA	Slope
BACK					
MIDDLE	9	2538	34		
FRONT					

Club Pro: No
Payment: Cash only
Tee Times: No
Fee 9 Holes: Weekday: $20 **Weekend:** $20
Fee 18 Holes: Weekday: $30 **Weekend:** $30
Twilight Rates: No **Discounts:** None
Cart Rental: $3/pull **Driving Range:** Members only
Lessons: No **Schools:** No **Junior Golf:** No
Membership: Yes **Architect/Yr Open:** Don Blakely/1920
Other: Snack Bar **GPS:**

The course is considered an easy walker. Recommended for beginners and senior citizens. Members only after 5:30pm. New state-of-the-art irrigation system.

	1	2	3	4	5	6	7	8	9
PAR	4	3	4	4	4	4	3	4	4
YARDS	358	170	340	330	325	255	155	295	310
PAR									
YARDS									

Directions: Take Route 6 to Exit 0 or 10. Take Route 28 to South Street. Course 200 yards.

SE
MA/
CAPE

Heather Hill Country Club

149 West Bacon Street
Plainville, MA (508) 695-0309

Tees	Holes	Yards	Par	USGA	Slope
BACK	27/18	6335	72	67.8	117
MIDDLE	27/18	6034	72	66.5	115
FRONT	27/18	4986	70	67.1	111

Club Pro: Mike Cosentino, PGA
Payment: Cash, Check
Tee Times: 1 week adv.
Fee 9 Holes: Weekday: $16　**Weekend:** $20
Fee 18 Holes: Weekday: $25　**Weekend:** $32
Twilight Rates: No　**Discounts:** None
Cart Rental: $26/18, $13/9 per cart　**Driving Range:** No
Lessons: $25/half hour　**Schools:** No　**Junior Golf:** No
Membership: No　**Architect/Yr Open:** 1955
Other: Clubhouse / Snack Bar / Bar-Lounge　**GPS:**

27-hole course: Middle and South courses play for 18. North course is 9 holes, 3368 yards. Open year round.

	1	2	3	4	5	6	7	8	9
PAR	3	4	4	5	4	4	5	3	4
YARDS	340	397	489	373	274	419	197	173	339
	10	11	12	13	14	15	16	17	18
PAR	3	4	4	5	4	4	5	3	4
YARDS	388	169	518	334	317	367	183	413	315

Directions: Take I-495 to Exit 15, follow Route 1A South to Route 106; take right on West Bacon Street in Plainville Center. Course is on right.

Hidden Hollow Country Club

30 Pierce Lane
Rehoboth, MA (508) 252-9392

Tees	Holes	Yards	Par	USGA	Slope
BACK					
MIDDLE	9	2905	35		
FRONT					

Club Pro: No
Payment: Cash only
Tee Times: No
Fee 9 Holes: Weekday: No　**Weekend:** No
Fee 18 Holes: Weekday: $17　**Weekend:** $21
Twilight Rates: No　**Discounts:** None
Cart Rental: $10pp/18, $6pp/9　**Driving Range:** No
Lessons: No　**Schools:** No　**Junior Golf:**
Membership: No　**Architect/Yr Open:** William B. Clark/1962
Other: Snack Bar / Bar-Lounge / Clubhouse　**GPS:**

Old-style, picturesque short course. Popular preference of female golfers.

	1	2	3	4	5	6	7	8	9
PAR	4	4	3	4	4	5	4	3	4
YARDS	341	307	187	382	400	481	313	233	261
PAR									
YARDS									

Directions: I-195 to MA Exit 2. North off exit to Davis Street. Left on Pleasant. Course is 1 mile on left.

Highland Links

25

Highland Road
North Truro, MA (508) 487-9201

Club Pro: Jim Knowles, PGA
Payment: Visa, MC
Tee Times: Yes
Fee 9 Holes: Weekday: $33
Fee 18 Holes: Weekday: $55
Twilight Rates: No
Cart Rental: $16pp/18, $8pp/9
Lessons: $45/half hour **Schools:** No
Membership: Yes, $575
Other: Clubhouse / Snack Bar

Tees	Holes	Yards	Par	USGA	Slope
BACK					
MIDDLE	9	2720	35	65.0	103
FRONT	9	2294	36	66.6	109

Weekend: $33
Weekend: $55
Discounts: None
Driving Range: No
Junior Golf: Yes
Architect/Yr Open: Isiah M. Small/1892
GPS:

SE MA/ CAPE

Off-season rates available. The oldest links in New England. Wind, water, and a layout tucked into a natural site. See golf the way it was played in the old days. "Every golfer should make a journey here. Don't expect anything fancy, but it is a treat to play." –JD Improved irrigation and rebuilt #9 tee.

	1	2	3	4	5	6	7	8	9
PAR	4	5	3	4	4	5	3	4	3
YARDS	250	460	160	346	380	464	171	353	136
PAR									
YARDS									

Directions: Take Route 6 to Truro. Course is just past the Truro elementary school. (Look for signs on Route 6.)

Hillside Country Club

26

82 Hillside Avenue
Rehoboth, MA (508) 252-9761
www.hillsidecountryclub.com

Club Pro:
Payment: Visa, MC, Disc, Cash
Tee Times:
Fee 9 Holes: Weekday: $15, $22 ride
Fee 18 Holes: Weekday: $23, $32 ride
Twilight Rates: No
Cart Rental: $14pp/18, $7pp/9, $3/pull
Lessons: No **Schools:** No
Membership: Yes
Other: Full Food and Beverage / Functions

Tees	Holes	Yards	Par	USGA	Slope
BACK	18				
MIDDLE	9	6065	71	69.5	126
FRONT	9	5422	74	72.8	124

Weekend: $15, $22 ride
Weekend: $23, $32 ride
Discounts: None
Driving Range: No
Junior Golf: No
Architect/Yr Open: George Cardono/1975
GPS:

Back to 9 holes since 2006. Play Blue tees on the front, White on the back. Two sets of tees mean change of par on the second 9.

	1	2	3	4	5	6	7	8	9
PAR	5	3	4	3	4	4	5	4	4
YARDS	437	175	440	155	312	338	470	331	370
	10	11	12	13	14	15	16	17	18
PAR	4	3	5	3	4	4	4	4	4
YARDS	415	164	488	183	316	336	420	355	360

Directions: Take Route 24 South to Route 44 West Taunton. Right onto Danforth Street. 1 mile West of intersection of Routes 118 & 44. Take first left onto River Street and first right onto Hillside Avenue.

Holly Ridge Golf Club

✪✪½ **27** ►

121 Country Club Road, Box 1021
South Sandwich, MA
(508) 428-5577
www.hollyridgegolf.com

Tees	Holes	Yards	Par	USGA	Slope
BACK	18	2952	54	55.4	74
MIDDLE	18	2715	54	54.1	N/A
FRONT	18	2194	54	54.8	N/A

Club Pro: Jean Enright
Payment: Visa, MC, Amex
Tee Times: 7 days
Fee 9 Holes: Weekday: $21   **Weekend:** $21
Fee 18 Holes: Weekday: $34   **Weekend:** $34
Twilight Rates: After 3:30pm   **Discounts:** Senior & Junior
Cart Rental: $10pp/18, $6pp/9   **Driving Range:** $10/lg, $7/med, $4/sm
Lessons: $50/half hour **Schools:** Yes   **Junior Golf:** Yes
Membership: No   **Architect/Yr Open:** Geoffrey Cornish/1967
Other: Restaurant / Bar-Lounge / Outings   **GPS:**

COUPON

Player Comments: "Awesome course. Very pro female." Open year round.

	1	2	3	4	5	6	7	8	9
PAR	3	3	3	3	3	3	3	3	3
YARDS	163	183	142	158	120	184	187	130	202
	10	11	12	13	14	15	16	17	18
PAR	3	3	3	3	3	3	3	3	3
YARDS	124	167	183	128	189	188	211	138	155

Directions: Take Route 3 South over Sagamore Bridge, follow Route 6 east to Exit 2. Go South on Route 130 for 1.6 miles, take left onto Cotuit Road for 1.4 miles, and left onto Farmersville Road for 1.6 miles. Follow signs for HRGC.

Hyannis Golf Club

✪✪½ **28** ►

Route 132
Hyannis, MA (508) 362-2606
www.hyannisgc.com

Tees	Holes	Yards	Par	USGA	Slope
BACK	18	6711	71	69.4	121
MIDDLE	18	6002	71	68.2	115
FRONT	18	5149	72	69.7	125

Club Pro: Mike Ghelfi, PGA
Payment: Cash, Check, Visa, MC
Tee Times: 12 months
Fee 9 Holes: Weekday: **Weekend:**
Fee 18 Holes: Weekday: $60 M-Th   **Weekend:** $60 F/S/S
Twilight Rates: After 4pm $30   **Discounts:** Sr. Days, M-Th
Cart Rental: $18pp/18   **Driving Range:** $7/lg, $5/sm bucket
Lessons: $70-$100/hour **Schools:** Jr. & Sr.   **Junior Golf:** Yes
Membership: Yes   **Architect/Yr Open:** Cornish and Robinson/1965
Other: 3 practice greens / Restaurant / Bar-Lounge / Snack Bar / Lockers/ Outings

COUPON

Home of Cape Cod's Open and Senior Open. Some of the Cape's most memorable holes. Lots of elevation changes from tees to fairways and back up to greens.

	1	2	3	4	5	6	7	8	9
PAR	4	4	4	4	5	4	3	3	4
YARDS	342	388	326	392	528	332	144	195	406
	10	11	12	13	14	15	16	17	18
PAR	5	3	4	4	5	3	4	4	4
YARDS	455	125	367	315	515	138	308	338	388

Directions: Take Route 6 (Mid-Cape Highway) to Exit 6 (Route 132). Go south on Route 132 for 1/4 mile and golf course is on left.

John F. Parker Municipal GC

17 Fisher Street
Taunton, MA (508) 822-1797

Tees	Holes	Yards	Par	USGA	Slope
BACK					
MIDDLE	9	3068	35	69.8	117
FRONT					

Club Pro: Hank Wojtkunski, PGA
Payment: Cash Only
Tee Times: No
Fee 9 Holes: Weekday: $18   **Weekend:** $21
Fee 18 Holes: Weekday: $21   **Weekend:** $24
Twilight Rates: No   **Discounts:** Senior
Cart Rental: $14pp/18, $7pp/9   **Driving Range:** $4/lg bucket
Lessons: Yes **Schools:**   **Junior Golf:** Yes
Membership: Yes   **Architect/Yr Open:** 1938
Other: Snack Bar / Bar-Lounge   **GPS:**

Reseeded fairways. Bunkers redone in 2008. Another 9 holes planned for 2010. Fun course to play, good for all skill levels, and great friendly staff.

	1	2	3	4	5	6	7	8	9
PAR	4	4	4	5	4	3	4	4	3
YARDS	360	412	350	478	345	168	330	390	235
PAR									
YARDS									

Directions: Route 24 to Route 140. Go West on Route 140 to center of Taunton. Pick up Route 44 West out of city. Go to 2nd set of traffic lights at Highland Street. Go right on Highland to the course.

Lakeville Country Club

Clear Pond Road
Lakeville, MA (508) 947-6630
www.lakevillecc.com

Tees	Holes	Yards	Par	USGA	Slope
BACK	18	6335	72	70.6	125
MIDDLE	18	5890	72	68.6	123
FRONT	18	4863	72	67.4	111

Club Pro: No
Payment: Visa, MC
Tee Times: 1 week adv.
Fee 9 Holes: Weekday: $26 M-Th $41/cart **Weekend:** $27 F/S/S $42/cart
Fee 18 Holes: Weekday: $40 M-Th $55/cart **Weekend:** $45 F/S/S $60/cart
Twilight Rates: After 2pm   **Discounts:** Senior
Cart Rental: $15pp/18, $10pp/9   **Driving Range:** No
Lessons: No **Schools:** No   **Junior Golf:** No
Membership: No   **Architect/Yr Open:** Roger Beach/1970
Other: Restaurant / Clubhouse / Snack Bar / Bar-Lounge

Early-bird special before 8:30am. Enthusiastic, friendly staff. Course is in good shape. Public course with private conditions.

	1	2	3	4	5	6	7	8	9
PAR	4	3	4	4	5	5	3	5	3
YARDS	334	216	351	432	533	538	216	521	166
	10	11	12	13	14	15	16	17	18
PAR	4	4	5	4	5	4	3	3	4
YARDS	339	380	500	324	463	335	139	178	370

Directions: I-495 to Exit 5. Go South on Route 18. Take left at first light to Route 79, then first right onto Clear Pond. Entrance is 1/2 mile on right.

Little Harbor Country Club

NR 31 ▶

Little Harbor Road
Wareham, MA (508) 295-2617
www.littleharborcountryclub.com

Club Pro: Shawn Lapworth
Payment: Visa, MC, Cash
Tee Times: 3 days adv.
Fee 9 Holes: Weekday: $16
Fee 18 Holes: Weekday: $27
Twilight Rates: After 3pm
Cart Rental: $21pp/18, $10.50pp/9
Lessons: $70 **Schools:** No
Membership: No
Other: Clubhouse / Snack Bar

Tees	Holes	Yards	Par	USGA	Slope
BACK					
MIDDLE	18	3038	56	54.4	79
FRONT	18	2692	56	51.9	72

Weekend: $17
Weekend: $30
Discounts: Senior & Junior
Driving Range: No
Junior Golf: Yes
Architect/Yr Open: Richard Bowler/1963
GPS:

COUPON

Holes range from 110 yards to 315 yards. Course and greens are in great condition. Open year round.

	1	2	3	4	5	6	7	8	9
PAR	3	3	3	3	3	4	4	3	3
YARDS	100	135	142	138	225	291	275	162	189
	10	**11**	**12**	**13**	**14**	**15**	**16**	**17**	**18**
PAR	3	3	3	3	3	3	3	3	3
YARDS	205	125	140	132	183	100	156	132	208

Directions: Take Route 6 to Depot Street. Follow Great Neck Road 2.5 miles. Go right on Stockton shortcut.

Locust Valley Golf Course

NR 32 ▶

106 Locust Street
Attleboro, MA (508) 222-1500

Club Pro: No
Payment: Visa, MC
Tee Times: No
Fee 9 Holes: Weekday:
Fee 18 Holes: Weekday: $11 unlimited
Twilight Rates: No
Cart Rental: $14pp/18
Lessons: No **Schools:** No
Membership: Yes
Other: Snack Bar / Bar-Lounge

Tees	Holes	Yards	Par	USGA	Slope
BACK					
MIDDLE	9	3065	36	69.8	124
FRONT	9	2615	36	NA	NA

Weekend:
Weekend: $15 unlimited
Discounts: Senior & Junior (M-F)
Driving Range: No
Junior Golf: No
Architect/Yr Open: 1939
GPS:

Special $7.50 weekday fee: Monday, Juniors and Thursday, Ladies. Wide open and an easy walker. Saturday and Sunday $10 after 2pm.

	1	2	3	4	5	6	7	8	9
PAR	5	5	4	4	4	3	4	3	4
YARDS	465	485	360	335	375	150	373	160	362
PAR									
YARDS									

Directions: I-95 to Exit 3A to Route 123. Proceed on Route 123, at second light continue straight for 1 mile and follow to the end of road. Take a right onto Route 152 and an immediate left onto Tyler Street. Road ends at course.

Marion Golf Course

10 South Drive
Marion, MA (508) 748-0199

Tees	Holes	Yards	Par	USGA	Slope
BACK	9	2695	34	67.1	121
MIDDLE	9	2695	34	67.1	121
FRONT	9	2089	35	66.0	117

Club Pro: No
Payment: Cash Only
Tee Times: No
Fee 9 Holes: Weekday: $15
Fee 18 Holes: Weekday: $22
Twilight Rates:
Cart Rental: $10pp/9, $20pp/18
Lessons: No **Schools:** No
Membership: Yes
Other: Club Rentals

Weekend: $17
Weekend: $24.50
Discounts: Sr./Jr. $2 off for 18 holes
Driving Range: No
Junior Golf: No
Architect/Yr Open: George Thomas/1904
GPS:

COUPON

European-style links. Open year round. "Several greens are defended by stone walls and cross bunkers. A wonderful 9 for the golf purist." –AP

	1	2	3	4	5	6	7	8	9
PAR	4	4	3	5	4	4	4	3	3
YARDS	315	290	175	460	365	430	365	180	115

PAR
YARDS

Directions: I-495 to I-195 East. Go to Exit 20. Bear right off exit onto Route 105. Follow to lights, bear left onto Route 6. Follow to next set of lights, bear right onto Point Road. Follow approximately 1.5 miles. Course on right.

MGA Links at Mamantapett

300 West Main Street (Route 123)
Norton, MA
(508) 222-0555
www.mgalinks.org

Tees	Holes	Yards	Par	USGA	Slope
BACK					
MIDDLE	18	2421	54		
FRONT	18	2321	56		

Club Pro: Pete Walsh, PGA
Payment: Cash, Credit Cards, Checks
Tee Times: No
Fee 9 Holes: Weekday: $15
Fee 18 Holes: Weekday: $20
Twilight Rates: No
Cart Rental: $3/18, $2/9 pull carts only
Lessons: No **Schools:** No
Membership: Yes
Other: Lounge

Weekend: $15
Weekend: $20
Discounts: Junior $7/9, $10/18
Driving Range: No
Junior Golf: Yes
Architect/Yr Open: 1972
GPS:

Good course for women, seniors, short game and irons practice. First Tee and MGA ForeKids Program Monday through Thursday. Available for adult public play daily. Open year round.

	1	2	3	4	5	6	7	8	9
PAR	3	3	3	3	3	3	3	3	3
YARDS	117	135	82	140	93	91	115	136	108
	10	**11**	**12**	**13**	**14**	**15**	**16**	**17**	**18**
PAR	3	3	3	3	3	3	3	3	3
YARDS	131	138	125	203	141	113	147	233	173

Directions: Take I-495 to Exit 10 (Route 123 West). Go approximately 4 miles. Course is on left.

Miacomet Golf Club

★★ 35

12 West Miacomet Road
Nantucket, MA (508) 325-0333
miacometgolf.com

Club Pro: Phillip Truono
Payment: Visa, MC, Amex, Disc
Tee Times: 4 days adv.

Tees	Holes	Yards	Par	USGA	Slope
BACK	18	6831	72	73.0	123
MIDDLE	18	6127	72	69.5	118
FRONT	18	5159	72	69.6	118

Fee 9 Holes: Weekday: $62
Fee 18 Holes: Weekday: $105
Twilight Rates: After 4pm $40
Cart Rental: $20.50pp/18, $12pp/9
Lessons: $125/hour **Schools:** Yes
Membership: Waitlist
Other: Restaurant / Clubhouse / Snack Bar / Bar-Lounge

Weekend: $62
Weekend: $105
Discounts: Senior
Driving Range: $10/lg, $5/sm bucket
Junior Golf: Yes
Architect/Yr Open: Ralph Marble/1962

Entire back 9 newly renovated. Resident, non-resident rates. Pace of play is 4 hours and 20 minutes. "A course for all golfers."

	1	2	3	4	5	6	7	8	9
PAR	4	4	3	5	5	4	4	3	4
YARDS	373	321	173	464	453	350	389	210	330
	10	11	12	13	14	15	16	17	18
PAR	4	4	3	4	5	3	4	4	5
YARDS	369	351	167	388	431	152	374	393	439

Directions: Nantucket is an island 25 miles off the coast of Cape Cod. Airport and ferry boat dock are in Hyannis.

Middlebrook Country Club

NR 36

149 Pleasant Street
Rehoboth, MA (508) 252-9395

Club Pro: No
Payment: Visa, MC
Tee Times: Weekends

Tees	Holes	Yards	Par	USGA	Slope
BACK					
MIDDLE	9	2784	35	67.0	122
FRONT	9	2509	35	N/A	108

Fee 9 Holes: Weekday: $14
Fee 18 Holes: Weekday: $18
Twilight Rates: No
Cart Rental: $20/18, $12/9 per cart, $2.50/pull
Lessons: No **Schools:** No
Membership: Currently full
Other: Snack Bar / Bar-Lounge / Clubhouse

Weekend: $17
Weekend: $22
Discounts: Senior
Driving Range: No
Junior Golf: No
Architect/Yr Open: 1950
GPS:

Open April 1 - November 1.

	1	2	3	4	5	6	7	8	9
PAR	4	4	4	4	5	3	3	4	4
YARDS	340	360	301	350	500	213	130	300	290
PAR									
YARDS									

Directions: Take I-195 to MA Exit 2. North off exit to Davis Street. Right on Davis to Pleasant Street. Left on Pleasant. Course is one mile on right.

Mink Meadows Golf Course ○○ 37

320 Golf Club Road
Vineyard Haven, MA
(508) 693-0600
www.minkmeadowsgc.com

Club Pro: Chet Nowak
Payment: Visa, MC, Amex, Disc, Check
Tee Times: 2 days adv.

Tees	Holes	Yards	Par	USGA	Slope
BACK					
MIDDLE	9	3078	35	69.9	126
FRONT	9	2729	35	71.7	123

Fee 9 Holes: Weekday: $50
Fee 18 Holes: Weekday: $75
Twilight Rates: $35 Sun-Th after 5pm
Cart Rental: $15pp/18, $10pp/9
Lessons: $45/half hour **Schools:** No
Membership: Yes
Other: Snack Bar

Weekend: $50
Weekend: $75
Discounts: Junior membership discount only
Driving Range: $6/lg, $3/sm bucket
Junior Golf: Yes
Architect/Yr Open: Wayne Stiles/1939
GPS:

Easy to walk, beautiful, challenging course. Off-season rates.

	1	2	3	4	5	6	7	8	9
PAR	4	4	4	4	3	4	3	5	4
YARDS	349	328	355	424	186	394	166	500	376
PAR									
YARDS									

Directions: From ferry, proceed to Main Street in Vineyard Haven. Take 2nd left and proceed to 2nd right (Franklin Street). Go 1.25 miles down Franklin Street to club entrance on left.

Norton Country Club ○○½ 38

188 Oak Street
Norton, MA (508) 285-2400
www.nortoncountryclub.com

Club Pro: Scott Hickey
Payment: Most Major Credit Cards
Tee Times: 5 days adv.

Tees	Holes	Yards	Par	USGA	Slope
BACK	18	6545	71	72.2	137
MIDDLE	18	6201	71	69.9	132
FRONT	18	5040	71	71.0	124

Fee 9 Holes: Weekday: $25 M-Th
Fee 18 Holes: Weekday: $39 M-Th
Twilight Rates: After 4pm
Cart Rental: $14pp/18, $8pp/9
Lessons: $40/half hour **Schools:** No
Membership: Yes
Other: Clubhouse / Lockers / Showers / Snack Bar / Bar-Lounge

Weekend: $25 F/S/S
Weekend: $62 F/S/S
Discounts: Lunch specials M-Th
Driving Range: No
Junior Golf: Yes
Architect/Yr Open: Cornish & Silva/1989

COUPON

Course is for serious golfers. "Beautiful course, great condition." "Not too long but tough. Course management a must, especially for first 6 holes."

	1	2	3	4	5	6	7	8	9
PAR	4	4	3	5	5	4	3	4	4
YARDS	346	426	143	500	492	419	105	383	313
	10	11	12	13	14	15	16	17	18
PAR	4	4	3	4	5	4	3	4	4
YARDS	328	344	138	298	489	414	120	358	389

Directions: Take Route 123 (Exit 10) off I-495. Take 123 West toward Norton Center to Oak Street. Club is 1 mile on the left.

Olde Barnstable Fairgrounds GC ✪✪✪ ▶ 39

Route 149
Marstons Mills, MA
(508) 420-1141
www.obfgolf.com

Club Pro: Merry Holway, PGA
Payment: Cash, MC, Visa
Tee Times: Yes
Fee 9 Holes: Weekday:
Fee 18 Holes: Weekday: $60 M-Th
Twilight Rates: After 4pm
Discounts: Jr. (18 & under) after 12pm $20
Cart Rental: $18pp/18
Lessons: $35/half hour **Schools:** Ladies
Membership: For residents and non-residents
Other: Restaurant / Clubhouse / Bar-Lounge

Tees	Holes	Yards	Par	USGA	Slope
BACK	18	6479	71	70.7	123
MIDDLE	18	6113	71	69.1	120
FRONT	18	5122	71	69.2	118

Weekend:
Weekend: $60 F/S/S

Driving Range: $7/lg, $5/sm bucket
Junior Golf: Yes
Architect/Yr: Cornish, Silva, Mungeam/1992
GPS:

COUPON

Player Comments: "From 1st tee to 18th green, a great test of golf. Great Cape Cod conditions."
Rates subject to change. Home to the 2007 Cape Cod Open.

	1	2	3	4	5	6	7	8	9
PAR	5	3	5	3	4	4	4	4	4
YARDS	485	140	503	158	365	351	430	317	385
	10	11	12	13	14	15	16	17	18
PAR	5	4	3	4	4	3	4	3	5
YARDS	510	335	157	340	380	172	395	155	535

Directions: Sagamore Bridge to Route 6, Exit 5, take right off ramp. Bear right on Route 149.
Course is 1/2 mile on left.

Paul Harney Golf Club ✪✪✪ ▶ 40

74 Club Valley Drive
East Falmouth, MA
(508) 563-3454
www.paulharneygolf.com

Club Pro: Mike Harney, PGA
Payment: Cash, Visa, MC
Tee Times: No
Fee 9 Holes: Weekday: $40 M-Th
Fee 18 Holes: Weekday: $40 M-Th
Twilight Rates: After 2pm, $25
Cart Rental: $14pp/18, $7pp/9
Lessons: $40/half hour, $75/hour **Schools:** Yes
Membership: No
Other: Bar-Lounge / Snack Bar

Tees	Holes	Yards	Par	USGA	Slope
BACK	18	3570	59	58.9	91
MIDDLE	18	3315	59	56.7	89
FRONT	18	3200	61	61.0	89

Weekend: $40 F/S/S
Weekend: $40 F/S/S
Discounts: None
Driving Range: Yes
Junior Golf: Yes
Architect/Yr Open: Paul Harney/1968
GPS:

COUPON

A true test for all golfers. Executive-style course. Paul Harney inducted into PGA Hall of Fame in 2005.
Family-friendly and fun for all levels and abilities.

	1	2	3	4	5	6	7	8	9
PAR	4	3	3	3	3	3	4	3	3
YARDS	345	155	160	235	155	180	260	160	170
	10	11	12	13	14	15	16	17	18
PAR	3	3	3	3	4	4	3	3	4
YARDS	185	225	150	90	250	270	165	175	255

Directions: From Bourne Bridge take Route 28 East. Then take Route 151 toward Mashpee. Go 3-4
miles and take a left onto Fordham Road. Take left onto Club Valley Road to clubhouse.

Pine Valley Golf Club

136 Providence Street
Rehoboth, MA (508) 336-9815

Tees	Holes	Yards	Par	USGA	Slope
BACK					
MIDDLE	9	3015	35		118
FRONT	9	2375	35		113

SE MA/ CAPE

Club Pro: Bob Pachaco
Payment: Visa, MC
Tee Times: No
Fee 9 Holes: Weekday: $29 ride
Fee 18 Holes: Weekday:
Twilight Rates: Yes
Cart Rental: Included
Lessons: No **Schools:** No
Membership: No
Other: Snack Bar / Bar-Lounge

Weekend: $31 ride
Weekend:
Discounts: Senior wkdys $13
Driving Range: No
Junior Golf: No
Architect/Yr Open: 1945
GPS:

Player Comments: "Shorter course. Players need to be creative. Big greens. 2 practice greens." "Narrow and challenging fairways."

	1	2	3	4	5	6	7	8	9
PAR	4	3	4	5	4	3	4	4	4
YARDS	387	172	397	568	306	218	383	301	283
PAR									
YARDS									

Directions: I-95 to I-195 East, take Exit 2 Route 136 North, left onto Davis, turn right at end of road.

Poquoy Brook Golf Course

20 Leonard Street
Lakeville, MA (508) 947-5261
www.poquoybrook.com

Tees	Holes	Yards	Par	USGA	Slope
BACK	18	6817	72	72.4	128
MIDDLE	18	6291	72	69.9	125
FRONT	18	5415	73	71.0	114

Club Pro: Gary Cardoza, PGA
Payment: Cash, All Major Credit Cards
Tee Times: M-F, 7 days adv., S/S, 5 days
Fee 9 Holes: Weekday: $24
Fee 18 Holes: Weekday: $40
Twilight Rates: After 5pm
Cart Rental: $16pp/18, $11pp/9
Lessons: Yes **Schools:** Yes
Membership: Yes
Other: Clubhouse / Lockers / Showers / Snack Bar / Restaurant / Bar-Lounge

Weekend: $27
Weekend: $49
Discounts: Junior under 18
Driving Range: $5/lg, $3/sm
Junior Golf: Yes
Architect/Yr Open: Geoffrey Cornish/1962

COUPON

Player Comments: "Good conditions, good staff, nice clubhouse." "Interesting layout with great holes." Open year round. Grows on you with each replay. 2 new tees completed and a great new website.

	1	2	3	4	5	6	7	8	9
PAR	4	4	3	4	5	4	4	3	5
YARDS	351	390	176	307	518	326	381	180	485
	10	11	12	13	14	15	16	17	18
PAR	4	4	3	4	5	3	4	4	5
YARDS	372	336	185	366	436	173	426	428	455

Directions: I-495 South - take Exit 5, Route 18 South. Bear right off exit. Take first right (Taunton Street) and then first left onto Leonard Street. Course on right.

Quashnet Valley Country Club ✪✪½ ▶ 43

309 Old Barnstable Road
Mashpee, MA (508) 477-4412
www.quashnetvalley.com

Tees	Holes	Yards	Par	USGA	Slope
BACK	18	6601	72	71.7	132
MIDDLE	18	6093	72	69.1	121
FRONT	18	5094	72	70.3	119

Club Pro: Bob Chase, PGA
Payment: Visa, MC, Disc
Tee Times: 1 week, prepay 6 months
Fee 9 Holes: Weekday: $20 M-Th $25 F   **Weekend:** $30 S/S/H
Fee 18 Holes: Weekday: $40 M-Th $50 F   **Weekend:** $60 S/S/H
Twilight Rates: After 1pm; varies   **Discounts:** None
Cart Rental: $17pp/18 $9pp/9   **Driving Range:** Irons only
Lessons: $40/half hour **Schools:** Yes   **Junior Golf:** Yes
Membership: Limited   **Architect/Yr Open:** Cornish & Robinson/1973
Other: Clubhouse / Showers / Snack Bar / Bar-Lounge / Banquet Facilities

COUPON

The experience begins and ends with challenging par 5s. Very natural setting with only one set parallel fairways on the course. No visible homes until the 10th hole. Ponds and streams abound. Player Comments: "Excellent layout. Great shape. Must play when on Cape. Friendly staff. Beautiful setting through old cranberry bogs."

	1	2	3	4	5	6	7	8	9
PAR	5	3	4	4	3	4	5	3	4
YARDS	505	135	328	310	153	420	488	173	349
	10	**11**	**12**	**13**	**14**	**15**	**16**	**17**	**18**
PAR	4	4	4	5	4	4	4	3	5
YARDS	302	390	322	530	354	360	339	155	480

Directions: Take Route 6 East to Exit 2. Take right onto Route 130 South, follow 7.2 miles then take a right onto Great Neck Road. Follow 1.6 miles, take right onto Old Barnstable Road. Course is on left at the end.

Rehoboth Country Club NR ▶ 44

155 Perryville Road
Rehoboth, MA (508) 252-6259
www.rehobothcountryclub.com

Tees	Holes	Yards	Par	USGA	Slope
BACK	18	6760	72	71.4	124
MIDDLE	18	6340	72	69.3	121
FRONT	18	5490	72	70.6	114

Club Pro: No
Payment: Visa, MC
Tee Times: 7 days adv.
Fee 9 Holes: Weekday: $19   **Weekend:** $25 after 2pm
Fee 18 Holes: Weekday: $30   **Weekend:** $35
Twilight Rates: After 2pm   **Discounts:** Senior & Junior
Cart Rental: $14pp/18, $7pp/9   **Driving Range:** Yes
Lessons: No **Schools:** No   **Junior Golf:** Yes
Membership: No   **Architect/Yr Open:** Geoffrey Cornish/1966
Other: Snack Bar / Clubhouse / Restaurant / Bar-Lounge
GPS: Yes

COUPON

Noted for large true greens and use of every club in bag. New tees and new bunkers. 20 minutes outside Providence, RI.

	1	2	3	4	5	6	7	8	9
PAR	4	5	3	5	4	4	4	3	4
YARDS	380	500	155	550	400	310	300	155	410
	10	**11**	**12**	**13**	**14**	**15**	**16**	**17**	**18**
PAR	5	4	3	4	4	4	3	5	4
YARDS	500	345	205	380	330	270	170	540	440

Directions: From Providence: East on Route 44 to Route 118, turn left and 1st left to course. From Taunton: West on Route 44 to Route 118. Turn right, 1st left to course. From Attleboro: East on Route 118, right on Fairview to Homestead. Right, then 1st left onto Perryville.

Rochester Golf Club

323 Rounseville Road
Rochester, MA (508) 763-5155
www.rochestergolfclub.net

Club Pro: Rusty Gunnerson, PGA
Payment: Cash Only
Tee Times: Sat, Sun, & holidays
Fee 9 Holes: Weekday: $15
Fee 18 Holes: Weekday: $25
Twilight Rates: No
Cart Rental: $20/18, $10/9 per cart
Lessons: Private **Schools:** No
Membership: No
Other: Snack Bar

Tees	Holes	Yards	Par	USGA	Slope
BACK	18	5250	69	66	115
MIDDLE	18	4830	69	64	107
FRONT	18	4032	69	58	100

Weekend: $15
Weekend: $25
Discounts: None
Driving Range: No
Junior Golf: Yes
Architect/Yr Open: 1969
GPS:

Course is challenging with beautiful scenery. New sandtraps. Accuracy at premium, not long but tight. "Heavy forest and water on 14 holes define the challenge. Think twice about pulling out the big dawg." –AP

	1	2	3	4	5	6	7	8	9
PAR	3	4	4	4	3	5	4	4	3
YARDS	156	386	258	252	128	435	250	312	116
	10	11	12	13	14	15	16	17	18
PAR	4	3	4	4	3	4	4	4	5
YARDS	280	110	272	290	180	260	280	373	492

Directions: I-195 to Rochester exit, follow Route 105 approximately 4 miles North on right.

Sandwich Hollows Golf Club ✪✪ 46

1 Round Hill Road,
East Sandwich, MA
(508) 888-3384x0
www.sandwichhollows.com

Club Pro: Jesse Schechtman, PGA
Payment: MC, Visa, Check
Tee Times: 3 week adv.
Fee 9 Holes: Weekday: $20, $29 ride
Fee 18 Holes: Weekday: $37.95 M/T/Th w/cart
Twilight Rates: After 2 $30 w/c, after 4 $24 w/c
Cart Rental: Included
Lessons: $40/half hour **Schools:** Adult Intro.
Membership: Full and Seasonal (wkdays only)
Other: Clubhouse / Restaurant / Lounge / Function Facilities

Tees	Holes	Yards	Par	USGA	Slope
BACK	18	6220	71	70.4	124
MIDDLE	18	5891	71	68.6	120
FRONT	18	4894	71	68.1	115

COUPON

Weekend: $22, $31 ride
Weekend: $62 w/cart
Discounts: None
Driving Range: $5 bucket, all grass tees
Junior Golf: Yes
Architect/Yr Open: Richard Cross/1972

The course is hilly. Accurate shots are essential. Open year round. All-day special on Wednesday includes green fee and cart. Pleasant views of Cape Cod Bay.

	1	2	3	4	5	6	7	8	9
PAR	5	4	3	4	4	5	3	4	4
YARDS	485	325	120	305	347	570	177	340	401
	10	11	12	13	14	15	16	17	18
PAR	4	4	3	4	5	3	4	4	4
YARDS	300	380	175	285	520	160	340	355	330

Directions: Located between Exits 3 and 4 on Route 6 (Mid-Cape Highway) on service road.

Shadow Brook Golf Course ✪✪

754 Newport Avenue
South Attleboro, MA
(508) 399-8918
www.atlanticgolfcenter.com

Tees	Holes	Yards	Par	USGA	Slope
BACK					
MIDDLE	9	752	27		
FRONT					

Club Pro: Al Vallente, PGA
Payment: Most Major
Tee Times: 7 days adv.
Fee 9 Holes: Weekday: $10   **Weekend:** $10
Fee 18 Holes: Weekday: $14   **Weekend:** $14
Twilight Rates: No   **Discounts:** None
Cart Rental: No   **Driving Range:** $10/jumbo, $8/lg., $6/med.
Lessons: Yes **Schools:** Jr./Sr.   **Junior Golf:** Yes
Membership: Value cards   **Architect/Yr Open:**
Other: Vending Machines   **GPS:**

COUPON

"Perfect for all level players to practice wedge game." –RW

	1	2	3	4	5	6	7	8	9
PAR	3	3	3	3	3	3	3	3	3
YARDS	82	62	70	81	75	64	65	95	83
PAR									
YARDS									

Directions: I-95 to Exit 2B. Course is 1 mile on right.

Stone-E-Lea Golf Course

1411 County Street
Attleboro, MA (508) 222-9735

Tees	Holes	Yards	Par	USGA	Slope
BACK	18	6251	69	69.5	116
MIDDLE	18	6030	69	67.8	112
FRONT					

Club Pro: No
Payment: Cash only
Tee Times: No
Fee 9 Holes: Weekday: $15   **Weekend:** $19
Fee 18 Holes: Weekday: $22   **Weekend:** $30
Twilight Rates: No   **Discounts:** Senior M-F before 2
Cart Rental: $22/18, $11/9 per cart   **Driving Range:** No
Lessons: No **Schools:** No   **Junior Golf:** No
Membership: No   **Architect/Yr Open:**
Other: Snack Bar / Bar / ATM on-site   **GPS:**

Discounts for seniors over 62 after 2pm Monday through Friday. Open year round. Clubhouse is newly renovated.

	1	2	3	4	5	6	7	8	9
PAR	4	4	4	3	4	4	3	4	4
YARDS	360	350	310	185	330	420	175	380	430
	10	11	12	13	14	15	16	17	18
PAR	5	4	4	4	4	3	4	4	3
YARDS	490	390	410	390	265	190	390	325	240

Directions: I-95 to Exit 3 to 123 West. At first light take left onto Tiffany Street. Next light take right onto County Street. Course is at top of hill on right.

Sun Valley Golf Course

329 Summer Street
Rehoboth, MA (508) 336-8686

SE
MA/
CAPE

Club Pro: No
Payment: Cash only
Tee Times: No
Fee 9 Holes: Weekday: $20
Fee 18 Holes: Weekday: $25
Twilight Rates: After 2pm
Cart Rental: $26/18, $14/9 per cart
Lessons: No **Schools:** No
Membership: No
Other: Restaurant / Clubhouse / Bar-Lounge / Lockers / Snack Bar / Showers

Tees	Holes	Yards	Par	USGA	Slope
BACK	18	6734	71	71.0	118
MIDDLE	18	6383	71	71.0	118
FRONT	18	5654	71	71.0	N/A

Weekend:
Weekend: $30
Discounts: Seniors play for $18
Driving Range:
Junior Golf: No
Architect/Yr Open: Benjamin J. Wihry/1961

COUPON

Sig. hole: #12, dogleg right, green to the left, brook runs through it. Flat, willow-tree-lined, large fairways (wide); some brooks, greens excellent. Open March - November.

	1	2	3	4	5	6	7	8	9
PAR	4	4	5	3	4	3	5	4	4
YARDS	345	336	475	180	380	155	510	415	400
	10	11	12	13	14	15	16	17	18
PAR	4	5	4	3	4	4	3	4	4
YARDS	365	450	425	172	380	400	195	385	415

Directions: Route I-195 West to Route 114A to Route 44 East for 3 miles. Take right on Lake Street. Go 1 mile to course.

Swansea Country Club

○○½ 50

299 Market Street
Swansea, MA (508) 379-9886
www.swanseacountryclub.com

Club Pro: Shane Drury, PGA
Payment: Most Major Cards, No Checks
Tee Times: Wed noon for weekend
Fee 9 Holes: Weekday: $23
Fee 18 Holes: Weekday: $31
Twilight Rates: After 6pm
Cart Rental: $13pp/18, $7pp/9
Lessons: Yes **Schools:** Yes
Membership: No
Other: Clubhouse / Snack Bar / Restaurant / Bar-Lounge / Outdoor Patio & Tent Seating 200 for outings overlooking golf course. Junior golf.

Tees	Holes	Yards	Par	USGA	Slope
BACK	18	6840	72	72.8	126
MIDDLE	18	6429	72	70.9	125
FRONT	18	5598	72	69.4	113

Weekend: $27
Weekend: $41
Discounts: Senior & Junior
Driving Range: Yes, grass tees
Junior Golf: No
Architect/Yr Open: Geoffrey Cornish/1963

COUPON

Great value, excellent course conditions highly underrated by *New England Golf Guide*. Just 10 minutes outside Providence.

	1	2	3	4	5	6	7	8	9
PAR	4	5	4	3	4	3	4	5	4
YARDS	331	496	415	206	353	118	366	475	419
	10	11	12	13	14	15	16	17	18
PAR	4	3	4	5	4	3	4	5	4
YARDS	323	170	366	615	291	203	300	478	436

Directions: I-195 East or West to Exit #2 (Massachusetts). South on Route 136 for 1 mile. Golf course on right.

Swansea Executive Par 3

★★ **51** ▶

299 Market Street
Swansea, MA (508) 379-9886
www.swanseacountryclub.com

Club Pro: Shone Drury/Ryan Porter
Payment: Most Major Cards, No Checks
Tee Times:
Fee 9 Holes: Weekday: $10
Fee 18 Holes: Weekday: $16
Twilight Rates: No
Cart Rental: $10pp/18, $5/9
Lessons: Yes **Schools:** Yes
Membership: Yes
Other:

Tees	Holes	Yards	Par	USGA	Slope
BACK	9	1378	27	54.8	84
MIDDLE	9	1196	27	54..8	84
FRONT	9	957	27	57.0	89

Weekend: $10
Weekend: $16
Discounts: None
Driving Range: Yes
Junior Golf: Yes
Architect/Yr Open: L. Doyle/1997
GPS:

A fine track in the beautiful setting of Narragansett Bay. Inquire about member rates: Family, Adult, Junior. Single-rider cart rates. 10 min. to downtown Providence.

	1	2	3	4	5	6	7	8	9
PAR	3	3	3	3	3	3	3	3	3
YARDS	153	115	160	128	134	141	101	122	142
PAR									
YARDS									

Directions: MA Exit 2 off I-195. Course is 1 mile South of freeway.

Touisset Country Club

NR **52** ▶

221 Pearse Road
Swansea, MA (508) 679-9577
www.touissetcc.com

Club Pro: Les Brigham
Payment: Cash, Visa, MC, Disc
Tee Times: No
Fee 9 Holes: Weekday: $19
Fee 18 Holes: Weekday: $21
Twilight Rates: After 4pm
Cart Rental: $13.50pp/18, $7.25pp/9
Lessons: $19/half hour **Schools:** Yes
Membership: Yes
Other: Snack Bar / Restaurant / Bar-Lounge / Clubhouse / Lockers / Practice Area and Putting Greens

Tees	Holes	Yards	Par	USGA	Slope
BACK	9	3182	36	69.1	111
MIDDLE	9	3024	35	69.1	111
FRONT	9	2776	36	71.1	114

Weekend: $21
Weekend: $26
Discounts: Senior & Junior
Driving Range: No
Junior Golf: Yes
Architect/Yr Open: Raymond H. Brigham/1961

9 hole course with 4 sets of tees. Fairly flat but challenging. Open year round, weather permitting.

	1	2	3	4	5	6	7	8	9
PAR	4	4	4	4	3	4	3	5	4
YARDS	324	291	373	388	118	448	160	534	388
PAR									
YARDS									

Directions: Exit 3 off I-195, Route 6 West. Left at first traffic light onto Maple Street. Straight 3/4 mile to 221 Pearse Road.

Twin Brooks Golf Course ✪✪✪

 53

35 Scudder Avenue
Hyannis, MA (508) 862-6980
www.twinbrooksgolf.net

Club Pro:
Payment: Visa, MC, Amex, Diner's, Cash
Tee Times: Call
Fee 9 Holes: Weekday:
Fee 18 Holes: Weekday: $28 M-Th
Twilight Rates: After 3pm M-Th $25
Cart Rental: $12pp/18, $4/pull
Lessons: Available **Schools:** No
Membership: Yes
Other: Restaurant / Hotel / Bar-Lounge / Showers

Weekend:
Weekend: $33 F/S/S
Discounts: Sr. $25, Jr. $25
Driving Range: No
Junior Golf: No
Architect/Yr Open: Cornish & Robinson/1965
GPS:

Tees	Holes	Yards	Par	USGA	Slope
BACK					
MIDDLE	18	2621	54		
FRONT					

COUPON

Very challenging. Open year round. Rates subject to change. Guest rates available. Pull carts and rental bags available.

	1	2	3	4	5	6	7	8	9
PAR	3	3	3	3	3	3	3	3	3
YARDS	135	90	165	144	110	102	175	140	135
	10	**11**	**12**	**13**	**14**	**15**	**16**	**17**	**18**
PAR	3	3	3	3	3	3	3	3	3
YARDS	190	140	150	115	170	215	150	160	135

Directions: Take Route 6 to Exit 6 (Hyannis), follow Route 132 to Hyannis, follow signs to West End Hyannis. At rotary, you will see the resort and confence center.

Wampanoag Golf Club

NR ▶ **54**

168 Old Providence Road
North Swansea, MA
(508) 379-9832
www.wampanoaggolfcouse.com

Club Pro: No
Payment: Cash Only
Tee Times: No
Fee 9 Holes: Weekday: $15
Fee 18 Holes: Weekday: $20
Twilight Rates: No
Cart Rental: $14pp/18, $7pp/9
Lessons: No **Schools:** No
Membership: Yes
Other: Snack Bar / Bar-Lounge

Weekend: $20
Weekend: $25
Discounts: Senior & Junior
Driving Range: No
Junior Golf: No
Architect/Yr Open: Aljenon Barney/1931
GPS:

Tees	Holes	Yards	Par	USGA	Slope
BACK					
MIDDLE	9	2775	35	69.5	112
FRONT	9	2439	37	69.5	112

COUPON

Good mix of long par 3s and short par 5s. Long ball hitters have a definite advantage. Play front and back tees for an enjoyable 18 holes. Open year round. Yardage markers, superb greens & improved drainage.

	1	2	3	4	5	6	7	8	9
PAR	4	3	4	4	4	3	5	4	4
YARDS	305	115	343	400	397	150	417	301	343
PAR									
YARDS									

Directions: Take I-95 to Exit 2 (Warren/Newport), turn right onto Route 6. Turn left at Mason Street. At stop sign turn right on Old Providence Road.

Wentworth Hills Golf Club

⭐⭐½ 55

27 Bow Street
Plainville, MA (508) 699-9406
www.wentworthhillsgolf.com

Club Pro: David Sibley, PGA
Payment: Visa, MC, Amex
Tee Times: 14 days adv.
Fee 9 Holes: Weekday: $28
Fee 18 Holes: Weekday: $42
Twilight Rates: After 3pm
Cart Rental: $19pp/18, $11pp/9
Lessons: Yes **Schools:** Yes
Membership: Yes
Other: Restaurant / Clubhouse / Bar-Lounge

Tees	Holes	Yards	Par	USGA	Slope
BACK	18	6202	71	71.0	128
MIDDLE	18	5817	71	68.0	125
FRONT	18	5325	71	65.3	120

Weekend: $28
Weekend: $52
Discounts: Senior & Junior
Driving Range: Yes
Junior Golf: Yes
Architect/Yr Open: Howard Maurer/2001
GPS:

COUPON

Player comment: "Several interesting holes, immaculate conditioning, flawless greens, and friendly staff make this a must-play."

	1	2	3	4	5	6	7	8	9
PAR	4	4	5	4	4	5	3	3	4
YARDS	406	336	468	256	272	462	153	140	380
	10	11	12	13	14	15	16	17	18
PAR	4	3	4	4	5	4	4	3	4
YARDS	358	138	384	374	488	366	314	142	380

Directions: From Route 495, take Route 1A/Wrentham-Plainville exit. Follow 1A South for .7 miles, right onto Green Street. Follow .3 miles, left onto High Street. Follow 1 mile, right onto Hancock Street. Follow .4 miles, left onto Bow Street. Follow Bow to entrance.

Whaling City Golf Course

NR 56

581 Hathaway Road
New Bedford, MA (508) 996-9393
www.johnsongolfmanagement.com

Club Pro: Bill Allan, PGA
Payment: Cash, Credit Cards
Tee Times: 7 days adv.
Fee 9 Holes: Weekday: $17
Fee 18 Holes: Weekday: $29
Twilight Rates: No
Cart Rental: $15pp/18, $8pp/9
Lessons: Yes **Schools:** No
Membership: Yes
Other: Snack Bar / Restaurant / Bar-Lounge

Tees	Holes	Yards	Par	USGA	Slope
BACK	18	6780	72	73	131
MIDDLE	18	6527	72	70.2	126
FRONT	18	6457	74	70.1	118

Weekend: $19
Weekend: $33
Discounts: Junior and Resident
Driving Range: Yes
Junior Golf: No
Architect/Yr Open: Donald Ross/1946
GPS:

New tees. Municipal course. Managed by Johnson Management. This course is a hidden gem of Southeastern Massachusetts!

	1	2	3	4	5	6	7	8	9
PAR	4	4	4	4	3	4	5	3	5
YARDS	448	382	409	343	190	381	530	140	453
	10	11	12	13	14	15	16	17	18
PAR	5	4	4	3	5	4	4	3	4
YARDS	535	379	436	163	499	333	356	179	331

Directions: Take Route 140 in New Bedford to Exit 3. Bear right.

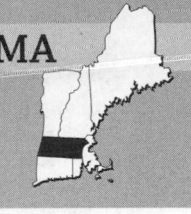

A map of Central & Western Massachusetts with numbered golf course locations near North Adams, Greenfield, Gardner, Leominster, Pittsfield, Northampton, Springfield, Southwick, and Worcester.

Course	No.	Course	No.	Course	No.
Agawam Municipal CC	1	Groton Country Club	32	Quail Hollow Golf & CC	63
Amherst Golf Club	2	Hampden Country Club	33	Ranch Golf Club, The	64
Ashfield Community Golf Club	3	Hemlock Ridge GC	34	Red Tail Golf Club	65
Bas Ridge Golf Course	4	Heritage Country Club	35	Scottish Meadow Golf Club	66
Bay Path Golf Course	5	Hickory Ridge CC	36	Shaker Farms CC	67
Beaver Brook Country Club	6	Highfields Golf & CC	37	Shaker Hills Golf Club	68
Bedrock Golf Club	7	Hillcrest Country Club	38	Skyline Country Club	69
Blackstone National Golf Club	8	Holden Hills CC	39	Southampton CC	70
Blissful Meadows GC	9	Holyoke Country Club	40	Southwick CC	71
Cherry Hills GC	10	Hopedale CC	41	St. Anne Country Club	72
Chicopee Municipal GC	11	Indian Meadows Golf Club	42	St. Mark's Golf Club	73
Clearview Golf Course	12	Juniper Hill GC (Lakeside)	43	Taconic Golf Club	74
Country Club of Greenfield	13	Juniper Hill GC (Riverside)	44	Tekoa Country Club	75
Country Club of Wilbraham	14	Kettle Brook Golf Club	45	Templewood Golf Course	76
Cranwell Resort, Spa & GC	15	Ledges Golf Club	46	The Meadows Golf Club	77
Crumpin-Fox Club	16	Leicester Country Club	47	Thomas Memorial Golf & CC	78
Cyprian Keyes Golf Club	17	Links at Lancaster Golf, The	48	Townsend Ridge CC	79
Cyprian Keyes GC, Par 3	18	Maplewood Golf Course	49	Twin Springs Golf Club	80
Dudley Hill Golf Club	19	Mill Valley Links	50	Tyngsboro CC	81
Dunroamin CC	20	Monoosnock CC	51	Veteran's Golf Club	82
East Mountain CC	21	North Adams CC	52	Wachusett CC	83
Edge Hill GC	22	Northfield CC	53	Wahconah CC	84
Edgewood Golf Club	23	Oak Ridge GC-Feeding Hills	54	Waubeeka Golf Links	85
Egremont Country Club	24	Oak Ridge GC-Gill	55	Westborough CC	86
Ellinwood CC	25	Pakachoag Golf Course	56	Westminster CC	87
Forest Park CC	26	Petersham CC	57	Westover Golf Course	88
Franconia Muni. GC	27	Pine Grove Golf Club	58	Winchendon School CC	89
Gardner Municipal GC	28	Pine Knoll Par 3	59	Woods of Westminster CC	90
GEAA Golf Club	29	Pine Ridge Country Club	60	Worthington GC	91
Green Hill Municipal GC	30	Pontoosuc Lake CC	61		
Greenock Country Club	31	Quaboag Country Club	62		

KEY TO THE STAR RATINGS:
5✪= Outstanding 4✪= Excellent 3✪= Very Good 2✪= Good 1✪= Average NR = Not Rated

Agawam Municipal Country Club NR

128 Southwick Street (Route 57)
Feeding Hills, MA
(413) 786-2194
www.agawamgc.com

Club Pro: Ron Dunn, PGA
Payment: Cash, Visa, MC
Tee Times: 7 days adv.

Tees	Holes	Yards	Par	USGA	Slope
BACK					
MIDDLE	18	6119	71	67.0	110
FRONT	18	5345	71	71.2	110

Fee 9 Holes: Weekday: $13
Fee 18 Holes: Weekday: $17
Twilight Rates: After 12pm
Cart Rental: $13pp/18, $7pp/9
Lessons: Private & Group **Schools:** No
Membership: No
Other: Snack Bar / Bar-Lounge

Weekend: $15
Weekend: $20
Discounts: Senior & Junior
Driving Range: No
Junior Golf: Yes
Architect/Yr Open: Richard Leao/1929
GPS:

A friendly course. No water holes but 1 creek and 8 sand traps. Total irrigation. The 9th hole is referred to as "Cardiac Hill," and for good reason. Weekend specials before 8am and after 12pm. Fees subject to change.

	1	2	3	4	5	6	7	8	9
PAR	5	4	3	4	3	4	4	5	3
YARDS	480	375	144	465	121	360	385	560	175
	10	**11**	**12**	**13**	**14**	**15**	**16**	**17**	**18**
PAR	5	4	4	3	4	3	5	5	3
YARDS	475	395	348	160	322	145	554	475	180

Directions: I-90 (Mass Pike) to I-91 to Route 57 (Agawam). Go West on Route 57. Club is in the town of Feeding Hills.

Amherst Golf Club ✪✪ 2

365 South Pleasant Street
Amherst, MA (413) 256-6894

Club Pro: Dave Twohig, PGA
Payment: Visa, MC
Tee Times: No

Tees	Holes	Yards	Par	USGA	Slope
BACK					
MIDDLE	9	3055	35	68.9	117
FRONT	9	2774	36	68.9	122

Fee 9 Holes: Weekday: $25
Fee 18 Holes: Weekday: $25
Twilight Rates: No
Cart Rental: $25/18 per cart
Lessons: $45/half hour **Schools:** No
Membership: Wait list
Other: Clubhouse / Lockers / Showers / Snack Bar

Weekend: $25
Weekend: $25
Discounts: None
Driving Range: No
Junior Golf: No
Architect/Yr Open: Walter Hatch/1900

COUPON

Sig. Hole #9 is a long, uphill par 3 with a sloping green. Collared shirts. Course is short in length with small greens, but in good shape. Old New England course.

	1	2	3	4	5	6	7	8	9
PAR	4	4	4	3	4	4	5	4	3
YARDS	390	375	405	160	350	340	525	310	200
PAR									
YARDS									

Directions: Take Mass Pike to Route 181 to Route 9 into Amherst. Course is located by Amherst College.

Ashfield Community Golf Club

NR

143 Norton Hill Road
Ashfield, MA (413) 628-4413

Club Pro: No
Payment: Cash or Check
Tee Times: Not needed
Fee 9 Holes: Weekday: $10
Fee 18 Holes: Weekday: $12
Twilight Rates: No
Cart Rental: Pull carts only
Lessons: No **Schools:** No
Membership: Yes
Other: Clubhouse / Snack Bar

Tees	Holes	Yards	Par	USGA	Slope
BACK					
MIDDLE	9	4187	66		
FRONT	9	3458	66		

Weekend: $12
Weekend: $16
Discounts: None
Driving Range: No
Junior Golf: Yes
Architect/Yr Open: 1927
GPS:

CTRL/
WEST
MA

Honor system for play during the week, instructions for payment on clubhouse door. Attendant on weekends and holidays.

	1	2	3	4	5	6	7	8	9
PAR	4	4	3	4	3	4	4	4	3
YARDS	286	289	201	317	102	200	185	341	156
	10	11	12	13	14	15	16	17	18
PAR	4	4	3	4	3	4	4	4	3
YARDS	286	289	201	317	122	200	185	354	156

Directions: I-91 to Exit 19. Right off ramp. Go straight at intersection onto Damon Road. Go straight through next intersection onto Bridge Road. At stop sign, turn right onto Route 9, go 14 miles. Turn right onto Route 112 for 6 miles. Go right on Route 116 East to center of Ashfield. Turn right at Norton Hill Road.

Bas Ridge Golf Course

NR 4

Plunkett Street
Hinsdale, MA
(413) 655-2605
www.basridge.tripod.com

Club Pro:
Payment: Cash Only
Tee Times: Recommended
Fee 9 Holes: Weekday: $12
Fee 18 Holes: Weekday: $15
Twilight Rates: After 4pm
Cart Rental: $11pp/18, $5.50pp/9
Lessons: No **Schools:**
Membership: Limited
Other: Clubhouse / Bar-Lounge

Tees	Holes	Yards	Par	USGA	Slope
BACK					
MIDDLE	18	5051	70	63.7	111
FRONT	18	4369	70	65.9	110

Weekend: $15
Weekend: $20
Discounts: Senior weekdays
Driving Range: No
Junior Golf: Yes
Architect/Yr Open: Rowland Armacost/1998
GPS:

Player Comments: "Each hole is more beautiful and the greens are incredible." –BB A shorter course, but fun. Open April 1 - November 1. Voted #1 - Best of the Berkshires Golf Course 2007 *(Berkshire Eagle)*

	1	2	3	4	5	6	7	8	9
PAR	4	4	3	4	3	4	4	4	4
YARDS	335	269	193	280	170	224	233	331	276
	10	11	12	13	14	15	16	17	18
PAR	4	4	3	4	5	3	5	4	4
YARDS	270	336	187	313	451	112	466	278	327

Directions: Take Mass Pike to Lee exit, go East on Route 20 about 8 miles. Left onto Route 8 North about 10 miles to Plunkett Street and the course.

Bay Path Golf Course

NR 5

193 North Brookfield Road
East Brookfield, MA
(508) 867-8161

Tees	Holes	Yards	Par	USGA	Slope
BACK	9	2952	36	67.4	109
MIDDLE	9	2640	36	66.0	107
FRONT	9	2298	36	67.6	107

Club Pro: None
Payment: Visa, MC
Tee Times: No
Fee 9 Holes: Weekday: $15　　　**Weekend:** $17
Fee 18 Holes: Weekday: $21　　**Weekend:** $26
Twilight Rates: No　　　**Discounts:** Junior w/adult player
Cart Rental: $15pp/18, $10pp/9　　**Driving Range:** No
Lessons: No **Schools:** No　　**Junior Golf:** No
Membership: Yes, limited　　**Architect/Yr Open:** John Hoenig/1962
Other: Clubhouse / Snack Bar / Bar-Lounge　**GPS:**

Player Comments: "Great deal for the money. Nice friendly staff and lounge." Very flat and easy to walk. Open April - November 15. Proper attire required.

	1	2	3	4	5	6	7	8	9
PAR	4	4	5	4	3	5	4	3	4
YARDS	297	273	456	305	131	426	270	151	331
PAR									
YARDS									

Directions: Mass. Pike to Route 20 East (Sturbridge exit). Then take Route 20 East to Route 49 North to Route 9 West to Route 67 North (North Brookfield Road). Course is approximately 1/4 mile on left.

Beaver Brook Country Club

NR 6

Route 9
Main Street, Haydenville, MA
(413) 268-7229

Tees	Holes	Yards	Par	USGA	Slope
BACK					
MIDDLE	9	3046	36	68.1	110
FRONT	9	2480	36	67.7	107

Club Pro: Hiro Shi
Payment: Most Major
Tee Times: Anytime
Fee 9 Holes: Weekday: $15　　**Weekend:** $16
Fee 18 Holes: Weekday: $23　　**Weekend:** $24
Twilight Rates: After 4pm, Sunday　**Discounts:** Senior, $1 off
Cart Rental: $14pp/18, $7pp/9　　**Driving Range:** No
Lessons: No **Schools:** No　　**Junior Golf:** Yes
Membership: Yes　　**Architect/Yr Open:** 1964
Other: Clubhouse / Snack Bar / Bar-Lounge　**GPS:**

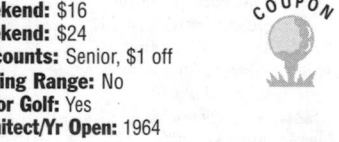

Beautifully laid out and maintained 9-hole course. The course sports 2 brooks and 4 ponds. Special Mon-Sat: 2 players w/cart 9 holes $37, 18 holes $58 until 2pm.

	1	2	3	4	5	6	7	8	9
PAR	4	4	5	3	4	4	4	3	5
YARDS	403	323	496	146	361	370	290	167	490
PAR									
YARDS									

Directions: I-91 to Exit 19 North. Continue to end; make right. Course is 2 miles on State Road (Route 9 West).

Bedrock Golf Club

87 Barre Paxton Road
Rutland, MA (508) 886-0202
www.bedrockgolfclub.com

Club Pro: Joe Carr, PGA
Payment: Visa, MC, Cash, Amex
Tee Times: Weekends
Fee 9 Holes: Weekday: $15
Fee 18 Holes: Weekday: $25
Twilight Rates: After 12pm $15/$25 wknds
Cart Rental: $20pp/18, $10pp/9
Lessons: No **Schools:** No
Membership: Yes
Other: Clubhouse / Bar-Lounge / Snack Bar

Tees	Holes	Yards	Par	USGA	Slope
BACK					
MIDDLE	9	3131	36	69.8	127
FRONT					

Weekend: $25
Weekend: $40
Discounts: Junior, wkdays $12/18
Driving Range: No
Junior Golf: No
Architect/Yr Open: Green & Whitehead/1992
GPS:

COUPON

New tees. Gently rolling, narrow landing areas. Small, undulating greens, challenging. Collared shirts required. "Absolutely loved it." April - November.

	1	2	3	4	5	6	7	8	9
PAR	4	5	4	3	4	5	3	4	4
YARDS	340	460	380	184	355	487	166	348	411
PAR									
YARDS									

Directions: I-90 (Mass Pike) to Auburn Exit (10). Then take Route 20 West to Route 56 North to Route 122 In Paxton. Course is 4 miles on left.

Berlin Country Club

25 Carr Road
Berlin, MA (978) 838-2733

Club Pro:
Payment: Cash Only
Tee Times: No
Fee 9 Holes: Weekday:
Fee 18 Holes: Weekday:
Twilight Rates:
Cart Rental: $17pp/18, $12pp/9
Lessons: Schools:
Membership:
Other:

Tees	Holes	Yards	Par	USGA	Slope
BACK	9	2433	33	32	108
MIDDLE	9	2072	33	31.4	104
FRONT					

Weekend: $15
Weekend: $25
Discounts:
Driving Range: Yes
Junior Golf:
Architect/Yr Open: 1957
GPS:

Mildly sloping fairways with challenging greens. Golf shirts and golf shoes required. Open March - November.

	1	2	3	4	5	6	7	8	9
PAR	4	4	4	3	4	4	3	4	3
YARDS	312	326	332	127	264	349	108	282	133
PAR									
YARDS									

Directions: From I-495 take Exit 26 to Route 62 West to Berlin Center. Take a right at Center Street and continue onto Highland Street. Turn left at Randall Road, then right at Carr Road, and follow to course.

Blackstone National GC ✪✪✪✪½

227 Putnam Hill Road
Sutton, MA (508) 865-2111
www.bngc.net

Club Pro: Matt Stephens, PGA
Payment: Visa, MC, Amex, Disc
Tee Times: 5 days adv.
Fee 9 Holes: Weekday: $40
Fee 18 Holes: Weekday: $71
Twilight Rates: After 1:30pm
Cart Rental: $19pp/18, $10pp/9
Lessons: Yes **Schools:** Yes
Membership: Yes **GPS:** Yes
Other: Full Restaurant / Clubhouse / Lockers / Showers / Bar-Lounge /
Henry-Griffitts Precision Golf Club Fitting

Tees	Holes	Yards	Par	USGA	Slope
BACK	18	6909	72	73.5	132
MIDDLE	18	6396	72	71.2	127
FRONT	18	5203	72	70.0	122

Weekend: $50
Weekend: $91
Discounts: Junior
Driving Range: Yes
Junior Golf: Yes
Architect/Yr Open: Rees Jones/2000

Player Comments: "Fun to play. Great condition. Excellent greens." "Elevated tees and greens call for lots of club decisions—pick the right tees or you'll wish you did." "Wonderfully built and kept." "Great scenery." "One of New England's premier tracks." –JD

	1	2	3	4	5	6	7	8	9
PAR	4	5	3	4	4	4	3	5	4
YARDS	331	575	154	393	346	425	196	480	363
	10	11	12	13	14	15	16	17	18
PAR	4	3	4	3	4	4	5	4	5
YARDS	396	160	358	190	387	481	568	372	480

Directions: Mass Pike to Exit 10A to Route 146 South. Go 6 miles and take Central Turnpike toward Oxford 3 miles, to 4-way stop. Take left. Course on top of hill.

Blissful Meadows Golf Club ✪✪✪½ 10

801 Chockalog Road
Uxbridge, MA (508) 278-6113
www.blissfulmeadows.com

Club Pro: Matthew Griffith, PGA
Payment: Visa, MC, Amex, Disc
Tee Times: 7 days adv.
Fee 9 Holes: Weekday: $20 M-Th
Fee 18 Holes: Weekday: $31 M-Th
Twilight Rates: After 3:30pm
Cart Rental: $17pp/18, $10pp/9
Lessons: Yes **Schools:** No
Membership: Yes
Other: Meadowview Tavern / Clubhouse / Bar-Lounge / Available for Outings

Tees	Holes	Yards	Par	USGA	Slope
BACK	18	6700	72	73.4	136
MIDDLE	18	6210	72	71.3	131
FRONT	18	5065	72	70.0	126

Weekend: $30 Fri $24
Weekend: $51 Fri $39
Discounts: Sr. & Jr. lunch specials
Driving Range: $7/lg., $4.50/sm.
Junior Golf: Yes
Architect/Yr Open: Brian Silva/1992

COUPON

Bent grass greens and tees. Many holes quite isolated. Front 9 gently rolling with lots of character, back 9 wild and very hilly. The 3 finishing holes are great. Each replay you'll enjoy it more. Scenic and challenging.

	1	2	3	4	5	6	7	8	9
PAR	4	3	5	4	3	4	4	5	4
YARDS	325	148	520	343	132	368	312	572	350
	10	11	12	13	14	15	16	17	18
PAR	5	4	4	3	4	3	5	4	4
YARDS	499	343	375	155	306	176	525	375	398

Directions: Take Route 146 to Route 16 West. Take first left onto West Street. Follow signs 3 miles. Take right at dead end.

Cherry Hills Golf Course

325 Montague Road
Amherst, MA (413) 256-4071
www.cherryhillgolf.org

Club Pro:
Payment: Visa/MC
Tee Times: No
Fee 9 Holes: Weekday: $15
Fee 18 Holes: Weekday: $20
Twilight Rates: No
Cart Rental: $24/18, $13/9 per cart
Lessons: No **Schools:** No
Membership: Yes
Other: Snack Bar

Tees	Holes	Yards	Par	USGA	Slope
BACK	9	2944	36	65.7	101
MIDDLE	9	2778	36	65.7	101
FRONT	9	2470	36	N/A	N/A

Weekend: $17
Weekend: $22
Discounts: Senior & Junior
Driving Range: No
Junior Golf: No
Architect/Yr Open: Dave Maxon/1963
GPS:

COUPON

A great course for everyone, beautiful views of the Berkshires and excellent greens.

	1	2	3	4	5	6	7	8	9
PAR	5	3	4	4	4	4	5	4	3
YARDS	555	159	298	341	406	291	415	296	183
PAR									
YARDS									

Directions: Take I-91 to Hadley exit, right on Route 9 into Amherst. Go North on Route 16 for 3 miles, turn right at light onto Pine Street and onto Route 63. Course is 1/2 mile on right.

Chicopee Municipal Golf Course ◐◐½

1290 Burnett Road
Chicopee, MA (413) 594-9295

Club Pro: Thomas DiRico, PGA
Payment: Cash, Credit Cards
Tee Times: Yes
Fee 9 Holes: Weekday: $15
Fee 18 Holes: Weekday: $25 (7 day, non-res.)
Twilight Rates: After 2pm
Cart Rental: $12pp/18
Lessons: Yes **Schools:** No
Membership: No
Other: Clubhouse / Snack Bar

Tees	Holes	Yards	Par	USGA	Slope
BACK	18	6742	71	73.0	126
MIDDLE	18	6109	71	70.4	120
FRONT	18	5123	71	72.4	115

Weekend: $18
Weekend: $25
Discounts: Senior residents
Driving Range: Yes
Junior Golf: No
Architect/Yr Open: Geoffrey Cornish/1965
GPS:

Player Comments: "Course provides the opportunity to hit every club. "A solid test of your skills from tee to green. Between the design and condition, this is one of the region's very best values." –JD
Voted by *Golf Digest* and *USA Today* Best Value In Massachusetts.

	1	2	3	4	5	6	7	8	9
PAR	4	5	3	4	4	4	5	3	4
YARDS	382	481	173	316	433	354	535	193	285
	10	11	12	13	14	15	16	17	18
PAR	4	3	3	4	4	5	3	5	4
YARDS	362	157	160	340	391	473	173	534	367

Directions: I-90 (Mass Pike) to Exit 6, turn right at light; course is 2.5 miles on left.

Clearview Golf Course

66 Park Hill Avenue
Millbury, MA (508) 754-5654

Club Pro: Bill Chisholm
Payment: Visa, MC, Cash
Tee Times: 1 week adv.

Tees	Holes	Yards	Par	USGA	Slope
BACK					
MIDDLE	9	2724	35	66.3	107
FRONT	9	2362	35	67.7	112

Fee 9 Holes: Weekday: $10 9am-1pm   **Weekend:** $18 9am-2pm
Fee 18 Holes: Weekday: $15 9am-2pm   **Weekend:** $26 9am-2pm
Twilight Rates: **Discounts:** None
Cart Rental: $14pp/18, $7pp/9   **Driving Range:** No
Lessons: Yes **Schools:** No   **Junior Golf:** No
Membership: Yes   **Architect/Yr Open:** 1962
Other: Snack Bar / Bar-Lounge   **GPS:**

"Best greens in Central Mass." Pre-9am discounts available: $6 for 9 holes. Between 9am and 1pm: $10 for 9 holes. (Specials are only M-F, no holidays.)

	1	2	3	4	5	6	7	8	9
PAR	3	5	5	3	5	3	4	4	3
YARDS	147	472	484	192	477	135	348	290	179
PAR									
YARDS									

Directions: I-90 (Mass Pike) to Exit 10A (Route 146). Look for Route 20 East. At first traffic light, go right onto Park Hill Avenue. Course is 1/2 mile on left.

Country Club of Greenfield

Country Club Road
Greenfield, MA
(413) 773-7530
www.countryclubofgreenfield.net

Club Pro: Kevin Piecuch, PGA
Payment: Cash, Visa
Tee Times: No

Tees	Holes	Yards	Par	USGA	Slope
BACK	18	6450	72	70.1	117
MIDDLE	18	6210	72	68.6	114
FRONT	18	5444	73	70.6	119

COUPON

Fee 9 Holes: Weekday: $25   **Weekend:** $30
Fee 18 Holes: Weekday: $35   **Weekend:** $45
Twilight Rates: No   **Discounts:** Senior & Junior
Cart Rental: $27pp/18, $13.50pp/9   **Driving Range:** Yes
Lessons: Yes **Schools:** No   **Junior Golf:** Yes
Membership: Yes   **Architect/Yr Open:** R. Alex Findlay/1896
Other: Full Restaurant / Clubhouse / Bar-Lounge / Snack Bar / Showers

Built in 1896. Easy drive from all over New England.

	1	2	3	4	5	6	7	8	9
PAR	4	3	4	4	3	5	4	5	4
YARDS	380	144	421	380	130	565	283	455	362
	10	11	12	13	14	15	16	17	18
PAR	4	3	5	4	5	3	4	4	4
YARDS	357	185	470	280	570	145	315	387	320

Directions: I-91, take Exit 27. Turn right at Route 5 and 10. Take right at first set of lights onto Silver Street. Country Club Road is fourth street on right.

Country Club of Wilbraham ✪✪½ 15

859 Stony Hill Road
Wilbraham, MA (413) 596-8887
www.countryclubofwilbraham.com

Tees	Holes	Yards	Par	USGA	Slope
BACK	18	6380	72	71.2	130
MIDDLE	18	5967	72	68.9	125
FRONT	18	5168	72	65.4	115

Club Pro: Pete Chapman, Andrew Michaels
Payment: Cash, Credit Card
Tee Times: No
Fee 9 Holes: Weekday: $40/res, $50/non-res, $18/guest
Weekend: $45/res, $55/non-res
Fee 18 Holes: Weekday: $40/res, $30/guest **Weekend:** $45/res
Twilight Rates: After 6pm weekdays; after 5pm weekends $25
Discounts: Senior discount Mondays $23
Cart Rental: $14pp/18, $7pp/9
Lessons: $50/half hour **Schools:** No
Membership: Yes
Other: Clubhouse / Practice Green

Driving Range: Yes
Junior Golf: For residents
Architect/Yr Open: Willie Org/1927
GPS:

Semi-private. Residents of Wilbraham after 3pm, or as a guest with a member. Challenging even from the middle tees.

	1	2	3	4	5	6	7	8	9
PAR	4	3	4	4	3	5	4	5	4
YARDS	375	162	364	416	142	481	258	528	359
	10	11	12	13	14	15	16	17	18
PAR	3	5	4	4	3	4	4	4	5
YARDS	136	445	383	304	167	327	295	350	475

Directions: Take I-90 (Mass Pike) West to Exit 7, Belchertown/Ludlow. Turn left at end of ramp. Take Route 21 South. Follow signs to Wilbraham. Go left on Route 20 to Stony Hill Road.

Cranwell Resort, Spa, and GC ✪✪✪½ 16

55 Lee Road
Lenox, MA (413) 637-2563
www.cranwell.com

Tees	Holes	Yards	Par	USGA	Slope
BACK	18	6346	70	70	123
MIDDLE	18	6169	70	69.4	120
FRONT	18	5602	72	70.2	121

Club Pro: David Strawn, PGA
Payment: Visa, MC, Amex, Disc
Tee Times: 1 week adv.
Fee 9 Holes: Weekday: $49 M-Th Spg/Fall **Weekend:** $55 F/S/S Spg/Fall
Fee 18 Holes: Weekday: $94 M-Th Sum **Weekend:** $99 F/S/S Sum
Twilight Rates: After 3pm/Sum, after 2pm Spg/Fall **Discounts:** Junior 18 under, $30
Cart Rental: Included **Driving Range:** $5/bucket
Lessons: $50/half hour, $100/hour **Schools:** Yes **Junior Golf:** No
Membership: Yes **Architect/Yr Open:** Stiles & Van Kleek/1926
Other: Hotel / Lockers / Showers / Snack Bar / Restaurant / Bar-Lounge/ Major Golf School

Scottish-style course with heavy rough and panoramic mountain views. Reworked sandtraps and cart path in 2007. Exceptional golf school. Seasonal rates.

	1	2	3	4	5	6	7	8	9
PAR	4	5	3	4	3	4	4	4	4
YARDS	384	463	144	373	218	370	360	340	405
	10	11	12	13	14	15	16	17	18
PAR	4	4	3	4	4	5	3	4	4
YARDS	263	390	195	426	315	495	148	315	375

Directions: I-90 (Mass Pike) to Exit 2, take Route 20 West. Course is 10 minutes up the road.

Crumpin-Fox Club

◊◊◊◊¹⁄₂  17

Parmenter Road
Bernardston, MA (413) 648-9101
www.golfthefox.com

Tees	Holes	Yards	Par	USGA	Slope
BACK	18	7007	72	73.8	141
MIDDLE	18	6508	72	71.3	136
FRONT	18	5432	72	71.5	131

Club Pro: Michael Zaranek
Payment: Visa, MC, Amex, Disc
Tee Times: golfthefox.com
Fee 9 Holes: Weekday: $45 w/cart
Fee 18 Holes: Weekday: $87 w/cart
Twilight Rates: After 4pm
Cart Rental: Included
Lessons: $45/half hour **Schools:** Jr. & Sr.
Membership: Yes

Weekend: $48 w/cart
Weekend: $92 w/cart
Discounts: Senior & Junior
Driving Range: $5/bag
Junior Golf: Yes
Architect/Yr Open: Roger Rulewich/1978

Other: Restaurant / Clubhouse / Hotel / Bar-Lounge / Lockers / Snack Bar / Showers / Tennis Courts / Pond

COUPON

Player Comments: "Must play." –JD "Variety of holes." "You really need to think before you hit." "Beautiful landscape." "Great staff and atmosphere." "Immaculate." "The rustic clubhouse and pro shop, the tall trees surrounding the entrance—it just doesn't get any better." –LB

	1	2	3	4	5	6	7	8	9
PAR	4	4	3	4	5	4	4	5	3
YARDS	386	338	165	345	501	402	353	568	177
	10	11	12	13	14	15	16	17	18
PAR	4	3	4	4	5	3	4	5	4
YARDS	394	150	374	370	506	172	410	508	389

Directions: I-91 to Exit 28A (between Brattleboro, VT and Greenfield, MA). Follow Route 10 North for 1 mile; take left on Parmenter Road and follow signs to club.

Cyprian Keyes Golf Club

◊◊◊◊ 18

284 East Temple Street
Boylston, MA (508) 869-9900
www.cypriankeyes.com

Tees	Holes	Yards	Par	USGA	Slope
BACK	18	6871	72	74.4	136
MIDDLE	18	6134	72	72.4	132
FRONT	18	5029	72	71.2	126

Club Pro: Terry O'Hara, PGA
Payment: Visa, MC, Amex, Disc
Tee Times: 5 days adv.
Fee 9 Holes: Weekday:
Fee 18 Holes: Weekday: $56 M-Th
Twilight Rates: After 3pm
Cart Rental: $18pp/18, $12pp/9
Lessons: Yes **Schools:** Yes
Membership: Yes

Weekend:
Weekend: $66 F/S/S/H
Discounts: Senior & Junior
Driving Range: $7/bucket
Junior Golf: Yes
Architect/Yr Open: Mark Mungeam/1997

COUPON

Other: Restaurant / Function Facilities / Golf School / Custom Club Fitting

Among many great holes, the short, risky 13th and the challenging 11th. Exceptional dining room and outdoor patio. Great pro shop and learning center. Home of New England's only Callaway Performance Center.

	1	2	3	4	5	6	7	8	9
PAR	4	4	5	5	4	3	4	4	3
YARDS	332	367	510	476	376	180	357	369	155
	10	11	12	13	14	15	16	17	18
PAR	5	3	4	4	4	4	3	4	5
YARDS	486	175	350	318	406	348	162	297	470

Directions: Route 290 to Exit 23B (Route 140 North). Go 1 mile and take third right onto East Temple Street.

Cyprian Keyes Golf Club, Par 3 ✪✪✪

19

284 East Temple Street
Boylston, MA (508) 869-9900
www.cypriankeyes.com

Club Pro: Terry O'Hara, PGA
Payment: Visa, MC, Amex, Disc
Tee Times: 5 days
Fee 9 Holes: Weekday: $15 M-Th
Fee 18 Holes: Weekday:
Twilight Rates: No
Cart Rental: Pull carts
Lessons: Yes **Schools:** Yes
Membership: Juniors
Other: Clubhouse / Restaurant/ Function Facilities / Golf School / Custom Club Fitting

Tees	Holes	Yards	Par	USGA	Slope
BACK					
MIDDLE	9	1230	27		
FRONT					

Weekend: $18 F/S/S/H
Weekend:
Discounts: Jr. and Sr.
Driving Range: $7 bucket
Junior Golf: Yes
Architect/Yr Open: Mark Mungeam/1997

Sig. Hole: #9 is a picturesque 165-yard hole framed by trees with water to the left. It provides the golfer with many options. Player comments: "There are some great holes here. They could be part of any full-sized course." –JD Home of New England's only Callaway Performance Center.

	1	2	3	4	5	6	7	8	9
PAR	3	3	3	3	3	3	3	3	3
YARDS	155	85	165	105	135	120	155	145	165
PAR									
YARDS									

Directions: Route 290 to Exit 23B (Route 140 North). Go 1 mile and take third right onto East Temple Street.

Dudley Hill Golf Club ✪✪½

20

80 Airport Road
Dudley, MA (508) 943-4538
www.dudleyhill.org

Club Pro:
Payment: Visa, MC
Tee Times: Weekends
Fee 9 Holes: Weekday: $20
Fee 18 Holes: Weekday: $30 M-Th
Twilight Rates: No
Cart Rental: $12pp/18, $6pp/9
Lessons: No **Schools:** No
Membership: Yes
Other: Snack Bar / Bar-Lounge

Tees	Holes	Yards	Par	USGA	Slope
BACK					
MIDDLE	9	3279	36	71.4	123
FRONT	9	2848	36	71.3	115

Weekend: $20
Weekend: $35 F/S/S
Discounts: Junior
Driving Range: No
Junior Golf: Yes
Architect/Yr Open: Devereux Emmett/1926
GPS:

Hidden secret, semi-private. Open to public weekdays and after 1pm on weekends. Weekdays before 12pm, $20 for 9 holes with cart and lunch, $35 for 18 holes with cart and lunch. Distances below from back tees.

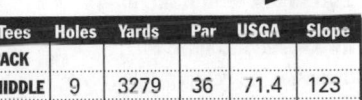

	1	2	3	4	5	6	7	8	9
PAR	4	4	3	4	4	3	4	5	5
YARDS	373	380	164	398	321	186	428	509	474
PAR									
YARDS									

Directions: I-395 to Exit 2 (West) in Webster, MA. Head East approximately 4.5 miles (Dudley) to Airport Road. Course is on right at Cumberland Farms.

Dunroamin Country Club

NR 21 ▶

Lower Road
Gilbertville, MA (413) 477-0004

Tees	Holes	Yards	Par	USGA	Slope
BACK					
MIDDLE	9	2863	35	68.6	117
FRONT	9	2401	35	66.8	106

Club Pro: Bob Lemoine
Payment: Cash or Credit Card
Tee Times: Weekends/Holidays
Fee 9 Holes: Weekday: $15
Fee 18 Holes: Weekday: $30
Twilight Rates: No
Cart Rental: $16pp/18, $8pp/9
Lessons: Yes **Schools:** No
Membership: Yes
Other: Clubhouse / Lockers / Showers / Snack Bar / Bar-Lounge

Weekend: $15
Weekend: $30
Discounts: Junior
Driving Range: $2.50/bucket
Junior Golf: Yes
Architect/Yr Open: Manuel Francis/1966

Come try us.

	1	2	3	4	5	6	7	8	9
PAR	3	4	4	5	4	4	4	3	4
YARDS	204	331	393	493	322	310	367	166	277
PAR									
YARDS									

Directions: Mass Pike, Exit 8. Route 32 North for 15 miles.

East Mountain Country Club

NR 22 ▶

1458 East Mountain Road
Westfield, MA (413) 568-1539
www.eastmountaincc.com

Tees	Holes	Yards	Par	USGA	Slope
BACK	18	6118	71	69.4	120
MIDDLE	18	5819	71	68.3	113
FRONT	18	4564	71	65.4	104

Club Pro: Ted Perez Jr., PGA
Payment: Visa, MC, Amex, Cash
Tee Times: 1 week adv.
Fee 9 Holes: Weekday: $15
Fee 18 Holes: Weekday: $23
Twilight Rates: After 5pm
Cart Rental: $13.50pp/18, $7.50pp/9
Lessons: Yes **Schools:** Yes
Membership: Full or Associate
Other: Clubhouse / Snack Bar / Lounge

Weekend: $16
Weekend: $26
Discounts: Sr. & Jr: $16 wkdys $9.50/9 holes
Driving Range: Yes
Junior Golf: Yes
Architect/Yr Open: Ted Perez Sr./1963
GPS:

SR 7200 Velvet Bent Greens seeded in 2003 – fantastic putting surface. Fees subject to change.

	1	2	3	4	5	6	7	8	9
PAR	4	4	3	5	4	4	4	4	3
YARDS	305	361	149	495	372	426	319	352	175
	10	11	12	13	14	15	16	17	18
PAR	3	5	5	3	4	5	4	3	4
YARDS	159	492	481	168	394	536	429	174	331

Directions: I-90 (Mass Pike) to Exit 3, follow Route 202 North to East Mountain Road. Course is 1.5 miles on right.

Edge Hill Golf Club

298 Barnes Road
Ashfield, MA (413) 625-6018
www.edgehillgolfcourse.com
Club Pro:
Payment: Cash, Visa, MC
Tee Times:
Fee 9 Holes: Weekday: $13
Fee 18 Holes: Weekday: $17
Twilight Rates: N/R
Cart Rental: $12.50pp/18, $6.25pp/9
Lessons: $40/45 min. **Schools:** No
Membership: Yes
Other: Full Restaurant / Clubhouse / Bar-Lounge

Tees	Holes	Yards	Par	USGA	Slope
BACK	9	3250	36	69.2	123
MIDDLE	9	3110	36	67.6	119
FRONT	9	2990	36	66.0	115

Weekend: $16
Weekend: $20
Discounts: None
Driving Range: $5/lg., $2.50/sm.
Junior Golf: No
Architect/Yr Open: Mark Graves/1994

Very challenging course demands playing positional golf. Open May - November. Construction has started on the back 9; completion date is 2009.

	1	2	3	4	5	6	7	8	9
PAR	5	4	3	4	4	3	5	4	4
YARDS	520	300	150	320	370	160	520	370	400
PAR									
YARDS									

Directions: Heading I-91 Southbound, take Exit 26 (Route 2 West) to Route 112 South. Left on Route 116 to course. Follow signs. From I-91 Northbound, take Exit 25 (Route 116/South Deerfield) to Conway-Ashfield. Turn right in Ashfield at Baptist Corner Road. Follow signs.

Edgewood Golf Club

161 Sheep Pasture Road
Southwick, MA (413) 569-6826
www.edgewood4golf.com
Club Pro: Mike Grigley, PGA
Payment: Visa, MC
Tee Times: 4 days adv.
Fee 9 Holes: Weekday: $13.50
Fee 18 Holes: Weekday: $21
Twilight Rates: After 6pm $6/M-F, after 5pm $10/weekend
Discounts: Senior & Junior
Cart Rental: $15pp/18, $8.50pp/9
Lessons: $40/half hour **Schools:** No
Membership: Yes
Other: Clubhouse / Showers / Snack Bar / Restaurant / Bar-Lounge

Tees	Holes	Yards	Par	USGA	Slope
BACK	18	6510	71	69.1	115
MIDDLE	18	6050	71	67.6	113
FRONT	18	5580	71	71.8	109

Weekend: $17
Weekend: $25
Driving Range: $7/lg, $4/sm bucket
Junior Golf: Yes, clinics
Architect/Yr Open: Geoffrey Cornish/1963

Picturesque, easy walk, fairly open.

	1	2	3	4	5	6	7	8	9
PAR	5	4	4	5	4	3	4	3	4
YARDS	450	415	315	523	385	170	390	205	340
	10	11	12	13	14	15	16	17	18
PAR	4	3	4	3	5	5	4	3	4
YARDS	295	160	375	150	545	480	355	160	340

Directions: I-90 (Mass Pike) to Exit 3 (Springfield). Route 57 to Southwick. Route 57 goes through Routes 10 and 202. Go through center of town. Take a left on Depot. Right onto Sheep Pasture Road, follow it around to the right.

CTRL/ WEST MA

Egremont Country Club

NR **25**

Route 23
Great Barrington, MA
(413) 528-4222
www.egremontcountryclub.com

Club Pro:
Payment: Cash, Visa, MC
Tee Times: 7 days adv.
Fee 9 Holes: Weekday: $15
Fee 18 Holes: Weekday: $25
Twilight Rates: After 4pm
Cart Rental: $16pp/18, $8pp/9
Lessons: Yes **Schools:** No
Membership: Yes
Other: Clubhouse / Lockers / Showers / Snack Bar / Restaurant / Bar-Lounge

Weekend: $25
Weekend: $45
Discounts: Senior, Thurs.
Driving Range: $7/lg, $5/sm
Junior Golf: Yes
Architect/Yr Open: 1920

Tees	Holes	Yards	Par	USGA	Slope
BACK	18	6036	71	68.7	122
MIDDLE	18	5771	71	67.5	120
FRONT	18	4894	71	68.1	113

COUPON

Sig. Hole: #18 Double-tiered, elevated tee area, framed by large maples. Some claim the feel of #18th hole 'chute' at Augusta. Green guarded by 2 bunkers. Accurate approach shots a must. Tanglewood nearby.

	1	2	3	4	5	6	7	8	9
PAR	4	4	3	4	5	3	4	4	3
YARDS	335	245	175	389	497	140	320	325	151
	10	11	12	13	14	15	16	17	18
PAR	4	4	5	5	3	4	4	4	4
YARDS	338	275	532	538	152	320	325	353	361

Directions: I-90 (Mass Pike) to Exit 2 (Lee) Route 7. Follow Route 102 West to Route 7 South. Turn right on Route 23 for 3 miles.

Ellinwood Country Club

✪✪½ **26**

1928 Pleasant Street
Athol, MA (978) 249-7460
www.ellinwoodcc.com

Club Pro: Jim LeBlanc, PGA
Payment: Visa, MC, Cash
Tee Times: Yes
Fee 9 Holes: Weekday: $22
Fee 18 Holes: Weekday: $32
Twilight Rates: After 5pm
Cart Rental: Yes
Lessons: Yes **Schools:** No
Membership: Yes
Other: Clubhouse / Snack Bar / Bar-Lounge / Banquet Hall

Weekend: $24
Weekend: $40
Discounts: Junior
Driving Range: No
Junior Golf: Yes
Architect/Yr Open: Ross/1929; Cornish/1968

Tees	Holes	Yards	Par	USGA	Slope
BACK	18	6195	71	69.5	123
MIDDLE	18	5891	71	68.8	119
FRONT	18	5515	73	69.1	118

COUPON

Immaculate, fast greens. No back and forth holes. Every hole offers a different challenge. 9 holes by Donald Ross in 1929. 9 holes by Geoff Cornish in 1968. Fully irrigated in 2004.

	1	2	3	4	5	6	7	8	9
PAR	4	4	3	5	5	3	4	3	4
YARDS	400	321	148	477	426	173	405	161	369
	10	11	12	13	14	15	16	17	18
PAR	3	4	3	5	3	4	5	4	5
YARDS	215	278	150	441	136	398	472	416	517

Directions: Route 2 to Exit 17. Take right off exit, follow 1/2 mile on right to Woodlawn Road. Go all the way to the end; clubhouse is on the right.

Forest Park Country Club

1928 Pleasant Street
Adams, MA (413) 743-3311

Tees	Holes	Yards	Par	USGA	Slope
BACK					
MIDDLE	9	2555	34	63.8	110
FRONT	9	2323	34	63.8	110

Club Pro: No
Payment: Cash/Check only
Tee Times: No
Fee 9 Holes: Weekday: $14   **Weekend:** $14
Fee 18 Holes: Weekday: $19   **Weekend:** $19
Twilight Rates: No   **Discounts:** None
Cart Rental: $11.50pp/18, $6pp/9   **Driving Range:** No
Lessons: No **Schools:** No   **Junior Golf:** Yes
Membership: Yes   **Architect/Yr Open:** Alex Findlay/1900
Other: Clubhouse / Lockers / Showers / Snack Bar / Bar-Lounge/ Banquet Hall

COUPON

Sig. Hole: #5 is a 157-yard par 3: all carry, well bunkered, small sloping green. Tricky to birdie. Ongoing clubhouse renovations. Scenic 9 holes at the foot of Mt. Greylock.

	1	2	3	4	5	6	7	8	9
PAR	4	4	3	4	3	4	4	4	4
YARDS	270	341	157	327	147	333	314	389	277
PAR									
YARDS									

Directions: I-90 (Mass Pike) to Exit 2 (Lee). Take Route 20 East to Route 8 to Adams. Take left at statue on Park Street to Maple Street. Take first left onto Forest Park Avenue.

Franconia Municipal Golf Course

618 Dwight Road
Springfield, MA (413) 734-9334

Tees	Holes	Yards	Par	USGA	Slope
BACK	18	6153	71	68.7	118
MIDDLE	18	5825	71	67.1	115
FRONT	18	5348	71	67.1	115

Club Pro: Kevin Kennedy, PGA
Payment: Most Major Credit Cards
Tee Times: Weekends
Fee 9 Holes: Weekday: No   **Weekend:** No
Fee 18 Holes: Weekday: $21   **Weekend:** $22
Twilight Rates: After 3pm   **Discounts:** Sr. & Jr. Weekdays
Cart Rental: $26/18, $14/9 per cart   **Driving Range:** No
Lessons: $24/half hour **Schools:** No   **Junior Golf:** Yes
Membership: Yes   **Architect/Yr Open:** Stiles & Van Kleek/1929
Other: Clubhouse / Snack Bar / Restaurant / Bar-Lounge

Rates are for all-day play. Several challenging par 5s. Good mix of holes. Discount for town residents. Great shape. Re-landscaped in 2001. Well maintained.

	1	2	3	4	5	6	7	8	9
PAR	4	4	4	5	3	4	4	3	4
YARDS	314	307	349	557	124	412	360	162	387
	10	11	12	13	14	15	16	17	18
PAR	5	4	5	4	3	4	4	3	4
YARDS	491	307	468	368	132	350	282	173	282

Directions: I-91 to Longmeadow exit. At 2nd light take a left onto Converse Street. At end, take left onto Dwight Road. Follow to course.

Gardner Municipal Golf Course ✪✪½

29

152 Eaton Street
Gardner, MA (978) 632-9703
www.gardner-ma.gov

Tees	Holes	Yards	Par	USGA	Slope
BACK	18	6106	71	68.9	124
MIDDLE	18	5857	71	67.6	120
FRONT	18	5557	75	71.7	122

Club Pro: Mike Egan, PGA
Payment: Cash Only
Tee Times: Weekends, Holidays
Fee 9 Holes: Weekday: $15   **Weekend:**
Fee 18 Holes: Weekday: $30   **Weekend:** $35
Twilight Rates: After 4pm weekday; after 3pm weekend
Discounts: Junior
Cart Rental: $13.50pp/18, $8pp/9   **Driving Range:** Yes
Lessons: $40/half hour **Schools:**   **Junior Golf:** Yes
Membership: Yes   **Architect/Yr Open:** 1936
Other: Clubhouse / Snack Bar / Restaurant / Bar-Lounge

New tee on #8, provides new angle of approach to green, requires carry over bunker. Player Comments:
"Lesser known to those outside the area, but well worth the trip."

	1	2	3	4	5	6	7	8	9
PAR	4	4	3	4	5	3	5	3	4
YARDS	320	297	215	316	525	137	530	142	406
	10	11	12	13	14	15	16	17	18
PAR	4	5	4	4	3	5	3	4	4
YARDS	300	450	323	370	136	478	207	352	353

Directions: Route 2 to Exit 24B (Route 140 North). Follow signs to Mount Wachusett Community College. Course is across street from front of college.

GEAA Golf Club NR

303 Crane Avenue
Pittsfield, MA (413) 443-5746

Tees	Holes	Yards	Par	USGA	Slope
BACK	9	3180	36	70.0	118
MIDDLE	9	3079	36	69.6	115
FRONT	9	2637	36	69.4	110

Club Pro: Jay Abir, PGA
Payment: All
Tee Times: All
Fee 9 Holes: Weekday: $14   **Weekend:** $14
Fee 18 Holes: Weekday: $22   **Weekend:** $22
Twilight Rates: No   **Discounts:** None
Cart Rental: $22pp/18, $14pp/9   **Driving Range:** For members
Lessons: Yes **Schools:** No   **Junior Golf:** Yes
Membership: Yes   **Architect/Yr Open:** Rowland Armacost/1930
Other: Restaurant / Clubhouse / Snack Bar / Bar-Lounge / Lockers / Showers

Gently rolling hills and windy all year round. Tree-lined fairways with beautiful view of Mt. Greylock.

	1	2	3	4	5	6	7	8	9
PAR	3	4	4	4	5	5	4	3	4
YARDS	170	379	348	276	443	539	332	134	391
PAR									
YARDS									

Directions: I-90 (Mass Pike) to Lee exit. Follow Route 7 North through Lee and Lenox. 1/2 mile past Reed Middle School is Crane Street; take right to the course.

Green Hill Municipal Golf Course ✪✪✪

2 Marsh Avenue
Worcester, MA (508) 799-1359
www.greenhillgc.com

Tees	Holes	Yards	Par	USGA	Slope
BACK	18	6455	72	71.4	130
MIDDLE	18	6054	72	69.6	127
FRONT	18	5255	71	71.0	120

Club Pro: Matthew Moison, PGA
Payment: Visa, MC, Cash
Tee Times: 2 days (508) 799-1545
Fee 9 Holes: Weekday: $20   **Weekend:** $25
Fee 18 Holes: Weekday: $30   **Weekend:** $35
Twilight Rates: No   **Discounts:** None
Cart Rental: $13pp/18, $8pp/9   **Driving Range:** No
Lessons: $40/hour **Schools:** Yes   **Junior Golf:** Yes
Membership: Yes   **Architect/Yr Open:** Ted Robinson/1929
Other: Clubhouse / Lockers / Showers / Snack Bar

CTRL/ WEST MA

Underappreciated muni, excellent shape, interesting holes, great value for the money. Brand-new renovations for the clubhouse, new pro shop, grill room, function facilities, and expansive deck. New women's tee boxes and expanded blue tees for total of 5 sets.

	1	2	3	4	5	6	7	8	9
PAR	4	4	5	4	4	3	4	3	5
YARDS	375	334	418	347	342	190	330	157	452
	10	11	12	13	14	15	16	17	18
PAR	4	3	4	5	4	3	5	4	4
YARDS	358	198	328	482	385	140	458	371	389

Directions: I-290 to Exit 20. Take left onto Lincoln Street, take right onto Marsh Avenue.

Greenock Country Club ✪✪✪

32

220 West Park Street
Lee, MA (413) 243-3323
www.greenockcc.com

Tees	Holes	Yards	Par	USGA	Slope
BACK					
MIDDLE	9	3070	35	68.9	120
FRONT	9	2843	37	72.2	123

Club Pro: Bob Mucha, PGA
Payment: Visa, MC, Cash, Check
Tee Times: Sat. and Sun., call
Fee 9 Holes: Weekday: $18   **Weekend:** $25
Fee 18 Holes: Weekday: $26   **Weekend:** $42
Twilight Rates: After 5pm wkdys   **Discounts:** None
Cart Rental: $9.50pp/18, $7.50pp/9   **Driving Range:** No
Lessons: $55/hour **Schools:** No   **Junior Golf:** Yes
Membership: Yes   **Architect/Yr Open:** Donald Ross/1927
Other: Clubhouse / Lockers / Showers / Snack Bar / Restaurant / Bar-Lounge

Postage stamp-size greens. Donald Ross design, one of the first 100 courses built in the United States. New irrigation.

	1	2	3	4	5	6	7	8	9
PAR	4	3	4	4	4	5	3	4	4
YARDS	330	158	391	300	423	464	168	360	364
PAR									
YARDS									

Directions: I-90 (Mass Pike) to Exit 2 (Lee). Take right on Housatonic Street to the center of Lee. Come to the stop sign next to town park. Take West Park Street up the hill over the RR tracks. Course on right.

Groton Country Club

94 Lovers Lane
Groton, MA (978) 448-2564
www.grotoncountryclub.com

Club Pro: Rod Van Guilder
Payment: Most Major Credit Cards
Tee Times: 7 days adv.

Tees	Holes	Yards	Par	USGA	Slope
BACK	9	3003	35	66.5	116
MIDDLE	9	2709	35	66.5	116
FRONT	9	2409	36		

Fee 9 Holes: Weekday: $17   **Weekend:** $19
Fee 18 Holes: Weekday: $24   **Weekend:** $30
Twilight Rates: No   **Discounts:** Senior & Junior
Cart Rental: $14pp/18, $8pp/9   **Driving Range:**
Lessons: Yes **Schools:** Yes   **Junior Golf:** Yes
Membership: Yes   **Architect/Yr Open:** 1950
Other: Full Restaurant / Clubhouse / Bar-Lounge / Snack Bar / Showers

COUPON

Resident-discounted rates. Collared shirts are required. Open April - November.

	1	2	3	4	5	6	7	8	9
PAR	4	4	4	3	3	4	4	5	4
YARDS	330	260	325	140	210	326	335	450	300
PAR									
YARDS									

Directions: I-495 to Route 119 West to Groton.

Hampden Country Club

128 Wilbraham Road
Hampden, MA (413) 566-8010
www.hampdencountryclub.com

Club Pro: Thomas E. Smith, Bill Tragakis
Payment: Visa, MC, Amex, Cash
Tee Times: 7 days adv.

Tees	Holes	Yards	Par	USGA	Slope
BACK	18	6833	72	73.6	134
MIDDLE	18	6349	72	70.4	129
FRONT	18	5283	72	71.8	126

Fee 9 Holes: Weekday: $18   **Weekend:** $20
Fee 18 Holes: Weekday: $25   **Weekend:** $36
Twilight Rates: After 1pm   **Discounts:** Jr.; Ladies on Tues, Sr. on Wed
Cart Rental: $15pp/18, $8pp/9   **Driving Range:** $6/large
Lessons: Yes **Schools:** No   **Junior Golf:** Yes
Membership: No   **Architect/Yr Open:** 1975
Other: Clubhouse / Bar-Lounge / Snack Bar / Lockers / Showers / Banquet Hall

Moderately hilly; challenging; water comes into play on 7 holes. Immaculate condition. Fees subject to change. Expansive patio overlooks beautiful scenic views.

	1	2	3	4	5	6	7	8	9
PAR	4	5	3	4	4	4	4	5	3
YARDS	323	533	201	359	364	374	368	517	150
	10	**11**	**12**	**13**	**14**	**15**	**16**	**17**	**18**
PAR	4	5	3	4	5	3	4	4	4
YARDS	362	555	185	350	529	163	319	347	350

Directions: I-91, Exit 1 (Longmeadow). Second set of lights, left onto Converse Street. Follow to end, take right on Dwight Road, then immediate left at intersection onto Maple Street. 2 miles to 83 South, turn right, 1 mile. Left onto Hampden Road, 5 miles to club on right.

Hemlock Ridge GC

NR  35 ▶

220 Holland Road
Fiskdale, MA (508) 347-9935
www.hemlockridgegolfcourse.com

Club Pro: No
Payment: Visa, MC
Tee Times: Weekends Only
Fee 9 Holes: Weekday: $15
Fee 18 Holes: Weekday: $22
Twilight Rates: No
Cart Rental: $9pp/18, $7pp/9
Lessons: No **Schools:** No
Membership: Yes
Other: Clubhouse / Snack Bar / Showers

Tees	Holes	Yards	Par	USGA	Slope
BACK					
MIDDLE	9	3136	36	70.6	117
FRONT	9	2603	36	69.0	109

Weekend: $17
Weekend: $25
Discounts: Senior $1 off
Driving Range: No
Junior Golf: Yes
Architect/Yr Open: Philip Wogan/1965
GPS:

CTRL/
WEST
MA

Hilly and scenic. Conditions good for both fairways and greens. No dress code. Open April 1 - November 1.

	1	2	3	4	5	6	7	8	9
PAR	4	4	3	4	4	5	4	3	5
YARDS	308	382	154	449	370	471	317	170	515
PAR									
YARDS									

Directions: Route 20 West through Sturbridge to Holland Road, turn left. Course is 1 mile up Holland Road.

Heritage Country Club

  36 ▶

85 Sampson Road
Charlton, MA (508) 248-5111
www.heritagecountryclub.com

Club Pro: Liz Farland, PGA
Payment: Cash, Credit Cards
Tee Times: 7 days adv.
Fee 9 Holes: Weekday: $21
Fee 18 Holes: Weekday: $33
Twilight Rates: After 4pm
Cart Rental: $13pp/18, $8pp/9
Lessons: $40/half hour **Schools:** No
Membership: Yes
Other: Clubhouse / Lockers / Showers / Snack Bar / Bar-Lounge

Tees	Holes	Yards	Par	USGA	Slope
BACK	18	6677	71	69.3	118
MIDDLE	18	6138	71	67.3	113
FRONT	18	5415	72	70.3	114

Weekend: $25 after 3pm
Weekend: $41
Discounts: Senior & Junior
Driving Range: $5/bucket
Junior Golf: Yes
Architect/Yr Open: Don Hoeing/1963

COUPON

"Good value. Hilly but fun and fair. Enjoy the views." Early-bird and late-afternoon specials. Weekend after 6pm $10 walk, $15 ride, unlimited. New 1,000,000 sq ft pond and new trees, bunkers, and tees. "Worth a new visit."

	1	2	3	4	5	6	7	8	9
PAR	4	4	3	4	4	5	3	4	4
YARDS	345	360	155	382	320	510	165	320	420
	10	11	12	13	14	15	16	17	18
PAR	4	4	5	3	4	4	3	5	4
YARDS	393	365	565	140	280	355	152	555	365

Directions. Located on Route 20 in Charlton. 3 miles East of Old Sturbridge Village. Easy to reach from Worcester, Boston, Springfield, Hartford, or Providence.

Hickory Ridge Country Club ✪✪✪

191 West Pomeroy Lane
S. Amherst, MA (413) 253-9320
www.hickoryridgecc.com
Club Pro: Rick Fleury, PGA
Payment: Cash, Visa, Amex, MC
Tee Times: 7 day adv.

Tees	Holes	Yards	Par	USGA	Slope
BACK	18	6794	72	72.8	130
MIDDLE	18	6427	72	71.1	126
FRONT	18	5340	74	71.1	122

Fee 9 Holes: Weekday: $33 ride, $25 walk   **Weekend:** $33 ride
Fee 18 Holes: Weekday: $50 ride, $35 walk   **Weekend:** $55 ride
Twilight Rates: No   **Discounts:** Junior
Cart Rental: $15pp/18, $8pp/9   **Driving Range:** $4/sm.
Lessons: $35/half hour **Schools:** No   **Junior Golf:** Yes
Membership: Indiv. $1575; Family $2375   **Architect/Yr Open:** Cornish & Robinson/1970
Other: Clubhouse / Lockers / Showers / Snack Bar / Restaurant / Bar-Lounge

COUPON

Improvements include enhanced practice facility. Open April - October. Worth the drive from anywhere.

	1	2	3	4	5	6	7	8	9
PAR	5	4	4	4	3	5	4	3	4
YARDS	500	375	325	380	201	510	345	174	435
	10	11	12	13	14	15	16	17	18
PAR	4	5	4	4	4	3	5	3	4
YARDS	365	451	410	340	352	144	481	183	444

Directions: I-91 to Route 9 East from Northampton to Route 116 in Amherst. Go South on Route 116 for 2.5 miles to West Pomeroy Lane. Right onto West Pomeroy for 1/2 mile.

Highfields Golf & Country Club ✪✪✪

38

150 Magill Drive (off Route 122)
Grafton, MA (508) 839-1945
www.highfieldsgolfcc.com
Club Pro: Roger Adams
Payment: Cash, Visa, MC, Disc
Tee Times: Yes

Tees	Holes	Yards	Par	USGA	Slope
BACK	18	7021	72	74.5	140
MIDDLE	18	6474	72	72.2	136
FRONT	18	6024	72	69.9	131

Fee 9 Holes: Weekday: $28 walk, $36 ride   **Weekend:** $28 walk, $36 ride
Fee 18 Holes: Weekday: $54 ride   **Weekend:** $61 ride
Twilight Rates: **Discounts:** Senior & Junior
Cart Rental: Included   **Driving Range:** Yes
Lessons: Yes **Schools:** Yes   **Junior Golf:** Yes
Membership: Many levels   **Architect/Yr:** Cornish, Silva, & Mungeam/2002
Other:

COUPON

Cornish, Silva, and Mungeam design complements a beautiful residential project. Breathtaking views all around. Playable for all levels and abilities. Well manicured. New 18,000 sq ft clubhouse.

	1	2	3	4	5	6	7	8	9
PAR	5	3	4	4	3	4	4	4	5
YARDS	516	138	399	365	218	389	383	339	570
	10	11	12	13	14	15	16	17	18
PAR	4	3	4	4	4	5	4	3	5
YARDS	411	145	325	385	321	501	441	121	507

Directions: I-90 (Mass Pike) to Exit 11 (Route 122). Go right off ramp (122 South). 4.5 miles to Magill Drive on left. Follow Magill Drive 1.5 miles to clubhouse on left.

Hillcrest Country Club

325 Pleasant Street
Leicester, MA (508) 892-0963

Tees	Holes	Yards	Par	USGA	Slope
BACK	9	3068	35	67.1	103
MIDDLE	9	3138	35	67.1	103
FRONT	9	2388	36	67.2	113

Club Pro: No
Payment: Cash Only
Tee Times: Suggested
Fee 9 Holes: Weekday: **Weekend:**
Fee 18 Holes: Weekday: $20 (Special Mondays $25/18 holes riding)
Weekend: $22
Twilight Rates: No
Cart Rental: $10pp/18, $6pp/9 weekends
Lessons: No **Schools:** No
Membership: No
Other: Clubhouse / Snack Bar / Restaurant / Bar-Lounge

Discounts: Junior
Driving Range: No
Junior Golf: No
Architect/Yr Open: Robert B. Harris/1964

Ongoing improvements. Friendly staff and personnel. Under new management.

	1	2	3	4	5	6	7	8	9
PAR	5	4	4	4	3	5	3	3	4
YARDS	500	402	345	340	355	475	110	136	475
PAR									
YARDS									

Directions: I-90 (Mass Pike) to Exit 10 (Auburn). Take right onto Route 12, follow 3 miles. Take right onto Route 20, follow 3 miles; take right onto Route 56, 4 miles.

Holden Hills Country Club

✪✪ 40 ▶

1800 Main Street
Jefferson, MA (508) 829-3129
www.holdenhillsgolf.com

Tees	Holes	Yards	Par	USGA	Slope
BACK	18	6022	71	71.9	126
MIDDLE	18	5826	71	71.9	125
FRONT	18	5241	74	74.9	116

Club Pro: Jeff Bailey
Payment: MC, Visa
Tee Times: Weekends, 1 week adv.
Fee 9 Holes: Weekday: $20
Fee 18 Holes: Weekday: $30
Twilight Rates: After 3pm
Cart Rental: $15pp/18, $8pp/9
Lessons: **Schools:** No
Membership: Yes
Other: Clubhouse / Snack Bar / Restaurant / Bar-Lounge

Weekend: $25
Weekend: $40
Discounts: Senior special M-F $20/walking
Driving Range: No
Junior Golf: Yes
Architect/Yr Open: William F. Mitchell/1957

Picturesque course set among hills, ponds, and streams. New cart path and bunkers. While not long, the holes demand good placement and are challenging. Early-bird before 8am. Golf and cart special M-F before 1:30pm.

	1	2	3	4	5	6	7	8	9
PAR	4	5	3	4	4	3	4	5	4
YARDS	354	592	163	309	312	147	340	478	348
	10	11	12	13	14	15	16	17	18
PAR	3	4	4	5	4	4	4	4	3
YARDS	164	269	278	433	359	341	414	327	216

Directions: I-290 to Route 190 North. Take second exit (Holden). Go straight through lights, then bear right. Bear left at next light, up hill. Right on Main Street to Route 122A North. Course is 5 miles on right.

Holyoke Country Club

NR ► 41

Route 5 at Delaney House
Holyoke, MA (413) 534-1933
www.holyokecountryclub.com

Tees	Holes	Yards	Par	USGA	Slope
BACK					
MIDDLE	9	3495	36	71	118
FRONT	9	2723	37	N/A	N/A

Club Pro: Via Whightman, PGA
Payment: Visa, MC
Tee Times: S/S Members
Fee 9 Holes: Weekday: $12   **Weekend:** $12
Fee 18 Holes: Weekday: $20   **Weekend:** $20
Twilight Rates: No   **Discounts:** Please call
Cart Rental: $18pp/18, $9pp/9 **Driving Range:** No
Lessons: $30/45 minutes **Schools:** Yes **Junior Golf:** Yes
Membership: No   **Architect/Yr Open:** 1896
Other: Clubhouse / Lockers / Showers / Snack Bar / Restaurant / Bar-Lounge

Second hole is difficult with a quick green, hitting up 2 levels. If you are on the top level of the green, and flag is on the bottom, easy to bogey or double bogey.

	1	2	3	4	5	6	7	8	9
PAR	4	4	4	4	5	4	4	3	4
YARDS	343	356	409	292	472	407	323	121	347
PAR									
YARDS									

Directions: I-91 to Exit 17A to traffic light. Turn left onto Route 5, approximately 2 1/2 miles. At the Delaney Restaurant go through entrance, past restaurant 50 yards, then turn left to country club.

Hopedale Country Club

✪✪ ► 42

Mill Street
Hopedale, MA
(508) 473-9876
www.hopedalecc.com

Tees	Holes	Yards	Par	USGA	Slope
BACK	9	3050	35	69	125
MIDDLE	9	2972	35	69	118
FRONT	9	2741	35	70.8	121

Club Pro: Joe Potty, PGA
Payment: Visa, MC, Cash
Tee Times: No
Fee 9 Holes: Weekday: $20 before 3pm,   **Weekend:** No public play
Fee 18 Holes: Weekday: $35 before 1pm M-Th **Weekend:** No public play
Twilight Rates: No   **Discounts:** None
Cart Rental: $20pp/18, $10pp/9 per person **Driving Range:** No
Lessons: $40/half hour **Schools:** No **Junior Golf:** Yes
Membership: Yes   **Architect/Yr Open:** Geoffrey Cornish/1953
Other: Clubhouse / Bar-Lounge / Snack Bar **GPS:**

New clubhouse. 9 holes, 2 sets of tees. Public play welcome on weekdays, except holidays.

	1	2	3	4	5	6	7	8	9
PAR	4	5	3	4	4	4	4	4	3
YARDS	374	508	140	371	362	316	304	381	216
PAR									
YARDS									

Directions: I-495 to Route 85 Milford. Turn right onto Route 85 and right onto Route 16 through center of Milford to Hopedale. At lights go left onto Hopedale Street to end. Take right onto Green Street to course.

Indian Meadows Golf Club NR 43

275 Turnpike Road
Westboro, MA (508) 836-5460
www.indianmeadowsgolf.com

Tees	Holes	Yards	Par	USGA	Slope
BACK	9	3265	36	71.7	124
MIDDLE	9	3019	36	69.4	119
FRONT	9	2468	36	67.0	107

Club Pro: Art Billingham
Payment: Cash, Check
Tee Times: 1 day adv.
Fee 9 Holes: Weekday: $20   **Weekend:** $22
Fee 18 Holes: Weekday: $30   **Weekend:** $32
Twilight Rates: After 6pm   **Discounts:** Senior & Junior
Cart Rental: $16pp/18, $8pp/9   **Driving Range:** No
Lessons: Yes **Schools:** No   **Junior Golf:** Yes
Membership: Yes   **Architect/Yr Open:** Art Billingham/1990
Other: Restaurant / Clubhouse / Bar-Lounge / Snack Bar

Great atmosphere. Water on every hole. Shirts with collars required. Open April - December. Semi-private.

	1	2	3	4	5	6	7	8	9
PAR	5	4	4	4	3	5	4	3	4
YARDS	451	340	420	316	136	455	415	173	313
PAR									
YARDS									

Directions: I-495 to Route 9 West (Turnpike Road). Follow Route 9 for 3 miles West to Westboro.

Juniper Hill Golf Club (Lakeside) ✪✪✪½ 44

202 Brigham Street
Northboro, MA (508) 393-2444
www.juniperhillgc.com

Tees	Holes	Yards	Par	USGA	Slope
BACK					
MIDDLE	18	6282	71	70.9	130
FRONT	18	4778	71	68.5	115

Club Pro: Ken Chrzan, PGA
Payment: Visa, MC, Cash, Check
Tee Times: 7 days adv.
Fee 9 Holes: Weekday: $22 Mon-Thur   **Weekend:** $25 F/S/S/H
Fee 18 Holes: Weekday: $39 Mon -Thur   **Weekend:** $44 F/S/S/H
Twilight Rates: No   **Discounts:** Before 1pm, Sr. (M-Th) & Jr. (M-Th)
Cart Rental: $17pp/18, $11pp/9   **Driving Range:** Practice green
Lessons: Yes **Schools:** Jr. & Sr.   **Junior Golf:** Yes
Membership: No   **Architect/Yr:** Phil Wogan, Homer Darling/1991
Other: Clubhouse / Lockers / Showers / Snack Bar / Bar-Lounge / Teaching Facility

18 holes of championship caliber with a lot of character. Collared shirts required. Noted for golf professional and friendly staff. Better year after year.

	1	2	3	4	5	6	7	8	9
PAR	3	5	4	4	3	4	5	3	4
YARDS	187	524	313	392	169	314	522	146	307
	10	11	12	13	14	15	16	17	18
PAR	4	4	4	4	3	5	4	5	3
YARDS	377	365	336	420	206	482	441	602	179

Directions: I-90 (Mass Pike) to I-495 North. Exit to Route 9 West and continue onto Route 135 West. Follow for 1.4 miles. Right onto Brigham Street. Follow for 1.3 miles to course.

Juniper Hill Golf Club (Riverside) ✪✪✪½ ▶ 45

202 Brigham Street
Northboro, MA (508) 393-2444
www.juniperhillgc.com

Tees	Holes	Yards	Par	USGA	Slope
BACK					
MIDDLE	18	6245	71	70.5	126
FRONT	18	5272	71	70.5	118

Club Pro: Ken Chrzan, PGA
Payment: Visa, MC, Cash, Check
Tee Times: 7 days adv.
Fee 9 Holes: Weekday: $22 Mon-Thur **Weekend:** $25 F/S/S/H
Fee 18 Holes: Weekday: $39 Mon-Thur **Weekend:** $44 F/S/S/H
Twilight Rates: No
Cart Rental: $17pp/18, $11pp/9
Lessons: Yes **Schools:** Jr. & Sr.
Membership: No
Discounts: Before 1pm, Sr. & Jr. (M-Th)
Driving Range: Practice green
Junior Golf: Yes
Architect/Yr Open: Homer Darling & Geoff Cornish/1931
Other: Clubhouse / Lockers / Showers / Snack Bar / Bar-Lounge / Teaching Facility

Player comments: "36 holes well-maintained for public play." "Some open fairways are inviting for your driver. Lots of variety." "Short overall but that doesn't mean easy. Number 17 is a dangerous and daunting par 3." Continually upgrading the facilities.

	1	2	3	4	5	6	7	8	9
PAR	4	4	5	4	3	4	3	4	4
YARDS	370	336	495	387	193	330	156	405	350
	10	11	12	13	14	15	16	17	18
PAR	5	4	4	4	4	3	4	3	5
YARDS	490	391	367	381	371	157	391	220	476

Directions: I-90 (Mass Pike) to I-495 North. Exit to Route 9 West and continue onto Route 135 West. Follow for 1.4 miles. Right onto Brigham Street. Follow for 1 mile to course.

Kettle Brook Golf Club ✪✪✪ ▶ 46

136 Marshall Street
Paxton, MA (508) 799-4653
www.kettlebrookgolfclub.com

Tees	Holes	Yards	Par	USGA	Slope
BACK	18	6912	72	73.1	125
MIDDLE	18	6203	72	70.3	121
FRONT	18	5105	72	70.2	118

Club Pro: Lee Danielian
Payment: Visa, MC, Amex, Cash, Checks
Tee Times: 7 days adv.
Fee 9 Holes: Weekday: $30 **Weekend:**
Fee 18 Holes: Weekday: $55 w/cart M-Th **Weekend:** $60 w/cart
Twilight Rates: After 3pm
Cart Rental: $14pp
Lessons: No **Schools:** No
Membership: Inner club
Discounts: Senior & Junior
Driving Range: No
Junior Golf: No
Architect/Yr Open: Brian Silva/1999
Other: Clubhouse / Bar / Snack Bar / Function Room for Outings

Player Comments: "Very good course—another Brian Silva gem. 3 of the best opening holes and 2 of the best closing holes anywhere." "Challenging but fun. Playable and friendly." "Awesome test of golf. Plays tougher than the slope rating. All they lack is a practice range."

	1	2	3	4	5	6	7	8	9
PAR	4	5	4	4	4	3	5	3	4
YARDS	366	522	359	327	339	170	485	132	452
	10	11	12	13	14	15	16	17	18
PAR	4	5	3	4	5	4	4	3	4
YARDS	346	485	164	251	481	338	379	196	411

Directions: I-290, exit to Route 9 to Worcester Center. Follow signs to Worcester airport. Take left off of Route 122 into airport rotary. First right to Bailey Street. Go 3 miles on right. See website.

Ledges Golf Club

$\star\star\frac{1}{2}$ | 47 ►

18 Mulligan Drive
South Hadley, MA (413) 532-2307
www.ledgesgc.com
Club Pro: Paul Ryiz, PGA
Payment: Visa, MC, Amex, Disc
Tee Times: 7 days adv.

Tees	Holes	Yards	Par	USGA	Slope
BACK	18	6507	72	72.2	133
MIDDLE	18	6110	72	70.9	129
FRONT	18	5001	72	69.5	125

Fee 9 Holes: Weekday: $16
Fee 18 Holes: Weekday: $24
Twilight Rates: After 3pm
Cart Rental: $14pp/18, $9pp/9
Lessons: Yes **Schools:** Yes
Membership: Yes
Other: Snack Bar / Bar / Restaurant

Weekend: $19
Weekend: $32
Discounts: Senior & Junior
Driving Range: No
Junior Golf: Yes
Architect/Yr Open: Howard Maurer/2001
GPS:

COUPON

Picturesque championship golf course. 78 strategically placed bunkers, 4 sets of tees. Well-maintained with thick rough and fast greens. New pro shop and a full-service restaurant.

	1	2	3	4	5	6	7	8	9
PAR	4	4	3	4	5	4	3	4	5
YARDS	386	424	96	276	456	300	123	349	528
	10	11	12	13	14	15	16	17	18
PAR	5	4	3	4	3	4	4	4	5
YARDS	564	405	215	397	176	270	273	372	500

Directions: I-91 to Exit 16. Follow signs for Route 202 toward South Hadley. At rotary, take 3rd right onto West Summit Street. Follow signs.

CTRL/
WEST
MA

Leicester Country Club

$\star\star$ | 48 ►

1430 Main Street
Leicester, MA
(508) 892-1390 Ext. 12
www. leicestercc.com
Club Pro: Cheryl Orrico, PGA
Payment: Visa, MC, Amex
Tee Times: 7 days adv.

Tees	Holes	Yards	Par	USGA	Slope
BACK					
MIDDLE	18	6026	70	69.8	126
FRONT	18	4559	70	67.4	121

Fee 9 Holes: Weekday: $17
Fee 18 Holes: Weekday: $24
Twilight Rates: After 6pm
Cart Rental: $16pp/18, $8pp/9
Lessons: No **Schools:** No
Membership: No
Other: Snack Bar / Bar-Lounge / Banquet Facility

Weekend: $20
Weekend: $30
Discounts: Senior & Junior
Driving Range: No
Junior Golf: Yes
Architect/Yr Open: 1864

COUPON

Previous improvements in tees and fairways have taken hold. More new front tees. Noted for excellent green conditions. New superintendent. New online reservation system.

	1	2	3	4	5	6	7	8	9
PAR	4	5	3	4	4	4	3	4	3
YARDS	437	489	201	345	371	328	179	309	173
	10	11	12	13	14	15	16	17	18
PAR	4	4	3	4	5	4	5	3	4
YARDS	314	317	165	411	545	403	515	183	341

Directions: I-90 (Mass Pike) to Exit 10 (Auburn). Take Route 12 West to Route 20 to Route 56 North. Follow Route 56 for 7 miles to Route 9. Turn left (west) at the light and continue for 1 mile. Club is on the right at the top of the hill 1/4 mile past the Castle Restaurant.

Links at Lancaster Golf, The NR 49 ▶

438 Old Union Turnpike
Lancaster, MA (978) 537-8922
www.lancastergolfcenter.com

Club Pro: Dennis Lanciani
Payment: Visa, MC, Amex, Disc, Checks
Tee Times:
Fee 9 Holes: Weekday: $10
Fee 18 Holes: Weekday: $13
Twilight Rates: No
Cart Rental:
Lessons: $45/half hour **Schools:**
Membership: Yes
Other:

Tees	Holes	Yards	Par	USGA	Slope
BACK					
MIDDLE	9	1057	27		
FRONT					

Weekend: $13
Weekend: $16
Discounts: Senior & Junior
Driving Range: Yes
Junior Golf: League & Summer Program
Architect/Yr Open: Gurall and Cronin/1996
GPS:

COUPON

Seniors pay 1/2 price green fees Monday until 3pm. Women pay 1/2 price green fees Tuesday until 3pm. Junior rate $8 M-F. Excellent range.

	1	2	3	4	5	6	7	8	9
PAR	3	3	3	3	3	3	3	3	3
YARDS	65	69	98	64	150	206	170	105	130
PAR									
YARDS									

Directions: Exit 34 off Route 2

Maplewood Golf Course NR 50 ▶

994 Northfield Road
Lunenburg, MA (978) 582-6694

Club Pro: Joe Benevento, PGA
Payment: Visa, MC
Tee Times: Weekends only
Fee 9 Holes: Weekday: $14
Fee 18 Holes: Weekday: $20
Twilight Rates: No
Cart Rental: $8pp/9, $3/pull
Lessons: No **Schools:** No
Membership: No
Other: Clubhouse / Snack Bar

Tees	Holes	Yards	Par	USGA	Slope
BACK					
MIDDLE	9	2685	35	63.9	106
FRONT	9	2520	35	66.5	105

Weekend: $16
Weekend: $25
Discounts: Senior & Ladies
Driving Range: No
Junior Golf: No
Architect/Yr Open: 1961
GPS:

Affordable and enjoyable golf. Irrigation system redone. Proper golf attire required. Open April - November (Thanksgiving).

	1	2	3	4	5	6	7	8	9
PAR	4	4	4	4	3	4	5	4	3
YARDS	350	320	310	340	175	350	480	230	130
PAR									
YARDS									

Directions: Route 2 to Route 13 North. Go past Whalom Park to stop sign. Take right, 1/8 mile to top of hill. Take left back on Route 13 North, go 2 miles to Northfield Road. Take left, go 1/2 mile. Clubhouse on right.

Meadows Golf Club, The

NR

398 Deerfield Street
Greenfield, MA (413)773-9047

Club Pro:
Payment: Visa, MC
Tee Times: No
Fee 9 Holes: Weekday: $13
Fee 18 Holes: Weekday: $18
Twilight Rates: No
Cart Rental: $12pp/18, $8pp/9, $2 pull
Lessons: No **Schools:** No
Membership: Yes
Other: Bar-Lounge / Restaurant Open All Year

Tees	Holes	Yards	Par	USGA	Slope
BACK	9	5716	72	66.6	106
MIDDLE	9	5600	72	66.6	106
FRONT	9	5094	72	66.6	106

Weekend: $16
Weekend: $22
Discounts: Seniors every day
Driving Range: No
Junior Golf: No
Architect/Yr Open: 1933
GPS:

Player Comments: "Great condition. Pretty elevation changes which also make for a challenging round. Extremely friendly and helpful staff." Rates may change.

	1	2	3	4	5	6	7	8	9
PAR	5	3	4	4	4	3	5	4	4
YARDS	475	155	320	280	255	135	470	365	345
	10	11	12	13	14	15	16	17	18
PAR	5	3	4	4	4	3	5	4	4
YARDS	475	163	320	280	255	135	470	365	345

Directions: I-91 to Route 2. Take Route 5 South, through Greenfield center. Course is 1.5 - 2 miles on right after center.

Mill Valley Links

⊙⊙ 52

380 Mill Valley Road
Belchertown, MA (413) 323-4079
www.millvalleygolflinks.com

Club Pro:
Payment: Cash, MC, Visa
Tee Times: Weekends
Fee 9 Holes: Weekday: $15
Fee 18 Holes: Weekday: $20
Twilight Rates: No
Cart Rental: $12pp/18, $6/9
Lessons: No **Schools:** Yes
Membership: Yes
Architect/Yr Open: Armstrong Golf Associates/1963
Other: Restaurant / Bar-Lounge / Snack Bar / Keno / Lottery
GPS: Garmin

Tees	Holes	Yards	Par	USGA	Slope
BACK	18	6583	72	72.2	131
MIDDLE	18	6076	72	70.5	125
FRONT	18	5546	72	72.0	131

Weekend: $15
Weekend: $25
Discounts: None
Driving Range: No
Junior Golf: Yes

Challenging and scenic. Every hole is tree-lined with beautiful greens. New pond on #8.

	1	2	3	4	5	6	7	8	9
PAR	3	4	4	4	4	4	5	4	4
YARDS	206	319	382	316	468	362	552	422	323
	10	11	12	13	14	15	16	17	18
PAR	5	5	4	4	3	4	4	4	3
YARDS	500	517	331	311	240	321	400	400	172

Directions: I-90 (Mass Pike) to Route 32 to Route 181 North. Course is about 2 miles on right.

Monoosnock Country Club

NR 53 ▶

40 Monoosnock Avenue
Leominster, MA (978) 537-1872
www.monoosnockcountryclub.com

Club Pro: John M. Novak
Payment: Visa, MC
Tee Times: No
Fee 9 Holes: Weekday: $16
Fee 18 Holes: Weekday: $26
Twilight Rates: No
Cart Rental: $16pp/18, $8pp/9
Lessons: $35/45 min. **Schools:** Night classes
Membership: Yes
Other: Clubhouse / Restaurant / Bar-Lounge

Tees	Holes	Yards	Par	USGA	Slope
BACK					
MIDDLE	9	3051	35	69.5	120
FRONT	9	2823	36	71.0	115

Weekend: No
Weekend: No
Discounts: None
Driving Range: $11/jumbo, $6/large
Junior Golf: Yes
Architect/Yr Open: 1919
GPS:

Course is open to public play on Monday - Friday until 3pm (except holidays). The fairways are narrow and brooks cross through 5 holes. 2 new bunkers on 5th hole and greens are in great shape. Full practice area with grass tees. Open April 1 - November 30.

	1	2	3	4	5	6	7	8	9
PAR	4	5	4	3	3	5	4	3	4
YARDS	335	515	378	158	235	450	387	214	379
PAR									
YARDS									

Directions: Route 2 to Route 13 North. Go North 1 mile and take right onto Monoosnock Avenue. Follow to pro shop.

North Adams Country Club

✪✪ 54 ▶

641 River Road
Clarksburg, MA (413) 664-7149
www.northadamscountryclub.com

Club Pro: Gary Cyr
Payment: Cash, Check
Tee Times: Weekends & Holidays
Fee 9 Holes: Weekday: $14
Fee 18 Holes: Weekday: $22
Twilight Rates: No
Cart Rental: $16pp/18, $8pp/9
Lessons: Yes **Schools:** No
Membership: Yes
Other: Snack Bar / Bar-Lounge

Tees	Holes	Yards	Par	USGA	Slope
BACK	9	2899	36	67.0	119
MIDDLE	9	2782	36	67.0	119
FRONT	9	2503	36	68.4	122

Weekend: $14
Weekend: $22
Discounts: M-Sat, 7am-11am
Driving Range: No
Junior Golf: Yes
Architect/Yr Open: Orrin E. Smith/1903
GPS:

COUPON

Traditional course in the midst of the Berkshires features small, fast greens requiring a good short game. Well-conditioned course with a great value for the price. Near the Mass MOCA museum.

	1	2	3	4	5	6	7	8	9
PAR	4	3	4	4	5	4	4	3	5
YARDS	339	143	364	257	484	360	273	143	419
PAR									
YARDS									

Directions: Route 2 to Route 8; go North 2 miles. Course is on left side.

Northfield Country Club

NR  55

31 Holten Street
East Northfield, MA
(413) 498-2432
www.northfieldcountryclub.com

Club Pro:
Payment: Visa, MC, Amex
Tee Times: No
Fee 9 Holes: Weekday: $12
Fee 18 Holes: Weekday: $20
Twilight Rates: No
Cart Rental: $24pp/18, $12pp/9
Lessons: No **Schools:** No
Membership: Yes
Other: Snack Bar / Clubhouse

Weekend: $15
Weekend: $25
Discounts: None
Driving Range: Net hitting area
Junior Golf: Yes
Architect/Yr Open: 1898
GPS:

Tees	Holes	Yards	Par	USGA	Slope
BACK					
MIDDLE	9	2760	36	66.2	121
FRONT	9	2405	36	68.0	121

Challenging layout. Very difficult to shoot the course rating. Open April - November.

	1	2	3	4	5	6	7	8	9
PAR	5	4	4	4	5	3	3	4	4
YARDS	430	300	370	260	450	170	130	270	380
PAR									
YARDS									

Directions: I-91 to Route 2 East to Routes 10 and 63 North, 1 mile North of the center of Northfield. Take Holton Street, turn right into parking lot.

Oak Ridge Golf Club-Feeding Hills ✪✪½ 56

850 South Westfield Street
Feeding Hills, MA (413) 789-7307
www.oakridgegolf.com

Club Pro: Eric Nelson, PGA
Payment: Cash, MC, Visa, Amex
Tee Times: 1 wk/wkdays: Wed/wkends
Fee 9 Holes: Weekday: $16
Fee 18 Holes: Weekday: $30
Twilight Rates: No
Cart Rental: $15pp/18
Lessons: $40/45 min **Schools:** No
Membership: Yes
Other: Clubhouse / Lockers / Showers / Bar-Lounge / Snack Bar

Weekend:
Weekend: $38
Discounts: Senior weekdays
Driving Range:
Junior Golf: Yes
Architect/Yr Open: Tom Fazio/1974

Tees	Holes	Yards	Par	USGA	Slope
BACK	18	6702	70	72.2	124
MIDDLE	18	6390	70	70.2	121
FRONT	18	5297	70	70.8	124

Excellent condition, flowers throughout course make for a real New England beauty. Open March 1 to December 1. Reduced rates after 2pm on weekends.

	1	2	3	4	5	6	7	8	9
PAR	4	4	4	3	4	5	4	3	4
YARDS	379	379	395	191	378	570	385	151	387
	10	**11**	**12**	**13**	**14**	**15**	**16**	**17**	**18**
PAR	4	3	5	3	4	4	5	3	4
YARDS	431	195	559	176	352	363	403	200	406

Directions: I-91 to Exit 3 Agawam/Southwick. Take Route 57 West to end. Take left onto Route 187 South then first left at Oak Ridge sign. Course 1/4 mile on right.

Oak Ridge Golf Club-Gill

NR 57

231 West Gill Road
Gill, MA (413) 863-9693
www.oakridgegolfclub.net

Club Pro:
Payment: Visa, MC
Tee Times: No

Tees	Holes	Yards	Par	USGA	Slope
BACK	9	2952	36	68.7	117
MIDDLE	9	2861	36	68.7	117
FRONT	9	5190	36	70.0	117

Fee 9 Holes: Weekday: $14   **Weekend:** $16
Fee 18 Holes: Weekday: $18   **Weekend:** $22
Twilight Rates: No   **Discounts:** Senior & Junior
Cart Rental: $10pp/18, $7pp/9; wknd: $12pp/18, $8pp/9
Driving Range: No
Lessons: No **Schools:** No   **Junior Golf:** No
Membership: Yes   **Architect/Yr Open:** 1963
Other: Full Restaurant/Clubhouse / Bar-Lounge / New Deck for Patio Dining

Scenic rolling hills, well groomed. Special rates for seniors (60+) and weekdays prior to 11am. Open March - November.

	1	2	3	4	5	6	7	8	9
PAR	4	4	5	4	4	4	4	4	3
YARDS	290	319	481	364	300	329	410	240	128
PAR									
YARDS									

Directions: I-91 to Exit 27 East and follow signs to golf course.

Pakachoag Golf Course

NR 58

Upland Street
Auburn, MA (508) 755-3291
www.johnsongolfmanagement.com

Club Pro:
Payment: Cash or Credit Card
Tee Times: Weekends & Holidays am only

Tees	Holes	Yards	Par	USGA	Slope
BACK					
MIDDLE	9	3255	36	70.0	119
FRONT					

Fee 9 Holes: Weekday: $14   **Weekend:** $16
Fee 18 Holes: Weekday: $24   **Weekend:** $28
Twilight Rates: No   **Discounts:** Senior & Junior
Cart Rental: $30pp/18, $15pp/9   **Driving Range:** No
Lessons: Yes **Schools:** No   **Junior Golf:** Yes
Membership: Yes   **Architect/Yr Open:** 1932
Other: Snack Bar   **GPS:**

Sig. Hole: #9, a dogleg left, has 3 ways to play. Short hitters - right of pond. Medium hitters - 180 yard carry. Big hitters - 270 yards over stone wall.

	1	2	3	4	5	6	7	8	9
PAR	4	4	4	3	5	4	4	3	5
YARDS	376	329	395	143	563	372	377	189	511
PAR									
YARDS									

Directions: From Route 20 to Greenwood Street to Upland Street. From I-290 use Auburn Street exit to Route 12 (Southbridge Street). Left at lights. 1/4 mile right, take Burnap Street up hill to Pakachoag Street and go left. 2 miles to Upland Street.

Petersham Country Club

240 North Main Street
Petersham, MA (978) 724-3388
www.petershamcc.com

Club Pro: Tim Bishop, PGA
Payment: Visa, MC
Tee Times: Weekends, 2 days adv.
Fee 9 Holes: Weekday: $16
Fee 18 Holes: Weekday: $20
Twilight Rates: No
Cart Rental: $16pp/18, $10pp/9
Lessons: Yes **Schools:** No
Membership: Yes
Other: Clubhouse / Lockers / Showers / Snack Bar / Bar-Lounge

Tees	Holes	Yards	Par	USGA	Slope
BACK	9	3004	35	68.9	116
MIDDLE	9	2955	35	66.4	114
FRONT	9	2516	36	69.1	114

Weekend: $18
Weekend: $26
Discounts: Junior $5
Driving Range: No
Junior Golf: Yes
Architect/Yr Open: Donald Ross/1922

Donald Ross design from 1922. Worth a drive if you haven't been here recently.

	1	2	3	4	5	6	7	8	9
PAR	4	3	4	4	5	4	4	3	4
YARDS	328	205	344	422	475	365	376	124	316
PAR									
YARDS									

Directions: I-91 to Route 2 to Petersham/Athol Exit 17, take right onto Route 32, and follow 6 miles. Course is on left.

Pine Grove Golf Club

254 Wilson Road
Northampton, MA
(413) 584-4570

Club Pro: None
Payment: Cash Only
Tee Times: Yes
Fee 9 Holes: Weekday: $13
Fee 18 Holes: Weekday: $20
Twilight Rates: No
Cart Rental: $28pp/18, $14pp/9 per cart
Lessons: Yes **Schools:** No
Membership:
Other: Clubhouse / Snack Bar / Bar-Lounge

Tees	Holes	Yards	Par	USGA	Slope
BACK					
MIDDLE	18	6115	72	68.8	121
FRONT	18	4890	72	67.3	114

Weekend: $17
Weekend: $24
Discounts: Senior & Junior
Driving Range: No
Junior Golf: No
Architect/Yr Open: 1972
GPS:

Open April 1 - December 1.

	1	2	3	4	5	6	7	8	9
PAR	4	5	5	3	4	3	4	4	4
YARDS	315	475	500	140	350	165	370	385	335
	10	11	12	13	14	15	16	17	18
PAR	4	3	4	4	5	3	4	5	4
YARDS	375	125	370	330	470	140	360	000	310

Directions: I-91 to Exit 18 Left off exit, Route 5 North about 1.5 miles to light. Left onto Route 9 West to next light. Straight through light, then bear left onto Route 66 for 3 miles, and bear left onto Wilson Road.

Pine Knoll Par 3 Golf Course

NR 61 ▶

380 Porter Road
East Longmeadow, MA
(413) 525-4444

Tees	Holes	Yards	Par	USGA	Slope
BACK					
MIDDLE	18	1567	54		
FRONT					

Club Pro: Robert Lake, PGA
Payment: Cash or Credit
Tee Times: No
Fee 9 Holes: Weekday: $8.50   **Weekend:** $10
Fee 18 Holes: Weekday: $9   **Weekend:** $10
Twilight Rates: No   **Discounts:** Senior & Junior
Cart Rental: $1.50/pull
Driving Range: $10/jumbo, $7/lg, $5.50/med, $3.75/sm bucket
Lessons: Yes **Schools:** No   **Junior Golf:** No
Membership: No   **Architect/Yr Open:** Ralph Fisk/1940
Other: First Tee Facility   **GPS:**

COUPON

Easy walker. Great for short game practice. Very scenic. Open March - November. First Tee facility. At Fenway Batting cages complex.

	1	2	3	4	5	6	7	8	9
PAR	3	3	3	3	3	3	3	3	3
YARDS	86	64	80	92	78	60	72	60	102
	10	11	12	13	14	15	16	17	18
PAR	3	3	3	3	3	3	3	3	3
YARDS	74	96	48	130	114	124	115	85	87

Directions: I-91 to Exit 4. Sumner Avenue (Route 21) East. Go to end of Summer Avenue, bear right by McDonald's onto Allen Street. 1/2 mile to Porter Road. Left turn onto Porter to course entrance on left.

Pine Ridge Country Club

✪✪½ 62 ▶

28 Pleasant Street
North Oxford, MA (508) 892-9188
www.pineridgegolf.net

Tees	Holes	Yards	Par	USGA	Slope
BACK	18	6002	71	69.7	120
MIDDLE	18	5763	71	68.3	117
FRONT	18	5307	72	69.6	117

Club Pro: Betty Donovan, LPGA
Payment: Visa, MC, Amex, Disc
Tee Times: 7 days adv.
Fee 9 Holes: Weekday: $17   **Weekend:** $20
Fee 18 Holes: Weekday: $29   **Weekend:** $38
Twilight Rates: After 3pm   **Discounts:** Senior & Junior
Cart Rental: $15pp/18, $9pp/9   **Driving Range:** No
Lessons: $50/hour **Schools:** Yes   **Junior Golf:** No
Membership: Yes   **Architect/Yr Open:** Phil Wogan/1969
Other: Clubhouse / Lockers / Showers / Snack Bar / Restaurant / Bar-Lounge

COUPON

Tournament friendly. Great value. New outdoor patio with access to the lounge. Great course for business outings with complete amenities.

	1	2	3	4	5	6	7	8	9
PAR	4	3	4	3	4	5	4	4	3
YARDS	295	144	437	161	382	390	330	358	148
	10	11	12	13	14	15	16	17	18
PAR	4	3	5	4	5	3	4	4	5
YARDS	270	188	431	403	482	166	354	344	480

Directions: I-90 (Mass Pike) Exit 10 or I-290 Exit 6B. Route 20 West to Route 56 North, go right. Take Route 56 North for 1 mile, club on left.

Pontoosuc Lake Country Club

NR 63

Kirkwood Drive
Pittsfield, MA (413) 445-4217
www.plcc.biz

Club Pro: Bob Dastoli, PGA
Payment: Cash, Check
Tee Times: Weekends & Holidays
Fee 9 Holes: Weekday: $14
Fee 18 Holes: Weekday: $22 all day
Twilight Rates: After 5pm
Cart Rental: $23pp/18, $11.50pp/9
Lessons: Yes Schools: No
Membership: Yes
Other: Snack Bar / Bar-Lounge / Hot Dogs

Tees	Holes	Yards	Par	USGA	Slope
BACK					
MIDDLE	18	6207	70	68.1	114
FRONT					

Weekend: $17
Weekend: $25 all day
Discounts: Jr. & Sr., weekdays only
Driving Range: No
Junior Golf: No
Architect/Yr Open: A.W. Tillinghast/1920
GPS:

Sig. Hole: #9 links hole with large mounds and hills leading to a highly elevated green. Considered moderately difficult. No one under 14 unless accompanied by an adult. Prices subject to change.

	1	2	3	4	5	6	7	8	9
PAR	4	4	5	3	4	4	4	3	4
YARDS	367	295	597	137	372	284	404	223	361
	10	11	12	13	14	15	16	17	18
PAR	4	3	4	4	3	5	3	4	5
YARDS	411	152	386	355	173	593	196	360	541

Directions: I-90 (Mass Pike) to Route 7 North to Hancock Road (left). Approximately 1 mile to Ridge Avenue (right), turn left on Kirkwood Dr.

Quaboag Country Club

NR 64

Route 32
Monson, MA (413) 267-5294
www.quaboagcountryclub.com

Club Pro: Greg Farland
Payment: Cash, Credit
Tee Times: 7 days adv.
Fee 9 Holes: Weekday: $17
Fee 18 Holes: Weekday: $24
Twilight Rates: No
Cart Rental: $10pp/9, $14pp/18
Lessons: $40/half hour Schools: No
Membership: $875/year
Other: Bar-Lounge / Banquet / Snack Bar / Lockers / Showers

Tees	Holes	Yards	Par	USGA	Slope
BACK					
MIDDLE	9	2880	34	67.2	116
FRONT	9	2610	35	69.2	113

Weekend: $29 w/cart
Weekend: $43 w/cart
Discounts: Senior & Junior
Driving Range: No
Junior Golf: Yes
Architect/Yr Open: 1900

Course is over 100 years old. Brimfield Flea Market and the Big "E" are area attractions.

	1	2	3	4	5	6	7	8	9
PAR	4	3	4	4	4	4	4	3	4
YARDS	350	225	435	430	360	350	250	130	350
PAR									
YARDS									

Directions: I-90 to Exit 8 in Palmer. Turn right onto Route 32 South. Go 2 lights, turn left. Go 3 miles to golf course on right.

Quail Hollow Golf & Country Club NR 65

1822 Old Turnpike Road
Oakham, MA (508) 882-5516
www.quailhollowgolf.net

Club Pro:
Payment: Visa, MC, Cash
Tee Times: Recommended
Fee 9 Holes: Weekday: $10
Fee 18 Holes: Weekday: $20
Twilight Rates: After 3pm
Cart Rental: $15pp/18, $8pp/9
Lessons: No **Schools:** No
Membership: Yes
Other: Clubhouse/ Bar-Lounge / Snack Bar

Tees	Holes	Yards	Par	USGA	Slope
BACK	18	5896	70	68.6	123
MIDDLE	18	5567	70	67.0	120
FRONT	18	4839	71	68.9	120

Weekend: $15
Weekend: $25
Discounts: Senior & Junior
Driving Range: $7/lg, $5/md, $3/sm
Junior Golf: Yes
Architect/Yr Open: Philip Wogan/1990
GPS:

COUPON

Cart paths are complete. Beautiful view. Hole #10 is a great short par 4.

	1	2	3	4	5	6	7	8	9
PAR	4	4	4	3	5	3	4	4	4
YARDS	296	290	230	174	500	140	415	299	310
	10	**11**	**12**	**13**	**14**	**15**	**16**	**17**	**18**
PAR	4	3	4	4	4	4	5	3	4
YARDS	324	178	361	340	347	408	511	115	320

Directions: I-290 to Worcester to Route 122 North to Oakham to Old Turnpike Road. Course is 3.5 miles off Route 122.

Ranch Golf Club, The ✪✪✪✪ 66

65 Sunnyside Road
Southwick, MA (413) 569-9333
www.theranchgolfclub.com

Club Pro: Hope Kelley, PGA
Payment: Visa, MC, Amex, Checks, Cash
Tee Times: 14 days adv.
Fee 9 Holes: Weekday:
Fee 18 Holes: Weekday: $100 M-Th
Twilight Rates: After 2pm
Cart Rental: Included
Lessons: $45/30min. $80/50min. **Schools:** Jr.
Membership: Yes
Other: Clubhouse / Lockers / Showers / Bar-Lounge

Tees	Holes	Yards	Par	USGA	Slope
BACK	18	6556	72	75.4	143
MIDDLE	18	6103	72	72.6	138
FRONT	18	4983	72	70.8	130

Weekend:
Weekend: $110 F/S/S/H
Discounts: Junior
Driving Range: Yes
Junior Golf: Yes
Architect/Yr Open: Damian Pascuzzo/2001
GPS: Yes

COUPON

"This club gets it right in all aspects: practice facilities; Course layout and beauty; setting; conditions; service; and little extras that make for a fantastic day. Must-play." –JD *NE GolfGuide* 2001 Best New Course. Real estate available.

	1	2	3	4	5	6	7	8	9
PAR	5	4	4	4	3	4	4	3	5
YARDS	484	341	375	404	146	334	369	180	502
	10	**11**	**12**	**13**	**14**	**15**	**16**	**17**	**18**
PAR	4	4	3	5	4	4	5	3	4
YARDS	406	366	181	540	419	357	578	170	404

Directions: I-90 (Mass Pike) to Exit 3. Go South on Routes 10/202 to Southwick. After Southwick CC, take right on Sunnyside Road. Club 1 mile on left.

Red Tail Golf Club

$\bigcirc\bigcirc\bigcirc\bigcirc$½

67

15 Bulge Road
Devens, MA (978) 772-3273
www.redtailgolf.net

Club Pro: Jim Pavlik, PGA
Payment: Visa, MC, Amex, Disc, Checks
Tee Times: Yes
Fee 9 Holes: Weekday:
Fee 18 Holes: Weekday: $95 cart incl. M-Th
Twilight Rates: After 2pm
Cart Rental: Yes
Lessons: Yes **Schools:** Sr. & Jr.
Membership: Yes
Other: Bar-Lounge

Tees	Holes	Yards	Par	USGA	Slope
BACK	18	7006	72	73.9	138
MIDDLE	18	6379	72	70.5	130
FRONT	18	5049	72	69.4	120

Weekend:
Weekend: $105 cart incl. F/S/S
Discounts: None
Driving Range: Yes
Junior Golf: Yes
Architect/Yr: Cornish, Silva, Mungeam/2002
GPS:

"One of New England's Top 5. Great variety and memorability of holes. Hard to pick a favorite hole—it changes every time I play it." –JD Site of the 2009 USGA Women's Amateur Public Links Championship.

	1	2	3	4	5	6	7	8	9
PAR	4	5	3	5	3	4	4	4	4
YARDS	354	516	170	512	161	331	425	306	417
	10	11	12	13	14	15	16	17	18
PAR	5	3	4	4	4	3	4	4	5
YARDS	507	154	352	342	399	181	368	385	499

Directions: I-495 to Route 2 West to Jackson Road, Devens exit. North on Jackson Road to Patton Road. Right on Patton Road to Bulge Road. Left on Bulge to clubhouse.

Scottish Meadow Golf Club

NR

68

361 Little Rest Road (Route 19)
Warren, MA (413) 436-5108
www.scottishmeadowgolfolub.com

Club Pro:
Payment: Visa, MC, Disc
Tee Times: Yes, 7 days
Fee 9 Holes: Weekday: $14
Fee 18 Holes: Weekday: $24
Twilight Rates: No
Cart Rental: $14pp/18, $9pp/9
Lessons: Yes **Schools:** No
Membership: Yes
Other: Clubhouse / Snack Bar

Tees	Holes	Yards	Par	USGA	Slope
BACK	9	3334	36		
MIDDLE	9	3118	36		
FRONT	9	2557	36		

Weekend: $20
Weekend: $30
Discounts: Senior
Driving Range: Yes
Junior Golf: Yes
Architect/Yr: Cornish, Silva, Mungeam/2000
GPS:

COUPON

Links-style. Viewable from Mass Pike, between Palmer and Sturbridge. Back 9 under constuction, 2 holes completed. Mark Mungeam design. Currently 9 holes with 2 sets of tees.

	1	2	3	4	5	6	7	8	9
PAR	4	3	4	4	3	5	4	4	5
YARDS	396	170	419	346	155	492	300	340	500
PAR									
YARDS									

Directions: I-90 to Exit 9 (Sturbridge, I-84). Take first exit onto Route 20 West. 7 miles to Brimfield Center, turn right onto Route 19 North for 2.5 miles, turn right just after the Entering Warren sign, onto Walkeen Kozial Road. Course is on left.

Shaker Farms Country Club ✪✪ 69

866 Shaker Road
Westfield, MA (413) 562-2770
www.shakerfarmscc.com

Tees	Holes	Yards	Par	USGA	Slope
BACK	18	6285	72	69.4	119
MIDDLE	18	6096	72	68.3	116
FRONT	18	5271	72	70.2	119

Club Pro:
Payment: Visa, MC, Amex, Disc
Tee Times: 1-7 days adv.
Fee 9 Holes: Weekday: $13 walk, $21 ride **Weekend:** $15 walk, $25 ride
Fee 18 Holes: Weekday: $20 walk, $29 ride **Weekend:** $25 walk, $36 ride
Twilight Rates: After 5pm **Discounts:** Junior
Cart Rental: Included **Driving Range:** Yes
Lessons: Yes **Schools:** No **Junior Golf:** Yes
Membership: Yes **Architect/Yr Open:** Geoffrey Cornish/1953
Other: **GPS:**

COUPON

Each hole has its own personality with natural slopes, breathtaking scenery, doglegs, and strategically placed bunkers. The back 9 is Cornish at his very best.

	1	2	3	4	5	6	7	8	9
PAR	5	4	4	5	4	5	3	4	3
YARDS	510	340	329	461	388	577	215	375	156
	10	**11**	**12**	**13**	**14**	**15**	**16**	**17**	**18**
PAR	4	4	3	4	3	4	4	5	4
YARDS	311	360	140	314	137	342	405	447	290

Directions: I-90 (Mass Pike) to Exit 3 Westfield. Follow Routes 10 and 202 South to Route 20. Stay on Route 20 East passing Westfield shops. Turn right on Route 187 at blinking light. Follow to course.

Shaker Hills Golf Club ✪✪✪✪ 70

146 Shaker Road
Harvard, MA (978) 772-2227
www.shakerhills.com

Tees	Holes	Yards	Par	USGA	Slope
BACK	18	6850	71	74	137
MIDDLE	18	6394	71	71.2	129
FRONT	18	5914	71	69.4	124

Club Pro: Michael G. Herrick, PGA
Payment: MC, Visa, Cash
Tee Times: 7 days in advance
Fee 9 Holes: Weekday: $40 **Weekend:** No
Fee 18 Holes: Weekday: $75 M-Th **Weekend:** $85 F/S/S
Twilight Rates: After 2pm **Discounts:** Senior & Junior
Cart Rental: Included **Driving Range:** Included in fee
Lessons: $40-$45/half hour **Schools:** Yes **Junior Golf:** Yes
Membership: Call golf shop **Architect/Yr Open:** Silva & Mungeam/1991
Other: Clubhouse / Snack Bar / Function Rooms **GPS:**

COUPON

Player Comments: "An established regional favorite." "Great conditions. Challenging but fair. Friendly staff. Great price for what you get." New 90-degree cart rule.

	1	2	3	4	5	6	7	8	9
PAR	4	5	3	4	5	3	4	4	4
YARDS	342	507	186	449	558	172	333	390	347
	10	**11**	**12**	**13**	**14**	**15**	**16**	**17**	**18**
PAR	4	4	4	3	4	5	3	4	4
YARDS	396	378	380	149	300	538	224	315	430

Directions: I-495 to Exit 30 (Route 2A West). 4 miles to Shaker Road on left. Course is 1/2 mile on left.

Skyline Country Club

405 South Main Street (Route 7)
Lanesborough, MA (413) 445-5584
www.skyline-cc.com

Club Pro: Jim Mitus
Payment: MC, Visa, Cash
Tee Times: 1 week adv.
Fee 9 Holes: Weekday: $16
Fee 18 Holes: Weekday: $25
Twilight Rates: After 3pm
Cart Rental: $15pp/18, $8pp/9 per cart
Lessons: $40/half hour **Schools:** No
Membership: Yes
Other: Snack Bar / Bar-Lounge

Tees	Holes	Yards	Par	USGA	Slope
BACK	18	6250	71	68.8	117
MIDDLE	18	6100	72	66.9	113
FRONT	18	4900	71	67.5	114

Weekend: $17
Weekend: $27
Discounts: None
Driving Range: Yes
Junior Golf: Yes
Architect/Yr Open: Rowland Armacost/1962
GPS:

COUPON

The course is somewhat hilly; considered moderately difficult.

	1	2	3	4	5	6	7	8	9
PAR	4	5	3	4	4	4	3	5	4
YARDS	369	487	127	331	363	390	196	540	379
	10	**11**	**12**	**13**	**14**	**15**	**16**	**17**	**18**
PAR	4	3	5	4	4	3	5	4	4
YARDS	395	167	490	343	295	167	432	362	379

Directions: I-90 (Mass Pike) to Exit 2 (Lee). Go North on Route 7. Course is approximately 20 miles on right.

Southampton Country Club

329 College Highway (Route 10)
Southampton, MA (413) 527-9815

Club Pro:
Payment: Cash, Check
Tee Times: S/S 1 wk. adv.
Fee 9 Holes: Weekday: $12
Fee 18 Holes: Weekday: $18
Twilight Rates: After 4pm
Cart Rental: $13pp/18, $8pp/9
Lessons: No **Schools:** No
Membership: Yes
Other: Snack Bar / Restaurant / Bar-Lounge

Tees	Holes	Yards	Par	USGA	Slope
BACK	18	6585	72	72.6	126
MIDDLE	18	6135	72	69.1	120
FRONT	18	5422	72	66.6	116

Weekend: $15
Weekend: $20
Discounts: None
Driving Range: No
Junior Golf: No
Architect/Yr Open: John Strychary/1950
GPS:

Sig. Hole: #4, 165-yard par 3. This meticulously maintained course is moderately easy with large greens, rolling hills and panoramic views. Rated 3 1/2 stars by *Golf Digest*. New website for 2009 season.

	1	2	3	4	5	6	7	8	9
PAR	4	3	4	3	4	5	4	4	5
YARDS	325	165	380	165	310	455	400	390	460
	10	**11**	**12**	**13**	**14**	**15**	**16**	**17**	**18**
PAR	3	5	5	3	4	4	4	4	4
YARDS	140	485	460	200	340	365	405	325	365

Directions: I-90 (Mass Pike) to Exit 3 West (Westfield exit). Take left onto Route 10/Route 202, Course is 5 miles on right.

Southwick Country Club

NR **73**

789 College Highway
Southwick, MA (413) 569-0136

Club Pro: No
Payment: Cash, Credit Cards
Tee Times: 1 day adv.
Fee 9 Holes: Weekday: $15
Fee 18 Holes: Weekday: $22
Twilight Rates: After 6pm
Cart Rental: $13pp/18, $8pp/9
Lessons: Yes **Schools:** No
Membership: Yes
Other: Snack Bar / Restaurant / Lounge / Weekday Specials

Weekend: $20
Weekend: $26
Discounts: Senior & Junior
Driving Range: No
Junior Golf: Yes
Architect/Yr Open: 1928

Tees	Holes	Yards	Par	USGA	Slope
BACK					
MIDDLE	18	6100	71	64.8	102
FRONT	18	5570	71	64.7	103

COUPON

The course is flat and wide open; considered an easy walker. "Crowned greens are fun." –FP Greens and course in excellent condition.

	1	2	3	4	5	6	7	8	9
PAR	4	5	3	4	4	3	4	4	4
YARDS	410	525	175	400	430	120	325	300	355
	10	11	12	13	14	15	16	17	18
PAR	5	4	4	4	3	4	4	4	4
YARDS	490	290	320	315	125	450	415	310	345

Directions: I-90 (Mass Pike) Exit 3, Westfield; turn right onto Route 202. Course is approximately 4 miles South of Westfield.

St. Anne Country Club

NR **74**

781 Shoemaker Lane
Feeding Hills, MA
(413) 786-2088
www.stannecc.com

Club Pro: Douglas Goodrich, USGTF
Payment: Most Major
Tee Times: 1 week adv.
Fee 9 Holes: Weekday: $16
Fee 18 Holes: Weekday: $21
Twilight Rates: No
Cart Rental: $28/18, $14/9 per cart
Lessons: Yes **Schools:** No
Membership: Open
Other: Snack Bar / Bar-Lounge

Weekend: $20
Weekend: $25
Discounts: Senior
Driving Range: No
Junior Golf: No
Architect/Yr Open: Joe Napolitan/1963
GPS:

Tees	Holes	Yards	Par	USGA	Slope
BACK	18	6608	72	70.8	120
MIDDLE	18	5927	72	69.5	118
FRONT	18	5566	72	70.0	118

	1	2	3	4	5	6	7	8	9
PAR	4	4	3	4	5	4	4	5	3
YARDS	385	312	141	342	500	381	394	420	171
	10	11	12	13	14	15	16	17	18
PAR	4	3	4	4	4	3	5	4	5
YARDS	310	133	315	315	273	185	467	360	523

Directions: I-91 to Route 57 West to Route 187. Turn right. First right is Shoemaker Lane. The club is 1/2 mile on the right.

St. Mark's Golf Club

32 Cordaville Road
Southborough, MA (508) 460-0946
www.newenglandgolfcorp.com

Club Pro:
Payment: Most Major Credit Cards
Tee Times: Weekends, Holidays
Fee 9 Holes: Weekday: $18
Fee 18 Holes: Weekday: $28
Twilight Rates: No
Cart Rental: $15pp/18, $9pp/9
Lessons: Yes **Schools:** No
Membership: Yes
Other: Leagues welcome

Tees	Holes	Yards	Par	USGA	Slope
BACK					
MIDDLE	9	2905	35	67.1	117
FRONT	9	2670	35	67.1	117

Weekend: $21
Weekend: $31
Discounts: Senior & Junior
Driving Range: Practice area
Junior Golf: No
Architect/Yr Open: 1895
GPS:

Scottish links styling, rolling terrain, long grass and sand pot bunkers, adjacent to scenic Sudbury reservoir. All tees redone in 2006. Under new management.

	1	2	3	4	5	6	7	8	9
PAR	4	3	5	4	4	4	3	4	4
YARDS	325	155	445	345	375	335	195	320	410
PAR									
YARDS									

Directions: Route 9 to Route 85 North. Course is .8 mile after intersection.

Taconic Golf Club

19 Meachum Street
Williamstown, MA (413) 458-3997
www.taconicgolf.com

Club Pro: Rick Pohle, PGA
Payment: Credit Cards, Checks
Tee Times: 7 days adv.
Fee 9 Holes: Weekday: No
Fee 18 Holes: Weekday: $145 (incl. cart)
Twilight Rates: No
Cart Rental: Included in greens fee
Lessons: $50/45 min. **Schools:**
Membership: No
Other: Clubhouse / Lockers / Showers / Snack Bar / Bar-Lounge

Tees	Holes	Yards	Par	USGA	Slope
BACK	18	6640	71	71.7	127
MIDDLE	18	6230	71	69.9	124
FRONT	18	5202	71	69.9	123

Weekend: No
Weekend: $145 (incl. cart)
Discounts: None
Driving Range: Yes
Junior Golf: Yes
Architect/Yr Open: Stiles & Van Kleek/1896

Players' Comments: "Outstanding course. Worth high rating. Nice people. Course was in super shape." "If you come to golf in Western New England or Eastern New York, you need to come to Taconic." –ER

	1	2	3	4	5	6	7	8	9
PAR	5	4	4	4	3	4	4	4	3
YARDS	475	391	409	358	172	361	402	394	188
	10	11	12	13	14	15	16	17	18
PAR	5	4	4	4	3	4	4	3	5
YARDS	506	470	363	391	173	420	430	221	510

Directions: Route 2 to Williamstown; left on Route 43 South; 3rd street on right.

CTRL/ WEST MA

Tekoa Country Club

459 Russell Road
Westfield, MA (413) 568-1064
www.tekoacc.com

Tees	Holes	Yards	Par	USGA	Slope
BACK	18	6215	71	70.1	123
MIDDLE	18	6022	71	69.2	121
FRONT	18	5169	71	69.3	112

Club Pro: E.J. Altobello
Payment: Visa, MC, Amex, Disc
Tee Times: 7 days adv.
Fee 9 Holes: Weekday: $14   **Weekend:** $18
Fee 18 Holes: Weekday: $22   **Weekend:** $27
Twilight Rates: After 5pm   **Discounts:** Senior & Junior
Cart Rental: $13pp/18, $7pp/9   **Driving Range:** No
Lessons: $35/half hour, $50/hour   **Schools:** No   **Junior Golf:** Yes
Membership: Yes   **Architect/Yr Open:** Donald Ross/1923
Other: Clubhouse / Restaurant / Sports Bar / Banquet Facilities

COUPON

Donald Ross design. Scenic views of Tekoa Mountain and Westfield River. Easy walking, short but challenging.

	1	2	3	4	5	6	7	8	9
PAR	4	4	3	5	4	3	5	4	4
YARDS	356	398	157	461	342	202	445	377	346
	10	**11**	**12**	**13**	**14**	**15**	**16**	**17**	**18**
PAR	4	3	5	4	5	4	3	4	3
YARDS	361	146	477	389	479	339	145	415	187

Directions: Take Mass Pike to Exit 3. Bear right onto Routes 10/202 South. Travel 2 miles into the center of Westfield. Bear right onto Route 20 West. Course is 2 miles on the right.

Templewood Golf Course

★★½ 78

160 Brooks Road
Templeton, MA (978) 939-5031
www.templewoodgolfcourse.com

Tees	Holes	Yards	Par	USGA	Slope
BACK	18	6067	70		
MIDDLE	18	5691	70		
FRONT	18	4882	70		

Club Pro: John Ross
Payment: Visa, MC, Cash
Tee Times: Weekends
Fee 9 Holes: Weekday: $18   **Weekend:** $32
Fee 18 Holes: Weekday: $28   **Weekend:** $36
Twilight Rates: Yes   **Discounts:** Senior
Cart Rental: $12pp/18, $8pp/9 weekends   **Driving Range:** Practice net
Lessons: Yes **Schools:** No   **Junior Golf:** Yes
Membership: No   **Architect/Yr Open:** Cornish/Maurer/1988
Other: Clubhouse / Lounge / New Pavillion / Practice Net

COUPON

Player Comments: "Inspiring views of surrounding terrain. Panoramic view of Mt. Monadnock. Friendly staff seek input after play." 18 holes now open.

	1	2	3	4	5	6	7	8	9
PAR	5	3	4	3	5	4	3	4	4
YARDS	515	135	375	135	455	405	135	245	345
	10	**11**	**12**	**13**	**14**	**15**	**16**	**17**	**18**
PAR	5	3	4	4	3	4	3	4	5
YARDS	479	158	373	262	154	382	186	400	552

Directions: Route 2 to Exit 20. Follow Trailblazing signs.

Thomas Memorial Golf & CC

29 Country Club Lane
Turners Falls, MA (413) 863-8003
www.tmgcc.net

Club Pro:
Payment: Visa, MC, Disc
Tee Times: No
Fee 9 Holes: Weekday: $12
Fee 18 Holes: Weekday: $18
Twilight Rates: No
Cart Rental: $24pp/18, $15pp/9 per cart
Lessons: Schools: No
Membership: Yes
Other: Bar-Lounge / Snack Bar

Tees	Holes	Yards	Par	USGA	Slope
BACK					
MIDDLE	9	2539	35	66.0	113
FRONT	9	2317	35	68.0	113

Weekend: $15
Weekend: $22
Discounts: None
Driving Range: No
Junior Golf: Yes
Architect/Yr Open: Walter B. Hatch/1959
GPS:

Course layout is interesting: hilly, several blind holes, narrow fairways, and some water hazards, 2 holes have 2 separate greens.

	1	2	3	4	5	6	7	8	9
PAR	4	4	4	4	5	4	3	4	3
YARDS	360	323	235	280	460	352	128	256	145
PAR									
YARDS									

Directions: Route 2 to lights at Turners Falls. Turn South on Avenue A to Turners Falls, left on 3rd Street. Right on L Street. At fork, bear left onto Montague. Right onto Griswold. Course .25 mile on right.

Townsend Ridge Country Club

40 Scales Lane
Townsend, MA (978) 597-8400
www.townsendridge.com

Club Pro: Derick Fors
Payment: Visa, MC, Amex
Tee Times: 7 days adv.
Fee 9 Holes: Weekday: $16
Fee 18 Holes: Weekday: $31
Twilight Rates: After 3pm wkdys, 1pm wknds
Cart Rental: $17pp/18
Lessons: $40/half hour **Schools:** Yes
Membership: Yes
Other: Clubhouse / 19th Hole Lounge / Full Bar / Outings encouraged!

Tees	Holes	Yards	Par	USGA	Slope
BACK	18	6188	70	70.2	125
MIDDLE	18	5814	70	68.5	123
FRONT	18	4709	71	68.3	115

Weekend: $23
Weekend: $43, cart req. before 12pm
Discounts: Sr. & Jr.
Driving Range: $5/bucket
Junior Golf: Yes
Architect/Yr: T. Manning & Mary Mills/1996

COUPON

Noted for condition and target golf. Challenging, popular course. Very outing-friendly staff. Number 9 & 18 share a huge green, and both are risk/reward birdie opportunities. Prices subject to change.

	1	2	3	4	5	6	7	8	9
PAR	4	4	3	4	5	4	3	4	4
YARDS	312	375	126	383	457	308	156	349	351
	10	11	12	13	14	15	16	17	18
PAR	4	4	5	4	4	3	4	3	4
YARDS	375	377	460	328	429	135	359	170	364

Directions: I-495 to Exit 31. Go West on Route 119 for 15 miles. Take first left after Townsend Ford onto Scales Lane.

Twin Springs Golf Club

NR 81

460 William Street
Bolton, MA (978) 779-5020
www.twinspringsgolf.com

Tees	Holes	Yards	Par	USGA	Slope
BACK					
MIDDLE	9	2592	34	64.8	113
FRONT	9	2432	35	67.2	106

Club Pro: Robert Keene, PGA
Payment: MC, Visa, Amex
Tee Times: 1 week adv.
Fee 9 Holes: Weekday: $16   **Weekend:** $18
Fee 18 Holes: Weekday: $24   **Weekend:** $28
Twilight Rates: No   **Discounts:** Sr. & Jr. wkdy; Jr. wknd
Cart Rental: $12.75pp/18, $7.75pp/9
Driving Range: S-$3.50, M-$7, Jumbo $10.50
Lessons: $60/hour **Schools:** Yes   **Junior Golf:** Yes
Membership: Senior & Junior   **Architect/Yr Open:** 1932
Other: Snack Bar/ Range   **GPS:**

Sig. Hole: #4 is a devilish par 3 with a great view of Wachusett Mountain, fronted by a creek.

	1	2	3	4	5	6	7	8	9
PAR	4	4	4	3	3	4	4	4	4
YARDS	327	294	300	140	161	318	368	320	384
PAR									
YARDS									

Directions: I-495 to Exit 27 to Route 117 West into center of Bolton. Go straight for .7 mile. Turn left up hill at Wilder Road. Course is 2 miles on right.

Tyngsboro Country Club

NR 82

48 Sherburne Avenue
Tyngsboro, MA
(978) 649-7334

Tees	Holes	Yards	Par	USGA	Slope
BACK	9	2590	35	65.2	104
MIDDLE	9	2397	35	63.2	104
FRONT	9	2023	35	62.6	97

Club Pro: Allan Pottle
Payment: Cash Only
Tee Times: Weekends 5 days
Fee 9 Holes: Weekday: $17   **Weekend:** $19
Fee 18 Holes: Weekday: $28   **Weekend:** $31
Twilight Rates: No   **Discounts:** None
Cart Rental: $25pp/18, $14pp/9 per cart   **Driving Range:** No
Lessons: No **Schools:** Yes   **Junior Golf:** No
Membership: 7 day/5 day   **Architect/Yr Open:** 1933
Other: Snack Bar / Bar-Lounge   **GPS:**

The course requires accurate shots and is easy to walk. Dress code required. Specials: Wednesday after 2pm, $12 for 9 holes; Tuesday, Thursday, and Friday, after 6pm, $15 for 9 holes; Saturday and Sunday after 2pm, $15 for 9 holes.

	1	2	3	4	5	6	7	8	9
PAR	4	4	3	5	3	5	4	4	3
YARDS	320	314	216	446	160	463	282	249	140
PAR									
YARDS									

Directions: I-95 to Route 3 North to Exit 35; onto Route 113 East; approximately 2.5 miles.

Veteran's Memorial Golf Course ○○

83

1059 South Branch Pkwy
Springfield, MA (413) 787-6449
www.springfieldcityhall.com/Park

Club Pro: Kevin Kennedy, PGA
Payment: Cash, Visa, MC
Tee Times: Sat, Sun
Fee 9 Holes: Weekday:
Fee 18 Holes: Weekday: $21
Twilight Rates: After 3pm
Cart Rental: $13pp/18, $7pp/9 per cart
Lessons: Call **Schools:**
Membership: No
Other: Snack Bar

Tees	Holes	Yards	Par	USGA	Slope
BACK	18	6350	72	69.9	116
MIDDLE	18	6115	72	69.9	116
FRONT	18	5884	72	70.2	112

Weekend:
Weekend: $22
Discounts: Senior & Junior
Driving Range: No
Junior Golf: No
Architect/Yr Open: Geoffrey Cornish/1963
GPS:

	1	2	3	4	5	6	7	8	9
PAR	4	4	5	4	3	4	3	4	5
YARDS	290	381	496	350	200	332	143	292	498
	10	**11**	**12**	**13**	**14**	**15**	**16**	**17**	**18**
PAR	4	4	5	4	5	3	4	4	3
YARDS	373	421	510	360	490	173	300	334	172

Directions: Call course for directions.

Wachusett Country Club ✪✪✪

84

187 Prospect Street
West Boylston, MA
(508) 835-2264
www.wachusettcc.com

Club Pro: Nick Marrone, PGA
Payment: Visa, MC, Amex
Tee Times: 7 days adv.

Tees	Holes	Yards	Par	USGA	Slope
BACK	18	6608	72	71.4	124
MIDDLE	18	6206	72	71.7	123
FRONT	18	6216	73	70.0	120

Fee 9 Holes: Weekday: $20/walk, $30/ride M-Th after 3pm only
Fee 18 Holes: Weekday: $40/walk, $57/ride   **Weekend:** $45/walk, $62/ride
Twilight Rates: After 3pm & before 9am M-F **Discounts:** Jr. after 3pm M-F
Cart Rental: **Driving Range:** Yes
Lessons: Schools: No   **Junior Golf:** Yes
Membership: Yes, wait list   **Architect/Yr Open:** Donald Ross/1927
Other: Snack Bar / Bar-Lounge / Banquet Facilities

Donald Ross design. Reduced rates after 3pm on weekdays. New improvements to holes 5 and 16.

	1	2	3	4	5	6	7	8	9
PAR	4	5	4	3	5	3	4	4	4
YARDS	388	518	380	145	507	175	360	436	426
	10	**11**	**12**	**13**	**14**	**15**	**16**	**17**	**18**
PAR	5	4	4	3	4	5	4	4	3
YARDS	494	430	426	203	330	508	316	374	192

Directions: I-90 (Mass Pike) to I-290 to I-190, Exit 4 onto Route 12 North. Approximately 2 miles to Franklin Street, turn left. At end of road turn left onto Prospect.

Wahconah Country Club ✪✪✪ ⬛ 85

15 Orchard Road
Dalton, MA (413) 684-1333
www.wahconahcountryclub.com

Tees	Holes	Yards	Par	USGA	Slope
BACK	18	6553	71	72.5	135
MIDDLE	18	6229	71	71.6	132
FRONT	18	5831	73	73	128

Club Pro: James Underdown, PGA
Payment: Cash, Check, Visa, MC
Tee Times: 1 week adv.
Fee 9 Holes: Weekday: **Weekend:**
Fee 18 Holes: Weekday: $70   **Weekend:** $80
Twilight Rates: No   **Discounts:** None
Cart Rental: $26pp/18, 2 riders   **Driving Range:** $6/lg., $4/med., $3/sm.
Lessons: $40/half hour **Schools:** Yes   **Junior Golf:** Yes
Membership: No waiting list   **Architect/Yr Open:** Wayne Stiles/1930
Other: Clubhouse / Restaurant / Bar-Lounge / Landscaped Patio

A beautiful, very challenging, semi-private course with fast greens. Considered to be moderately difficult. "Excellent conditions." –FP Open April 15 - November 15.

	1	2	3	4	5	6	7	8	9
PAR	4	3	4	4	4	3	5	4	4
YARDS	382	206	398	300	360	147	476	390	388
	10	11	12	13	14	15	16	17	18
PAR	4	4	4	3	5	4	4	3	5
YARDS	368	340	371	203	480	349	430	177	458

Directions: I-90 (Mass Pike) to Exit 2. Follow Route 9 North from Amherst into Dalton. In Dalton, take left onto Orchard Road. Course is approximately 1/2 mile on left.

Waubeeka Golf Links NR ⬛ 86

137 New Ashford Road (Route 7)
South Williamstown, MA
(413) 458-8355
www.waubeeka.com

Tees	Holes	Yards	Par	USGA	Slope
BACK	18	6394	72	70.6	126
MIDDLE	18	6024	72	69.5	122
FRONT	18	5023	72	69.6	119

Club Pro: Erik Tiele, PGA
Payment: Most Major Credit Cards
Tee Times: Yes
Fee 9 Holes: Weekday: $20, $29 w/cart   **Weekend:** $25, $34 w/cart
Fee 18 Holes: Weekday: $39, $55 w/cart   **Weekend:** $49, $65 w/cart
Twilight Rates: After 4pm, S/S/M/T   **Discounts:** Junior weekdays
Cart Rental: $16pp/18, $9pp/9   **Driving Range:** Yes
Lessons: $30/45 min., $125/5 lessons
Schools: Jr./Women   **Junior Golf:** Yes
Membership: Yes   **Architect/Yr Open:** Rowland Armacost/1966
Other: Clubhouse / Lockers / Showers / Snack Bar / Restaurant / Bar-Lounge

Cart paths added to every hole. Well-groomed, scenic, Audubon Society member. Open April - November. Dress code.

	1	2	3	4	5	6	7	8	9
PAR	4	4	4	4	3	5	3	5	4
YARDS	351	370	330	286	132	482	161	473	318
	10	11	12	13	14	15	16	17	18
PAR	4	4	3	5	4	4	3	5	4
YARDS	348	405	167	480	410	342	169	453	347

Directions: I-90 (Mass Pike) to Exit 2 (Lee) to Route 20 North to Route 7 North. Go North about 45 minutes. Course is on left.

Westborough Country Club

121 West Main Street
Westborough, MA
(508) 366-9947

Club Pro: Jack A. Negoshian
Payment: Visa, MC, Cash
Tee Times: Weekends, 1 day
Fee 9 Holes: Weekday: $18
Fee 18 Holes: Weekday: $30
Twilight Rates: No
Cart Rental: $15pp/18, $8pp/9
Lessons: Limited **Schools:** No
Membership: Waiting list
Other: Restaurant / Bar-Lounge

Open April - November.

Tees	Holes	Yards	Par	USGA	Slope
BACK	9	3163	36	35.5	125
MIDDLE	9	2973	36	34.7	122
FRONT	9	2574	36	35.6	124

Weekend:
Weekend: $32
Discounts: Senior & Junior
Driving Range: No
Junior Golf: No
Architect/Yr Open: Bill Spence/1921
GPS:

CTRL/ WEST MA

	1	2	3	4	5	6	7	8	9
PAR	5	4	5	4	3	4	3	4	4
YARDS	412	265	491	322	168	346	149	405	415
PAR									
YARDS									

Directions: Route 9 to Route 30 toward Westborough. Take a right at the stop sign. Course is 1 mile past center of town on the right.

Westminster Country Club

51 Ellis Road
Westminster, MA (978) 874-5938
www.westminstercountryclub.com

Club Pro: Michael Leblanc, Chris Shepard
Payment: Most Major
Tee Times: 3 days adv.
Fee 9 Holes: Weekday: $15
Fee 18 Holes: Weekday: $30
Twilight Rates: No
Cart Rental: $16pp/18, $8pp/9
Lessons: Yes **Schools:** No
Membership: Yes
Other: Clubhouse / Lockers / Showers / Snack Bar / Restaurant / Bar-Lounge

Tees	Holes	Yards	Par	USGA	Slope
BACK	18	6491	71	70.9	133
MIDDLE	18	6223	71	69.5	123
FRONT	18	5453	71	70.0	115

Weekend: $18
Weekend: $35
Discounts: Srs. M-F, varies by time
Driving Range: No
Junior Golf: Yes
Architect/Yr Open: LeBlanc and Francis/1957

COUPON

Player Comments: "Moderately easy to walk. Carts not required." Open April 15 - November 30.

	1	2	3	4	5	6	7	8	9
PAR	4	4	4	4	4	4	4	4	3
YARDS	422	396	344	384	353	316	333	312	173
	10	**11**	**12**	**13**	**14**	**15**	**16**	**17**	**18**
PAR	3	4	3	4	5	4	5	3	5
YARDS	131	381	224	452	532	314	548	157	451

Directions: Route 2 to Route 140 East. Take an immediate right after bridge, through Westminster Center. Follow 2 miles. Left onto Nichols. Bear right at fork onto Ellis. Course is 1 mile on right.

Westover Golf Course

89

488 Chapin Street
Granby, MA (413) 547-8610
www.westovergolfcourse.com

Tees	Holes	Yards	Par	USGA	Slope
BACK	18	7025	72	74.0	131
MIDDLE	18	6610	72	71.9	129
FRONT	18	5580	72	71.9	115

Club Pro: Bill Kubinski, PGA
Payment: Cash, Card
Tee Times: 7 days in advance
Fee 9 Holes: Weekday: $15   **Weekend:** $19
Fee 18 Holes: Weekday: $22   **Weekend:** $25
Twilight Rates: After 4pm   **Discounts:** Senior & Junior
Cart Rental: $20pp/18, $12pp/9 **Driving Range:** $8/lg., $5/sm. bucket
Lessons: $45/50 min **Schools:** No   **Junior Golf:** Yes
Membership: Range Memberships   **Architect/Yr Open:** Al Zikorus/1957
Other: Clubhouse / Lockers / Showers / Snack Bar / Restaurant / Bar-Lounge

Player's Comment: "A great challenge for a reasonable price." Fantastic layout, very challenging. Dress code: no cutoffs or tank tops. Lessons for all ages and abilities. Open April 1 - December.

	1	2	3	4	5	6	7	8	9
PAR	4	4	4	3	4	4	5	3	5
YARDS	390	410	335	207	396	419	489	163	532
	10	11	12	13	14	15	16	17	18
PAR	3	4	5	3	4	4	4	4	5
YARDS	160	422	490	160	364	405	373	354	541

Directions: I-90 to Exit 5. Go left on Route 33 North, follow for approximately 5 miles to New Ludlow Road. Take right and go 3 miles to South Street.

Winchendon School Country Club NR

90

435 Spring Street
Winchendon, MA (978) 297-9897
www.winchgolf.com

Tees	Holes	Yards	Par	USGA	Slope
BACK	18	5512	70	67.8	122
MIDDLE	18	5348	70	67.2	119
FRONT	18	4693	72	70.5	124

Club Pro: Tom Borden, PGA
Payment: All major
Tee Times: 3 days adv.
Fee 9 Holes: Weekday: $14, $21 ride   **Weekend:** $16, $23 ride
Fee 18 Holes: Weekday: $25, $39 ride   **Weekend:** $30, $44 ride
Twilight Rates: After 4pm   **Discounts:** None
Cart Rental: Yes   **Driving Range:** Yes
Lessons: Pro **Schools:** No   **Junior Golf:** Yes
Membership: Yes   **Architect/Yr Open:** Donald Ross/1926
Other: Clubhouse / Bar-Lounge / Snack Bar / Banquets / Outings Welcome

COUPON

Improvements include a new clubhouse and pro shop. New driving range. Distances below from back tees.

	1	2	3	4	5	6	7	8	9
PAR	4	5	4	4	3	4	3	3	4
YARDS	278	423	242	288	245	233	211	175	314
	10	11	12	13	14	15	16	17	18
PAR	5	4	4	4	4	3	3	5	3
YARDS	472	388	381	377	372	285	161	502	165

Directions: Route 2 to Route 140 North to Route 12 North. 1/2 mile down on your left.

Woods of Westminster CC

90 Bean Porridge Hill Rd.
Westminster, MA (978) 874-0500
www.woodsofwestminster.com

Club Pro: Dan Bartkus
Payment: Visa, MC, Amex, Disc
Tee Times: 5 days adv.
Fee 9 Holes: Weekday: $16
Fee 18 Holes: Weekday: $28
Twilight Rates: No
Cart Rental: $16pp/18, $10pp/9
Lessons: Yes **Schools:** Yes
Membership: Yes
Other: Full Restaurant / Clubhouse / Bar

Tees	Holes	Yards	Par	USGA	Slope
BACK	18	6060	72	67.2	121
MIDDLE	18	5505	72	65.7	117
FRONT	18	4765	72	66.6	111

Weekend: $19
Weekend: $34
Discounts: Senior & Junior
Driving Range: $6/lg., $4/sm.
Junior Golf: Yes
Architect/Yr Open: Al Zikorus/1998
GPS:

Player Comments: "Best value insider secret: Mon-Thurs. before noon." Magnificent mountain views. Open year round. Noted for lunch and dinner packages. "A fun place to play just off 495 year after year."

	1	2	3	4	5	6	7	8	9
PAR	5	4	5	4	4	3	4	3	4
YARDS	460	275	525	295	345	175	405	145	320
	10	11	12	13	14	15	16	17	18
PAR	5	4	4	5	3	4	3	4	4
YARDS	345	220	330	435	145	315	130	300	340

Directions: I-495 to Rt 2 West. Exit 27 off Route 2 onto Depot Road. Go right to stop sign. Take right onto Route 2A to first left (S. Ashburn Road). Go 1.2 miles to Bean Porridge Hill Road on right (#90).

Worthington Golf Course NR 92

113 Ridge Road
Worthington, MA (413) 238-4404
www.worthingtongolfclub.net

Club Pro: Karl Enroth, PGA
Payment: Cash, Credit
Tee Times: 1 week adv.
Fee 9 Holes: Weekday: $13
Fee 18 Holes: Weekday: $26
Twilight Rates: No
Cart Rental: $30pp/18, $18pp/9 per cart
Lessons: Yes **Schools:** Yes
Membership: Yes
Other: Clubhouse / Snack Bar / Restaurant / Bar-Lounge

Tees	Holes	Yards	Par	USGA	Slope
BACK	9	2782	35	33.3	115
MIDDLE	9	2797	70	66.8	116
FRONT	9	2797	35	33.5	121

Weekend: $17
Weekend: $30
Discounts: None
Driving Range: Yes
Junior Golf: Yes
Architect/Yr Open: A.P. Taylor/1904

Sig. Hole: #6, par 3, 2 trees guarding fairway. 2 sand traps in front and 2-tiered green. Call ahead for tee times. 2 sets of tees makes an interesting 18. The 8th hole is the highest elevated golf hole in all of Massachusetts.

	1	2	3	4	5	6	7	8	9
PAR	4	4	4	4	3	3	5	5	3
YARDS	333	322	340	301	201	148	528	476	148
PAR									
YARDS									

Directions: I-91 to Northampton. Exit 19, Depart Route 9 West toward Williamsburg, turn left onto Route 143 West. Follow to the traffic light at Worthington Four Corners. Go straight through intersection up Buffington Hill Road. Turn left onto Ridge Road to the course.

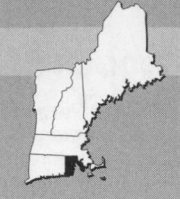

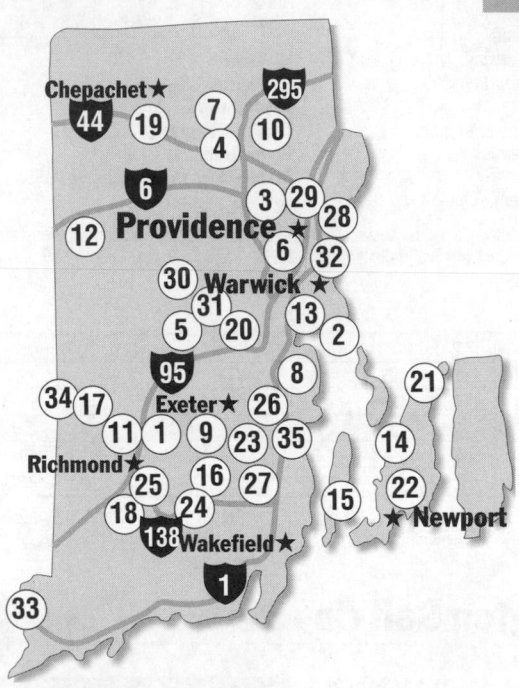

Beaver River Golf Club	1	Goddard State Park GC	13	Richmond Country Club	25
Bristol Golf Club	2	Green Valley CC	14	Rolling Greens GC	26
Button Hole	3	Jamestown Golf & CC	15	Rose Hill Golf Course	27
Country View Golf Club	4	Laurel Lane Country Club	16	Silver Spring Golf Club	28
Coventry Pines Golf Club	5	Lindhbrook GC	17	Triggs Memorial GC	29
Cranston Country Club	6	Meadow Brook GC	18	Washington Village GC	30
Crystal Lake GC of R I	7	Melody Hill Golf Course	19	West Warwick CC, The	31
East Greenwich CC	8	Midville Country Club	20	Windmill Hill Golf Course	32
Exeter Country Club	9	Montaup Country Club	21	Winnapaug Golf Course	33
Fairlawn Golf Course	10	Newport National Golf Club	22	Wood River Golf	34
Fenner Hill Golf Club	11	North Kingstown Muni.	23	Woodland Greens GC	35
Foster Country Club	12	Pinehurst CC	24		

Beaver River Golf Club

✪✪½

343 Kingstown Road
Richmond, RI (401) 539-2100
www.beaverrivergolf.com

Club Pro: Brian Forster
Payment: Visa, MC
Tee Times: 7 days adv.

Tees	Holes	Yards	Par	USGA	Slope
BACK	18	6086	70	67.1	123
MIDDLE	18	5802	70	65.7	123
FRONT	18	5410	70	70.8	115

Fee 9 Holes: Weekday: $19 M-Th   **Weekend:** $21
Fee 18 Holes: Weekday: $34 M-Th   **Weekend:** $40
Twilight Rates: M-Th $41/18 w/cart, $38 Sr.   **Discounts:** Senior and Military
Cart Rental: $15pp/18, $7.50pp/9   **Driving Range:** No
Lessons: No   **Schools:**   **Junior Golf:** Yes
Membership: Yes   **Architect/Yr Open:** Michael Weremay/2001
Other: Clubhouse / Bar-Lounge   **GPS:**

COUPON

Bent grass from tee to green. Excellent conditions and service. South County course. New cosmetic improvements. Scenic fall views.

	1	2	3	4	5	6	7	8	9
PAR	5	4	3	4	4	5	3	4	4
YARDS	477	334	150	326	318	485	201	411	332
	10	11	12	13	14	15	16	17	18
PAR	4	3	4	4	4	3	4	4	4
YARDS	328	146	433	379	300	170	265	367	380

Directions: I-95 to Exit 3A. Take Route 138, 3 miles East.

Bristol Golf Club

NR 2

95 Tupelo Road
Bristol, RI (401) 253-9844

Club Pro: No
Payment: Cash Only
Tee Times: No

Tees	Holes	Yards	Par	USGA	Slope
BACK					
MIDDLE	9	2273	33	69.9	118
FRONT					

Fee 9 Holes: Weekday: $10   **Weekend:** $12
Fee 18 Holes: Weekday: $10   **Weekend:** $12
Twilight Rates: No   **Discounts:** None
Cart Rental: $10pp/18, $5/pull   **Driving Range:** No
Lessons: No   **Schools:** No   **Junior Golf:** No
Membership: Yes   **Architect/Yr Open:** 1964
Other: Snack Bar / Bar-Lounge   **GPS:**

A good course for beginners.

	1	2	3	4	5	6	7	8	9
PAR	3	4	3	3	3	4	5	4	4
YARDS	137	254	148	130	167	337	480	320	300
PAR									
YARDS									

Directions: I-195 East to Exit 2, follow Route 136 to Tupelo Street, take right and course is on left.

RI

Button Hole

1 Button Hole Drive
Providence, RI (401) 421-1664
www.buttonhole.org

Club Pro:
Payment: Visa, MC, Amex
Tee Times: Yes
Fee 9 Holes: Weekday: $10
Fee 18 Holes: Weekday: $15
Twilight Rates: No
Cart Rental: $3/pull
Lessons: Yes* **Schools:** Yes
Membership: Range + Course
Other: Clubhouse / Patio / Snacks / 16,000 sq ft Putting Green / Chipping area

Tees	Holes	Yards	Par	USGA	Slope
BACK	9	1035	27		50.9
MIDDLE	9	780	27		48.6
FRONT					

Weekend: $10
Weekend: $15
Discounts: Senior & Junior
Driving Range: Yes $9/lg., $5/sm.
Junior Golf: Yes
Architect/Yr Open: Ron Pritchard, P.B. Dye/1998

Short course and teaching center designed to lower cost, provide easy access and playing time. "Not just a beginner's layout. Shots and putts have to be made to score." –R.W.

*Lessons priced according to age. Inquire!

	1	2	3	4	5	6	7	8	9
PAR	3	3	3	3	3	3	3	3	3
YARDS	70	118	60	90	95	62	110	90	85
PAR									
YARDS									

Directions: I-95 to Route 6 West to Route 6A West-Hartford Avenue exit. Take left (East) on Hartford Avenue. Go .7 miles and take right on Glenbridge Avenue. Go .3 miles and take left on Button Hole Drive. Facility on right.

Country View Golf Club

NR ▶ 4

49 Club Lane
Harrisville, RI (401) 568-7157
www.countryviewgolf.net

Club Pro: Rick Finlayson, PGA
Payment: Visa, MC, Disc
Tee Times: 7 days adv.
Fee 9 Holes: Weekday: $18
Fee 18 Holes: Weekday: $30
Twilight Rates: After 5pm
Cart Rental: $15pp/18, $9pp/9
Lessons: $35/half hour **Schools:** No
Membership: Yes
Other: Clubhouse / Lockers / Showers / Snack Bar / Restaurant / Bar-Lounge

Tees	Holes	Yards	Par	USGA	Slope
BACK	18	6067	70	68.2	117
MIDDLE	18	5721	70	66.5	113
FRONT	18	5060	70	67.4	108

Weekend: $25
Weekend: $37
Discounts: Senior & Junior
Driving Range: No
Junior Golf: No
Architect/Yr Open: Carl Dexter/1965

COUPON

Sig. Hole: #3 is a par 5. Long hitters have a chance to go for it in 2, but most players have to lay up to a downhill lie for the third shot. After 4pm on Sat and Sun, juniors are free with one paid adult fee. The 9s have been reversed.

	1	2	3	4	5	6	7	8	9
PAR	4	4	5	3	4	4	4	3	4
YARDS	379	281	485	178	332	392	386	184	367
	10	**11**	**12**	**13**	**14**	**15**	**16**	**17**	**18**
PAR	4	3	4	4	4	5	3	4	4
YARDS	318	126	341	347	315	461	137	344	348

Directions: I-295 to Exit 8 (Route 7 North). Follow 5 miles, take left onto Mattity Road. Follow to end. Take left onto Tarkiln Road 600 yards. Take left onto Colewell Road, 1/2 mile on right.

Coventry Pines Golf Club

NR **5**

Harkney Hill Road
Coventry, RI (401) 397-9482

Tees	Holes	Yards	Par	USGA	Slope
BACK					
MIDDLE	9	3170	36	68.0	113
FRONT	9	3120	36	70.0	113

Club Pro: No
Payment: Cash Only
Tee Times: No
Fee 9 Holes: Weekday: $13   **Weekend:** $17
Fee 18 Holes: Weekday: $23   **Weekend:** $26
Twilight Rates: After 6pm   **Discounts:** Senior M-F
Cart Rental: $32/18, $16/9 per cart   **Driving Range:** Practice field
Lessons: No **Schools:** No   **Junior Golf:** No
Membership: No   **Architect/Yr Open:** 1959
Other: Snack Bar   **GPS:**

A very scenic course with rolling hills and tree-lined fairways. 3 water holes. Noted for the par 5 sixth which has 2 different greens, men's and women's. South County course. Open March - December.

	1	2	3	4	5	6	7	8	9
PAR	4	4	3	5	4	5	4	3	4
YARDS	375	308	169	484	408	520	357	187	362
PAR									
YARDS									

Directions: I-95 to RI Exit 6 (Route 3). Continue North on Route 3 for 1 mile. Take a left on Harkney Hill Road. The course is 2 miles on the left.

Cranston Country Club

★★½ **6**

69 Burlingame Road
Cranston, RI (401) 826-1683
www.cranstoncc.com

Tees	Holes	Yards	Par	USGA	Slope
BACK	18	6914	71	73.5	130
MIDDLE	18	6493	71	70.8	125
FRONT	18	6109	71	69.1	122

Club Pro: Edward Hanley
Payment: Visa, MC, Cash
Tee Times: Yes
Fee 9 Holes: Weekday: $27   **Weekend:** $27
Fee 18 Holes: Weekday: $38   **Weekend:** $44
Twilight Rates: After 3pm on weekends/$25   **Discounts:** Senior
Cart Rental: $17pp/18, $9pp/9   **Driving Range:** Grass
Lessons: Yes **Schools:** Yes   **Junior Golf:** Yes
Membership: Yes   **Architect/Yr Open:** Geoffrey Cornish/1974
Other: Clubhouse / Lockers / Showers / Snack Bar / Bar / Banquet Facilities

Hole #8 is an island green. Scenic country setting. W-i-d-e fairways. Lots of room to hit driver. 4 finishing holes are a fun challenge!

	1	2	3	4	5	6	7	8	9
PAR	5	4	4	3	4	4	4	3	4
YARDS	529	348	375	180	338	346	344	173	410
	10	**11**	**12**	**13**	**14**	**15**	**16**	**17**	**18**
PAR	4	4	3	5	4	3	4	5	4
YARDS	345	377	125	475	349	166	369	545	355

Directions: I-95 to Route 37 West (Exit 14). Go to end of Route 37, turn left. Go .2 mile to intersection, turn right; .4 mile to stop sign, bear right. Proceed .2 mile to crossroads and turn left (Phoenix Avenue). 2 miles to golf course.

Crystal Lake Golf Course of RI ✪✪½

100 Broncos Highway (Route 102)
Harrisville, RI (401) 567-4500
www.crystallakegolfclub.com

Club Pro: Tony DiGiorgio, Pro
Payment: Cash, MC, Visa, Amex
Tee Times: 6 days adv.

Tees	Holes	Yards	Par	USGA	Slope
BACK	18	6349	71	70.0	120
MIDDLE	18	5892	71	68.2	116
FRONT	18	5035	71	69.9	115

Fee 9 Holes: Weekday: $18
Fee 18 Holes: Weekday: $32
Twilight Rates: After 6pm
Cart Rental: $20pp/18, $9pp/9
Lessons: Yes **Schools:** Yes
Membership: Yes
Other: Clubhouse / Restaurant / Bar / Function Facility

Weekend: $24
Weekend: $44 ($30 Friday)
Discounts:
Driving Range: Yes
Junior Golf: Yes
Architect/Yr Open: Howard Maurer/2003

Clubhouse with 4-star restaurant. Great views and better greens. "18-hole course with great variety of holes wrapped around Crystal Lake. Lots of elevation changes and doglegs make for interesting round." –JD

	1	2	3	4	5	6	7	8	9
PAR	4	3	4	4	5	5	4	3	4
YARDS	347	165	375	358	535	450	415	170	292
	10	11	12	13	14	15	16	17	18
PAR	4	3	4	4	5	3	4	4	4
YARDS	407	178	295	275	460	130	315	372	353

Directions: 146 North or South to Route 102 West, 8 miles to Crystal Lake on right.

East Greenwich Country Club ✪✪

1646 Division Street
East Greenwich, RI (401) 884-5656
www.rigolf.com/eg

Club Pro: Larry Rittmann
Payment: Cash Only
Tee Times: No

Tees	Holes	Yards	Par	USGA	Slope
BACK	9	3315	36		127
MIDDLE	9	3125	36		124
FRONT	9	2875	36		119

Fee 9 Holes: Weekday: $17
Fee 18 Holes: Weekday: $27
Twilight Rates: After 5pm
Cart Rental: $22pp/18, $12pp/9
Lessons: Yes **Schools:** Yes
Membership: Yes
Other: Snack Bar / Bar-Lounge

Weekend: $20
Weekend: $30
Discounts: Senior
Driving Range: No
Junior Golf: Yes
Architect/Yr Open: Michael Kroian/1963
GPS:

Rated as one of the more challenging 9-hole courses in N.E. Private club conditions. Fantastic greens, trees, and scenic ponds.

	1	2	3	4	5	6	7	8	9
PAR	4	4	5	4	4	3	5	4	3
YARDS	365	325	500	360	385	160	475	380	175
PAR									
YARDS									

Directions: I-95 to Exit 8 (East Greenwich). Take right off exit (Route 2). Head South for 300 yards to traffic light. Take right (Division Road). Course is 1/2 mile on left.

Exeter Country Club

320 Pen Rod Road
Exeter, RI (401) 295-8212
www.exetercc.com

Club Pro: No
Payment: Visa, MC $15 Minimum
Tee Times: 1 day, call after 8am

Tees	Holes	Yards	Par	USGA	Slope
BACK	18	6919	72	72.3	123
MIDDLE	18	6390	72	69.9	116
FRONT	18	5733	72	72.1	115

Fee 9 Holes: Weekday: $20 M-Th 1pm   Weekend: $25 F/S/S/H 3:30pm
Fee 18 Holes: Weekday: $35 walk/$50 ride   Weekend: $40walk/$55 ride F/S/S/H
Twilight Rates: After 4pm   Discounts: Junior
Cart Rental: $15pp/18, $9pp/9   Driving Range: $8/lg., $5/med.
Lessons: No Schools: No   Junior Golf: No
Membership: Yes, waiting list   Architect/Yr Open: Geoffrey Cornish/1969
Other: Clubhouse / Snack Bar / Lockers / Bar-Lounge / Full Restaurant

Course has a beautiful layout with strategically placed hazards. Wide fairways – bring your driver. Friendly staff. Open March - November. South County course.

	1	2	3	4	5	6	7	8	9
PAR	4	5	3	5	3	4	4	4	4
YARDS	350	530	190	510	180	360	420	370	400
	10	11	12	13	14	15	16	17	18
PAR	4	3	4	4	5	4	4	3	5
YARDS	400	150	330	310	480	350	370	200	490

Directions: I-95 to Route 4 (Exit 5B South) into Exeter (approximately 4-5 mile), take Route 102 North. Course is on left 2.5 miles. From South, take I-95 North to Exit 4 on Route 3 North, At intersection of Route 102, go right. Course is 5 miles on right side.

Fairlawn Golf Course

NR

3 Sherman Avenue
Lincoln, RI (401) 334-3937
www.fairlawngolfcourse.com

Club Pro: No
Payment: Cash Only
Tee Times: No

Tees	Holes	Yards	Par	USGA	Slope
BACK					
MIDDLE	9	2534	27	52.2	N/A
FRONT					

Fee 9 Holes: Weekday: $13   Weekend: $15
Fee 18 Holes: Weekday: $18   Weekend: $20
Twilight Rates: Discounts: Senior
Cart Rental: $3/pull   Driving Range: No
Lessons: No Schools: No   Junior Golf: No
Membership: Yes   Architect/Yr Open: Adams/1963
Other: Clubhouse / Beer and Wine   GPS:

COUPON

Beautiful and affordable course.

	1	2	3	4	5	6	7	8	9
PAR	3	3	3	3	3	3	3	3	3
YARDS	133	181	121	167	91	110	110	161	193
PAR									
YARDS									

Directions: I-95 North to Route 146 North to Sherman Avenue exit. Course is on right. You can't miss it.

Fenner Hill Golf Club

33 Wheeler Lane
Hope Valley, RI (401) 539-8000
www.fennerhill.com

Tees	Holes	Yards	Par	USGA	Slope
BACK	18	6600	72	71.7	134
MIDDLE	18	6260	72	70.1	125
FRONT	18	5100	72	68.8	117

Club Pro: No
Payment: Visa, MC
Tee Times: 3 days adv.
Fee 9 Holes: Weekday: $21
Fee 18 Holes: Weekday: $34
Twilight Rates: After 3pm
Cart Rental: $16pp/18, $10pp/9
Lessons: No **Schools:** No
Membership: Yes
Weekend: $23
Weekend: $42
Discounts: Sr. & Jr. Weekdays
Driving Range: $6/lg., $3/med.
Junior Golf: No
Architect/Yr Open: Ron & Dennis Levesque/1999
Other: Restaurant / Bar-Lounge / Banquet Facilities / Corporate Outings

Player Comments: "Looks easy from the road, but watch out. Walkable." The beauty of the landscape pleases and challenges all levels. Greens #16 and #18 have been rebuilt. Foxwoods nearby.

	1	2	3	4	5	6	7	8	9
PAR	4	4	5	3	4	3	4	5	4
YARDS	366	347	486	152	352	158	394	520	355
	10	11	12	13	14	15	16	17	18
PAR	5	3	4	4	5	4	3	4	4
YARDS	468	164	440	338	525	309	166	297	425

Directions: I-95 to Exit 2. Bear right to stop sign, take right, 3/4 mile on right. I-95 North to Exit 2. From North, left off exit to stop sign. Take a right, 3/4 mile on right.

Foster Country Club

67 Johnson Road
Foster, RI (401) 397-7750
www.fostercountryclub.com

Tees	Holes	Yards	Par	USGA	Slope
BACK					
MIDDLE	18	6187	72	71.5	117
FRONT	18	5499	72	70.0	112

Club Pro: Brian Benson
Payment: Visa, MC
Tee Times: 7 days adv.
Fee 9 Holes: Weekday: $17
Fee 18 Holes: Weekday: $27
Twilight Rates: After 2pm
Cart Rental: $14pp/18, $7pp/9
Lessons: Yes **Schools:** No
Membership: Yes
Weekend: $20
Weekend: $36
Discounts: Junior weekdays
Driving Range: Practice nets
Junior Golf: No
Architect/Yr Open: Geoffrey Cornish/1962
Other: Clubhouse / Snack Bar / Restaurant / Bar-Lounge / 180-Seat Banquet Hall

"Best-kept secret in Western Rhode Island. " Added length in 2005. Open April - November.

	1	2	3	4	5	6	7	8	9
PAR	4	4	3	5	4	4	3	5	4
YARDS	356	340	241	595	295	425	130	485	310
	10	11	12	13	14	15	16	17	18
PAR	4	4	5	4	5	4	4	3	3
YARDS	405	310	495	375	450	295	315	170	195

Directions: Take I-95 to Route 102 North to Route 14. Left on Route 14 to Moosup Valley Road (on right) to Johnson Road (on right). Follow to course.

Goddard State Park Golf Course NR 13

Ives Road
Warwick, RI (401) 884-9834
www.riparks.com

Club Pro: No
Payment: Cash or Check
Tee Times: No
Fee 9 Holes: Weekday: $12
Fee 18 Holes: Weekday:
Twilight Rates: No
Cart Rental: $14pp/9
Lessons: No **Schools:** No
Membership: No

Tees	Holes	Yards	Par	USGA	Slope
BACK	9	3250	36	34.2	111
MIDDLE	9	3032	36	33.8	109
FRONT					

Weekend: $14
Weekend:
Discounts: Senior 1/2 price
Driving Range: No
Junior Golf: No
Architect/Yr Open: 1939

Other: Clubhouse / Snack Bar / Picnic Facilities / Beach / Showers

The course, located inside Goddard State Park, is open and very walkable. Horse paths and jogging trails are also available. 300 trees have been added to the course, resulting in more of a challenge.

	1	2	3	4	5	6	7	8	9
PAR	5	4	3	4	5	4	3	4	4
YARDS	503	377	180	292	500	301	168	390	321
PAR									
YARDS									

Directions: I-95 to Route 4 cutoff, take first exit (East Greenwich). Take Route 401 and follow signs to course.

Green Valley Country Club ★★½ 14

Union Street
Portsmouth, RI (401) 847-9543
www.greenvalleyccofri.com

Club Pro: Gary P. Dorsi, PGA
Payment: Visa, MC, Amex
Tee Times: 3 days adv.
Fee 9 Holes: Weekday: No
Fee 18 Holes: Weekday: $45, $64 w/cart
Twilight Rates: After 3pm
Cart Rental: $16pp/18
Lessons: $35/half hour **Schools:** Yes
Membership: Yes, Junior
Other: Snack Bar / Clubhouse / Outings

Tees	Holes	Yards	Par	USGA	Slope
BACK	18	6830	71	72.1	125
MIDDLE	18	6721	71	71.6	122
FRONT	18	5459	71	69.5	120

Weekend: No
Weekend: $64 w/cart
Discounts: None
Driving Range: $3/bucket
Junior Golf: Yes
Architect/Yr Open: Manuel Raposa/1957
GPS:

Hosted USGA Qualifiers, RI Amateur, RI Open. May book large or small outings. Nice character with old stone walls. Ideal for tournaments and outings and an afternoon of golf.

	1	2	3	4	5	6	7	8	9
PAR	4	4	4	5	3	4	4	3	4
YARDS	361	454	386	541	175	392	354	201	424
	10	11	12	13	14	15	16	17	18
PAR	5	3	3	4	4	4	4	5	4
YARDS	605	220	125	327	440	334	394	540	308

Directions: I-195 to Route 24 South, follow Route 114 South, Raytheon Corp is on right. Take left on Union Street (2nd light after Raytheon Corp.).

RI

Jamestown Golf Course

NR   15

245 Conanicus Ave
Jamestown, RI (401) 423-9930
www.jamestowngolf.com

Club Pro: No
Payment: All types
Tee Times: No
Fee 9 Holes: Weekday: $17
Fee 18 Holes: Weekday: $27
Twilight Rates: No
Cart Rental: $12pp/18, $7pp/9
Lessons: No **Schools:** No
Membership: No
Other: Clubhouse / Snack Bar / Bar-Lounge

Weekend: $19
Weekend: $29
Discounts: None
Driving Range: No
Junior Golf: Yes
Architect/Yr Open: 1901
GPS:

Tees	Holes	Yards	Par	USGA	Slope
BACK	9	3048	36	69.7	110
MIDDLE	9	2751	36	69.7	110
FRONT	9	2421	38		

Course is completely watered by irrigation. Open April - November.

	1	2	3	4	5	6	7	8	9
PAR	4	5	4	4	3	5	3	4	4
YARDS	270	484	279	375	114	379	141	368	328
PAR									
YARDS									

Directions: I-95 to Route 138 East. Go over Jamestown Bridge. Cross the island and follow signs to the Newport Bridge. When toll booths are in sight, take last exit before toll. Course on right.

Laurel Lane Country Club

★★½   16

309 Laurel Lane
West Kingston, RI (401) 783-3844
www.laurellanecountryclub.com

Club Pro: Pat O'Brien, PGA
Payment: Cash, Visa, MC
Tee Times: 7 days adv.
Fee 9 Holes: Weekday: $21
Fee 18 Holes: Weekday: $33
Twilight Rates: After 3pm
Cart Rental: $16pp/18, $9pp/9
Lessons: Yes **Schools:** Jr.
Membership: Yes
Other: Clubhouse / Snack Bar / Bar-Lounge

Weekend: $25
Weekend: $42
Discounts: Senior & Junior
Driving Range: Yes
Junior Golf: Yes
Architect/Yr Open: Holley, Sr; Thoren; Bota/1961
GPS:

Tees	Holes	Yards	Par	USGA	Slope
BACK	18	6250	71		120
MIDDLE	18	6077	71	68.1	114
FRONT	18	5301	70	70.8	115

COUPON

Home course for URI. New clubhouse now open. New tees on #1, #3, and #8; new 9th green in 2006. New putting course open: July 2007.

	1	2	3	4	5	6	7	8	9
PAR	4	5	3	4	4	4	3	4	4
YARDS	295	485	260	370	340	260	206	370	380
	10	11	12	13	14	15	16	17	18
PAR	4	4	4	4	4	3	5	3	5
YARDS	395	335	320	340	385	150	485	161	540

Directions: I-95 to Exit 3A. Go approximately 6 miles East on Route 138. Right on Laurel Lane.

Lindhbrook Golf Course

NR 17

299 Woodville Alton Road
Hope Valley, RI (401) 539-8700
www.rigolf.com/lindhbrook

Club Pro: Bill Patnoad
Payment: Visa, MC, Amex
Tee Times: Yes
Fee 9 Holes: Weekday: $15
Fee 18 Holes: Weekday: $20
Twilight Rates: After 5:30pm
Cart Rental: $18pp/18, $12pp/9
Lessons: Yes **Schools:** No
Membership: Yes
Other: Snack Bar / Restaurant / Bar-Lounge

Tees	Holes	Yards	Par	USGA	Slope
BACK	18	3000	54		
MIDDLE	18	2869	54		
FRONT	18	2600	54		

Weekend: $15
Weekend: $25
Discounts: Senior & Junior
Driving Range: No
Junior Golf: Yes
Architect/Yr Open: 1954
GPS:

South County course.

RI

	1	2	3	4	5	6	7	8	9
PAR	3	3	3	3	3	3	3	3	3
YARDS	132	146	171	172	150	168	158	175	125
	10	11	12	13	14	15	16	17	18
PAR	3	3	3	3	3	3	3	3	3
YARDS	139	143	127	180	181	192	143	183	184

Directions: I-95 to Exit 2. If Northbound, bear right; if Southbound, turn left. Course 800 yards from I-95 on right.

Meadow Brook Golf Club

NR 18

153 Kingstown Road
Richmond, RI (401) 539-8491
www.rigolf.com/meadowbrook

Club Pro: No
Payment: Cash Only
Tee Times: No
Fee 9 Holes: Weekday: $10
Fee 18 Holes: Weekday:
Twilight Rates: After 5pm
Cart Rental: $20pp/18
Lessons: No **Schools:** No
Membership: No
Other: Clubhouse / Snack Bar

Tees	Holes	Yards	Par	USGA	Slope
BACK					
MIDDLE	18	6075	71	70.1	118
FRONT	18	5605	73	N/A	N/A

Weekend: $12
Weekend:
Discounts: None
Driving Range: No
Junior Golf: No
Architect/Yr Open: W. Bradlee/1929
GPS:

The course is very level and well laid out. South County course. Under construction, now only a 9 hole course.

	1	2	3	4	5	6	7	8	9
PAR	4	3	4	4	3	5	4	4	5
YARDS	300	175	350	335	155	535	300	365	505
	10	11	12	13	14	15	16	17	18
PAR	3	4	4	5	4	4	4	4	3
YARDS	180	385	350	485	395	385	340	305	140

Directions: I-95 to Exit 3A in RI. Continue on Route 138 East. Course is 1 mile East of I-95.

Melody Hill Golf Course

NR **19** ▶

55 Melody Hill Lane
Harmony, RI (401) 949-9851
www.thegolfcourses.net

Club Pro: Lynn Molhan, USGTF
Payment: Cash Only
Tee Times: No
Fee 9 Holes: Weekday: $18
Fee 18 Holes: Weekday: $26
Twilight Rates: After 5pm
Cart Rental: $25pp/18, $17pp/9
Lessons: Yes **Schools:** No
Membership: No
Other: Clubhouse / Snack Bar / Bar-Lounge

Tees	Holes	Yards	Par	USGA	Slope
BACK	18	6004	71	68.4	109
MIDDLE	18	5801	71	67.5	108
FRONT	18	5363	71	70.4	113

Weekend: $19
Weekend: $30
Discounts: Senior $21pp/18, $17pp/9 (M-F)
Driving Range: No
Junior Golf: No
Architect/Yr Open: Sam Mitchell/1967
GPS:

Lessons by certified teacher of golf. Twilight rates: 9 holes only $15 after 5pm weekdays, $17 after 4pm weekends. Seniors M-F 9 holes $17, 18 holes $21.

	1	2	3	4	5	6	7	8	9
PAR	4	4	4	3	4	3	4	5	4
YARDS	360	315	385	95	465	145	425	500	235
	10	11	12	13	14	15	16	17	18
PAR	5	4	5	3	4	3	4	4	4
YARDS	445	405	535	185	360	165	355	400	410

Directions: Route 44 West toward CT, take first left after fire station in Harmony Center onto Saw Mill Road.

Midville Country Club

NR **20** ▶

100 Lombardi Lane
West Warwick, RI (401) 828-9215

Club Pro: No
Payment: Visa, MC, Disc
Tee Times: No
Fee 9 Holes: Weekday: $24
Fee 18 Holes: Weekday: $35
Twilight Rates: No
Cart Rental: $18pp/18, $9pp/9
Lessons: No **Schools:** No
Membership: No
Other: Clubhouse / Snack Bar / Bar-Lounge

Tees	Holes	Yards	Par	USGA	Slope
BACK	9	2970	35	68.3	115
MIDDLE	9	2779	70	68.2	114
FRONT	9	2340	35		

Weekend: $25
Weekend: $39
Discounts: Senior
Driving Range: No
Junior Golf: Yes
Architect/Yr Open: Carmine Lombardi/1962
GPS:

COUPON

Scenic 9-hole layout. Well-conditioned public course. April - December.

	1	2	3	4	5	6	7	8	9
PAR	4	4	4	4	3	5	3	4	4
YARDS	334	314	327	346	145	523	145	309	336
	10	11	12	13	14	15	16	17	18
PAR	4	4	4	4	3	5	3	4	4
YARDS	359	321	343	378	171	540	168	346	344

Directions: I-95 to Route 113 West exit. Go straight through 3 sets of lights. Cross bridge, bear right and then straight through the 4th light. Course is 1 mile on left.

Montaup Country Club

 ✪✪✪½ **21**

500 Anthony Road
Portsmouth, RI (401) 683-0955
www.montaupcountryclub.com

Club Pro: Steve Diemoz
Payment: Cash, Credit Card, Check
Tee Times: 3 days adv.

Tees	Holes	Yards	Par	USGA	Slope
BACK	18	6513	71	71.3	130
MIDDLE	18	6250	71	70.3	125
FRONT	18	5417	73	71.4	118

Fee 9 Holes: Weekday: Weekend:
Fee 18 Holes: Weekday: $45 Weekend: $45
Twilight Rates: After 3:30pm wkends only **Discounts:** None
Cart Rental: $18pp/18 **Driving Range:** No
Lessons: $30/half hour **Schools:** No **Junior Golf:** Yes
Membership: Yes **Architect/Yr Open:** 1929
Other: Clubhouse / Snack Bar / Restaurant / Bar-Lounge

Player Comments: "Always in excellent shape and great to walk." "Excellent greens, lots of room to hit away." Open April - December.

	1	2	3	4	5	6	7	8	9
PAR	4	4	3	4	5	4	5	3	4
YARDS	406	404	213	384	491	349	533	135	344
	10	**11**	**12**	**13**	**14**	**15**	**16**	**17**	**18**
PAR	3	4	3	5	3	4	5	4	4
YARDS	149	392	173	493	163	418	517	399	297

Directions: I-195 to Route 24 South to Anthony Road. Exit right off ramp; course is visible from ramp.

Newport National Golf Club

 ✪✪✪✪ **22**

324 Mitchell's Lane
Middletown, RI (401) 848-9690
www.newportnational.com

Club Pro: David Johnson, PGA
Payment: Cash, All Major Cards
Tee Times: Yes

Tees	Holes	Yards	Par	USGA	Slope
BACK	18	7244	72	74.4	138
MIDDLE	18	6553	72	71.9	130
FRONT	18	5217	71	68.8	119

Fee 9 Holes: Weekday: Weekend:
Fee 18 Holes: Weekday: $125 w/cart Weekend: $150 w/cart
Twilight Rates: After 3pm **Discounts:** RI residents
Cart Rental: Included **Driving Range:** None
Lessons: Schools: **Junior Golf:** Yes
Membership: Yes **Architect/Yr Open:** Arthur Hill, Drew Rogers/2002
Other: Clubhouse / Lodging Partners **GPS:**

Dramatic holes, great challenges. Links-style; fescue rough; bent grass fairways, tees, and greens. R.I. resident rates. Strong junior golf program. "My favorite course in New England." –BC

	1	2	3	4	5	6	7	8	9
PAR	5	4	3	3	4	4	4	5	4
YARDS	486	400	168	154	296	449	444	495	348
	10	**11**	**12**	**13**	**14**	**15**	**16**	**17**	**18**
PAR	4	5	4	3	5	4	3	4	4
YARDS	383	505	326	148	523	396	212	430	381

Directions: I-195 to MA Route 24 South or RI 138 or RI 114 South. Follow signs to Newport. Take 138 South (East Main Road) through Portsmouth. Watch for Mitchell's Lane on the left. Newport Airport? You went too far.

North Kingstown Muni. GC ✪✪✪  23

615 Callahan Road
North Kingstown, RI (401) 294-0684
www.nkgc.com

Tees	Holes	Yards	Par	USGA	Slope
BACK	18	6161	70	69.3	123
MIDDLE	18	5848	70	67.8	121
FRONT	18	5227	70	69.5	115

Club Pro: John Rainone, head pro
Payment: Cash, Visa, MC
Tee Times: 2 days adv.
Fee 9 Holes: Weekday: $21 **Weekend:**
Fee 18 Holes: Weekday: $31 **Weekend:** $39
Twilight Rates: 2-4pm and after 4pm $22 (weekends only)
Discounts: Senior
Cart Rental: $30/18, $16/9 per cart **Driving Range:** $8/lg, $5/sm
Lessons: Yes **Schools:** Yes **Junior Golf:** Yes
Membership: Yes **Architect/Yr Open:** Walter Johnson/1943
Other: Restaurant / Lounge / Clubhouse **GPS:**

Player Comments: "Just plain enjoyable. Redefines what a muncipal can be." Hosted 2006 US Open Qualifier. Links-style overlooking Narragansett Bay. South County course.

	1	2	3	4	5	6	7	8	9
PAR	4	4	3	5	4	4	5	3	4
YARDS	369	411	185	499	375	353	545	197	283
	10	11	12	13	14	15	16	17	18
PAR	3	5	4	4	3	4	4	4	3
YARDS	171	559	333	403	194	413	398	315	158

Directions: I-95 South to Route 45. Exit 7A off Route 45 (403E). Follow approximately 4.5 miles. Go left at 1st light. First right. Clubhouse on the right.

Pinecrest Golf Course ✪✪½ 24

25 Pinehurst Drive
Carolina, RI (401) 364-8600
www.pinehurstgolfri.com

Tees	Holes	Yards	Par	USGA	Slope
BACK	9	2900	35	67.7	131
MIDDLE	9	2611	35	66.2	123
FRONT	9	2309	35	69.4	123

Club Pro:
Payment: Visa, MC
Tee Times: Wed. for nonmembers
Fee 9 Holes: Weekday: $20 **Weekend:** $22
Fee 18 Holes: Weekday: $30 **Weekend:** $32
Twilight Rates: After 3pm **Discounts:** Senior & Junior
Cart Rental: $12pp/18, $7pp/9 **Driving Range:** No
Lessons: No **Schools:** No **Junior Golf:** No
Membership: Yes
Architect/Yr Open: Beakman-Wermy/Intergolf Design/2002
Other: Bar / Grille / Clubhouse

"Short 9 holes with one par 5. Very playable for all levels of golfing ability. 9th is the signature hole." –RW

	1	2	3	4	5	6	7	8	9
PAR	4	5	3	4	4	3	4	4	4
YARDS	348	540	129	382	337	145	314	320	385
PAR									
YARDS									

Directions: I-95 to Exit 3 to Route 138 East to Route 112. 2.4 miles to Pinehurst Drive on left.

Richmond Country Club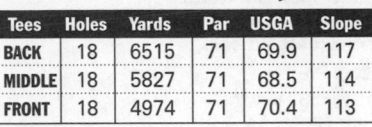

74 Sandy Pond Road
Richmond, RI (401) 364-9200
www.richmondcountryclub.net

Club Pro: No
Payment: Visa, MC
Tee Times: 2 days adv.

Tees	Holes	Yards	Par	USGA	Slope
BACK	18	6515	71	69.9	117
MIDDLE	18	5827	71	68.5	114
FRONT	18	4974	71	70.4	113

Fee 9 Holes: Weekday: $18 after 3pm
Fee 18 Holes: Weekday: $33
Twilight Rates: After 3pm
Cart Rental: $30/18, $15/9
Lessons: No **Schools:** No
Membership: No
Weekend:
Weekend: $40
Discounts: Senior
Driving Range: Yes
Junior Golf: No
Architect/Yr Open: Cornish & Silva/1992
Other: Restaurant / Clubhouse / Bar-Lounge / Banquet Facilities

Player Comments: "Plush fairways. Pure greens. Aesthetically pleasant." South County course.

	1	2	3	4	5	6	7	8	9
PAR	4	4	3	5	3	4	5	4	4
YARDS	318	353	204	504	165	428	450	277	285
	10	11	12	13	14	15	16	17	18
PAR	4	5	3	4	4	3	5	3	4
YARDS	320	431	184	408	368	176	474	154	328

Directions: I-95 to Exit 3B; follow 2 miles. Left at flashing light onto Mechanic Street. 2.5 miles, turn right onto Sandy Pond Road.

Rolling Greens Golf Course   NR 26

1625 Pen Rod Road
North Kingstown, RI
(401) 294-9859
www.rollinggreensri.com

Club Pro:
Payment: Cash Only
Tee Times: No

Tees	Holes	Yards	Par	USGA	Slope
BACK					
MIDDLE	9	3072	35		
FRONT					

Fee 9 Holes: Weekday: $16
Fee 18 Holes: Weekday: $22
Twilight Rates: No
Cart Rental: $20pp/18, $12pp/9
Lessons: No **Schools:** No
Membership: Yes
Weekend: $18
Weekend: $25
Discounts: None
Driving Range: No
Junior Golf: No
Architect/Yr Open: 1969
Other: Clubhouse / Snack Bar / Restaurant / Bar-Lounge

The course is hilly and has just 1 water hole. South County course.

	1	2	3	4	5	6	7	8	9
PAR	4	4	4	3	5	4	4	3	4
YARDS	339	353	383	147	550	325	315	220	440
PAR									
YARDS									

Directions: I-95 to Route 4, North Kingston. Get onto Route 102 West toward Exeter. Course is 1.25 miles on right.

Rose Hill Golf Club ✪✪ 27 ▶

222 Rose Hill Road
Wakefield, RI (401) 788-1088
www.rosehillri.com

Tees	Holes	Yards	Par	USGA	Slope
BACK	9	1206	27		
MIDDLE	9	1206	27		
FRONT	9	981	27		

Club Pro:
Payment: Visa, MC
Tee Times: No
Fee 9 Holes: Weekday: $12 **Weekend:** $12
Fee 18 Holes: Weekday: $18 **Weekend:** $18
Twilight Rates: No **Discounts:** Senior & Junior
Cart Rental: $10pp/9, $15pp/18, $3 pullcart **Driving Range:** No
Lessons: Yes **Schools:** Sr. & Jr. **Junior Golf:** Yes
Membership: Yes **Architect/Yr Open:** Beckman, Weremay/2001
Other: New Bistro / Restaurant / Pub / Clubhouse / League Play

COUPON

"Sophisticated design for a 9-holer that circles a pond situated in the middle of the course. Excellent greens." –RW Family-friendly environment. South County course.

	1	2	3	4	5	6	7	8	9
PAR	3	3	3	3	3	3	3	3	3
YARDS	144	140	74	101	143	168	129	178	129
PAR									
YARDS									

Directions: Route 1 to Route 138 West 2.5 miles, and turn left onto Rose Hill Road. Course is 9/10 mile on right.

Silver Spring Golf Club NR 28 ▶

3301 Pawtucket Avenue
East Providence, RI
(401) 434-9697

Tees	Holes	Yards	Par	USGA	Slope
BACK					
MIDDLE	4	1668	23	N/A	N/A
FRONT					

Club Pro: No
Payment: Cash Only
Tee Times: No
Fee 9 Holes: Weekday: **Weekend:**
Fee 18 Holes: Weekday: $17 **Weekend:** $17
Twilight Rates: **Discounts:** None
Cart Rental: $14/cart **Driving Range:** No
Lessons: No **Schools:** No **Junior Golf:** No
Membership: Yes **Architect/Yr Open:**
Other: No **GPS:**

6-hole course, fairly hilly with tree-lined fairways. Good practice course. Can play 6, 12, or 18 holes at various rates. Open May - December.

	1	2	3	4	5	6	7	8	9
PAR	4	5	3	3	5	3			
YARDS	315	433	173	123	411	122			
PAR									
YARDS									

Directions: I-195 to RI Exit 4. Go South on Veterans Memorial Parkway. Course is 3 miles on Route 103 South.

Triggs Memorial Golf Course ✿✿✿ ▶29

1533 Chalkstone Avenue
Providence, RI (401) 521-8460
www.triggs.us

Tees	Holes	Yards	Par	USGA	Slope
BACK	18	6522	72	72.8	128
MIDDLE	18	6302	72	71.7	125
FRONT	18	5392	72	73.1	123

Club Pro: Mike Ryan, PGA
Payment: Visa, MC, Cash
Tee Times: 2 weeks adv.
Fee 9 Holes: Weekday: $23 **Weekend:** $23
Fee 18 Holes: Weekday: $38 **Weekend:** $40
Twilight Rates: No **Discounts:** Senior $23/18 weekday
Cart Rental: $18pp/18, $9pp/9 **Driving Range:** No
Lessons: No **Schools:** No **Junior Golf:** Yes
Membership: Yes **Architect/Yr Open:** Donald Ross/1933
Other: Full Kitchen and Lounge **GPS:**

Player Comments: "Solid layout. No easy holes, quick greens, very challenging. Course maintenance has improved." Classic Ross design.

	1	2	3	4	5	6	7	8	9
PAR	4	4	4	3	4	5	3	4	4
YARDS	379	411	445	184	316	437	185	332	391
	10	11	12	13	14	15	16	17	18
PAR	5	4	3	5	3	5	4	4	4
YARDS	502	340	195	447	140	496	302	401	399

Directions: I-95 to Exit 23. Go right at exit. Right on Douglas Avenue. First red light is Chalkstone, turn left. Go 2 miles. I-95 South take Exit 21. Right onto Atwell at light, right at Dean Street, at 5th light, take left onto Chalkstone. Go 1.5 miles.

Washington Village Golf Course NR ▶30

2 Fairway Drive
Coventry, RI
(401) 823-0010

Tees	Holes	Yards	Par	USGA	Slope
BACK					
MIDDLE	9	2525	33	N/A	N/A
FRONT	9	1993	33		

Club Pro: Jeremy Votolato, GM, head pro
Payment: Visa, MC
Tee Times: No
Fee 9 Holes: Weekday: $14 **Weekend:** $15
Fee 18 Holes: Weekday: $19 **Weekend:** $20
Twilight Rates: No **Discounts:** Senior & Junior
Cart Rental: $14pp/18, $7pp/9 **Driving Range:** No
Lessons: $25/half hour **Schools:** No **Junior Golf:** Yes
Membership: Yes **Architect/Yr Open:** Carl Augenstein/1970
Other: Bar-Lounge / Snack Bar **GPS:**

COUPON

Course is well-kept and is easy to walk. South County course. New ownership. New carts for upcoming year. Great for beginners and families.

	1	2	3	4	5	6	7	8	9
PAR	3	4	3	4	5	3	4	3	4
YARDS	175	360	150	310	470	200	360	200	300
PAR									
YARDS									

Directions: I-95 to Route 117 West. Follow 5 miles into Coventry; follow signs.

West Warwick Country Club, The NR  31

335 Wakefield Street
West Warwick, RI
(401) 821-9789

Club Pro: No
Payment: Most Major
Tee Times: No
Fee 9 Holes: Weekday: $25
Fee 18 Holes: Weekday: $39
Twilight Rates: No
Cart Rental: $8pp/9, $16pp/18
Lessons: No **Schools:** No
Membership: Yes
Other: Bar-Lounge / Snacks / Restaurant / Banquet Facilities

Tees	Holes	Yards	Par	USGA	Slope
BACK					
MIDDLE	9	3015	35	67.6	120
FRONT					

Weekend: $25
Weekend: $39
Discounts: None
Driving Range: No
Junior Golf: No
Architect/Yr Open: McGregor/1941

Road divides course: First 4 holes are hilly, back 5 are parallel and flat. Public play limited to weekends after 2:30pm.

	1	2	3	4	5	6	7	8	9
PAR	4	4	3	4	4	4	4	3	5
YARDS	419	338	140	390	360	363	333	162	510
PAR									
YARDS									

Directions: I-95 to Route 113 West for 1 mile. At intersection of Route 2, go straight through, onto East Avenue for 1/2 mile. Turn right onto River Street for 1/4 mile. River Street becomes Wakefield Street at light. Club is 1.5 miles up on top of hill.

Windmill Hill Golf Course NR 32

35 Schoolhouse Road
Warren, RI (401) 245-1463
www.windmillhillgolfri.com

Club Pro: No
Payment: Most Major
Tee Times: Weekend only
Fee 9 Holes: Weekday: $15
Fee 18 Holes: Weekday: $21
Twilight Rates: No
Cart Rental: $28pp/18, $15pp/9 per cart
Lessons: Available **Schools:** No
Membership: Yes
Other: Clubhouse / Showers / Restaurant / Bar-Lounge / Banquet Facilities / Decks

Tees	Holes	Yards	Par	USGA	Slope
BACK	9	1432	27		
MIDDLE	9	1191	27		
FRONT	9	891	27		

Weekend: $16
Weekend: $22
Discounts: Senior & Junior
Driving Range: No
Junior Golf: No
Architect/Yr Open: Beckman, Weremay/2000

Pleasant challenge for all levels. Course makes you use all your clubs. Lush greens and fairways.

	1	2	3	4	5	6	7	8	9
PAR	3	3	3	3	3	3	3	3	3
YARDS	91	129	167	120	136	150	162	125	111
PAR									
YARDS									

Directions: I-195 to Exit 2. Follow signs for Route 136 South, 2 miles. Turn left onto Schoolhouse Road. Entrance is .3 miles on right.

Winnapaug Golf Course ⊙⊙ ▶33

184 Shore Road
Westerly, RI (401) 596-1237
www.winnapaugcountryclub.com

Tees	Holes	Yards	Par	USGA	Slope
BACK	18	6361	72	70.6	124
MIDDLE	18	5944	72	68.6	119
FRONT	18	5183	72	69.2	118

Club Pro: Jeff Beaupre, PGA
Payment: Cash, Check, Charge
Tee Times: 1 week adv.
Fee 9 Holes: Weekday: $20
Fee 18 Holes: Weekday: $40
Twilight Rates: After 4pm
Cart Rental: $16pp/18, $9pp/9
Lessons: Yes **Schools:** Yes
Membership: Yes
Other: Clubhouse / Restaurant / Bar-Lounge / Beverage Cart

Weekend:
Weekend: $60 w/cart & lunch (June)
Discounts: Senior & Junior
Driving Range: Practice range
Junior Golf: No
Architect/Yr Open: Donald Ross/1922

Donald Ross design with tight, short fairways and demanding greens. Open year-round. South County course. New green on #1, 30 yards longer. Close to the Misquamicot Beaches.

	1	2	3	4	5	6	7	8	9
PAR	4	5	3	4	4	3	4	4	5
YARDS	319	484	156	402	270	106	344	322	508
	10	11	12	13	14	15	16	17	18
PAR	4	4	3	5	4	5	3	4	4
YARDS	395	348	141	472	383	451	140	376	302

Directions: I-95 to Exit 92, take right onto Route 2, follow to Route 78, follow signs for beaches. Turn left onto Route 1A, course is 1 mile on left.

Wood River Golf NR ▶34

78A Woodville Alton Road
Hope Valley, RI (401) 364-0700
www.woodrivergolf.com

Tees	Holes	Yards	Par	USGA	Slope
BACK					
MIDDLE	18	5273	69		
FRONT	18	4452	69		

Club Pro:
Payment: Cash, Checks, Credit Cards
Tee Times: No
Fee 9 Holes: Weekday: $14 (11 holes)
Fee 18 Holes: Weekday: $22, $30 all day
Twilight Rates: After 3pm
Cart Rental: $16 per cart, $10pp
Lessons: Schools:
Membership: No
Other: Pub and Restaurant / Clubhouse

Weekend: $14 (11 holes)
Weekend: $22
Discounts: None
Driving Range: No
Junior Golf: No
Architect/Yr Open: Weston Thompson/2000
GPS:

COUPON

Natural setting, links-style course. South county course. Improvements on 15th, 16th, 17th. Course more user-friendly. 20 minutes from local beaches and casino.

	1	2	3	4	5	6	7	8	9
PAR	5	3	4	3	5	4	3	4	4
YARDS	453	152	332	185	445	315	217	331	315
	10	11	12	13	14	15	16	17	18
PAR	3	4	4	4	4	4	4	4	3
YARDS	153	305	315	300	265	400	330	305	155

Directions: I-95 to Exit 2. 3.5 miles along Woodville Alton Roads, course on the left.

Woodland Greens Golf Club

655 Old Baptist
North Kingstown, RI
(401) 294-2872
www.woodlandgc.com

Club Pro: No
Payment: Visa, MC
Tee Times: No
Fee 9 Holes: Weekday: $21
Fee 18 Holes: Weekday: $28
Twilight Rates: No
Cart Rental: $30pp/18, $15pp/9
Lessons: No **Schools:** No
Membership: Yes
Other: Snack Bar / Bar-Lounge

Tees	Holes	Yards	Par	USGA	Slope
BACK					
MIDDLE	9	3023	35	69.2	126
FRONT	9	2872	35	68.3	124

Weekend: $23
Weekend: $31
Discounts: Senior M-F, 7am-1pm
Driving Range: No
Junior Golf: No
Architect/Yr Open: Geoffrey Cornish/1963
GPS:

Player Comments: "The course has tight fairways and fast greens." Open March - December. South County course.

	1	2	3	4	5	6	7	8	9
PAR	4	5	3	5	3	4	4	3	4
YARDS	360	413	198	505	152	330	297	203	414
PAR									
YARDS									

Directions: I-95 to Route 4 South. Take left at 2nd light onto Stony Lane. At 1st intersection take left onto Old Baptist Road. Course is 1/8 mile on left.

NEW ENGLAND GOLFGUIDE®
2009

THE PERFECT GIFT!

For your boss, your employees, your husband, your wife, your kids, your best friend, your father, mother, father-in-law, mother-in-law, your brother, brother-in-law, sister, sister-in-law, your significant other, and for **ANY GOLFER ON YOUR GIFT LIST!**

And you can get **20% OFF**
See the New England GolfGuide coupon on page 434.

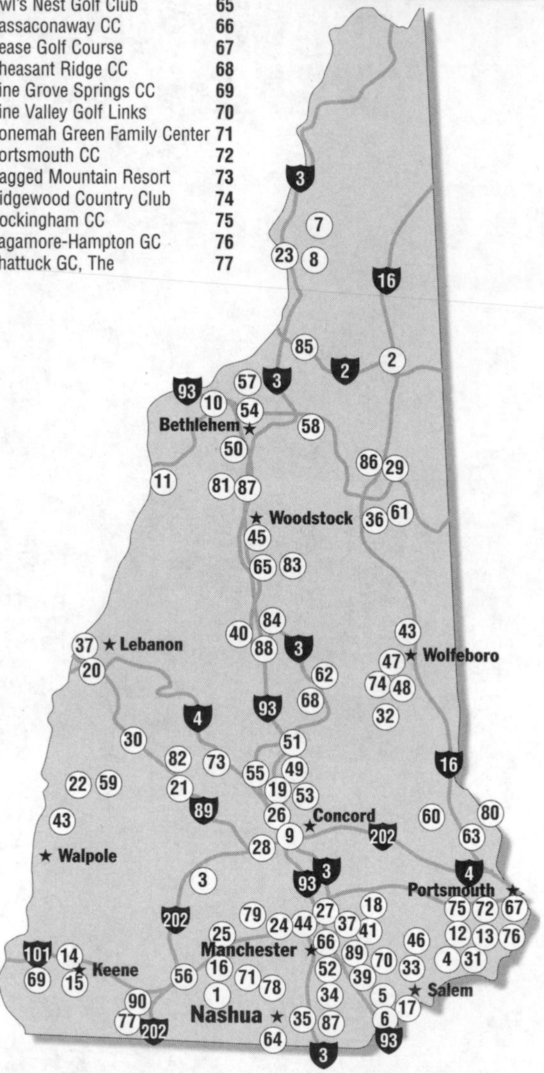

KEY TO THE STAR AND VALUE RATINGS:
5◉= Outstanding 4◉= Excellent 3◉= Very Good 2◉= Good 1◉= Average **NR** = Not Rated
EV = Excellent Value **GV** = Good Value **V** = Value

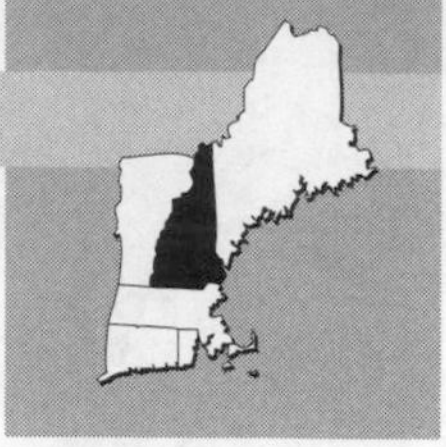

Amherst Country Club ✪✪ ▶ 1

72 Ponemah Road
Amherst, NH (603) 673-9908
www.amherstcountryclub.com

Tees	Holes	Yards	Par	USGA	Slope
BACK	18	6543	72	70.7	123
MIDDLE	18	6036	72	68.4	117
FRONT	18	5615	74	71.7	118

Club Pro:
Payment: Visa, MC, Cash, Check
Tee Times: 5 day adv.
Fee 9 Holes: Weekday: $23   **Weekend:** $25
Fee 18 Holes: Weekday: $36   **Weekend:** $48
Twilight Rates: After 6pm   **Discounts:** Senior & Junior
Cart Rental: $15pp/18   **Driving Range:** Yes
Lessons: Yes **Schools:** No   **Junior Golf:** Yes
Membership: Yes   **Architect/Yr Open:** William Mitchell/1965
Other: Lounge / Cafe / Outings / Functions   **GPS:**

Updated course layout. Player Comments: "Relatively flat, open course with few bunkers but interesting to all levels of play." –GG

	1	2	3	4	5	6	7	8	9
PAR	4	5	3	5	4	4	3	4	4
YARDS	300	475	188	460	370	338	183	412	373
	10	11	12	13	14	15	16	17	18
PAR	4	4	4	3	5	3	5	4	4
YARDS	350	260	344	135	455	135	508	391	359

Directions: Route 3 North to Exit 8. Follow to Route 101A North. Go 8 miles to Route 122 North. Take a right and go 1/4 mile.

Androscoggin Valley CC ✪✪½ ▶ 2

2 Main Street (Route 2)
Gorham, NH (603) 466-9468
www.avccgolf.com

Tees	Holes	Yards	Par	USGA	Slope
BACK	18	6110	70	67.9	118
MIDDLE	18	5715	70	66.5	115
FRONT	18	5131	70	71.0	122

Club Pro: Gary A. Riff
Payment: Visa, MC, Amex, Disc
Tee Times: 1 day adv.
Fee 9 Holes: Weekday: $20   **Weekend:** $25
Fee 18 Holes: Weekday: $30   **Weekend:** $35
Twilight Rates: After 1pm   **Discounts:** Junior
Cart Rental: $40/18, $20/9 per cart   **Driving Range:** $5/lg, $3/sm
Lessons: $50/hour **Schools:**   **Junior Golf:** Yes
Membership:
Architect/Yr Open: Alex Chisolm & Horace Smith/2004
Other: Clubhouse / Snack Bar / Bar-Lounge / Lockers / Showers

COUPON

Scenic, open layout with good greens makes this a joy to play and score on. Some holes border the Androscoggin River. Open May 1 - October 31.

	1	2	3	4	5	6	7	8	9
PAR	5	4	3	5	4	3	3	4	5
YARDS	475	375	165	475	310	190	170	325	520
	10	11	12	13	14	15	16	17	18
PAR	4	4	4	3	5	3	4	3	4
YARDS	375	370	350	145	480	155	290	195	350

Directions: I-93 to Route 3 through Twin Mountain to Route 115 East to Route 2. Take Route 2 to Gorham. At light, take a right through town. Cross bridge, club is on left.

Angus Lea Golf Course

NR 3

126 West Main Street
Hillsboro, NH (603) 464-5404
www.anguslea.com

Club Pro: Curtis R. Niven, PGA
Payment: Visa, MC
Tee Times: Weekends/Holidays

Tees	Holes	Yards	Par	USGA	Slope
BACK					
MIDDLE	9	2319	33	60.0	94
FRONT	9	2097	33	65.6	101

Fee 9 Holes: Weekday: $18   **Weekend:** $18
Fee 18 Holes: Weekday: $32   **Weekend:** $32
Twilight Rates: No
Discounts: M-Th 11-2pm $15, Student (college w/ID or younger) $14
Cart Rental: $28/18, $16/9 per cart   **Driving Range:** No
Lessons: $35/hour **Schools:** No   **Junior Golf:** Yes
Membership: Yes   **Architect/Yr Open:** Ed Bedell/1964
Other: Snack Bar / Bar-Lounge / Tennis Courts   **GPS:**

Bordered by the Contoocook River, the course plays around water and through the woods. Beautiful view from large screened porch.

	1	2	3	4	5	6	7	8	9
PAR	4	3	3	4	4	4	4	3	4
YARDS	283	150	160	300	310	435	245	161	275
PAR									
YARDS									

Directions: I-89 to Exit #5. Located on Main Street (Route 202/9) in Hillsboro. 1/2 mile on left after traffic light in downtown.

Apple Hill Golf Club

NR 4

69 East Road (Route 107)
E. Kingston, NH (603) 642-4414
www.applehillgolf.com

Club Pro: Steve Lundquist, PGA
Payment: Visa, MC, Checks
Tee Times: 1 week adv.

Tees	Holes	Yards	Par	USGA	Slope
BACK	18	6311	70	70.4	134
MIDDLE	18	6003	70	69.1	131
FRONT	18	5006	70	69..8	122

Fee 9 Holes: Weekday: $18   **Weekend:** $20
Fee 18 Holes: Weekday: $30   **Weekend:** $35
Twilight Rates: No   **Discounts:** Senior & Junior
Cart Rental: $17pp/18, $9pp/9   **Driving Range:** No
Lessons: Yes **Schools:** No   **Junior Golf:** Yes
Membership: Yes   **Architect/Yr Open:**
Other: Clubhouse / Snack Bar / Bar-Lounge   **GPS:**

COUPON

Now 27 holes, including Apple Hill 9-hole par 3 course, 715 yards. (Rates $10 every day.) Both courses are well maintained.

	1	2	3	4	5	6	7	8	9
PAR	4	3	4	3	5	4	4	4	4
YARDS	365	145	377	165	479	415	368	358	357
	10	11	12	13	14	15	16	17	18
PAR	5	4	4	4	3	4	4	3	4
YARDS	458	374	363	414	169	294	356	136	410

Directions: I-95 to Exit 1 in New Hampshire (Route 107). The course is 6 miles on right. From Route 125 Kingston, take Route 107 South, 3 1/2 miles.

Applewood Golf Links

5

55 Range Road
Windham, NH (603) 898-6793
www.heavyhittersgolf.com

Club Pro: Ray Kelm, PGA
Payment: Cash, MC, Visa
Tee Times: No
Fee 9 Holes: Weekday: $14
Fee 18 Holes: Weekday: $24
Twilight Rates: No
Cart Rental: $20pp/18, $10pp/9
Lessons: $45/half hour **Schools:** Jr. & Sr.
Membership: Jr. & Sr.
Other:

Tees	Holes	Yards	Par	USGA	Slope
BACK	9	1867	27	56.0	82
MIDDLE	9	1367	27	56.0	82
FRONT					

Weekend: $14
Weekend: $24
Discounts: Sr. & Jr. weekdays only
Driving Range: $10/lg bucket
Junior Golf: Yes
Architect/Yr Open: Peter Chulack/1992
GPS:

COUPON

Player Comments: "An impeccably maintained par 3 that's pure fun to play." Noted improvement: driving range has heated bays for winter usage. Attention given to senior and women golfers.

	1	2	3	4	5	6	7	8	9
PAR	3	3	3	3	3	3	3	3	3
YARDS	179	150	136	170	123	129	158	147	175
PAR									
YARDS									

Directions: I-93 to Exit 3 in NH. Right at end of ramp onto Route 111 East. First light, go left. First right is huge parking lot.

NH

Atkinson Resort and CC

⊛⊛⊛⊛

6

85 Country Club Drive
Atkinson, NH (603) 362-8700
www.atkinsonresort.com

Club Pro: Peter Doherty, PGA
Payment: Visa, MC, Amex, Checks
Tee Times: 5 days adv.
Fee 9 Holes: Weekday: $28
Fee 18 Holes: Weekday: $52
Twilight Rates: After 5:30pm
Cart Rental: $18pp/18, $10pp/9
Lessons: Yes **Schools:** Yes
Membership: Yes
Other: Snack Bar / New Clubhouse / Restaurant / Function Facility / 16 Guest Rooms
GPS: Yes

Tees	Holes	Yards	Par	USGA	Slope
BACK	18	6580	72	73.1	135
MIDDLE	18	6088	72	70.3	131
FRONT	18	4867	72	68.6	117

Weekend: $33
Weekend: $62
Discounts: Senior & Junior
Driving Range: Yes
Junior Golf: Yes
Architect/Yr Open: Lewis Builders/1996

COUPON

Player Comments: "A demanding, difficult, but fair course." Upscale public golf resort. GPS system on carts. Spectacular views. Changed holes 15 & 16 to make more user-friendly.

	1	2	3	4	5	6	7	8	9
PAR	4	5	3	4	4	5	4	3	4
YARDS	310	485	180	350	400	481	366	185	380
	10	11	12	13	14	15	16	17	18
PAR	4	3	5	4	3	4	5	4	4
YARDS	346	144	477	317	127	370	466	370	334

Directions: I-95 to Exit 50 (Route 97). Left off exit, follow 4 miles, take right onto Hampstead Road. 2.0 miles on right.

Balsams Panorama Golf Club ✪✪✪½

1000 Cold Spring Road
Dixville Notch, NH (603) 255-4961
www.thebalsams.com

Club Pro: Douglas A. Ruttle, PGA
Payment: Visa, MC, Amex, Disc
Tee Times:
Fee 9 Holes: Weekday:
Fee 18 Holes: Weekday: $70
Twilight Rates: After 2pm
Cart Rental: $19 per cart
Lessons: $85/hour **Schools:** Yes
Membership: Yes

Tees	Holes	Yards	Par	USGA	Slope
BACK	18	6804	72	72.8	130
MIDDLE	18	6097	72	69.1	122
FRONT	18	5069	72	67.8	115

Weekend:
Weekend: $70
Discounts: None
Driving Range: $5/lg.
Junior Golf: No
Architect/Yr Open: Donald Ross/1912

COUPON

Other: Clubhouse / Restaurant / Bar-Lounge / Resort Hotel

Player Comments: "Great view. Friendly staff. Always interesting." Donald Ross design. Built in 1912. Dine at Panorama Grill.

	1	2	3	4	5	6	7	8	9
PAR	4	5	4	4	3	5	3	4	4
YARDS	366	457	376	363	175	463	157	346	316
	10	11	12	13	14	15	16	17	18
PAR	4	4	4	4	3	5	3	4	5
YARDS	320	302	323	423	191	501	173	365	480

Directions: 1) Take I-93 North to Exit 35, Route 3 North to Colebrook, east on Route 26 for 10 miles, or 2) Take I-91 to exit at St. Johnsbury, Route 2. Go East on Route 2 to Lancaster. Take Route 3 North to Colebrook, and East on Route 26 for 10 miles.

Balsams-Coashaukee Golf Course ✪✪

1000 Cold Spring Road
Dixville Notch, NH (603) 255-4961
www.thebalsams.com

Club Pro: Douglas A. Ruttle
Payment: MC, Visa, Disc, Amex
Tee Times: None required
Fee 9 Holes: Weekday:
Fee 18 Holes: Weekday: $25
Twilight Rates: No
Cart Rental: $25pp/18, $17pp/9
Lessons: Yes **Schools:** Sr.
Membership: Yes
Other:

Tees	Holes	Yards	Par	USGA	Slope
BACK					
MIDDLE	9	1917	32	59.1	87
FRONT					

Weekend:
Weekend: $25
Discounts: None
Driving Range: No
Junior Golf: No
Architect/Yr Open: James Smith/1965
GPS:

COUPON

A 9-hole executive layout adjacent to the Balsams Resort Hotel. New pro-PGA director, Douglas A. Ruttle. Dine at Panorama Grill.

	1	2	3	4	5	6	7	8	9
PAR	4	3	3	4	4	4	3	4	3
YARDS	304	147	174	223	265	236	145	313	110
PAR									
YARDS									

Directions: 1) Take I-93 North to Exit 35, Route 3 North to Colebrook, East on Route 26 for 10 miles, or 2) Take I-91 to exit at St. Johnsbury, Route 2. Go East on Route 2 to Lancaster. Take Route 3 North to Colebrook, and East on Route 26 for 10 miles.

Beaver Meadow Golf Club ✪✪½ 🚩9

1 Beaver Meadow Drive
Concord, NH (603) 228-8954
beavermeadowgolfcourse.com

Club Pro: E. Deshaies
Payment: Visa, MC
Tee Times: Weekends, 2 days adv.
Fee 9 Holes: Weekday: $25
Fee 18 Holes: Weekday: $40
Twilight Rates: After 3pm
Cart Rental: $16pp/18, $8pp/9
Lessons: $50/45 minutes **Schools:** No
Membership: Yes
Other: Clubhouse / Snack Bar / Bar-Lounge

Tees	Holes	Yards	Par	USGA	Slope
BACK	18	6356	72	70.8	127
MIDDLE	18	6034	72	69.2	121
FRONT	18	6519	72	71.8	123

Weekend: $25
Weekend: $40
Discounts: Srs. on annual basis
Driving Range: Yes
Junior Golf: City Rec. Dept.
Architect/Yr Open: Willie Campbell/1896
GPS:

COUPON

Newly renovated practice facility with grass tee. Host site 2009 USI Championship. An official event on the Duramed Futures Tour, road to the LPGA.

	1	2	3	4	5	6	7	8	9
PAR	4	5	3	5	4	3	4	4	4
YARDS	341	480	153	474	336	138	366	414	315
	10	11	12	13	14	15	16	17	18
PAR	5	4	4	3	4	4	5	3	4
YARDS	527	320	301	130	347	400	560	156	276

Directions: I-93 to Exit 15 West (North Main Street). At second light, take right onto Route 3 North. Course is 3.1 miles on right.

Bethlehem Country Club NR 🚩10

1901 Main Street
Bethlehem, NH (603) 869-5745
www.bethlehemccnhgolf.com

Club Pro:
Payment: Visa, MC, Cash
Tee Times: Required
Fee 9 Holes: Weekday: $17 (12 holes)
Fee 18 Holes: Weekday: $25
Twilight Rates: After 4pm
Cart Rental: $14pp/18, $10pp/12
Lessons: $35/half hour **Schools:** No
Membership: Yes
Other: Restaurant/ Snack Bar / Retail

Tees	Holes	Yards	Par	USGA	Slope
BACK	18	5808	70	67.9	110
MIDDLE	18	5586	70	66.6	110
FRONT	18	5008	70	63.0	98

Weekend: $22 (12 holes)
Weekend: $30
Discounts: Junior
Driving Range: No
Junior Golf: Yes
Architect/Yr: W. Lilywhite/1898; D. Ross/1910
GPS:

COUPON

Player Comments: "Generous fairways and light rough will have you blasting your driver on all long holes. Accuracy is required on the 4 par 3 holes." –AP

	1	2	3	4	5	6	7	8	9
PAR	4	4	3	4	4	4	3	4	4
YARDS	413	319	210	264	402	399	157	328	288
	10	11	12	13	14	15	16	17	18
PAR	3	5	3	4	4	5	4	4	4
YARDS	95	487	153	417	260	501	270	296	360

Directions: I-93 to Exit 40 East. 2.5 miles on Route 302 East.

NH

Blackmount Country Club ✪✪ ▶11

400 Clark Pond Road
North Haverhill, NH (603) 787-6564
www.blackmountcountryclub.com

Club Pro: Bill Grimes
Payment: Cash or Check
Tee Times: No
Fee 9 Holes: Weekday: $12
Fee 18 Holes: Weekday: $20
Twilight Rates: No
Cart Rental: $24/18, $15/9 per cart
Lessons: Yes **Schools:** No
Membership: Yes
Other: Clubhouse / Snack Bar / Gazebo / Beer & Wine

Tees	Holes	Yards	Par	USGA	Slope
BACK	9	3015	36	34.8	114
MIDDLE	9	2658	36	33.3	110
FRONT	9	2316	36	35.7	121

Weekend: $16
Weekend: $24
Discounts: Senior, Junior, Ladies
Driving Range: Yes
Junior Golf: No
Architect/Yr Open: Robert Stoddard

COUPON

Outstanding greens. Beautiful course. Play & Stay package with the Hayloft Inn B&B adjacent to 1st hole.

	1	2	3	4	5	6	7	8	9
PAR	3	5	4	5	4	4	4	3	4
YARDS	150	400	333	383	217	317	350	142	366
PAR									
YARDS									

Directions: I-91 to Bradford, VT. Exit to NH Route 10 to village of North Haverhill, NH. Turn onto Clark Pond Road, across from Aldrich's General Store. Bear right for 1.5 miles.

Bramber Valley Golf Course ✪✪ ▶12

75 Bramber Valley Drive
Greenland, NH 03840
(603) 436-4288
www.BramberValleygolf.com

Club Pro: Scott Marceau
Payment: Cash, Check, Credit Cards
Tee Times: No
Fee 9 Holes: Weekday: $20
Fee 18 Holes: Weekday: $32
Twilight Rates: Fall only, after 2pm
Cart Rental: $24pp/18, $14pp/9
Lessons: Yes **Schools:** Jr.
Membership: No
Other: Clubhouse / Bar-Lounge

Tees	Holes	Yards	Par	USGA	Slope
BACK					
MIDDLE	9	2114	32	61.4	103
FRONT					

Weekend: $20
Weekend: $32
Discounts: Senior & Junior
Driving Range: $8/lg., $4/sm.
Junior Golf: Yes
Architect/Yr Open: James Petropolus/1994
GPS:

COUPON

Great playing surfaces, friendly staff, wonderful practice facility, and low prices. Improvements ongoing. Full-service restaurant and bar. Beaches nearby.

	1	2	3	4	5	6	7	8	9
PAR	3	4	3	4	3	4	4	3	4
YARDS	133	333	107	312	160	260	315	180	314
PAR									
YARDS									

Directions: I-95 to Exit 3A. Go West on Route 33 for about 3 miles. Blue sign for club is after Golf & Ski Warehouse.

Breakfast Hill Golf Club ✪✪✪½ 13 ▶

399 Breakfast Hill Road
Greenland, NH (603) 436-5001
www.breakfasthill.com

Club Pro: Nathan Bridges
Payment: Visa, MC, Disc
Tee Times: 5 days adv.

Tees	Holes	Yards	Par	USGA	Slope
BACK	18	6493	71	70.8	134
MIDDLE	18	5981	71	68.7	124
FRONT	18	4994	72	64.7	108

Fee 9 Holes: Weekday: $30 M-F   **Weekend:** $30 after 2pm
Fee 18 Holes: Weekday: $47 M-Th, $50 F   **Weekend:** $57
Twilight Rates: After 5pm   **Discounts:** None
Cart Rental: $15pp/18, $10pp/9   **Driving Range:** Yes
Lessons: Yes **Schools:** Yes   **Junior Golf:** Yes
Membership: Yes, Season Pass   **Architect/Yr Open:** Brian Silva/2000
Other: Restaurant / Clubhouse / Bar-Lounge   **GPS:**

COUPON

18 unique holes with rolling fairways and contoured greens. Brian Silva design. New clubhouse open. Rated Top Five in state by *Golf Week*.

	1	2	3	4	5	6	7	8	9
PAR	4	5	4	3	5	3	4	4	4
YARDS	350	465	365	149	489	124	364	332	350
	10	11	12	13	14	15	16	17	18
PAR	4	4	5	4	3	4	4	3	4
YARDS	309	460	526	296	165	322	378	143	394

Directions: I-95 to Exit 3 (Greenland/Portsmouth). Left onto Route 33. Left onto Route 151 South for 1.4 miles. Go left onto Breakfast Hill Road. Course is 1 mile on left.

Bretwood Golf Course (North) ✪✪✪½ 14 ▶

635 East Surry Road
Keene, NH (603) 352-7626
www.bretwoodgolf.com

Club Pro: Matt Barrett, PGA
Payment: Visa, MC, Disc
Tee Times: Weekends, 3 days adv.

Tees	Holes	Yards	Par	USGA	Slope
BACK	18	6974	72	73.7	136
MIDDLE	18	6434	72	71.5	131
FRONT	18	5822	72	68.9	125

Fee 9 Holes: Weekday: $20   **Weekend:** $24
Fee 18 Holes: Weekday: $35   **Weekend:** $42
Twilight Rates: No   **Discounts:** None
Cart Rental: $13pp/18, $8pp/9   **Driving Range:** $6/lg., $5/med., $4/sm.
Lessons: To be arranged **Schools:** No   **Junior Golf:** Yes
Membership: Yes   **Architect/Yr Open:** Hugh Barrett/1968
Other: Clubhouse / Snack Bar   **GPS:**

Player Comments: "Gets better every year. Favorite hole # 13 island green." "Scenic. Great layouts." "Excellent fairways and greens. River meanders through course and comes into play often. Covered bridges, great value." –GG

	1	2	3	4	5	6	7	8	9
PAR	4	5	3	4	5	4	5	3	4
YARDS	413	552	187	340	505	390	480	138	400
	10	11	12	13	14	15	16	17	18
PAR	4	4	4	3	4	4	3	5	4
YARDS	400	340	372	130	380	379	154	501	373

Directions: I-91 North to Route 9 East to Keene. Follow hospital signs to Court Street. East Surry Road is off Upper Court Sreet. 1.5 miles to course.

NH

Bretwood Golf Course (South) ✪✪✪ 15 ▶

635 East Surry Road
Keene, NH (603) 352-7626
www.bretwoodgolf.com
Club Pro: Matt Barrett, PGA
Payment: Visa, MC, Disc
Tee Times: Weekends, 3 days adv.
Fee 9 Holes: Weekday: $20
Fee 18 Holes: Weekday: $35
Twilight Rates: No
Cart Rental: $13pp/18, $8pp/9
Lessons: Yes **Schools:** No
Membership: Yes
Other: Clubhouse / Snack Bar

Tees	Holes	Yards	Par	USGA	Slope
BACK	18	6952	72	73.2	133
MIDDLE	18	6345	72	70.7	124
FRONT	18	5645	70	68.0	119

Weekend: $24
Weekend: $42
Discounts: None
Driving Range: $8/lg., $6/med., $4/sm. bucket
Junior Golf: Yes
Architect/Yr: Geoffrey Cornish, Hugh Barrett/1968
GPS: Yes

Parkland course in excellent condition. Newer than the North course, but maturing nicely. Wider and straighter than the North, but challenging nonetheless.

	1	2	3	4	5	6	7	8	9
PAR	5	5	3	4	4	4	3	4	4
YARDS	477	530	168	364	288	305	181	394	383
	10	11	12	13	14	15	16	17	18
PAR	5	4	3	5	4	4	3	4	4
YARDS	472	372	133	536	371	340	176	410	445

Directions: I-91 North to Route 9 East to Keene. Follow hospital signs to Court Street. East Surry Road is off Upper Court Sreet. 1.5 miles to course.

Buckmeadow Golf Club NR 16 ▶

30 Route 101A
Amherst, NH
(603) 673-7077
Club Pro:
Payment: Cash, Check
Tee Times: Public/ Members
Fee 9 Holes: Weekday: $14
Fee 18 Holes: Weekday: $26
Twilight Rates: No
Cart Rental: $14pp/18, $7pp/9
Lessons: Yes **Schools:** No
Membership: Limited/100 max.
Other: Bar-Lounge / Snack Bar

Tees	Holes	Yards	Par	USGA	Slope
BACK	9	2425	33	61.8	101
MIDDLE	9	2340	33	60.9	100
FRONT	9	2280	34	66.2	103

Weekend: $16
Weekend: $28
Discounts: Senior & Junior
Driving Range: No
Junior Golf: No
Architect/Yr Open: M.E. Young/1979
GPS:

"Six dogleg par 4s and 3 interesting 1-shot holes make for a challenging round on this nicely maintained venue." –AP

	1	2	3	4	5	6	7	8	9
PAR	4	3	4	4	4	3	4	3	4
YARDS	320	120	190	335	345	175	330	185	340
PAR									
YARDS									

Directions: Route 3 to Route 101A West. Course is 1.5 miles off Route 101 outside of Milford.

Campbell's Scottish Highlands ✪✪✪½   ▶ 17

79 Brady Avenue
Salem, NH (603) 894-4653
www.scottishhighlandsgolf.com

Tees	Holes	Yards	Par	USGA	Slope
BACK	18	6249	71	69.3	124
MIDDLE	18	5746	71	67.6	116
FRONT	18	5056	71	68.9	116

Club Pro: Geoff Williams
Payment: Visa, MC, Disc
Tee Times: 5 days adv.
Fee 9 Holes: Weekday: $22   **Weekend:** $27
Fee 18 Holes: Weekday: $39   **Weekend:** $49
Twilight Rates: Yes   **Discounts:** Senior & Junior
Cart Rental: $15pp/18, $10pp/9   **Driving Range:** Yes
Lessons: $50/half hour **Schools:**   **Junior Golf:** Yes
Membership: No   **Architect/Yr:** MHF Design & G. Sargent/1994
Other: Clubhouse / Bar-Lounge / Lockers / Shower / Snack Bar

COUPON

NGCOA - Beginner-friendly certified. Noted for friendly staff, well-maintained turf. Open, rolling fairways and 'true rolling' velvet greens, some of them very large. Links-style course with well-placed hazards.

	1	2	3	4	5	6	7	8	9
PAR	4	5	3	4	5	4	3	4	4
YARDS	341	454	185	418	482	358	167	260	352
	10	**11**	**12**	**13**	**14**	**15**	**16**	**17**	**18**
PAR	4	3	4	4	4	3	4	4	5
YARDS	295	162	330	322	395	125	303	305	492

Directions: I-93 to Exit 2. Bear right off ramp. Right onto South Policy Street. Next light, right onto Route 38. Straight through next set of lights, left on to Brady Avenue for .5 miles.

Candia Woods ✪   ▶ 18

313 South Road
Candia, NH (603) 483-2307
www.candiawoods.com

Tees	Holes	Yards	Par	USGA	Slope
BACK	18	6540	71	70.9	118
MIDDLE	18	6317	71	69.8	117
FRONT	18	5367	71	69.8	116

Club Pro: Ted Bishop, PGA
Payment: Visa, MC, Disc, Amex
Tee Times: 5 days adv.
Fee 9 Holes: Weekday: $30   **Weekend:** $35
Fee 18 Holes: Weekday: $50   **Weekend:** $60
Twilight Rates: After 6pm, $20   **Discounts:** Senior & Junior
Cart Rental: $16pp/18, $9pp/9   **Driving Range:** $5/sm., $8/lg. bucket
Lessons: $50/half hour **Schools:** No   **Junior Golf:** Yes
Membership: Yes   **Architect/Yr Open:** Phil Wogan/1964
Other: Restaurant / Bar-Lounge / Lockers / Showers / Snack Bar / Pavilion / Outings

10 minutes from Manchester Airport and Mall of NH. Multiple tees allow for all skill levels, user-friendly layout. Private club conditions and service.

	1	2	3	4	5	6	7	8	9
PAR	4	4	4	4	3	4	4	3	5
YARDS	409	359	355	389	183	357	382	195	521
	10	**11**	**12**	**13**	**14**	**15**	**16**	**17**	**18**
PAR	5	4	4	4	4	3	5	3	4
YARDS	464	443	394	309	308	158	540	146	405

Directions: I-93, Exit 7 to Route 101 East. Take Exit 3. Straight at stop sign, right at next stop sign. Club is 1/8 mile on left at top of hill.

NH

Canterbury Woods Country Club ✪✪✪

15 West Road
Canterbury, NH (603) 783-9400
www.canterburywoodscc.com

Tees	Holes	Yards	Par	USGA	Slope
BACK	18	6650	72	71.7	136
MIDDLE	18	6134	72	69.2	130
FRONT	18	5535	72	66.1	118

Club Pro: Laura Shanahan-Rowe
Payment: Visa, MC
Tee Times: 5 days adv.
Fee 9 Holes: Weekday: $20 walk, $30 ride after 12pm
　　　　　　　Weekend: $25 walk, $35 ride after 12pm
Fee 18 Holes: Weekday: $35 walk, $50 ride **Weekend:** $42 walk, $58 ride
Twilight Rates: Yes　　　　　　　**Discounts:** Senior & Junior
Cart Rental: $15pp/18, $10pp/9　　**Driving Range:** Yes
Lessons: Yes **Schools:** Yes　　　**Junior Golf:** Clinics
Membership: Yes　　　　　　　　　**Architect/Yr Open:** Ross Forbes/2003
Other: Restaurant / Clubhouse/ Snack Bar / Bar-Lounge

COUPON

Site of the 2006 NH State Amateur Championshop. Bent grass greens, tees, and fairways. Outstanding playing conditions. New tee box #7 and drainage in fairways.

	1	2	3	4	5	6	7	8	9
PAR	4	5	4	5	4	3	4	3	4
YARDS	394	488	364	518	264	128	353	208	347
	10	11	12	13	14	15	16	17	18
PAR	5	3	4	3	4	5	5	3	4
YARDS	456	180	381	176	340	516	474	138	409

Directions: I-93 to Exit 18. Turn left on to West Road. Continue left at fork 1/2 mile from exit ramp. Course entrance is on the left just beyond Sloping Acres Farm (approximately 1/2 mile) from fork.

Carter Country Club

257 Mechanic Street
Lebanon, NH
(603) 448-4483

Tees	Holes	Yards	Par	USGA	Slope
BACK	9	2800	36	68.1	116
MIDDLE	9	2760	36	66.1	114
FRONT	9	2565	36	71.7	127

Club Pro: Rich Parker, PGA
Payment: Most Major
Tee Times: No
Fee 9 Holes: Weekday: $15　　　**Weekend:** $15
Fee 18 Holes: Weekday: $24　　　**Weekend:** $24
Twilight Rates: No　　　　　　　**Discounts:** None
Cart Rental: $13pp/18, $7pp/9　　**Driving Range:** No
Lessons: Yes **Schools:** No　　　**Junior Golf:** Yes
Membership: Yes　　　　　　　　**Architect/Yr Open:** Donald Ross/1923
Other: Restaurant / Clubhouse / Bar-Lounge　**GPS:**

Semi-hilly course, very scenic, especially nice in the Fall, small greens, very sloped. Men's League on Thursday. Open April - November. New drainage makes the course much drier.

	1	2	3	4	5	6	7	8	9
PAR	4	3	5	4	4	5	4	4	3
YARDS	350	155	470	365	280	480	265	285	110
PAR									
YARDS									

Directions: Just a short pitch off I-89, Exit 19.

Claremont Country Club

NR 21

Maple Avenue
Claremont, NH (603) 542-9550

Tees	Holes	Yards	Par	USGA	Slope
BACK					
MIDDLE	9	2647	34	64.7	104
FRONT	9	2415	34		

Club Pro:
Payment: Cash or Check
Tee Times: No
Fee 9 Holes: Weekday: $16 **Weekend:** $18
Fee 18 Holes: Weekday: $25 **Weekend:** $28
Twilight Rates: No **Discounts:** None
Cart Rental: $25pp/18, $15pp/9 **Driving Range:** Yes
Lessons: **Schools:** No **Junior Golf:** Yes
Membership: Yes **Architect/Yr Open:** 1917
Other: Clubhouse / Bar-Lounge / Snack Bar / Lockers / Showers

Old-style course. Small greens. Hilly, with woods.

	1	2	3	4	5	6	7	8	9
PAR	4	4	4	4	4	3	4	3	4
YARDS	420	328	273	262	275	174	434	169	312
PAR									
YARDS									

Directions: I-91 to Claremont exit. Follow signs to downtown Claremont. Take Pleasant Street to Maple Avenue. Right onto Maple. Course is 1/2 mile down.

Colebrook Country Club

NR 22

15 Abenaki Lane
Colebrook, NH (603) 237-5566
www.colebrookcountryclub.com

Tees	Holes	Yards	Par	USGA	Slope
BACK					
MIDDLE	9	2891	36	67.5	114
FRONT	9	2184	37	72.3	114

Club Pro: No
Payment: Visa, MC, Amex, Disc
Tee Times: No
Fee 9 Holes: Weekday: $18 **Weekend:** $22
Fee 18 Holes: Weekday: $18 **Weekend:** $22
Twilight Rates: After 5pm **Discounts:** Senior, Junior, Women
Cart Rental: $25pp/18, $20pp/9 **Driving Range:** No
Lessons: No **Schools:** **Junior Golf:** Yes
Membership: Yes **Architect/Yr Open:** 1927
Other: Restaurant / Bar-Lounge / Motel **GPS:**

COUPON

Beautifully maintained. Hole #5 is 612 yards. Discounts after 5pm daily and on Mondays and Wednesdays. 9 holes with 2 sets of tees. Hole #7 has been rebuilt in June 2007.

	1	2	3	4	5	6	7	8	9
PAR	4	4	3	4	6	3	5	3	4
YARDS	345	328	191	289	612	186	518	122	300
PAR									
YARDS									

Directions: From I-93 or I-91, take Route 3 North from Littleton, NH. When in Colebrook, take right onto Route 26 East about 1/2 mile. Club is on left.

NH

Country Club of New Hampshire ✪✪½ 23 ▶

Kearsarge Road
North Sutton, NH (603) 927-4246
www.playgolfne.com

Club Pro: Kevin Gibson
Payment: Visa, MC, Amex, Disc
Tee Times: 1 week adv.

Tees	Holes	Yards	Par	USGA	Slope
BACK	18	6743	72	72.5	134
MIDDLE	18	6256	72	70.3	126
FRONT	18	5416	72	71.7	127

Fee 9 Holes: Weekday: $18   **Weekend:** $25
Fee 18 Holes: Weekday: $35   **Weekend:** $43
Twilight Rates: After 2pm   **Discounts:** None
Cart Rental: $30pp/18, $18pp/9   **Driving Range:** $12/lg., $6/sm.
Lessons: $40/half hour **Schools:** No   **Junior Golf:** No
Membership: Yes   **Architect/Yr Open:** Stiles & Van Kleek/1930
Other: Clubhouse / Showers / Snack Bar / Restaurant / Bar-Lounge / Hotel

COUPON

The front 9 is level, the back is hilly. Home of the N.E. Senior Open. Golf Management LLC Company.

	1	2	3	4	5	6	7	8	9
PAR	4	3	5	4	4	3	4	5	4
YARDS	380	160	495	330	346	169	376	452	380
	10	11	12	13	14	15	16	17	18
PAR	4	3	4	5	4	3	4	4	5
YARDS	410	124	351	471	366	169	412	400	465

Directions: One mile off I-89 at Exit 10. Follow signs to Winslow State Park.

Countryside Golf Club   NR 24 ▶

20 Country Club Drive (Route 13)
Dunbarton, NH (603) 774-5031
www.countrysidegolfnh.com

Club Pro:
Payment: Visa, MC, Disc
Tee Times: Weekends only

Tees	Holes	Yards	Par	USGA	Slope
BACK	9	3157	36	69.3	128
MIDDLE	9	3001	36	69.2	126
FRONT	9	2758	36	71.5	126

Fee 9 Holes: Weekday: $15   **Weekend:** $18
Fee 18 Holes: Weekday: $25   **Weekend:** $28
Twilight Rates: After 3pm wknds, 2pm wkdys **Discounts:** Senior & Junior on weekends
Cart Rental: $25/18, $15/9 per cart   **Driving Range:** Yes
Lessons: Yes **Schools:** No   **Junior Golf:** No
Membership: Yes   **Architect/Yr Open:** Bill Mitchell/1964
Other: Clubhouse / Snack Bar / Bar-Lounge / Function Room / Deck

New paved cart paths and new irrigation. Scenic views and friendly staff under new management.

	1	2	3	4	5	6	7	8	9
PAR	4	4	3	5	4	4	4	3	5
YARDS	305	369	138	485	386	365	344	143	466
PAR									
YARDS									

Directions: Route 101 to Route 114 toward Goffstown. Take Route 13 North at Sully's Superette. 4 miles. Club on left.

Crotched Mountain Golf Club ✪✪ ▶25

740 2nd NH Turnpike North (Rt. 47)
Francestown, NH (603) 588-2923
www.shellvacationsclub.com

Club Pro: Ken Hamel, PGA
Payment: Visa, MC, Amex
Tee Times: 7 days adv.

Tees	Holes	Yards	Par	USGA	Slope
BACK	18	6111	71	69.2	125
MIDDLE	18	5530	71	66.7	118
FRONT	18	4604	71	67.4	117

Fee 9 Holes: Weekday: $22
Fee 18 Holes: Weekday: $34
Twilight Rates: After 3pm
Cart Rental: $15pp/18, $10pp/9
Lessons: Yes **Schools:** Yes
Membership: Yes
Other: Restaurant / Clubhouse / Bar-Lounge / Snack Bar

Weekend: $28
Weekend: $45
Discounts: Senior & Junior M-Th
Driving Range: $8/lg., $5/sm.
Junior Golf: Yes
Architect/Yr Open: Donald Ross/1929

COUPON

Beautiful mountain views, spectacular greens, and first-rate hospitality. A 1929 Donald Ross original. Owned by Shell Vacation Club. Renovations start 2009.

	1	2	3	4	5	6	7	8	9
PAR	4	4	3	5	4	3	5	4	4
YARDS	338	310	145	479	339	184	416	333	374
	10	11	12	13	14	15	16	17	18
PAR	4	4	4	5	4	4	3	4	3
YARDS	347	289	342	383	328	277	186	290	170

Directions: Route 101 East, to Route 114 North (Goffstown), to Route 13 South (New Boston). Take Route 136 North (Francestown), and then Route 47 North for 4 miles. Resort on right.

Den Brae Golf Course NR ▶26

80 Prescott Road
Sanbornton, NH (603) 934-9818
www.denbrae.com

Club Pro: Tom Gilley
Payment: Visa, MC
Tee Times: Weekends, Holidays

Tees	Holes	Yards	Par	USGA	Slope
BACK	9	3095	36		
MIDDLE	9	2959	36	67.0	112
FRONT	9	2663	36	70.0	123

Fee 9 Holes: Weekday: $15
Fee 18 Holes: Weekday: $25
Twilight Rates: After 3pm
Cart Rental: $14pp/18, $8pp/9
Lessons: $27/hour **Schools:** No
Membership: Yes
Other: Clubhouse / Snack Bar / Bar-Lounge

Weekend: $16
Weekend: $27
Discounts: None
Driving Range: $6.50/lg., grass tees
Junior Golf: Yes
Architect/Yr Open: Henry Homan/1958
GPS:

COUPON

New 6500-square-foot 7th green is pure putting purgatory! Open April - October. New women's tees make course more woman-friendly. New greens on course. New target greens on driving range.

	1	2	3	4	5	6	7	8	9
PAR	4	4	3	5	4	4	4	4	4
YARDS	380	241	170	490	270	370	288	355	395
PAR									
YARDS									

Directions: I-93 to Exit 22, go South on Route 127 for 1.1 miles. Right on Prescott Road, 0.3 mile on left.

NH

Derryfield Country Club

625 Mammoth Road
Manchester, NH (603) 669-0235
www.derryfieldgolf.com

Club Pro: Mike Ryan, PGA
Payment: Cash, Visa, MC
Tee Times: S/S/H

Tees	Holes	Yards	Par	USGA	Slope
BACK	18	6143	70	69.0	1126
MIDDLE	18	5852	70	67.5	124
FRONT	18	5233	70	70.4	114

Fee 9 Holes: Weekday: $22
Fee 18 Holes: Weekday: $37
Twilight Rates: No
Cart Rental: $14pp/18, $8pp/9
Lessons: $40/half hour **Schools:** No
Membership: Yes
Other: Snack Bar / Restaurant / Bar-Lounge

Weekend: $22
Weekend: $37
Discounts: None
Driving Range: No
Junior Golf: Yes
Architect/Yr Open: 1932
GPS:

Because course is hilly with small greens, approach shots are key. Wide-open fairways let you open up. Voted one of the best places to play by 2008 *Golf Digest*. New half-million-dollar drainage project for 6 holes completed in 2008.

	1	2	3	4	5	6	7	8	9
PAR	4	4	3	4	4	4	4	3	4
YARDS	302	386	176	349	361	363	349	159	313
	10	**11**	**12**	**13**	**14**	**15**	**16**	**17**	**18**
PAR	4	4	3	4	4	4	4	5	4
YARDS	312	409	146	238	327	327	320	504	374

Directions: I-93 to Exit 8. Bear right at the bottom of the ramp. At second set of lights, take a left. Course is on the left.

Duston Country Club

40 Country Club Road
Hopkinton, NH (603) 746-4234
www.dustoncc.com

Club Pro:
Payment: Visa, MC
Tee Times: Weekends & Holidays

Tees	Holes	Yards	Par	USGA	Slope
BACK					
MIDDLE	9	2109	32	59.9	99
FRONT	9	2083	33	63.8	107

Fee 9 Holes: Weekday: $14
Fee 18 Holes: Weekday: $20
Twilight Rates: After Labor Day
Cart Rental: $24pp/18, $15pp/9
Lessons: Schools: No
Membership: Yes
Other: Clubhouse / Grill / Bar-Lounge

Weekend: $15
Weekend: $22
Discounts: Senior & Junior
Driving Range: No
Junior Golf: Yes
Architect/Yr Open: 1926
GPS:

Scottish-style bunkers and lush greens. Some hills. Greens are small to medium in size. Open April - November. Family run.

	1	2	3	4	5	6	7	8	9
PAR	4	3	4	3	4	4	3	4	3
YARDS	295	117	353	133	265	299	194	273	180
PAR									
YARDS									

Directions: I-89 to Exit 5 onto Routes 202 & 9 for 3 miles. Take Country Club Road exit.

Eagle Mountain House

Carter Notch Road
Jackson, NH (603) 383-9090
www.eaglemt.com

Tees	Holes	Yards	Par	USGA	Slope
BACK					
MIDDLE	9	2154	32	61.0	102
FRONT	9	1620	32		

Club Pro: Bob McGraw PGA
Payment: Cash, Visa, MC, Amex, Disc
Tee Times: 1 week adv.
Fee 9 Holes: Weekday: $20 | **Weekend:** $25
Fee 18 Holes: Weekday: $30 | **Weekend:** $37
Twilight Rates: After 3pm | **Discounts:** Junior
Cart Rental: $18pp/18, $12pp/9 (weekdays); $22pp/18, $18pp/9 (weekends)
Driving Range: Full
Lessons: Yes **Schools:** No
Membership: Yes | **Junior Golf:** Yes
Other: Hotel / Lockers / Showers / Snack Bar / Restaurant / Bar-Lounge | **Architect/Yr Open:** Patrick Markey/1912

Breathtaking views of mountains and river. Grass driving range. Always improving. *Cart rentals vary weekdays and weekends. Open late May - late October.

	1	2	3	4	5	6	7	8	9
PAR	4	3	4	5	3	3	3	3	4
YARDS	255	190	310	395	146	192	170	208	288
PAR									
YARDS									

Directions: I-95 to Route 16 North. 9 miles North of North Conway. Continue through covered bridge into Jackson, 1/2 mile up Carter Notch Road.

Eastman Golf Links

6 Clubhouse Lane
Grantham, NH (603) 863-4500
www.eastmangolflinks.com

Tees	Holes	Yards	Par	USGA	Slope
BACK	18	6731	71	73.5	131
MIDDLE	18	6338	71	71.7	127
FRONT	18	5499	73	71.9	125

Club Pro: Mark Larrabee, PGA
Payment: Visa, MC, Amex, Disc
Tee Times: Up to 5 days adv.
Fee 9 Holes: Weekday: $34 | **Weekend:** $34
Fee 18 Holes: Weekday: $58 | **Weekend:** $58
Twilight Rates: After 4pm | **Discounts:** Junior after 4pm
Cart Rental: $16pp/18, $11pp/9 | **Driving Range:** $6/bucket
Lessons: $30/half hour **Schools:** No | **Junior Golf:** Yes
Membership: Yes | **Architect/Yr Open:** Geoffrey Cornish/1973
Other: Clubhouse / Snack Bar / Restaurant / Bar-Lounge

Pro's Comment: "Fantastic shape!" –DT. Best conditions in 25 years; many renovations. Carts required Friday, Saturday, and Sunday until 2pm. New restaurant.

	1	2	3	4	5	6	7	8	9
PAR	4	5	3	4	4	4	3	5	4
YARDS	354	544	167	353	389	409	189	493	395
	10	**11**	**12**	**13**	**14**	**15**	**16**	**17**	**18**
PAR	4	4	4	3	4	3	5	4	4
YARDS	322	384	443	189	384	113	441	305	384

Directions: Take I-89 to Exit 13; left off ramp from North, right off ramp from South. 1/4 mile on right is entrance to course.

Exeter Country Club

⊛⊛ **31**

58 Jady Hill Avenue
Exeter, NH (603) 772-4752
www.exetercountryclub.com

Tees	Holes	Yards	Par	USGA	Slope
BACK	9	2721	35	68.9	114
MIDDLE	9	2553	35	70.1	117
FRONT					

Club Pro: Joel Jenkins, PGA
Payment: Visa, MC, Disc
Tee Times: Yes
Fee 9 Holes: Weekday: $20   **Weekend:** $25
Fee 18 Holes: Weekday: $35   **Weekend:** $40
Twilight Rates: After 5pm   **Discounts:** None
Cart Rental: $18pp/18, $9pp/9   **Driving Range:** yes
Lessons: $35/half hour **Schools:** Yes   **Junior Golf:** Yes
Membership: Yes $333   **Architect/Yr Open:** 1889; M. Francis/1950
Other: Restaurant / Clubhouse / Snack Bar / Showers / Bar-Lounge

COUPON

Player Comments: "A placement course. Makes you think about each shot." Rolling terrain with a variety of challenges. Not overly difficult. Open April 1 - December 1.

	1	2	3	4	5	6	7	8	9
PAR	4	3	5	4	4	4	4	3	4
YARDS	379	160	460	361	365	250	281	165	300
PAR									
YARDS									

Directions: I-95 to Hampton, NH exit to Route 101 West, exit to Route 108 to Stratham, Exeter. Bear left. Go right at 3rd light, take 1st left, then the next right.

Farmington Country Club

NR **32**

181 Main Street (Route 153)
Henry Wilson Highway
Farmington, NH
(603) 755-2412
www.farmingtoncountryclubnh.com

Tees	Holes	Yards	Par	USGA	Slope
BACK					
MIDDLE	9	3108	36	70.0	127
FRONT	9	2753	36	70.8	116

Club Pro: James Pollini, PGA
Payment: Visa, MC
Tee Times: Weekends
Fee 9 Holes: Weekday: $17   **Weekend:** $21
Fee 18 Holes: Weekday: $25   **Weekend:** $31
Twilight Rates: No   **Discounts:** None
Cart Rental: $25/18, $17/9 per cart **Driving Range:** Yes
Lessons: $40/half hour **Schools:** Yes **Junior Golf:** Yes
Membership: Yes   **Architect/Yr Open:** 1924, 1996
Other: Clubhouse / Snack Bar/ Bar-Lounge / Beverage Cart

Challenging redesigned course. 9 holes, 2 sets of tees.

	1	2	3	4	5	6	7	8	9
PAR	4	4	3	5	4	3	5	4	4
YARDS	350	350	140	491	375	135	516	406	345
PAR									
YARDS									

Directions: Exit 15 off Spaulding Turnpike (Route 16). Route 11 West to Farmington 5 miles, take right at lights, Route 153, 1 mile on right.

Granite Fields Golf Club ✪✪½ 33 ▶

7 Route 125
Kingston, NH (603) 642-9977
www.granitefields.com

Club Pro:
Payment: Most Major Credit Cards
Tee Times: 5 days adv.

Tees	Holes	Yards	Par	USGA	Slope
BACK	18	6518	72	71.6	131
MIDDLE	18	6018	72	68.7	124
FRONT	18	4695	72		

Fee 9 Holes: Weekday: $18   **Weekend:** $20
Fee 18 Holes: Weekday: $30   **Weekend:** $35
Twilight Rates: **Discounts:** Senior & Junior
Cart Rental: $15pp/18, $10pp/9 **Driving Range:** Yes
Lessons: Yes **Schools:** No   **Junior Golf:**
Membership: Yes   **Architect/Yr Open:** Steve Cummings/2005
Other: Clubhouse / Bar-Lounge **GPS:**

COUPON

Has matured into a real winner. Very scenic and challenging, too. Distances below are from the Blue tees.

	1	2	3	4	5	6	7	8	9
PAR	4	3	4	3	5	5	4	4	4
YARDS	353	158	404	202	503	511	436	344	403
	10	11	12	13	14	15	16	17	18
PAR	4	4	4	3	4	5	4	3	5
YARDS	390	360	310	175	385	520	375	190	499

Directions: I-495 to Exit 51B. North on Route 125. 5.3 miles on right. From 101: take 125 South.
Approximately 11 miles on left.

Green Meadow GC #1, The Prairie ✪✪ 34 ▶

59 Steele Road
Hudson, NH
(603) 889-1555
www.greenmeadowgolfclub.com

Club Pro: Brian Doyle, PGA
Payment: Cash, MC, Visa, Disc, Amex
Tee Times: Weekends, 1 week adv.

Tees	Holes	Yards	Par	USGA	Slope
BACK	18	6160	70	68.4	113
MIDDLE	18	5810	70	66.7	110
FRONT	18	4877	70	66.6	106

Fee 9 Holes: Weekday: $21   **Weekend:**
Fee 18 Holes: Weekday: $32   **Weekend:** $39
Twilight Rates: Noon, 2pm, 5pm **Discounts:** Junior
Cart Rental: $14pp/18, $9pp/9   **Driving Range:** $5/lg. bucket
Lessons: $35/half hour **Schools:** No **Junior Golf:** Yes
Membership: No   **Architect/Yr Open:** Philip Friel/1952
Other: Snack Bar / Bar-Lounge / Showers **GPS:**

Lots of room and very forgiving. Junior discounts S/S after 3pm. Senior playbook available.

	1	2	3	4	5	6	7	8	9
PAR	4	4	3	4	4	3	5	4	4
YARDS	334	328	141	376	341	169	471	411	364
	10	11	12	13	14	15	16	17	18
PAR	4	3	4	3	4	4	4	4	5
YARDS	353	158	324	153	329	410	313	329	506

Directions: Take Route 3 to Exit 2. Follow the signs toward Hudson, NH. At the end of the bridge
bear to the right onto Route 3A South. At the third set of lights, which is Steele Road, take a right.
This road leads directly into the Green Meadow parking lot.

NH

Green Meadow GC #2, The Jungle ✪✪½ ▶ 35

59 Steele Road
Hudson, NH
(603) 889-1555

Tees	Holes	Yards	Par	USGA	Slope
BACK	18	6940	72	71.5	124
MIDDLE	18	6394	72	68.9	120
FRONT	18	5352	72	69.7	114

Club Pro: Brian Doyle, PGA
Payment: Cash, MC, Visa, Disc, Amex
Tee Times: Weekends, 1 week adv.
Fee 9 Holes: Weekday: $21
Fee 18 Holes: Weekday: $35
Twilight Rates: Noon, 2pm, 5pm
Cart Rental: $14pp/18, $9pp/9
Lessons: $35/half hour **Schools:** No
Membership: No
Other: Snack Bar / Bar-Lounge / Showers

Weekend:
Weekend: $46
Discounts: Senior & Junior
Driving Range: $5/lg.
Junior Golf: Yes
Architect/Yr Open: Philip Friel/1952
GPS:

Junior discounts on weekends after 3pm. Senior playbook available. Course set along the Merrimac River. More challenging than the Prairie Course. Junior discounts S/S after 3pm.

	1	2	3	4	5	6	7	8	9
PAR	4	4	5	3	4	4	4	3	5
YARDS	368	341	513	164	351	405	366	185	479
	10	11	12	13	14	15	16	17	18
PAR	4	3	4	5	4	4	3	4	5
YARDS	358	137	370	538	382	368	142	415	512

Directions: Take Route 3 to Exit 2. Follow the signs toward Hudson, NH. At the end of the bridge bear to the right onto Route 3A South. At the third set of lights, which is Steele Road, take a right. This road leads directly into the Green Meadow parking lot.

Hales Location Golf Course ✪✪½ ▶ 36

87 Fairway Drive
West Side Road, North Conway, NH
(603) 356-2140
www.whitemountainhotel.com

Tees	Holes	Yards	Par	USGA	Slope
BACK	9	3025	36	68.8	122
MIDDLE	9	2816	36	66.8	115
FRONT	9	2508	36	67.4	113

Club Pro: Julie Rivers
Payment: All Major Cards
Tee Times: May 1st for season
Fee 9 Holes: Weekday: $30
Fee 18 Holes: Weekday: $42
Twilight Rates: After 3pm
Cart Rental: $16pp/18, $10pp/9
Lessons: Yes **Schools:** Yes
Membership: Yes
Other: Clubhouse / Hotel / Restaurant / Bar-Lounge / Snack Bar / Lockers / Showers

Weekend: $33
Weekend: $45
Discounts: None
Driving Range: No
Junior Golf: Yes
Architect/Yr Open: Al Zikorus/1990

COUPON

Special holes: #1 and #9. Great 9-hole layout with breathtaking views of the White Mountains. Bent grass fairways and greens. Golf rates vary seasonally. Open May-November.

	1	2	3	4	5	6	7	8	9
PAR	5	4	3	4	5	3	4	4	4
YARDS	458	312	148	256	468	130	334	368	342
PAR									
YARDS									

Directions: Route 16 to traffic light in Conway. Turn onto Washington Street, then right onto West Side Road; 5 miles on left.

Hanover Country Club ✪✪✪½ ⯈ 37

Rope Ferry Road
Hanover, NH (603) 646-2000
www.dartmouth.edu/~hccweb

Tees	Holes	Yards	Par	USGA	Slope
BACK	18	6472	71	70.8	131
MIDDLE	18	6142	71	70.8	131
FRONT	18	5330	72	71.5	128

Club Pro: Alex Kirk, PGA
Payment: Visa, MC, Amex
Tee Times: 3 days adv.
Fee 9 Holes: Weekday:
Fee 18 Holes: Weekday: $49
Twilight Rates: After 3pm $30
Cart Rental: $16pp/18
Lessons: $40/half hour **Schools:** No
Membership: Yes
Other: Clubhouse / Snack Bar / Leagues

Weekend:
Weekend: $59
Discounts: Junior
Driving Range: Yes
Junior Golf: Yes
Architect/Yr Open: O. Smith/1899
GPS:

COUPON

Home of Dartmouth golf team. "Course greens in great shape, fast, challenging, and fun." Parkland-style with old-growth trees.

	1	2	3	4	5	6	7	8	9
PAR	4	4	4	3	3	4	4	4	5
YARDS	400	408	290	115	183	341	405	283	572
	10	11	12	13	14	15	16	17	18
PAR	4	4	3	4	3	4	4	5	5
YARDS	385	315	177	308	142	425	358	467	457

Directions: I-91 to bridge into Hanover. 1st left after lights, then 2nd left onto Maynard Street. Next right onto Rope Ferry Road. Follow to end.

Hidden Creek Golf Course NR ⯈ 38

17 Morgan Road
Litchfield, NH (603) 262-9275
www.hiddencreekgolfnh.com

Tees	Holes	Yards	Par	USGA	Slope
BACK	9	3251	36	70.5	
MIDDLE	9	3114	36	68.5	
FRONT	9	2858	36	68.0	

Club Pro: Matthew J. Madore
Payment: Visa, MC
Tee Times: Yes
Fee 9 Holes: Weekday: $28
Fee 18 Holes: Weekday: $37
Twilight Rates: After 4pm
Cart Rental: $14pp/18, $9pp/9
Lessons: Yes **Schools:** No
Membership: Yes
Other:

Weekend: $31
Weekend: $44
Discounts: Senior & Junior
Driving Range: Yes
Junior Golf: No
Architect/Yr Open: 2005
GPS:

Opened late 2006. Sister course to Passaconaway.

	1	2	3	4	5	6	7	8	9
PAR	4	4	3	5	4	4	3	5	4
YARDS	371	345	190	565	330	283	140	500	390
PAR									
YARDS									

Directions: I-93 North to Exit 5 (Route 28). Go South 1.3 miles, turn right at Stonehenge Road. Go left at Bartley Hill Road for 3.5 miles (becomes Corning Road). Turn left at Charles Bancroft Highway (Route 3A), turn left at Albuquerque Avenue and left at Morgan Road.

NH

Hidden Valley Golf Course

NR  **39**

81 Damren Road
Derry, NH (603) 887-7888
www.hiddenvalleygolfpark.com

Club Pro: No
Payment: Visa, MC, Cash
Tee Times: 7 days adv.
Fee 9 Holes: Weekday: $15
Fee 18 Holes: Weekday: $25
Twilight Rates: After 4pm
Cart Rental: Yes
Lessons: Yes **Schools:** No
Membership: Yes
Other: RV Campsites

Tees	Holes	Yards	Par	USGA	Slope
BACK	18	6310	72	70.8	126
MIDDLE	18	5838	72	67.8	124
FRONT	18	5200	72	65.3	109

Weekend: $20
Weekend: $35
Discounts: Senior
Driving Range: No
Junior Golf: No
Architect/Yr Open: Ed Simonsen/1993
GPS:

RV sites at course. Nice big greens. Added 9-hole par 3 courses. Southern NH's most scenic, well-maintained 18-hole championship course. Friendly staff, leagues, tournaments.

	1	2	3	4	5	6	7	8	9
PAR	3	4	3	5	4	4	4	5	4
YARDS	150	310	155	420	355	345	345	505	275
	10	11	12	13	14	15	16	17	18
PAR	5	4	3	5	4	4	3	4	4
YARDS	420	325	190	530	365	308	155	355	330

Directions: I-93 to Exit 4. East to rotary. Take East Derry Road for 4.5 miles. Sign on right. 1 mile to course.

Highlands Links Golf Club

✪✪ **40**

Mt. Prospect Road
Plymouth, NH (603) 536-3452
www.highlandlinks.net

Club Pro: Joe Clark Sr., PGA
Brian Desilets, Pro
Payment: Cash, Credit
Tee Times: No
Fee 9 Holes: Weekday: $14
Fee 18 Holes: Weekday: $20
Twilight Rates: No
Cart Rental: $25/18, $15/9 per cart
Lessons: Yes, inquire! **Schools:** Yes
Membership: Yes
Other: Clubhouse / Custom Club Fitting

Tees	Holes	Yards	Par	USGA	Slope
BACK					
MIDDLE	9	1485	27	59.0	97
FRONT	9	2710	64		

Weekend: $14
Weekend: $20
Discounts: Junior
Driving Range: No
Junior Golf: Yes
Architect/Yr Open:
GPS:

Sig. Hole: #8, 190-yard par 3 called "Ballybunion." Elevated tee with rolling fairway — outstanding Southwest view.

	1	2	3	4	5	6	7	8	9
PAR	3	3	3	3	3	3	3	3	3
YARDS	210	185	140	165	145	130	165	190	155
PAR									
YARDS									

Directions: I-93 to Exit 25, turn left at end of ramp. Follow 1/4 mile to Route 175 South, at stop sign. Opposite Holderness Prep School, take left onto Mt. Prospect Road, follow 1.5 mile to course.

Hoodkroft Country Club

NR **41**

121 East Broadway
Derry, NH (603) 434-0651
www.hoodkroftcc.com

Tees	Holes	Yards	Par	USGA	Slope
BACK	9	3263	36	35.5	128
MIDDLE	9	3238	72	71.4	128
FRONT	9	2626	36	63.8	109

Club Pro: R. Berberian, PGA & L. Ward, PGA
Payment: Visa, MC, Disc
Tee Times: Tues for weekend
Fee 9 Holes: Weekday: $21   **Weekend:** $22
Fee 18 Holes: Weekday: $33   **Weekend:** $36
Twilight Rates: After 4pm   **Discounts:** Senior, weekdays only
Cart Rental: $15pp/18, $8pp/9   **Driving Range:** No
Lessons: $35/half hour **Schools:** No   **Junior Golf:** Yes
Membership: Waiting list   **Architect/Yr Open:** Philip Wogan/1971
Other: Clubhouse / Bar-Lounge / Snack Bar / Showers

Mostly flat, open fairways, lots of water. Large open greens. New chipping area. Open April 1 - November 30 (or snow).

	1	2	3	4	5	6	7	8	9
PAR	4	4	3	5	4	4	4	3	5
YARDS	335	430	187	555	355	400	340	180	456
	10	11	12	13	14	15	16	17	18
PAR	4	4	3	5	4	4	4	3	5
YARDS	355	420	224	538	375	380	360	155	456

Directions: I-93 to Exit 4 in NH, head East on Route 102. Go about 2 miles. Golf course is on right-hand side.

Hooper Golf Club

⭐⭐ **42**

166 Prospect Hill
Walpole, NH
(603) 756-4020

Tees	Holes	Yards	Par	USGA	Slope
BACK					
MIDDLE	9	3033	71	68.9	123
FRONT	9	2709	36	71.2	121

Club Pro: Jay Clace
Payment: Visa, MC
Tee Times: No
Fee 9 Holes: Weekday: $18   **Weekend:** $18
Fee 18 Holes: Weekday: $34   **Weekend:** $34
Twilight Rates: No   **Discounts:** None
Cart Rental: $14pp/18, $9pp/9   **Driving Range:** No
Lessons: No **Schools:** No   **Junior Golf:** Yes
Membership: $590/Adult, $130/Junior   **Architect/Yr Open:** Stiles & Van Kleek/1927
Other: Full Restaurant / Clubhouse / Bed and Breakfast Hotel - $90/night for 2, $80-single.

Historic clubhouse and bed & breakfast. Call ahead to this busy course. Open April - October. On weekends opens at 10:30 to non-members. Newly decorated clubhouse and B&B.

	1	2	3	4	5	6	7	8	9
PAR	5	4	4	3	5	3	4	4	4
YARDS	456	427	285	155	474	194	311	381	350
	10	11	12	13	14	15	16	17	18
PAR	4	4	4	3	5	3	4	4	4
YARDS	435	427	275	155	481	194	311	381	336

Directions: I-91 to Exit 5. Take Route 5 South to 1st left, onto Route 123 to Route 12. Turn right onto Route 12 South, take 1st left onto South Street to Prospect Hill Road, 3/4 mile on Prospect. Golf course on right.

NH

Indian Mound Golf Club ✪✪ ▶ 43

Old Route 16
Center Ossipee, NH
(603) 539-7733
www.indianmoundgc.com

Club Pro: Jonathan Rivers
Payment: Most Major Credit Cards
Tee Times: Yes
Fee 9 Holes: Weekday: $20-27
Fee 18 Holes: Weekday: $30-41
Twilight Rates: After 3pm
Cart Rental: $14pp/18, $8pp/9
Lessons: Yes **Schools:** No
Membership: Yes
Other: Clubhouse / Restaurant / Bar-Lounge

Tees	Holes	Yards	Par	USGA	Slope
BACK	18	5675	70	68.1	120
MIDDLE	18	5360	70	67.1	118
FRONT	18	4713	70	67.5	117

Weekend: $20-29
Weekend: $30-48
Discounts: Several specials
Driving Range: No
Junior Golf: Yes
Architect/Yr Open: Philip Wogan/1968
GPS: Golf Logic

COUPON

Player Comments: "This course is a gem. Expensive feel at reasonable rates." Off-season specials. Under new ownership and management. Group and tournament outings welcome.

	1	2	3	4	5	6	7	8	9
PAR	4	5	4	3	4	4	4	3	4
YARDS	295	465	355	118	288	276	295	170	365
	10	11	12	13	14	15	16	17	18
PAR	4	3	4	4	5	4	3	5	3
YARDS	340	113	303	400	433	360	104	495	185

Directions: From West or East, Route 25 or Route 28 to Route 16 to Center Ossipee exit. Course is .5 mile on left.

Intervale Country Club ✪✪ ▶ 44

1491 Front Street
Manchester, NH (603) 647-6811
www.intervalecc.com

Club Pro: Matt Thibeault, PGA
Payment: Cash or Personal Check
Tee Times: No
Fee 9 Holes: Weekday: $23
Fee 18 Holes: Weekday: $32
Twilight Rates: No
Cart Rental: $22pp/18, $12pp/9
Lessons: $50/hour **Schools:** No
Membership: Yes
Architect/Yr Open: A. Findlay/1903; W.B. Booth/2004
Other: Restaurant / Bar-Lounge

Tees	Holes	Yards	Par	USGA	Slope
BACK					
MIDDLE	9	3099	36	68.2	108
FRONT	9	2774	36	71..7	120

Weekend: $23
Weekend: $32
Discounts: None
Driving Range: No
Junior Golf: Yes

COUPON

Semi-private. Call for details. Open April - November. New tees on 1st, 6th, and 10th for 2008-09. Classic design, course is over 100 years old. New green added over water hazard.

	1	2	3	4	5	6	7	8	9
PAR	3	4	4	5	4	4	4	3	5
YARDS	222	338	334	485	441	342	284	137	516
PAR									
YARDS									

Directions: I-293 North to Exit 7. Course is 1/2 mile on right. Exit 10 off I-93, left and course is 2 miles on left.

Jack O'Lantern Resort

○○ 45

Route 3
Woodstock, NH (603) 745-3636
www.jackolanternresort.com

Club Pro: James Gelunas
Payment: Visa, MC, Amex, Disc
Tee Times: 24 hours adv.
Fee 9 Holes: Weekday: $25
Fee 18 Holes: Weekday: $45
Twilight Rates: After 3pm
Cart Rental: $18pp/18, $11pp/9
Lessons: $30/half hour **Schools:** Yes
Membership: Yes
Other: Restaurant / Hotel / Bar-Lounge / Snack Bar

Tees	Holes	Yards	Par	USGA	Slope
BACK					
MIDDLE	18	6003	70	68.6	117
FRONT	18	4917	71	67.0	113

Weekend: $30
Weekend: $48
Discounts: Junior
Driving Range: No
Junior Golf: Yes
Architect/Yr Open: Bob Keating/1948

COUPON

Player Comments: "Great resort for golf and fun." "Good golf package." Carts required on Friday, Saturday, and Sunday. New golf carts. Pristine greens. Authentic covered bridge, 360-degree views of the White Mountains. Many return year after year, and so will you.

	1	2	3	4	5	6	7	8	9
PAR	4	4	4	4	3	4	4	4	3
YARDS	370	365	414	362	175	421	335	395	160
	10	11	12	13	14	15	16	17	18
PAR	5	4	4	3	4	5	4	3	4
YARDS	519	292	305	140	410	520	320	175	325

Directions: I-93 to Exit 30, right there on the right!

NH

Kingston Fairways

NR 46

65 Depot Road (Route 107)
Kingston, NH (603) 642-7722

Club Pro: Mike Andersen
Payment: Cash, Visa, MC
Tee Times: No
Fee 9 Holes: Weekday: $16
Fee 18 Holes: Weekday: $27
Twilight Rates: After 5pm
Cart Rental: $28/18, $14/9 per cart
Lessons: No **Schools:** No
Membership: No
Other: Clubhouse / Snack Bar

Tees	Holes	Yards	Par	USGA	Slope
BACK					
MIDDLE	18	5710	71	67.4	114
FRONT	18	2669	72		

Weekend: $19
Weekend: $33
Discounts: Senior & Junior
Driving Range: No
Junior Golf: Yes
Architect/Yr Open: Frank Colanton/1994
GPS:

Now 18 holes. Large chipping and putting area. Twilight golf after 5pm, $10.

	1	2	3	4	5	6	7	8	9
PAR	3	5	4	4	4	4	4	4	4
YARDS	125	505	315	329	347	300	300	330	381
	10	11	12	13	14	15	16	17	18
PAR	3	4	4	3	4	4	5	4	4
YARDS	154	429	300	135	240	380	470	252	378

Directions: Route 107 off Route 125 in Kingston, 1/4 of a mile. Or Exit 1 in Seabrook off of Route I-95. Go 10 miles West on Route 107.

Kingswood Golf Club

✪✪½ ▶ 47

37 Kingswood Road
Wolfeboro, NH (603) 569-3569
www.kingswoodgolfclub.com

Club Pro: Dan Botelho, PGA
Payment: Visa, MC, Amex, Disc
Tee Times: 5 days adv.
Fee 9 Holes: Weekday: $27
Fee 18 Holes: Weekday: $46
Twilight Rates: After 2pm
Cart Rental: $21pp/18, $12pp/9
Lessons: $60/hour, $35/half hour **Schools:** No
Membership: Yes
Other: Snack Bar / Bar-Lounge

Tees	Holes	Yards	Par	USGA	Slope
BACK	18	6366	72	71.1	125
MIDDLE	18	5934	72	68.8	122
FRONT	18	5448	72	73.1	130

Weekend: $27
Weekend: $46
Discounts: None
Driving Range: $4/bucket
Junior Golf: Yes
Architect/Yr Open: Donald Ross/1915
GPS:

COUPON

The course is hilly with 5 ponds. Has an excellent iron practice range with a green to hit with short irons (190-yard range). Reduced fees after 2pm without cart. Open April - October 31.

	1	2	3	4	5	6	7	8	9
PAR	4	5	3	4	4	3	4	4	4
YARDS	380	420	163	372	310	138	367	297	337
	10	11	12	13	14	15	16	17	18
PAR	4	5	4	3	4	4	5	4	4
YARDS	334	461	367	175	349	284	464	360	356

Directions: Route 28 North .25 mile past Kingswood High School. Turn left onto Kingswood Road.

Kona Mansion Inn

NR ▶ 48

Moultonborough Neck Road
Moultonboro, NH
(603) 253-4900
www.konamansioninn.com

Club Pro:
Payment: Visa, MC, Disc
Tee Times: No
Fee 9 Holes: Weekday: $15
Fee 18 Holes: Weekday: $15
Twilight Rates: No
Cart Rental: $3/pull
Lessons: No **Schools:** No
Membership: Yes-seasonal
Other: Hotel / Full-Service Restaurant

Tees	Holes	Yards	Par	USGA	Slope
BACK					
MIDDLE	9	1170	27		
FRONT					

Weekend: $15
Weekend: $15
Discounts: None
Driving Range:
Junior Golf: No
Architect/Yr Open: N.P. Nelson/1903
GPS:

A resort on Lake Winnipesaukee. Par 3 course. New driving range.

	1	2	3	4	5	6	7	8	9
PAR	3	3	3	3	3	3	3	3	3
YARDS	105	150	130	135	128	150	162	125	85
PAR									
YARDS									

Directions: I-93 to Exit 23 and follow to the end in Meredith, 11 miles, left on Route 3 to lights, right on Route 25. 9 miles to Moultonboro Neck Road on right. Go right, 2.5 miles to Kona Road on right. Follow signs.

Lakeview Golf Club

89 Ladd Hill Road
Belmont, NH (603) 524-2220

Club Pro: No
Payment: Cash or Check
Tee Times: No
Fee 9 Holes: Weekday: $15
Fee 18 Holes: Weekday: $22
Twilight Rates: After 3pm $12pp/9 M-F
Cart Rental: $10pp/18, $6pp/9
Lessons: No **Schools:** No
Membership: Yes

Tees	Holes	Yards	Par	USGA	Slope
BACK					
MIDDLE	9	3615	35	69	
FRONT	9	2270	37	72.0	

Weekend: $15
Weekend: $22
Discounts: None
Driving Range: No
Junior Golf: No
Architect/Yr Open: 1925

Beautiful 9-hole golf course overlooks a panorama of lakes and mountains. Good walking course. Dress code. Twilight rates for 9 holes after 3pm - $12.

	1	2	3	4	5	6	7	8	9
PAR	5	4	4	4	3	4	3	5	3
YARDS	505	315	290	425	220	435	175	550	195
PAR									
YARDS									

Directions: I-93 North to Exit 20, then East toward Laconia on Routes 3 & 11. Cross Winnisquam bridge and follow 1 mile to set of lights. Take right, across from Belknap Mall.

Lisbon Village Country Club

NR 50

621 Bishop Road
Lisbon, NH (603) 838-6004
www.lisbongolf.com
Club Pro: Steve Schultz
Payment: Cash or Check
Tee Times: Suggested
Fee 9 Holes: Weekday: $17
Fee 18 Holes: Weekday: $25
Twilight Rates: After 4pm
Cart Rental: $16pp/18, $9pp/9
Lessons: Yes **Schools:** No
Membership: Yes
Other: Club House/ Bar-Lounge / Snack Bar

Tees	Holes	Yards	Par	USGA	Slope
BACK					
MIDDLE	9	2900	36	69.7	126
FRONT	9	2466	36	70.6	127

Weekend: $20
Weekend: $28
Discounts: Junior
Driving Range: $5/lg, $3/sm
Junior Golf: Yes
Architect/Yr Open: Ralph Barten/1927
GPS:

COUPON

Scenic White Mt. course that is the epitome of target golf, noted for elevated tees and greens. 9 holes with 18 different tees. Par will change on some holes. Requires a deft touch with irons and woods. Juniors under 7 play for free. Open mid-April through October.

	1	2	3	4	5	6	7	8	9
PAR	4	5	4	4	3	4	5	4	3
YARDS	255	535	310	397	211	248	440	350	148
PAR									
YARDS									

Directions: Route 302 West from I-93 interchange approximately 9 miles to Lyman Road on right. Take Bishop Road .25 mile on left. Entrance to golf course .5 mile on right.

Lochmere Golf & Country Club ✪✪✪½ ▶ 51

Route 3
Tilton, NH (603) 528-4653
www.lochmeregolf.com

Club Pro: Vic Stanfield, PGA
Payment: Visa, MC
Tee Times: 7 days adv.
Fee 9 Holes: Weekday: $18
Fee 18 Holes: Weekday: $32, $47 w/cart
Twilight Rates: After 4pm
Cart Rental: $15pp/18, $9pp/9
Lessons: $25/half hour **Schools:** No
Membership: Yes

Tees	Holes	Yards	Par	USGA	Slope
BACK	18	6660	72	71.7	128
MIDDLE	18	6190	72	69.4	123
FRONT	18	5227	72	68.9	120

Weekend: $23
Weekend: $45, $60 w/cart
Discounts: Seasonal specials
Driving Range: $4/bucket
Junior Golf: Yes
Architect/Yr Open: Wogan & Sargent/1992

COUPON

Other: Restaurant / Clubhouse / Bar-Lounge / Snack Bar / Function Room / Gazebo
GPS: Yes

Player Comments: "Great challenging course, friendly staff." Renovated hole #5 has greater landing area.
Tuesday is senior citizen day. Four-Star *Golf Digest* facility.

	1	2	3	4	5	6	7	8	9
PAR	4	4	3	4	4	4	5	3	4
YARDS	330	340	140	350	368	363	480	163	390
	10	11	12	13	14	15	16	17	18
PAR	4	5	4	4	3	4	4	4	5
YARDS	350	500	310	373	160	401	377	323	472

Directions: I-93 to Exit 20 (Laconia/Tilton). Go 1.5 miles East on Route 3. Course is on left.

Londonderry Country Club NR ▶ 52

Kimball Road
Londonderry, NH (603) 432-9789
londonderrycountryclub.com

Club Pro: Dan Gillis, PGA
Payment: Cash, Visa, MC
Tee Times: Thurs. am for weekend
Fee 9 Holes: Weekday: $19
Fee 18 Holes: Weekday: $28
Twilight Rates: No
Cart Rental: $11pp/18, $11pp/9
Lessons: Yes **Schools:** No
Membership: No
Other: Nuttfield Lounge and Snack Bar

Tees	Holes	Yards	Par	USGA	Slope
BACK					
MIDDLE	18	3897	62	60.7	102
FRONT	18	3258	62	58.5	92

Weekend: $23
Weekend: $32
Discounts: Senior & Junior
Driving Range: Netted area
Junior Golf: Yes
Architect/Yr Open: Forrest & Tom Kimball/1969
GPS:

Lots of improvements in last two years. Beautiful condition due to the new improvements! Friendly staff.

	1	2	3	4	5	6	7	8	9
PAR	3	3	4	4	3	3	3	3	3
YARDS	210	165	235	215	135	165	177	123	165
	10	11	12	13	14	15	16	17	18
PAR	3	3	4	4	4	4	4	4	3
YARDS	155	115	300	310	340	235	370	345	135

Directions: I-93 to Exit 4, left onto Route 102 West, follow to Route 128. Take right onto Route 128
North, follow 4 miles to blinking light. Left on Litchfield Road. Go 1.7 miles, take left onto Kimball
Road. Club is 1 mile on right.

Loudon Country Club

NR 53 ▶

853 Route 106
Loudon, NH 03301
(603) 783-3372
www.loudoncc.com

Tees	Holes	Yards	Par	USGA	Slope
BACK	18	6288	72	70.4	120
MIDDLE	18	5926	72	68.7	115
FRONT	18	4913	72	67	112

Club Pro: Bob Bean, PGA
Payment: Most Major Credit Cards
Tee Times: 7 days in advance
Fee 9 Holes: Weekday: $19   **Weekend:** $22
Fee 18 Holes: Weekday: $33   **Weekend:** $40
Twilight Rates: After 3:30pm   **Discounts:** Senior & Junior
Cart Rental: $14pp/18, $8pp/9   **Driving Range:** $7/lg., $5/sm.
Lessons: Yes **Schools:** Yes   **Junior Golf:** Yes
Membership: Yes   **Architect/Yr Open:** William Leombruno/1993
Other: Full Restaurant / Bar-Lounge / Clubhouse

Challenging, but very playable for all abilities.

	1	2	3	4	5	6	7	8	9
PAR	4	5	4	3	4	5	4	3	5
YARDS	271	497	365	169	389	484	381	168	429
	10	11	12	13	14	15	16	17	18
PAR	4	3	5	3	4	4	4	4	4
YARDS	339	210	485	166	298	359	482	415	381

Directions: I-93 to I-393. Take Exit 3 from 393, left at lights to Route 106 North for 7.5 miles. Course is on left.

Maplewood Golf Club

★★ 54 ▶

Route 302
Bethlehem, NH (603) 869-3335
www.maplewoodgolfresort.com

Tees	Holes	Yards	Par	USGA	Slope
BACK	18	6200	72	69.2	125
MIDDLE	18	6001	72	69.2	123
FRONT	18	5013	71	68.8	113

Club Pro: Trevor Howard, Golf Dir.
Payment: Most Major Credit Cards
Tee Times: Yes
Fee 9 Holes: Weekday: $22   **Weekend:** $28
Fee 18 Holes: Weekday: $39   **Weekend:** $49
Twilight Rates: After 4pm wkdy, 5pm wknd   **Discounts:** Junior
Cart Rental: $16pp/18, $10pp/9   **Driving Range:**
Lessons: No **Schools:** No   **Junior Golf:** No
Membership: Yes   **Architect/Yr Open:** Donald Ross/1914
Other: 1890 Restored Clubhouse / Showers / Lockers / Bar-Lounge / Hotel

COUPON

Recently restored classic Donald Ross course. Stay and Play packages. Ladies' Day on Wednesday. Cart required 8am - 2pm on weekends. New tees on holes 3 and 6.

	1	2	3	4	5	6	7	8	9
PAR	5	4	4	4	4	4	4	3	4
YARDS	445	399	277	388	367	373	319	150	355
	10	11	12	13	14	15	16	17	18
PAR	4	3	3	4	4	5	6	4	3
YARDS	355	163	201	321	279	527	651	287	144

Directions: I-93 Exit 40 onto Route 302 East. Approximately 5 miles.

Mojalaki Golf Club & Academy NR 55

321 Prospect Street
Franklin, NH (603) 934-3033
www.mojalaki.com

Tees	Holes	Yards	Par	USGA	Slope
BACK	9	3096	36	35.1	115
MIDDLE	9	2795	36	34.0	112
FRONT	9	2066	36	32.2	106

Club Pro: Curt Mahoney
Payment: Visa, MC, Disc
Tee Times: 5 days adv.
Fee 9 Holes: Weekday: $14
Fee 18 Holes: Weekday: $20
Twilight Rates: After 3pm
Cart Rental: $15pp/18, $9pp/9
Lessons: Yes **Schools:** Yes
Membership: Yes
Other: Complete Function Facility holds 180 / Snack Bar / Large Outings Welcome

Weekend: $15
Weekend: $22
Discounts: Senior & Junior
Driving Range: Yes
Junior Golf: Yes
Architect/Yr Open: Stiles & Sargent/1920; 2003

COUPON

Beautiful views and a combination of contemporary and traditional design with tees to complement every skill level. New golf academy, driving range, 5-hole quickie course, practice putting and chipping greens.

	1	2	3	4	5	6	7	8	9
PAR	4	4	3	5	4	4	5	3	4
YARDS	258	312	140	478	407	319	454	179	387
PAR									
YARDS									

Directions: I-93 to Exit 19 traveling North, Exit 20 traveling South. Route 3 South to downtown Franklin, left onto Prospect Street. Golf course 1 mile on right.

Monadnock Country Club NR 56

49 High Street
Peterborough, NH (603) 924-7769
www.monadnockcc.com

Tees	Holes	Yards	Par	USGA	Slope
BACK					
MIDDLE	9	1576	29	54.0	76
FRONT	9	1576	32	54.0	76

Club Pro: Dana Hennessey
Payment: Visa, MC
Tee Times: No
Fee 9 Holes: Weekday: $15
Fee 18 Holes: Weekday: $25
Twilight Rates: After 4pm
Cart Rental: $26/18, $15/9 per cart
Lessons: Yes **Schools:** No
Membership: Yes
Other: Clubhouse / Snack Bar / Bar-Lounge / 2 Tennis Courts / Banquet Facility

Weekend: $15
Weekend: $25
Discounts: Senior & Junior
Driving Range: Cage, $2.50/bucket
Junior Golf: Yes
Architect/Yr Open: S. Anderson & Son/1901

While the men's par is 29 and the women's 32, don't be fooled. This course can be challenging for both veterans and beginners. The scenic beauty alone is worth the trip. Clubhouse recently renovated.

	1	2	3	4	5	6	7	8	9
PAR	4	3	3	3	3	4	3	3	3
YARDS	241	108	205	150	166	257	134	162	153
PAR									
YARDS									

Directions: From East or West, Route 101. From North or South, Route 202. Located on High Street.

Mountain View Grand Resort & Spa   NR   57

Mountain View Road
Whitefield, NH (866)484-3843
www.mountainviewgrand.com

Club Pro: David Tetreault
Payment: Visa, MC, Amex
Tee Times: 1 day
Fee 9 Holes: Weekday: $18
Fee 18 Holes: Weekday: $28
Twilight Rates: After 3pm
Cart Rental: $12pp/18, $6 pp/9
Lessons: Yes **Schools:**
Membership: Yes

Tees	Holes	Yards	Par	USGA	Slope
BACK	9	2930	35	66	112
MIDDLE	9	2873	35	66	112
FRONT					

Weekend: $20
Weekend: $34
Discounts: Junior
Driving Range: No
Junior Golf:
Architect/Yr Open: Ralph Barton/1900

Other: Restaurant / Clubhouse / Hotel / Bar / Lounge / Tennis

Challenging course in the heart of the White Mountains. Majestic views and great accommodations. Historic 9 holes completely renovated in 1998. Additional holes in planning stage.

	1	2	3	4	5	6	7	8	9
PAR	4	4	5	4	4	3	4	3	4
YARDS	449	398	472	326	316	126	342	123	321
PAR									
YARDS									

Directions: I-93 North to Exit 35. 21 miles North on Route 3.

Mt. Washington Hotel Golf Course ✪✪✪   58

210 Mt. Washington Hotel Road
Bretton Woods, NH (603) 278-4653
www.mountwashington.com

Club Pro: Michael Carroll
Payment: Visa, MC, AMEX, Disc, Checks
Tee Times: 1 week in adv.
Fee 9 Holes: Weekday:
Fee 18 Holes: Weekday: $135
Twilight Rates: After 3pm, $75
Cart Rental: Included
Lessons: Private and Group **Schools:** Yes
Membership: Yes

Tees	Holes	Yards	Par	USGA	Slope
BACK	18	6974	72		
MIDDLE	27	6378	72	68.0	113
FRONT	27/18	5336	71	69.7	116

Weekend:
Weekend: $135
Discounts: None
Driving Range: Yes
Junior Golf: Yes

Architect/Yr Open: Donald Ross/1915, Cornish & Silva 9-hole course/1989
Other: Resort / Golf Packages / Restaurant / Clubhouse / Bar-Lounge / Lockers / Showers

Surrounded by White Mountain National Forest, the course provides "mountain golf at its greatest," according to Brian Silva, who restored the course based on the original Ross design of 1915. Re-opened Aug. '08. New Spa and Conference Center in Winter '08/'09.

	1	2	3	4	5	6	7	8	9
PAR	4	4	4	4	3	5	4	4	4
YARDS	377	373	374	309	143	501	318	410	394
	10	11	12	13	14	15	16	17	18
PAR	5	5	4	4	3	4	3	4	4
YARDS	522	508	313	374	204	293	100	371	351

Directions: I-93 to Exit 35 to Route 302 East to Bretton Woods.

Newport Country Club ✪✪ 59

Unity Road
Newport, NH (603) 863-7787
www.newport-golf.com

Club Pro: Jeff Peabody
Payment: Visa, MC, Cash
Tee Times: 3 days adv.

Tees	Holes	Yards	Par	USGA	Slope
BACK	18	6509	71	72.7	126
MIDDLE	18	6083	71	70.4	125
FRONT	18	4738	71	62.7	108

Fee 9 Holes: Weekday: $20
Fee 18 Holes: Weekday: $34
Twilight Rates: After 2pm
Cart Rental: $15pp/18, $10pp/9
Lessons: $35/half hour **Schools:** No
Membership: Yes
Other: Clubhouse / Snack Bar / Bar-Lounge / Lockers

Weekend: $38 includes cart
Weekend: $59 includes cart
Discounts: Junior
Driving Range: 2006
Junior Golf: Yes
Architect/Yr Open: Raph Barton/1922

COUPON

Improvements: recently completed full renovations. New hole number 5. Area attractions include, Mt. Sunapee, great hiking, and stream fishing.

	1	2	3	4	5	6	7	8	9
PAR	5	4	4	3	4	4	3	4	4
YARDS	511	326	388	179	373	375	145	269	369
	10	11	12	13	14	15	16	17	18
PAR	5	3	4	4	4	4	3	4	5
YARDS	477	138	387	379	375	341	169	375	507

Directions: I-91 North or South to Exit 8. East to Claremont, then Route 11 toward Newport, take right onto Unity Road at Hilltop Motel, 3/4 mile on the left. Or, I-89 North to Exit 9. Follow Route 103 to Route 11 to center of town on Route 11 & 10 to lights, take right toward Claremont, first left after next light onto Unity Road, 3/4 mile on left.

Nippo Lake Golf Club ✪✪✪ 60

550 Province Road
Barrington, NH (603) 664-7616
www.nippolake.com

Club Pro: Rick Rogers
Payment: Visa, MC
Tee Times: Recommended

Tees	Holes	Yards	Par	USGA	Slope
BACK	18	5627	70	67.3	123
MIDDLE	18	5336	70	65.9	120
FRONT	18	4573	70	62.0	106

Fee 9 Holes: Weekday: $20
Fee 18 Holes: Weekday: $35
Twilight Rates: No
Cart Rental: $15pp/18, $9pp/9
Lessons: $45/45 min. **Schools:** Jr.
Membership: Yes
Other: Clubhouse / Snack Bar / Restaurant / Bar-Lounge / Video instruction

Weekend: $24
Weekend: $42
Discounts: Junior
Driving Range: Yes
Junior Golf: Yes
Architect/Yr Open:

COUPON

Course is noted for scenic mountain views and friendly atmosphere. Rates subject to change. Changed tees, elevated some. Bow Lake, Nippo Lake area attractions.

	1	2	3	4	5	6	7	8	9
PAR	4	5	3	5	4	3	4	4	3
YARDS	314	515	145	491	358	121	316	335	135
	10	11	12	13	14	15	16	17	18
PAR	5	4	3	4	4	4	4	3	4
YARDS	452	312	151	293	305	341	331	166	253

Directions: Spaulding Turnpike North to Exit 13 (Route 202 North). Take right onto Route 126. Go 1/4 mile, then take a left onto Province Road.

North Conway Country Club ✪✪½ 61

Main Street (Route 16)
North Conway, NH (603) 356-9391
www.northconwaycountryclub.com

Club Pro: Larry Gallagher, PGA
Payment: Visa, MC, Amex
Tee Times: 7 days adv.

Tees	Holes	Yards	Par	USGA	Slope
BACK	18	6659	71	71.9	125
MIDDLE	18	6266	71	70.3	121
FRONT	18	5530	71	70.7	118

Fee 9 Holes: Weekday:
Fee 18 Holes: Wkdy: $46 walk, $60 ride, M-Th
Twilight Rates: After 4pm
Cart Rental: $28pp/18
Lessons: By appointment **Schools:** Junior
Membership: Yes
Other: Restaurant / Bar-Lounge / Public Dining

Weekend:
Weekend: $70 w/cart F/S/S/H
Discounts: Senior after 1pm M-Th
Driving Range: Yes, natural grass
Junior Golf: Yes
Architect/Yr: Alex Findlay & Phil Wogan/1895
GPS:

Player Comments: " Great condition and layout. Scenic. Worth the green fees." Hosted NH PGA
Championship, State Amateur, NH Open. Top Pro. Seasonal rates. Friendly staff.

	1	2	3	4	5	6	7	8	9
PAR	4	4	4	3	4	4	3	5	4
YARDS	406	399	354	130	328	362	208	497	376
	10	11	12	13	14	15	16	17	18
PAR	4	5	4	3	4	3	4	5	4
YARDS	349	475	385	150	420	147	357	528	337

Directions: Route 16 to Main Street, North Conway. Next to scenic railroad station.

NH

Oak Hill Golf Course NR 62

159 Pease Road
Meredith, NH (603) 279-4438
www.oakhillgc.com

Club Pro: No
Payment: Cash, Visa, MC
Tee Times: No

Tees	Holes	Yards	Par	USGA	Slope
BACK	9	2347	34	62.2	98
MIDDLE	9	2210	34	60.7	96
FRONT	9	1890	34	62.6	94

Fee 9 Holes: Weekday: $14
Fee 18 Holes: Weekday: $24
Twilight Rates: After 3pm
Cart Rental: $24/18, $14/9 per cart
Lessons: No **Schools:** No
Membership: Yes
Other: Snack Bar / Bar-Lounge

Weekend: $14
Weekend: $24
Discounts: None
Driving Range: No
Junior Golf: No
Architect/Yr Open: Harry Page/1963
GPS:

COUPON

Short regulation New England course with 5 greens blind from tee. Good challenge for your irons.
Wooded and scenic. No tank tops. Open late April to November.

	1	2	3	4	5	6	7	8	9
PAR	4	3	4	4	3	4	3	4	5
YARDS	255	136	258	298	159	229	118	300	457
PAR									
YARDS									

Directions: I-93 to Exit 23 Route 104 East, 7.5 miles to stop light. Turn right onto Pease Road
1.5 miles. Parking on left, golf course on right.

Oaks Golf Links, The ✪✪✪½ 63

100 Hideaway Place
Somersworth, NH (603) 692-6257
theoaksgolflinks.com

Tees	Holes	Yards	Par	USGA	Slope
BACK	18	6711	71	72.1	126
MIDDLE	18	6104	71	69.4	123
FRONT	18	4899	71		

Club Pro: Rick Altham, head pro
Payment: Most Major Credit Cards
Tee Times: 5 days
Fee 9 Holes: Weekday: $30　**Weekend:** $35
Fee 18 Holes: Weekday: $50　**Weekend:** $60
Twilight Rates: Yes, varies　**Discounts:** Senior & Junior
Cart Rental: $18pp/18, $9pp/9　**Driving Range:** Yes
Lessons: Yes **Schools:** Yes　**Junior Golf:**
Membership: Yes　**Architect/Yr Open:** Brad Booth/2005
Other: Restaurant, with Bar and Grille　**GPS:**

"Very interesting layout, cut nicely through the woods. Plan your layups and approaches carefully. Great-looking clubhouse overlooking the 10th hole." –FP New cart paths, reduced hazards. 2007-2008 "NH Top Ten" –*Golf Digest*.

	1	2	3	4	5	6	7	8	9
PAR	4	4	3	5	3	4	4	4	4
YARDS	346	315	167	555	149	398	398	324	380
	10	11	12	13	14	15	16	17	18
PAR	4	5	4	3	4	4	3	4	5
YARDS	333	510	306	135	359	326	148	393	562

Directions: I-95 in Portsmouth to Route 16 North (Spaulding Turnpike) to Exit 9. Bear right off ramp and then move to left lane at Weeks Crossings intersection (about .3 miles). North on Route 108 for 3.6 miles; club on right.

Overlook Golf Club ✪✪✪ 64

5 Overlook Drive
Hollis, NH (603) 465-2909
www.overlookgolfclub.com

Tees	Holes	Yards	Par	USGA	Slope
BACK	18	6624	71	70.2	126
MIDDLE	18	6103	71	68.2	119
FRONT	18	5255	72	73.4	131

Club Pro: Dan Diskin
Payment: Visa, MC, Amex, Disc
Tee Times: 7 days adv.
Fee 9 Holes: Weekday: $23　**Weekend:** $30
Fee 18 Holes: Weekday: $38　**Weekend:** $49
Twilight Rates: After 1pm　**Discounts:** Senior & Junior
Cart Rental: $15pp/18, $10pp/9　**Driving Range:** No
Lessons: Yes **Schools:** Yes, group rates　**Junior Golf:** Yes
Membership: Inner Club　**Architect/Yr Open:** 1989
Other: Clubhouse / Snack Bar / Bar-Lounge　**GPS:**

Player Comments: "Enjoyable for all abilities." "Use all clubs in bag." The front 9 are fairly hilly, back 9 are somewhat flat. New 6th hole. Front and back women's tees. Friendly atmosphere, great conditions. Nice practice area with bunkers and huge putting green.

	1	2	3	4	5	6	7	8	9
PAR	5	4	4	4	3	4	4	3	4
YARDS	535	299	433	390	177	345	292	167	326
	10	11	12	13	14	15	16	17	18
PAR	5	4	4	4	3	4	4	3	5
YARDS	522	350	346	390	164	341	320	138	516

Directions: Route 3 to Exit 5W (Route 111 West). Continue 4 miles. Course is on the right.

Owl's Nest Golf Club ✪✪✪½ ▶65

1 Clubhouse Lane
Campton, NH (603) 726-3076
www.owlsnestgolf.com

Tees	Holes	Yards	Par	USGA	Slope
BACK	18	6818	72	74.0	133
MIDDLE	18	6110	72	69.7	124
FRONT	18	5174	72	67.8	117

Club Pro: Charles Wheeler
Payment: Visa, MC, Amex
Tee Times: 7 days, 1-888-OWL-NEST
Fee 9 Holes: Weekday: $34   **Weekend:** $34
Fee 18 Holes: Weekday: $64   **Weekend:** $64
Twilight Rates: After 4pm   **Discounts:** Junior 50% M-Th
Cart Rental: $16pp   **Driving Range:** $6/lg., $4/sm.
Lessons: $40/half hour **Schools:** No   **Junior Golf:** Yes
Membership: Yes   **Architect/Yr Open:** Cornish & Mungeam/1998
Other: Off-season rates as low as $44/18   **GPS:**

COUPON

Player Comments: "Great greens" "Nice layout, well-maintained, courteous staff." "Excellent customer service." "A true destination course." Discount rates in early and late seasons (call ahead). One of the best layouts in New England. Best scenic view around; staff will make you feel welcome.

	1	2	3	4	5	6	7	8	9
PAR	4	4	4	5	3	4	3	4	5
YARDS	370	366	395	503	160	311	174	335	483
	10	11	12	13	14	15	16	17	18
PAR	3	4	4	5	3	4	4	5	4
YARDS	127	316	391	489	160	259	435	488	348

Directions: I-93 to Exit 28, West on Route 49, then North on Owl Street.

Passaconaway Country Club ✪✪✪½ ▶66

12 Midway Avenue (Route 3A)
Litchfield, NH (603) 424-4653
passaconawaycc.com

Tees	Holes	Yards	Par	USGA	Slope
BACK	18	6855	71	73.0	132
MIDDLE	18	6462	71	71.0	128
FRONT	18	5369	71	70.3	118

Club Pro: Joe Healey
Payment: Cash, Visa, MC
Tee Times: 5 days adv.
Fee 9 Holes: Weekday: $30   **Weekend:** $32 after 10:30am only
Fee 18 Holes: Weekday: $43   **Weekend:** $54
Twilight Rates: After 6pm   **Discounts:** Sr., Jr., & Ladies wkdys
Cart Rental: $15pp/18, $110pp/9   **Driving Range:** $6/lg, $3/sm
Lessons: $45/half hour **Schools:** No   **Junior Golf:** Yes
Membership: Yes, Inner Club   **Architect/Yr Open:** Cornish & Silva/1989
Other: Restaurant / Showers   **GPS:**

Player Comments: "Links-style. Clubhouse staff very friendly. Course is well-maintained, very plush, greens outstanding and true. Plenty of water on the course. Bring the driver: long par 4's."

	1	2	3	4	5	6	7	8	9
PAR	5	3	4	3	5	4	4	4	4
YARDS	532	150	424	172	556	454	443	379	307
	10	11	12	13	14	15	16	17	18
PAR	4	4	4	3	5	4	4	3	4
YARDS	352	327	395	203	502	348	321	189	428

Directions: Route 93 North to Exit 4. Left on Route 102 for 5.5 miles to yellow blinking light. Take right on West Road, for 3 miles to the end. Left on Hillcrest for 3 miles, the course is straight ahead.

NH

Pease Golf Course

✪✪ ▶ 67

200 Grafton Road
Portsmouth, NH (603) 433-1331
www.peasegolf.com

Club Pro: Tim Riese, PGA
Payment: Visa, MC, Amex, Cash
Tee Times: 7 days adv.
Fee 9 Holes: Weekday: $22
Fee 18 Holes: Weekday: $40
Twilight Rates: After 4pm
Cart Rental: $14pp/18, $8pp/9
Lessons: $35-$50/half hour **Schools:** Jr.
Membership: Yes

Tees	Holes	Yards	Par	USGA	Slope
BACK	27/18	6346	71	70.3	126
MIDDLE	27/18	5901	71	68.8	120
FRONT	27/18	5243	71	69.5	124

Weekend: $25
Weekend: $44
Discounts: Senior & Junior
Driving Range: $11/lg., $4/sm.
Junior Golf: Yes
Architect/Yr Open: Arthur Findlay/1901

COUPON

Other: Clubhouse / Bar-Lounge / Snack Bar / Showers / Lockers

27 holes available. Blue course 9 demanding for all levels: rating, 35.0/slope/120. Carts mandatory only for new 9. Scorecard below from the middle tees Red and White courses.

	1	2	3	4	5	6	7	8	9
PAR	5	5	3	4	4	4	4	4	3
YARDS	465	471	160	315	343	310	370	364	150
	10	11	12	13	14	15	16	17	18
PAR	4	3	4	5	3	5	3	4	4
YARDS	322	185	385	535	143	481	162	365	375

Directions: I-95 North to Exit 3, at light turn left, take 1st right. From Route I-95 South take Exit 3A, at stop sign turn right.

Pheasant Ridge Country Club

✪✪ ▶ 68

140 Country Club Road
Gilford, NH (603) 524-7808
www.playgolfne.com

Club Pro: Jim Swarthout, PGA
Payment: Visa, MC, Disc, Amex
Tee Times: 7 days adv.
Fee 9 Holes: Weekday: $20
Fee 18 Holes: Weekday: $32
Twilight Rates: After 2pm
Cart Rental: $30/18 per cart
Lessons: $70/Hour **Schools:** No
Membership: No

Tees	Holes	Yards	Par	USGA	Slope
BACK	18	6402	70	69.3	115
MIDDLE	18	6004	70	67.2	112
FRONT	18	5192	70	68.6	112

Weekend: $25
Weekend: $43
Discounts: None
Driving Range: Yes, grass tee
Junior Golf: No
Architect/Yr Open: Geoffrey Cornish/1962

COUPON

Other: Snack Bar / Bar-Lounge / 400-seat Function Hall

"Course reflects both the late Phil Friel's skill as a golfer and as a developer." –Paul Harber. Beautiful views. A Golf Management Company course.

	1	2	3	4	5	6	7	8	9
PAR	4	3	4	4	4	5	4	3	4
YARDS	340	150	370	410	290	535	329	163	370
	10	11	12	13	14	15	16	17	18
PAR	5	4	4	3	4	4	4	4	3
YARDS	480	385	380	190	340	360	360	376	176

Directions: I-93 to Exit 20 (3 North), follow 9 miles onto Laconia Bypass. Take 2nd exit, right off ramp then next right onto Country Club Road. Course is 1/2 mile up hill on left.

Pine Grove Springs Country Club NR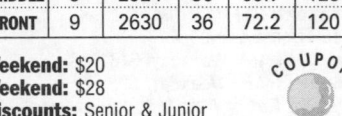

292 Route 9A
Spofford, NH (603) 363-4433
www.pgscc.com

Club Pro:
Payment: Disc, Visa, MC, Cash
Tee Times: No
Fee 9 Holes: Weekday: $14
Fee 18 Holes: Weekday: $22
Twilight Rates: After 5pm
Cart Rental: $28pp/18, $16pp/9
Driving Range: No - practice area. 9-hole pitch 'n putt course
Lessons: Yes **Schools:** No
Membership: Yes
Other: Snack Bar / Bar-Lounge

Tees	Holes	Yards	Par	USGA	Slope
BACK					
MIDDLE	9	2924	36	69.7	128
FRONT	9	2630	36	72.2	120

Weekend: $20
Weekend: $28
Discounts: Senior & Junior

Junior Golf: Yes
Architect/Yr Open: 1900

Sig. Hole: #3 is a par 5 with 3 water hazards, dogleg right, rolling fairways, and elevated green. Open April - October. Plus 5-hole pitch and putt course.

	1	2	3	4	5	6	7	8	9
PAR	4	4	5	4	3	4	5	4	3
YARDS	269	368	541	345	148	347	420	318	168
PAR									
YARDS									

Directions: I-91 to Exit 3, 6 miles East of Brattleboro, VT.

Pine Valley Golf Links NR 70

246 Old Gage Hill Road
Pelham, NH
(603) 635-7979, (603) 635-8305
www.pinevalleygolflinks.com

Club Pro: Shawn Logan, PGA
Payment: Visa, MC, Disc
Tee Times: Wkdays, Holidays before 12pm
Fee 9 Holes: Weekday: $16
Fee 18 Holes: Weekday: $21
Twilight Rates: After 3pm
Cart Rental: $12pp/18, $8pp/9
Lessons: Yes **Schools:** No
Membership: Yes
Other: Snack Bar / Bar-Lounge

Tees	Holes	Yards	Par	USGA	Slope
BACK	9	3015	35	90	128
MIDDLE	9	2805	35	66.8	113
FRONT	9	2705	36	70	125

Weekend: $18
Weekend: $36
Discounts: None
Driving Range: No
Junior Golf: Yes
Architect/Yr Open: Todd Madden/1960
GPS:

Course is well-trapped and wooded. Easy to walk. Dress code. Inquire about rates for twilight and all-day play.

	1	2	3	4	5	6	7	8	9
PAR	4	3	5	4	4	4	4	4	3
YARDS	290	200	510	295	335	410	320	320	125
PAR									
YARDS									

Directions: I-93 to Exit 1 (Rockingham Park). Follow signs to Route 38 South (Pelham). Course is located 4 miles up on left.

NH

Ponemah Green Family Center   NR

55 Ponemah Road
Amherst, NH (603) 672-4732
www.amherstcountryclub.com

Club Pro:
Payment: Visa, MC, Disc
Tee Times: 5 days

Tees	Holes	Yards	Par	USGA	Slope
BACK	9	2210	34	62.4	110
MIDDLE	9	2160	34	61.4	107
FRONT	9	1804	34	71.0	106

Fee 9 Holes: Weekday: $16
Fee 18 Holes: Weekday: $25
Twilight Rates: After 4pm, weekends only
Cart Rental: $9pp/9
Lessons: $69/hour, $40/half hour **Schools:** No
Membership: Yes
Other: Clubhouse / Snack Shop

Weekend: $16
Weekend: $25
Discounts: Junior
Driving Range: $5/sm., $8/lg.
Junior Golf: Yes
Architect/Yr Open: Geoffrey Cornish/1989
GPS:

Executive 9-hole golf course with small undulating greens. Accuracy a must. Open April until first snow. Now with mini-golf.

	1	2	3	4	5	6	7	8	9
PAR	3	3	4	4	4	4	4	4	4
YARDS	111	129	252	238	394	251	292	229	314
PAR									
YARDS									

Directions: I-293, to Route 101 West to Amherst. Then take Route 122 to the course located 1/2 mile past Amherst Country Club.

Portsmouth Country Club   ✪✪✪½   72

80 Country Club Lane
Greenland, NH (603) 436-9719
www.portsmouthcc.net

Club Pro: Bill Andrews, PGA
Payment: Visa, MC, Disc, Cash
Tee Times: 3 day adv.

Tees	Holes	Yards	Par	USGA	Slope
BACK	18	7072	72	73.6	123
MIDDLE	18	6649	72	71.8	121
FRONT	18	5511	75	72.1	120

Fee 9 Holes: Weekday:
Fee 18 Holes: Weekday: $85 Summer rate
Twilight Rates: No
Cart Rental: $18pp/18, $13pp/9
Lessons: $80/hour **Schools:** No
Membership: Yes
Other: Clubhouse / Snack Bar / Bar-Lounge

Weekend:
Weekend: $85 Summer rate
Discounts: None
Driving Range: $5/lg., $3/sm.
Junior Golf: No
Architect/Yr Open: Robert Trent Jones Jr./1957
GPS:

COUPON

Hosted State Amateur. Architect, Robert Trent Jones Jr., links, designed to be open, with gently rolling hills, nice bunkers, and large fast greens. 7 holes play alongside the very scenic Great Bay and the course interacts with the water. Constant sea breeze creates a challenge. Ask about other seasonal rates.

	1	2	3	4	5	6	7	8	9
PAR	4	4	4	5	3	4	5	3	4
YARDS	386	425	375	494	157	412	504	219	371
	10	11	12	13	14	15	16	17	18
PAR	4	5	4	3	5	4	3	4	4
YARDS	418	511	452	152	490	329	143	401	420

Directions: I-95 to Route 33 West (Greenland exit). Follow (tiny) signs. Course is approximately 2 miles from I-95.

Ragged Mountain Resort ✪✪

620 Ragged Mountain Road
Danbury, NH (603) 768-3600
raggedmountainresort.com

Club Pro: Tom Gilly
Payment: Visa, MC
Tee Times: 7 adv.

Tees	Holes	Yards	Par	USGA	Slope
BACK	18	6482	72	72.5	136
MIDDLE	18	5762	72	69.3	125
FRONT	18	4963	72	65.1	118

Fee 9 Holes: Weekday: $35 ride   **Weekend:** $35 ride
Fee 18 Holes: Weekday: $49 ride   **Weekend:** $59 ride
Twilight Rates: After 3pm $35/18 or 9   **Discounts:** None
Cart Rental: Included   **Driving Range:** $4.50/bucket
Lessons: Schools: No   **Junior Golf:** No
Membership: No   **Architect/Yr Open:** Jeff Julian/1999
Other: Full Restaurant / Clubhouse / Bar Lounge

Player Comments: "Great mountain course. Beautiful setting." Spectacular views under 2 hours from Boston.
4 sets of tees. 2-year major renovation project to begin Spring of 2009. Ask about early season rates.

	1	2	3	4	5	6	7	8	9
PAR	4	5	4	4	3	4	3	5	4
YARDS	305	432	377	290	143	302	112	497	302
	10	11	12	13	14	15	16	17	18
PAR	4	5	4	3	4	3	4	5	4
YARDS	342	438	307	136	349	188	412	500	330

Directions: Route 93 North to Exit 23. Take Route 104 West for 20 minutes, through town of Bristol.
Follow signs for Ragged Mountain access road on left. Follow road for 2 miles to course.

Ridgewood Country Club NR

258 Gov. Wentworth Highway
Moultonborough, NH
(603) 476-5930
www.ridgewoodcc.net

Club Pro: Louis Rivers, PGA
Payment: Visa, MC, Amex
Tee Times: 5 days adv.

Tees	Holes	Yards	Par	USGA	Slope
BACK	18	6548	72	71.6	128
MIDDLE	18	6059	72	69.2	124
FRONT	18	4627	72	67.7	114

Fee 9 Holes: Weekday: $29   **Weekend:** $32
Fee 18 Holes: Weekday: $40   **Weekend:** $45
Twilight Rates: After 4pm   **Discounts:** Senior
Cart Rental: $17pp/18, $11pp/9   **Driving Range:** $8/lg., $5/sm. bucket
Lessons: $50/45 min. **Schools:** Jr. & Lady   **Junior Golf:** Yes
Membership: Yes, yearly and monthly   **Architect/Yr Open:** John Ponko/1998
Other: Full-Service Restaurant   **GPS:**

18 championship holes, full-service golf shop, custom club fitting, short game practice area.

	1	2	3	4	5	6	7	8	9
PAR	4	4	5	4	3	4	3	4	5
YARDS	307	341	470	393	173	371	178	288	535
	10	11	12	13	14	15	16	17	18
PAR	3	5	4	4	4	4	4	3	5
YARDS	173	517	347	350	361	340	349	128	438

Directions: Route I-93, Exit 23 to Route 104. Left at Route 3 in Meredith to Route 25 East
Moultonboro to Route 109 South. 1.5 mile on right. Please see website.

NH

Rockingham Country Club

NR 75

200 Exeter Road
Newmarket, NH (603) 659-9956
www.rockinghamgolf.com

Tees	Holes	Yards	Par	USGA	Slope
BACK					
MIDDLE	9	2875	35	65.3	104
FRONT	9	2622	37	69.4	104

Club Pro: No
Payment: Visa, MC, Disc, Cash
Tee Times: 7 days adv. (non-members)
Fee 9 Holes: Weekday: $20   **Weekend:** $20
Fee 18 Holes: Weekday: $29   **Weekend:** $29
Twilight Rates: Play before 7am M-F, $13/9 only
Discounts: Senior & Juniors weekdays
Cart Rental: $30/18, $15/9 per cart   **Driving Range:** No
Lessons: No **Schools:** No   **Junior Golf:** No
Membership: No   **Architect/Yr Open:** 1933
Other: $1.50 a hole during the week (M-F), no holidays.

The course is level and well-kept with 2 water holes.

	1	2	3	4	5	6	7	8	9
PAR	4	4	3	4	4	4	3	4	5
YARDS	386	315	175	393	315	380	125	306	480
PAR									
YARDS									

Directions: I-95 to Hampton Exit (Route 101 West) to Route 108. North to course.

Sagamore-Hampton Golf Club ✪✪

76

101 North Road
North Hampton, NH (603) 964-5341
www.sagamoregolf.com

Tees	Holes	Yards	Par	USGA	Slope
BACK	18	6041	71	69.2	122
MIDDLE	18	5647	71	67.4	118
FRONT	18	4886	71	67.5	112

Club Pro: Brian O'Hearn
Payment: Visa, MC, Amex
Tee Times: 1 week adv.
Fee 9 Holes: Weekday: $23   **Weekend:** $26
Fee 18 Holes: Weekday: $39   **Weekend:** $45
Twilight Rates: After 5pm wkdays, 3pm wkends   **Discounts:** Senior & Junior
Cart Rental: $16pp/18, $10pp/9   **Driving Range:** Yes, off course
Lessons: Yes **Schools:** Yes   **Junior Golf:** Yes
Membership: No   **Architect/Yr Open:** Christopher Luff/1962
Other: Frequent player discounts / E-mail specials / Bar-Lounge

COUPON

Offering an enjoyable layout for all abilities at affordable prices. Portsmouth and Newburyport nearby. Considered by many to be the best golf value on the seacoast. Newly redesigned 2nd and 9th greens. See website for coupons and loyalty programs.

	1	2	3	4	5	6	7	8	9
PAR	4	4	4	3	4	5	3	5	3
YARDS	291	325	352	135	300	463	192	424	166
	10	11	12	13	14	15	16	17	18
PAR	5	3	4	5	3	4	5	3	4
YARDS	527	172	380	446	125	284	456	190	419

Directions: I-95 to Exit 2, right to 101 West. First exit, go right onto 111 East, then follow 2.5 miles. Left onto 151 North, follow 1 mile, right onto North Road.

Shattuck Golf Course, The ✪✪½ ▸77

53 Dublin Road
Jaffrey, NH (603) 532-4300
www.sterlinggolf.com

Tees	Holes	Yards	Par	USGA	Slope
BACK	18	6764	71	73.5	153
MIDDLE	18	6077	71	70.9	141
FRONT	18	4632	71	73.1	135

Club Pro: Jim Deutsch
Payment: MC, Visa, Amex, Cash
Tee Times: 7 days adv.
Fee 9 Holes: Weekday: $25   **Weekend:** $32
Fee 18 Holes: Weekday: $40   **Weekend:** $46
Twilight Rates: After 5pm   **Discounts:** Senior & Junior
Cart Rental: $16pp/18, $10pp/9   **Driving Range:** $5/lg.
Lessons: Yes **Schools:** Yes   **Junior Golf:** Yes
Membership: Yes   **Architect/Yr Open:** Brian Silva/1991
Other: Bar-Lounge / Weddings / Large Functions

COUPON

Player Comments: "Every-club-in-the-bag course. Very challenging." "Believe the slope rating—this is a monster. Helpful Player's Guide on website. Uncrowded." Under Sterling Golf Management. Brian Silva course designed in 1991.

	1	2	3	4	5	6	7	8	9
PAR	4	3	4	4	5	5	3	4	4
YARDS	357	146	343	312	551	508	183	373	356
	10	**11**	**12**	**13**	**14**	**15**	**16**	**17**	**18**
PAR	4	4	3	4	3	5	4	4	4
YARDS	394	407	155	303	121	508	367	313	380

Directions: I-90 (Mass Pike) to 495 North to Route 2 West. Take Exit 24B Route 140 North to Route 12 North. Take a left, Go .9 mile. Go right, Route 202 North to Jaffrey, NH. Go left on Route 124. Follow West 2.2 miles. Go right at Mount Monadnock sign. Club is on the left.

Souhegan Woods Golf Club ✪✪½ ▸78

65 Thornton's Ferry Road
Amherst, NH (603) 673-0200
www.playgolfne.com

Tees	Holes	Yards	Par	USGA	Slope
BACK	18	6507	72	70	118
MIDDLE	18	6122	72	68.3	115
FRONT	18	5286	71/69	70.6	123

Club Pro: Bill Meier, PGA
Payment: Most Major
Tee Times: 7 days adv.
Fee 9 Holes: Weekday: $23   **Weekend:**
Fee 18 Holes: Weekday: $35   **Weekend:** $45
Twilight Rates: After 3pm   **Discounts:** Senior & Junior
Cart Rental: $14pp/18, $9pp/9   **Driving Range:** $8/lg, $5/sm bucket
Lessons: $80/hour **Schools:** No   **Junior Golf:** No
Membership: No   **Architect/Yr Open:** Phil Friel/1992
Other: Clubhouse / Bar-Lounge / Snack Bar / Showers

COUPON

Designed to challenge all golfers. In very good condition and well spread out. Open April - November. A Golf Management Company course.

	1	2	3	4	5	6	7	8	9
PAR	4	4	3	5	4	5	4	3	4
YARDS	375	312	168	445	402	501	337	149	355
	10	**11**	**12**	**13**	**14**	**15**	**16**	**17**	**18**
PAR	4	3	4	4	5	4	4	3	5
YARDS	312	153	343	368	510	310	400	166	469

Directions: Route 3 (Everett Turnpike) to Exit 11 (Merrimack). Left off ramp from South, 4.3 miles on Amherst Road.

NH

Stonebridge Country Club ✪✪✪½ 79

161 Gorham Pond Road
Goffstown, NH (603) 497-8633
www.golfstonebridgecc.com

Club Pro: Matt Madore
Payment: Visa, MC, Amex, Disc
Tee Times: 5 days adv.

Tees	Holes	Yards	Par	USGA	Slope
BACK	18	6808	72	72.9	136
MIDDLE	18	6388	72	71.0	133
FRONT	18	4747	72	67.6	116

Fee 9 Holes: Weekday: $27   **Weekend:** $35
Fee 18 Holes: Weekday: $44   **Weekend:** $55
Twilight Rates: After 3pm   **Discounts:** Jr., M-Th before 3pm
Cart Rental: $11pp/9, $16pp/18   **Driving Range:** $7/bucket
Lessons: $40/half hour **Schools:** No   **Junior Golf:** Yes
Membership: Yes   **Architect/Yr Open:** Phil Wogan/1998
Other: Full Restaurant / Clubhouse / Lockers / Showers / Bar-Lounge

COUPON

Player Comments: "Challenging greens. Beautiful landscape." "Demanding layout from middle and back tees." Newly paved cart paths, new carts, and other renovations completed in 2008. Hole no. 6, the short but dangerous par 3, was voted number 1 golf hole in NH by WMUR-TV viewers.

	1	2	3	4	5	6	7	8	9
PAR	5	4	4	3	4	3	4	4	4
YARDS	480	398	370	152	366	136	332	408	417
	10	11	12	13	14	15	16	17	18
PAR	5	4	4	3	5	4	3	5	4
YARDS	496	325	349	193	526	369	150	521	400

Directions: I-93 to Route 101 West to Route 114 North for 9 miles, through Goffstown center. After Sully's Superette, go 1.5 mile and take right onto Parker Station Road. Immediate right onto Gorham Pond Road. Course is 3/4 mile on left.

Sunningdale Golf Course NR 80

301 Green Street
Somersworth, NH (603) 742-8056

Club Pro: Kevin Rillivick
Payment: Visa, MC, Cash, Check
Tee Times: Yes

Tees	Holes	Yards	Par	USGA	Slope
BACK	9	3505	36	71.8	125
MIDDLE	9	3170	36	71.8	125
FRONT	9	3170	36	74.4	121

Fee 9 Holes: Weekday: $10   **Weekend:** $18
Fee 18 Holes: Weekday: $18   **Weekend:** $28
Twilight Rates: No   **Discounts:** Junior
Cart Rental: $10pp/18, $5/9   **Driving Range:** $4
Lessons: Yes **Schools:** No   **Junior Golf:** Yes
Membership: Yes   **Architect/Yr Open:** Geoffrey Cornish/1962
Other: Bar-Lounge   **GPS:**

Under new management. Hilly and fairly narrow. Fairways in great shape. Improving every day.

	1	2	3	4	5	6	7	8	9
PAR	4	4	3	5	4	5	3	4	4
YARDS	385	335	200	500	325	470	185	350	420
PAR									
YARDS									

Directions: Exit 9 off Spaulding Turnpike. Straight through intersection on Route 9. Right on Stackpole Road just past Wal-mart. Right onto Green Street. 1/3 mile on right.

Sunset Hill Golf Course

NR 81

234 Sunset Hill Road
Sugar Hill, NH (603) 823-7244
www.sunsethillgolf.com

Tees	Holes	Yards	Par	USGA	Slope
BACK	9	1977	33		81
MIDDLE	9	1953	33	58.2	81
FRONT					

Club Pro:
Payment: Visa, MC, Amex, Disc, Checks
Tee Times: Yes
Fee 9 Holes: Weekday: $15 **Weekend:** $20
Fee 18 Holes: Weekday: $20 **Weekend:** $30
Twilight Rates: After 5pm **Discounts:** Junior
Cart Rental: $25pp/18; weekday $15pp/9, $30pp/18; weekend $20pp/9
Driving Range: No
Lessons: $30/half hour **Schools:** Yes
Membership: Yes **Junior Golf:** Yes
Architect/Yr Open: Ted Bonar/1897
Other: Snack Bar / Restaurant / Hotel Along 1st Hole / Functions

COUPON

"Particularly friendly for families, beginners, and seniors. Hassle-free golf the way we remember it." Oldest 9-hole course in NH, built in 1897. Antique clubhouse restored in 2007. A really fun place to play golf.

	1	2	3	4	5	6	7	8	9
PAR	4	4	4	4	3	4	3	4	3
YARDS	233	286	231	229	169	210	157	260	178
PAR									
YARDS									

Directions: I-93 to Exit 38. Go left at bottom of ramp, take right at blinking light. Go 1/2 mile then left on Route 117. Go uphill for 2 miles and turn left onto Sunset Hill Road. Course is on the left in 1/2 mile.

Twin Lake Villa Golf Course

NR 82

164 Twin Lake Villa Road
New London, NH (603) 526-6460
www.twinlakevillage.com

Tees	Holes	Yards	Par	USGA	Slope
BACK	9	1515	27		
MIDDLE	9	1356	27		
FRONT	9	1149	27		

Club Pro:
Payment: Personal Checks
Tee Times: 3 days adv.
Fee 9 Holes: Weekday: $12 **Weekend:** $12
Fee 18 Holes: Weekday: $16 **Weekend:** $16
Twilight Rates: No **Discounts:** Senior, $2 off
Cart Rental: No Carts **Driving Range:** No
Lessons: Arranged off-site **Schools:** No **Junior Golf:** No
Membership: Yes **Architect/Yr Open:** Henry Kidder/1948
Other: **GPS:**

Open May 1 - October 31.

	1	2	3	4	5	6	7	8	9
PAR	3	3	3	3	3	3	3	3	3
YARDS	141	113	118	109	190	197	180	177	131
PAR									
YARDS									

Directions: I-89 to Exit 12. Go East 2 miles to New London. At blinking light, turn left onto Country Road. At first stop sign, turn left onto Little Sunapee Road for 1 mile. Bear right onto Twin Lake Villa Road and follow up hill to Hotel and Golf Shop.

NH

Waterville Valley

NR **83** ▶

Route 49
Waterville, NH (603) 236-4805
www.waterville.com

Tees	Holes	Yards	Par	USGA	Slope
BACK					
MIDDLE	9	2404	32	63	105
FRONT					

Club Pro: John Wood, PGA
Payment: Visa, MC, Amex, Disc
Tee Times: 48 hours adv.
Fee 9 Holes: Weekday: $25
Fee 18 Holes: Weekday: $35
Twilight Rates: No
Cart Rental: $24pp/18, $17pp/9
Lessons: $45/half hour **Schools:** No
Membership: Yes
Other: Clubhouse / Snack Bar / Club Storage / Resort

Weekend: $25
Weekend: $35
Discounts: None
Driving Range: No
Junior Golf: Yes
Architect/Yr Open: 1898

Interesting, newly designed golf course with 3 holes on the top of the hill. Spectacular view. Mountain resort. Open May 27 - October 15. Inquire about junior clinics. New clubhouse.

	1	2	3	4	5	6	7	8	9
PAR	4	3	3	4	3	3	4	4	4
YARDS	371	124	150	410	220	150	251	377	351
PAR									
YARDS									

Directions: I-93 to Exit 28; follow Route 49 for 12 miles.

Waukewan Golf Club

✪✪½ **84** ▶

166 Waukewan Road
Center Harbor, NH (603) 279-6661
www.waukewan.com

Tees	Holes	Yards	Par	USGA	Slope
BACK	18	5885	72	68.7	118
MIDDLE	18	5415	72	68.3	117
FRONT	18	4695	72	64.6	113

Club Pro: Chuck Yeager
Payment: Cash or Credit Card
Tee Times: Up to 7 days adv. 6am-3pm
Fee 9 Holes: Weekday: $25
Fee 18 Holes: Weekday: $40
Twilight Rates: After 3pm $15
Cart Rental: $16pp/18, $10pp/9
Lessons: Available **Schools:** Yes
Membership: Yes
Other: Clubhouse / Snack Bar / Bar-Lounge

Weekend: $30
Weekend: $45
Discounts: None
Driving Range: $6/lg, $3/sm bucket
Junior Golf: Yes
Architect/Yr Open: Melvin D. Hale Sr./1958
GPS:

COUPON

Located in the Lakes Region of New Hampshire, this scenic course is nestled within a beautiful mountain range. The redsigned 13th green is our latest accomplishment. The friendly staff will only add to your relaxing golf experience.

	1	2	3	4	5	6	7	8	9
PAR	4	4	3	4	4	5	3	5	4
YARDS	360	305	130	230	230	530	160	430	370
	10	**11**	**12**	**13**	**14**	**15**	**16**	**17**	**18**
PAR	4	3	4	4	4	5	3	5	4
YARDS	260	180	245	400	280	440	180	430	215

Directions: I-93 to Exit 23. Route 104 to Meredith, Route 3 North toward Plymouth 3 miles from Meredith traffic junction, left turn onto Waukewan Road.

Waumbek Country Club, The

Route 2
Jefferson, NH (603) 586-7777
www.playgolfne.com

Tees	Holes	Yards	Par	USGA	Slope
BACK	18	6128	71	67.0	117
MIDDLE	18	5792	71	65	111
FRONT	18	4772	71	67.8	111

Club Pro: Larry Fellows
Payment: Visa, MC, Amex
Tee Times: Weekends
Fee 9 Holes: Weekday: $16   **Weekend:** $19
Fee 18 Holes: Weekday: $25   **Weekend:** $31
Twilight Rates: After 3pm, $15   **Discounts:** Junior
Cart Rental: $13pp/18   **Driving Range:**
Lessons: Yes **Schools:** Yes   **Junior Golf:** Yes
Membership: Yes   **Architect/Yr Open:** Willy Norton/1895
Other: Snack Bar   **GPS:**

COUPON

Challenging course in great shape. The oldest 18-hole course in New Hampshire. Ball 'magnetizes' toward Cherry Mountain — don't aim for the hole, aim for the mountain.

	1	2	3	4	5	6	7	8	9
PAR	4	4	5	4	4	4	4	3	3
YARDS	333	370	500	310	320	390	290	200	195
	10	11	12	13	14	15	16	17	18
PAR	4	5	4	4	3	4	4	5	3
YARDS	310	465	387	280	110	340	335	490	170

Directions: I-93 to Exit 35 (Route 3 North). Follow Route 3 for 12 miles, then take a right onto Route 115 North. Follow Route 115 North for 6.7 miles. Take a left onto Route 115A. Golf course is 4 miles down on the right.

Wentworth Resort GC

Route 16A
Jackson, NH (603) 383-9641
www.wentworthgolf.com

Tees	Holes	Yards	Par	USGA	Slope
BACK					
MIDDLE	18	5581	69	66.0	115
FRONT	18	5087	70	66.7	114

Club Pro: Kevin Walker PGA
Payment: MC, Visa, Amex, Disc
Tee Times: Anytime
Fee 9 Holes: Weekday: **Weekend:**
Fee 18 Holes: Weekday: $35   **Weekend:** $45 F/S/S/H
Twilight Rates: After 3pm   **Discounts:** Junior
Cart Rental: $15pp/18, $9pp/9   **Driving Range:** No
Lessons: $45/45 min **Schools:** No   **Junior Golf:** Yes
Membership: Yes   **Architect/Yr:** Wayne Stiles/1895, Arthur Hill/1998
Other: Snack Bar / Restaurant / Bar-Lounge   **GPS:**

COUPON

Challenging course situated in Jackson Village. Enjoy the rolling hills and the covered bridge crossing the Ellis River on the White Mountains' 2nd oldest course.

	1	2	3	4	5	6	7	8	9
PAR	4	4	4	3	3	4	4	4	5
YARDS	305	337	349	304	147	411	291	307	479
	10	11	12	13	14	15	16	17	18
PAR	4	4	4	4	3	5	3	3	4
YARDS	333	359	336	365	185	464	100	144	295

Directions: I-95 to Spaulding Turnpike. Take Route 16 North to Jackson Village. Or I-93 to Route 25 to Route 16 North to Jackson Village.

NH

Whip-Poor-Will Golf Club

NR **87**

55 Marsh Road
Hudson, NH (603) 889-9706

Tees	Holes	Yards	Par	USGA	Slope
BACK	9	3015	36	67.8	120
MIDDLE	9	2990	36	67.8	120
FRONT	9	2547	36	69.9	119

Club Pro: Al Levesque, mgr.
Payment: Visa, MC, Amex, Disc
Tee Times: 7 days in advance
Fee 9 Holes: Weekday: $21 **Weekend:** $24
Fee 18 Holes: Weekday: $30 **Weekend:** $35
Twilight Rates: After 3pm wknds **Discounts:** Senior & Junior
Cart Rental: $12.50pp/18, $8pp/9 **Driving Range:** No
Lessons: Schools: No **Junior Golf:** No
Membership: No **Architect/Yr Open:** Manuel Francis/1959
Other: Clubhouse / Snack Bar / Bar Lounge **GPS:**

COUPON

An enjoyable well-maintained 9-hole course, perfect for an early afternoon off. A Golf Management Company course.

	1	2	3	4	5	6	7	8	9
PAR	4	3	4	4	5	4	4	5	3
YARDS	330	170	345	315	485	402	280	498	165
PAR									
YARDS									

Directions: I-93 to Exit 4 to Route 102 West approximately 7 miles. Course is on left at Marsh Road just after Alverine High School.

White Mountain Country Club ✪✪½ **88**

North Ashland Road
Ashland, NH
(603) 536-2227

Tees	Holes	Yards	Par	USGA	Slope
BACK	18	6428	71	70.4	122
MIDDLE	18	5963	112	67.9	119
FRONT	18	5350	72	69.6	118

Club Pro: Gregg Sufat
Payment: Visa, MC
Tee Times: 1 week adv.
Fee 9 Holes: Weekday: $20 **Weekend:** $32
Fee 18 Holes: Weekday: $32 **Weekend:** $43
Twilight Rates: After 3pm **Discounts:** None
Cart Rental: $16pp/18, $9pp/9 **Driving Range:** $8/lg, $4/sm bucket
Lessons: $30/half hour, $50/hour **Schools:** No **Junior Golf:** No
Membership: No **Architect/Yr Open:** Cornish & Silva/1975
Other: Bar-Lounge / Snack Bar / Townhouse Rentals

COUPON

Player Comments: "Great course in the Fall." Golfer-friendly, challenging, well-cared-for. Expanded driving range and recent reversal of dogleg on hole #2. A Golf Management Company course.

	1	2	3	4	5	6	7	8	9
PAR	4	4	4	3	5	4	3	5	4
YARDS	327	334	325	174	524	300	172	508	312
	10	**11**	**12**	**13**	**14**	**15**	**16**	**17**	**18**
PAR	4	3	4	4	4	4	4	4/5	4
YARDS	356	154	356	374	321	301	359	410	356

Directions: I-93 North to Exit 24, left off ramp for 1 mile. Right onto North Ashland Road, 2.5 miles on left.

Windham Country Club ✪✪✪ 89 ▶

Country Club Road
Windham, NH (603) 434-2093
www.windhamcc.com

Tees	Holes	Yards	Par	USGA	Slope
BACK	18	6442	72	71.2	135
MIDDLE	18	6033	72	69.1	129
FRONT	18	5584	72	67.4	122

Club Pro: Joanne Flynn, PGA
Payment: Visa, MC
Tee Times: 7 days a week, 5 days in adv.
Fee 9 Holes: Weekday: $22   **Weekend:** $28
Fee 18 Holes: Weekday: $42   **Weekend:** $50
Twilight Rates: After 6pm wkdys, 4pm wknds   **Discounts:** Senior & Junior
Cart Rental: $16pp/18, $8pp/9   **Driving Range:** $8/lg., $5/sm.
Lessons: $50/half hour   **Schools:** Yes   **Junior Golf:** Yes
Membership: No   **Architect/Yr Open:** William Flynn/1995
Other: Full Restaurant / Clubhouse / Bar-Lounge / Snack Bar

COUPON

Noted for condition and challenging layout. Open year round (when possible). New superintendent, and great overall condition.

	1	2	3	4	5	6	7	8	9
PAR	5	4	3	4	5	3	4	4	3
YARDS	522	374	158	365	578	136	398	369	165
	10	11	12	13	14	15	16	17	18
PAR	4	4	5	4	3	5	4	4	4
YARDS	280	354	440	304	166	444	382	335	306

Directions: I-93 to Exit 3. Take Route 111 West 1.5 miles. Then right on Church Street to fire station, then right onto North Lowell for 1 mile. Left onto Londonderry Road .5 mile and left on Country Club Road.

Woodbound Inn Golf Course NR 90 ▶

247 Woodbound Road
Jaffrey, NH (603) 532-8341
www.woodbound.com

Tees	Holes	Yards	Par	USGA	Slope
BACK					
MIDDLE	9	1956	27		
FRONT					

Club Pro: No
Payment: Visa, MC, Amex, Cash
Tee Times: No
Fee 9 Holes: Weekday: $15   **Weekend:** $15
Fee 18 Holes: Weekday: $15   **Weekend:** $15
Twilight Rates: After 6pm   **Discounts:** Senior & Junior
Cart Rental: Pull carts   **Driving Range:** No
Lessons: No   **Schools:** No   **Junior Golf:** No
Membership: Yes   **Architect/Yr Open:** Ed Brummer/1963
Other: Snack Bar / Restaurant / Gift Shop / Bar-Lounge

COUPON

A course that is great for families, seniors, beginners, corporate outings, or short game. 18 different tee boxes. Resident rates.

	1	2	3	4	5	6	7	8	9
PAR	3	3	3	3	3	3	3	3	3
YARDS	114	138	94	128	109	79	142	117	131
PAR									
YARDS									

Directions: I-495 to Route 202 West, 10 miles from NH border. Follow signs to course.

NH

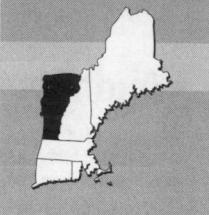

Burlington ★

Newport ★

★ Stowe
★ Montpelier

★ St. Johnsbury

★ Warren

White River Junction ★

★ Rutland

★ Manchester

★ Bennington

Champlain Country Club	13	Okemo Valley GC	37
Copley Country Club	14	Orleans Country Club	38
Country Club of Barre	15	Proctor Pittsford CC	39
Crown Point CC	16	Prospect Bay CC	40
Enosburg Falls CC	17	Ralph Myhre GC	41
Equinox Country Club	18	Richford CC	42
Essex Country Club	19	Rocky Ridge GC	43
Farm Resort GC	20	Rutland CC	44
Green Mt. National GC	21	Sitzmark GC	45
Haystack Golf Club	22	St. Johnsbury CC	46
Jay Peak Resort GC	23	Stamford Valley CC	47
John P. Larkin CC	24	Stonehedge GC	48
Killington Golf Resort	25	Stowe Country Club	49
Kwiniaska Golf Club	26	Stratton Moutain GC	50
Lake Morey CC	27	Sugarbush Golf Club	51
Lake St. Catherine CC	28	Tater Hill Golf Club	52
Links at Lang Farm	29	West Bolton Golf Club	53
Montague Golf Club	30	White River Golf Club	54
Montpelier CC	31	Wilcox Cove GC	55
Mount Snow Golf Club	32	Williston Golf Club	56
Mt. Anthony CC	33	Woodbury GC	57
Neshobe Golf Club	34	Woodstock Inn	58
Newport CC	35		
Northfield CC	36		

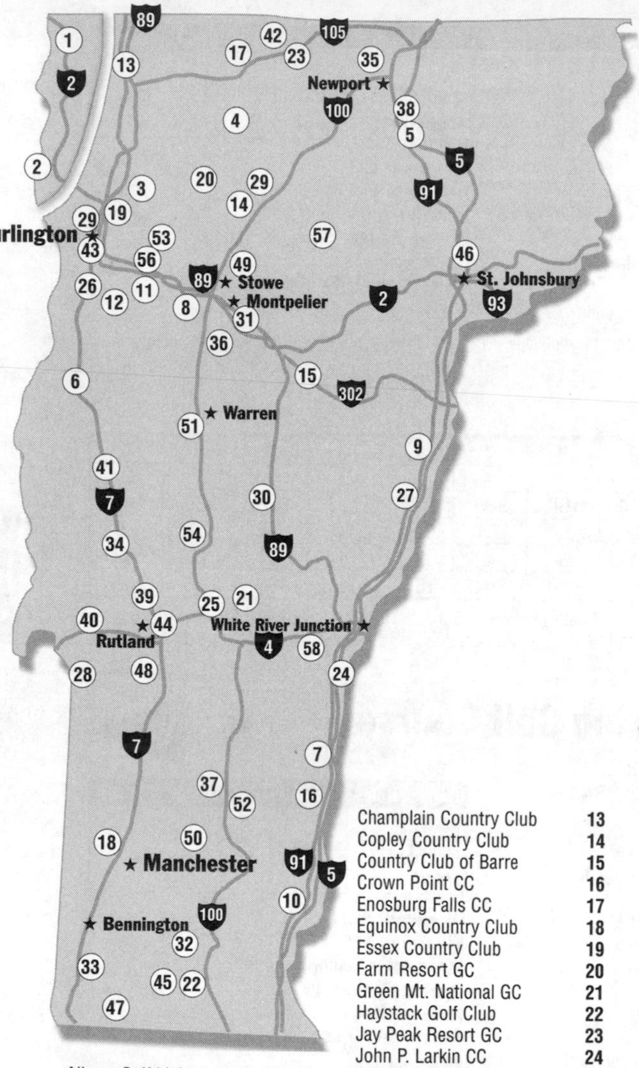

Alburg Golf Links	1
Apple Island Resort GC	2
Arrowhead GC	3
Bakersfield CC	4
Barton Golf Club	5
Basin Harbor Club	6
Bellows Falls CC	7
Blush Hill CC	8
Bradford Golf Course	9
Brattleboro CC	10
Catamount Golf Course	11
Cedar Knoll CC	12

Alburg Golf Links ⊗⊙ 1

230 Route 129
Alburg, VT (802) 796-4248
www.alburggolflinks.com

Club Pro: No
Payment: Visa, MC
Tee Times: Sat/Sun/Holidays
Fee 9 Holes: Weekday: $17
Fee 18 Holes: Weekday: $27.50
Twilight Rates: After 1pm
Cart Rental: $15pp/18, $11pp/9
Lessons: Yes **Schools:** No
Membership: Yes

Tees	Holes	Yards	Par	USGA	Slope
BACK	18	6450	72	70.1	121
MIDDLE	18	5803	72	67.3	115
FRONT	18	5044	72	66.4	105

Weekend: $22
Weekend: $37
Discounts: None
Driving Range: $10 unlimited
Junior Golf: Yes
Architect/Yr Open: Dick Ellison/1967

Other: Clubhouse / Snack Bar / Bar-Lounge / 1 Week & 2 Week Vacation Specials

A good vacation course, moderately challenging. Driving range, unlimited balls, $10/Sr., $5/Jr.

	1	2	3	4	5	6	7	8	9
PAR	4	4	4	4	3	4	5	4	3
YARDS	320	360	387	355	120	362	459	143	344
	10	11	12	13	14	15	16	17	18
PAR	5	3	4	5	4	4	3	5	4
YARDS	467	167	404	488	296	286	140	447	322

Directions: Take I-89 to Exit 17; take Route 2 to Champlain Islands North to Alburg; take Route 129 to course.

Apple Island Resort Golf Course NR 2

VT

71 Route 2
South Hero, VT (802) 372-9600
www.appleislandresort.com/golf.html

Club Pro: No
Payment: Cash, Checks
Tee Times: No
Fee 9 Holes: Weekday: $14.75
Fee 18 Holes: Weekday:
Twilight Rates: After 5:30pm
Cart Rental: $2/pull
Lessons: No **Schools:** No
Membership: Yes
Other: Resort

Tees	Holes	Yards	Par	USGA	Slope
BACK					
MIDDLE	9	1108	27		
FRONT					

Weekend: $16.75
Weekend:
Discounts: None
Driving Range: No
Junior Golf: No
Architect/Yr Open: Walter Barcomb/1977
GPS:

Course in great shape and all tees have been redone. No one under 5 years allowed. Open May 1 - October 20. Extended tee off boxes holes #3 & #5.

	1	2	3	4	5	6	7	8	9
PAR	3	3	3	3	3	3	3	3	3
YARDS	100	90	158	184	158	108	84	96	130
PAR									
YARDS									

Directions: Exit 17 off I-89. Go 6 miles, on left. Must drive through campground to reach course.

Arrowhead Golf Course ✪✪ ▶3

350 Murray Avenue
Milton, VT (802) 893-0234

Tees	Holes	Yards	Par	USGA	Slope
BACK	9	1542	27	56.6	80
MIDDLE	9	1330	27	56.0	79
FRONT	9	1005	27	48.8	55

Club Pro:
Payment: Cash, Check, Credit
Tee Times: No
Fee 9 Holes: Weekday: $14
Fee 18 Holes: Weekday: $18
Twilight Rates: No
Cart Rental: $10pp/18, $7pp/9
Lessons: No **Schools:** No
Membership: Yes $215
Other: Clubhouse

Weekend: $16
Weekend: $20
Discounts: None
Driving Range: $7/lg., $4/sm. bucket
Junior Golf: No
Architect/Yr Open: T.F. Goodwin/1997
GPS:

This 9-hole, par 3 golf course consists of gently rolling fairways, unique design characteristics, excellent greens, sand bunkers, water hazards, and natural hazards. 3rd hole is very challenging. New range mats.

	1	2	3	4	5	6	7	8	9
PAR	3	3	3	3	3	3	3	3	3
YARDS	165	148	195	90	119	195	136	104	178
PAR									
YARDS									

Directions: Exit 18 from I-89. Go South on Route 7 approximately 1/2 mile. Turn right onto Ballard Road for 1/2 mile, take left onto Old Stage Road for 1 mile, then right onto Murray Avenue for 1.6 miles. Course is on left.

Bakersfield Country Club NR ▶4

Boston Post Road
Bakersfield, VT (802) 933-5100

Tees	Holes	Yards	Par	USGA	Slope
BACK	18	6222	72		
MIDDLE	18	5881	72	69.0	115
FRONT	18	5006	72	68.7	108

Club Pro:
Payment: Visa, MC, Amex
Tee Times: Yes
Fee 9 Holes: Weekday: $18
Fee 18 Holes: Weekday: $23
Twilight Rates: After 4:15pm
Cart Rental: $13pp/18, $8pp/9
Lessons: Inquire **Schools:** No
Membership: Junior
Other: Snack Bar / Restaurant / Bar-Lounge

Weekend: $18
Weekend: $26
Discounts: None
Driving Range: No
Junior Golf: No
Architect/Yr Open: John Watson/1987
GPS:

	1	2	3	4	5	6	7	8	9
PAR	4	4	5	3	4	3	4	5	4
YARDS	273	357	424	128	445	155	350	460	375
	10	11	12	13	14	15	16	17	18
PAR	4	3	4	4	5	3	5	3	5
YARDS	360	155	345	290	468	150	392	155	599

Directions: Route 108 through Bakersfield. Take right onto Boston Post Road. Follow signs.

Barton Golf Club

NR ▶ **5**

548 Telfer Hill Road
Barton, VT (802) 525-1126
www.bartongolfclub.com

Club Pro: Bill King
Payment: Visa, MC, Disc
Tee Times: Yes
Fee 9 Holes: Weekday: $13
Fee 18 Holes: Weekday: $21
Twilight Rates: After 6pm
Cart Rental: $14pp/18, $7pp/9
Lessons: No **Schools:** No
Membership: Yes
Other: Light Fare Menu

Tees	Holes	Yards	Par	USGA	Slope
BACK	18	6000	70	66.8	114
MIDDLE	18	5304	70	65.3	104
FRONT	18	4500	69		

Weekend: $13
Weekend: $21
Discounts: None
Driving Range: No
Junior Golf: No
Architect/Yr Open: Brian King/1991
GPS:

COUPON

Scenic 18 holes in the heart of Vermont's Northeast Kingdom. New layout due to the replacement of 7 holes. Spectacular views.

	1	2	3	4	5	6	7	8	9
PAR	4	5	4	3	4	4	3	5	4
YARDS	256	465	303	120	304	396	160	440	365
	10	11	12	13	14	15	16	17	18
PAR	4	3	5	4	3	3	5	3	4
YARDS	268	130	450	385	140	150	502	135	335

Directions: I-91 to Exit 25. Take Route 16 into Barton. Go right on Water Street. Cross Route 5. Left on High Street. Club is 1 mile on right.

Basin Harbor Club

✪✪✪ ▶ **6**   VT

4800 Basin Harbor Road
Vergennes, VT (802) 475-2309
www.basinharbor.com

Club Pro: Doug Slusser, PGA
Payment: Visa, MC
Tee Times: Anytime for current season
Fee 9 Holes: Weekday: $36
Fee 18 Holes: Weekday: $53
Twilight Rates: After 1pm
Cart Rental: $18pp/18, $12pp/9
Lessons: $40/half hour **Schools:** Yes
Membership: Yes
Other: Clubhouse / Snack Bar / Restaurant / Bar-Lounge / Hotel

Tees	Holes	Yards	Par	USGA	Slope
BACK	18	6513	72	70.7	120
MIDDLE	18	6232	72	69.5	118
FRONT	18	5745	72	66.2	114

Weekend: $36
Weekend: $53
Discounts: None
Driving Range: $4 or $7.50/bucket
Junior Golf: Yes
Architect/Yr Open: Alex Campbell/1927

Fairly flat, located on Lake Champlain. Collared shirt required. No cutoffs. Open May 1 - mid-October. 18-hole rate reduced after 1pm, free cart after 3. New women's tee boxes. Improved playability through bunker work, tree removal and tees. Resort guests have reduced rates.

	1	2	3	4	5	6	7	8	9
PAR	4	4	4	4	3	4	3	5	5
YARDS	360	361	398	328	103	323	150	458	475
	10	11	12	13	14	15	16	17	18
PAR	4	4	5	3	4	4	3	5	4
YARDS	387	376	500	181	324	414	175	510	409

Directions: Route 7 to Vergennes exit. Straight through town on Route 22A. Cross over bridge, take right at sign to Basin Harbor. 1 mile to Basin Harbor Road, take right, 6 miles to course.

Bellows Falls Country Club

Rockingham Road
Route 103, Rockingham, VT
(802) 463-9809
www.bellowsfallscountryclub.com

Club Pro:
Payment: Visa, MC, Cash
Tee Times: No
Fee 9 Holes: Weekday: $16
Fee 18 Holes: Weekday: $27
Twilight Rates: After 4pm
Cart Rental: $30/18, $20/9 per cart
Lessons: Yes **Schools:** No
Membership: Yes
Other: Restaurant / Bar

Tees	Holes	Yards	Par	USGA	Slope
BACK					
MIDDLE	9	2892	35	65.8	117
FRONT	9	2569	35	65.8	110

Weekend: $20
Weekend: $30
Discounts: Senior
Driving Range: No
Junior Golf: No
Architect/Yr Open: 1923
GPS:

COUPON

Open May 1 - November 1. Vermont Country Store, Bellows Falls and Chester Village nearby!

	1	2	3	4	5	6	7	8	9
PAR	4	5	3	3	4	4	4	3	5
YARDS	389	513	178	155	381	370	320	158	428
PAR									
YARDS									

Directions: I-91 to Exit 6. Route 103 North. Turn right onto Country Club Road. Across from Vermont Country Store.

Blush Hill Country Club

✪✪ 8

Blush Hill Road
Waterbury, VT (802) 244-8974
www.blushhillcountryclub.com

Club Pro:
Payment: Visa, MC
Tee Times: Encouraged
Fee 9 Holes: Weekday: $19 M-Th
Fee 18 Holes: Weekday: $25 M-Th
Twilight Rates: No
Cart Rental: $28pp/18, $18pp/9
Lessons: $40/half hour **Schools:** No
Membership: Yes
Other: Clubhouse / Lockers / Showers / Snack Bar / Restaurant / Bar-Lounge

Tees	Holes	Yards	Par	USGA	Slope
BACK					
MIDDLE	9	2416	33	62.7	113
FRONT	9	2275	33	66.2	114

Weekend: $22 F/S/S
Weekend: $28 F/S/S
Discounts: None
Driving Range: $5/lg., $3/sm.
Junior Golf: Yes
Architect/Yr Open: Andrew Freeland/1926

COUPON

One of the most extraordinary scenic views in Vermont. Course kept in excellent shape. Open May 1 - October 15. Ben & Jerry's right around the corner.

	1	2	3	4	5	6	7	8	9
PAR	4	4	4	3	4	3	3	4	4
YARDS	377	350	206	171	266	146	157	377	302
PAR									
YARDS									

Directions: 1/2 mile off I-89 North, on Route 100. 1000 feet left on Blush Hill Road, 3/4 mile beyond Best Western on Blush Hill Road.

Bradford Golf Course ✪✪ ▶9

Bradford, VT
(802) 222-5207
www.bradfordgolfclubinc.com

Tees	Holes	Yards	Par	USGA	Slope
BACK	9	2155	32		
MIDDLE	9	2052	32		
FRONT					

Club Pro: No
Payment: Cash, Visa, MC
Tee Times: No
Fee 9 Holes: Weekday: $16
Fee 18 Holes: Weekday: $21
Twilight Rates: After 5pm $12+tax
Cart Rental: $15pp/18, $10pp/9
Lessons: No **Schools:** No
Membership: Yes
Other: Snacks

Weekend: $16
Weekend: $24
Discounts: None
Driving Range: No
Junior Golf: No
Architect/Yr Open: 1927
GPS:

"Greens usually in fine shape." –JS Par 32, 18 sets of tees.

	1	2	3	4	5	6	7	8	9
PAR	3	4	3	3	4	3	5	4	3
YARDS	174	239	160	115	304	185	431	294	150

PAR									
YARDS									

Directions: From I-91, take Exit 16, turn right and go 3/4 of a mile. Turn left, go 1 mile North. Turn right, go by Bradford Academy to bottom of hill.

Brattleboro Country Club ✪✪½ ▶10

Upper Dummerston Road
Brattleboro, VT (802) 257-7380
www.brattleborogolf.com

Tees	Holes	Yards	Par	USGA	Slope
BACK	18	6508	71	71.0	123
MIDDLE	18	6073	71	69.3	118
FRONT	18	5059	71	70.0	116

Club Pro: Eric Sandstrum, PGA
Payment: Visa, MC, Amex
Tee Times: 3 days adv.
Fee 9 Holes: Weekday: $26
Fee 18 Holes: Weekday: $45
Twilight Rates: No
Cart Rental: $18pp/18, $11pp/9
Lessons: Yes **Schools:** Yes
Membership: Yes
Other: Restaurant / Bar-Lounge

Weekend: $32
Weekend: $59
Discounts: Senior
Driving Range: Yes
Junior Golf: Yes
Architect/Yr Open: Wayne Stiles/1912
GPS:

Player Comments: "Wide fairways, greens in good condition, rustic setting, friendly staff. Still relatively unknown." "Great value." Recent expansion to 18 holes. Inquire about special offers. 10 new holes with range. First golf course in Vermont when travelling I-91 North. Hidden gem! Many new hotels and restaurants in Brattleboro area.

	1	2	3	4	5	6	7	8	9
PAR	4	5	4	3	4	4	5	3	4
YARDS	405	504	359	155	397	243	455	155	363
	10	**11**	**12**	**13**	**14**	**15**	**16**	**17**	**18**
PAR	5	4	4	3	4	4	3	4	4
YARDS	492	378	376	172	340	386	152	346	389

Directions: I-91 North or South to Exit 2. Left off exit, go 1/2 mile to Cedar Street. Turn left, follow to bottom of hill. Left on Route 30. Left at Upper Dumerston Road. Club 1/2 mile on left.

Catamount Golf Course

NR 11

1400 Mountain View Drive
Williston, VT (802) 878-7227
www.catamountgolf.com

Club Pro: Lou Jarvis, PGA
Payment: Cash, Visa, MC
Tee Times:
Fee 9 Holes: Weekday: $16
Fee 18 Holes: Weekday: $32
Twilight Rates: No
Cart Rental: $16pp/18, $8pp/9
Lessons: Schools: Yes
Membership: Yes
Other: Snack Bar

Tees	Holes	Yards	Par	USGA	Slope
BACK					
MIDDLE	9	3040	35		
FRONT					

Weekend: $16
Weekend: $32
Discounts: None
Driving Range: $9/lg., $5/sm., double-decker
Junior Golf: Yes
Architect/Yr Open: Marty Keene/1999
GPS:

$130 discount card available for 10 9-hole rounds. Course landscaped to provide visual depiction of the route to play this links-style course.

	1	2	3	4	5	6	7	8	9
PAR	4	3	4	3	5	3	5	4	4
YARDS	385	160	380	185	520	170	485	365	390
PAR									
YARDS									

Directions: I-89 to Exit 12 (Route 2A). Go North on Route 2A for about 2.5 miles. Turn right on Mountain View Drive, go 1.5 miles. Course will be on your right.

Cedar Knoll Country Club

NR 12

13020 Route 116
Hinesburg, VT (802) 482-3186
www.cedarknollgolf.com

Club Pro: Barry Churchill
Payment: Visa, MC, Amex
Tee Times: Yes
Fee 9 Holes: Weekday: $20
Fee 18 Holes: Weekday: $32
Twilight Rates: After 5pm
Cart Rental: $16pp/18, $10pp/9
Lessons: Yes **Schools:** No
Membership: Yes
Other: Restaurant / Clubhouse / Bar-Lounge / Lockers / Showers / Snack Bar

Tees	Holes	Yards	Par	USGA	Slope
BACK	27/18	6541	72	72.5	117
MIDDLE	27/18	6144	72	72.5	117
FRONT	27/18	5360	72	69.5	108

Weekend: $20
Weekend: $32
Discounts: None
Driving Range: $3/sm., $6/lg. bucket
Junior Golf: No
Architect/Yr Open: Raymond Ayer/1994

Now 27 holes. Rolling hills. 250 acres allows for nice spacing of holes. Beautiful scenery. Cedar Knoll South 9-hole addition is also open. 9-hole rate, $20.

	1	2	3	4	5	6	7	8	9
PAR	5	3	4	4	5	3	4	4	4
YARDS	500	156	315	358	505	170	392	313	438
	10	11	12	13	14	15	16	17	18
PAR	5	3	4	4	3	4	4	4	5
YARDS	494	169	298	333	156	291	341	315	536

Directions: I-89 to Exit 12; follow 5 miles to intersection of Routes 2A and 116. Take left and go 5 miles on 116. Course on right.

Champlain Country Club

Route 7
Swanton, VT (802) 527-1187
www.champlaincountryclub.com

Tees	Holes	Yards	Par	USGA	Slope
BACK	18	6237	70	69.9	123
MIDDLE	18	5959	70	68.8	121
FRONT	18	5366	70	70.4	117

Club Pro: Michael Swim
Payment: MC, Visa, Disc
Tee Times: Weekends, Holidays
Fee 9 Holes: Weekday: $25   **Weekend:** $30
Fee 18 Holes: Weekday: $35   **Weekend:** $40
Twilight Rates: **Discounts:** When playing with member
Cart Rental: $15pp/18, $10/9   **Driving Range:** Free balls
Lessons: $25/half hour **Schools:**   **Junior Golf:** Yes
Membership: Yes   **Architect/Yr Open:** Duer Irving Sewall/1915
Other: Clubhouse / Lockers / Showers / Snack Bar / Restaurant / Bar-Lounge
GPS: Yes

Overlooking Lake Champlain. Nice views. New tees.

	1	2	3	4	5	6	7	8	9
PAR	4	5	3	4	4	4	3	4	4
YARDS	359	472	152	377	353	347	135	350	342
	10	11	12	13	14	15	16	17	18
PAR	4	4	3	4	3	5	4	4	4
YARDS	303	444	142	370	167	526	328	415	315

Directions: I-89 to Exit 20; take Route 7 North 1/2 mile to course.

Copley Country Club

Maple Road
Morrisville, VT (802) 888-3013
www.copleygolfcourse.com

Tees	Holes	Yards	Par	USGA	Slope
BACK	9	3000	35	67.4	112
MIDDLE	9	2775	35	67.4	112
FRONT	9	2510	35	68.0	104

Club Pro: No
Payment: Visa, MC
Tee Times: Required
Fee 9 Holes: Weekday: $19   **Weekend:** $19
Fee 18 Holes: Weekday: $29.50   **Weekend:** $29.50
Twilight Rates: No   **Discounts:** None
Cart Rental: $13pp/18, $9pp/9   **Driving Range:** No
Lessons: No **Schools:** No   **Junior Golf:** Yes
Membership: Yes   **Architect/Yr Open:** 1936
Other: Clubhouse / Lockers / Snack Bar / Restaurant / Bar-Lounge

Ideal conditions. The course is level with a handful of tree-lined holes.

	1	2	3	4	5	6	7	8	9
PAR	4	3	4	4	3	5	4	4	4
YARDS	310	218	326	296	171	526	395	270	262
	10	11	12	13	14	15	16	17	18
PAR									
YARDS									

Directions: I-89 to Waterbury exit, follow 18 miles to Morrisville.

Country Club of Barre ✪✪½ ▸ 15

Plainsfield Road
Barre, VT (802) 476-7658
www.ccofbarre.com

Tees	Holes	Yards	Par	USGA	Slope
BACK	18	6315	71	70.4	123
MIDDLE	18	5938	71	68.9	121
FRONT	18	5126	71	70.3	121

Club Pro: Roger King, PGA
Payment: Visa, MC, Amex
Tee Times: 5 days adv.
Fee 9 Holes: Weekday: $26   **Weekend:** $26
Fee 18 Holes: Weekday: $47   **Weekend:** $47
Twilight Rates: After 4pm on weekends   **Discounts:** None
Cart Rental: $23pp/18, $12pp/9   **Driving Range:** $3/lg.
Lessons: $35/40 min. **Schools:** No   **Junior Golf:** For members
Membership: Yes   **Architect/Yr Open:** Wayne Stiles/1924
Other: Clubhouse / Lockers / Showers / Snack Bar / Restaurant / Bar-Lounge

COUPON

Player Comments: "One of the hidden gems in Vermont." Semi-private, call for tee times.

	1	2	3	4	5	6	7	8	9
PAR	4	4	4	3	5	4	3	4	4
YARDS	368	383	285	190	455	339	142	370	368
	10	11	12	13	14	15	16	17	18
PAR	5	4	4	3	4	5	3	4	4
YARDS	492	372	314	170	431	439	125	343	352

Directions: I-89 to Exit 7, to Barre. Follow Route 14 North 3.9 miles, take right onto East Hill Road, take a left at the T, go 2 miles.

Crown Point Country Club ✪✪½ ▸ 16

Weathersfield Center Road
Springfield, VT (802) 885-1010
crownpointcc.com

Tees	Holes	Yards	Par	USGA	Slope
BACK	18	6602	72	71.2	128
MIDDLE	18	6120	72	69.1	122
FRONT	18	5542	72	73.0	124

Club Pro: Paul Politano, PGA
Payment: Visa, MC, Cash
Tee Times: Recommended
Fee 9 Holes: Weekday: $25   **Weekend:** $28
Fee 18 Holes: Weekday: $45   **Weekend:** $55
Twilight Rates: After 2pm & 4pm   **Discounts:** Senior & Junior
Cart Rental: Yes   **Driving Range:** Yes
Lessons: Yes **Schools:** No   **Junior Golf:** Yes
Membership: Yes   **Architect/Yr Open:** William Mitchell/1953
Other: Clubhouse / Showers / Restaurant / Bar-Lounge

COUPON

Course noted for smooth fast greens. Great views. Open April 15 - November 1 (weather permitting).

	1	2	3	4	5	6	7	8	9
PAR	4	5	4	4	3	4	5	4	3
YARDS	370	426	344	337	168	365	487	376	154
	10	11	12	13	14	15	16	17	18
PAR	4	5	4	3	4	5	4	4	3
YARDS	344	463	390	158	344	459	381	371	183

Directions: I-91 North to Exit 7; turn right and follow to center of Springfield. Turn right onto Valley Street. Course 3 miles on left.

Enosburg Falls Country Club

NR 17

53 Elm Street
Enosburg Falls, VT
(802) 933-2296
www.efccvt.com

Tees	Holes	Yards	Par	USGA	Slope
BACK	18	5580	72	67.4	116
MIDDLE	18	5418	72	66.8	115
FRONT	18	4633	72	63.4	108

Club Pro: Rick Marckres, head pro
Payment: MC, Visa
Tee Times: Yes
Fee 9 Holes: Weekday: $19   **Weekend:** $19
Fee 18 Holes: Weekday: $30   **Weekend:** $30
Twilight Rates: After 3pm   **Discounts:** Junior
Cart Rental: $28/18, $15/9 per cart   **Driving Range:** Irons range
Lessons: Yes   **Schools:** No   **Junior Golf:** Yes
Membership: Yes   **Architect/Yr Open:** 1963
Other: Restaurant / Clubhouse / Lockers / Showers

Course has some great birdie opportunities. Variety of rates for special memberships. Upgrading course with new bunkers. Open May - October.

	1	2	3	4	5	6	7	8	9
PAR	4	5	4	4	4	3	4	5	3
YARDS	249	498	337	251	350	115	331	552	119
	10	11	12	13	14	15	16	17	18
PAR	4	3	4	5	5	3	4	4	4
YARDS	272	140	335	490	478	112	267	255	267

Directions: I-89 to St. Albans Exit to Route 105 North; follow to Enosburg Falls. Take left at junction of Routes 108 and 105 to course.

Equinox Country Club

✪✪✪ 18 VT

3567 Main Street (Route 7A)
Manchester, VT (802) 362-3223
www.playequinoxresort.com

Tees	Holes	Yards	Par	USGA	Slope
BACK	18	6423	71	70.8	129
MIDDLE	18	6069	71	69.2	125
FRONT	18	5082	71	64.3	113

Club Pro: Joan McDonald, LPGA
Payment: MC, Visa, Amex, Disc
Tee Times: 7 days adv.
Fee 9 Holes: Weekday: $60   **Weekend:** $70
Fee 18 Holes: Weekday: $100   **Weekend:** $120
Twilight Rates: After 3pm   **Discounts:** None
Cart Rental: $20pp   **Driving Range:** No
Lessons: $60/half hour   **Schools:** No   **Junior Golf:** No
Membership: Yes   **Architect/Yr Open:** Walter Travis/1926
Other: Restaurant / Clubhouse / Snack Bar / Bar-Lounge / Hotel / Lockers / Showers

Player Comments: "A great place to stay and play while on a New England vacation." "Wonderful challenge." "Elegant surroundings, impeccable fairways. The views make you forget the score."

	1	2	3	4	5	6	7	8	9
PAR	4	4	4	3	4	4	5	4	4
YARDS	334	385	346	141	316	323	502	380	344
	10	11	12	13	14	15	16	17	18
PAR	4	4	4	4	3	5	3	4	4
YARDS	336	361	347	401	112	462	181	403	395

Directions: Located on Route 7A in Manchester.

Essex Country Club

NR 19 ▶

332 Old Stage Road
Essex Junction, VT (802) 879-3232
www.essexccvt.com

Club Pro: Mike Morelli, assistant pro
Lou Jarvis, PGA
Payment: Visa, MC, Amex
Tee Times: Weekends

Tees	Holes	Yards	Par	USGA	Slope
BACK	18	6475	72	70.0	117
MIDDLE	18	6315	72	70.0	117
FRONT	18	5500	72	69.1	112

Fee 9 Holes: Weekday: $20 **Weekend:** $20
Fee 18 Holes: Weekday: $30 **Weekend:** $30
Twilight Rates: After 4pm
Discounts: Mon: Men's day $19, Tues: Seniors' day $19, Wed: Ladies' day $19
Cart Rental: $15pp/18, $8pp/9 **Driving Range:** $5/sm., $6/med., $7/lg. bucket
Lessons: Yes **Schools:** No **Junior Golf:** Yes
Membership: Yes **Architect/Yr Open:** Joe Chastaney/1988
Other: **GPS:**

Ongoing improvements. Monday, Tuesday and Wednesday specials. Upgraded irrigation. 14 of the 18 holes are fully irrigated. New putting green and practice range.

	1	2	3	4	5	6	7	8	9
PAR	4	3	4	4	5	4	5	4	3
YARDS	365	155	400	330	450	335	530	315	190
	10	11	12	13	14	15	16	17	18
PAR	5	4	4	3	4	5	3	4	4
YARDS	580	320	355	130	360	530	170	350	450

Directions: I-89 to Exit 12. Williston exit Route 2A to Essex 5 corner; then take Route 15 to Old Stage Road 3 miles North to course.

Farm Resort & Golf Course

NR 20 ▶

Route 100
Morrisville, VT (802) 888-3525
www.farmresortgolf.com

Club Pro: Eileen Kask, PGA
Payment: Visa, MC
Tee Times: Yes

Tees	Holes	Yards	Par	USGA	Slope
BACK	9	3019	36	69.4	108
MIDDLE	9	2909	36	68.3	108
FRONT	9	2599	36	68.9	113

Fee 9 Holes: Weekday: $20 **Weekend:** $22
Fee 18 Holes: Weekday: $29 **Weekend:** $31
Twilight Rates: After 4pm **Discounts:** Junior
Cart Rental: $13.50pp/18, $9pp/9 **Driving Range:** $7.50/lg, $4.50/med
Lessons: Yes **Schools:** Yes **Junior Golf:** Yes
Membership: Yes **Architect/Yr Open:** Geoffrey Cornish/1969
Other: Camp **GPS:**

COUPON

Great course for golfers of all abilities. Play & stay at 1 location. Open May - October. Bunker and greens improvements! Montreal and Stow, VT close by.

	1	2	3	4	5	6	7	8	9
PAR	4	4	5	3	3	5	4	3	5
YARDS	331	290	460	147	142	556	391	142	450
PAR									
YARDS									

Directions: I-89 to Route 100 North approximately 15 miles to Stowe. Take Route 108 North 5.5 miles to Cape Cod Road. Follow signs.

Green Mountain National GC ✪✪✪✪ 21 ▶

Barrows Towne Road (Route 100)
Killington, VT (802) 422-GOLF
www.greenmountainnational.com

Tees	Holes	Yards	Par	USGA	Slope
BACK	18	6589	71	72.1	138
MIDDLE	18	6164	71	70.2	133
FRONT	18	4740	71	68.9	118

Club Pro: David Soucy, PGA
Payment: Visa, MC, AMEX, Disc
Tee Times: 7 days adv.
Fee 9 Holes: Weekday: $46.78 w/cart   **Weekend:** $49.78 w/cart
Fee 18 Holes: Weekday: $80.20 w/cart   **Weekend:** $90.20 w/cart
Twilight Rates: After 3pm $49 weekday, $52 Sat/Sun
Discounts: Junior
Cart Rental: Included   **Driving Range:** $7/lg., $4/sm. bucket
Lessons: $60-80/hour **Schools:** Adult   **Junior Golf:** Yes
Membership: Resident/Non-Resident passes   **Architect/Yr Open:** Gene Bates/1996
Other: Bar / Lounge / Snack Bar   **GPS:** Yes

Player Comments: "Unbelievable in the fall. Incredibly challenging. Great layout, conditions and friendly personnel." Several stay-and-play partners.

	1	2	3	4	5	6	7	8	9
PAR	5	4	4	4	3	5	3	4	4
YARDS	494	387	381	406	152	492	145	348	419
	10	11	12	13	14	15	16	17	18
PAR	4	4	4	3	4	5	4	3	4
YARDS	396	350	375	157	326	437	359	169	371

Directions: I-91 to Exit 6. Turn left onto Route 103 North for about 30 minutes. Take right onto Route 100 North. Go by Killington Mountain Road. Course is 2 miles on left. Travel time from I-91 is about 1 hour.

Haystack Golf Club ✪✪✪½ 22 ▶   VT

Mann Road
Wilmington, VT (802) 464-8301
www.haystackgolf.com

Tees	Holes	Yards	Par	USGA	Slope
BACK	18	6549	72	71.7	128
MIDDLE	18	6164	72	69.3	125
FRONT	18	5396	74	71.4	122

Club Pro: Jack Tosone, PGA
Payment: Visa, MC, Amex, Disc
Tee Times: Call
Fee 9 Holes: Weekday: $35 w/cart   **Weekend:** $55 w/cart
Fee 18 Holes: Weekday: $49 w/cart   **Weekend:** $79 w/cart
Twilight Rates: After 2pm   **Discounts:** Sr. Day M $35 w/cart
Cart Rental: Included   **Driving Range:** $5/bucket Irons only
Lessons: Yes **Schools:** Junior   **Junior Golf:** Yes
Membership: Yes   **Architect/Yr Open:** Desmond Muirhead/1972
Other: Clubhouse / Lockers / Showers / Restaurant / Bar-Lounge / Snack Bar/ Hotel

COUPON

The Desmond Muirhead-designed championship layout offers manicured fairways and challenging 9 greens. Shot-making is in order as you go from a front side with gently rolling terrain to a back 9 with breathtaking mountain views and dramatic elevation changes.

	1	2	3	4	5	6	7	8	9
PAR	4	4	5	3	4	4	3	5	4
YARDS	348	389	460	181	347	291	166	505	380
	10	11	12	13	14	15	16	17	18
PAR	4	5	4	3	5	4	3	4	4
YARDS	328	509	352	160	516	343	165	301	423

Directions: I-91 to Brattleboro, take Route 9 West to Wilmington. At light head North on Route 100 (3 miles). Look for signs, turn left on Coldbrook Road (2 miles). Take left on Mann Road (1.5 miles) to gate.

Jay Peak Resort Golf Course
NR **23** ▶

4850 Route 242
Jay, VT (802) 988-2611
www.jaypeakresort.com

Club Pro: R. Vacca
Payment: Visa, MC, Amex, Disc, Checks
Tee Times: Yes
Fee 9 Holes: Weekday: $49 w/cart
Fee 18 Holes: Weekday: $79 w/cart
Twilight Rates: After 3pm
Cart Rental: Included
Lessons: Yes **Schools:** Yes
Membership: Yes
Other:

Tees	Holes	Yards	Par	USGA	Slope
BACK	18	6908	72	73.1	138
MIDDLE	18	6330	72	71.0	133
FRONT	18	5094	72	69.1	120

Weekend:
Weekend: $99 w/cart
Discounts: Senior & Junior
Driving Range: Yes
Junior Golf:
Architect/Yr Open: Graham Cooke/2006
GPS: Yes

COUPON

Front 9 wraps its way around Eastern edge of the resort. Back 9 course design by Graham Cooke. Outstanding championship course in the Northeast kingdom. Spectacular course is a must-play.

	1	2	3	4	5	6	7	8	9
PAR	4	3	4	5	3	4	5	4	4
YARDS	410	133	422	538	167	347	472	380	367
	10	11	12	13	14	15	16	17	18
PAR	4	5	3	5	3	4	5	3	4
YARDS	399	474	129	513	196	335	486	155	407

Directions: I-91 to Exit 26 (Orleans). Go North via Route 5 to Route 14 North. Then go South on Route 100. Take a right in center of Troy onto 101 North. Left onto Route 242. Follow to entrance on right.

John P. Larkin Country Club
NR **24** ▶

Route 5
Windsor, VT (802) 674-6491
www.clublarkin.com

Club Pro:
Payment: Visa, MC
Tee Times: Wknds/M/T/Hldy
Fee 9 Holes: Weekday: $15
Fee 18 Holes: Weekday: $18
Twilight Rates: No
Cart Rental: $25/18, $15/9 per cart
Lessons: Yes **Schools:** No
Membership: Yes
Other: Restaurant / Clubhouse / Snack Bar / Bar-Lounge / Lockers / Showers

Tees	Holes	Yards	Par	USGA	Slope
BACK					
MIDDLE	9	2670	34	65.1	105
FRONT	9	2462	36	68.2	109

Weekend: $25
Weekend: $28
Discounts: None
Driving Range: No
Junior Golf: Yes
Architect/Yr Open: 1921

Course has views of Mt. Ascutney and Connecticut River. New irrigation. New Hampshire is out of bounds.

	1	2	3	4	5	6	7	8	9
PAR	4	3	4	4	4	3	3	5	4
YARDS	332	215	333	309	383	176	140	442	340
PAR									
YARDS									

Directions: I-91 to Exit 9, left on Route 5, course is 3.5 miles down.

Killington Golf Resort ✪✪✪ 25 ▶

4763 Killington Road
Killington, VT (802) 422-6700
www.killingtongolf.com

Tees	Holes	Yards	Par	USGA	Slope
BACK	18	6168	72	70.3	129
MIDDLE	18	5876	72	68.9	124
FRONT	18	4803	72	68.3	119

Club Pro: Dave Pfannenstein, PGA
Payment: Most Major
Tee Times: Recommended
Fee 9 Holes: Weekday: $30   **Weekend:** $30
Fee 18 Holes: Weekday: $52   **Weekend:** $57
Twilight Rates: After 3pm   **Discounts:** Senior & Junior
Cart Rental: $19pp/18; $11pp/9   **Driving Range:** $3.50/bucket
Lessons: $60/hour **Schools:** Jr. & Sr.   **Junior Golf:** Yes
Membership: Yes   **Architect/Yr Open:** Geoffrey Cornish/1983
Other: Hotel / Clubhouse / Snack Bar / Restaurant / Bar-Lounge

Player Comments: "Great mountain course. Beautiful setting."

	1	2	3	4	5	6	7	8	9
PAR	4	5	3	4	5	3	5	4	4
YARDS	354	485	163	395	452	138	480	321	270
	10	11	12	13	14	15	16	17	18
PAR	4	5	4	4	3	4	4	3	4
YARDS	334	485	300	355	174	370	360	150	290

Directions: I-89 to Exit 1 onto Route 4 West to Killington Road. Turn left onto Killington Road. Go 3.5 miles and look for signs.

Kwiniaska Golf Club ✪✪ 26 ▶

5531 Spear Street
Shelburne, VT (802) 985-3672
www.kwiniaska.com

Tees	Holes	Yards	Par	USGA	Slope
BACK	18	6848	72	72.7	129
MIDDLE	18	6601	72	71.7	126
FRONT	18	5246	72	70.6	115

Club Pro: Michael Bailey, PGA
Payment: Visa, MC, Disc
Tee Times: Weekends & Holidays
Fee 9 Holes: Weekday: **Weekend:**
Fee 18 Holes: Weekday: $36   **Weekend:** $36
Twilight Rates: After 4pm $24   **Discounts:** None
Cart Rental: $16pp/18, $9pp/9   **Driving Range:** Yes
Lessons: Yes **Schools:** No   **Junior Golf:** Yes
Membership: Yes/limited   **Architect/Yr Open:** A. Bradford Caldwell/1996
Other: Clubhouse / Locker Room Facilities / Showers / Snack Bar

Course is framed with trees that are spectacular during foliage. Course plays tougher than it looks. 3rd longest course in the state.

	1	2	3	4	5	6	7	8	9
PAR	4	3	5	3	4	4	4	4	5
YARDS	425	186	467	181	446	375	407	374	541
	10	11	12	13	14	15	16	17	18
PAR	4	4	3	5	4	3	5	4	4
YARDS	307	341	169	495	399	193	490	328	417

Directions: I-89 to Exit 14 West. Follow signs to Spear Street, then 5 miles South.

Lake Morey Country Club ●● 27

Spear Road
Fairlee, VT (802) 333-4800
www.lakemoreycc.com

Tees	Holes	Yards	Par	USGA	Slope
BACK	18	6024	70	69.4	120
MIDDLE	18	5807	70	68.4	118
FRONT	18	4942	70	68.0	116

Club Pro: B. Ross Jr., golf dir.
Payment: Visa, MC, Disc
Tee Times: 4 days adv.
Fee 9 Holes: Weekday: $23   **Weekend:** $23
Fee 18 Holes: Weekday: $34   **Weekend:** $43
Twilight Rates: After 3pm $23, after 4pm $16   **Discounts:** Senior, M-T $23
Cart Rental: $15.57pp/18, $10pp/9   **Driving Range:** $3/bucket
Lessons: $40/45 minutes **Schools:** No   **Junior Golf:** Yes
Membership: Yes   **Architect/Yr Open:** 1915; Geoffrey Cornish/1989
Other: Clubhouse / Showers / Snack Bar / Restaurant / Bar-Lounge / Hotel

Player Comment: A flat course with multiple stay-and-play packages. Home of Vermont Open for 53 years. Recently completed work on tees.

	1	2	3	4	5	6	7	8	9
PAR	3	5	4	4	4	3	3	4	4
YARDS	213	460	356	337	334	158	114	395	321
	10	11	12	13	14	15	16	17	18
PAR	4	4	5	5	4	3	4	3	4
YARDS	324	369	504	517	373	188	371	160	313

Directions: I-91 North to Exit 15, take left off ramp and follow signs. 25 minutes North of White River Junction.

Lake St. Catherine Country Club NR 28

Route 30
Poultney, VT (802) 287-9341
www.lsccc.net

Tees	Holes	Yards	Par	USGA	Slope
BACK	18	6204	72	69.0	125
MIDDLE	18	5840	72	67.3	118
FRONT	18	4899	72	62.0	107

Club Pro: Jack Sodoma
Payment: Visa, MC, Cash
Tee Times: 1 week in adv.
Fee 9 Holes: Weekday: $19   **Weekend:** $29
Fee 18 Holes: Weekday: $29   **Weekend:** $36
Twilight Rates: After 1pm wkdys; after 2pm wknds **Discounts:** Senior
Cart Rental: $18pp/18, $11pp/9   **Driving Range:** Yes
Lessons: $40/45min **Schools:** No   **Junior Golf:** Yes
Membership: Yes   **Architect/Yr Open:** 1925
Other: Snack Bar / Bar-Lounge / Full-Service Restaurant

Player Comments: "15th and 16th holes most scenic in state." Open April - October. Brand-new clubhouse opened 2006.

	1	2	3	4	5	6	7	8	9
PAR	4	4	3	4	4	4	5	3	5
YARDS	391	340	156	405	354	333	517	186	444
	10	11	12	13	14	15	16	17	18
PAR	5	4	4	4	3	4	3	4	5
YARDS	522	343	327	320	125	374	166	388	513

Directions: Directly on Route 30 South of Poultney, easily accessible from Route 4 to 30 South.

Links at Lang Farm

29

○○½

39 Essex Way
Essex Junction, VT (802) 878-0298
www.linksatlangfarm.com

Tees	Holes	Yards	Par	USGA	Slope
BACK	18	3809	60	59.8	102
MIDDLE	18	3444	60	58	96
FRONT	18	2884	60		

Club Pro: Steve Gonsalves, PGA/dir. of golf
     Jon Milne, head pro
Payment: Visa, MC, Disc, Check, Cash
Tee Times: 7 day adv.
Fee 9 Holes: Weekday: $21
Fee 18 Holes: Weekday: $31
Twilight Rates: After 5pm
Cart Rental: $14pp/18, $7pp/9
Lessons: Yes **Schools:** Yes
Membership: Yes
Other: Inn / Lodging Partner / Stay and Play

Weekend: $21
Weekend: $31
Discounts: Senior
Driving Range: Yes
Junior Golf: Yes
Architect/Yr Open: Michael Asmundson/2002
GPS: Yes

Appealing to all levels of play. Exceptional conditions. Call ahead for times. Golf packages available with The Inn at Essex. New clubhouse coming Spring 2009.

	1	2	3	4	5	6	7	8	9
PAR	3	3	3	4	3	4	3	3	3
YARDS	158	167	155	295	124	307	133	180	156
	10	11	12	13	14	15	16	17	18
PAR	3	3	4	3	4	3	3	4	4
YARDS	156	147	273	126	258	102	152	231	324

Directions: I-89 to Exit 11. Follow Route 117, 6 miles to VT 289. Exit 10, Turn Left.

Montague Golf Club

30

○○

VT

Randolph Avenue
Randolph, VT (802) 728-3806
www.montaguegolf.com

Tees	Holes	Yards	Par	USGA	Slope
BACK	18	6200	69	66.9	116
MIDDLE	18	5438	70	65.5	114
FRONT	18	5025	71	63.3	108

Club Pro: Bob Hanlon, PGA
Payment: Visa, MC
Tee Times: Yes
Fee 9 Holes: Weekday: $15
Fee 18 Holes: Weekday: $27
Twilight Rates: After 3:30pm
Cart Rental: $15pp/18, $8pp/9
Lessons: Yes, PGA **Schools:** No
Membership: Yes
Other: Clubhouse / Snack Bar / Putting Green

Weekend: $20
Weekend: $32
Discounts: Sr. (M), Jr. (w/adult)
Driving Range: Yes
Junior Golf: Yes
Architect/Yr Open: 1913/Geoffrey Cornish
GPS:

Links-style course. New back tees for holes #6, #11, #13, #14 make course over 6200 yards long.

	1	2	3	4	5	6	7	8	9
PAR	4	4	4	3	4	4	3	4	3
YARDS	312	365	332	196	415	368	140	317	155
	10	11	12	13	14	15	16	17	18
PAR	3	5	4	4	5	4	4	4	4
YARDS	198	486	298	300	475	276	375	376	307

Directions: I-89 North to Exit 4. Follow Route 66 into downtown Randolph on Route 12 South. Take left on Merchant Road. Go straight onto Randolph Avenue — end of road, take left.

Montpelier Country Club

NR **31** ▶

Country Club Road
Montpelier, VT (802) 223-7457

Tees	Holes	Yards	Par	USGA	Slope
BACK	9	2564	35	67.0	117
MIDDLE	9	2739	35	66.6	114
FRONT	9	2383	35	67.9	112

Club Pro: No
Payment: Cash, Credit
Tee Times: Weekends, 1 day adv.
Fee 9 Holes: Weekday: $15   **Weekend:** $15
Fee 18 Holes: Weekday: $22   **Weekend:** $22
Twilight Rates: No   **Discounts:** None
Cart Rental: $15pp/18, $11pp/9   **Driving Range:** No
Lessons: Private and Group **Schools:** No **Junior Golf:** Yes
Membership: Yes   **Architect/Yr Open:** 1902
Other: Clubhouse / Lockers / Showers / Snack Bar / Restaurant / Bar-Lounge

The course is relatively short but made challenging by the hilly terrain. Open April 1 - October 31.

	1	2	3	4	5	6	7	8	9
PAR	4	3	5	5	4	3	4	3	4
YARDS	358	155	422	459	226	149	325	191	279
PAR									
YARDS									

Directions: I-89 to Route 2 exit, follow signs for Montpelier.

Mount Snow Golf Club

✪✪✪ **32** ▶

Country Club Road
Mount Snow, VT (802) 464-4254
www.mountsnow.com

Tees	Holes	Yards	Par	USGA	Slope
BACK	18	6943	72	73.7	129
MIDDLE	18	6539	72	71.9	125
FRONT	18	5384	72	70.4	117

Club Pro: Jay Morelli, PGA
Payment: Visa, MC, Amex, Disc
Tee Times: Yes
Fee 9 Holes: Weekday: $36 w/cart   **Weekend:**
Fee 18 Holes: Weekday: $44 w/cart   **Weekend:** $75 w/cart
Twilight Rates: After 2pm   **Discounts:** Senior & Junior
Cart Rental: Included   **Driving Range:** Yes
Lessons: $40/half hour **Schools:** Yes **Junior Golf:** Yes
Membership: Yes   **Architect/Yr Open:** Geoffrey Cornish/1967
Other: Clubhouse / Snack Bar / Restaurant / Bar-Lounge / Hotel / Spa

Home of the Original Golf School, headed by Jay Morelli, MSGC offers breathtaking views and challenging golf for all ability levels. Gold Tees for seniors in 2005. New ladies' tees. Rates subject to change.

	1	2	3	4	5	6	7	8	9
PAR	4	5	3	4	4	3	5	4	4
YARDS	372	593	160	407	432	150	480	400	396
	10	11	12	13	14	15	16	17	18
PAR	4	4	3	4	5	3	5	4	4
YARDS	394	364	143	354	479	187	542	323	163

Directions: I-91 to Exit 2 in Brattleboro to Route 9 West, 20 miles to Wilmington. Turn right at the stop light onto Route 100 North. About 6 miles, take a left on Crosstown Road. At top of hill on left.

Mt. Anthony Country Club ✪✪✪ ▶33

180 Country Club Drive
Bennington, VT (802) 447-7079
www.golfingvermont.com

Tees	Holes	Yards	Par	USGA	Slope
BACK	18	6200	71	75.0	125
MIDDLE	18	6000	71	69.2	125
FRONT	18	5200	71	67.7	106

Club Pro: John Cleanthes, PGA
Payment: Visa, MC, Amex
Tee Times: Yes
Fee 9 Holes: Weekday: **Weekend:**
Fee 18 Holes: Weekday: $45   **Weekend:** $55
Twilight Rates: No   **Discounts:** Junior
Cart Rental: $18pp/18   **Driving Range:** $7/bucket
Lessons: Call for rates **Schools:** Junior   **Junior Golf:** Yes
Membership: Yes   **Architect/Yr Open:** Jay Jerome/1897
Other: Snack Bar / Restaurant / Bar-Lounge / Lockers / Showers

Player Comments: "Good price. Scenic. Great services. Well-maintained." Open April - October. Under new ownership, many improvements being made to the clubhouse and course.

	1	2	3	4	5	6	7	8	9
PAR	4	3	5	3	5	4	4	4	4
YARDS	366	182	474	104	538	369	338	331	304
	10	11	12	13	14	15	16	17	18
PAR	4	4	4	3	3	4	5	4	4
YARDS	344	368	348	156	182	304	435	406	351

Directions: From Route 7 go to Bennington Center. Turn onto West Main Street (Route 9 West). 1/4 mile after Paradise Motel take first right onto Convent Avenue. Follow to end and take left. Course is down on the right.

Neshobe Golf Club ✪✪✪ ▶34

224 Town Farm Road
Brandon, VT (802) 247-3611
www.neshobe.com

Tees	Holes	Yards	Par	USGA	Slope
BACK	18	6349	72	71.6	125
MIDDLE	18	5865	72	68.7	122
FRONT	18	5046	71	64.9	115

Club Pro: Rodney Bicknell, PGA
Payment: MC, Visa
Tee Times: Yes
Fee 9 Holes: Weekday: $20   **Weekend:** $25
Fee 18 Holes: Weekday: $35   **Weekend:** $40
Twilight Rates: After 4pm   **Discounts:** Junior
Cart Rental: $16pp/18, $8pp/9   **Driving Range:** Yes
Lessons: $60/hour **Schools:** No   **Junior Golf:** Yes
Membership: Yes   **Architect/Yr Open:** Steve Durkee/1958
Other: Clubhouse / Lockers / Showers / Snack Bar / Restaurant / Bar-Lounge / Horseshoes / Billiards / Card Room

COUPON

Player Comments: "A challenging course in very good shape." "Best buy in the area." Very scenic course, classic Vermont scenery.

	1	2	3	4	5	6	7	8	9
PAR	4	4	4	4	5	3	4	5	4
YARDS	309	317	339	389	508	132	384	458	272
	10	11	12	13	14	15	16	17	18
PAR	3	5	3	4	5	4	4	3	4
YARDS	102	491	148	343	522	357	243	117	344

Directions: Route 7 to Route 73 East. Follow for 1.5 miles East of Brandon Center.

VT

Newport Country Club ✪✪½

35

Pine Hill Road
Newport, VT (802) 334-2391
www.newportscountryclub.com

Club Pro: Carl Fitz III, PGA
Payment: MC, Visa
Tee Times: 2 day adv.
Fee 9 Holes: Weekday: $20
Fee 18 Holes: Weekday: $36
Twilight Rates: No
Cart Rental: $18pp/18, $10pp/9
Lessons: $40/half hour **Schools:**
Membership: Yes
Other: Restaurant / Clubhouse / Bar-Lounge / Lockers / Showers / Snack Bar

Tees	Holes	Yards	Par	USGA	Slope
BACK	18	6491	72	70.4	117
MIDDLE	18	6228	72	68.6	114
FRONT	18	5274	72	71	114

Weekend: $20
Weekend: $36
Discounts: Junior under 10 yrs/$5
Driving Range: $5/bucket
Junior Golf: Yes
Architect/Yr Open: Ralph Barton

COUPON

Very friendly. Improvements continuing. Nicer greens.

	1	2	3	4	5	6	7	8	9
PAR	4	3	4	5	4	3	4	4	5
YARDS	354	172	356	484	326	150	397	335	469
	10	11	12	13	14	15	16	17	18
PAR	5	4	4	3	4	4	4	3	5
YARDS	479	374	387	144	375	395	314	142	464

Directions: I-91 to Exit 27. Head toward Newport about 1/2 mile. Take left and follow signs.

Northfield Country Club NR

36

Route 12A
Northfield, VT
(802) 485-4515
www.northfieldcountryclub.com

Club Pro: Joe Dingledine, PGA
Payment: Visa, MC, Cash, Checks
Tee Times: Required
Fee 9 Holes: Weekday: $15 M-Th
Fee 18 Holes: Weekday: $21 M-Th
Twilight Rates: No
Cart Rental: $15pp/18, $9pp/9
Lessons: Private and Group **Schools:** No
Membership: Yes
Other: Restaurant / Bar / Clubhouse / Showers

Tees	Holes	Yards	Par	USGA	Slope
BACK	18	5972	70	69.0	122
MIDDLE	18	5768	70	68.0	120
FRONT	18	5140	70	63.1	119

Weekend: $20 F/S/S
Weekend: $28 F/S/S
Discounts: Junior and under free
Driving Range: Netted practice area
Junior Golf: Yes
Architect/Yr Open: Les Heon/1927
GPS:

Player Comments: "Old-fashioned, wonderful and friendly course." Known for 'The Volcano' hole #4.

	1	2	3	4	5	6	7	8	9
PAR	4	4	4	3	4	5	4	3	4
YARDS	348	314	276	148	377	532	336	183	367
	10	11	12	13	14	15	16	17	18
PAR	4	4	3	3	5	5	4	3	4
YARDS	340	352	175	148	465	532	325	183	367

Directions: I-89 to Exit 5, follow to bottom of hill. Go straight .75 mile to a T. Turn left on 12A and go 2.5 miles. Clubhouse on right.

Okemo Valley Golf Club ✪✪✪✪ ▶ 37

77 Okemo Ridge Road
Ludlow, VT (802) 228-1396
www.okemo.com

Tees	Holes	Yards	Par	USGA	Slope
BACK	18	6400	70	71.1	130
MIDDLE	18	6104	70	69.6	128
FRONT	18	5105	70	67.6	118

Club Pro:
Payment: Visa, MC, Amex
Tee Times: 2 days adv.
Fee 9 Holes: Weekday: $40 **Weekend:** $40
Fee 18 Holes: Weekday: $79 **Weekend:** $79
Twilight Rates: No **Discounts:** Junior
Cart Rental: $21pp/18, $11pp/9 **Driving Range:** Yes
Lessons: $70/hour **Schools:** Adult **Junior Golf:** No
Membership: Waiting list **Architect/Yr Open:** Steve Durkee/1999
Other: Full Restaurant / Clubhouse / Hotel / Inn / Lockers / Showers / Bar

NE GolfGuide Pick: "Vermont's Best Course, 2005. "Visually splendid, strategically challenging." –JD
"Beautiful greens. Friendly people."

	1	2	3	4	5	6	7	8	9
PAR	4	5	4	3	4	3	5	3	4
YARDS	381	522	352	175	368	167	487	173	347
	10	**11**	**12**	**13**	**14**	**15**	**16**	**17**	**18**
PAR	4	5	4	4	3	4	4	3	4
YARDS	305	502	371	304	205	396	435	196	418

Directions: Just North of Ludlow about 1 mile on Route 103. Right onto Fox Lane (signs on highway).

Orleans Country Club ✪✪ ▶ 38

316 Country Club Lane
Orleans, VT (802) 754-2333
www.orleanscc.com

Tees	Holes	Yards	Par	USGA	Slope
BACK	18	6191	72	69.3	121
MIDDLE	18	5980	72	68.5	119
FRONT	18	5515	73	66.7	116

Club Pro: Robert Silvester, PGA
Payment: MC, Visa
Tee Times: 3 days in adv.
Fee 9 Holes: Weekday: $16 **Weekend:** $17
Fee 18 Holes: Weekday: $32 **Weekend:** $34
Twilight Rates: No **Discounts:** Mondays, except holidays
Cart Rental: $16pp/18 **Driving Range:** $6/lg, $4/sm bucket
Lessons: $40/half hour **Schools:** No **Junior Golf:** Yes
Membership: Yes **Architect/Yr Open:** Alex Reid/1928
Other: Clubhouse / Restaurant / Snack Bar / Bar Lounge / Complete Practice Facility
GPS: Yes

The course has scenic mountain views on most holes. Considered challenging. Newly renovated clubhouse and new tees. Course is in excellent condition and very popular.

	1	2	3	4	5	6	7	8	9
PAR	5	4	3	5	4	4	4	3	4
YARDS	442	319	152	439	368	356	290	180	370
	10	**11**	**12**	**13**	**14**	**15**	**16**	**17**	**18**
PAR	3	5	4	3	4	4	5	4	4
YARDS	202	479	359	134	426	292	495	285	392

Directions: I-91 to Exit 26. Follow Route 58 1.5 miles East, turn right onto Country Club Lane.

VT

Proctor Pittsford Country Club ✪✪

Cornhill Road
Pittsford, VT (802) 483-9379
www.proctor-pittsford.com

Tees	Holes	Yards	Par	USGA	Slope
BACK	18	6052	70	69.4	121
MIDDLE	18	5728	70	67.9	118
FRONT	18	5446	72	66.1	115

Club Pro: Merle Schoenfeld
Payment: MC, Visa
Tee Times: 2 days adv.
Fee 9 Holes: Weekday: $22   **Weekend:** $22
Fee 18 Holes: Weekday: $38   **Weekend:** $38
Twilight Rates: After 4pm $20   **Discounts:** None
Cart Rental: $16pp/18, $8pp/9   **Driving Range:** $5/lg., $3/sm.
Lessons: Yes **Schools:** No   **Junior Golf:** Yes
Membership: No   **Architect/Yr Open:** Henry Collin/1927
Other: Restaurant / Lounge   **GPS:**

COUPON

Beautiful views, excellent greens and fairways, good test of golf. Open April 15 - October 31. Brand-new driving range. Full-service restaurant. Check out the marble clubhouse.

	1	2	3	4	5	6	7	8	9
PAR	4	4	4	5	4	4	3	4	3
YARDS	325	386	308	489	370	326	133	281	219
	10	11	12	13	14	15	16	17	18
PAR	4	3	5	4	4	4	4	3	4
YARDS	409	144	468	377	332	301	388	163	309

Directions: Take Route 7 for 4 miles North, take left after Nissan dealer. Go 1/2 mile, take right at "T," 3 miles on Cornhill Road.

Prospect Bay Country Club

Prospect Point Road
Route 30, Bomoseen, VT
(802) 468-5581

Tees	Holes	Yards	Par	USGA	Slope
BACK	9	2635	35	65.2	115
MIDDLE	9	2557	35	64.6	114
FRONT	9	2294	35	65.4	114

Club Pro:
Payment: MC, Visa
Tee Times: No
Fee 9 Holes: Weekday: $15, $23/ride   **Weekend:** $17, $26/ride
Fee 18 Holes: Weekday: $22, $30/ride   **Weekend:** $26, $36/ride
Twilight Rates: After 4pm weekdays   **Discounts:** None
Cart Rental: $13.50pp/18, $9pp/9   **Driving Range:** No
Lessons: No **Schools:** No   **Junior Golf:** Yes
Membership: Yes   **Architect/Yr Open:** 1981
Other: Clubhouse / Snack Bar   **GPS:**

The course is hilly and scenic. Great shape. Open April - November.

	1	2	3	4	5	6	7	8	9
PAR	5	3	4	4	4	4	4	4	3
YARDS	405	155	311	283	268	335	298	370	132
PAR									
YARDS									

Directions: Route 4 to Exit 4; follow Route 30 North for 2 miles to course entrance.

Ralph Myhre Golf Course ✪✪

41

317 Golf Course Road
Middlebury, VT (802) 443-5125
www.middlebury.edu

Tees	Holes	Yards	Par	USGA	Slope
BACK	18	6379	71	70.8	124
MIDDLE	18	6014	71	69.2	121
FRONT	18	5337	71	66.9	120

Club Pro: Jim Dayton
Payment: Cash, Visa, MC
Tee Times: Recommended
Fee 9 Holes: Weekday: $20   **Weekend:** $20
Fee 18 Holes: Weekday: $37   **Weekend:** $37
Twilight Rates: After 5pm   **Discounts:** Student
Cart Rental: $18pp/18, $9pp/9   **Driving Range:** Yes
Lessons: Yes **Schools:** No   **Junior Golf:** Yes
Membership: Yes   **Architect/Yr Open:** Ralph Myhre/1920
Other: Clubhouse / Snack Bar / Showers   **GPS:** Yes

COUPON

Open fairways with moderate hills. Well-kept and tees sodded. Owned by Middlebury College. Any student (any school) pays $15.

	1	2	3	4	5	6	7	8	9
PAR	5	4	4	3	4	4	3	4	4
YARDS	479	341	311	166	356	370	141	353	365
	10	11	12	13	14	15	16	17	18
PAR	4	5	3	4	3	4	5	4	4
YARDS	404	525	152	325	126	363	512	351	377

Directions: Route 7 to Route 30 South. Course is just beyond Middlebury College Field House.

Richford Country Club NR

42

1964 King Road
Route 106, Richford, VT
(802) 848-3527

Tees	Holes	Yards	Par	USGA	Slope
BACK					
MIDDLE	9	2908	36	68.2	116
FRONT	9	2326	36	72.0	118

Club Pro: No
Payment: Visa, MC
Tee Times: No
Fee 9 Holes: Weekday: $14 M-Th   **Weekend:** $18 F/S/S
Fee 18 Holes: Weekday: $16 M-Th   **Weekend:** $22 F/S/S
Twilight Rates: Wed. after 3pm   **Discounts:** None
Cart Rental: $12.50pp/18, $18.50pp/9   **Driving Range:** No
Lessons: No **Schools:** No   **Junior Golf:** Yes
Membership: Yes   **Architect/Yr Open:** 1915
Other: Clubhouse / Snack Bar / Bar-Lounge.   **GPS:**

Excellent views of the Green Mountains. New clubhouse. "Vermont's most scenic golf course." Open April - October.

	1	2	3	4	5	6	7	8	9
PAR	4	5	3	4	5	3	4	4	4
YARDS	283	453	170	400	453	175	309	376	289
PAR									
YARDS									

Directions: I-89 to St. Albans exit. Follow Route 105 North to Richford (28 miles).

Rocky Ridge Golf Club ✪✪ 43

7470 Route 116
St. George, VT
(802) 482-2191
www.rockyridge.com

Club Pro: Ed Coleman
Payment: Visa, MC
Tee Times: 48 hours in advance

Tees	Holes	Yards	Par	USGA	Slope
BACK	18	6282	72	70.3	126
MIDDLE	18	6000	72	69.1	124
FRONT	18	5230	72	69.9	117

Fee 9 Holes: Weekday: **Weekend:**
Fee 18 Holes: Weekday: $32   **Weekend:** $37
Twilight Rates: After 5pm $21   **Discounts:** None
Cart Rental: $16pp   **Driving Range:** Yes
Lessons: Yes **Schools:**   **Junior Golf:** Yes
Membership: Yes   **Architect/Yr Open:** E. Farrington/1963
Other: Clubhouse / Lockers / Restaurant / Bar-Lounge

A challenging and very scenic country setting for all skill levels. Online course review.

	1	2	3	4	5	6	7	8	9
PAR	4	5	3	5	4	4	4	3	4
YARDS	270	542	195	576	314	251	339	191	345
	10	11	12	13	14	15	16	17	18
PAR	4	4	4	4	3	4	5	3	5
YARDS	395	289	312	367	156	315	460	163	513

Directions: I-89 to Exit 12. Go 5 miles West. Course is at intersection of Routes 2A and 116.

Rutland Country Club ✪✪✪ 44

North Grove Street
Rutland, VT (802) 773-3254
www.rutlandcountryclub.com

Club Pro: Greg Nelson, PGA
Payment: Visa, MC
Tee Times: 48 hours adv.

Tees	Holes	Yards	Par	USGA	Slope
BACK	18	6135	70	69.7	125
MIDDLE	18	5758	70	67.9	122
FRONT	18	5368	71	71.6	125

Fee 9 Holes: Weekday: **Weekend:**
Fee 18 Holes: Weekday: $91, cart incl.   **Weekend:** $91 after 12pm
Twilight Rates: No   **Discounts:** Junior
Cart Rental: Included   **Driving Range:** No
Lessons: Yes **Schools:** No   **Junior Golf:** Yes
Membership: Yes   **Architect/Yr Open:** George Low/1902
Other: Clubhouse / Lockers / Showers / Snack Bar / Restaurant / Bar-Lounge

Player Comments: "Great greens and great values. Worth the money." Open May - October. Added cart paths.

	1	2	3	4	5	6	7	8	9
PAR	4	4	3	5	3	4	4	4	4
YARDS	379	381	125	463	215	366	322	368	300
	10	11	12	13	14	15	16	17	18
PAR	4	4	3	5	4	3	4	4	4
YARDS	296	316	193	513	347	121	351	326	376

Directions: I -89 to Exit 1. Take Route 4 West to Rutland. Take right onto Grove Street and follow signs to course.

Sitzmark Golf Course

NR 45 ▶

Route 100
Wilmington, VT
(802) 464-3384

Club Pro: Tom Cohen
Payment: Visa, MC
Tee Times: No

Tees	Holes	Yards	Par	USGA	Slope
BACK					
MIDDLE	18	2300	54		
FRONT					

Fee 9 Holes: Weekday: **Weekend:**
Fee 18 Holes: Weekday: $18 **Weekend:** $18
Twilight Rates: No **Discounts:** None
Cart Rental: $15 **Driving Range:** No
Lessons: No **Schools:** Yes **Junior Golf:** No
Membership: Yes
Architect/Yr Open: Robert Miller & Charles Rotollo/1979
Other: Snack Bar / Bar-Lounge

An 18-hole par 3, plus 2 long shots. Generally considered an "iron course," it provides a challenge for the experienced golfer and an excellent introduction for the beginner.

	1	2	3	4	5	6	7	8	9
PAR	3	3	3	3	3	3	3	3	3
YARDS	105	95	105	125	155	90	115	127	115
	10	11	12	13	14	15	16	17	18
PAR	3	3	3	3	3	3	3	3	3
YARDS	90	110	105	126	120	90	105	90	115

Directions: I-91 to Brattleboro, get on Route 9 to Wilmington, take Route 100 to course (5 miles).

St. Johnsbury Country Club

 ✪✪½ 46 ▶ VT

Route 5
St. Johnsbury, VT (802) 748-9894
www.stjohnsburycountryclub.com

Club Pro: Colin Gillies, PGA
Payment: Cash, Credit Card
Tee Times: 1 week adv.

Tees	Holes	Yards	Par	USGA	Slope
BACK	18	6373	70	70.4	129
MIDDLE	18	5860	70	68.6	125
FRONT	18	5480	70	71.3	120

Fee 9 Holes: Weekday: $35 w/cart before 4 **Weekend:** $43 w/cart before 4
Fee 18 Holes: Weekday: $61 w/cart before 4 **Weekend:** $68 w/cart before 4
Twilight Rates: After 4pm **Discounts:** Junior
Cart Rental: $19pp/18, $11pp/9 **Driving Range:** $5/med., $3/sm.
Lessons: 3 lessons/$125 **Schools:** No **Junior Golf:** Yes
Membership: Yes **Architect/Yr Open:** Willie Park Jr./1923
Other: Clubhouse / Snack Bar / Renovated Restaurant / Bar-Lounge

COUPON

Player Comments: "Great value." Front 9, wide open. Back 9, narrow and challenging. Lots of hills and blind shots. Not for the timid." Prices subject to change.

	1	2	3	4	5	6	7	8	9
PAR	4	4	3	4	3	5	3	5	4
YARDS	314	363	168	434	232	578	188	473	434
	10	11	12	13	14	15	16	17	18
PAR	5	4	3	4	4	3	5	3	4
YARDS	496	385	176	398	395	195	575	203	366

Directions: I-91 North to Exit 23 (US Route 5); follow 3 miles. From I-91 South to Exit 22 to Route 5; follow 4 miles.

Stamford Valley Country Club NR 47

194 Phelene Lane (Route 9)
Stamford, VT
(802) 694-9144

Club Pro: No
Payment: Cash, Visa, MC
Tee Times: Recommended

Tees	Holes	Yards	Par	USGA	Slope
BACK					
MIDDLE	9	2709	36	66.6	104
FRONT					

Fee 9 Holes: Weekday: $14   **Weekend:** $14
Fee 18 Holes: Weekday: $20   **Weekend:** $20
Twilight Rates: No   **Discounts:** None
Cart Rental: $12pp/18, $7pp/9   **Driving Range:** No
Lessons: No **Schools:** No   **Junior Golf:** No
Membership: Yes   **Architect/Yr Open:** Stan & Leroy Lawrence/1964
Other: Full Restaurant   **GPS:**

Great foliage and wonderful mountain views. Over 20 new bunkers and brand-new clubhouse with complete restaurant facility. A course for all ages.

	1	2	3	4	5	6	7	8	9
PAR	4	4	4	5	4	4	3	4	4
YARDS	232	288	342	392	330	320	215	355	235
PAR									
YARDS									

Directions: Route 8 North (out of North Adams), about 5 miles over Stamford line.

Stonehedge Golf Course NR 48

216 Squire Road
North Clarendon, VT
(802) 773-2666
www.stonehedgegolf.com

Club Pro:
Payment: Visa, MC, Cash, Check
Tee Times: Yes

Tees	Holes	Yards	Par	USGA	Slope
BACK					
MIDDLE	9	1107	27		
FRONT					

Fee 9 Holes: Weekday: $11.50   **Weekend:** $12.50
Fee 18 Holes: Weekday: $15.50   **Weekend:** $17.50
Twilight Rates: No   **Discounts:** Senior Wednesdays
Cart Rental: $9.50pp/18, $6.50pp/9   **Driving Range:** No
Lessons: No **Schools:** No   **Junior Golf:** No
Membership: No   **Architect/Yr Open:** Robert Matson/1995
Other: Snacks and Soft Drinks   **GPS:**

Challenging par 3 with pretty views — excellent greens, water and sand traps — easy course to walk.

	1	2	3	4	5	6	7	8	9
PAR	3	3	3	3	3	3	3	3	3
YARDS	153	84	181	152	86	77	180	93	101
PAR									
YARDS									

Directions: Located 3 miles South of Rutland (no interstate nearby) at the junction of Routes 7 and 103.

Stowe Country Club ○○½ 49 ▶

5781 Mountain Road
Stowe, VT (802) 253-4893
www.stowe.com

Club Pro: Dan Lehmann, PGA
Payment: Visa, MC, Amex, Disc
Tee Times: Anytime
Fee 9 Holes: Weekday:
Fee 18 Holes: Weekday: $90-$105 w/cart
Twilight Rates: After 2pm
Cart Rental: Included
Lessons: Yes **Schools:** Golf School
Membership: Yes
Other: Clubhouse / Lockers / Showers / Restaurant / Bar/ Hotel / Beverage Cart

Tees	Holes	Yards	Par	USGA	Slope
BACK	18	6213	72	69.3	117
MIDDLE	18	5851	72	67.5	114
FRONT	18	5365	74	68.5	112

Weekend:
Weekend: $90-$105 w/cart
Discounts: None
Driving Range: $5/lg bucket
Junior Golf: Yes
Architect/Yr Open: Walter Barcomb/1950

Player Comments: "Beautiful course. Friendly staff." Excellent stay & play golf package. Open May - mid-October. Fees vary with season and time of day.

	1	2	3	4	5	6	7	8	9
PAR	5	3	5	3	4	5	4	3	4
YARDS	482	152	450	153	367	472	381	135	370
	10	11	12	13	14	15	16	17	18
PAR	3	5	4	4	5	3	4	4	4
YARDS	170	445	371	327	447	158	352	341	279

Directions: I-89 to Exit 10. Follow Route 100 for 10 miles to blinking light in center of Stowe Village, turn left onto Route 108. Turn right directly past Whiskers Restaurant onto Cape Cod Road. Course straight ahead.

Stratton Mtn. (Lake, Forest, Mtn)○○○ 50 ▶   VT

Rural Route 1
Stratton Mountain, VT
(802) 297-4114
www.stratton.com

Club Pro:
Payment: Most Major Credit Cards
Tee Times: Up to 7 days adv.
Fee 9 Holes: Weekday:
Fee 18 Holes: Wkdy: $69-$79 (M-Th) w/cart
Twilight Rates: After 5pm
Cart Rental: Cart included
Lessons: $40/half hour **Schools:** Yes
Membership: Yes
Other: Clubhouse / Lockers-Showers / Snack Bar / Restaurant / Bar-Lounge / Hotel

Tees	Holes	Yards	Par	USGA	Slope
BACK	27/8	6526	72	71.2	125
MIDDLE	27/8	6044	72	69.4	122
FRONT	27/8	5155	74	69.8	123

Weekend:
Wknd: $89-$99 incl. cart F/S/S/H
Discounts: Junior
Driving Range: $7/lg., $4/sm.
Junior Golf: No
Architect/Yr Open: Geoffrey Cornish/1959

COUPON

Player Comments: 27-hole complex—Forest & Lake 9s below. "1st-class services really makes a golfer feel special." Cornish design features. Rates vary by season.

	1	2	3	4	5	6	7	8	9
PAR	4	4	4	3	5	4	3	5	4
YARDS	372	387	305	129	467	295	140	504	379
	10	11	12	13	14	15	16	17	18
PAR	4	4	4	3	4	5	3	4	5
YARDS	353	395	328	164	269	466	193	390	508

Directions: Take I-91 to Brattleboro exit, follow Route 30 East for 30 miles to Bondville; look for signs to Stratton Mountain.

Sugarbush Golf Club ✪✪✪½ ▶ 51

1840 Sugarbush Access Road
Warren, VT (802) 583-6725
www.sugarbush.com

Tees	Holes	Yards	Par	USGA	Slope
BACK	18	6464	72	71.7	128
MIDDLE	18	5922	70	69.0	122
FRONT	18	5231	72	70.5	129

Club Pro: Ron Philo Jr., PGA
Payment: Visa, MC, Amex, Disc
Tee Times: Yes
Fee 9 Holes: Weekday:
Fee 18 Holes: Weekday: $90
Twilight Rates: After 2pm
Cart Rental: $18pp/9, $30pp/18
Lessons: Yes **Schools:** No
Membership: Yes
Weekend:
Weekend: $100
Discounts: Senior & Junior
Driving Range: Yes
Junior Golf: Yes
Architect/Yr Open: Robert Trent Jones Sr./1962
Other: Restaurant / Clubhouse / Hotel / Bar-Lounge / Lockers / Snack Bar / Showers / Schools
GPS: Yes

COUPON

Breathtaking views. Dramatic elevation changes. Many blind shots.

	1	2	3	4	5	6	7	8	9
PAR	4	4	4	4	3	4	4	3	4
YARDS	322	372	396	355	164	374	433	166	353
	10	11	12	13	14	15	16	17	18
PAR	5	3	4	4	5	4	3	4	4
YARDS	504	118	395	325	449	352	157	329	322

Directions: From I-89 South: Exit 10 to Route 100 South to Sugarbush Access Road. From I-89 North: take Exit 9 to Route 100B South to Route 100 South.

Tater Hill Golf Club ✪✪✪ ▶ 52

6802 Popple Dungeon Road
North Windham, VT
(802) 875-2517
www.taterhillgolfclub.com

Tees	Holes	Yards	Par	USGA	Slope
BACK	18	6048	70	71.4	129
MIDDLE	18	5426	72	68.7	125
FRONT	18	4475	70	68.1	112

Club Pro: John Pawlak, PGA
Payment: Visa, MC, Amex
Tee Times: 5 days adv.
Fee 9 Holes: Weekday: $35
Fee 18 Holes: Weekday: $57
Twilight Rates: After 4pm
Cart Rental: $19pp/18, $10pp/9
Lessons: $40/half hour **Schools:** No
Membership: Yes
Other: Clubhouse / Bar-Lounge / Restaurant
Weekend: $35
Weekend: $77 w/cart
Discounts: Junior
Driving Range: $3/30 balls
Junior Golf: Yes
Architect/Yr Open: Don Warner/1963
GPS:

Reconstructed front 9 in 2005. "Very well maintained, greens are fantastic, terrific staff." "Better every year." –KL Sister course to Okemo.

	1	2	3	4	5	6	7	8	9
PAR	5	3	3	4	3	5	4	4	5
YARDS	473	133	193	352	160	470	397	305	450
	10	11	12	13	14	15	16	17	18
PAR	3	4	4	4	4	3	5	4	5
YARDS	168	388	414	373	324	148	462	295	530

Directions: I-91 to Exit 6; take left onto Route 103, turns into 11 West; 7 miles outside Chester look for signs to course.

West Bolton Golf Club

● ● 53

5161A Stage Road, West Bolton
Jericho, VT (802) 434-4321
www.westboltongolfclub.com

Club Pro: Ken Stavisky
Payment: Visa, MC, Cash, Check
Tee Times: 1 week adv.
Fee 9 Holes: Weekday: $20
Fee 18 Holes: Weekday: $27
Twilight Rates: After 3pm
Cart Rental: $14pp/18, $7/9
Lessons: Yes **Schools:** Junior
Membership: Yes
Other: Clubhouse / Snack Bar

Tees	Holes	Yards	Par	USGA	Slope
BACK					
MIDDLE	18	5761	72	66.8	115
FRONT	18	5165	72	72.5	111

Weekend: $20
Weekend: $27
Discounts: Srs., Jrs., Ladies
Driving Range: No
Junior Golf: Yes
Architect/Yr Open: Ken Wheeler/1983
GPS:

Unique 18-hole course nestled in the Green Mountains. The fairway trees are small, but the mountains surrounding the course are grand.

	1	2	3	4	5	6	7	8	9
PAR	4	5	3	4	4	3	4	4	4
YARDS	303	481	149	248	353	191	329	359	295
	10	11	12	13	14	15	16	17	18
PAR	3	5	4	5	3	5	4	4	4
YARDS	128	430	392	451	180	458	273	323	418

Directions: I-89 to Exit 11 toward Richmond. Left at light (Four Corners). Go about 7 miles and take a right at the West Bolton Golf Course sign. Continue for 4 miles.

White River Golf Club

NR 54

VT

3070 Route 100
Rochester, VT
(802) 767-4653
www.whiterivergolf.com

Club Pro:
Payment: Cash, MC, Visa
Tee Times: Recommended
Fee 9 Holes: Weekday: $20
Fee 18 Holes: Weekday: $30
Twilight Rates: M/T/Th/F after 3:30pm
Cart Rental: $10pp/18
Lessons: Schools: Yes
Membership: Yes
Other: Clubhouse / Bar-Lounge / Snack Bar

Tees	Holes	Yards	Par	USGA	Slope
BACK	9	2657	34	65.6	115
MIDDLE	9	2345	34	64.6	112
FRONT	9	1988	34	60.2	104

Weekend: $21
Weekend: $31
Discounts: Junior
Driving Range: Yes
Junior Golf: Yes
Architect/Yr Open: Peter McGowan/1972
GPS:

COUPON

9-hole panoramic from every hole. Recent design changes have made a true test of skill for the experienced golfer while still appealing to the novice golfer. Open May - October. 10-play ticket available.

	1	2	3	4	5	6	7	8	9
PAR	3	5	4	3	3	4	4	4	4
YARDS	175	485	248	115	118	385	218	332	269
PAR									
YARDS									

Directions: I-89 to Route 107 West to Route 100 North. Course is 10 miles North on Route 100. Approximately halfway between Killington and Sugarbush.

Wilcox Cove Golf Course

3 Camp Vermont Court
Highway 314, Grand Isle, VT
(802) 372-8343

Club Pro:
Payment: Cash, Check
Tee Times: No
Fee 9 Holes: Weekday: $15
Fee 18 Holes: Weekday: $15
Twilight Rates: After 6pm
Cart Rental: $3/pull
Lessons: No **Schools:** No
Membership: Yes
Other: No

Tees	Holes	Yards	Par	USGA	Slope
BACK					
MIDDLE	9	1732	32		
FRONT					

Weekend: $18
Weekend: $18
Discounts: None
Driving Range: No
Junior Golf:
Architect/Yr Open: Michael Hurzdan/1947
GPS:

An executive-type course on the West shore of Grand Isle, looking over Lake Champlain to the Adirondack Mountains of New York. A fairly level course. Twilight weekend rates.

	1	2	3	4	5	6	7	8	9
PAR	4	4	4	3	4	3	4	3	3
YARDS	240	210	254	120	245	190	185	193	95
PAR									
YARDS									

Directions: I-89 to Exit 17 (Route 2 North). Take Route 314 past Grand Isle ferry.

Williston Golf Club

 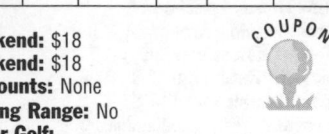

424 Golf Course Road
Williston, VT (802) 878-3747
www.willistongolfclub.com

Club Pro: Todd Trono
Payment: Visa, MC
Tee Times: Weekends and Holidays
Fee 9 Holes: Weekday:
Fee 18 Holes: Weekday: $33
Twilight Rates: After 4pm
Cart Rental: $15pp/18
Lessons: Yes **Schools:** No
Membership: Yes
Other: 19th-hole Resturant / Old Duffers Tavern

Tees	Holes	Yards	Par	USGA	Slope
BACK	18	6621	69	N/R	N/R
MIDDLE	18	5262	69	66.6	113
FRONT	18	4716	71	64	106

Weekend:
Weekend: $33
Discounts: None
Driving Range: Nearby
Junior Golf: Yes
Architect/Yr Open: Ben Murray/1927
GPS: Yes

Player Comments: "Play it at least twice a season. Very well kept. Always friendly." Fully irrigated. Open May - November 1.

	1	2	3	4	5	6	7	8	9
PAR	4	4	4	4	4	3	4	4	5
YARDS	316	390	289	272	260	184	267	382	445
	10	11	12	13	14	15	16	17	18
PAR	4	3	3	4	4	3	3	4	5
YARDS	325	160	212	254	395	151	90	360	510

Directions: I-89 to Exit 11 or 12; Route 2 East to North Williston Road. Course is 1/2 mile on right. 7 miles east of Burlington, Vermont.

Woodbury Golf Course NR 57 ▶

2120 East Hill Road
South Woodbury, VT
(802) 456-7421
www.woodburygolf.com

Tees	Holes	Yards	Par	USGA	Slope
BACK					
MIDDLE	9	1264	27		
FRONT					

Club Pro: Darwin Thompson
Payment: Visa, MC, Checks
Tee Times: (802) 456-1250
Fee 9 Holes: Weekday: $11 **Weekend:** $11
Fee 18 Holes: Weekday: $16.50 **Weekend:** $16.50
Twilight Rates: No
Discounts: Juniors 12 and under free w/paying adult
Cart Rental: $10/9 per cart **Driving Range:** No
Lessons: No **Schools:** No **Junior Golf:**
Membership: Yes **Architect/Yr Open:** Thompson Family/2004

COUPON

Great for your short game or a quick round with the family.

	1	2	3	4	5	6	7	8	9
PAR	3	3	3	3	3	3	3	3	3
YARDS	120	145	128	185	147	118	125	129	167
PAR									
YARDS									

Directions: I-89 to Route 2 East. Take Route 14 North. Right onto Easthill Road in South Woodbury. 2 miles on right.

Woodstock Inn & Resort ✪✪✪½ 58 ▶

Fourteen, The Green
Route 106 South, Woodstock, VT
(802) 457-6674
www.woodstockinn.com

Tees	Holes	Yards	Par	USGA	Slope
BACK	18	6052	70	69.7	123
MIDDLE	18	5619	70	68.0	117
FRONT	18	4924	71	69.0	113

Club Pro: Jim Gunnare
Payment: Cash, MC, Visa, Amex
Tee Times: Yes
Fee 9 Holes: Weekday: **Weekend:**
Fee 18 Holes: Weekday: $85 **Weekend:** $95
Twilight Rates: After 4pm **Discounts:** None
Cart Rental: $20pp/18 **Driving Range:** $4/lg bucket
Lessons: $50/half hour **Schools:** Jr. & Sr. **Junior Golf:** Yes
Membership: Yes **Architect/Yr Open:** William H. Tucker/1895
Other: Clubhouse / Lockers / Showers / Restaurant / Bar-Lounge / Hotel / Snack Bar

Renovated clubhouse restaurant, ballroom, dining room, and new deck. Hosting annual Northeast PGA seniors championship. Updated by Robert Trent Jones in 1962. Driving range with new tee boxes.

	1	2	3	4	5	6	7	8	9
PAR	5	3	4	4	3	5	3	4	4
YARDS	465	162	346	382	134	503	162	356	386
PAR									
YARDS									

Directions: I-89 to Exit 1 (VT), Route 4 West to Woodstock - South on Route 106 (1 mile).

VT

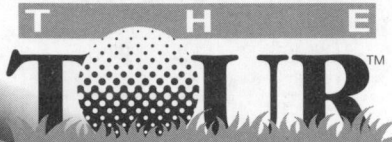

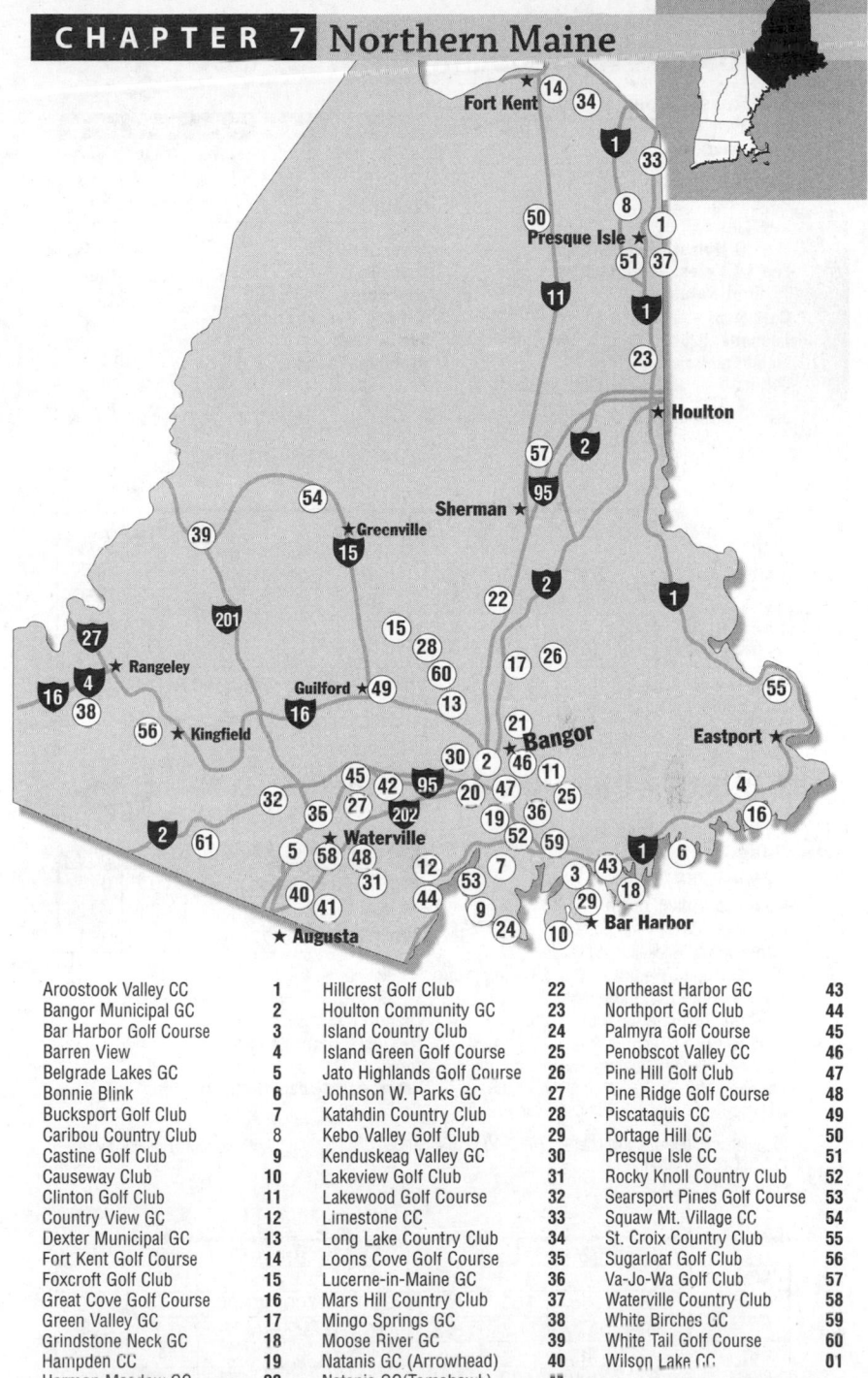

Aroostook Valley CC	1	Hillcrest Golf Club	22	Northeast Harbor GC	43
Bangor Municipal GC	2	Houlton Community GC	23	Northport Golf Club	44
Bar Harbor Golf Course	3	Island Country Club	24	Palmyra Golf Course	45
Barren View	4	Island Green Golf Course	25	Penobscot Valley CC	46
Belgrade Lakes GC	5	Jato Highlands Golf Course	26	Pine Hill Golf Club	47
Bonnie Blink	6	Johnson W. Parks GC	27	Pine Ridge Golf Course	48
Bucksport Golf Club	7	Katahdin Country Club	28	Piscataquis CC	49
Caribou Country Club	8	Kebo Valley Golf Club	29	Portage Hill CC	50
Castine Golf Club	9	Kenduskeag Valley GC	30	Presque Isle CC	51
Causeway Club	10	Lakeview Golf Club	31	Rocky Knoll Country Club	52
Clinton Golf Club	11	Lakewood Golf Course	32	Searsport Pines Golf Course	53
Country View GC	12	Limestone CC	33	Squaw Mt. Village CC	54
Dexter Municipal GC	13	Long Lake Country Club	34	St. Croix Country Club	55
Fort Kent Golf Course	14	Loons Cove Golf Course	35	Sugarloaf Golf Club	56
Foxcroft Golf Club	15	Lucerne-in-Maine GC	36	Va-Jo-Wa Golf Club	57
Great Cove Golf Course	16	Mars Hill Country Club	37	Waterville Country Club	58
Green Valley GC	17	Mingo Springs GC	38	White Birches GC	59
Grindstone Neck GC	18	Moose River GC	39	White Tail Golf Course	60
Hampden CC	19	Natanis GC (Arrowhead)	40	Wilson Lake GC	61
Hermon Meadow GC	20	Natanis GC (Tomahawk)	41		
Hidden Meadows GC	21	Newport CC	42		

KEY TO THE STAR AND VALUE RATINGS:
5◐= Outstanding 4◐= Excellent 3◐= Very Good 2◐= Good 1◐= Average NR = Not Rated
EV = Excellent Value GV = Good Value V = Value

Aroostook Valley Country Club ✪✪✪

235 Russell Road
Fort Fairfield, ME (207) 476-8083
www.avcc.ca

Tees	Holes	Yards	Par	USGA	Slope
BACK	18	6304	72	69.6	117
MIDDLE	18	5957	72	68.4	113
FRONT	18	5373	72	74.1	119

Club Pro: Steven Leitch, CPGA
Payment: Visa, MC
Tee Times: 7 days adv.
Fee 9 Holes: Weekday: $23   **Weekend:** $23
Fee 18 Holes: Weekday: $45   **Weekend:** $45
Twilight Rates: After 2pm   **Discounts:** Junior $20
Cart Rental: $17pp/18, $8.50pp/9   **Driving Range:** $5/bucket
Lessons: $25/half hour **Schools:** No   **Junior Golf:** Yes
Membership: Yes   **Architect/Yr Open:**
Other: Clubhouse / Snack Bar / Bar-Lounge / Lockers / Showers

COUPON

Very beautiful course; difficult inclines on back 9 make it challenging. White silica sand in bunkers.

	1	2	3	4	5	6	7	8	9
PAR	4	4	5	3	5	4	4	3	4
YARDS	375	327	478	132	440	308	334	139	365
	10	11	12	13	14	15	16	17	18
PAR	4	4	5	3	5	3	4	3	5
YARDS	382	322	489	189	510	156	383	134	494

Directions: I-95 to last exit; take left onto Route 1 to Fort Fairfield, cross bridge. Take first right.
Follow Russell Road to course.

Bangor Municipal Golf Course ✪✪½

278 Webster Avenue
Bangor, ME (207) 941-0232
www.bangorgc.com

Tees	Holes	Yards	Par	USGA	Slope
BACK	18	6345	71	69.2	115
MIDDLE	18	6150	71	67.9	112
FRONT	18	5172	71	69.1	111

Club Pro: Brian Enman
Payment: Cash, Visa, MC
Tee Times: Weekends, Holidays
Fee 9 Holes: Weekday: $14, $9 before 11am **Weekend:** $14
Fee 18 Holes: Weekday: $28   **Weekend:** $28
Twilight Rates: After 4pm $17/18   **Discounts:** Yes
Cart Rental: $12pp/18, $6pp/9   **Driving Range:** $4/bucket
Lessons: $45/45 minutes **Schools:** Yes   **Junior Golf:** Yes
Membership: Yes   **Architect/Yr Open:** Geoffrey Cornish/1964
Other: Restaurant / Clubhouse / Bar-Lounge   **GPS:**

27 holes includes a 9-hole course with 3215 yards, par 36, USGA rating 69.6/113 slope. Hosted USGA
Public Links Qualifier.

	1	2	3	4	5	6	7	8	9
PAR	4	4	3	5	4	3	4	4	4
YARDS	335	395	165	530	330	200	400	410	415
	10	11	12	13	14	15	16	17	18
PAR	4	3	4	4	4	5	3	4	5
YARDS	400	200	400	315	410	470	165	340	480

Directions: I-95 to Exit 183 (Hammond Street). Turn right and then immediate right onto Norway
Road. Go to stop sign and turn right - 1/2 mile on left.

Bar Harbor Golf Course

51 Jordan River Road, Route 204
Trenton, ME (207) 667-7505
www.barharborgolfcourse.com

Club Pro: No
Payment: Visa, MC
Tee Times: No
Fee 9 Holes: Weekday: $25
Fee 18 Holes: Weekday: $40
Twilight Rates: No
Cart Rental: $15pp/18, $8pp/9
Lessons: No **Schools:** No
Membership: Yes
Other: Clubhouse / Snack Bar / Bar-Lounge

Tees	Holes	Yards	Par	USGA	Slope
BACK	18	6680	71	71.1	125
MIDDLE	18	6450	71	69.8	121
FRONT	18	5428	73	70.4	115

Weekend: $25
Weekend: $40
Discounts: None
Driving Range: No
Junior Golf: No
Architect/Yr Open: Philip Wogan/1967
GPS: Yes

COUPON

One of the best-kept secrets in the state. Links-style tract was designed by Phil Wogan. Located adjacent to the ocean, it is challenging and picturesque.

	1	2	3	4	5	6	7	8	9
PAR	4	4	5	3	4	4	4	3	4
YARDS	427	388	520	156	402	408	368	172	343
	10	11	12	13	14	15	16	17	18
PAR	4	3	4	5	4	4	4	3	5
YARDS	428	155	295	589	374	318	405	158	544

Directions: Route 3 toward Bar Harbor. Course is located at intersection of Route 3 and Route 204 in Trenton.

Barren View

NR 4

1354 Route 1
Jonesboro, ME (207) 434-6531
www.barrenview.com

Club Pro: No
Payment:
Tee Times: Open
Fee 9 Holes: Weekday: $15
Fee 18 Holes: Weekday: $25
Twilight Rates:
Cart Rental: $14pp/18, $8pp/9
Lessons: Yes **Schools:**
Membership: Yes
Other:

Tees	Holes	Yards	Par	USGA	Slope
BACK	9	2741	34	64.9	112
MIDDLE	9	2613	34	32.5112	112
FRONT	9	2321	34	64.9	112

Weekend: $15
Weekend: $25
Discounts: Junior 12 and under $10
Driving Range: $4/bucket
Junior Golf:
Architect/Yr Open: 2003
GPS:

**N
ME**

Links-style course for all levels. Opened 2003. Holes #8 & 9 worth the trip alone.

	1	2	3	4	5	6	7	8	9
PAR	4	3	5	3	3	4	4	4	4
YARDS	369	129	406	201	143	280	292	361	430
PAR									
YARDS									

Directions: I-95 North to I-395 East to Route 1A. Exit toward Bar Harbor/Ellsworth. Take Route 1 out of Ellsworth toward Machias. Course is on right.

Belgrade Lakes Golf Club ✪✪✪✪

5

West Road
Belgrade Lakes, ME 207-495-GOLF
www.belgradelakesgolf.com

Tees	Holes	Yards	Par	USGA	Slope
BACK	18	6723	71	72.2	135
MIDDLE	18	6285	71	69.9	131
FRONT	18	5168	71	64.1	126

Club Pro: No
Payment: Visa, MC, Amex
Tee Times: 7 days adv.
Fee 9 Holes: Weekday: **Weekend:**
Fee 18 Holes: Weekday: $120 in season   **Weekend:** $120 in season
Twilight Rates: No   **Discounts:** None
Cart Rental: $20pp/18   **Driving Range:** Hitting net
Lessons: No **Schools:** No   **Junior Golf:** Yes
Membership: No   **Architect/Yr Open:** Clive Clark/1997
Other: Snack Bar   **GPS:** Yes

Player Comments: "Every hole different and spectacularly beautiful." Improvements: enlarged and lengthened several tees. Walking encouraged. Caddies available for a fee plus tip.
Golf Magazine 'Top 100 Courses You Can Play.'

	1	2	3	4	5	6	7	8	9
PAR	4	3	5	4	3	5	4	3	4
YARDS	424	156	450	424	161	485	384	186	376
	10	**11**	**12**	**13**	**14**	**15**	**16**	**17**	**18**
PAR	4	4	5	3	4	4	5	3	4
YARDS	346	395	568	203	344	311	530	171	371

Directions: I-95 to Exit 112B. Turn right onto Route 27. Go for 12 miles to town of Belgrade Lakes. Turn left at the Sunset Grille onto West Road. Course is 1/4 mile on left.

Bonnie Blink Golf Links ✪✪

6

185 East Side Road
Sorrento, ME (207) 422-3930

Tees	Holes	Yards	Par	USGA	Slope
BACK					
MIDDLE	9	2520	36	65	112
FRONT					

Club Pro: None
Payment: Cash or Check
Tee Times:
Fee 9 Holes: Weekday: $20 all day   **Weekend:** $30 all day
Fee 18 Holes: Weekday: $20 all day   **Weekend:** $30 all day
Twilight Rates: No   **Discounts:** None
Cart Rental: $2/pull   **Driving Range:** No
Lessons: No **Schools:**   **Junior Golf:**
Membership: Yes   **Architect/Yr Open:**
Other: **GPS:**

Player Comments: "Undiscovered gem. Breathtaking views, right on the ocean." Sorrento Village Improvement Association Yacht Club members only Friday morning until noon. Great for a quick 9.

	1	2	3	4	5	6	7	8	9
PAR	4	4	3	5	5	4	3	4	4
YARDS	350	270	180	510	490	310	120	290	330
PAR									
YARDS									

Directions: 48 miles from Bangor. Route Alternate 1 to Ellsworth (23 miles). Stay on Route 1 to Hancock. Then in Sullivan, go right on Route 185 (East Side Road) and proceed 2 miles. Course is on left.

Bucksport Golf Club

39 / State Route 46
Bucksport, ME (207) 469-7612

Tees	Holes	Yards	Par	USGA	Slope
BACK	9	3890	37	72.5	
MIDDLE	9	3373	37	72.5	136
FRONT	9	5972	74	72.2	128

Club Pro: Wayne Hand, PGA
Payment: Visa, MC
Tee Times: No
Fee 9 Holes: Weekday: $20   **Weekend:** $20
Fee 18 Holes: Weekday: $30   **Weekend:** $30
Twilight Rates: No   **Discounts:** Junior
Cart Rental: $35/18, $25/9 per cart   **Driving Range:** $5/lg., $3.50/sm.
Lessons: Yes **Schools:** No   **Junior Golf:** Yes
Membership: Yes   **Architect/Yr Open:** Phil Wogan/1967
Other: Bar-Lounge / Snack Bar / Lockers / Showers
GPS: Yes

COUPON

9 holes with 2 sets of tees — 6780 yards, par 74, when you play both. Natural state of land emphasized in design.

	1	2	3	4	5	6	7	8	9
PAR	4	5	3	4	5	3	4	4	5
YARDS	330	500	147	407	504	163	408	354	560
PAR									
YARDS									

Directions: From Augusta: Route 3 to Belfast. Route 1 North to Bucksport. From Bangor take Route 1A to Route 46. Course is 3 miles from Downtown Bucksport.

Caribou Country Club

Sweden Road
Caribou, ME (207) 493-3933

Tees	Holes	Yards	Par	USGA	Slope
BACK		3215	36		
MIDDLE	9	3160	36	69.0	124
FRONT	9	2816	36	69.6	116

Club Pro: Jeff Jose
Payment: Visa, MC, Amex, Disc
Tee Times: No
Fee 9 Holes: Weekday: $15   **Weekend:** $15
Fee 18 Holes: Weekday: $22   **Weekend:** $22
Twilight Rates: No   **Discounts:** Junior memberships
Cart Rental: $22pp/18, $15pp/9   **Driving Range:** $7/lg, $3/sm bucket
Lessons: Yes **Schools:** No   **Junior Golf:** Yes
Membership: Yes   **Architect/Yr Open:** Geoffrey Cornish/1970
Other: Restaurant / Clubhouse / Bar-Lounge / Snack Bar / Lockers / Showers

COUPON

N ME

The course has a beautiful log cabin clubhouse. 9-hole layout with 2 sets of tees. Toughness of holes varies with each 9. Open May 1 - October 15.

	1	2	3	4	5	6	7	8	9
PAR	4	5	3	4	4	4	3	5	4
YARDS	340	515	195	330	360	340	150	530	400
PAR									
YARDS									

Directions: Route 161 North; follow 1.5 miles outside Caribou; course is on right side.

Castine Golf Club

200 Battle Avenue
Castine, ME (207) 326-8844
www.castinegolfclub.com

Club Pro: Bob Flanders, PGA
Payment: Cash, Most Major Credit Cards, Check
Tee Times: Yes
Fee 9 Holes: Weekday: $20
Fee 18 Holes: Weekday: $35
Twilight Rates: After 4pm
Cart Rental: $25pp/18, $15pp/9
Lessons: Yes **Schools:** No
Membership: Yes
Other: Clubhouse - Members only

Tees	Holes	Yards	Par	USGA	Slope
BACK					
MIDDLE	9	2994	35	67.5	112
FRONT	9	2678	35	71.3	121

Weekend: $20
Weekend: $35
Discounts: Junior, call
Driving Range: Yes
Junior Golf: Yes
Architect/Yr Open: Willie Park Jr./1921
GPS: Yes

Old-style links flavor, designed by Will Park Jr. Ocean view on 1 hole. Often not busy. Discounts Spring and Fall.

	1	2	3	4	5	6	7	8	9
PAR	4	3	4	3	4	4	5	4	4
YARDS	400	175	402	152	376	342	466	316	365
PAR									
YARDS									

Directions: Routes 1 & 3 through Bucksport. Turn right onto Route 175 to Route 166. Course is on right.

Causeway Club

Fernald Road
S.W. Harbor, ME (207) 244-3780
www.thecausewayclub.org

Club Pro:
Payment: Visa, MC
Tee Times: No
Fee 9 Holes: Weekday: $35
Fee 18 Holes: Weekday: $45
Twilight Rates: After 4pm
Cart Rental: $25/18, $18/9 per cart
Lessons: No **Schools:** No
Membership: Yes
Other: Clubhouse / Lockers / Snacks

Tees	Holes	Yards	Par	USGA	Slope
BACK					
MIDDLE	9	2302	32	60.9	95
FRONT	9	2085	32	63.9	102

Weekend: $35
Weekend: $45
Discounts: Junior
Driving Range: No
Junior Golf: Yes
Architect/Yr Open:
GPS: Yes

On S.W. Harbor with scenic views. Closed to public after 6:30pm. Near Acadia National Park. New practice facility. 9-hole executive course with 2 sets of tees. Two 9s equal 4718 yards, par 65.

	1	2	3	4	5	6	7	8	9
PAR	4	4	4	4	4	3	3	3	3
YARDS	390	270	298	278	390	140	228	175	133
PAR									
YARDS									

Directions: I-95 to ALT Route 1 to Ellsworth. Follow Route 3 to Mt. Desert Island. Take Route 102 to Southwest Harbor.

Clinton Golf Club ✪✪✪ ► 11

510 Hill Road
Clinton, ME (207) 426-8795
www.clintongolfcourse.com

Club Pro: No
Payment: Most Major Credit Cards
Tee Times: Call ahead
Fee 9 Holes: Weekday: $25
Fee 18 Holes: Weekday: $50
Twilight Rates: No
Cart Rental: $20pp/18, $10pp/9
Lessons: No **Schools:** No
Membership: No
Other: Snack Bar

Tees	Holes	Yards	Par	USGA	Slope
BACK	9	3240	36	71.2	140
MIDDLE	9	3002	36	68.8	138
FRONT	9	2348	36		

Weekend: $25
Weekend: $50
Discounts: None
Driving Range: No
Junior Golf: No
Architect/Yr Open: Steve Brown/2001
GPS:

Family-owned, -built, and -run. Limited access. Teetimes every half hour. 9 holes with 2 sets of tees. "Very well kept, great way to spend a day." –GD

	1	2	3	4	5	6	7	8	9
PAR	4	4	4	3	5	4	3	5	4
YARDS	392	374	334	168	514	359	182	506	411
PAR									
YARDS									

Directions: I-95 to Exit 138 (Hinckley Road) to 100 North. Follow 100 to Railroad Street. Go left onto Railroad, and then left onto Hill Road.

Country View Golf Course NR ► 12

178 Moose Head Trail
(Route 7) Brooks, ME
(207) 722-3161

Club Pro: No
Payment: Most Major
Tee Times: No
Fee 9 Holes: Weekday: $17
Fee 18 Holes: Weekday: $25
Twilight Rates: No
Cart Rental: $26pp/18 , $16pp/9
Lessons: No **Schools:** No
Membership: Yes
Other: Snack Bar

Tees	Holes	Yards	Par	USGA	Slope
BACK	9	3000	36		115
MIDDLE	9	2885	36		115
FRONT	9	2480	36		105

Weekend: $17
Weekend: $25
Discounts: None
Driving Range: Yes
Junior Golf: No
Architect/Yr Open:
GPS:

All irrigated. 12 miles to Belfast and coast. Tourist attractions.

	1	2	3	4	5	6	7	8	9
PAR	4	4	5	3	4	5	4	4	3
YARDS	330	335	450	125	345	480	340	335	145
PAR									
YARDS									

Directions: I-95 (in Fairfield) to Route 139 all the way to Brooks. Turn left to Route 7 North 1.5 miles.

Dexter Municipal Golf Course ○○½ 13 ▶

35 Sunrise Avenue
Dexter, ME (207) 924-6477

Tees	Holes	Yards	Par	USGA	Slope
BACK	9	2640	35	65.7	115
MIDDLE	9	2586	70	65.7	115
FRONT	9	2392	35		

Club Pro:
Payment: Visa, MC
Tee Times: No
Fee 9 Holes: Weekday: $10 M-Th
Fee 18 Holes: Weekday: $14 M-Th
Twilight Rates: After 5pm
Cart Rental: $20pp/18, $10pp/9
Lessons: No **Schools:** No
Membership: Yes
Other: Clubhouse / Restaurant

Weekend: $12 F/S/S
Weekend: $20 F/S/S
Discounts: Junior
Driving Range: Yes
Junior Golf: Yes
Architect/Yr Open: 1968
GPS:

Not too long, but full of challenges. Lots of hills and ponds — fun course to play. Open April 15 - October 15.

	1	2	3	4	5	6	7	8	9
PAR	4	4	4	4	3	4	4	3	5
YARDS	275	285	338	242	173	260	390	179	444
	10	11	12	13	14	15	16	17	18
PAR	4	4	4	4	3	4	4	3	5
YARDS	305	290	340	248	180	265	395	184	448

Directions: I-95 to Exit 157 (Newport exit) follow Route 7 North to Dexter (14 miles). Take left on Liberty Street (across from Rite Aid). Take a left at the second stop sign. Course is second driveway on right.

Fort Kent Golf Course NR 14 ▶

Route 161
Fort Kent, ME (207) 834-3149

Tees	Holes	Yards	Par	USGA	Slope
BACK					
MIDDLE	9	3122	35	69.0	111
FRONT	9	2681	36	69.0	111

Club Pro: Kelly O'Leary, PGA
Payment: Visa, MC
Tee Times: No
Fee 9 Holes: Weekday: $16
Fee 18 Holes: Weekday: $25
Twilight Rates: No
Cart Rental: $25pp/18, $16pp/9 per cart
Lessons: $35/lesson **Schools:** No
Membership: Yes **GPS:** Yes
Other: Restaurant / Clubhouse / Bar-Lounge / Lockers / Showers

Weekend: $16
Weekend: $25
Discounts:
Driving Range: Yes
Junior Golf: Yes
Architect/Yr Open: Ben Gray/1966

COUPON

The course, located a chip shot from the Canadian border, sports many challenges: bunkers, water hazards, and hills. Expanded water on hole #9.

	1	2	3	4	5	6	7	8	9
PAR	4	4	3	4	3	4	4	4	5
YARDS	406	302	160	322	151	390	412	437	542
PAR									
YARDS									

Directions: Route 161 to Fort Kent; follow 3 miles to course.

Foxcroft Golf Club

NR 15

84 Foxcroft Center Road
Dover Foxcroft, ME
(207) 564-8887
www.foxcroftgolfclub.com

Tees	Holes	Yards	Par	USGA	Slope
BACK	9	3136	36	66.1	109
MIDDLE	9	2968	36	66.1	107
FRONT	9	2753	37	67.0	101

Club Pro: Jessica Bentz
Payment: Personal Checks, Cash
Tee Times: No
Fee 9 Holes: Weekday: $15
Fee 18 Holes: Weekday: $24
Twilight Rates: After 4pm
Cart Rental: $15pp/18, $10pp/9
Lessons: Yes **Schools:** No
Membership:
Other: Snack Bar/ Clubhouse

Weekend: $15
Weekend: $24
Discounts: None
Driving Range: No
Junior Golf: No
Architect/Yr Open:
GPS:

Recently lengthened first tee. New White tees on #7 and #9.

	1	2	3	4	5	6	7	8	9
PAR	5	4	4	3	4	4	3	4	5
YARDS	474	430	380	102	328	267	168	381	488
PAR									
YARDS									

Directions: I-95 to Exit 39 (Newport exit). Follow Route 7 into Dover-Foxcroft. Turn left. Go right at traffic light. Take 2nd right, Route 16. Take Route 16 from the post office 1.3 miles to Foxcroft Center Road. Sign is at corner of Milo Road.

Great Cove Golf Course

NR 16

387 Great Cove Road
Roque Bluffs, ME (207) 434-7200
greatcovegolf.com

Tees	Holes	Yards	Par	USGA	Slope
BACK					
MIDDLE	9	1709	30	59.1	100
FRONT					

Club Pro: No
Payment: Cash Only
Tee Times: No
Fee 9 Holes: Weekday: $9
Fee 18 Holes: Weekday: $18
Twilight Rates: No
Cart Rental: $10/9 per cart
Lessons: No **Schools:** No
Membership: Yes
Other: Clubhouse / Snack Bar

Weekend: $9
Weekend: $18
Discounts: None
Driving Range: $6/lg., $4/sm.
Junior Golf: Yes
Architect/Yr Open: Paul Browne/1977
GPS:

Several tricky par 3s with natural hazards.

	1	2	3	4	5	6	7	8	9
PAR	4	3	4	3	4	3	3	3	3
YARDS	304	185	245	193	228	103	137	177	137
PAR									
YARDS									

Directions: 3 miles off Route 1 from Jonesboro. Located on Great Cove Road.

Green Valley Golf Course

1886 Main Road (Route 2)
West Enfield, ME (207) 732-3006

Tees	Holes	Yards	Par	USGA	Slope
BACK	9	3032	35		
MIDDLE	9	2852	35	67.8	120
FRONT	9	2299	35		

Club Pro: Michael Clendenning
Payment: Cash, Visa, MC, Disc, Amex
Tee Times: Yes
Fee 9 Holes: Weekday: $14
Fee 18 Holes: Weekday: $18 all day
Twilight Rates: No
Cart Rental: $20/18, $16/9 per cart
Lessons: Yes **Schools:** Yes
Membership: Yes
Other: Clubhouse / Snack Bar

Weekend: $14
Weekend: $18 all day
Discounts: Jr., 10 & under free w/paid adult
Driving Range: $3/bucket
Junior Golf: Yes
Architect/Yr Open:
GPS:

Relatively easy to walk. Attractions include those of Lincoln Lakes area. Under new ownership.

	1	2	3	4	5	6	7	8	9
PAR	5	3	4	4	4	4	3	4	4
YARDS	490	172	288	238	355	405	156	366	382
PAR									
YARDS									

Directions: I-95 to Exit 217, go right. Go 3/4 of a mile to stop sign. Take a right. Go 3/4 of a mile to stop sign. Take left on Route 2. Go 4 miles, course is located off Route 2 on right.

Grindstone Neck Golf Course ✪✪✪

Grindstone Avenue
Winter Harbor, ME (207) 963-7760
www.grindstonegolf.com

Tees	Holes	Yards	Par	USGA	Slope
BACK					
MIDDLE	9	3095	36		
FRONT	9	2550	36		

Club Pro: Kevin Conley
Payment: Visa, MC
Tee Times: No
Fee 9 Holes: Weekday: $24
Fee 18 Holes: Weekday: $36
Twilight Rates: After 4:30pm
Cart Rental: $25/18, $15/9 per cart, $4/pull
Lessons: No **Schools:** No
Membership: Yes
Other: No

Weekend: $28
Weekend: $45
Discounts: College & Juniors
Driving Range: No
Junior Golf: No
Architect/Yr Open: Alex Handy/1891
GPS:

Player Comments: "Could not be more beautiful." Located on Frenchman's Bay. Enjoy cool sea breezes, spectacular ocean views.

	1	2	3	4	5	6	7	8	9
PAR	4	4	4	3	4	4	5	4	4
YARDS	345	340	317	138	413	335	457	343	407
PAR									
YARDS									

Directions: Route 1 to Route 186. Route 186 to Main Street. Right on Main for 1 mile to Grindstone Avenue.

Hampden Country Club

25 Thomas Road
Hampden, ME (207) 862-9999
hampdencountryclub.net

Club Pro: No
Payment: Most Major Credit Cards
Tee Times: No
Fee 9 Holes: Weekday: $12
Fee 18 Holes: Weekday: $20
Twilight Rates: After 5pm
Cart Rental: $20pp/18, $10pp/9
Lessons: No **Schools:** No
Membership: Yes
Other: Snack Bar

Tees	Holes	Yards	Par	USGA	Slope
BACK	9	2570	36		
MIDDLE	9	2737	36	66.0	108
FRONT	9	2550	36		112

Weekend: $15
Weekend: $25
Discounts: Senior, Vets, Ladies' Day
Driving Range: No
Junior Golf: No
Architect/Yr Open:
GPS:

The course is fairly wide open, friendly for beginners and seniors. Considered an easy walker. Tuesday is Ladies Day for $15 all day. Thursday is Senior Citizens and Veterans Day for $15 all day.

	1	2	3	4	5	6	7	8	9
PAR	4	3	4	4	4	3	5	4	5
YARDS	320	170	330	295	257	195	450	310	410
PAR									
YARDS									

Directions: I-95 to Exit 174, follow Route 69 East for 1.5 miles. Take Route 9 East for 2 miles; course is on right.

Hermon Meadow Golf Club

281 Billings Road
Bangor, ME (207) 848-3741
www.hermonmeadow.com

Club Pro: Thea Davis
Payment: Most Major Credit Cards
Tee Times: No
Fee 9 Holes: Weekday: $15
Fee 18 Holes: Weekday: $27 all day
Twilight Rates: After 3pm
Cart Rental: $15pp/18, $8.50pp/9
Lessons: Yes **Schools:** Jr.
Membership: $200
Other: Clubhouse / Snack Bar / Bar-Lounge

Tees	Holes	Yards	Par	USGA	Slope
BACK	18	6329	72	69.4	117
MIDDLE	18	5895	72	67.7	113
FRONT	18	5395	72	70.9	120

Weekend: $15
Weekend: $27 all day
Discounts: Junior
Driving Range: $4/bucket
Junior Golf: Yes
Architect/Yr Open:
GPS:

The greens are small and fast; back 9 is heavily wooded. Driving range has largest bent grass tees in Maine. Call for daily specials.

	1	2	3	4	5	6	7	8	9
PAR	4	4	3	5	4	5	4	3	4
YARDS	350	385	130	460	270	545	350	165	350
	10	11	12	13	14	15	16	17	18
PAR	4	4	3	5	4	5	3	4	4
YARDS	265	310	160	430	320	510	135	370	390

Directions: Take Union Street 4 miles past airport in Bangor, take left on Billings Road, course is 2 miles on left.

Hidden Meadows Golf Course

240 West Old Town Road
Old Town, ME (207) 827-4779
www.oldtowngolf.com

Tees	Holes	Yards	Par	USGA	Slope
BACK					
MIDDLE	9	2974	35	66.5	112
FRONT	9	2481	35	66.4	109

Club Pro:
Payment: Cash, Visa, MC, Disc
Tee Times: No
Fee 9 Holes: Weekday: $12 **Weekend:** $12
Fee 18 Holes: Weekday: $20 **Weekend:** $20
Twilight Rates: No
Discounts: Senior discounts M/Th, $12/18 walking, $10/18 cart
Cart Rental: $24/18, $15/9 per cart **Driving Range:** No
Lessons: Yes **Schools:** Yes **Junior Golf:** Yes
Membership: Yes **Architect/Yr Open:** Jeffrey P. Dufour/1995
Other: Open May to October **GPS:**

New clubhouse with full-service lounge. Continuous major improvements, new women's tees.

	1	2	3	4	5	6	7	8	9
PAR	4	4	4	3	5	4	4	3	4
YARDS	389	323	339	148	547	335	394	167	332
PAR									
YARDS									

Directions: I-95 to Exit 197. West on Route 43 toward Hudson. Golf course is 1/4 mile from interstate on left.

Hillcrest Golf Club

59 Grove Street
Millinocket, ME (207) 723-8410

Tees	Holes	Yards	Par	USGA	Slope
BACK					
MIDDLE	9	2477	33	63.2	104
FRONT					

Club Pro: Carolyn Simone
Payment: Visa, MC
Tee Times: No
Fee 9 Holes: Weekday: $12 **Weekend:** $12
Fee 18 Holes: Weekday: $18 all day **Weekend:** $18 all day
Twilight Rates: No **Discounts:** None
Cart Rental: $20pp/18, $10pp/9 **Driving Range:** No
Lessons: Yes **Schools:** No **Junior Golf:** Yes
Membership: Yes **Architect/Yr Open:**
Other: Clubhouse / Snack Bar / Bar-Lounge **GPS:**

Player Comments: "Great shape." "Sits at bottom of Mt. Katahdin. Very nice short course, very tight with narrow, tree-lined fairways." Open April - October.

	1	2	3	4	5	6	7	8	9
PAR	4	3	4	4	4	4	3	3	4
YARDS	359	152	364	287	265	401	221	153	275
PAR									
YARDS									

Directions: I-95 to Medway Exit 244, left off ramp onto Route 157. Follow 12 miles to Millinocket. Past McDonald's to bottom of hill. Follow signs at right.

Houlton Community Golf Course NR  23

Nickerson Lake Road
Houlton, ME (207) 532-2662
www.houltongolf.com

Club Pro:
Payment: Cash, Check, Credit Cards
Tee Times: No
Fee 9 Holes: Weekday: $15
Fee 18 Holes: Weekday: $23
Twilight Rates: No
Cart Rental: $14pp/9
Lessons: $30/half hour **Schools:** No
Membership: Yes
Other: Clubhouse / Snack Bar / Bar-Lounge

Tees	Holes	Yards	Par	USGA	Slope
BACK					
MIDDLE	9	2993	36	68.9	117
FRONT	9	2705	38	73.6	109

Weekend: $15
Weekend: $23
Discounts: Senior & Junior
Driving Range: Yes
Junior Golf: Yes
Architect/Yr Open:
GPS:

COUPON

The course is adjacent to beautiful Nickerson Lake. Hilly, but other than a scenic view of the lake, has few water hazards. 2 sets of tees means a change of par on some holes on 2nd round. Open May - September.

	1	2	3	4	5	6	7	8	9
PAR	4	5	3	4	4	5	4	3	4
YARDS	325	475	150	260	425	455	345	175	383
PAR									
YARDS									

Directions: I-95 to Houlton Exit 305 (last US exit on I-95 North), follow signs to course

Island Country Club NR 24

442 Sunset Drive
Sunset, ME (207) 348-2379
www.islandcountryclub.net

Club Pro: Shaun Webb
Payment: Visa, MC
Tee Times: No
Fee 9 Holes: Weekday: $20
Fee 18 Holes: Weekday: $30
Twilight Rates: No
Cart Rental: $24pp/18, $12pp/9
Lessons: $85/hr **Schools:** No
Membership: Yes, $550
Other: Clubhouse / Snack Bar

Tees	Holes	Yards	Par	USGA	Slope
BACK					
MIDDLE	9	1949	62	60.2	108
FRONT					

Weekend: $20
Weekend: $30
Discounts: Junior
Driving Range: No
Junior Golf: Yes, $120
Architect/Yr Open: Stiles & Van Kleek/1918
GPS:

Hilly, fast greens. Contoured fairways, fully irrigated. Alcohol served on premises. Lunch 11-2 Tuesday-Sunday. Beaches, boating, tennis, fine dining, art galleries and shopping close by.

	1	2	3	4	5	6	7	8	9
PAR	4	4	3	3	3	3	3	4	4
YARDS	315	246	118	146	161	116	205	318	321
	10	11	12	13	14	15	16	17	18
PAR	4	4	3	3	3	3	3	4	4
YARDS	315	201	110	140	161	116	205	279	321

Directions: Route 15 to Deer Isle, then Route 15A to Sunset. Club is about 3 miles on the left.

Island Green Golf Course

NR **25**

1 Main Road
Holden, ME (207) 989-9909

Tees	Holes	Yards	Par	USGA	Slope
BACK	9	2461	35	63.6	101
MIDDLE	9	2261	35	62.8	97
FRONT	9	1667	33	63.6	101

Club Pro: Bill Curtis
Payment: Visa, MC
Tee Times: Preferred
Fee 9 Holes: Weekday: $14   **Weekend:** $14
Fee 18 Holes: Weekday: $20   **Weekend:** $20
Twilight Rates: Early-bird
Discounts: Senior Day Monday $10, Ladies' Day Wednesday $10
Cart Rental: $10pp/18, $7pp/9   **Driving Range:** $8/lg., $6/sm.
Lessons: Yes **Schools:** Yes   **Junior Golf:** Yes
Membership: Yes   **Architect/Yr Open:**
Other: Restaurant / Lounge / Night-Lit Driving Range

COUPON

Plays par 33 from Whites and par 35 from the Blues. Great risk/reward course. Although a short course, the greens are regulation size. A challenge for all levels. Easy walker. Also try our mini-golf and mini-putt.

	1	2	3	4	5	6	7	8	9
PAR	4	4	4	4	4	5	3	3	4
YARDS	255	190	305	345	185	447	109	129	296
PAR									
YARDS									

Directions: I-395 to Holden. Exit Route 1A. 2 miles South, course on right.

Jato Highlands Golf Course

NR **26**

175 Town Farm Road
Lincoln, ME (207) 794-2433
www.jatohighlands.com

Tees	Holes	Yards	Par	USGA	Slope
BACK	18	5715	72	68	123
MIDDLE	18	5491	71	67	121
FRONT	18	4916	72	64.1	108

Club Pro: Jaymis Dugams
Payment: Visa, MC, Cash, Check
Tee Times: Yes
Fee 9 Holes: Weekday: $20   **Weekend:** $20
Fee 18 Holes: Weekday: $30   **Weekend:** $30
Twilight Rates: No   **Discounts:** Junior, $10
Cart Rental: $15pp/18, $10pp/9   **Driving Range:** Yes
Lessons: Yes **Schools:** No   **Junior Golf:** Yes
Membership: Yes   **Architect/Yr Open:** Tom Gardner/1999
Other: Restaurant / Clubhouse / Bar-Lounge   **GPS:**

COUPON

Player Comments: "A hidden gem. Well maintained. A demanding challenge from any tees."

	1	2	3	4	5	6	7	8	9
PAR	4	3	4	4	3	4	4	4	5
YARDS	345	138	399	365	218	389	383	339	570
	10	11	12	13	14	15	16	17	18
PAR	4	3	4	4	4	5	4	3	5
YARDS	411	145	325	385	321	501	441	121	507

Directions: I-95 to Lincoln exit. Left on Route 2, 6 miles on Town Farm Road on right.

Johnson W. Parks Golf Course

94 Hartland Avenue
Pittsfield, ME (207) 487-5545
www.jwparksgolf.com

Club Pro: Michael Dugas, PGA
Payment: Most Major
Tee Times: No
Fee 9 Holes: Weekday: $14
Fee 18 Holes: Weekday: $18
Twilight Rates: After 5pm
Cart Rental: $14pp/18, $7pp/9
Lessons: $25/30 half hour **Schools:** No
Membership: Yes
Other: Clubhouse / Sports Bar

Tees	Holes	Yards	Par	USGA	Slope
BACK	9	2927	35	34.1	120
MIDDLE	9	2678	35	35.1	120
FRONT	9	2554	35	35.0	120

Weekend: $16
Weekend: $22
Discounts: Junior, 1/2 price
Driving Range: Yes
Junior Golf: Yes
Architect/Yr Open:
GPS:

Tall pines, narrow fairways and a series of streams add to the challenge at one of central Maine's most popular courses. Fully irrigated. Open April 25 - October 31. Twilight rates after 3pm and 5pm include cart.

	1	2	3	4	5	6	7	8	9
PAR	4	4	5	3	4	4	4	3	4
YARDS	375	405	531	227	308	268	322	160	331
PAR									
YARDS									

Directions: I-95 to Pittsfield Exit 150, go East off ramp. Take a left onto Route 152. 1/2 mile on the loft.

Katahdin Country Club

80 Park Street
Milo, ME (207) 943-8734

Club Pro: No
Payment: Cash Only
Tee Times: No
Fee 9 Holes: Weekday: $14 all day
Fee 18 Holes: Weekday: $14 all day
Twilight Rates: No
Cart Rental: $11pp/18, $5.50pp/9
Lessons: No **Schools:**
Membership: Yes
Other: Clubhouse / Snack Bar

Tees	Holes	Yards	Par	USGA	Slope
BACK					
MIDDLE	9	2968	36	65.8	103
FRONT					

Weekend: $14 all day
Weekend: $14 all day
Discounts: None
Driving Range: No
Junior Golf: Yes
Architect/Yr Open:
GPS:

Wide-open fairways, short-cut rough and no water hazards. Largest sand trap around. Open April 15 - November.

	1	2	3	4	5	6	7	8	9
PAR	4	3	4	4	3	5	5	4	4
YARDS	327	150	322	257	180	485	519	447	281
PAR									
YARDS									

Directions: I-95 North to LaGrange-Milo exit, follow signs to course.

Kebo Valley Golf Club

☆☆☆½ **29**

136 Eagle Lake Road
Bar Harbor, ME (207) 288-3000
www.kebovalleyclub.com

Club Pro: Peiter K. DeVos, PGA
        Jay Blackwell, PGA
Payment: Cash, Visa, MC, Amex
Tee Times: 6 days adv.
Fee 9 Holes: Weekday: $50
Fee 18 Holes: Weekday: $85
Twilight Rates: After 3:30pm
Cart Rental: $25pp/18, $15pp/9
Lessons: Yes **Schools:** No
Membership: Yes
Other: Restaurant / Bar-Lounge / Lockers

Tees	Holes	Yards	Par	USGA	Slope
BACK	18	6131	70	69.0	124
MIDDLE	18	5933	70	69.0	122
FRONT	18	5440	72	72	121

Weekend: $50
Weekend: $85
Discounts: None
Driving Range: No
Junior Golf: Yes
Architect/Yr Open: H.C. Leeds/1891
GPS: Yes

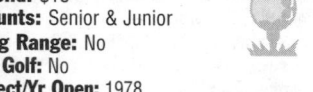
COUPON

8th-oldest club in the country. Majestic views of Acadia National Park. 17th hole restored to its original beauty. Clubhouse overlooks the golf course.

	1	2	3	4	5	6	7	8	9
PAR	4	4	4	3	5	3	4	4	3
YARDS	388	438	336	143	500	165	322	413	194
	10	**11**	**12**	**13**	**14**	**15**	**16**	**17**	**18**
PAR	4	4	4	4	5	3	4	4	4
YARDS	338	400	283	390	530	146	258	349	340

Directions: I-95 to Bangor, 395 to Route 1A, Route 1A to Route 3, Route 3 to Route 233. Look for signs to course.

Kenduskeag Valley Golf Course

NR **30**

947 Grant Road
Kenduskeag, ME (207) 884-7330

Club Pro: No
Payment: Cash, Check, Credit Card
Tee Times: No
Fee 9 Holes: Weekday: $13
Fee 18 Holes: Weekday: $18
Twilight Rates: No
Cart Rental: $20pp/18, $14pp/9
Lessons: No **Schools:** No
Membership: Yes
Other: Clubhouse / Snack Bar

Tees	Holes	Yards	Par	USGA	Slope
BACK	9	2613	35	63.8	98
MIDDLE	9	2575	35	68	98
FRONT	9	2339	35	61.7	96

Weekend: $13
Weekend: $18
Discounts: Senior & Junior
Driving Range: No
Junior Golf: No
Architect/Yr Open: 1978
GPS:

COUPON

An easy but pretty course. Rolling, wooded and stream scenery. Appropriate dress. Open May 1 - October 31. New clubhouse.

	1	2	3	4	5	6	7	8	9
PAR	4	4	5	3	4	3	5	3	4
YARDS	320	343	483	110	285	143	465	154	310
PAR									
YARDS									

Directions: I-95 to Exit 185. Right to Route 15 Broadway North, 12 miles to course. Left onto Grant Road.

Lakeview Golf Club

NR **31**

21 Reynolds Lane
Burnham, ME (207) 948-5414

Tees	Holes	Yards	Par	USGA	Slope
BACK	9	3016	36	68.0	107
MIDDLE	9	2950	36	65.9	107
FRONT	9	2698	36	69.9	114

Club Pro:
Payment: Visa, MC
Tee Times: No
Fee 9 Holes: Weekday: $12
Fee 18 Holes: Weekday: $18
Twilight Rates: No
Cart Rental: $25pp/18, $13pp/9
Lessons: No **Schools:** No
Membership: Yes
Other: Cafe / Clubhouse / Lockers

Weekend: $15
Weekend: $20
Discounts: Junior
Driving Range: No
Junior Golf: No
Architect/Yr Open:
GPS:

COUPON

Beautiful 9-hole course nestled on the shores of scenic Lake Winnecook. Friendly staff and great food. An excellent walking course with level fairways. Highly recommended for senior citizens. All-day passes available — $25 during the week and $30 on weekends.

	1	2	3	4	5	6	7	8	9
PAR	4	4	3	3	4	5	5	4	4
YARDS	381	298	120	159	328	503	485	351	325
PAR									
YARDS									

Directions: I-95 to Fairfield exit. Take Route 139 from Fairfield to Burnham West. Take Prairie Road off 139, clubhouse is on right.

Lakewood Golf Course

NR **32**

Route 201
Madison, ME (207) 474-5955

Tees	Holes	Yards	Par	USGA	Slope
BACK					
MIDDLE	18	6278	72	70.1	128
FRONT	18	5490	74	71.9	120

Club Pro:
Payment: Visa, MC
Tee Times: Weekends & Holidays only
Fee 9 Holes: Weekday: $19
Fee 18 Holes: Weekday: $29
Twilight Rates: After 5 pm
Cart Rental: $31pp/18, $19pp/9
Lessons: Yes **Schools:** No
Membership: Yes
Other: Snack Bar / Bar-Lounge / Hall Rental

Weekend: $19
Weekend: $29
Discounts: Junior
Driving Range: No
Junior Golf: Yes
Architect/Yr Open:
GPS:

Beautiful views overlooking Sugarloaf and the lake. Classic layout, built in 1926. Practice, chipping, and putting areas. #12 is a par 6. Open April - November.

	1	2	3	4	5	6	7	8	9
PAR	4	4	3	5	4	3	4	4	5
YARDS	365	435	160	471	285	141	325	410	510
	10	11	12	13	14	15	16	17	18
PAR	3	4	6	4	4	4	4	4	3
YARDS	130	350	660	410	370	350	360	394	152

Directions: Route 201, go 6 miles past Showhegan toward Bingham.

Limestone Country Club

★★½ ▶ **33**

487 West Gate Road
Limestone, ME (207) 328-7277
www.limestonecountryclub.com

Club Pro:
Payment: Visa, MC
Tee Times: No
Fee 9 Holes: Weekday: $14
Fee 18 Holes: Weekday: $22
Twilight Rates: No
Cart Rental: $22/18, $14/9 per cart
Lessons: No **Schools:** No
Membership: Yes
Other: Clubhouse / Bar / Lounge / Snack Bar / Restaurant

Tees	Holes	Yards	Par	USGA	Slope
BACK					
MIDDLE	9	3355	36	70.4	114
FRONT	9	2870	36	71.4	116

Weekend: $14
Weekend: $22
Discounts: Senior & Junior
Driving Range: Yes
Junior Golf: No
Architect/Yr Open: William Mitchell/1961

COUPON

Course is sited to capture the wind. Fairways lined with evergreens and hardwoods. Elevated greens at different angles. Long- and short-term accomodations are available. Golf packages. New carts.

	1	2	3	4	5	6	7	8	9
PAR	4	5	3	4	4	3	4	5	4
YARDS	415	525	160	370	355	225	390	515	400
PAR									
YARDS									

Directions: I-95 North to Holton, then Route 1 North to Caribou. From Caribou take Route 89 East to Loring/Limestone. Take a left on West Gate Road for 2.5 miles and club is located on the right.

Long Lake Country Club

NR ▶ **34**

744 Lake Shore Road
Madawaska, ME (207) 895-6957
www.longlakegolfcourse.com

Club Pro: Al Hebert
Payment: Credit Card, Check, Cash
Tee Times: No
Fee 9 Holes: Weekday: $15
Fee 18 Holes: Weekday: $25
Twilight Rates: No
Discounts: Junior 12 and under $7.50/9holes
Cart Rental: $10pp/9
Lessons: Yes **Schools:** No
Membership: Yes
Other: Bar-Lounge / Restaurant / Indoor Simulator

Tees	Holes	Yards	Par	USGA	Slope
BACK	9	2955	35		
MIDDLE	9	2760	35		
FRONT	9	2565	36		

Weekend: $12
Weekend: $20

Driving Range: Yes
Junior Golf: No
Architect/Yr Open: Ben Gray/1961

COUPON

Very pretty course located next to Long Lake. 2 new bunkers #4, new sand in others.

	1	2	3	4	5	6	7	8	9
PAR	4	4	4	4	3	4	5	4	3
YARDS	265	345	395	290	160	385	475	290	155
PAR									
YARDS									

Directions: I-95 North to Houlton - Route 1, to Beaulieu Road, Madawaska to Lakeshore Road.

Loons Cove Golf Course

NR ▶ 35

Route 201
Skowhegan, ME (207) 474-9550
www.loonscovegolfcourse.com

Club Pro: No
Payment: Cash or Check
Tee Times: No
Fee 9 Holes: Weekday: $8
Fee 18 Holes: Weekday: $12
Twilight Rates: No
Cart Rental: $18/18, $10/9 per cart
Lessons: Yes **Schools:** No
Membership: Yes
Other: Snacks / Beverages / Lunch Counter

Weekend: $8
Weekend: $12
Discounts: For members
Driving Range: Yes
Junior Golf: Yes
Architect/Yr Open:
GPS:

Tees	Holes	Yards	Par	USGA	Slope
BACK					
MIDDLE	9	1214	27		
FRONT					

Host of the Special Olympics Skills Program.

	1	2	3	4	5	6	7	8	9
PAR	3	3	3	3	3	3	3	3	3
YARDS	142	162	125	160	110	125	128	115	147
PAR									
YARDS									

Directions: I-95 to Route 201. 6 miles to Skowhegan.

Lucerne-in-Maine Golf Course

●● ▶ 36

Route 1A
Dedham, ME (207) 843-6282
www.lucernegolf.com

Club Pro: No
Payment: Cash, Check, Visa, MC
Tee Times: 7 days adv.
Fee 9 Holes: Weekday: $20
Fee 18 Holes: Weekday: $30
Twilight Rates: After 3pm
Cart Rental: $15pp/18, $8pp/9
Lessons: Yes **Schools:**
Membership: Yes
Other: Snack Bar / Lodging Available at Lucerne Inn

Weekend: $20
Weekend: $30
Discounts: None
Driving Range: Warm-up range
Junior Golf: No
Architect/Yr Open: Donald Ross/1926

Tees	Holes	Yards	Par	USGA	Slope
BACK	9	3205	36	70.6	119
MIDDLE	9	2845	36	67.4	119
FRONT	9	2650	36	69.5	116

COUPON

Donald Ross course features tree-lined fairways, ample landing areas and small greens guarded by pot bunkers. Recently put back original bunkers that had been removed.

	1	2	3	4	5	6	7	8	9
PAR	5	3	4	4	4	3	4	5	4
YARDS	450	155	235	360	305	150	340	485	365
PAR									
YARDS									

Directions: I-95 to Exit 45A (Route I-395). Course is 8 miles on left, halfway between Bangor and Ellsworth on Route 1A.

Mars Hill Country Club

NR ▶ 37

75 Country Club Road
Mars Hill, ME (207) 425-4802
www.golfmhcc.com

Tees	Holes	Yards	Par	USGA	Slope
BACK	18	6043	72		
MIDDLE	18	5742	72	68.7	125
FRONT	18	5159	72		

Club Pro: No
Payment: Visa, MC
Tee Times: No
Fee 9 Holes: Weekday: $13
Fee 18 Holes: Weekday: $26
Twilight Rates: No
Cart Rental: $16pp/18, $8pp/9
Lessons: Limited **Schools:** No
Membership: Yes
Other: Clubhouse / Full Snack Bar / Beer

Weekend: $13
Weekend: $26
Discounts: None
Driving Range: $3/sm bucket
Junior Golf: Yes
Architect/Yr Open: A. McQuade/1991
GPS: Yes

COUPON

6th hole par 3, with a 162-foot vertical drop, is amazing. Moose, deer, and/or bear seen on course almost daily. Near New England's largest wind farm.

	1	2	3	4	5	6	7	8	9
PAR	4	5	4	5	4	3	4	3	4
YARDS	350	481	257	470	326	145	313	130	300
	10	11	12	13	14	15	16	17	18
PAR	4	4	5	3	4	3	4	5	4
YARDS	398	380	470	163	363	125	309	447	315

Directions: I-95 to Route US1 to Mars Hill. Then North 1/2 mile on Route 1A. Turn right onto Boynton Road, then left onto Country Club Road.

Mingo Springs Golf Course

✪✪½ ▶ 38

43 Country Club Road
Rangeley, ME (207) 864-5021
www.mingosprings.com

Tees	Holes	Yards	Par	USGA	Slope
BACK					
MIDDLE	18	6014	70	65.5	114
FRONT	18	5158	70	67.4	110

Club Pro: William Ladd
Payment: Visa, MC, Disc, Cash
Tee Times: Please call
Fee 9 Holes: Weekday: $32 M-Th
Fee 18 Holes: Weekday: $42 M-Th
Twilight Rates: After 4pm*
Cart Rental: $20/18, $12/9 per cart
Lessons: Yes **Schools:** No
Membership: Yes
Other: Snack Bar / Bar-Lounge

Weekend: $36 F/S/S
Weekend: $46 F/S/S
Discounts: Junior
Driving Range: Irons only
Junior Golf: Yes
Architect/Yr Open:
GPS:

New green on #16, new tee on #13. Noted for being a challenging old-fashioned course, yet family- and beginner-friendly. Exceptionally scenic views of Rangeley Mountains.
*Twilight rate excludes Tuesday & Saturday.

	1	2	3	4	5	6	7	8	9
PAR	4	4	4	3	4	4	3	4	5
YARDS	350	375	378	173	360	391	177	318	470
	10	11	12	13	14	15	16	17	18
PAR	3	5	3	4	4	4	4	4	4
YARDS	152	522	133	400	360	277	419	363	396

Directions: I-95 to Exit 12 (Auburn). Pick up Route 4. Go through Farmington to Rangeley Village. 2 miles toward Oquossoc, left on Mingo Loop Road. Follow signs to course.

Moose River Golf Course

39

701 Main Street (Route 201)
Moose River, ME (207) 668-5331
www.jackman.com

Club Pro: Wade Turmel
Payment: Cash Only
Tee Times: No
Fee 9 Holes: Weekday: $14
Fee 18 Holes: Weekday: $22
Twilight Rates: No
Cart Rental: $18/18, $13/9 per cart
Lessons: No Schools: No
Membership: Yes
Other:

Tees	Holes	Yards	Par	USGA	Slope
BACK					
MIDDLE	9	1976	31		
FRONT					

Weekend: $14
Weekend: $22
Discounts: None
Driving Range: No
Junior Golf: No
Architect/Yr Open:
GPS:

Open May 15 - October 15. Rate subject to change. Interesting 9-hole course. Very fun to play. Greens are in good condition compared to past years. Great place for family and friends to get together.

	1	2	3	4	5	6	7	8	9
PAR	3	3	4	4	4	3	3	3	4
YARDS	204	168	213	248	259	168	171	169	376
PAR									
YARDS									

Directions: I-95 to Fairfield exit, follow Route 201 North about 85 miles to Moose River.

Natanis Golf Course (Arrowhead) ✪✪½ 40

Webber Pond Road
Vassalboro, ME (207) 622-3561
www.natanisgc.com

Club Pro: Richard Browne, PGA
Payment: Visa, MC, Cash
Tee Times: 1 week adv.
Fee 9 Holes: Weekday: $20
Fee 18 Holes: Weekday: $35
Twilight Rates: After 4pm
Cart Rental: $15pp/18, $9pp/9
Lessons: $35/half hour Schools: No
Membership: Yes
Other: Clubhouse / Lockers / Snack Bar

Tees	Holes	Yards	Par	USGA	Slope
BACK	18	6338	72	70.0	117
MIDDLE	18	5847	72	67.8	116
FRONT	18	5019	72	68.7	117

Weekend: $20
Weekend: $35
Discounts: None
Driving Range: $4.50/lg., $3.50/sm. bucket
Junior Golf: Yes
Architect/Yr Open: Phil Wogan/1974
GPS:

Player Comments: "36 holes of top-notch golf. Challenging." Improved cart paths. State of Maine Museum and Fieldstone Gardens nearby. Distance below is from back tees. Come play both courses.

	1	2	3	4	5	6	7	8	9
PAR	5	4	4	5	3	4	3	4	4
YARDS	500	400	350	461	200	255	190	365	240
	10	11	12	13	14	15	16	17	18
PAR	3	4	3	4	4	5	4	5	4
YARDS	185	380	165	403	424	530	441	439	410

Directions: I-95 to Augusta/Winthrop exit onto Route 201 to Webber Pond Road. Follow signs.

Natanis Golf Course (Tomahawk) ✪✪✪ ▶41

Webber Pond Road
Vassalboro, ME (207) 622-3561
www.natanisgc.com

Tees	Holes	Yards	Par	USGA	Slope
BACK	18	6607	72	70.6	132
MIDDLE	18	6060	72	67.3	123
FRONT	18	5034	72	63.8	104

Club Pro: Richard Browne, PGA
Payment: Visa, MC, Cash
Tee Times: 1 week adv.
Fee 9 Holes: Weekday:
Fee 18 Holes: Weekday: $45
Twilight Rates: After 4pm
Cart Rental: $15pp/18
Lessons: $35/half hour **Schools:** No
Membership: Yes
Other: Clubhouse / Lockers / Snack Bar

Weekend:
Weekend: $45
Discounts: None
Driving Range: $4.50/lg., $3.50/sm. bucket
Junior Golf: Yes
Architect/Yr Open: Dan Maples/2002
GPS:

The tougher of this pair, the Dan Maples design has more length and more challenges. Distance below is from middle tees.

	1	2	3	4	5	6	7	8	9
PAR	5	4	5	3	4	4	3	4	4
YARDS	490	342	526	124	358	362	121	354	359
	10	11	12	13	14	15	16	17	18
PAR	3	4	4	3	5	5	4	4	4
YARDS	130	320	373	163	481	503	311	365	378

Directions: I-95 to Augusta/Winthrop exit onto Route 201 to Webber Pond Road. Follow signs.

Newport Country Club NR ▶42

170 Golf Course Road
Newport, ME (207) 368-5600

Tees	Holes	Yards	Par	USGA	Slope
BACK					
MIDDLE	9	2520	35		
FRONT					

Club Pro: Jeff Peabody, PGA
Payment: Cash Only
Tee Times: Yes
Fee 9 Holes: Weekday: $12
Fee 18 Holes: Weekday: $18
Twilight Rates: No
Cart Rental: $10pp/9
Lessons: Yes **Schools:** Yes
Membership: Yes
Other: Clubhouse / Snack Bar

Weekend: $12
Weekend: $18
Discounts: Senior & Junior
Driving Range: Yes
Junior Golf: Yes
Architect/Yr Open:
GPS:

	1	2	3	4	5	6	7	8	9
PAR	3	3	5	4	4	5	4	3	4
YARDS	155	135	430	380	255	450	290	190	235
PAR									
YARDS									

Directions: I-95 to Exit 157 to Route 7 to right turn on Golf Course Road in Newport.

Northeast Harbor Golf Club ✪◔½ ▸43

15 Golf Club Road
N.E. Harbor, ME (207) 276-5335
www.nehgc.com

Club Pro: R. Gardner, PGA
Payment: Visa, MC, Amex, Disc
Tee Times: No
Fee 9 Holes: Weekday: $25
Fee 18 Holes: Weekday: $45
Twilight Rates: No
Cart Rental: $24pp/18, $12pp/9
Lessons: Private, Group, Jr. Clinic **Schools:** Yes
Membership: Yes
Other: Clubhouse/ Lockers

Tees	Holes	Yards	Par	USGA	Slope
BACK	18	5504	69	66.7	128
MIDDLE	18	5324	69	65.9	124
FRONT	18	4558	71	66.9	124

Weekend: $25
Weekend: $45
Discounts: None
Driving Range: Members only
Junior Golf: Yes
Architect/Yr Open: J.G. Thorpe./1895
GPS:

Classic Donald Ross design. Complete irrigation. Located on Mt. Desert Island. Close to Acadia National Park. Open to the public May - June and September - October. Members only July and August.

	1	2	3	4	5	6	7	8	9
PAR	4	4	3	4	4	3	4	3	5
YARDS	325	320	149	425	305	127	284	155	457
	10	11	12	13	14	15	16	17	18
PAR	5	4	3	4	3	4	4	4	4
YARDS	495	310	175	337	187	415	281	338	239

Directions: I-95 to Bangor exit (Route 1A), follow to Ellsworth, take Route 3 to Mt. Desert Island. Right at light at head of island on Route 198. Left at next light (still 198), right on Sargent Drive. NEHGC on left.

Northport Golf Club ✪✪✪½ ▸44

Off Route 1
Belfast, ME (207) 338-2270

Club Pro: Peter Hodgkins, PGA
Payment: Visa, MC, AMEX
Tee Times: Weekends & Holidays
Fee 9 Holes: Weekday: $22
Fee 18 Holes: Weekday: $30
Twilight Rates: No
Cart Rental: $15pp/18, $18pp/9
Lessons: $45/half hour **Schools:** No
Membership: Yes
Other: Clubhouse / Snack Bar

Tees	Holes	Yards	Par	USGA	Slope
BACK					
MIDDLE	9	3047	36	34.2	112
FRONT	9	2747	37	35.7	113

Weekend: $22
Weekend: $30
Discounts: Spring/Fall
Driving Range: Yes
Junior Golf: Yes
Architect/Yr Open: William Jennings/1916
GPS:

COUPON

Whole course now fully irrigated. New tee on #2, and new practice green. Built in 1916 — rare velvet bentgrass fairways and greens.

	1	2	3	4	5	6	7	8	9
PAR	4	4	3	4	5	4	5	4	3
YARDS	290	377	157	310	483	412	530	338	150
PAR									
YARDS									

Directions: I-95 to Augusta. Exit onto Route 3 East to Belfast/Bar Harbor. Stay on Route 3 to Route 1 South 2 miles. Left at Dos Amigos restaurant.

Palmyra Golf Course ✪✪½ ▶ 45

147 Lang Hill Road
Palmyra, ME (207)938-4947
www.palmyra-me.com

Tees	Holes	Yards	Par	USGA	Slope
BACK	18	6617	72	70.1	120
MIDDLE	18	6367	72	69.0	118
FRONT	18	5464	72	69.0	118

Club Pro: None
Payment: Visa, MC, Disc
Tee Times: Recommended
Fee 9 Holes: Weekday: $14   **Weekend:** $16
Fee 18 Holes: Weekday: $24   **Weekend:** $28
Twilight Rates: After 6pm   **Discounts:** None
Cart Rental: $24pp/18, $12pp/9, $4/pull   **Driving Range:** $3.50/45 balls
Lessons: Yes **Schools:** No   **Junior Golf:** Yes
Membership: Yes   **Architect/Yr Open:**
Other: Snack Bar / RV Facility with 100 Full Hookup Sites

COUPON

Complete renovation and extensive changes in 2005 and '06. Course noted for excellent value and high quality. Course awarded for programs advancing junior golf.

	1	2	3	4	5	6	7	8	9
PAR	4	4	5	3	4	4	4	3	5
YARDS	430	281	575	153	400	407	400	129	476
	10	11	12	13	14	15	16	17	18
PAR	4	3	4	4	5	4	4	3	5
YARDS	386	150	350	387	487	373	304	198	481

Directions: I-95 to Exit 157 (Newport). Route 2 West, approximately 5 miles. Right at white church. Course is on top of hill.

Penobscot Valley Country Club ✪✪✪ ▶ 46

366 Main Street
Orono, ME (207) 866-2423
www.penobscotvalleycc.com

Tees	Holes	Yards	Par	USGA	Slope
BACK	18	6445	72	71.2	128
MIDDLE	18	6301	72	70.5	126
FRONT	18	5796	74	73.9	128

Club Pro: Dick Harris, PGA
Payment: Most Major Credit Cards
Tee Times: Up to 1 week in adv.
Fee 9 Holes: Weekday: $30   **Weekend:** $30
Fee 18 Holes: Weekday: $60   **Weekend:**
Twilight Rates: No   **Discounts:** None
Cart Rental: $12pp/18, $7pp/9   **Driving Range:** $5/bag
Lessons: $35/half hour **Schools:** Yes   **Junior Golf:** Yes
Membership: Yes   **Architect/Yr Open:** Donald Ross/1924
Other: Clubhouse / Lockers / Showers / Snack Bar / Restaurant / Bar-Lounge

This Donald Ross course holds many amateur tournaments. A shotmaker's course, it is in great shape. The course is very challenging and hilly with scenic views.

	1	2	3	4	5	6	7	8	9
PAR	4	4	5	3	4	3	5	4	4
YARDS	396	396	471	143	354	163	443	337	384
	10	11	12	13	14	15	16	17	18
PAR	5	4	4	4	3	5	3	4	4
YARDS	490	390	371	424	143	455	193	323	425

Directions: I-95 to Exit 189. Right to dead end. Right 1/4 mile to club.

Pine Hill Golf Club

NR 47

11 Pine Hill Drive
Brewer, ME (207) 989-3824

Tees	Holes	Yards	Par	USGA	Slope
BACK	9	2979	36	66	100
MIDDLE	9	2749	36	66	100
FRONT	9	2580	36	67	99

Club Pro:
Payment: Visa, MC
Tee Times: No
Fee 9 Holes: Weekday: $13   **Weekend:** $13.50
Fee 18 Holes: Weekday: $15.50 all day   **Weekend:** $15.50 all day
Twilight Rates: No   **Discounts:** Ladies Monday
Cart Rental: $21/18, $13/9 per cart   **Driving Range:** $3.50/med.
Lessons: Yes **Schools:** No   **Junior Golf:** No
Membership: Yes   **Architect/Yr Open:**
Other: Clubhouse / Snack Bar   **GPS:**

Mostly level. Very scenic. Good course for beginners and intermediates. Open April - October.

	1	2	3	4	5	6	7	8	9
PAR	4	4	4	4	3	5	4	5	3
YARDS	292	333	326	339	166	498	320	495	210
PAR									
YARDS									

Directions: I-395 to South Main Street/Brewer exit, follow signs to course.

Pine Ridge Golf Course

NR

97 West River Road
Waterville, ME (207) 873-0474

Tees	Holes	Yards	Par	USGA	Slope
BACK					
MIDDLE	9	2570	27		
FRONT					

Club Pro:
Payment: Cash or Check
Tee Times: No
Fee 9 Holes: Weekday: $11   **Weekend:** $13
Fee 18 Holes: Weekday: **Weekend:**
Twilight Rates: No   **Discounts:** Sr. & Jr. memberships
Cart Rental: $5/pull   **Driving Range:** No
Lessons: No **Schools:** No   **Junior Golf:** No
Membership: Yes   **Architect/Yr Open:**
Other: Restaurant / Bar-Lounge   **GPS:**

Well-built and -maintained par 3. Great for beginners, seniors and people with little time.

	1	2	3	4	5	6	7	8	9
PAR	3	3	3	3	3	3	3	3	3
YARDS	160	135	110	125	220	100	125	175	135
PAR									
YARDS									

Directions: I-95 (Maine Turnpike) to Waterville exit. Follow signs for Thomas College.

Piscataquis Country Club

17 Country Club Lane (Route 15)
Guilford, ME (207) 876-3203

Tees	Holes	Yards	Par	USGA	Slope
BACK	9	2844	36	66.0	115
MIDDLE	9	2582	36	64.3	106
FRONT	9	2417	36	69.7	123

Club Pro: No
Payment: Visa, MC, Check
Tee Times: No
Fee 9 Holes: Weekday: $12
Fee 18 Holes: Weekday: $20
Twilight Rates: After 4pm $10
Cart Rental: $20pp/18, $10pp/9
Lessons: Schools: No
Membership: Yes
Other: Clubhouse / Kitchen

Weekend: $12
Weekend: $20
Discounts: Junior
Driving Range: No
Junior Golf: Yes
Architect/Yr Open: 1926
GPS:

Number 5 is now a par 5, all uphill. All-day rates for juniors. Prices subject to change.

	1	2	3	4	5	6	7	8	9
PAR	4	4	4	4	5	3	4	4	4
YARDS	352	324	251	290	470	164	268	348	377
PAR									
YARDS									

Directions: I-95 to Newport exit, Route 7 to Route 23 North, to Route 15. Course is 1/10 mile from the intersection.

Portage Hill Country Club

Route 11
Portage, ME (207) 435-8221
www.ainop.com/portagehillscc

Tees	Holes	Yards	Par	USGA	Slope
BACK					
MIDDLE	9	3109	36	69.5	110
FRONT	9	2796	37	71.5	113

Club Pro:
Payment: Most Major Credit Cards
Tee Times: No
Fee 9 Holes: Weekday: $15
Fee 18 Holes: Weekday: $25
Twilight Rates: No
Cart Rental: $12pp/cart
Lessons: No **Schools:**
Membership: Yes
Other: Clubhouse / Snack Bar / Bar-Lounge

Weekend: $15
Weekend: $25
Discounts: None
Driving Range: No
Junior Golf: No
Architect/Yr Open:
GPS:

The course is well-maintained, hilly and scenic. Open from mid-May to mid-September. Rates subject to change.

	1	2	3	4	5	6	7	8	9
PAR	4	4	4	4	5	3	4	5	3
YARDS	432	323	321	343	478	128	388	504	165
PAR									
YARDS									

Directions: I-95, to Sherman exit, Route 11. Follow Route 11 North approximately 65 miles.

Presque Isle Country Club ✪✪ ▶ 51

Route 205
Presque Isle, ME (207) 764-0430
www.picountryclub.com

Tees	Holes	Yards	Par	USGA	Slope
BACK	18	6751	72	70.8	118
MIDDLE	18	6217	72	69.2	113
FRONT	18	5387	72	72.2	122

Club Pro: Barry Madore
Payment: Cash, Visa, MC, Amex, Disc
Tee Times: No
Fee 9 Holes: Weekday: $18
Fee 18 Holes: Weekday: $36
Twilight Rates: $40 w/cart
Cart Rental: $15pp/18, $9pp/9
Lessons: $25/35 min. **Schools:** No
Membership: Yes
Other: Clubhouse / Lockers / Showers / Restaurant/Lounge

Weekend: $18
Weekend: $36
Discounts: None
Driving Range: $7/lg., $3.50/sm.
Junior Golf: Yes
Architect/Yr Open: Ben Gray/1959

COUPON

Player Comments: "Friendly and challenging." A very picturesque golf course. Home of the Spudland Open amateur golf tournament.

	1	2	3	4	5	6	7	8	9
PAR	4	4	4	3	4	4	5	3	5
YARDS	322	400	367	155	410	394	473	146	465
	10	11	12	13	14	15	16	17	18
PAR	4	4	5	4	4	5	3	3	4
YARDS	376	334	510	364	387	476	105	191	342

Directions: From Presque Isle, take Route 167 to Route 205. You can't miss it, but if you do, call course for directions.

Rocky Knoll Country Club NR ▶ 52

94 River Rd.
Orrington, ME (207) 989-0109
www.rockyknollcc.com

Tees	Holes	Yards	Par	USGA	Slope
BACK					
MIDDLE	9	3055	36	65.9	94
FRONT	9	2653	36		

Club Pro: Mark Hall, PGA
Payment: Visa, MC, Amex, Disc, Checks
Tee Times: No
Fee 9 Holes: Weekday: $13
Fee 18 Holes: Weekday: $18
Twilight Rates: No
Discounts: Senior, Wed. Junior & Ladies' discounts
Cart Rental: $25pp/18, $15pp/9
Lessons: $35/hour **Schools:** No
Membership: Yes
Other: Restaurant / Clubhouse

Weekend: $15
Weekend: $20

Driving Range: Yes
Junior Golf: No
Architect/Yr: Dan K. & Howard F. Grover/1999
GPS: Yes

Easy to walk. Water comes into play on 2 holes. Lovely pond on #8—try to avoid it!

	1	2	3	4	5	6	7	8	9
PAR	5	4	4	5	3	4	3	4	4
YARDS	479	351	401	452	147	406	154	287	345
PAR									
YARDS									

Directions: I-395 to South Main Street exit, Brewer. Turn left onto Route 15 for about 3 miles. Course is on left.

Searsport Pines Golf Course ✪✪ ▶53

240 Mt. Ephraim Road
Searsport, ME (207) 548-2854
www.searsportpines.com

Tees	Holes	Yards	Par	USGA	Slope
BACK					
MIDDLE	9	2695	36	65.9	122
FRONT	9	2366	35/36	68.7	116

Club Pro:
Payment: Cash, Visa, MC, Check
Tee Times: Not required
Fee 9 Holes: Weekday: $20   **Weekend:** $20
Fee 18 Holes: Weekday: $30   **Weekend:** $30
Twilight Rates: No   **Discounts:** Senior & Junior
Cart Rental: $16pp/18, $11pp/9   **Driving Range:** Yes
Lessons: No **Schools:** No   **Junior Golf:** Yes
Membership: Yes   **Architect/Yr Open:** Bert Witten/1997
Other: Food Concession / Beer / Wine / Club Rentals / Practice Area

COUPON

Plush greens,manicured fairways, meticulously maintained and fully integrated. Friendly staff and scenic atmosphere. Easy-walking and enjoyable for all levels of players. Numerous antique shops, Penobscot Marine Museum, restaurants, lodging nearby. 10 minutes from Belfast.

	1	2	3	4	5	6	7	8	9
PAR	4	4	4	4	5	3	4	5	3
YARDS	285	353	313	316	390	150	295	464	129
PAR									
YARDS									

Directions: Route 1 to Searsport Center. Turn left at Tozier's Market in Searsport onto Mt. Ephraim Road. Course is 2 miles on left.

Squaw Mt. Village Country Club NR ▶54

Route 15
Greenville Junction, ME
(207) 695-3609

Tees	Holes	Yards	Par	USGA	Slope
BACK					
MIDDLE	9	2341	34	70	113
FRONT					

Club Pro: No
Payment: Cash Only
Tee Times: No
Fee 9 Holes: Weekday: $15   **Weekend:** $15
Fee 18 Holes: Weekday: $25   **Weekend:** $25
Twilight Rates: No   **Discounts:** Junior
Cart Rental: $20pp/18, $12pp/9   **Driving Range:** No
Lessons: No **Schools:** No   **Junior Golf:** Yes
Membership: Yes   **Architect/Yr Open:**
Other: **GPS:**

Discount on membership for juniors, seniors, and families.

	1	2	3	4	5	6	7	8	9
PAR	4	3	5	4	4	3	4	3	4
YARDS	359	121	458	288	267	109	317	119	303
PAR									
YARDS									

Directions: I-95 South to Exit 217. Follow Route 6 toward Dover. Stay on 6 to Greenville. Or I-95 South, Exit 185 Bangor, stay on Route 15 North to Greenville. At blinking light in Greenville, go left on Route 15. Course is 3.2 miles on right.

St. Croix Country Club

River Road
Calais, ME (207) 454-8875
www.stcroixcc.com

Club Pro: Mike Ellis, PGA
Payment: Visa, MC
Tee Times: No
Fee 9 Holes: Weekday: $14
Fee 18 Holes: Weekday: $22
Twilight Rates: No
Cart Rental: $16pp/18, $10pp/9
Lessons: $30/half hour **Schools:** No
Membership: Yes
Other: Clubhouse / Showers / Bar-Lounge

Tees	Holes	Yards	Par	USGA	Slope
BACK					
MIDDLE	9	2797	35	65.2	107
FRONT	9	2647	36	64.8	119

Weekend: $14
Weekend: $22
Discounts: Senior
Driving Range: No
Junior Golf: Yes
Architect/Yr Open:
GPS:

Easternmost golf course in U.S.A. Watch eagles train their young, eagle's nest on hole #7 on river. Call ahead for league or tournament times. Open May 1 - October 31.

	1	2	3	4	5	6	7	8	9
PAR	3	5	4	4	5	3	4	3	4
YARDS	162	495	319	405	495	126	295	188	312
PAR									
YARDS									

Directions: Head East on Route 1.2 miles outside of Calais.

Sugarloaf Golf Club

5092 Access Road (Route 27)
Carrabassett Valley, ME
(207) 237-2000
www.sugarloaf.com

Club Pro: J. Scott Hoisington
Payment: Cash or Credit Card
Tee Times: 14 days adv.
Fee 9 Holes: Weekday: $60
Fee 18 Holes: Weekday: $100 w/cart
Twilight Rates: After 3pm
Cart Rental: $20pp/18, $10pp/9
Lessons: $50/half hour **Schools:** Jr. & Sr.
Membership: Yes
Other: Snack Bar / Restaurant / Bar-Lounge / Health Club / Hotel

Tees	Holes	Yards	Par	USGA	Slope
BACK	18	6457	72	72.4	143
MIDDLE	18	5946	72	71.6	138
FRONT	18	5289	72	72.5	131

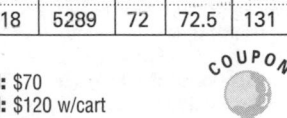

Weekend: $70
Weekend: $120 w/cart
Discounts: Junior 50%
Driving Range: Yes
Junior Golf: Yes
Architect/Yr Open: Robert Trent Jones Jr./1985

Player Comments: "Breathtaking resort course." "Challenging and picturesque." Discounted rates for guests. New pro shop in 2005.

	1	2	3	4	5	6	7	8	9
PAR	4	5	3	5	4	4	4	3	4
YARDS	372	510	168	466	358	337	331	153	363
	10	11	12	13	14	15	16	17	18
PAR	4	3	5	4	4	3	5	4	4
YARDS	255	166	495	359	333	132	458	339	351

Directions: Route 27. Located 36 miles North of Farmington on Route 27 at Sugarloaf Mountain Ski Resort.

Va-Jo-Wa Golf Club

⊘⊘½   **57**

**142 Walker Settlement Road
Island Falls, ME (207) 463-2128
www.vajowa.com**

Club Pro: David Krumenacker, PGA
Payment: MC, Visa, Disc
Tee Times:
Fee 9 Holes: Weekday: $20
Fee 18 Holes: Weekday: $35
Twilight Rates:
Cart Rental: $30pp/18, $20pp/9
Lessons: $25/half hour by appt. **Schools:** No
Membership: Yes
Other: Clubhouse / Snack Bar / Restaurant / Bar-Lounge / Condos / Bag Storage

Tees	Holes	Yards	Par	USGA	Slope
BACK	18	6223	72	70.4	125
MIDDLE	18	5862	72	69.1	121
FRONT	18	5065	72	69.6	115

Weekend: $20
Weekend: $35
Discounts: Junior
Driving Range: Yes
Junior Golf: July
Architect/Yr Open: Vaughn Waller/1964

COUPON

Only 18-hole course in 80-mile radius. Noted for scenic value and quality layout. Open May 1 - October 31. 16th hole and most of the back 9, great scenery including view of Mt. Katahdin.

	1	2	3	4	5	6	7	8	9
PAR	4	4	4	3	4	3	5	4	5
YARDS	308	445	283	207	378	116	517	354	531
	10	**11**	**12**	**13**	**14**	**15**	**16**	**17**	**18**
PAR	4	3	4	4	4	5	3	4	5
YARDS	315	138	381	458	387	478	161	371	524

Directions: I-95 to Exit 276; follow Route 2 East 3 miles; look for signs to Va-Jo-Wa.

Waterville Country Club

⊘⊘⊘   **58**

**Route 137
Oakland, ME (207) 465-9861**

Club Pro: Don Roberts, PGA
Payment: Cash, Visa, MC
Tee Times: Yes
Fee 9 Holes: Weekday: No
Fee 18 Holes: Weekday: $65
Twilight Rates: No
Cart Rental: $15pp/18
Lessons: $35/half hour **Schools:** No
Membership: Yes
Other: Snack Bar / Restaurant / Bar-Lounge

Tees	Holes	Yards	Par	USGA	Slope
BACK	18	6427	70	70.1	123
MIDDLE	18	6108	70	68.6	118
FRONT	18	5381	70	71.3	119

Weekend: No
Weekend: $65
Discounts: None
Driving Range: $3/bucket
Junior Golf: Yes
Architect/Yr Open: Cornish 1916/Orrin Smith
GPS: Yes

Excellent for all golfers. Semi-private.

	1	2	3	4	5	6	7	8	9
PAR	4	3	5	4	4	3	4	4	5
YARDS	350	140	455	378	430	170	300	385	505
	10	**11**	**12**	**13**	**14**	**15**	**16**	**17**	**18**
PAR	4	4	4	3	4	4	3	4	4
YARDS	435	410	370	200	355	330	185	370	340

Directions: I-95 North to Exit 127 to Route 137 West to Oakland. Waterville Country Club is 1.5 miles on left.

White Birches Golf Course

20 Thorsen Road
Ellsworth, ME (207) 667-3621
www.wbirches.com

Club Pro:
Payment: Visa, MC, Amex
Tee Times: No
Fee 9 Holes: Weekday: $11
Fee 18 Holes: Weekday: $20
Twilight Rates: No
Cart Rental: $20pp/18, $12pp/9
Lessons: Schools:
Membership: Yes
Other: Clubhouse / Bar-Lounge / Restaurant / Motel

Tees	Holes	Yards	Par	USGA	Slope
BACK					
MIDDLE	9	948	27		
FRONT					

Weekend: $11
Weekend: $20
Discounts: None
Driving Range: No
Junior Golf: No
Architect/Yr Open:

Come try us. Memberships available.

	1	2	3	4	5	6	7	8	9
PAR	3	3	3	3	3	3	3	3	3
YARDS	123	84	129	92	113	104	74	87	142
PAR									
YARDS									

Directions: I-95 to Route 182A exit, follow to Ellsworth on Route 1 East; course is 1.5 miles on left.

White Tail Golf Course

373 School Road
Charleston, ME (207) 285-7730
www.golfwhitetailinmaine.com

Club Pro: Scott Duthie
Payment: Cash and Checks
Tee Times: No
Fee 9 Holes: Weekday: $11
Fee 18 Holes: Weekday: $13
Twilight Rates: No
Cart Rental: $16/18, $10/9 per cart
Lessons: No **Schools:** No
Membership:
Other: Restaurant / Clubhouse

Tees	Holes	Yards	Par	USGA	Slope
BACK	9	2784	34	66.1	114
MIDDLE	9	2577	34	66.1	114
FRONT	9	2358	34	66.6	106

Weekend: $11
Weekend: $13
Discounts: None
Driving Range: No
Junior Golf:
Architect/Yr Open: 1997
GPS:

COUPON

Scenic, country setting. with rolling hills and 32 different tees, making it challenging and fun for all abilities.

	1	2	3	4	5	6	7	8	9
PAR	5	3	3	4	3	4	4	4	4
YARDS	494	136	176	235	150	329	330	370	357
PAR									
YARDS									

Directions: I-95 to Bangor, exit North on Route 15. Go approximately 30 miles. Course is at the corner of Route 15 and School Road in Charleston. Turn left.

Wilson Lake Country Club ✪✪✪ ▶ 61

Weld Road (Route 156)
Wilton, ME (207) 645-2016
www.wilsonlakecc.com

Club Pro:
Payment: Visa, MC
Tee Times: 1 day adv.
Fee 9 Holes: Weekday: $12
Fee 18 Holes: Weekday: $20
Twilight Rates: 4pm weekdays
Cart Rental: $20pp/18, $12pp/9
Lessons: Yes Schools: No
Membership: Yes

Tees	Holes	Yards	Par	USGA	Slope
BACK					
MIDDLE	9	3022	35	68.8	117
FRONT	9	2807	37	71.9	119

Weekend: $12
Weekend: $20
Discounts: Lung Card
Driving Range: No
Junior Golf: Yes
Architect/Yr Open: 1931

Other: Clubhouse / Bar-Lounge / Snack Bar / Lockers / Showers

Noted for having some of the best greens in the state. Hole #11, 210 yards, is one of the toughest par 3s in the state.

	1	2	3	4	5	6	7	8	9
PAR	4	3	5	4	4	4	3	4	4
YARDS	399	159	501	406	364	379	135	327	352
PAR									
YARDS									

Directions: Route 4 to Route 2 to Route 156 into Wilton. Course is on Weld Road in Wilton.

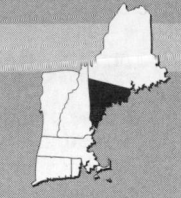

★ Bethel

★ Augusta

Rockport ★

Lewiston ★

Bridgton ★

★ Brunswick

Raymond ★

★ Portland

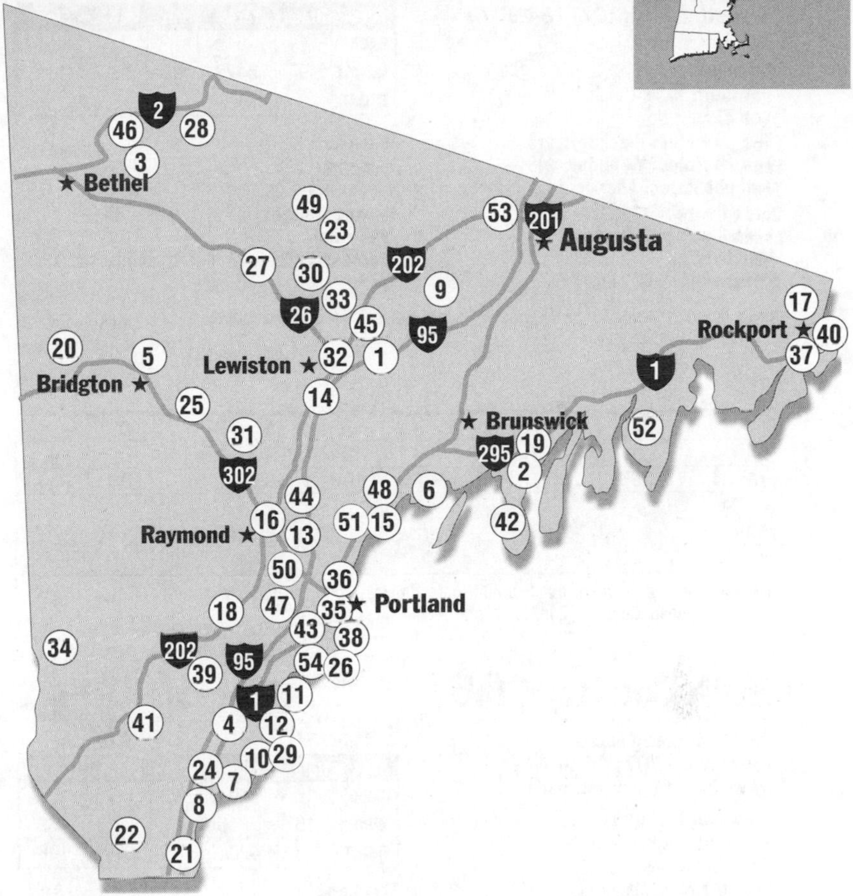

Apple Valley GC	1	Highland Green Golf Club	19	Rockland Golf Club	37
Bath Country Club	2	Lake Kezar CC	20	Sable Oaks Golf Club	38
Bethel Inn & CC	3	The Ledges Golf Club	21	Salmon Falls GC	39
Biddeford & Saco CC	4	The Links at Outlook	22	Samoset Resort GC	40
Bridgton Highlands CC	5	Maple Lane Inn and GC	23	Sanford Country Club	41
Brunswick Golf Club	6	Merriland Farm Par 3 GC	24	Sebasco Harbor Resort GC	42
Cape Arundel Golf Club	7	Naples Golf and CC	25	South Portland Muni.	43
Cape Neddick CC	8	Nonesuch River GC	26	Spring Meadows GC	44
Cobbossee Colony GC	9	Norway Country Club	27	Springbrook GC	45
Deep Brook Golf Course	10	Oakdale CC	28	Sunday River Golf Club	46
Dunegrass Golf Club	11	Old Marsh	29	Sunset Ridge	47
Dutch Elm Golf Course	12	Paris Hill Country Club	30	Toddy Brook Golf Course	48
Fairlawn Golf Club	13	Point Sebago Golf Club	31	Turner Highland GC	49
Fox Ridge Golf Club	14	Poland Spring CC	32	Twin Falls Golf Course	50
Freeport Country Club	15	Prospect Hill GC	33	Val Halla Golf Course	51
Frye Island Golf Course	16	Province Lake Golf Club	34	Wawenock CC	52
Goose River GC	17	River Meadow GC	35	Western View Golf Club	53
Gorham Country Club	18	Riverside Muni. GC	36	Willowdale Golf Club	54

KEY TO THE STAR AND VALUE RATINGS:
5✪= Outstanding 4✪= Excellent 3✪= Very Good 2✪= Good 1✪= Average **NR** = Not Rated
EV = Excellent Value **GV** = Good Value **V** = Value

Apple Valley Golf Club

NR **1** ▶

Pinewoods Road
Lewiston, ME (207) 784-9773

Tees	Holes	Yards	Par	USGA	Slope
BACK					
MIDDLE	9	2473	35	63.7	111
FRONT					

Club Pro: No
Payment: Cash, Credit
Tee Times: No
Fee 9 Holes: Weekday: $15   **Weekend:** $15
Fee 18 Holes: Weekday: $23   **Weekend:** $23
Twilight Rates: After 4pm   **Discounts:** Junior
Cart Rental: $12pp/18, $6pp/9   **Driving Range:** No
Lessons: Yes **Schools:**   **Junior Golf:**
Membership: **Architect/Yr Open:** Arthur David Chapman/1974
Other: Clubhouse / Snack Bar   **GPS:**

Open April 15 - November 15. New Apple Valley Estates golf residential community being built. Homes available Spring '08.

	1	2	3	4	5	6	7	8	9
PAR	4	4	3	5	3	4	4	4	4
YARDS	235	256	147	445	108	333	299	300	350
PAR									
YARDS									

Directions: Maine Turnpike to Exit 80 (Route 196 East) for 4 miles. Right onto Dyer Road. Left onto Pinewoods Road. Course is 2 miles on left.

Bath Country Club

 2 ▶

387 Whiskeag Road
Bath, ME (207) 442-8411
www.skipworkplaygolf.com

Tees	Holes	Yards	Par	USGA	Slope
BACK	18	6301	70	70.8	130
MIDDLE	18	5840	70	68.3	129
FRONT	18	4708	70	67.9	108

Club Pro: Richard Carroll, PGA
Payment: Cash, Credit Cards
Tee Times: Yes
Fee 9 Holes: Weekday: $25   **Weekend:** $25
Fee 18 Holes: Weekday: $40   **Weekend:** $40
Twilight Rates: No   **Discounts:** None
Cart Rental: $13pp/18, $8pp/9   **Driving Range:** No
Lessons: Yes **Schools:** No   **Junior Golf:** Yes
Membership: Yes   **Architect/Yr Open:** Wayne Stiles/1932
Other: Clubhouse / Restaurant / Lounge / Lockers   **GPS:** Yes

Fairways are tight and tree-lined. Paved cart paths. 8th hole is an outstanding par 4. Series of lessons offered. Excellent course conditions and friendly staff.

	1	2	3	4	5	6	7	8	9
PAR	4	4	5	4	4	3	4	4	3
YARDS	338	375	500	370	325	160	420	425	178
	10	11	12	13	14	15	16	17	18
PAR	4	4	4	3	4	4	3	5	4
YARDS	258	326	275	115	352	356	163	525	352

Directions: I-295 to Route 1 North. From 1 North take New Meadows Road exit. Go right at stop sign. Go 1 1/4 miles to next stop sign. Go straight through onto Ridge Road for 1 1/4 miles to 18th tee. Go right.

Bethel Inn & Country Club ✪✪ ▶3

Broad Street
Bethel, ME (207) 824-6276
www.bethelinn.com

Club Pro: Chris Bourasso, PGA
Payment: MC, Visa, Amex, Cash
Tee Times: 2 days adv.

Tees	Holes	Yards	Par	USGA	Slope
BACK	18	6663	72	71.0	128
MIDDLE	18	6017	72	67.9	122
FRONT	18	5280	72	71.5	129

Fee 9 Holes: Weekday: $27
Fee 18 Holes: Weekday: $50
Twilight Rates: No
Cart Rental: $18pp/18, $13pp/9
Lessons: $50/half hour **Schools:** Yes
Membership: Yes
Weekend: $27
Weekend: $50 walk
Discounts: None
Driving Range: $5/lg. bucket
Junior Golf: Yes
Architect/Yr Open: Geoffrey Cornish, 1913

COUPON

Other: Clubhouse / Showers / Snack Bar / Restaurant / Bar / Lodging

The Guaranteed Performance School of Golf at this Cornish-designed course highlights the summer season. New draining and watering. "Great views. We were treated very well."

	1	2	3	4	5	6	7	8	9
PAR	4	4	3	4	5	3	4	5	4
YARDS	340	262	130	370	492	141	361	500	292
	10	**11**	**12**	**13**	**14**	**15**	**16**	**17**	**18**
PAR	4	5	3	4	4	4	3	5	4
YARDS	325	546	167	294	397	400	151	506	343

Directions: Maine Turnpike to Exit 63 Gray. Take Route 26 North to Bethel. Route 26 becomes Main Street in Bethel. Follow Main Street to the top. Course is on left behind Main Inn.

Biddeford & Saco Country Club ✪✪½ ▶4

101 Old Orchard Road
Saco, ME (207) 282-5883
www.biddefordsacocountryclub.com

Club Pro: Tim Angis, PGA
Payment: All Major
Tee Times: 3 days, June-Sept.

Tees	Holes	Yards	Par	USGA	Slope
BACK	18	6196	71	69.6	123
MIDDLE	18	5744	71	68.6	114
FRONT	18	5433	72	71.4	117

Fee 9 Holes: Weekday: No
Fee 18 Holes: Weekday: $45
Twilight Rates: No
Cart Rental: $15pp/18
Lessons: Call for details **Schools:** No
Membership: No
Weekend: No
Weekend: $50
Discounts: None
Driving Range: $4/bucket
Junior Golf: Yes
Architect/Yr Open: Donald Ross/1928

Other: Restaurant / Snack Bar / Bar-Lounge / Lockers / Showers

Designed by 2 great architects, Ross and Silva. Semi-private. Off-peak rates.

	1	2	3	4	5	6	7	8	9
PAR	4	3	5	4	4	4	4	3	4
YARDS	347	181	496	343	391	242	340	153	425
	10	**11**	**12**	**13**	**14**	**15**	**16**	**17**	**18**
PAR	3	4	5	4	4	3	4	5	4
YARDS	145	438	467	317	316	129	317	412	285

Directions: I-95 to Exit 36 Maine Turnpike. Straight to American Motorcycle on right. Take right on Old Orchard Road, course is 1/2 mile on left.

**S
ME**

Bridgton Highlands Country Club ✪✪ ▶ 5

Highland Ridge Road
Bridgton, ME (207) 647-3491
www.bridgtonhighlands.com

Club Pro: Wayne Hill, PGA
Payment: Cash, Check, Credit
Tee Times: 3 days adv.
Fee 9 Holes: Weekday: $24
Fee 18 Holes: Weekday: $34
Twilight Rates: After 3pm
Cart Rental: $16pp/18, $8pp/9
Lessons: $30/half hour **Schools:** No
Membership: Yes

Tees	Holes	Yards	Par	USGA	Slope
BACK	18	6335	72	70.4	128
MIDDLE	18	5796	72	69.0	123
FRONT	18	5378	7472	66.5	117

Weekend:
Weekend: $38
Discounts: Junior
Driving Range: No
Junior Golf: Yes
Architect/Yr: Geoffrey Cornish, Fred Ryan/1926

Other: Snack Bar / Restaurant / Bar-Lounge / Clubhouse

Noted for scenery and challenging design.

	1	2	3	4	5	6	7	8	9
PAR	4	3	4	5	4	4	5	3	4
YARDS	434	152	377	437	333	299	413	148	307
	10	**11**	**12**	**13**	**14**	**15**	**16**	**17**	**18**
PAR	3	4	4	3	4	5	4	4	5
YARDS	153	324	383	152	350	442	282	296	493

Directions: Route 302 in Bridgton to Highland Road. Course is 1.9 miles on the right.

Brunswick Golf Club   ✪✪½ ▶ 6

165 River Road
Brunswick, ME (207) 725-8224
www.brunswickgolfclub.com

Club Pro: Paddy Badcock
Payment: Visa, MC
Tee Times: Anytime
Fee 9 Holes: Weekday: $25
Fee 18 Holes: Weekday: $40
Twilight Rates: After 4pm
Cart Rental: $15pp/18, $10pp/9
Lessons: $65/hour **Schools:** No
Membership: Yes

Tees	Holes	Yards	Par	USGA	Slope
BACK	18	6609	72	69.9	126
MIDDLE	18	6251	72	70	123
FRONT	18	5772	74	71.6	123

Weekend: $25
Weekend: $50
Discounts: Junior
Driving Range: Yes, new
Junior Golf: Yes

Architect/Yr Open: Front: Cornish/1960; Back: Stiles & Van Cleek/1898
Other: Clubhouse / Deck / Snack Bar / Bar-Lounge / Lockers

A real classic layout, a must-play. Easiest, challenging course to walk in New England.

	1	2	3	4	5	6	7	8	9
PAR	4	5	5	3	3	4	4	4	5
YARDS	355	547	485	179	110	440	332	364	494
	10	**11**	**12**	**13**	**14**	**15**	**16**	**17**	**18**
PAR	4	3	4	4	4	3	5	4	4
YARDS	353	172	297	363	430	145	490	300	395

Directions: I-295 to Exit 28, Brunswick; at 2nd light take left onto River Road. Follow 1 mile to course on left.

Cape Arundel Golf Club   ○○½

19 River Road
Kennebunkport, ME (207) 967-3494
www.capearundelgolfclub.com

Tees	Holes	Yards	Par	USGA	Slope
BACK	18	5881	69	67.1	118
MIDDLE	18	5310	69	63.7	100
FRONT	18	5026	70	69.7	119

Club Pro: Ken Raynor
Payment: Visa, MC, Amex
Tee Times: 3 days adv.
Fee 9 Holes: Weekday: $45
Fee 18 Holes: Weekday: $65, $80 w/cart
Twilight Rates: After 4pm $35
Cart Rental: $15pp/18
Lessons: Yes **Schools:** No
Membership:
Other: Clubhouse / Lockers

Weekend: $45
Weekend: $65, $80 w/cart
Discounts: Voucher books available
Driving Range: No
Junior Golf: No
Architect/Yr Open: Walter Travis/1896
GPS:

Home course of President Bush's family. Members only 11am - 2:30pm daily. Twilight rates are not available during July and August.

	1	2	3	4	5	6	7	8	9
PAR	4	4	3	4	4	3	4	4	5
YARDS	375	311	154	398	350	118	381	370	480
	10	**11**	**12**	**13**	**14**	**15**	**16**	**17**	**18**
PAR	4	4	4	3	4	4	3	4	4
YARDS	345	320	409	165	387	322	220	365	394

Directions: From South I-95 to Wells Exit 19. Left to Route 1.2 miles to right on Route 9 to Kennebunkport. From North I-95 Exit 32.

Cape Neddick Country Club   ○○○

650 Shore Road
Ogunquit, ME (207) 361-2011
www.capeneddickgolf.com

Tees	Holes	Yards	Par	USGA	Slope
BACK	18	6066	70	69.3	119
MIDDLE	18	5698	70	67.5	116
FRONT	18	4904	71	69.1	121

Club Pro: David Perroni, PGA
Payment: Visa, MC
Tee Times: 5 days
Fee 9 Holes: Weekday: $35 M-Th
Fee 18 Holes: Weekday: $56 M-Th
Twilight Rates: No
Cart Rental: $15pp/18, $10pp/9
Lessons: $40/half hour **Schools:** No
Membership: Yes
Other: Restaurant / Clubhouse / Lockers / Bar-Lounge / Driving Range

Weekend: $38
Weekend: $63
Discounts: None
Driving Range: Yes
Junior Golf: Yes
Architect/Yr Open: Donald Ross/1920

COUPON

Player Comments: "Challenging; back 9 tougher than first 9. Fun for all skills." "Good summer vacation course. Nice ocean setting." Semi-private. Just 1 hour North of Boston. Best-conditioned course in Southern Maine!

	1	2	3	4	5	6	7	8	9
PAR	4	3	5	4	4	3	4	3	4
YARDS	340	168	577	302	305	122	300	151	326
	10	**11**	**12**	**13**	**14**	**15**	**16**	**17**	**18**
PAR	4	3	5	4	3	5	4	4	4
YARDS	432	153	518	384	170	540	324	268	318

Directions: From the South: I-95 to Exit 7 (York), go East .5 mile to U.S.1. Go North for 3.4 miles to River Road. East on River Road for 1 mile to Shore Road. Club is 2.8 miles North on Shore Road.

Cobbossee Colony Golf Course ✪✪ ▶9

885 Cobbossee Road
Monmouth, ME (207) 268-4182
www.golfcobbossee.com

Club Pro: No
Payment: Cash, Check, Visa, MC
Tee Times: No
Fee 9 Holes: Weekday: $12
Fee 18 Holes: Weekday: $17
Twilight Rates: After 5pm
Cart Rental: $20pp/18, $11pp/9
Lessons: Yes **Schools:** No
Membership: Yes
Other: Snack Bar/ Clubhouse

Tees	Holes	Yards	Par	USGA	Slope
BACK					
MIDDLE	9	2390	34	61.6	100
FRONT					

Weekend: $13
Weekend: $18
Discounts: Lung Card
Driving Range: Yes
Junior Golf: No
Architect/Yr Open: Sheep/1925
GPS:

COUPON

It's an easy walk, and fun. 2 new sand bunkers and 2 or 3 new tees should be ready for 2009.

	1	2	3	4	5	6	7	8	9
PAR	5	3	4	4	3	4	3	4	4
YARDS	450	140	246	312	216	331	108	293	294
PAR									
YARDS									

Directions: From Brunswick area, Exit 51 off I-295 Gardiner - Litchfield. Go approximately 5 miles West on Route 126. Right onto Hallowell Road for 1.5 miles. Left onto Hardscrabble Road. Course is about 1.5 miles on both sides of the road.

Deep Brook Golf Course NR ▶10

36 New County Road
Saco, ME (207) 283-3500
www.deepbrookgolfcourse.com

Club Pro:
Payment: Cash or Charge
Tee Times: 1 day adv.
Fee 9 Holes: Weekday: $18
Fee 18 Holes: Weekday: $28
Twilight Rates: After 5pm
Cart Rental: $12pp/18, $7pp/9
Lessons: Yes **Schools:**
Membership:
Other: Clubhouse / Snack Bar

Tees	Holes	Yards	Par	USGA	Slope
BACK	9	3076	36	70.0	129
MIDDLE	9	2831	36	67.8	127
FRONT	9	2312	36	67.6	111

Weekend: $20
Weekend: $30
Discounts: Senior & Junior
Driving Range: No
Junior Golf:
Architect/Yr Open: William Bradley Booth/2001
GPS:

COUPON

Challenging course, geographicaly accessible for daily play. Tee lengths change on back 9. Open April - Snow. "A work in progress. Nice finishing hole." –RW

	1	2	3	4	5	6	7	8	9
PAR	4	4	3	4	5	3	5	4	4
YARDS	389	399	150	287	566	119	472	352	342
	10	11	12	13	14	15	16	17	18
PAR									
YARDS									

Directions: Exit 5 from Maine Turnpike. Left at traffic light onto Industrial Park Road to first light; take left at light. Next light go right, then first left onto Garfield Street to end at light onto Route 5. Course is 1 mile on left.

Dunegrass Golf Club  ✪✪✪½

200 Wild Dunes Way
Old Orchard Beach, ME
(207) 934-4513
www.dunegrass.com

Tees	Holes	Yards	Par	USGA	Slope
BACK	18	6644	71	71.6	134
MIDDLE	18	6266	72	68.8	125
FRONT	18	4920	71	68.0	113

Club Pro: Mark G. Fogg, PGA
Payment: Cash, Visa, MC
Tee Times: 7 days adv.
Fee 9 Holes: Weekday: $35 w/cart
Fee 18 Holes: Weekday: $59 w/cart
Twilight Rates: After 1pm
Cart Rental: $17pp/18
Lessons: Yes **Schools:** No
Membership: Yes

Weekend: $45 w/cart F/S/S
Weekend: $79 w/cart F/S/S
Discounts: None
Driving Range: Yes
Junior Golf: Yes
Architect/Yr Open: Dan Maples/1999
Other: New Clubhouse / Restaurant / Lockers-Showers / Bar-Lounge / Hotel / Inn

Player Comments: "Great staff, fine conditions." "Visit once and you'll return. Super layout." –GD
Vacation packages.

	1	2	3	4	5	6	7	8	9
PAR	5	3	4	4	4	4	5	3	4
YARDS	539	140	387	301	368	348	526	163	333
	10	11	12	13	14	15	16	17	18
PAR	4	3	5	3	4	5	4	3	5
YARDS	376	168	500	175	395	443	410	170	524

Directions: I-95 to Exit 36 at I-195 to Exit 2 B (Route 1 North). Travel about .1 mile on Route 1 to
Ross Road on right. Take Ross Road for about 2 miles. See Wild Dunes Way and golf course on right.

Dutch Elm Golf Course   NR   12

5 Brimstone Road
Arundel, ME (207) 282-9850
www.dutchelmgolf.com

Tees	Holes	Yards	Par	USGA	Slope
BACK	18	6314	72	69.7	122
MIDDLE	18	5934	72	68.3	118
FRONT	18	5304	72	70.9	120

Club Pro: Norm Hevey
Payment: Cash, Visa, MC
Tee Times: Yes
Fee 9 Holes: Weekday: $25
Fee 18 Holes: Weekday: $35
Twilight Rates: After 3pm
Cart Rental: $16pp/18, $10pp/9
Lessons: $25/half hour **Schools:** No
Membership: Yes
Other: Bar-Lounge / Snack Bar

Weekend: $30
Weekend: $40
Discounts: Senior & Junior
Driving Range: Yes
Junior Golf: No
Architect/Yr Open: Lucien Bourque/1965
GPS:

COUPON

We put a premium on keeping the course manicured. Come try us. New green on #15 and #12.

	1	2	3	4	5	6	7	8	9
PAR	4	5	4	4	4	5	3	3	4
YARDS	300	494	276	347	326	493	202	182	357
	10	11	12	13	14	15	16	17	18
PAR	4	3	3	5	5	4	4	4	4
YARDS	356	156	150	440	486	411	300	342	357

Directions: Off Maine Turnpike, take Exit 32 (Biddeford). Turn right on Route 111, go 1 mile to
Valero Gas Station. Bear left, go 1 mile to stop sign. Turn right, course is on left.

Fairlawn Golf Club ✪✪ ▶ 13

434 Empire Road
Poland , ME (207) 998-4277
www.fairlawngolf.com

Tees	Holes	Yards	Par	USGA	Slope
BACK	18	3198	72	69.8	117
MIDDLE	18	2894	72	67.5	110
FRONT	18	2436	72	69.9	112

Club Pro: David Bartasius, PGA
Payment: Visa, MC
Tee Times: No
Fee 9 Holes: Weekday: **Weekend:**
Fee 18 Holes: Weekday: $28   **Weekend:** $30
Twilight Rates: After 4pm   **Discounts:** None
Cart Rental: $12/18, $7/9 per cart   **Driving Range:** Yes
Lessons: $30/half hour **Schools:** No   **Junior Golf:** No
Membership: Yes, waiting list   **Architect/Yr Open:**
Other: Clubhouse / Lockers / Showers / Snack Bar / Bar-Lounge

Open May 1 - until it snows. Condos on course available for rent.

	1	2	3	4	5	6	7	8	9
PAR	4	3	5	4	4	4	5	3	4
YARDS	323	205	544	409	364	357	497	182	317
	10	**11**	**12**	**13**	**14**	**15**	**16**	**17**	**18**
PAR	4	3	5	3	4	4	5	4	4
YARDS	394	133	491	154	358	363	535	341	333

Directions: From Maine Turnpike, Exit 75, take right off exit; take first right (Kittyhawk). Go to end of road and take left (Lewiston Junction Road). At first stop sign take right. Course on left. From West, take Route 26 South to Route 122. Take right onto Route 122 and follow signs.

Fox Ridge Golf Club ✪✪✪ ▶ 14

550 Penley Corner Road
Auburn, ME (207) 777-GOLF (4653)
www.foxridgegolfclub.com

Tees	Holes	Yards	Par	USGA	Slope
BACK	18	6814	72	72.0	132
MIDDLE	18	6297	72	70.1	126
FRONT	18	4959	72	69.4	123

Club Pro: Bob Darling Jr.
Payment: Visa, MC
Tee Times: Call anytime
Fee 9 Holes: Weekday: $25   **Weekend:** $27
Fee 18 Holes: Weekday: $36   **Weekend:** $44
Twilight Rates: After 3pm   **Discounts:** Sr. & Jr., Sr. discounts Wed
Cart Rental: $16pp/18, $9pp/9   **Driving Range:** Yes
Lessons: $40/half hour **Schools:** Jr.   **Junior Golf:**
Membership: **Architect/Yr Open:** C. Lennie Myshrall/2001
Other: Restaurant / Clubhouse / Bar-Lounge   **GPS:**

COUPON

A blend of St. Andrews and the Maine Seacoast: stone walls, stone bridges, and island greens. "Layout aesthetically magnificent, but severe on both greens and fairways." –RW Home of the Maine Open.

	1	2	3	4	5	6	7	8	9
PAR	4	4	3	5	3	4	4	4	5
YARDS	322	387	167	529	191	349	360	300	489
	10	**11**	**12**	**13**	**14**	**15**	**16**	**17**	**18**
PAR	4	5	4	3	4	4	3	5	4
YARDS	383	551	378	113	322	344	203	518	391

Directions: Maine Turnpike to Exit 75. Left on Washington, right on Danville Corner, left on Danville Road, right on Hammond Cooper.

Freeport Country Club

2 Old County Road
Freeport, ME (207) 865-0711
harrisgolfonline.com

Club Pro: Steve Hodgkins
Payment: Visa, MC, Amex, Disc
Tee Times: No
Fee 9 Holes: Weekday: $10
Fee 18 Holes: Weekday: $20
Twilight Rates: No
Cart Rental: $14pp/18, $7pp/9
Lessons: Yes **Schools:** No
Membership: Yes, $350
Other: Clubhouse / Snack Bar

Tees	Holes	Yards	Par	USGA	Slope
BACK					
MIDDLE	9	2939	36	69.0	116
FRONT	9	2544	36	69.1	108

Weekend: $10
Weekend: $20
Discounts: None
Driving Range: No
Junior Golf: Yes
Architect/Yr Open: 1965
GPS:

Links-style layout with open fairways. A great value. Good condition. Tee length changes on second 9. Located within 5 minutes of L.L. Bean, excellent alternative to shopping in Freeport.

	1	2	3	4	5	6	7	8	9
PAR	4	4	4	4	5	3	4	3	5
YARDS	378	320	403	250	418	177	306	156	531
PAR									
YARDS									

Directions: I-295 North to Exit 17, right on U.S.1 for 2 miles, left over the overpass, then 1st right to club.

Frye Island Golf Course

115 Cape Road Extension
Raymond, ME (207) 655-3551
www.fryeisland.com

Club Pro: No
Payment: Cash, Credit Cards
Tee Times: Weekends
Fee 9 Holes: Weekday: $20
Fee 18 Holes: Weekday: $20
Twilight Rates: After 5pm
Cart Rental: $13pp/18, $8pp/9
Lessons: Yes **Schools:** No
Membership: Yes
Other: Snack Bar / Lounge

Tees	Holes	Yards	Par	USGA	Slope
BACK	9	3139	36	70.0	123
MIDDLE	9	3023	36	69.4	121
FRONT	9	2651	36	72.4	126

Weekend: $30
Weekend: $30
Discounts: Junior
Driving Range: No
Junior Golf: No
Architect/Yr Open: Geoffrey Cornish/1972
GPS:

COUPON

This 9-hole course is narrow with water holes and tree-lined fairways. Open May 1 - November 1. Continuous improvement.

	1	2	3	4	5	6	7	8	9
PAR	4	5	4	3	4	4	5	3	4
YARDS	378	481	391	160	358	293	456	155	351
PAR									
YARDS									

Directions: Take Exit 48 (Westbrook) to Route 302 (2 miles) to Raymond Cape Road. Follow 20 miles to Frye Island Ferry Landing for 5 miles.

S ME

Goose River Golf Club

50 Park Street
Rockport, ME (207) 236-8488
www.gooserivergolf.com

Club Pro: Jim Blanchett, golf dir.
Payment: Cash, MC, Visa
Tee Times: Yes
Fee 9 Holes: Weekday: $25
Fee 18 Holes: Weekday: $40
Twilight Rates: No
Cart Rental: $15pp/18, $10pp/9
Lessons: Yes **Schools:** No
Membership: Yes
Other: Snack Bar

Tees	Holes	Yards	Par	USGA	Slope
BACK					
MIDDLE	9	3072	35	68.0	118
FRONT	9	2608	36	69.7	117

Weekend: $25
Weekend: $40
Discounts: Junior
Driving Range:
Junior Golf: Yes
Architect/Yr Open: 1965
GPS: Yes

COUPON

9 holes, 2 sets of tees. Area known for sailing, kayaking, and hiking. Attractions include: Camden Hills, 2 museums, Rockport and Camden harbors.

	1	2	3	4	5	6	7	8	9
PAR	5	4	4	4	5	3	4	3	3
YARDS	581	341	372	403	495	163	326	189	179
PAR									
YARDS									

Directions: North on I-95, North on Route 1. Follow Route 1 into Camden and follow signs.

Gorham Country Club

68 McLellan Road
Gorham, ME (207) 839-3490

Club Pro: Rick Altham, PGA
Payment: Cash, Check, Credit
Tee Times: Weekends/Holidays
Fee 9 Holes: Weekday: $20
Fee 18 Holes: Weekday: $30
Twilight Rates: After 3pm
Cart Rental: $15pp/18, $10pp/9
Lessons: Yes **Schools:** No
Membership: Yes
Other: Lockers / Showers / Snack Bar / Restaurant

Tees	Holes	Yards	Par	USGA	Slope
BACK	18	6552	71	69.0	118
MIDDLE	18	5884	71	68.2	117
FRONT	18	5426	72	70.5	117

Weekend: $22
Weekend: $32
Discounts: Senior & Junior
Driving Range: Yes
Junior Golf: Yes
Architect/Yr Open: Ernest Hawkes/1961

An 18-hole layout located on a game preserve. A beautiful and challenging course for all abilities.

	1	2	3	4	5	6	7	8	9
PAR	4	4	4	3	4	3	4	4	5
YARDS	324	344	369	160	406	141	391	378	488
	10	11	12	13	14	15	16	17	18
PAR	5	4	4	3	4	3	4	4	5
YARDS	561	427	365	155	424	168	358	375	500

Directions: I-95 to Exit 45. Follow Route 114 to Gorham. Take right onto McLellan Road.

Highland Green Golf Club

NR **19** ▶

114 Village Drive
Topsham, ME 207-725-4549
www.highlandgreenmaine.com

Club Pro: Dan Berry
Payment: Most Major Credit Cards
Tee Times: Yes

Tees	Holes	Yards	Par	USGA	Slope
BACK	9	2917	35		
MIDDLE	9	2518	35		
FRONT	9	2263	35		

Fee 9 Holes: Weekday: $18 walk
Fee 18 Holes: Weekday: $30 walk
Twilight Rates: Yes
Cart Rental: $18pp/18, $8pp/9
Lessons: Schools: No
Membership: Yes
Other: Snack Bar / Bar Lounge

Weekend: $23 walk
Weekend: $40 walk
Discounts: Senior & Junior
Driving Range:
Junior Golf: Yes
Architect/Yr Open: Jim Dodson/2001
GPS:

COUPON

Well-maintained. Traditional-style golf course on the coast of Maine. Proper attire required. No metal spikes.

	1	2	3	4	5	6	7	8	9
PAR	4	4	5	4	4	3	4	4	3
YARDS	330	335	410	295	300	150	365	400	180
PAR									
YARDS									

Directions: 1 minute from I-95 and Route 1, on the Coastal Connector in Topsham, Maine.

Lake Kezar Country Club

★★½ **20** ▶

Route 5
Lovell, ME (207) 925-2462
www.lakekezargolf.com

Club Pro: Richard Dennison, PGA
Payment: Visa, MC
Tee Times: 7 days adv. members

Tees	Holes	Yards	Par	USGA	Slope
BACK	18	5961	72	63.3	117
MIDDLE	18	5585	72	65.7	111
FRONT	18	5088	72	68.8	114

Fee 9 Holes: Weekday: $19 (M-Th)
Fee 18 Holes: Weekday: $28 (M-Th)
Twilight Rates: After 4pm
Cart Rental: $10pp/18, $6pp/9
Lessons: Please call **Schools:** No
Membership: Yes
Other: Snack Bar / Bar-Lounge

Weekend: $22 (F/S/S/H)
Weekend: $32 (F/S/S/H)
Discounts: None
Driving Range: No
Junior Golf: Yes
Architect/Yr Open: Donald Ross/1923
GPS:

Very scenic, pine trees, mountains, meandering brook, quiet. Design by Donald Ross. Clubhouse was 1-room schoolhouse.

	1	2	3	4	5	6	7	8	9
PAR	4	4	4	4	3	4	3	5	4
YARDS	292	305	299	291	136	383	201	498	272
	10	**11**	**12**	**13**	**14**	**15**	**16**	**17**	**18**
PAR	5	4	3	4	5	4	3	4	5
YARDS	450	278	123	334	481	326	153	282	526

Directions: I-95 to Route 302. At the base of Pleasant Mountain, take right onto Knights Hill Road, follow to Lovell Village. Go North on Route 5. Course is 2 miles up on Route 5.

Ledges Golf Club, The ✪✪✪½ ▶ 21

One Ledges Drive
York, ME (207) 351-3000
www.ledgesgolf.com

Club Pro: Matt Blasik
Payment: Visa, MC, Amex
Tee Times: 7 days adv.

Tees	Holes	Yards	Par	USGA	Slope
BACK	18	6981	72	74.0	137
MIDDLE	18	6357	72	71.2	131
FRONT	18	5960	72	69.2	130

Fee 9 Holes: Weekday: $35/$45 ride
Fee 18 Holes: Weekday: $60/75 ride
Twilight Rates: After 2pm
Cart Rental: $15pp before 2pm
Lessons: Yes **Schools:** No
Membership: Yes
Other: Bar-Lounge / Lodging Partner

Weekend: $35
Weekend: $65
Discounts: None
Driving Range: $5/lg., $3/sm.
Junior Golf: First Tee
Architect/Yr Open: William Bradley Booth/1998
GPS:

COUPON

"None better in Southern Maine. A must-play annual visit." –TM "I drive up from Boston every year for this one." –GD

	1	2	3	4	5	6	7	8	9
PAR	4	4	4	5	3	4	5	3	4
YARDS	405	313	344	542	148	391	493	196	333
	10	11	12	13	14	15	16	17	18
PAR	4	3	5	4	3	4	4	4	5
YARDS	388	179	470	356	131	315	377	429	547

Directions: I-95 North to Exit 7 in Maine. Take right to Route 1 South. In 1 mile take Route 91 for 5.1 miles. Club on right. Call for directions from Route 95 South.

Links at Outlook, The ✪✪✪ ▶ 22

Route 4
South Berwick, ME (207) 384-4653
www.outlookgolf.com

Club Pro: Dave Paskowski
Payment: Cash, Visa, MC
Tee Times: 7 days adv.

Tees	Holes	Yards	Par	USGA	Slope
BACK	18	6425	71	70.2	125
MIDDLE	18	6004	71	68.3	121
FRONT	18	5492	71	68.3	115

Fee 9 Holes: Weekday: $29 (M-Thur)
Fee 18 Holes: Weekday: $43 (M-Thur)
Twilight Rates: After 1pm
Cart Rental: $15pp/18, $10pp/9
Driving Range: Yes, grass tees w/target greens
Lessons: $40/half hour, $70/hour
Schools: Adult
Membership: Yes
Other: The Medalist Golf School & The Grille Room

Weekend:
Weekend: $50 (F/S/S)
Discounts: Sr. Mon & Tues only

COUPON

Junior Golf: Yes
Architect/Yr Open: Brian Silva/2000

Player Comments: GPS on all golf carts. "Excellent fairways. Great conditions overall" –FP
Most of the course has a links-like, wide-open feel. Southern Maine beaches nearby.

	1	2	3	4	5	6	7	8	9
PAR	5	4	3	5	4	4	4	3	4
YARDS	481	396	162	453	316	317	310	190	314
	10	11	12	13	14	15	16	17	18
PAR	4	3	4	4	3	4	4	5	4
YARDS	331	138	224	322	123	344	340	415	316

Directions: From Boston: I-95 North to Exit 3, South Berwick. Right on Route 236. Follow 11 miles to end and take right. After 1/4 miles, take right onto Route 4. Course is 1 mile up on right.
From Portland: I-95 South to Exit 2, Wells/Sanford. Take right past toll booths. Take next left onto Route 9. Follow Route 4 into South Berwick. Course on left.

Maple Lane Inn and Golf Club

NR 23

295 Maple Lane
Livermore, ME (207) 897-3770
www.maplelaneinn.com

Tees	Holes	Yards	Par	USGA	Slope
BACK	9	3019	35	65	118
MIDDLE	9	2797	35	62.8	114
FRONT	9	2665	35	65.8	118

Club Pro: Kevin Cullen
Payment: Visa, MC
Tee Times: Yes
Fee 9 Holes: Weekday: $10   **Weekend:** $10
Fee 18 Holes: Weekday: $18   **Weekend:** $18
Twilight Rates: After 4pm   **Discounts:** Senior
Cart Rental: $10pp/18, $5pp/9   **Driving Range:** No
Lessons: Yes **Schools:** Jr. & Sr.   **Junior Golf:** Yes
Membership: Yes   **Architect/Yr Open:** D.R. Grasso/1997
Other: Snack Bar/ Dining Room & Patio / Hotel   **GPS:**

COUPON

Stay-and-play packages start at $70 per couple per night.

	1	2	3	4	5	6	7	8	9
PAR	4	5	3	4	5	4	4	3	3
YARDS	356	347	555	370	155	170	348	540	168
PAR									
YARDS									

Directions: I-95 to Auburn Exit 75. Take Route 4 to Livermore/Livermore Falls town line. Take a right before bridge onto River Road. (From Augusta, take Route 17 South to 133 North.)

Merriland Farm Par 3 Golf

✪✪✪ 24

545 Coles Hill Road
Wells, ME (207) 646-0508
www.merrilandfarm.com

Tees	Holes	Yards	Par	USGA	Slope
BACK					
MIDDLE	9	838	27		
FRONT					

Club Pro: No
Payment: Cash, Visa, MC
Tee Times: No
Fee 9 Holes: Weekday: $13   **Weekend:** $13
Fee 18 Holes: Weekday: $20   **Weekend:** $20
Twilight Rates: No   **Discounts:** None
Cart Rental: No   **Driving Range:** No
Lessons: Yes **Schools:** No   **Junior Golf:** Yes
Membership: Yes   **Architect/Yr Open:** James Morrison/1992
Other: Cafe Serving Breakfast & Lunch / Raspberry, Blueberry Baked Specialties

COUPON

S ME

Player Comments: "A par 3 that lets you and the family enjoy the outing. Pleasant staff. Great muffins."

	1	2	3	4	5	6	7	8	9
PAR	3	3	3	3	3	3	3	3	3
YARDS	83	96	119	111	67	86	63	109	104
PAR									
YARDS									

Directions: I-95 to Exit 19 (Wells). Left onto Route 109, left onto Route 1 about 1.5 miles to Coles Hill Road on left. 1.5 miles up Coles Hill Road to course on right.

Naples Golf and Country Club ✪✪½ ▶ 25

Route 114
Naples, ME (207) 693-6424
www.naplesgolfcourse.com

Club Pro: Bob Caron II, PGA
Payment: Visa, MC
Tee Times: Required
Fee 9 Holes: Weekday: $20
Fee 18 Holes: Weekday: $31
Twilight Rates: After 11am & 3pm
Cart Rental: $16pp/18, $8pp/9
Lessons: $30/half hour **Schools:** No
Membership: Yes
Other: Full Restaurant / Clubhouse / Bar-Lounge

Tees	Holes	Yards	Par	USGA	Slope
BACK	18	6039	72	71.9	126
MIDDLE	18	5617	72	67.8	121
FRONT	18	5498	72	N/A	N/A

Weekend: $20
Weekend: $31
Discounts: None
Driving Range: Yes
Junior Golf: Yes
Architect/Yr Open: James Burnham/1921

COUPON

"Challenging for any level player. Friendly atmosphere. Beautiful setting." Located in the heart of the Sebago Lake Region. Area attractions center around Lake Region.

	1	2	3	4	5	6	7	8	9
PAR	5	4	4	4	4	4	4	4	3
YARDS	465	305	345	405	340	340	375	340	130
	10	11	12	13	14	15	16	17	18
PAR	4	3	4	4	5	4	3	4	5
YARDS	280	125	320	325	400	280	155	262	425

Directions: Exit 48 from Maine Turnpike. Turn right on Riverside Street. 3 miles to Route 302. Left on Route 302 for 30 miles to Naples. Take left on Route 114 in Naples Village. Course is 1 mile on left.

Nonesuch River Golf Club ✪✪✪ ▶ 26

304 Gorham Road
Scarborough, ME (888) 256-2717
www.nonesuchgolf.com

Club Pro: Jim Fairbanks
Payment: Visa, MC, Amex, Disc
Tee Times: 7 days adv.
Fee 9 Holes: Weekday: $22
Fee 18 Holes: Weekday: $32-$36
Twilight Rates: After 3pm $25
Cart Rental: $15pp/18
Lessons: Yes **Schools:** Yes
Membership: Yes
Other: Clubhouse / Food and Beverage, Full Service

Tees	Holes	Yards	Par	USGA	Slope
BACK	18	6324	70	69.0	120
MIDDLE	18	6003	70	67.3	114
FRONT	18	5611	70	63.4	115

Weekend: $25
Weekend: $40
Discounts: None
Driving Range: $5 per bucket
Junior Golf: Yes
Architect/Yr Open: Tom Walker/1996

COUPON

Player Comments: "Great shape, well-run, good package deal." Stay-and-play partner with several area hotels. Off-season rates in Spring and Fall. Course noted for conditions and great layout. Challenging to the best, fair to the rest.

	1	2	3	4	5	6	7	8	9
PAR	4	3	5	3	4	3	4	4	4
YARDS	389	180	539	214	362	173	348	413	431
	10	11	12	13	14	15	16	17	18
PAR	5	4	4	4	4	3	5	3	4
YARDS	492	375	365	397	381	160	496	174	435

Directions: Maine Turnpike to Exit 42. Turn left out of toll. Turn left at 2nd set of lights onto Route 114. Course is .5 miles on left.

Norway Country Club

NR 27

310 Waterford Road
Norway, ME (207) 743-9840

Tees	Holes	Yards	Par	USGA	Slope
BACK					
MIDDLE	9	2909	35	66.6	107
FRONT					

Club Pro: Dave Mazzeo, PGA
Payment: Most Major Credit Cards
Tee Times: No
Fee 9 Holes: Weekday: $16   **Weekend:** $16
Fee 18 Holes: Weekday: $22   **Weekend:** $24
Twilight Rates: After 4pm   **Discounts:** None
Cart Rental: $20pp/18, $10pp/9   **Driving Range:** $4/bucket
Lessons: $35/half hour **Schools:** Clinics   **Junior Golf:** Yes
Membership: Yes   **Architect/Yr Open:** George Dunn/1929
Other: Restaurant / Clubhouse / Snack Bar / Bar-Lounge

Greens in excellent condition. "Most scenic-9 hole course in Maine." –DM

	1	2	3	4	5	6	7	8	9
PAR	4	3	4	4	4	3	5	4	4
YARDS	375	187	327	300	430	167	450	420	253
PAR									
YARDS									

Directions: I-95 North to Exit 63. Take Route 26 to Norway. Follow Main Street/Route 118, 3 miles to the course.

Oakdale Country Club

NR 28

13 Country Club Road
Mexico, ME 04224
(207) 364-3951
www.oakdalecc.com

Tees	Holes	Yards	Par	USGA	Slope
BACK					
MIDDLE	18	6133	72	68.4	121
FRONT	18	5486	74	73.6	125

Club Pro: Dave Weston, PGA
Payment: Visa, MC, Disc
Tee Times: No
Fee 9 Holes: Weekday: $15   **Weekend:** $15
Fee 18 Holes: Weekday: $20   **Weekend:** $20
Twilight Rates: After 5pm   **Discounts:** None
Cart Rental: $14pp/18, $7pp/9   **Driving Range:** No
Lessons: None **Schools:** No   **Junior Golf:** Yes
Membership: Yes   **Architect/Yr Open:** 1923
Other: Clubhouse / Snack Bar / Cocktails   **GPS:**

COUPON

Course is noted for playability. Hilly fairways and challenging greens.

	1	2	3	4	5	6	7	8	9
PAR	4	5	4	3	4	4	4	4	4
YARDS	327	476	339	160	423	390	339	228	362
	10	11	12	13	14	15	16	17	18
PAR	4	5	4	3	5	4	4	3	4
YARDS	336	456	354	144	430	380	391	206	392

Directions: I-95 to Exit 75, Route 4 North to Route 108 toward Rumford. Then to Route 2 West to course.

S
ME

Old Marsh Country Club

○○○½

29

445 Clubhouse Road
Wells, ME (207) 251-4653
www.sundayrivergolf.com

Club Pro: Mark Robinson, PGA
Payment: Visa, MC, Disc
Tee Times: 7 days adv.

Tees	Holes	Yards	Par	USGA	Slope
BACK	18	6523	70	71.7	135
MIDDLE	18	6012	70	68.9	130
FRONT	18	4847	70	68.7	116

Fee 9 Holes: Weekday: $50   **Weekend:** $50
Fee 18 Holes: Weekday: $89   **Weekend:** $89
Twilight Rates: No   **Discounts:** Juniors
Cart Rental: Included   **Driving Range:** Not yet, but coming
Lessons: Yes **Schools:** No   **Junior Golf:** Yes
Membership: Yes   **Architect/Yr Open:** Brian Silva/2008
Other: Putting Green / Grille Room / Bar with All Amish-Made Furniture / Workout Area / Tennis Courts

New in 2008, upscale semi-private course. "My first visit was an absolute treat. We had to think our way around every single hole. The par 3s are wild." –MT Distances below are from the back tees.

	1	2	3	4	5	6	7	8	9
PAR	4	4	5	4	4	3	4	3	4
YARDS	413	375	530	350	410	185	465	209	390
	10	**11**	**12**	**13**	**14**	**15**	**16**	**17**	**18**
PAR	4	4	4	5	4	3	5	3	4
YARDS	353	390	359	535	296	175	523	215	427

Paris Hill Country Club

NR

30

Paris Hill Road
Paris, ME (207) 743-2371
www.parishillcc.com

Club Pro: Mike Cloutier
Payment: Cash, Visa, MC
Tee Times: No

Tees	Holes	Yards	Par	USGA	Slope
BACK					
MIDDLE	9	2305	33	62.1	102
FRONT					

Fee 9 Holes: Weekday: $13   **Weekend:** $13
Fee 18 Holes: Weekday: $18   **Weekend:** $18
Twilight Rates: After 4pm, $10 for as many holes as you can play
Cart Rental: $10pp/18, $8/9   **Driving Range:** No
Lessons: Yes **Schools:** Yes   **Junior Golf:**
Membership: Yes   **Architect/Yr Open:** 1899
Other: Clubhouse / Luncheonette / Bar / Dining Room

COUPON

Overlooks beautiful Oxford Hills and mountains. Open May - October. Great family-play golf course.

	1	2	3	4	5	6	7	8	9
PAR	4	4	4	3	4	3	4	3	4
YARDS	350	260	231	194	352	125	309	129	355
PAR									
YARDS									

Directions: I-95 to Exit 63 (Gray). Take Route 26 to South Paris.

Point Sebago Golf Club ✪✪✪

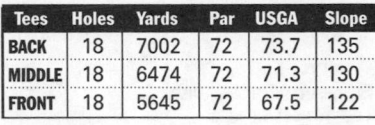

31

201 Point Sebago Road (Route 302)
Casco, ME (207) 655-2747
www.pointsebago.com

Club Pro:
Payment: Visa, MC, Disc
Tee Times: 7 days adv.
Fee 9 Holes: Weekday: $35
Fee 18 Holes: Weekday: $65
Twilight Rates: After 4pm
Cart Rental: Included
Lessons: $75/hour **Schools:** Yes
Membership: Yes
Architect/Yr Open: Philip Wogan & George Sargent/1996
Other: Resort / Restaurant / Snack Bar

Tees	Holes	Yards	Par	USGA	Slope
BACK	18	7002	72	73.7	135
MIDDLE	18	6474	72	71.3	130
FRONT	18	5645	72	67.5	122

Weekend: $35
Weekend: $65
Discounts: Senior & Junior
Driving Range: Yes
Junior Golf: Yes

COUPON

"Upscale layout with a nice variety of holes. Long distance between holes cut deep in the woods. Back tees and fast greens will challenge all players. Nice granite distance markers, and well-marked fairways help." –FP

	1	2	3	4	5	6	7	8	9
PAR	5	3	4	4	4	4	5	3	4
YARDS	502	154	388	375	335	383	549	181	418
	10	11	12	13	14	15	16	17	18
PAR	4	5	4	4	3	4	4	3	5
YARDS	390	533	380	370	163	302	361	183	507

Directions: Turn off Maine Turnpike at Exit 48 and follow signs to Route 302 West for approximately 22.5 miles. Look for Chute's Cafe in Casco. Take second left. Follow signs.

Poland Spring Country Club ✪✪✪

32

543 Main Street (Route 26)
Poland Spring, ME (207) 998-6002
www.polandspringresort.com

Club Pro: No
Payment: Cash or Credit Card
Tee Times: Yes
Fee 9 Holes: Weekday:
Fee 18 Holes: Weekday: $35
Twilight Rates: After 3pm
Cart Rental: $14pp/18
Lessons: No **Schools:** No
Membership: Yes
Other: Clubhouse / Lockers / Showers / Pool / Snack Bar / Restaurant / Bar-Lounge / Hotel

Tees	Holes	Yards	Par	USGA	Slope
BACK	18	6178	71	69.5	127
MIDDLE	18	5931	71	68.1	126
FRONT	18	5133	73	69.0	117

Weekend:
Weekend: $40
Discounts: None
Driving Range: No
Junior Golf: No
Architect/Yr Open: Donald Ross/1893

COUPON

Oldest 18-hole resort course in U.S. (1893) designed by Donald Ross. "Great value. Great views. Wide landing areas. Will definitely go back." –EP Open May 1 - November 1.

	1	2	3	4	5	6	7	8	9
PAR	4	4	4	4	4	3	4	3	4
YARDS	337	306	388	410	305	132	378	184	322
	10	11	12	13	14	15	16	17	18
PAR	4	5	4	3	4	4	5	4	4
YARDS	293	446	292	169	399	404	531	292	329

Directions: Take Maine Turnpike Exit 63 (Gray) to Route 26. Follow Route 26 North about 12 miles. Resort sign is on right.

S
ME

Prospect Hill Golf Course

NR **33** ▶

694 South Main Street
Auburn, ME (207) 782-9220

Club Pro: No
Payment: Visa, MC, Disc
Tee Times: Optional
Fee 9 Holes: Weekday: $17
Fee 18 Holes: Weekday: $25
Twilight Rates: After 4pm
Cart Rental: $15pp/18, $8pp/9
Lessons: No **Schools:** Yes
Membership: Yes
Other: Snack Bar / Bar-Lounge

Tees	Holes	Yards	Par	USGA	Slope
BACK					
MIDDLE	18	5846	71	69.9	110
FRONT	18	5227	71	69.9	111

Weekend: $17
Weekend: $25
Discounts: None
Driving Range: No
Junior Golf: Yes
Architect/Yr Open: 1957
GPS:

The front 9 are wide open with a few small creeks, while the back 9 have 4 ponds and tree-lined fairways. Spikeless course. Collared shirts required.

	1	2	3	4	5	6	7	8	9
PAR	5	4	3	4	3	4	4	4	4
YARDS	460	350	210	230	225	395	370	260	290
	10	11	12	13	14	15	16	17	18
PAR	4	4	5	4	4	3	4	4	4
YARDS	412	290	510	276	357	138	366	311	396

Directions: I-95 to Exit 75, left off ramp, look for signs.

Province Lake Golf Club

⊙⊙ **34** ▶

Route 153
Parsonfield, ME
(800) 325-4434
www.provincelakegolf.com

Payment: Visa, MC
Tee Times: 7 days adv.

Tees	Holes	Yards	Par	USGA	Slope
BACK	18	6277	71	69.8	123
MIDDLE	18	5904	71	68.1	115
FRONT	18	4935	71	69.2	116

Fee 9 Holes: Weekday: $24, $19 after 1pm **Weekend:** $34, $29 after 1pm/$16 after 4pm
Fee 18 Holes: Weekday: $39, $29 after 1pm **Weekend:** $49, $39 after 1pm/$24 after 4pm
Twilight Rates: After 6pm
Cart Rental: $16pp/18, $11pp/9
Lessons: $35/half hour **Schools:** Juniors
Membership: Yes
Other: Clubhouse / Snack Bar / Restaurant / Bar-Lounge / Function Room / Patio / 2 Decks / Childcare

Discounts: Junior
Driving Range: Mats/Turf, 300 yards
Junior Golf: Yes
Architect/Yr Open: Silva/1984

Playable for all. New beginners' tees — 2000 yards. Constantly improving course. Definitely family-friendly — $4/hr babysitter on site. 3rd year in a row named the number 1 golf course for women in New England by *Golf Magazine* July 2007.

	1	2	3	4	5	6	7	8	9
PAR	4	5	3	4	3	5	4	4	4
YARDS	378	438	201	378	144	525	369	376	309
	10	11	12	13	14	15	16	17	18
PAR	4	3	4	4	3	5	4	4	4
YARDS	338	146	295	337	142	483	383	331	331

Directions: I-95 to Route 16 (Spaulding Turnpike) to Route 153 North. Course is 15 miles North. Or access Route 153 South from Route 25.

River Meadow Golf Club

NR 35

216 Lincoln Street
Westbrook, ME (207) 854-1625

Club Pro: Dan Falcone
Payment: Visa, MC
Tee Times: Weekends & Holidays
Fee 9 Holes: Weekday: $20
Fee 18 Holes: Weekday: $28
Twilight Rates: No
Cart Rental: $16pp/18, $10pp/9
Lessons: No **Schools:** Yes
Membership: Yes
Other: Grill Room and Bar / Clubhouse / Snack Bar / Restaurant

Tees	Holes	Yards	Par	USGA	Slope
BACK	9	2915	35	67.0	112
MIDDLE	9	2759	35	67.0	112
FRONT	9	2605	36	67.0	112

Weekend: $22
Weekend: $30
Discounts: None
Driving Range: No
Junior Golf: Yes
Architect/Yr Open: Rufus Jordan/1958

COUPON

Open April - November 15th. Several holes upgraded in 2004-5.

	1	2	3	4	5	6	7	8	9
PAR	4	4	4	3	4	4	4	3	5
YARDS	371	411	248	139	350	350	295	150	445
PAR									
YARDS									

Directions: Maine Turnpike (Route 95), Exit 48 to Route 25 West into Westbrook (approximately 2 miles). Right turn onto Bridge Street (approximately 1/4 mile). Left onto Lincoln Street to course.

Riverside Municipal Golf Course ✪✪

36

1158 Riverside Street
Portland, ME (207) 797-3524
www.portlandmaine.gov

Club Pro: Ron Bibeau, PGA
Payment: Visa, MC, Cash
Tee Times: Required
Fee 9 Holes: Weekday: $22
Fee 18 Holes: Weekday: $30
Twilight Rates: No
Cart Rental: $16pp/18, $10pp/9
Lessons: $45/half hour **Schools:** No
Membership: Yes
Other: Clubhouse / Lockers / Showers / Snack Bar / Restaurant / Bar-Lounge

Tees	Holes	Yards	Par	USGA	Slope
BACK	18	6370	72	69.2	115
MIDDLE	18	6052	72	67.5	112
FRONT	18	5630	73	70.7	112

Weekend: $23
Weekend: $35
Discounts: Senior & Junior weekdays
Driving Range: $8/bucket
Junior Golf: Yes
Architect/Yr: Geoffrey Cornish & Bill Robinson/1932

27 holes available. South course is an additional 9-hole regulation course with 3102 yards. Wide fairways, medium-speed greens, only a little hilly. Open ASAP; close on first snow. "Best shape ever!" –RB

	1	2	3	4	5	6	7	8	9
PAR	5	4	3	5	4	3	4	4	4
YARDS	450	365	202	488	322	197	314	324	396
	10	11	12	13	14	15	16	17	18
PAR	5	4	4	3	4	4	4	4	4
YARDS	540	384	414	167	346	338	334	374	382

Directions: Maine Turnpike to Exit 48. Follow signs to course.

S

Rockland Golf Club

◆◆½

37

Old County Road
Rockland, ME (207) 594-9322
www.rocklandgolf.com

Club Pro: Keenan Flanagan, PGA
Payment: Most Major
Tee Times: 3 days adv.
Fee 9 Holes: Weekday: $25
Fee 18 Holes: Weekday: $50
Twilight Rates: No
Cart Rental: $20pp/18, $10pp/9
Lessons: $35/half hour **Schools:** No
Membership: Yes
Other: Clubhouse / Bar-Lounge / Snack Bar / Showers

Tees	Holes	Yards	Par	USGA	Slope
BACK	18	6041	70	67.6	122
MIDDLE	18	5831	70	66.9	120
FRONT	18	5457	73	71.8	119

Weekend:
Weekend:
Discounts: Junior
Driving Range: No
Junior Golf: Yes
Architect/Yr Open: Roger Sorrent/1930

COUPON

Player Comments: "Courteous, friendly staff." New irrigation system and new tee markers. Views of ocean and Rockland Harbor. Series of 5 1-hour lessons for $240. Punch and Play card. Opens early Spring.

	1	2	3	4	5	6	7	8	9
PAR	5	4	4	4	3	4	5	4	3
YARDS	521	378	268	359	136	303	485	398	215
	10	11	12	13	14	15	16	17	18
PAR	3	3	4	4	4	5	4	4	3
YARDS	176	210	282	425	357	582	341	232	163

Directions: I-95 to Coastal Route 1 through Thomaston. Left onto old Country Road to course 3.5 miles on left.

Sable Oaks Golf Club

◆◆◆½

38

505 Country Club Drive
South Portland, ME
(207) 775-6257
www.sableoaks.com

Club Pro: Roger E. Densmore III, PGA
Payment: Visa, MC, Disc, Amex
Tee Times: Recommended/7 days
Fee 9 Holes: Weekday: $30
Fee 18 Holes: Weekday: $40
Twilight Rates: After 4pm
Cart Rental: $15pp/18, $10pp/9
Lessons: $70/hour **Schools:** No
Membership: Yes
Other: Snack Bar / Bar-Lounge / Function Hall / Showers / Locker Room / Lodging

Tees	Holes	Yards	Par	USGA	Slope
BACK	18	6359	70	71.6	130
MIDDLE	18	5545	70	68.2	120
FRONT	18	4786	72	69.1	129

Weekend: $35
Weekend: $45
Discounts: Junior
Driving Range: No
Junior Golf: Yes
Architect/Yr Open: Cornish & Silva/1989

COUPON

You'll be treated to some challenging yet enjoyable golf, surrounded by woods and ponds, with soft fairways and gently rolling manicured greens. *Travel Golf Magazine* calls Sable Oaks "One of the most imaginative courses in the state." Sister course to Samoset Resort. Off-season rates, inquire.

	1	2	3	4	5	6	7	8	9
PAR	4	5	4	4	5	3	4	3	4
YARDS	389	460	419	398	442	170	319	138	394
	10	11	12	13	14	15	16	17	18
PAR	4	3	4	3	5	4	4	3	4
YARDS	378	159	437	171	443	384	383	164	408

Directions: I-95 to Exit 45 (Maine Mall, Jet Port). Take 1st exit off Exit 45. Go right at light. At 4th light, go left on Running Hill Road. Take the second right onto Country Club Drive.

Salmon Falls Golf Course

NR 39 ▶

52 Golf Course Lane
Hollis, ME
(207) 929-5233 or (800) 734-1616
www.salmonfalls-resort.com

Club Pro:
Payment: Visa, MC, Amex, Disc
Tee Times: Weekends and Holidays
Fee 9 Holes: Weekday: $40/2 players ride
Fee 18 Holes: Weekday: $50/2 players ride
Twilight Rates: No
Cart Rental: $11pp/18, $8.50pp/9
Lessons: No **Schools:** No
Membership: Yes
Other: Clubhouse / Snack Bar

Tees	Holes	Yards	Par	USGA	Slope
BACK	9	2965	36	67.7	113
MIDDLE	9	2883	72	67.7	113
FRONT					

Weekend: $45/2 players ride
Weekend: $60/2 players ride
Discounts: None
Driving Range: No
Junior Golf: No
Architect/Yr Open: Robert Trent Jones Sr./1966
GPS:

COUPON

Suggest beginners come after 1pm on weekends. Open March through November. Noted for beauty of Maine.

	1	2	3	4	5	6	7	8	9
PAR	4	4	3	5	5	3	4	4	4
YARDS	365	250	190	500	455	165	303	251	404
	10	11	12	13	14	15	16	17	18
PAR	4	4	3	5	5	3	4	4	4
YARDS	380	245	235	510	460	165	310	265	395

Directions: I-95 to Exit 36 (Saco), follow Route 112 North. Follow signs to course.

Samoset Resort Golf Course

✪✪✪✪ 40 ▶

220 Warrenton Street
Rockport, ME (207) 594-1431
www.samosetresort.com

Club Pro: Gary Soule
Payment: All Major Cards, Checks
Tee Times: Yes
Fee 9 Holes: Weekday: $60
Fee 18 Holes: Weekday: $110
Twilight Rates: After 2pm

Tees	Holes	Yards	Par	USGA	Slope
BACK	18	6617	70	70.7	130
MIDDLE	18	5615	70	68.9	124
FRONT	18	5145	72	71.2	125

Weekend: $60
Weekend: $110
Discounts: None
Driving Range: $5/half hour, $10/hour, included in green fee
Lessons: $70/half hour **Schools:** Yes **Junior Golf:** Yes
Cart Rental: Included **Membership:** Yes **Architect/Yr Open:** Bob Elder/1902
Other: Clubhouse / Snack Bar / Restaurant / Bar-Lounge / Resort / Indoor Golf Center

$3 million renovation in 2004. New 18th hole. Also multimillion-dollar hotel renovation. Noted for ocean views and spectacular condition. Range use included in green fee.

	1	2	3	4	5	6	7	8	9
PAR	4	4	3	5	3	4	3	4	4
YARDS	360	388	190	481	165	380	176	330	312
	10	11	12	13	14	15	16	17	18
PAR	4	3	5	3	5	4	4	4	4
YARDS	338	120	494	190	500	366	375	400	446

Directions: I-95 to I-295 to Exit 28 to Brunswick Coastal Route 1 North, through Rockland. Turn right onto Warrenton Street.

S
ME

Sanford Country Club ✪✪ 🚩 41

Route 4
Sanford, ME (207) 324-5462
www.sanfordcountryclub.com

Club Pro: Jon Eliis, PGA
Payment: Cash, Visa, MC
Tee Times: Yes
Fee 9 Holes: Weekday: $31   Weekend: $38
Fee 18 Holes: Weekday: $41   Weekend: $48
Twilight Rates: After 3pm   Discounts: None
Cart Rental: $24pp/18, $12pp/9   Driving Range: Yes
Lessons: Yes Schools: Jr.   Junior Golf: Yes
Membership: Yes
Architect/Yr Open: Alex Chisholm & Marvin Armstrong/1932
Other: Restaurant / Clubhouse / Bar-Lounge / Snack Bar
GPS: Yes

Tees	Holes	Yards	Par	USGA	Slope
BACK	18	6726	72	73.2	128
MIDDLE	18	6217	72	70.5	122
FRONT	18	5320	74	66.5	114

COUPON

Course has outstanding reviews. Stay-and-play packages available. Call pro shop for specials. Home of the 2005 Maine Amateur and qualifying site of the 2006 U.S. Amateur.

	1	2	3	4	5	6	7	8	9
PAR	4	4	5	3	4	4	3	4	5
YARDS	342	313	488	100	323	373	186	389	557

	10	11	12	13	14	15	16	17	18
PAR	4	4	3	5	5	4	4	3	4
YARDS	417	308	185	440	488	429	326	130	423

Directions: I-95 to Exit 2, head North on Route 109 for approximately 10 miles to Route 4 Intersection. Take left off 109 to Route 4 South for 2.5 miles. Located on left.

Sebasco Harbor Resort Golf Club ✪✪½ 🚩 42

844 Stevens Avenue (Route 217)
Sebasco Estates, ME
(207) 389-9060
www.sebasco.com

Club Pro: Rob McDonough, PGA
Payment: Visa, MC, Amex, Disc
Tee Times: Yes
Fee 9 Holes: Weekday: $33   Weekend: $33
Fee 18 Holes: Weekday: $48   Weekend: $48
Twilight Rates: After 4pm   Discounts: None
Cart Rental: $15pp/18, $10pp/9   Driving Range: Practice course
Lessons: $50/hour, $30/half hour Schools: Clinics Junior Golf: No
Membership: Yes   Architect/Yr Open: 1925
Other: Full Restaurant / Clubhouse / Hotel / Inn / Lockers / Showers / Bar-Lounge
GPS: Yes

Tees	Holes	Yards	Par	USGA	Slope
BACK	9	2987	36	69.1	125
MIDDLE	9	2794	36	67.3	122
FRONT	9	2364	36	68.2	127

Newly renovated course. #2 is a featured hole with beautiful ocean view. New 3-hole practice course. Discounted rates for guests and boaters.

	1	2	3	4	5	6	7	8	9
PAR	4	3	5	4	4	3	4	4	5
YARDS	370	140	467	309	339	179	387	316	480

PAR									
YARDS									

Directions: South of Bath on Route 209 for 10 miles. Turn right onto Route 217. Follow the Sebasco signs. Course 1/4 mile on left.

South Portland Municipal GC

NR **43**

155 Wescott Road
South Portland, ME
(207) 775-0005

Tees	Holes	Yards	Par	USGA	Slope
BACK					
MIDDLE	9	2071	32	59.0	92
FRONT					

Club Pro: No
Payment: Cash/Check Only
Tee Times: No
Fee 9 Holes: Weekday: $12   **Weekend:** $13
Fee 18 Holes: Weekday: **Weekend:**
Twilight Rates: No   **Discounts:** None
Cart Rental: $2/pull   **Driving Range:** No
Lessons: Group lessons **Schools:** No   **Junior Golf:** No
Membership: Yes, residents   **Architect/Yr Open:** Larry Rowe/1931
Other: Snack Bar   **GPS:**

Well-maintained, polite staff. Carts are not required. Pay once, play for 3 rounds. Clinics offered by recreation center.

	1	2	3	4	5	6	7	8	9
PAR	4	3	4	3	4	3	3	4	4
YARDS	340	140	238	132	372	167	122	285	275
PAR									
YARDS									

Directions: I-95 to Exit 3 (Westbrook Street). Go East on Westbrook Street (about 3/10 of a mile). Take a left onto Wescott Street. The clubhouse is on the left under Bradts Memorial Library.

Spring Meadows Golf Course

✪✪✪ **44**

Lewiston Road
Gray, ME (207) 657-2586
www.springmeadowsgolf.com

Tees	Holes	Yards	Par	USGA	Slope
BACK	18	6652	71	71.7	123
MIDDLE	18	6065	71	69.4	121
FRONT	18	5448	71	66.0	112

Club Pro: Ben Morey, PGA
Payment: Most Major
Tee Times: Up to 7 days
Fee 9 Holes: Weekday: $22   **Weekend:** $26
Fee 18 Holes: Weekday: $35   **Weekend:** $42
Twilight Rates: After 3pm   **Discounts:** None
Cart Rental: $16pp/18, $8pp/9   **Driving Range:** Yes
Lessons: $60/hour **Schools:** Junior   **Junior Golf:** No
Membership: Yes   **Architect/Yr Open:** William Bradley Booth/1999
Other: Refurbished Barn with Banquet Facilities Seating 220 / Player's Lounge
GPS: Yes

"Among the lushest courses anywhere in New England." –PB

	1	2	3	4	5	6	7	8	9
PAR	4	4	5	3	4	3	4	4	4
YARDS	367	283	500	148	341	135	280	367	303
	10	11	12	13	14	15	16	17	18
PAR	5	4	4	3	4	5	3	4	4
YARDS	464	340	263	97	268	404	100	388	351

Directions: Course is 1 mile from Exit 63 off Maine Turnpike, on Route 4/100/202 Northbound.

S
ME

Springbrook Golf Course

Route 202
Leeds, ME (207) 946-5900
www.springbrookgolfclub.com

Club Pro: Ed Balboni, PGA
Payment: Visa, MC
Tee Times: Weekends, Holidays
Fee 9 Holes: Weekday: $15
Fee 18 Holes: Weekday: $28 all day
Twilight Rates: After 4pm
Cart Rental: $30/18, $16/9 per person
Lessons: $45/45 min. **Schools:** No
Membership: Yes

Tees	Holes	Yards	Par	USGA	Slope
BACK	18	6408	71	68.1	119
MIDDLE	18	6163	71	64.7	111
FRONT	18	4989	74	61.4	96

Weekend: $15 after 2pm
Weekend: $28 all day
Discounts: Juniors, Seniors, Ladies
Driving Range: $2.50/sm., $4.50/lg. bucket
Junior Golf: Yes
Architect/Yr Open: Arnold Biondi/1966

Other: Clubhouse / Lockers / Showers / Snack Bar / Bar-Lounge / Discount Game Cards

Sig. Hole: #15 is a 219-yard, uphill par 3. Very difficult hole. Rolling hills and roughly reminiscent of a Scottish-style course.

	1	2	3	4	5	6	7	8	9
PAR	4	3	4	4	4	4	5	3	4
YARDS	415	160	410	350	335	385	520	168	340
	10	11	12	13	14	15	16	17	18
PAR	4	4	5	3	4	3	5	4	4
YARDS	420	290	460	180	350	206	480	325	365

Directions: Maine Turnpike to Lewiston exit to Route 202 East. Course is 10 miles outside of Lewiston-Auburn.

Sunday River Golf Club

Monkey Brook Road
Bethel, ME (207) 824-4653
www.sundayrivergolf.com

Club Pro: John Hickson, PGA
Payment: Visa, MC, Amex, Disc
Tee Times: 14 days adv.
Fee 9 Holes: Weekday: $60 w/cart
Fee 18 Holes: Weekday: $95 w/cart
Twilight Rates: No
Cart Rental: Included
Lessons: Yes **Schools:** Yes
Membership: Yes

Tees	Holes	Yards	Par	USGA	Slope
BACK	18	6558	72	72.3	140
MIDDLE	18	5828	72	68.5	129
FRONT	18	5006	72	65.2	118

Weekend: $70 w/cart
Weekend: $120 w/cart
Discounts: Yes
Driving Range: Yes
Junior Golf:
Architect/Yr Open: Robert Trent Jones Jr./2004

Other: Log Cabin Clubhouse / Pub / Full Banquet at Resort

Opened late 2004. Robert Trent Jones Jr. design. Each hole has 4 tee boxes. Yardage below is from the Blue tees. "1 of New England's top 10. A golf experience for the purist." –JD

	1	2	3	4	5	6	7	8	9
PAR	5	4	4	3	4	3	5	4	4
YARDS	499	384	332	175	425	178	440	410	339
	10	11	12	13	14	15	16	17	18
PAR	4	5	4	4	3	5	3	4	4
YARDS	385	565	412	316	185	483	142	428	414

Directions: Take Route 1 North to I-95 North to Maine Turnpike (I-495). Take Maine Turnpike (I-495) to Exit 11 (Gray). Take Route 26 North to Bethel. Follow Route 2 East for 2.6 miles. Take left onto Sunday River Road. Follow to the fork with Sunday River Ski Resort sign. Take right on Monkey Brook Road for 4 miles.

Sunset Ridge

771 Cumberland St.
Westbrook, ME (207) 854-9463
www.golfmaine.com

Tees	Holes	Yards	Par	USGA	Slope
BACK	9	3100	35	68.6	129
MIDDLE	9	2642	35	64.5	116
FRONT	9	2277	35	64.4	102

Club Pro:
Payment: Visa, MC, Amex, Disc
Tee Times: Yes
Fee 9 Holes: Weekday: $17 walk $25 w/cart M-Th
  Weekend: $20 walk $28 w/cart
Fee 18 Holes: Weekday: $25 walk $39 w/cart M-Th
  Weekend: $30 walk $44 w/cart

Twilight Rates: No **Discounts:** 10 days play
Cart Rental: $14pp/18 $8pp/9 **Driving Range:** $10/xlg., $8/lg., $6/sm.
Lessons: $35/half hour **Schools:** Yes **Junior Golf:** Yes
Membership: Yes **Architect/Yr Open:** Tom Emery/2000
Other: Snack Bar / Tennis Courts / Sports / Full Catering & Function Service

Construction under way on back 9. Affiliated with sports park, Westerly Winds.

	1	2	3	4	5	6	7	8	9
PAR	4	4	4	3	4	4	3	4	5
YARDS	257	273	287	172	307	312	162	388	490
PAR									
YARDS									

Directions: I-95 to Exit 48 Maine Turnpike West on Route 25 to Windham sign. 2 miles toward Windham. Approximately 5 minutes from Exit 48.

Toddy Brook Golf Course

925 Sligo Road
North Yarmouth, ME
(207) 829-5100
www.toddybrookgolf.com

Tees	Holes	Yards	Par	USGA	Slope
BACK	18	5886	71	68.9	124
MIDDLE	18	5173	71	65.6	116
FRONT	18	4409	36	65.1	108

Club Pro: Mel Strange, teaching pro
Payment: Visa, MC, Amex, Disc
Tee Times:
Fee 9 Holes: Weekday: $20 **Weekend:** $25
Fee 18 Holes: Weekday: $30 **Weekend:** $35
Twilight Rates: After 5:30pm **Discounts:** Junior (T/Th)
Cart Rental: $16pp/18, $10pp/9 **Driving Range:** Yes
Lessons: Schools: **Junior Golf:**
Membership: **Architect/Yr Open:** Robert Anderson/2002
Other: Restaurant / Clubhouse / Lockers / Showers / Bar-Lounge

COUPON

Beautiful layout with challenging tees. Each hole has unique design with plenty of sand & water to test your skills. New back 9 with beautiful views. Layout ends with a daunting island green. Back tees below.

	1	2	3	4	5	6	7	8	9
PAR	4	4	4	3	5	3	4	4	5
YARDS	307	357	366	151	453	184	350	314	506
	10	11	12	13	14	15	16	17	18
PAR	4	3	4	5	4	4	3	5	3
YARDS	363	150	309	400	371	380	133	546	112

Directions: I-95 to Yarmouth exit. Follow Route 1 to Route 115 exit. Take 115 West about 1/4 mile to Sligo Road on right. Go Approx. 3 1/8 miles. Course on right.

Turner Highland Golf Course

10 B Highland Avenue
Turner, ME (207) 224-7060
www.turnerhighlands.com

Club Pro:
Payment: Visa, MC, Amex, Disc
Tee Times: Yes
Fee 9 Holes: Weekday: $16
Fee 18 Holes: Weekday: $28
Twilight Rates: Yes
Cart Rental: $16pp/18, $8pp/9
Lessons: $25/half hour **Schools:** No
Membership: Yes
Other: Lockers / Showers / Snack Bar / Restaurant.

Weekend: $16
Weekend: $28
Discounts: None
Driving Range: $3/bucket
Junior Golf: No
Architect/Yr Open: Steve Leavitt/1993

Tees	Holes	Yards	Par	USGA	Slope
BACK					
MIDDLE	18	6033	71	68.6	115
FRONT	18	4705	71	67.5	113

COUPON

Player Comments: "A well-maintained local popular favorite." Now 18 holes. A scenic golf course situated high on a hill.

	1	2	3	4	5	6	7	8	9
PAR	4	5	4	3	4	5	4	3	4
YARDS	280	442	282	149	365	452	372	204	376
	10	11	12	13	14	15	16	17	18
PAR	3	4	4	4	5	3	5	4	3
YARDS	135	365	370	430	592	125	500	387	182

Directions: I-95 to Exit 75 toward Auburn. Get onto Route 4 North. Turn right onto Route 117. Stay on Route 117 for 8.5 miles. Course is on the right.

Twin Falls Golf Course

364 Spring Street
Westbrook, ME (207) 854-5397

Club Pro: No
Payment: Cash, Credit, Debit
Tee Times: No
Fee 9 Holes: Weekday: $16
Fee 18 Holes: Weekday: $21
Twilight Rates: After 5pm
Cart Rental: $11pp/18, $6pp/9
Lessons: No **Schools:** No
Membership: Yes
Other: Clubhouse / Snack Bar

Weekend: $16
Weekend: $21
Discounts: None
Driving Range: No
Junior Golf: No
Architect/Yr Open: Albert Young/1972
GPS:

Tees	Holes	Yards	Par	USGA	Slope
BACK					
MIDDLE	18	5061	68	61.3	90
FRONT					

"Fine public course for beginners. Keep your drive on #1 to the left of center as the brook hidden from view will come into play." –AP

	1	2	3	4	5	6	7	8	9
PAR	4	3	3	4	4	4	4	5	4
YARDS	334	152	110	343	351	260	275	498	298
	10	11	12	13	14	15	16	17	18
PAR	4	3	3	4	4	3	4	4	4
YARDS	364	165	137	374	408	185	248	301	258

Directions: I-95 to Exit 45, follow Maine Mall Road to Spring Street to course.

Val Halla Golf Course

✿✿✿

51

Val Halla Road
Cumberland, ME (207) 829-2225
www.valhallagolf.com

Tees	Holes	Yards	Par	USGA	Slope
BACK	18	6567	72	71.1	126
MIDDLE	18	6201	72	69.3	122
FRONT	18	5437	72	71.4	120

Club Pro: Cory Mansfield, PGA
Payment: Visa, MC
Tee Times: Yes
Fee 9 Holes: Weekday: $22
Fee 18 Holes: Weekday: $30
Twilight Rates: After 4pm
Cart Rental: $12.50pp/18, $7.50pp/9
Lessons: $40/half hour **Schools:** No
Membership: Yes
Other: Snack Bar / Lounge

Weekend: $24
Weekend: $35
Discounts: Senior & Junior
Driving Range: $4/bucket
Junior Golf: Yes
Architect/Yr Open: Phil Wogan/1965
GPS:

Consistently rated 1 of Maine's best public courses. Bent grass, good shape, wooded, hilly, scenic, brooks and streams, excellent layout. Open April 15 - November 1.

	1	2	3	4	5	6	7	8	9
PAR	4	3	5	4	4	4	4	3	5
YARDS	350	142	553	383	394	340	369	175	484
	10	11	12	13	14	15	16	17	18
PAR	4	4	3	5	5	4	4	3	4
YARDS	376	347	148	465	440	388	294	155	398

Directions: From Portland take 295 North to Exit 10. Follow Route 9 to Cumberland Center. The course is off Greely Road on Val Halla Road.

Wawenock Country Club

NR

52

Route 129
Walpole, ME (207) 563-3938
www.wawenockgolfclub.com

Tees	Holes	Yards	Par	USGA	Slope
BACK					
MIDDLE	9	3009	35	68.8	122
FRONT	9	2727	36	73.5	119

Club Pro: Lon Wanser
Payment: Cash, Check, Visa, MC, Amex, Disc
Tee Times: July - August
Fee 9 Holes: Weekday: $20
Fee 18 Holes: Weekday: $30
Twilight Rates: After 5pm
Cart Rental: $14pp/18, $11pp/9
Lessons: Yes **Schools:** No
Membership: Yes
Other: Clubhouse / Bar-Lounge / Snack Bar / Showers

Weekend: $20
Weekend: $30
Discounts: Junior
Driving Range: Yes
Junior Golf: No
Architect/Yr: Wayne Stiles & John Van Kleek/1928

COUPON

Fairly open course with small greens and hills, but challenging. Shoulder season rates. Open May - October. The only golf course on beautiful Pemaquid Peninsula.

	1	2	3	4	5	6	7	8	9
PAR	4	4	3	5	4	4	4	3	4
YARDS	329	398	233	477	415	296	357	134	370
PAR									
YARDS									

Directions: Route 1 to Route 129; follow for 7 miles. 5 miles from town of Damariscotta, Maine.

Western View Golf Club

189 Bolton Hill Road
Augusta, ME (207) 622-5309

Club Pro: Peter Matthews, PGA
Payment: Visa, MC, Amex, Disc
Tee Times: No
Fee 9 Holes: Weekday: $12
Fee 18 Holes: Weekday: $20
Twilight Rates: No
Cart Rental: $13pp/18, $8pp/9
Lessons: $30/half hour **Schools:** No
Membership: Yes
Other: Snack Bar / Clubhouse / Lounge / Restaurant / Range

Tees	Holes	Yards	Par	USGA	Slope
BACK					
MIDDLE	9	2700	35	64.5	107
FRONT	9	2506	36	68.0	110

Weekend: $15
Weekend: $22
Discounts: Junior membership
Driving Range: $3/bucket
Junior Golf: Yes
Architect/Yr Open: Archie Humphrey/1935

Fully irrigated: tees, greens, fairways. New easy access off I-95.

	1	2	3	4	5	6	7	8	9
PAR	4	3	4	3	5	4	4	4	4
YARDS	305	180	260	150	445	315	285	385	375
PAR									
YARDS									

Directions: I-95 Exit 113. Go about 5 miles through 4 sets of lights (on Route 3 East). Bolton Hill Road on right. 1 mile past 4th set of lights.

Willowdale Golf Club

52 Willowdale Road
Scarborough, ME (207) 883-9351
www.willowdalegolf.com

Club Pro:
Payment: Visa, Amex, MC, Disc, Checks
Tee Times: 5 days adv. for weekends
Fee 9 Holes: Weekday: $18
Fee 18 Holes: Weekday: $29
Twilight Rates: After 4pm
Cart Rental: $24pp/18, $14pp/9
Lessons: **Schools:** No
Membership: Yes
Other: Clubhouse / Snack Bar / Showers

Tees	Holes	Yards	Par	USGA	Slope
BACK					
MIDDLE	18	5881	70	67.7	115
FRONT	18	5049	70	68.9	116

Weekend: $20
Weekend: $31
Discounts: Junior memberships
Driving Range: No
Junior Golf: No
Architect/Yr Open: Eugene Wogan/1930
GPS:

Sig. Hole: #5 is a beautiful, 195-yard par 3. Water on 1 side, tree-lined on the other. Difficult shot for a par 3. Twilight rates offered 7 days a week. Pitching and putting green available.

	1	2	3	4	5	6	7	8	9
PAR	4	5	4	4	3	4	3	4	4
YARDS	357	487	386	349	197	367	163	342	325
	10	**11**	**12**	**13**	**14**	**15**	**16**	**17**	**18**
PAR	4	3	4	4	4	3	4	4	5
YARDS	393	185	367	382	280	150	374	288	489

Directions: Exit 36 off Maine Turnpike. US 95 to Route 1. Turn left onto Route 1 North. First light, turn right 1/4 miles.

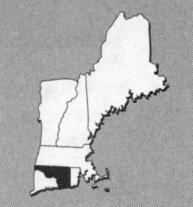

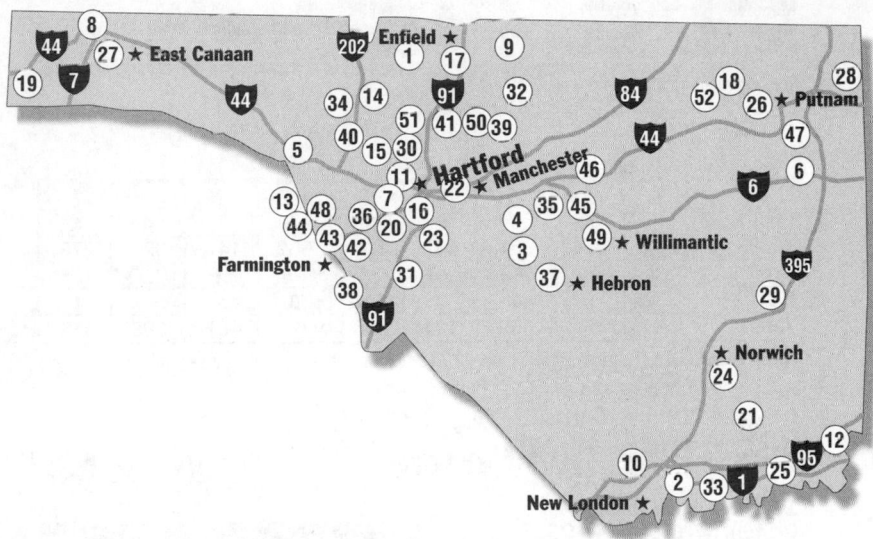

Airways Golf Course	1	Hotchkiss School GC	19	Tallwood Country Club	37
Birch Plain Golf Course	2	Keney Golf Club	20	Timberlin Golf Club	38
Blackledge CC - Anderson's	3	Lake of Isles GC & Resort	21	Topstone Golf Course	39
Blackledge CC - Gilead	4	Manchester CC	22	Tower Ridge GC	40
Blue Fox Run	5	Minnechaug GC	23	Tradition GC at Windsor	41
Brooklyn Golf Course	6	Norwich Golf Course	24	Tunxis Plan. CC (Green)	42
Buena Vista GC	7	Pequot Golf Club	25	Tunxis Plan. CC (White)	43
Canaan Country Club	8	Putnam Country Club	26	Tunxis Plan. GC (Red)	44
Cedar Knob GC	9	Quarryview Golf Course	27	Twin Hills CC	45
Cedar Ridge GC	10	Raceway Golf Club	28	Villa Hills Par 3	46
East Hartford GC	11	River Ridge Golf Course	29	Vineyard Valley Golf Club	47
Elmridge Golf Course	12	Rockledge CC	30	Westwoods Golf Course	48
Fairview Farm GC	13	Rolling Greens GC	31	Willimantic C. C.	49
Fox Run at Copper Hill	14	Rolling Meadows CC	32	Willow Brook Golf Course	50
Gillette Ridge Golf Club	15	Shennecosset GC	33	Wintonbury Hills GC	51
Goodwin Golf Course	16	Simsbury Farms GC	34	Woodstock Golf Course	52
Grassmere CC	17	Skungamaug River GC	35		
Harrisville GC	18	Stanley Golf Club	36		

KEY TO THE STAR AND VALUE RATINGS:
5✪= Outstanding 4✪= Excellent 3✪= Very Good 2✪= Good 1✪= Average NR = Not Rated
EV = Excellent Value GV = Good Value V = Value

Airways Golf Course

NR ▶ 1

1070 South Grand Street
West Suffield, CT (860) 668-4973
www.airwaysgolf.com

Tees	Holes	Yards	Par	USGA	Slope
BACK	18	5914	71	66.0	106
MIDDLE	18	5528	71	65.0	103
FRONT	18	5134	72	65.0	103

Club Pro: No
Payment: Visa, MC, Cash
Tee Times: 1 week adv.
Fee 9 Holes: Weekday: $12.50   **Weekend:** $13.50
Fee 18 Holes: Weekday: $21   **Weekend:** $24
Twilight Rates: No   **Discounts:** Senior
Cart Rental: $11pp/18, $5.50pp/9   **Driving Range:** No
Lessons: No **Schools:** No   **Junior Golf:** No
Membership: No   **Architect/Yr Open:** Geoffrey Cornish/1973
Other: Clubhouse / Snack Bar   **GPS:**

COUPON

Noted for great value. Easy to walk, beautiful course.

	1	2	3	4	5	6	7	8	9
PAR	4	4	4	5	4	4	3	4	4
YARDS	336	351	351	487	301	302	147	320	273
	10	**11**	**12**	**13**	**14**	**15**	**16**	**17**	**18**
PAR	3	5	4	3	4	3	5	4	4
YARDS	127	451	369	133	346	132	451	388	263

Directions: I-91 to Exit 40, exit for Route 20 West. At 4th light turn right, course 2 miles on the right. Check website.

Birch Plain Golf Course

NR ▶ 2

119 High Rock Road
Groton, CT (860) 445-9918
www.birchplaingolf.com

Tees	Holes	Yards	Par	USGA	Slope
BACK					
MIDDLE	18	2666	54		
FRONT					

Club Pro: Jeff Doerr, PGA
Payment: Visa, MC
Tee Times: No
Fee 9 Holes: Weekday: No   **Weekend:** No
Fee 18 Holes: Weekday: $21   **Weekend:** $25
Twilight Rates: After 5:30pm   **Discounts:** Senior, Junior, Military
Cart Rental: $10pp/18, $2.50/pull cart   **Driving Range:** $7.50/lg., $6.50/sm. bucket
Lessons: No **Schools:**   **Junior Golf:**
Membership: Yes   **Architect/Yr Open:** Armando Baldelli/1969
Other: Snacks   **GPS:**

A pleasant par 3. Good for beginners. Nearby attractions include Mystic Seaport area, and casinos.

	1	2	3	4	5	6	7	8	9
PAR	3	3	3	3	3	3	3	3	3
YARDS	107	170	148	228	206	124	113	137	129
	10	**11**	**12**	**13**	**14**	**15**	**16**	**17**	**18**
PAR	3	3	3	3	3	3	3	3	3
YARDS	105	187	108	147	136	164	150	155	156

Directions: I-95 to Route 349 (Clarence Sharp Highway). At second light, go left. At next light, go right. Follow signs for Groton/New London Airport. Course on right.

Blackledge CC - Anderson's Glen ✪✪½ 3

180 West Street
Hebron, OT (860) 228-0250
www.blackledgecc.com

Club Pro: K. J. Higgins, PGA & C. Morris
Payment: Visa, MC
Tee Times: 1 week adv.

Tees	Holes	Yards	Par	USGA	Slope
BACK	18	6787	72	72.0	128
MIDDLE	18	6137	72	68.9	122
FRONT	18	5458	72	71.7	123

Fee 9 Holes: Weekday: $18 walk, $26 ride Weekend: $21 walk, $28 ride
Fee 18 Holes: Weekday: $36 walk, $49 ride Weekend: $41 walk, $55 ride
Twilight Rates: After 5:30pm weekdays, after 1pm and 3pm on F/S/S
Discounts: Senior & Junior
Cart Rental: $24pp/18, $12pp/9 Driving Range: No
Lessons: $35/half hour Schools: No Junior Golf: No
Membership: Yes Architect/Yr Open: Geoffrey Cornish/1964
Other: Clubhouse / Snack Bar / Restaurant / Bar-Lounge

COUPON

Good walking course that tests every shot in your game. Fairways are in great shape. Greens are on the fast side. Open March - December. Please visit website.

	1	2	3	4	5	6	7	8	9
PAR	4	4	4	5	4	3	4	3	5
YARDS	375	365	389	480	350	153	318	170	485
	10	11	12	13	14	15	16	17	18
PAR	4	4	5	3	4	4	3	5	4
YARDS	316	408	465	142	383	369	179	425	365

Directions: Route 2 East to Exit 8. Left off ramp, go 9 miles. Take a right onto West Street. Course is on the right.

Blackledge CC - Gilead Highlands ✪✪½ 4

171 West Street
Hebron, CT (860) 228-0250
www.blackledgecc.com

Club Pro: Kevin J. Higgins, PGA
Payment: Visa, MC
Tee Times: 1 week adv.

Tees	Holes	Yards	Par	USGA	Slope
BACK	18	6129	72	69.8	121
MIDDLE	18	5714	72	68.0	116
FRONT	18	4951	72		

Fee 9 Holes: Weekday: $18 walk, $26 ride Weekend: $21 walk, $28 ride
Fee 18 Holes: Weekday: $36 walk, $49 ride Weekend: $41 walk, $55 ride
Twilight Rates: After 5:30pm weekdays, after 1pm and 3pm on F/S/S
Discounts: Senior & Junior
Cart Rental: $24pp/18, $12pp/9 Driving Range: No
Lessons: $35/half hour Schools: No Junior Golf: No
Membership: Yes Architect/Yr Open: Mark Mungeam/1974
Other: Clubhouse / Snack Bar / Restaurant / Bar-Lounge

COUPON

Player Comments: "Best course conditions ever." New improved website, please visit. Open March - December.

NE
CT

	1	2	3	4	5	6	7	8	9
PAR	4	3	5	4	4	4	5	3	4
YARDS	369	133	436	275	359	325	455	142	366
	10	11	12	13	14	15	16	17	18
PAR	5	3	5	3	4	4	4	4	4
YARDS	464	142	454	148	358	346	301	320	327

Directions: Route 2 East to Exit 8. Left off ramp, go 9 miles. Take a right onto West Street. Course is on the right.

Blue Fox Run

5

65 Nod Road
Avon, CT (860) 678-1679
www.bluefoxent.com

Club Pro: Sean Smedick, PGA
Payment: Visa, MC, Amex
Tee Times: Yes

Tees	Holes	Yards	Par	USGA	Slope
BACK	18	6779	71	72.0	125
MIDDLE	18	6116	71	69.2	121
FRONT	18	5232	72	70.2	124

Fee 9 Holes: Weekday: $20 M-Th   **Weekend:** $22 F/S/S/H
Fee 18 Holes: Weekday: $34 M-Th   **Weekend:** $44 F/S/S/H
Twilight Rates: After 5:30pm weekdays   **Discounts:** Senior & Junior
Cart Rental: $15pp/18 $9pp/9   **Driving Range:** $5 token
Lessons: $50/half hour, $100/hour **Schools:** Yes **Junior Golf:** Yes
Membership: No   **Architect/Yr Open:** Joe Brunoli/1974
Other: Restaurant / Bar-Lounge / Banquet Facilities **GPS:** Yes

Player Comments: "Course is in good shape. Very pretty in fall." Open March 1 - December 15.

	1	2	3	4	5	6	7	8	9
PAR	4	4	3	4	5	4	3	5	3
YARDS	335	305	148	334	486	374	202	512	170
	10	11	12	13	14	15	16	17	18
PAR	4	4	5	4	5	3	4	3	4
YARDS	388	392	512	414	513	136	365	150	380

Directions: I-84 Exit 39 to Route 4, Farmington Center. Turn right onto Waterville Road (Route 10 North). Go 5 miles, cross over Route 44 intersection to Nod Road. Club is 1/2 mile on left.

Brooklyn Golf Course

NR **6**

170 South Street
Brooklyn, CT (860) 779-9333

Club Pro:
Payment: Visa, MC
Tee Times: Weekends

Tees	Holes	Yards	Par	USGA	Slope
BACK	9	2880	35		
MIDDLE	9	2783	35		
FRONT					

Fee 9 Holes: Weekday: $11   **Weekend:** $13
Fee 18 Holes: Weekday: $20   **Weekend:** $22
Twilight Rates: After 5pm   **Discounts:** Senior & Junior
Cart Rental: $6pp/9   **Driving Range:** Yes
Lessons: Yes **Schools:** No   **Junior Golf:** Yes
Membership: Yes   **Architect/Yr Open:** 1960
Other: Clubhouse / Snack Bar / Bar-Lounge   **GPS:**

This course is now a municipal golf course and improvements are being made to its overall appearance. Driving range is lighted for evening use.

	1	2	3	4	5	6	7	8	9
PAR	4	4	4	4	5	3	4	3	4
YARDS	385	350	340	410	460	130	420	135	250
PAR									
YARDS									

Directions: I-395 to Route 6 West exit; take left onto Allen Hill Road. Take first left onto South Street, course is 1/2 mile on left.

Buena Vista Golf Course

Buena Vista Road
West Hartford, CT (860) 521-7359
www.west-hartford.com

Club Pro: Richard Crow, PGA
Payment: Cash or Check
Tee Times: No
Fee 9 Holes: Weekday: $12.50
Fee 18 Holes: Weekday: $24
Twilight Rates: No
Cart Rental: $12pp/9
Lessons: No **Schools:** No
Membership: West Hartford residents only
Other: Putting Green

Tees	Holes	Yards	Par	USGA	Slope
BACK					
MIDDLE	9	1977	31		
FRONT	9	1653	30		

Weekend: $13.50
Weekend: $25.50
Discounts: Sr. & Jr., W. Hartford residents only
Driving Range: No
Junior Golf: No
Architect/Yr Open: 1960
GPS:

A good mix of holes. Great for all levels of golfers. Open April-December. Additional tee boxes to accommodate a greater number of golfing abilities.

	1	2	3	4	5	6	7	8	9
PAR	4	4	4	3	3	3	3	3	4
YARDS	263	344	295	171	130	98	223	214	239
PAR									
YARDS									

Directions: I-84 to Exit 43 (Park Road); left off ramp; go through 3 lights, take left onto Buena Vista Road. Course on left. Parking lot shared with Cornerstone Pool

Canaan Country Club

74 South Canaan Road (Route 7)
Canaan, CT (860) 824-7683
www.canaancountryclub.com

Club Pro: Fran Marrello, PGA
Payment: Most Major Credit Cards
Tee Times: No
Fee 9 Holes: Weekday: $14
Fee 18 Holes: Weekday: $20
Twilight Rates: No
Cart Rental: $15pp/18, $7.50pp/9
Lessons: Yes **Schools:** No
Membership: Yes
Other: Snack Bar / Restaurant / Function Rooms

Tees	Holes	Yards	Par	USGA	Slope
BACK	9	2941	35	66.8	114
MIDDLE	9	2835	35	66.8	114
FRONT	9	2412	36	67	107

Weekend: $20
Weekend: $27
Discounts: Senior
Driving Range: No
Junior Golf: No
Architect/Yr Open: 1931
GPS:

The course is mostly flat with a few rolling hills. Considered a good walking course. New pro shop and irrigation systems. Set in beautiful Blackberry River Valley. New 5th hole par 3 replaced old 7th. All holes are now irrigated.

NE CT

	1	2	3	4	5	6	7	8	9
PAR	4	5	3	5	3	4	4	3	4
YARDS	317	490	184	450	132	356	371	180	355
PAR									
YARDS									

Directions: Route 8 North to Winsted, West on Route 44 to town of Canaan. South 1/2 mile on Route 7.

Cedar Knob Golf Course

NR 9

466 Billings Road
Somers, CT (860) 749-3550
www.cedarknobgolfcourse.com

Club Pro: Jeffrey Swanson
Payment: Most Major Credit Cards
Tee Times: 7 days
Fee 9 Holes: Weekday: $19
Fee 18 Holes: Weekday: $34
Twilight Rates: No
Cart Rental: $16pp/18, $8pp/9
Lessons: $40/45 min **Schools:** No
Membership: No
Other: Clubhouse / Snack Bar / Restaurant / Bar-Lounge

Tees	Holes	Yards	Par	USGA	Slope
BACK	18	6734	72	72.4	126
MIDDLE	18	6298	72	70.5	122
FRONT	18	5784	74	73.9	129

Weekend: $22
Weekend: $37
Discounts: Sr. & Jr. weekdays
Driving Range: Yes, must use own balls
Junior Golf: Yes
Architect/Yr Open: Geoffrey Cornish/1963

Dress code. Open year round (weather permitting). Call about specials.

	1	2	3	4	5	6	7	8	9
PAR	4	3	5	4	3	4	5	4	4
YARDS	384	154	482	397	209	319	478	327	328
	10	11	12	13	14	15	16	17	18
PAR	5	4	4	4	3	4	3	5	4
YARDS	490	370	410	350	170	350	210	470	400

Directions: I-91 to Exit 47 (East toward Somers). Right onto Route 83; right on Billings Road. Course is 1/2 mile on left.

Cedar Ridge GC

NR 10

34 Drabik Road
East Lyme, CT (860) 691-4568
www.cedarridgegolf.com

Club Pro: Chris Madeiros
Payment: Cash, Visa, MC
Tee Times: 7 days adv.
Fee 9 Holes: Weekday: $15
Fee 18 Holes: Weekday: $21
Twilight Rates: After 4pm
Cart Rental: $22pp/18, $11pp/9
Lessons: Yes **Schools:** No
Membership: Ticket Packets
Other: Snacks Only

Tees	Holes	Yards	Par	USGA	Slope
BACK					
MIDDLE	18	3025	54		
FRONT					

Weekend: $19
Weekend: $27
Discounts: Senior & Junior
Driving Range: No
Junior Golf: Yes
Architect/Yr Open: Chester Jenkins/1962
GPS:

Very challenging for the serious and pleasant for the casual player. Course in excellent condition, rolling hills, water hazards. Takes around 2 hours. Dress is casual. Open April - November.

	1	2	3	4	5	6	7	8	9
PAR	3	3	3	3	3	3	3	3	3
YARDS	157	160	177	103	191	160	122	150	166
	10	11	12	13	14	15	16	17	18
PAR	3	3	3	3	3	3	3	3	3
YARDS	155	130	250	145	196	218	215	203	127

Directions: I-95 to Exit 74, left on Route 161 North. 1 mile to Drabik Road on left.

East Hartford Golf Course

NR 11▶

130 Long Hill Street
East Hartford, CT (860) 528-5082

Tees	Holes	Yards	Par	USGA	Slope
BACK	18	6186	71	69.1	124
MIDDLE	18	6076	71	68.6	124
FRONT	18	5072	72	68.9	113

Club Pro: Kevin Tierney, PGA
Payment: Visa, MC, Disc
Tee Times: Weekends, 1 week adv.
Fee 9 Holes: Weekday: $17
Fee 18 Holes: Weekday: $23
Twilight Rates: After 6pm
Cart Rental: $14pp/18, $8pp/9
Lessons: $40/half hour **Schools:** No
Membership: No
Other: Restaurant

Weekend: $22
Weekend: $29
Discounts: Sr. & Jr. weekdays
Driving Range: No
Junior Golf: Yes
Architect/Yr Open: Al Zikorus/1927
GPS:

COUPON

Dress code: no tank tops or cutoffs. Pond recently added to #13; recent drainage work and sand trap renovations.

	1	2	3	4	5	6	7	8	9
PAR	4	4	4	3	5	4	4	3	4
YARDS	305	397	322	123	508	415	308	127	385
	10	11	12	13	14	15	16	17	18
PAR	5	3	4	4	4	3	4	4	5
YARDS	512	188	308	330	356	150	457	384	500

Directions: I-84 to Exit 60, onto Burnside Avenue toward East Hartford. Enter East Hartford, take a right at second traffic light onto Long Hill Street. Proceed through 3 stop signs, course on right.

Elmridge Golf Course

✪✪ 12▶

Elmridge Road
Pawcatuck, CT (860) 599-2248
www.elmridgegolf.com

Tees	Holes	Yards	Par	USGA	Slope
BACK	27/18	6347	71	70.8	115
MIDDLE	18	6014	71	69.3	112
FRONT	27/18	5430	71	69.0	109

Club Pro: Thomas Jones, PGA
Payment: Visa, MC, Amex
Tee Times: Mon/weekend, Fri/weekdays
Fee 9 Holes: Weekday: $24
Fee 18 Holes: Weekday: $37 (M-Th)
Twilight Rates: After 1pm
Cart Rental: $16pp/18, $9pp/9
Lessons: $40/45 min. **Schools:** No
Membership: Yes
Other: Clubhouse / Snack Bar / Restaurant / Bar-Lounge/ Outings

Weekend: $24 after 1pm
Weekend: $43 (F/S/S)
Discounts: None
Driving Range: Yes
Junior Golf: No
Architect/Yr Open: Joe & Charlie Rustici/1964

27 holes allow variety of play: Red South, White West, and Blue North courses. Scorecard below is Red South-White West. Located 7 miles from Foxwoods Casino.

	1	2	3	4	5	6	7	8	9
PAR	4	4	4	5	4	3	4	3	4
YARDS	366	335	360	462	149	324	167	385	268
	10	11	12	13	14	15	16	17	18
PAR	4	5	4	3	5	3	5	3	4
YARDS	365	485	342	149	576	340	365	206	370

Directions: I 95 North, Exit 92 in CT. From North, go left. From South go right. Take first right onto Elmridge Road. Course is 1 mile on left.

NE CT

Fairview Farm Golf Course ✪✪½ ▶ 13

300 Hill Road
Harwinton, CT (860) 689-1000
www.fairviewfarmgolfcourse.com
Club Pro: Bob Sparks, PGA
Payment: Visa, MC, Amex
Tee Times: 5 days
Fee 9 Holes: Weekday: $21
Fee 18 Holes: Weekday: $40
Twilight Rates: No
Cart Rental: $18pp/18, $9pp/9
Lessons: $90/hour **Schools:**
Membership: No
Other: Clubhouse / Restaurant / Bar-Lounge / Snacks
GPS: Yes

Tees	Holes	Yards	Par	USGA	Slope
BACK	18	6539	72	71.7	128
MIDDLE	18	6149	72	69.8	122
FRONT	18	4780	72	67.6	118

Weekend: $24
Weekend: $46
Discounts: None
Driving Range: Yes
Junior Golf: Yes
Architect/Yr Open: Bob Ferrarotti/2000

Player Comments: "Well kept. Well laid out." Challenging scenic layout. Fabulous views with scenic par 3s. Upscale public course. "First-class design." –RW

	1	2	3	4	5	6	7	8	9
PAR	4	4	5	3	4	5	3	4	4
YARDS	380	355	500	160	330	450	155	350	375
	10	11	12	13	14	15	16	17	18
PAR	3	4	3	4	4	4	5	4	5
YARDS	187	350	175	340	320	385	520	307	510

Directions: Route 8 to Exit 42 (Route 118), head East on Route 118, turn right onto Route 222. Course is 2 miles on the left. From Route 4 West to Route 118, take left on Route 222. Club is 2 miles on left.

Fox Run at Copper Hill NR ▶ 14

Griffin Road
East Granby, CT (860) 653-6191
www.bluefoxent.com
Club Pro: Sean Smedick, PGA
Payment: Visa, MC, Amex
Tee Times: 7 days a week
Fee 9 Holes: Weekday: $15
Fee 18 Holes: Weekday: $22
Twilight Rates: No
Cart Rental: $12pp/18, $8pp/9
Lessons: Yes **Schools:** Yes, Jr.
Membership: Yes, semi-private
Other: Clubhouse / Snack Bar / Restaurant / Bar-Lounge

Tees	Holes	Yards	Par	USGA	Slope
BACK					
MIDDLE	18	6004	72	68.6	116
FRONT	18	5090	72	68.1	124

Weekend: $16
Weekend: $23
Discounts: Senior & Junior
Driving Range: Across street
Junior Golf: Yes
Architect/Yr Open: Allen Bissette/1956

Improvements include full irrigation. New greens superintendent. Frequent Player card available. Visit our sister course, Blue Fox Run in Avon, CT.

	1	2	3	4	5	6	7	8	9
PAR	4	4	3	5	4	3	4	5	4
YARDS	331	313	163	437	241	164	308	426	376
	10	11	12	13	14	15	16	17	18
PAR	4	4	3	5	4	3	4	5	4
YARDS	336	356	176	473	261	178	361	459	402

Directions: I-91 to Exit 40 (Bradley Field exit). Follow Route 20 West to Newgate Road (6 lights). Turn right on Newgate Road. Go past old Newgate prison to stop sign. Turn left to course.

Gillette Ridge Golf Club ✪✪✪½ ▶15

1360 Hall Boulevard
Bloomfield, CT (860) 726-1430
www.gilletteridgegolf.com

Club Pro: Pat Aquaro, PGA
Payment: Most Major Credit Cards
Tee Times: 7 days adv.
Fee 9 Holes: Weekday:
Fee 18 Holes: Weekday: $50 w/cart
Twilight Rates: Yes
Cart Rental: Included
Lessons: Yes **Schools:**
Membership: Yes
Other: Clubhouse / Bar-Lounge / Showers / Lockers

Tees	Holes	Yards	Par	USGA	Slope
BACK	18	7191	72	74.8	135
MIDDLE	18	6703	72	72.2	133
FRONT	18	6133	72	67.2	117

Weekend:
Weekend: $65 w/cart
Discounts: None
Driving Range: $5/bucket
Junior Golf:
Architect/Yr Open: Arnold Palmer/2004

Opened July 2004. "Fairways are generous but approach to green narrows. This is a course that keeps coming at you. Many carries, especially to the green. Bring your aerial game. Great fun." –JD

	1	2	3	4	5	6	7	8	9
PAR	4	5	4	3	4	4	5	3	4
YARDS	379	418	380	162	283	336	555	157	389
	10	11	12	13	14	15	16	17	18
PAR	4	3	5	4	4	3	4	5	4
YARDS	377	155	528	242	326	156	383	502	405

Directions: I-91 to Exit 39B West. 218 West for approximately 6 miles. Route 218 becomes Cottage Grove Road.

Goodwin Golf Course ✪✪ ▶16

1130 Maple Avenue
Hartford, CT (860) 956-3601
www.americangolf.com

Club Pro: Mark Castelhano, GM
Payment: Visa, MC, Amex
Tee Times: 7 days adv.
Fee 9 Holes: Weekday: $15.50
Fee 18 Holes: Weekday: $23.50
Twilight Rates: After 5pm
Cart Rental: $24.50pp/18, $16pp/9
Lessons: $65/hour **Schools:** Yes
Membership: Yes
Other: Banquet Facility / Snack Bar

Tees	Holes	Yards	Par	USGA	Slope
BACK	18	5953	70	68.0	116
MIDDLE	18	5605	70	66.6	110
FRONT	18	5069	70	69.6	109

Weekend: $17
Weekend: $26.50
Discounts: Senior & Junior
Driving Range: Yes
Junior Golf: Yes
Architect/Yr Open: Everett Pyle/1930
GPS:

COUPON

New clubhouse renovations, full menu, bar, new banquet facilities. Renovated bunkers and cart paths. Good contrast between open and tight holes.

	1	2	3	4	5	6	7	8	9
PAR	5	4	4	4	4	4	3	3	4
YARDS	486	315	367	322	370	286	127	155	332
	10	11	12	13	14	15	16	17	18
PAR	4	3	5	4	4	3	4	4	4
YARDS	334	213	471	361	312	138	336	352	361

Directions: I-91 to Exit 28. Take Route 15, 5 South to Exit 85 (Route 99), follow ramp to first light. Right on Joran to right on Maple.

Grassmere Country Club

✪✪   **17**

130 Town Farm Road
Enfield, CT (860) 749-7740
www.grassmerecountryclub.com

Club Pro: No
Payment: Cash, Check, Credit Cards
Tee Times: Anytime
Fee 9 Holes: Weekday: $17
Fee 18 Holes: Weekday: $24
Twilight Rates: No
Cart Rental: $12pp/18, $7pp/9
Lessons: No **Schools:** No
Membership: Yes
Other: Clubhouse / Snack Bar / Banquet Facility

Weekend: $18
Weekend: $28
Discounts: Sr. & Jr. M-F until 3pm, Sat 12-close
Driving Range: No
Junior Golf: Yes
Architect/Yr Open: 1976
GPS:

Tees	Holes	Yards	Par	USGA	Slope
BACK					
MIDDLE	9	3065	35	69.1	111
FRONT	9	2673	70		

Emphasis on nice landscaping aound the holes. Open March 15 - December 31. Noted for friendly staff and beautifully manicured course.

	1	2	3	4	5	6	7	8	9
PAR	4	4	4	4	3	5	4	4	3
YARDS	360	390	405	415	160	475	320	360	180
PAR									
YARDS									

Directions: Route I-91 to Exit 45, Right onto Route 140 East. Merge with Route 191 East. Stay on 191 5.8 miles. Left on Town Farm Road. Course is on left.

Harrisville Golf Course

NR   **18**

125 Harrisville Road
Woodstock, CT (860) 928-6098
www.harrisvillegolfcourse.com

Club Pro: Michael Sosik, PGA apprentice
Payment: Cash, Check, Credit
Tee Times: Weekend mornings
Fee 9 Holes: Weekday: $12
Fee 18 Holes: Weekday: $18
Twilight Rates: No
Cart Rental: $14pp/18, $7pp/9
Lessons: Yes **Schools:** No
Membership: Yes
Other: Snack Bar

Weekend: $14
Weekend: $20
Discounts: Senior & Junior
Driving Range: No
Junior Golf:
Architect/Yr Open: Aimee Salvas/1929
GPS:

Tees	Holes	Yards	Par	USGA	Slope
BACK	9	2915	36	67.4	118
MIDDLE	9	2725	36	65.0	109
FRONT	9	2415	35	66.4	115

COUPON

Improvements include: 9 new tees, remodeled fairways, and new 9th hole. Enjoyable round, easy walk. Noted for small greens and rolling hills.

	1	2	3	4	5	6	7	8	9
PAR	4	3	5	4	4	5	4	4	3
YARDS	290	170	500	265	410	420	295	235	200
PAR									
YARDS									

Directions: I-395 to Exit 97. Take right onto Route 171 West. Take left at Public Golf Course sign (Citizens Bank). Follow signs (next 2 rights).

Hotchkiss School Golf Course ⚉⚉ ▶ 19

Route 112
Lakeville, CT (860) 435-4400
www.hotchkiss.org/AboutHotchkiss/
GolfCourse.asp

Club Pro: James Kennedy, PGA
Payment: Cash Only
Tee Times: No
Fee 9 Holes: Weekday: $14
Fee 18 Holes: Weekday: $20
Twilight Rates: No
Cart Rental: $30/18, $15/9 per cart
Lessons: Yes **Schools:** Yes
Membership: Yes
Other: Snack Bar

Tees	Holes	Yards	Par	USGA	Slope
BACK					
MIDDLE	9	3043	35	68.8	117
FRONT					

Weekend: $15
Weekend: $25
Discounts: None
Driving Range: No
Junior Golf: No
Architect/Yr: Seth Raynor & Charles Banks/1911
GPS:

COUPON

Good variety, mildly challenging.

	1	2	3	4	5	6	7	8	9
PAR	4	3	4	4	3	4	5	3	5
YARDS	420	192	401	370	128	347	500	165	520
PAR									
YARDS									

Directions: Route 7 to Route 112 West to course, or Route 44 to Route 112 East.

Keney Golf Club ⚆⚆ ▶ 20

280 Tower Avenue
Hartford, CT (860) 525-3656
www.americangolf.com

Club Pro:
Payment: Visa, MC, Amex, Disc, Checks
Tee Times: 7 days adv.
Fee 9 Holes: Weekday: $15.50
Fee 18 Holes: Weekday: $23.50
Twilight Rates: After 6pm
Cart Rental: $13.50pp/18, $11.50pp/9
Lessons: Yes **Schools:** Yes
Membership: Yes
Other: Clubhouse / Lockers / Snack Bar / Restaurant / Function

Tees	Holes	Yards	Par	USGA	Slope
BACK	18	6014	70	68.1	18115
MIDDLE	18	5739	70	66.8	113
FRONT	18	4967	70	68.9	116

Weekend: $17
Weekend: $26.50
Discounts: Senior & Junior
Driving Range: No
Junior Golf: Yes
Architect/Yr Open: Devereaux Emmet/1927

COUPON

Player Comments: "Tight course. Good challenge" "A sleeper." True links-style. The clubhouse is reminiscent of the grand architectural style of the late 20s. Resident rate. Early-bird rates. Open year round.

	1	2	3	4	5	6	7	8	9
PAR	4	5	3	4	4	3	4	4	4
YARDS	315	487	109	328	396	134	363	381	377
	10	11	12	13	14	15	16	17	18
PAR	5	3	4	3	5	4	4	4	3
YARDS	526	190	261	102	446	366	374	364	160

Directions: I-91 to Exit 34. Left at ramp, right at light. Course is 5 minutes North of downtown Hartford.

NE
CT

Lake of Isles GC and Resort ✪✪✪½ ▸ 21

One Lake of Isles Road
North Stonington, CT
(888) 475-3746
www.lakeofisles.com

Club Pro: Robbie Leming, Dir. of Golf
Payment: Visa, MC, Amex
Tee Times: 30 days adv.

Tees	Holes	Yards	Par	USGA	Slope
BACK	18	7252	72	76.6	146
MIDDLE	18	6304	72	71.5	135
FRONT	18	4937	72	68.9	127

Fee 9 Holes: Weekday: Weekend:
Fee 18 Holes: Weekday: $155 - $195   Weekend: $195
Twilight Rates: No   Discounts: Junior
Cart Rental: Included   Driving Range: Yes
Lessons: $110/hour, $60/half hour Schools: Yes Junior Golf: Yes
Membership: Yes   Architect/Yr Open: Rees Jones/2005
Other: Restaurant / Clubhouse / Bar & Lounge / Indoor Outdoor Practice Facility / Luxury Villas

Located around a 90-acre lake, Rees Jones design. Multiple tee locations offer a varied test for all levels. "Many carries; visually splendid. Expecting this to become one of New England's best." –JD

	1	2	3	4	5	6	7	8	9
PAR	5	3	4	4	5	4	3	4	4
YARDS	550	164	308	398	457	395	182	325	389
	10	11	12	13	14	15	16	17	18
PAR	4	3	5	4	4	5	3	4	4
YARDS	399	154	469	345	399	496	166	342	366

Directions: I-95 North to Exit 92 in CT. Turn left on Route 2 West. Lake of Isles is 8 miles on Route 2 West. Directly across the street from Foxwoods Resort.

Manchester Country Club ✪✪½ ▸ 22

305 South Main Street
Manchester, CT (860) 646-0226
www.mancc.com

Club Pro: Ralph DeNicolo, PGA
Payment: MC, Visa
Tee Times: 7 days adv.

Tees	Holes	Yards	Par	USGA	Slope
BACK	18	6285	72	70.8	125
MIDDLE	18	6167	72	69.7	123
FRONT	18	5610	73	72.0	120

Fee 9 Holes: Wkdy: $23 non-res./$21 res.   Weekend: $25 non-res./$23 res.
Fee 18 Holes: Wkdy: $41 non-res./$38 res.   Weekend: $43 non-res./$41 res.
Twilight Rates: No   Discounts: Senior & Junior
Cart Rental: $16pp/18, $8pp/9   Driving Range: Yes
Lessons: Call for rates Schools: No   Junior Golf: Yes
Membership: Yes   Architect/Yr Open: Devereux Emmet/1917
Other: Clubhouse / Lockers / Showers / Snack Bar / Restaurant / Bar-Lounge

Old-style golf course. Variety of elevation changes. Open April - December. Dress code.

	1	2	3	4	5	6	7	8	9
PAR	4	4	5	5	3	4	4	3	4
YARDS	308	333	507	500	144	406	331	143	348
	10	11	12	13	14	15	16	17	18
PAR	4	4	3	4	5	5	4	4	3
YARDS	294	340	135	335	520	510	397	362	182

Directions: I-84 to Route 384 East (Exit 3). Take left 1000 yards up onto South Main Street. Course is on the left.

Minnechaug Golf Course

NR ▶ 23

16 Fairway Crossing
Glastonbury, CT (860) 643-9914
www.minnechauggolfclub.com

Tees	Holes	Yards	Par	USGA	Slope
BACK	9	2654	35	67.4	112
MIDDLE	9	2527	35	66.5	110
FRONT	9	2186	35	62.7	102

Club Pro: John Dipollina
Payment: Cash or Credit
Tee Times: 1 week adv.
Fee 9 Holes: Weekday: $15   **Weekend:** $16
Fee 18 Holes: Weekday: $24   **Weekend:** $26
Twilight Rates: No   **Discounts:** Senior, Junior, Resident
Cart Rental: $12pp/18, $7pp/9   **Driving Range:** No
Lessons: Yes **Schools:** Yes   **Junior Golf:** No
Membership: No   **Architect/Yr Open:** Geoffrey Cornish/1959
Other: Restaurant/ Beer/ Snacks   **GPS:**

Reduced rates for residents, juniors and seniors, open year round.

	1	2	3	4	5	6	7	8	9
PAR	4	4	5	4	5	3	4	3	3
YARDS	311	307	464	327	437	161	269	116	135
PAR									
YARDS									

Directions: I-84 to Route 384 East, Exit 3. Left off exit on Route 83. Follow for 3 miles. Course on right.

Norwich Golf Course

✪✪ ▶ 24

New London Turnpike
Norwich, CT (860) 889-6973
www.norwichgolf.com

Tees	Holes	Yards	Par	USGA	Slope
BACK	18	6183	71	69.5	129
MIDDLE	18	5877	72	68.1	126
FRONT	18	5104	71	70.2	118

Club Pro: John Paesani, PGA
Payment: Visa, MC
Tee Times: 3 days adv.
Fee 9 Holes: Weekday: **Weekend:**
Fee 18 Holes: Weekday: $40 (rates may change) **Weekend:** $48 (rates may change)
Twilight Rates: After 5pm   **Discounts:** None
Cart Rental: $18pp/wknd, $16pp/wkdy   **Driving Range:** No
Lessons: $50/half hour **Schools:**   **Junior Golf:** Yes
Membership: Yes   **Architect/Yr Open:** Donald Ross/1926
Other: Clubhouse / Lockers / Showers / Restaurant / Bar-Lounge

Short but tricky course: overly aggressive play could lead to disaster. Designed by Donald Ross. Open April - November. Residents' rate. New bridges. Visit website for full listing of rates.

	1	2	3	4	5	6	7	8	9
PAR	4	4	4	4	5	4	4	4	3
YARDS	303	276	366	410	487	330	370	300	170
	10	11	12	13	14	15	16	17	18
PAR	4	4	5	3	5	4	4	4	3
YARDS	355	388	503	105	545	170	330	303	166

Directions: I-95 to I-395 North to Exit 80 East. Take right off ramp (West Main Street), follow to 5th light. Take right onto New London Turnpike. Course is 1/2 mile down on right.

Pequot Golf Club ✪✪ ▶ 25

127 Wheeler Road
Stonington, CT (860) 535-1898
www.pequotgolf.com

Club Pro: Joe Brucas, PGA
Payment: Visa, MC, Cash
Tee Times: 14 days adv.

Tees	Holes	Yards	Par	USGA	Slope
BACK					
MIDDLE	18	5903	70	68.7	118
FRONT	18	5246	71	69.4	112

Fee 9 Holes: Weekday: $19 M-Th
Fee 18 Holes: Weekday: $29 M-Th
Twilight Rates: After 1pm
Cart Rental: $15pp/18, $10pp/9
Lessons: Yes **Schools:** No
Membership: Yes
Other: Restaurant / Bar-Lounge

Weekend: $20 F/S/S
Weekend: $34 F/S/S
Discounts: Senior & Junior
Driving Range: No
Junior Golf: Yes
Architect/Yr Open: Wendell Ross/1959
GPS:

COUPON

Player Comments: "Beautiful course." Open March 1 - December 15. Historic Mystic Seaport and casinos nearby.

	1	2	3	4	5	6	7	8	9
PAR	4	4	4	4	4	3	4	4	3
YARDS	353	329	358	287	328	179	379	376	209
	10	11	12	13	14	15	16	17	18
PAR	4	4	3	5	4	4	4	3	5
YARDS	276	361	149	469	417	336	339	193	565

Directions: I-95 to Exit 91. Left off 95 South, right off 95 North. Go 1 mile. Take right onto Wheeler Road.

Putnam CC at Chase Farm ✪✪ ▶ 26

136 Chase Road
Putnam, CT (860) 928-7748
www.putnamcountryclub.com

Tees	Holes	Yards	Par	USGA	Slope
BACK	18	6169	71	70.1	124
MIDDLE	18	5819	71	69.1	119
FRONT	18	4961	71	68.8	114

Payment: Visa, MC, Amex, Disc
Tee Times: 5 days adv.
Fee 9 Holes: Weekday: $14
Fee 18 Holes: Weekday: $26
Twilight Rates: After 1pm
Cart Rental: $14pp/9
Lessons: Yes **Schools:** No
Membership: Yes
Other: Clubhouse / Snack Bar / Beer & Wine

Weekend: $20
Weekend: $35
Discounts: Senior & Junior wkdys
Driving Range: Yes
Junior Golf: Yes
Architect/Yr Open: Mike & Sally Donovan/1993

COUPON

Player Comments: "Awesome, small, fairly priced golf course. Pro shop staff willing to help with any request." New sand in bunkers and new tees coming! Open April 1 - November 30. Will be changing name to Connecticut National. All prices subject to change.

	1	2	3	4	5	6	7	8	9
PAR	5	4	4	3	4	5	3	4	3
YARDS	436	333	380	192	304	552	160	320	111
	10	11	12	13	14	15	16	17	18
PAR	4	3	5	4	4	3	4	4	5
YARDS	373	151	479	315	385	134	395	360	502

Directions: I-395 to Exit 97, East on Route 44. 3 1/2 miles to public course, sign on right. Right onto East Putnam Road. At 2nd stop sign, take a right (Chase Road). Course is 1 mile on right.

Quarryview Golf Course

NR 27 ▶

30 Allyndale Road
East Canaan, CT
(860) 824-4252

Tees	Holes	Yards	Par	USGA	Slope
BACK	9	1626	31		
MIDDLE	9	1576	31	59.0	93
FRONT	9	1532	31	58.0	89

Club Pro:
Payment: Visa, MC
Tee Times: No
Fee 9 Holes: Weekday: $11
Fee 18 Holes: Weekday: $17
Twilight Rates: No
Cart Rental: $10pp/18, $6pp/9
Lessons: Schools:
Membership: Yes
Other: Snack Bar

Weekend: $14
Weekend: $20
Discounts: None
Driving Range: Yes, grass
Junior Golf: Yes
Architect/Yr Open: Leonard Allyn/2002
GPS:

9 hole executive course, families welcome, with a full-service practice range. A work in progress. Also has a driving range.

	1	2	3	4	5	6	7	8	9
PAR	3	3	3	3	3	3	5	4	4
YARDS	95	188	150	125	120	128	385	200	220
PAR									
YARDS									

Directions: Route 44 in East Canaan to Allyndale Road.

Raceway Golf Club

NR 28 ▶

Route 31
Thompson, CT (860) 923-9591
www.racewaygolf.com

Tees	Holes	Yards	Par	USGA	Slope
BACK	18	6523	72	70.0	111
MIDDLE	18	6050	72	67.7	106
FRONT	18	5531	72	71.3	117

Club Pro: David Hall, PGA
Payment: Visa, MC, Disc
Tee Times: M-F 7 days, S/S 4 days
Fee 9 Holes: Weekday:
Fee 18 Holes: Weekday: $35 w/cart & lunch
Twilight Rates: After 5:30pm
Cart Rental: Included
Lessons: Yes **Schools:**
Membership:
Other: Clubhouse / Lockers/ Snack Bar / Restaurant / Bar-Lounge

Weekend:
Weekend: $42 w/cart
Discounts: None
Driving Range: 40 mats, grass $6
Junior Golf: Yes
Architect/Yr Open: Don Hoenig/1947

An enjoyable course. 6th hole has been lengthened. New 14th hole for 2009 season.

	1	2	3	4	5	6	7	8	9
PAR	4	4	4	3	5	5	4	4	3
YARDS	277	387	304	152	536	486	350	402	174
	10	11	12	13	14	15	16	17	18
PAR	5	4	4	5	3	4	4	3	4
YARDS	492	382	342	425	146	353	347	166	289

Directions: I-395 to Exit 99; go into Thompson Center, left at blinking light onto Route 193. Follow signs to Thompson Speedway which will lead to the course.

River Ridge Golf Course ✪✪½ ▶ 29

259 Poreston Road
Jewitt City, CT (860) 376-3268
www.riverridgegolf.com

Club Pro: Brian Morrow, PGA
Payment: Visa, MC, Amex
Tee Times: 10 days

Tees	Holes	Yards	Par	USGA	Slope
BACK	18	6871	72	71.8	124
MIDDLE	18	6474	72	69.8	122
FRONT	18	5393	72	70.4	119

Fee 9 Holes: Weekday: $20   **Weekend:** $20
Fee 18 Holes: Weekday: $35   **Weekend:** $42
Twilight Rates: After 2pm   **Discounts:** None
Cart Rental: $16pp/18, $9pp/9   **Driving Range:** No
Lessons: Yes **Schools:** No   **Junior Golf:** No
Membership: Yes   **Architect/Yr Open:** Joseph & Charlie Rustici/1999
Other: Full Restaurant / Bar-Lounge

Challenging course cut through trees with significant elevation changes. 24-hour automated tee time system. Voted one of the Top 5 Connecticut courses.

	1	2	3	4	5	6	7	8	9
PAR	4	4	5	3	5	3	4	4	5
YARDS	390	391	510	180	530	156	350	354	560
	10	11	12	13	14	15	16	17	18
PAR	4	3	4	4	4	5	4	3	4
YARDS	401	122	420	326	350	530	340	185	379

Directions: I-395 to Exit 85 to Route 164 South. 7/10 mile on right.

Rockledge Country Club ✪✪✪ ▶ 30

289 South Main Street
West Hartford, CT
(860) 521-3156
www.golfrockledge.com

Club Pro: Richard F. Crowe, PGA
Payment: Visa, MC, Cash
Tee Times: 7 days adv. (860) 521-6284

Tees	Holes	Yards	Par	USGA	Slope
BACK	18	6436	72	71.1	129
MIDDLE	18	6069	72	69.3	125
FRONT	18	5434	72	72.7	129

Fee 9 Holes: Weekday: $17.25   **Weekend:** $18.75
Fee 18 Holes: Weekday: $33   **Weekend:** $37
Twilight Rates: Yes, depends on sunset   **Discounts:** Senior & Junior
Cart Rental: $14pp/18, $8pp/9   **Driving Range:** $9/lg, $6.50/med, $3.75/sm
Lessons: $40/half hour **Schools:** No   **Junior Golf:** Yes
Membership: Yes   **Architect/Yr Open:** Al Zikorus/1940
Other: Clubhouse / Lockers / Showers / Snack Bar / Restaurant / Bar-Lounge

Player Comments: "Challenging layout. Always in great condition." Open April - December. Resident fees and tee times. Lottery for weekends.

	1	2	3	4	5	6	7	8	9
PAR	4	4	4	4	3	5	4	3	5
YARDS	334	286	394	395	177	450	299	181	448
	10	11	12	13	14	15	16	17	18
PAR	4	4	5	3	5	4	3	4	4
YARDS	404	302	465	136	515	357	152	381	393

Directions: I-84 to Exit 41. From West take a right off the exit, from East take a left off the exit. Course is 1/4 mile on left.

Rolling Greens Golf Club NR 31

600 Cold Spring Road
Rocky Hill, CT
(860) 257-9775

Tees	Holes	Yards	Par	USGA	Slope
BACK					
MIDDLE	9	3131	35	70.1	130
FRONT	9	2614	36	71.7	130

Club Pro: Gary Deep, PGA
Payment: Visa, MC
Tee Times: No
Fee 9 Holes: Weekday: $17   **Weekend:** $17
Fee 18 Holes: Weekday: $34   **Weekend:** $34
Twilight Rates: After 5:30pm   **Discounts:** Senior & Junior
Cart Rental: $16pp/18, $10pp/9   **Driving Range:** No
Lessons: $60   **Schools:** No   **Junior Golf:** No
Membership: Yes   **Architect/Yr Open:** Geoffrey Cornish/1973
Other: Clubhouse / Lockers / Showers / Restaurant / Bar-Lounge

Challenging! Shotmaker's course. Great shape. Dress code (no tank tops, T-shirts, or cutoff jeans). Open March - November.

	1	2	3	4	5	6	7	8	9
PAR	4	5	3	4	4	4	4	3	4
YARDS	360	553	191	315	379	440	373	180	340
PAR									
YARDS									

Directions: I-91 to Exit 23. Signs to Rolling Greens. Approximately 1 mile from exit.

Rolling Meadows Country Club ✪✪ 32

Route 140
Ellington, CT (860) 870-5328
www.rollingmeadowscountryclub.com

Tees	Holes	Yards	Par	USGA	Slope
BACK	18	6818	72	72.5	128
MIDDLE	18	6269	72	70	123
FRONT	18	5331	72	70.4	122

Club Pro: Jeff Swanson, PGA
Payment: Visa, MC, Disc
Tee Times: 3 days adv. (860) 749-3550
Fee 9 Holes: Weekday: $19   **Weekend:** $22
Fee 18 Holes: Weekday: $34   **Weekend:** $37
Twilight Rates: No   **Discounts:** Sr. & Jr. M-Th
Cart Rental: $8pp/9, $16pp/18   **Driving Range:** Yes
Lessons: Yes   **Schools:** Yes   **Junior Golf:** Yes
Membership: Yes   **Architect/Yr Open:** Al Zirokus/1997
Other: Restaurant / Bar / Beverage Cart   **GPS:**

Player Comments: " Getting better every year." Special 7am-1pm, Monday - Friday 1 player only $41 with cart, $38 military or senior.

	1	2	3	4	5	6	7	8	9
PAR	5	4	3	5	4	4	4	3	4
YARDS	488	316	166	491	390	366	335	186	346
	10	11	12	13	14	15	16	17	18
PAR	4	5	4	3	5	4	4	3	4
YARDS	383	473	366	163	490	433	345	190	342

Directions: I-91 to Route 140 or I-84 to 83 to Route 140 (across from Brookside Park, Ellington).

Shennecosset Golf Club ✪✪✪

33 ▶

Plant Street
Groton, CT (860) 445-0262
www.shennygolf.com

Tees	Holes	Yards	Par	USGA	Slope
BACK	18	6562	71	71.5	122
MIDDLE	18	6088	71	69.1	121
FRONT	18	5671	74	72.4	122

Club Pro: Todd Goodhue, PGA
Payment: Visa, MC
Tee Times: 3 days adv.
Fee 9 Holes: Weekday:
Fee 18 Holes: Weekday: $37
Twilight Rates: After 12
Cart Rental: $16pp/18
Lessons: $35/half hour **Schools:** No
Membership: Yes
Other: Clubhouse / Snack Bar / Restaurant / Bar-Lounge

Weekend:
Weekend: $42
Discounts: Junior
Driving Range: No
Junior Golf: Yes
Architect/Yr Open: Donald Ross

Player Comments: "Great old course. Newer holes along the river are terrific." Fully irrigated. Donald Ross-designed seaside course. Open year round. Mohegan Sun and Foxwoods Casino nearby.

	1	2	3	4	5	6	7	8	9
PAR	4	4	4	3	5	4	4	5	3
YARDS	350	368	361	195	488	145	433	367	418
	10	11	12	13	14	15	16	17	18
PAR	4	4	3	4	4	3	4	4	5
YARDS	400	160	460	542	323	116	343	362	311

Directions: I-95 to Exit 87 (Clarence Sharp Highway); take right at second light. Take left at next light, proceed past Pfizer; course is on left side.

Simsbury Farms Golf Club ✪✪

34 ▶

100 Old Farms Road
Simsbury, CT (860) 658-6246
www.simsburyfarms.com

Tees	Holes	Yards	Par	USGA	Slope
BACK	18	6509	72	71.0	122
MIDDLE	18	6119	72	69.0	119
FRONT	18	5400	72	70.8	122

Club Pro: John Verrengia, PGA
Payment: Cash, Check, Most Major
Tee Times: 7 days adv.
Fee 9 Holes: Weekday: $18.50
Fee 18 Holes: Weekday: $31
Twilight Rates: After 6:30pm
Cart Rental: $15pp/18, $9pp/9
Lessons: $50/45 min. **Schools:** No
Membership: Residents
Other: Restaurant / Clubhouse

Weekend: $21
Weekend: $35
Discounts: Senior & Junior
Driving Range: 8/lg, $6/med, $3.50/sm bucket
Junior Golf: Yes
Architect/Yr Open: Geoffrey Cornish/1934
GPS: Yes

Good challenge with a decent mix of holes. A nice hilly course. Continued drainage improvements. Open April - November.

	1	2	3	4	5	6	7	8	9
PAR	4	4	4	3	5	4	5	4	3
YARDS	341	381	361	135	487	361	535	279	178
	10	11	12	13	14	15	16	17	18
PAR	4	4	5	3	5	4	3	4	4
YARDS	346	335	533	169	465	325	200	302	386

Directions: Route 185 North to end. Take left on to 10 North. At 2nd light take left onto Stratton Brook Road. Through 2 traffic lights, course is 3/4 mile on the right.

Skungamaug River Golf Club ✪✪ ⏵35

104 Folly Lane
Coventry, CT (860) 742-9348
www.skungamauggolf.com

Tees	Holes	Yards	Par	USGA	Slope
BACK	18	5785	70	69.4	123
MIDDLE	18	5624	70	68.6	120
FRONT	18	4838	71	69.3	123

Club Pro: Rick Nelson, PGA
Payment: Visa, MC, Amex, Disc
Tee Times: M-F 7 days, S/S 6 days
Fee 9 Holes: Weekday: $18   **Weekend:** $19
Fee 18 Holes: Weekday: $35   **Weekend:** $37
Twilight Rates: After 6pm   **Discounts:** Senior
Cart Rental: $14pp/18, $7pp/9   **Driving Range:** $5/lg, $3/sm bucket
Lessons: $40/half hour **Schools:** No   **Junior Golf:** Yes
Membership: Yes   **Architect/Yr Open:** Chet Jenkins/1962
Other: Clubhouse / Snack Bar / Bar-Lounge   **GPS:**

COUPON

River runs along right side, large tree divides upper and lower levels of hole #15. No cutoffs or tank tops.
Open April - December.

	1	2	3	4	5	6	7	8	9
PAR	4	3	4	5	3	4	5	3	4
YARDS	339	154	291	438	139	332	461	158	351
	10	**11**	**12**	**13**	**14**	**15**	**16**	**17**	**18**
PAR	4	3	4	4	4	4	4	3	5
YARDS	376	171	363	371	395	290	323	189	483

Directions: I-84 to Exit 68. South on Route 195, 1/4 mile to light. Turn right onto Goose Lane, follow yellow, triangular arrows on telephone poles. 3 miles to club.

Stanley Golf Club ✪✪✪ ⏵36

245 Hartford Road
New Britain, CT (860) 827-8570
www.stanleygolf.com

Tees	Holes	Yards	Par	USGA	Slope
BACK	27/18	6452	72	70.8	115
MIDDLE	27	6107	72	69.1	114
FRONT	27/18	5434	73	71.3	115

Club Pro: Kyle Hedstrom
Payment: Most Major Credit Cards
Tee Times: Wknds, 3 days adv. (827-1362)
Fee 9 Holes: Weekday: $18.25   **Weekend:** $19.75
Fee 18 Holes: Weekday: $30.50   **Weekend:** $33
Twilight Rates: No   **Discounts:** Senior & Junior
Cart Rental: $29/18, $18/9 per cart   **Driving Range:** $9.50/lg, $7/med
Lessons: Yes **Schools:** No   **Junior Golf:** Yes
Membership: Season Pass   **Architect/Yr Open:** Orrin E. Smith/1930
Other: Clubhouse / Lockers / Showers / Restaurant / Bar-Lounge / Snack / Outings
GPS: Yes

27 holes. White to Red score card below. Improvements include 4 redesigned holes. New driving range.
Resident rates. New carts with GPS, new practice area and 9 Blue Green.

	1	2	3	4	5	6	7	8	9
PAR	5	4	3	4	4	4	3	4	5
YARDS	492	430	150	352	365	320	105	387	460
	10	**11**	**12**	**13**	**14**	**15**	**16**	**17**	**18**
PAR	4	3	5	4	4	4	3	4	5
YARDS	338	201	461	357	325	376	160	363	465

Directions: I-84 to Exit 39A, then right onto Route 9 South to Exit 30. Take right at end of ramp.
Course is 1/2 mile on left.

Tallwood Country Club

★★½ 37 ▶

91 North Street (Route 85)
Hebron, CT (860) 646-1151
www.ctgolfer.com/tallwoodcc

Tees	Holes	Yards	Par	USGA	Slope
BACK	18	6353	72	70.4	123
MIDDLE	18	6126	72	69.3	121
FRONT	18	5424	72	70.6	121

Club Pro: John Nowobilski, PGA
Payment: Visa, MC
Tee Times: M-F 7 days, S/S 5 days
Fee 9 Holes: Weekday: $18   **Weekend:** $19
Fee 18 Holes: Weekday: $35   **Weekend:** $38
Twilight Rates: After 4pm   **Discounts:** Senior & Junior
Cart Rental: $14pp/18, $7pp/9   **Driving Range:** $7/lg, $4/sm bucket
Lessons: $80/hour **Schools:** Yes, Jr.   **Junior Golf:** No
Membership: Yes   **Architect/Yr Open:** Mike Ovian/1970
Other: Restaurant / Clubhouse / Snack Bar   **GPS:**

Annual host of CTPGA, CSGA events. Open March - December.

	1	2	3	4	5	6	7	8	9
PAR	5	4	3	5	4	3	4	4	3
YARDS	528	287	176	483	400	158	341	359	167
	10	11	12	13	14	15	16	17	18
PAR	4	5	4	4	3	4	5	4	4
YARDS	296	500	361	346	157	364	460	377	366

Directions: I-84 East to I-384. Exit 5 off I-384, right off exit puts you on Route 85 South. Course is on right.

Timberlin Golf Club

★★½ 38 ▶

330 Southington Road
Berlin, CT (860) 828-3228
www.timberlingc.com

Tees	Holes	Yards	Par	USGA	Slope
BACK	18	6733	72	72.0	127
MIDDLE	18	6342	72	70.2	126
FRONT	18	5472	72	72.0	125

Club Pro: Jeffrey J. Coderre, PGA
Payment: Cash or Credit
Tee Times: 7 days wkdys, 3 days wknd
Fee 9 Holes: Weekday: $20   **Weekend:** $21
Fee 18 Holes: Weekday: $32   **Weekend:** $34.75
Twilight Rates: No   **Discounts:** Senior & Junior
Cart Rental: $15.50pp/18, $9pp/9   **Driving Range:** Yes
Lessons: $60/hour **Schools:** Yes   **Junior Golf:** Yes
Membership: Yes   **Architect/Yr Open:** Al Zikorus/1970
Other: Clubhouse / Showers / Snack Bar   **GPS:**

COUPON

Player Comments: "Friendly staff." "Challenging course in great shape." "Good value." Conservative layout with well-placed traps. Open April - November. Bunker and irrigation improvements complete.

	1	2	3	4	5	6	7	8	9
PAR	5	4	4	3	4	5	3	4	4
YARDS	550	340	360	170	360	526	150	342	377
	10	11	12	13	14	15	16	17	18
PAR	5	4	3	5	4	4	3	4	4
YARDS	492	361	160	477	362	400	163	359	393

Directions: Located off Route 71 which runs between I-691 and Route 372. Course is on Route 364, .6 mile from Route 71. Left onto Southlington Avenue.

Topstone Golf Course ✪✪✪ ▶ 39

516 Griffin Road
South Windsor, CT (860) 648-4653
www.topstonegc.com

Tees	Holes	Yards	Par	USGA	Slope
BACK	18	6549	72	70.7	124
MIDDLE	18	6199	72	69.0	121
FRONT	18	4987	72	68.2	109

Club Pro: Casey Morris
Payment: Visa, MC, Amex
Tee Times: 14/wkdys; 7/wknds
Fee 9 Holes: Weekday: $19.50   **Weekend:** $21.50
Fee 18 Holes: Weekday: $38   **Weekend:** $41
Twilight Rates: After 12:30pm & 2:30pm   **Discounts:** Senior & Junior
Cart Rental: $12pp/18, $6.50pp/9   **Driving Range:** No
Lessons: $40/half hour **Schools:** No   **Junior Golf:** Yes
Membership: Yes   **Architect/Yr Open:** Al Zikorus, Joe Kelley/1997
Other: Bar / Restaurant / Clubhouse   **GPS:**

Player Comments: "A good value for your golfing dollars." "Shows a great deal of maturity. Back 9 has more distinctive holes." "Well-kept course. Great greens." Challenging for all abilities with 5 sets of tees.

	1	2	3	4	5	6	7	8	9
PAR	4	5	4	3	5	4	4	3	4
YARDS	365	472	304	175	480	385	397	138	254
	10	11	12	13	14	15	16	17	18
PAR	5	4	3	4	4	3	5	4	4
YARDS	482	389	167	340	399	140	471	320	336

Directions: Take I-291 from either Routes 84 or 91. Take Exit 4 (Route 5). Go North on Route 5 for 4 miles, turn right onto Route 194 for .5 mile. Left onto Rye Street for 1.5 miles, Turn right onto Griffin Street for 1.25 miles.

Tower Ridge ✪✪✪½ ▶ 40

140 Nod Road
Simsbury, CT 06070
www.towerridge.com

Tees	Holes	Yards	Par	USGA	Slope
BACK	18	6443	71	71.5	132
MIDDLE	18	6124	71	70.0	129
FRONT	18	5164	72	76.3	133

Club Pro: Jay Thomas (860) 658-9767
Payment: Most Major Credit Cards
Tee Times: 7 days per week
Fee 9 Holes: Weekday: $27   **Weekend:** $32
Fee 18 Holes: Weekday: $45   **Weekend:** $55
Twilight Rates: After 1pm wknd, after 3pm wkdys   **Discounts:** Senior
Cart Rental: Included   **Driving Range:** Yes
Lessons: $100/hour **Schools:** Yes   **Junior Golf:** Yes
Membership: Yes   **Architect/Yr Open:** Geoffrey Cornish/1959
Other: Restauarant, Tennis Center & Swim Club for Members

COUPON

Former private now accepting public play. Partially flat, partially hilly. Several nice views from elevated tees. A challenging course for any level of player.

	1	2	3	4	5	6	7	8	9
PAR	4	4	3	4	4	4	4	4	4
YARDS	367	383	141	369	377	341	416	230	335
	10	11	12	13	14	15	16	17	18
PAR	5	4	3	4	5	4	3	4	4
YARDS	449	429	179	397	400	389	164	314	364

Directions: I-84 to exit Route 4 Farmington. At 2nd light, right on Route 10 North. Cross Route 44. Club is on right.

NE
CT

Tradition Golf Course at Windsor NR ▶ 41

147 Pigeon Hill Road
Windsor, CT (860) 688-2575
www.traditionalclubs.com

Tees	Holes	Yards	Par	USGA	Slope
BACK	18	6068	71	69.8	119
MIDDLE	18	5805	71	67.9	116
FRONT	18	4877	71	68.9	117

Club Pro: Mike Swanson, GM
Payment: Visa, MC, Amex, Disc
Tee Times: 7 days adv.
Fee 9 Holes: Weekday: $12   **Weekend:** $15
Fee 18 Holes: Weekday: $18   **Weekend:** $25
Twilight Rates: After 2pm   **Discounts:** Junior
Cart Rental: Incl. in riding rates, not listed above   **Driving Range:** Nearby
Lessons: Yes   **Schools:** Call   **Junior Golf:** Yes
Membership: Yes   **Architect/Yr Open:** Geoffrey Cornish/1963
Other: Clubhouse / Snack Bar / Restaurant / Patio Dining / Beverage Cart / Bag Drop

Player Comments: "Elevation changes in the front 9. Lots of decisions to make on the back 9."
Expanded golf shop and restaurant overlook course. Proper attire required. Rates may change.

	1	2	3	4	5	6	7	8	9
PAR	5	4	4	4	5	3	3	4	4
YARDS	451	335	358	346	486	147	197	395	285
	10	11	12	13	14	15	16	17	18
PAR	4	4	4	3	5	4	3	3	5
YARDS	399	289	325	168	451	350	140	202	481

Directions: I-91 to Exit 38. Left onto Route 75, 1 mile to Pigeon Hill Road. Turn right, course 1/4 mile on left.

Tunxis Plantation CC (Green) ✪✪✪ ▶ 42

87 Town Farm Road
Farmington, CT (860) 677-1367
www.tunxisgolf.com

Tees	Holes	Yards	Par	USGA	Slope
BACK	18	6446	70	70.9	125
MIDDLE	18	6027	70	69.0	121
FRONT	18	4883	70	71.0	115

Club Pro: Lou Pandolfi
Payment: Most Major Credit Cards
Tee Times: 1 week in advance
Fee 9 Holes: Weekday: $21   **Weekend:** $23
Fee 18 Holes: Weekday: $36   **Weekend:** $43
Twilight Rates: No   **Discounts:** Senior & Junior
Cart Rental: $30/18, $16.50/9 per cart   **Driving Range:** $4/bucket
Lessons: $40/half hour   **Schools:** No   **Junior Golf:** Yes
Membership: No   **Architect/Yr Open:** Al Zakoris/1962
Other: Restaurant / Clubhouse / Bar-Lounge / Lockers / Snack Bar / Showers

Very well run for such a complex. Fine staff. Wide-open fairways make for a forgiving layout. Great course for intermediate players. Open April 1 - November 20.

	1	2	3	4	5	6	7	8	9
PAR	4	5	4	4	3	4	4	3	4
YARDS	363	511	354	369	188	434	345	166	335
	10	11	12	13	14	15	16	17	18
PAR	4	4	3	4	4	4	4	5	3
YARDS	348	365	165	373	342	291	397	496	185

Directions: I-84 to Exit 39 (Route 4); first right over Farmington River.

Tunxis Plantation GC (Red) ✪✪✪ 43 ▶

87 Town Farm Road
Farmington, CT (860) 677-1367
www.tunxisgolf.com

Tees	Holes	Yards	Par	USGA	Slope
BACK	9	3219	35	35.1	125
MIDDLE	9	2999	35	34.1	121
FRONT	9	2872	35	35.8	117

Club Pro: Lou Pandolfi, PGA
Payment: Visa, MC, Amex
Tee Times: Yes, call in advance
Fee 9 Holes: Weekday: $21   **Weekend:** $23
Fee 18 Holes: Weekday: $36   **Weekend:** $43
Twilight Rates: No   **Discounts:** Senior & Junior
Cart Rental: $30/18, $16.50/9 per person   **Driving Range:** $4/bucket
Lessons: $40/half hour   **Schools:** No   **Junior Golf:** Yes
Membership: No   **Architect/Yr Open:** Al Zikorus/1962
Other: Restaurant / Clubhouse / Bar-Lounge / Lockers / Snack Bar / Showers

9-hole course in excellent condition located in Farmington Valley, next to Farmington River. Open April 1 - November 20.

	1	2	3	4	5	6	7	8	9
PAR	4	4	3	4	5	4	4	3	4
YARDS	348	395	141	322	483	396	366	177	371
PAR									
YARDS									

Directions: I-84 to Exit 39 (Route 4); first right over Farmington River.

Tunxis Plantation CC (White) ✪✪✪ 44 ▶

87 Town Farm Road
Farmington, CT (860) 677-1367
www.tunxisgolf.com

Tees	Holes	Yards	Par	USGA	Slope
BACK	18	6638	72	71.3	124
MIDDLE	18	6241	72	69.4	120
FRONT	18	5744	72	71.5	116

Club Pro: Lou Pandolfi, PGA
Payment: Visa, MC, Amex
Tee Times: Call in advance
Fee 9 Holes: Weekday: $21   **Weekend:** $23
Fee 18 Holes: Weekday: $36   **Weekend:** $43
Twilight Rates: No   **Discounts:** Senior & Junior
Cart Rental: $30/18, $16.50/9 per cart   **Driving Range:** $4/bucket
Lessons: $40/half hour   **Schools:** No   **Junior Golf:** Yes
Membership: No   **Architect/Yr Open:** Al Zikorus/1962
Other: Restaurant / Clubhouse / Bar-Lounge / Lockers / Snack Bar / Showers

Great course for intermediate players. Play from the Blue tees for a real challenge. Lake comes into play on seevral holes. Open April 1 - November 20. "Florida-style golf: water and sand provide challenges. Holes 5 & 13 really tough." –AR

	1	2	3	4	5	6	7	8	9
PAR	5	4	4	3	5	4	4	3	4
YARDS	526	407	343	153	476	366	358	147	332
	10	11	12	13	14	15	16	17	18
PAR	4	5	4	5	3	4	3	4	4
YARDS	334	508	368	515	176	413	154	357	318

Directions: I-84 to Exit 39 (Route 4); first right over Farmington River.

NE
CT

Twin Hills Country Club

NR 45

199 Bread and Milk Street
Coventry, CT (860) 742-9705
www.twinhillscountryclub.com

Club Pro: Eric DeStefano, PGA
    J. Nowobilski, dir.
Payment: Visa, MC
Tee Times: 7 days F/S/S/H
Fee 9 Holes: Weekday: $18
Fee 18 Holes: Weekday: $34
Twilight Rates: No
Cart Rental: Wknd: $26pp/18, $13pp/9
Lessons: No **Schools:** No
Membership: No
Other: Clubhouse / Snack Bar / Beer & Soda

Tees	Holes	Yards	Par	USGA	Slope
BACK	18	6275	71	69.8	123
MIDDLE	18	5954	71	68.9	117
FRONT	18	5249	71	69.5	116

Weekend: $19
Weekend: $37
Discounts: Senior & Junior
Driving Range: No
Junior Golf: Yes
Architect/Yr Open: George McDermott/1971
GPS:

A rustic, but interesting, layout. Number 3 is a fun par 5 with risk/reward chance for a birdie. Open March - December.

	1	2	3	4	5	6	7	8	9
PAR	4	4	5	3	5	4	4	3	4
YARDS	380	284	530	144	502	348	446	152	357
	10	11	12	13	14	15	16	17	18
PAR	4	4	4	3	4	5	3	4	4
YARDS	320	336	311	204	374	494	144	361	267

Directions: I-84 to Route 31 South; follow 4 miles. Course is on the right.

Villa Hills Par 3

NR 46

497 Middle Turnpike
Storrs, CT (860) 429-6421

Club Pro: Bernie Broder, owner
Payment: Cash, Visa, MC
Tee Times:
Fee 9 Holes: Weekday: $10
Fee 18 Holes: Weekday: $19
Twilight Rates: No
Cart Rental: $3/pull
Lessons: **Schools:** No
Membership:
Other: Restaurant/Snack Bar/Bar

Tees	Holes	Yards	Par	USGA	Slope
BACK					
MIDDLE	9	1158	27		
FRONT					

Weekend: $10
Weekend: $19
Discounts:
Driving Range:
Junior Golf: No
Architect/Yr Open: 1997
GPS:

Popular Par 3.

	1	2	3	4	5	6	7	8	9
PAR	3	3	3	3	3	3	3	3	3
YARDS	97	185	150	105	165	65	120	124	147
PAR									
YARDS									

Directions: I-384 to Route 44. Course is on left.

Vineyard Valley Golf Club

34 Brayman Hollow Road
Pomfret Center, CT (860) 974-2100
www.vineyardvalleygolfclub.com

Club Pro: Eric Sarette, PGA
Payment: Visa, MC, Amex, Disc
Tee Times: Yes

Tees	Holes	Yards	Par	USGA	Slope
BACK	9	3033	36	69.6	120
MIDDLE	9	2849	36	67.0	115
FRONT	9	2021	36	63.0	103

Fee 9 Holes: Weekday: $20   **Weekend:** $23
Fee 18 Holes: Weekday: $32   **Weekend:** $40
Twilight Rates: No
Discounts: Senior & Junior
Cart Rental: Included   **Driving Range:** Yes, grass
Lessons: $55/45 min. **Schools:**   **Junior Golf:** Yes
Membership: Yes   **Architect/Yr Open:**
Other: Restaurant / Snacks / Mulligan's Pub and Restaurant
GPS: Yes

COUPON

From hole #7, view of 4 states on a clear day. Adding drainage, irrigation and continuous improvements. #9 one of the area's top par 3s.

	1	2	3	4	5	6	7	8	9
PAR	5	3	4	4	4	5	4	4	3
YARDS	436	164	350	394	362	448	426	293	160
PAR									
YARDS									

Directions: From I-395 North/South, take Exit 97. Go West on Route 44 to Route 97 South. Take to Route 244 West. Course is .25 miles on left. From RI, take Route 44 West (same). From Hartford, I-84 East to Route 44 East. to Route 244 East, go 6 miles.

Westwoods Golf Course

Route 177
Farmington, CT (860) 675-2548
www.farmington.ct.org

Club Pro: Larry Graham, PGA
Payment: Most Major Credit Cards
Tee Times: Weekends, 7 days adv.

Tees	Holes	Yards	Par	USGA	Slope
BACK					
MIDDLE	18	4407	61	61.1	87
FRONT	18	3547	61	59.5	85

Fee 9 Holes: Weekday: $17.25   **Weekend:** $19.75
Fee 18 Holes: Weekday: $25.50   **Weekend:** $28
Twilight Rates: No   **Discounts:** Senior & Junior
Cart Rental: $29.68/18, $16.96/9 per cart **Driving Range:** Yes
Lessons: $60/hour, $40/half hour **Schools:** No **Junior Golf:** Yes
Membership: Yes   **Architect/Yr Open:** Geoffrey Cornish/1965
Other: Snack Bar / Bar-Lounge / Clubhouse / Restaurant / 20,000 sq. ft. Putting Green

Numerous par 3s make it an easy walker. Has some challenging water holes. Reduced rates for residents. League twilight play.

	1	2	3	4	5	6	7	8	9
PAR	5	3	3	3	4	3	3	4	3
YARDS	494	164	135	187	315	204	159	344	235
	10	11	12	13	14	15	16	17	18
PAR	4	3	3	4	3	4	3	3	3
YARDS	420	236	121	376	211	348	163	163	132

Directions: Take I-84 to Route 72 Plainville to Washington Street (177). Take right on 177 North. Follow 3 miles, cross Route 6 and then course is 200 yards on left.

Willimantic Country Club ✪✪½ ▶ 49

184 Club Road
Willimantic, CT (860) 456-1971
www.willigolf.com

Club Pro: Scott Potter, PGA
Payment: Visa, MC, Amex, Disc, Checks
Tee Times: M-Th, 7am-3pm

Tees	Holes	Yards	Par	USGA	Slope
BACK	18	6271	71	70.5	121
MIDDLE	18	6003	71	69.2	119
FRONT	18	5106	71	68.5	113

Fee 9 Holes: Weekday: $18
Fee 18 Holes: Weekday: $31
Twilight Rates: No
Cart Rental: $14pp/18, $8pp/9
Lessons: No **Schools:** No
Membership: Yes
Other: Full Restaurant / Clubhouse / Bar/Lounge / Lockers / Showers

Weekend: $20
Weekend: $36
Discounts: Jrs./Srs. $25/18 walking M-Th
Driving Range: No
Junior Golf: Yes
Architect/Yr Open: 1922

Open to public on weekdays and after 10am on weekends. Well worth the play. Play moves swiftly, long holes are compensated for by a number of short par 4s. Tee times required.

	1	2	3	4	5	6	7	8	9
PAR	4	4	4	4	4	5	3	4	4
YARDS	370	281	400	384	295	475	167	330	358
	10	11	12	13	14	15	16	17	18
PAR	3	4	4	5	4	5	3	4	3
YARDS	110	388	286	485	414	483	154	417	206

Directions: I-384 to Route 6 East. 11.6 miles to intersection of Route 6 and 66. Remain on Route 6 for 4.5 miles of Bypass Xpway. At end of bypass, turn left onto Route 66. Club is 1/2 mile on left.

Willow Brook Golf Course ✪✪ ▶ 50

124 Brookfield St.
South Windsor, CT (860) 648-2061
www.willowbrookgc.com

Club Pro: Jeff Bayer
Payment: Visa, MC
Tee Times:

Tees	Holes	Yards	Par	USGA	Slope
BACK	18	2985	60	56.2	79
MIDDLE	18	2613	60		
FRONT	18	2275	60		

Fee 9 Holes: Weekday: $13.50
Fee 18 Holes: Weekday: $26
Twilight Rates:
Cart Rental: $8pp/18, $4.50pp/9
Lessons: Yes **Schools:**
Membership:
Other: Restaurant / Bar / Snack Bar

Weekend: $15.50
Weekend: $28
Discounts: Senior & Junior
Driving Range: Yes
Junior Golf:
Architect/Yr Open: Joe Kelly/2002
GPS:

Par 60 with 6 par 4s. Player Comments: "Good for beginners. Intermediates can practice short game. Play 18 holes in 2.5 hours."

	1	2	3	4	5	6	7	8	9
PAR	3	3	4	3	3	4	4	3	3
YARDS	92	119	216	67	103	197	223	106	94
	10	11	12	13	14	15	16	17	18
PAR	3	4	3	4	3	3	3	3	4
YARDS	100	233	83	281	137	100	86	75	301

Directions: I-84 to Exit 62. Left off ramp onto Sullivan Road. Follow Sullivan 4 miles. Right onto Troy Street, then right on to Brookfield Street. Course is on the right.

Wintonbury Hills GC

◎◎◎◎ **51** ▶

206 Terry Plains Road
Bloomfield, CT (860) 242-1401
www.wintonburyhills.com

Tees	Holes	Yards	Par	USGA	Slope
BACK	18	6709	70	70.8	125
MIDDLE	18	6283	70	69.5	121
FRONT	18	5005	70	68.2	112

Club Pro: Doug Juhasz, dir. of golf
Payment: Visa, MC, Amex, Disc
Tee Times: 7 Days
Fee 9 Holes: Weekday:
Fee 18 Holes: Weekday: $69
Twilight Rates: After 2pm
Cart Rental: Included
Lessons: Yes **Schools:** Yes
Membership: Yes
Other: Bloomfield Resident Rates Available / GPS-Equipped Carts
GPS: Yes

Weekend:
Weekend: $79
Discounts: Sr. wkdy, Jr. wkdy/wknd
Driving Range: Yes
Junior Golf: Yes
Architect/Yr Open: Pete Dye & Tim Liddy/2003

Resident rates available. Playing conditions better than many private clubs. "Gorgeous holes, courteous staff, excellent condition." –RW "Has joined the ranks of New England's best." –JD

	1	2	3	4	5	6	7	8	9
PAR	4	4	3	5	4	4	3	5	3
YARDS	367	365	139	512	327	400	200	543	170
	10	**11**	**12**	**13**	**14**	**15**	**16**	**17**	**18**
PAR	4	4	3	5	4	4	4	3	4
YARDS	402	400	162	521	415	397	368	190	405

Directions: From East: I-291 West toward Windsor. Take Exit 1 – CT-218 West. Turn left onto CT-218 for 4 miles. Right onto Bloomfield Avenue/CT-189. Follow 189 until it turns right at a traffic light. DO NOT GO RIGHT, go straight onto Terry Plains Road. Follow Terry Plains Road. for 1 mile. See web for more.

Woodstock Golf Course

◎◎ **52** ▶

Roseland Golf Course
South Woodstock, CT
(860) 928-4130

Tees	Holes	Yards	Par	USGA	Slope
BACK					
MIDDLE	9	2413	34	32.6	107
FRONT	9	1822	34	66.8	103

Club Pro: Rob Moffa, PGA
Payment: Visa, MC, Amex
Tee Times: Weekend, holiday, 3 day adv.
Fee 9 Holes: Weekday: $13
Fee 18 Holes: Weekday: $20
Twilight Rates: No
Cart Rental: $11pp/18, $7pp/9
Lessons: Yes **Schools:** No
Membership: Yes
Other: Clubhouse / Snack Bar / Lockers / Showers

Weekend: $15
Weekend: $25
Discounts: Sr. & Jr. wkdys only
Driving Range: Yes
Junior Golf: Yes
Architect/Yr Open: 1896

Established 1896. Challenging, hilly course with small sloping greens. Target golf. Open April - November.

	1	2	3	4	5	6	7	8	9
PAR	3	4	4	4	4	4	3	4	4
YARDS	170	265	305	304	289	275	231	385	227
PAR									
YARDS									

Directions: I-395 to Route 44 (Exit 97). West on Route 44. Take Route 171 in Putnam, continue West. Follow 4.5 miles to Roseland Park Road, take right. Course 3/4 mile on left.

NE CT

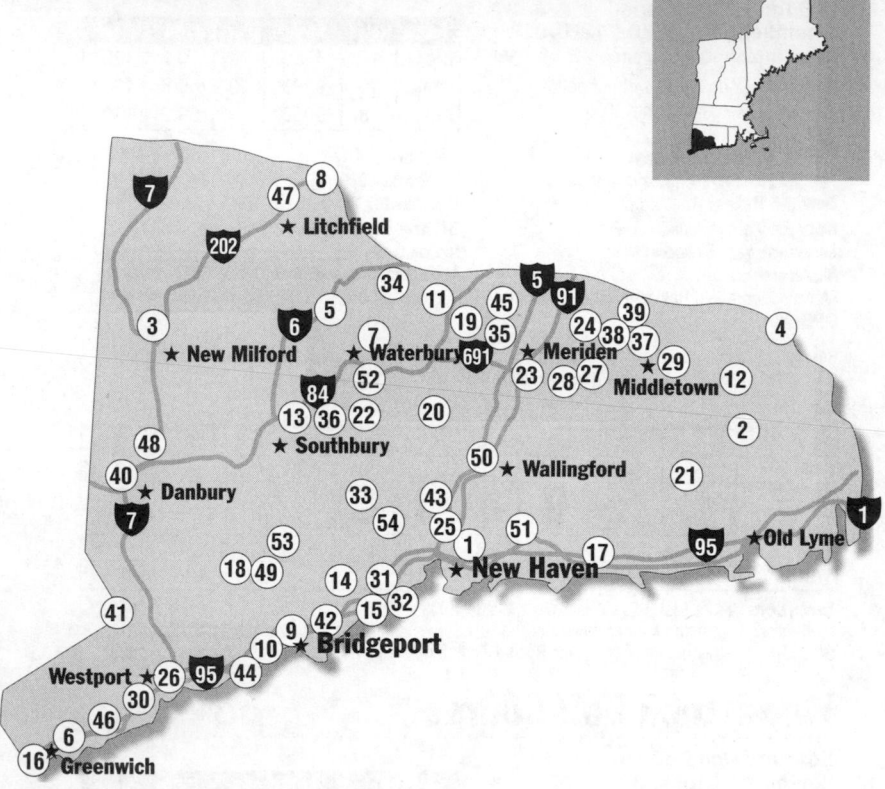

Alling Memorial GC	1	Hawk's Landing CC	19	Portland Golf Club	37
Banner Country Club	2	Highland Greens GC	20	Portland West Golf Club	38
Candlewood Valley CC	3	Hillside Links LLC	21	Quarry Ridge GC	39
Chanticlair Golf Course	4	Hop Brook CC	22	Richter Park GC	40
Crestbrook Park GC	5	Hunter Golf Club	23	Ridgefield Golf Club	41
E. Gaynor Brennan GC	6	Indian Springs GC	24	Short Beach Par 3 GC	42
East Mountain GC	7	Laurel View CC	25	Sleeping Giant GC	43
Eastwood CC	8	Longshore Park	26	South Pine Creek Par 3 GC	44
Fairchild Wheeler GC (Black)	9	Lyman Orchards GC (Jones)	27	Southington CC	45
Fairchild Wheeler GC (Red)	10	Lyman Orchards GC (Player)	28	Sterling Farms GC	46
Farmingbury Hills CC	11	Miner Hills Family Golf, LLC	29	Stonybrook GC	47
Fox Hopyard Country Club	12	Oak Hills Park G.C.	30	Sunset Hill GC	48
Gainfield Farms GC	13	Orange Hills CC	31	Tashua Knolls CC	49
Grassy Hill Country Club	14	Orchards Golf Course, The	32	Tradition GC at Wallingford	50
Great River Golf Club	15	Oxford Greens, The GC at	33	Twin Lakes GC	51
Griffith E. Harris GC	16	Pequabuck Golf Course	34	Western Hills GC	52
Guilford Lakes GC	17	Pine Valley Golf Course	35	Whitney Farms	53
H. Smith Richardson GC	18	Pomperaug Golf Club	36	Woodhaven CC	54

KEY TO THE STAR AND VALUE RATINGS:
5✪= Outstanding 4✪= Excellent 3✪= Very Good 2✪= Good 1✪= Average **NR** = Not Rated
EV = Excellent Value **GV** = Good Value **V** = Value

Alling Memorial Golf Course

NR

35 Eastern Street
New Haven, CT (203) 946-8014
www.allingmemorialgolfclub.com

Club Pro: Larry Thornhill, PGA
Payment: Cash, Visa, MC
Tee Times: Weekends, 3 day adv.

Tees	Holes	Yards	Par	USGA	Slope
BACK	18	6283	72	71.9	129
MIDDLE	18	5911	72	69.3	127
FRONT	18	5107	72	71.0	129

Fee 9 Holes: Weekday: $17 | **Weekend:** $18
Fee 18 Holes: Weekday: $25 | **Weekend:** $30
Twilight Rates: After 6pm | **Discounts:** Senior & Junior
Cart Rental: $26/18, $15/9 per cart | **Driving Range:** No
Lessons: Yes **Schools:** No | **Junior Golf:** Yes
Membership: Yes | **Architect/Yr Open:** McDonald/1929
Other: Lockers / Showers / Restaurant / Bar-Lounge

Appreciated by old, young, and new golfers alike. Excellent value for the money. Host to numerous CT state golf events. Resident rates.

	1	2	3	4	5	6	7	8	9
PAR	4	4	3	5	4	4	4	4	4
YARDS	380	313	168	474	231	344	366	274	305
	10	11	12	13	14	15	16	17	18
PAR	3	5	3	4	4	5	4	3	5
YARDS	158	475	180	337	408	493	331	203	471

Directions: I-91 to Exit 8, bear right to second light (Eastern Street), right 3/4 mile. Course on left.

Banner Country Club

⊙⊙

10 Banner Road
Moodus, CT (860) 873-9075
www.bannercountryclub.com

Club Pro: Bill Phaneuf
Payment: Cash, Check, MC, Visa, Amex, Disc
Tee Times: Call pro shop

Tees	Holes	Yards	Par	USGA	Slope
BACK					
MIDDLE	18	6015	72	68.9	118
FRONT	18	5776	74	73.7	123

Fee 9 Holes: Weekday: $12 | **Weekend:** $12
Fee 18 Holes: Weekday: $22 | **Weekend:** $22
Twilight Rates: | **Discounts:** Senior & Junior M-W
Cart Rental: $18/18, $8/9 per cart | **Driving Range:** $5/bucket
Lessons: $40/half hour **Schools:** Yes | **Junior Golf:** 11 and under free w/adult
Membership: Yes | **Architect/Yr Open:** Frank Gamberdella
Other: Clubhouse / Snack Bar / Restaurant | **GPS:**

COUPON

Course renamed in 2006. Management indicates many plans afoot including improved tees, fairways, and greens. Weekdays before noon, $30 for 18 holes with cart.

	1	2	3	4	5	6	7	8	9
PAR	4	4	4	4	3	5	5	3	4
YARDS	375	320	406	324	125	477	485	154	347
	10	11	12	13	14	15	16	17	18
PAR	5	4	4	4	4	3	5	3	4
YARDS	475	318	366	288	422	144	501	154	341

SW
CT

Directions: CT Route 9 to Exit 7; follow Route 82 East to Route 149 North. Continue to center of Moodus. Follow signs to course.

Candlewood Valley Country Club ✪✪

3

401 Danbury Road
New Milford, CT (860) 354-9359
www.candlewoodvalleygolf.com

Club Pro: Ed Slattery
Payment: Most Major
Tee Times: 4 days adv.

Tees	Holes	Yards	Par	USGA	Slope
BACK	18	6441	72	72.0	126
MIDDLE	18	6033	72	70.2	120
FRONT	18	5362	72	72.5	123

Fee 9 Holes: Weekday: **Weekend:**
Fee 18 Holes: Weekday: $35   **Weekend:** $42
Twilight Rates: After 3pm   **Discounts:** Senior & Junior
Cart Rental: $30/18, $16/9 per cart   **Driving Range:** No
Lessons: $45/half hour **Schools:** Yes   **Junior Golf:** Yes
Membership: Yes, Men's Club, Ladies' Club, Senior League
Architect/Yr Open: Cornish, Kay, & McNeil/1961
Other: Clubhouse / Lockers / Showers / Snack Bar / Restaurant / Bar-Lounge / Banquet Facilities

Take advantage of the Wednesday special: cart, 18 holes, lunch. Traps added. New cart paths.

	1	2	3	4	5	6	7	8	9
PAR	4	4	5	4	3	3	4	4	4
YARDS	301	315	448	370	152	160	350	447	402
	10	11	12	13	14	15	16	17	18
PAR	3	4	4	4	5	5	4	4	4
YARDS	210	413	390	418	530	459	366	386	316

Directions: I-84 to Exit 7 (Brookfield/ New Milford). Follow to end. Turn right at light onto Route 7 North. Follow 4.1 miles to CVCC on the right.

Chanticlair Golf Course   NR   **4**

Old Hebron Road
Colchester, CT (860) 537-3223

Club Pro: No
Payment: Cash, Visa, MC
Tee Times: 1 week adv.

Tees	Holes	Yards	Par	USGA	Slope
BACK					
MIDDLE	9	3061	35	69.8	117
FRONT	9	2501	35	69.1	112

Fee 9 Holes: Weekday: $17   **Weekend:** $18
Fee 18 Holes: Weekday: $26   **Weekend:** $27
Twilight Rates: No   **Discounts:** Senior & Junior
Cart Rental: $12pp/18, $6pp/9   **Driving Range:** No
Lessons: No **Schools:** No   **Junior Golf:** Yes
Membership: Yes   **Architect/Yr Open:** Hymie Stoloman/1973
Other: Clubhouse / Snacks / Beer / Soda   **GPS:**

The 4th hole has an elevated island green. Fairly flat; a good walking course.

	1	2	3	4	5	6	7	8	9
PAR	3	4	4	3	4	4	4	4	5
YARDS	205	390	375	138	387	385	350	380	451
	10	11	12	13	14	15	16	17	18
PAR									
YARDS									

Directions: Route 2 to State Police Barracks exit; take left off ramp and go up hill. Make left onto Old Hebron Road at firehouse. Course 1/4 mile on right.

Crestbrook Park Golf Course ✪✪½ 5

834 Northfield Road
Watertown, CT (860) 945-5249

Tees	Holes	Yards	Par	USGA	Slope
BACK	18	6915	71	73.6	128
MIDDLE	18	6098	71	69.9	121
FRONT	18	5696	75	73.8	128

Club Pro: Kenneth Gemmell, PGA
Payment: Cash Only
Tee Times: Weekends, 2 days adv.
Fee 9 Holes: Weekday: $19   **Weekend:** $21
Fee 18 Holes: Weekday: $33   **Weekend:** $36
Twilight Rates: No   **Discounts:** Senior & Junior M- F
Cart Rental: $14pp/18, $9/9   **Driving Range:** $6.50/lg, $5/md, $3.50/sm
Lessons: $35/half hour   **Schools:** No   **Junior Golf:** Yes
Membership: Yes   **Architect/Yr Open:** Geoffrey Cornish/1970
Other: Clubhouse / Snack Bar / Restaurant / Bar-Lounge / Pool / Tennis / Picnic

Player Comments: "Totally different 9s, front 9 tight, back 9 open and angled fairways." Cornish design. Resident rates.

	1	2	3	4	5	6	7	8	9
PAR	4	4	4	5	3	4	4	3	5
YARDS	370	447	411	515	152	384	405	194	536
	10	11	12	13	14	15	16	17	18
PAR	4	4	3	4	4	5	3	4	4
YARDS	357	401	160	337	333	463	210	308	393

Directions: Route 8 to Echo Lake Road (turn left). Take right at 2nd light (Buckingham); another right at stop sign (Northfield). Course is 1/4 mile on right on Northfield Road.

E. Gaynor Brennan Golf Course NR 6

451 Stillwater Road
Stamford, CT (203) 324-4185
www.brennangolf.com

Tees	Holes	Yards	Par	USGA	Slope
BACK	18	5931	71	69.5	121
MIDDLE	18	5814	71	68.0	118
FRONT	18	5180	73	72.3	124

Club Pro: V. Levin, A. Aulenti, golf dir.
Payment: Cash, Visa, MC
Tee Times: 7 days adv.
Fee 9 Holes: Weekday: $26   **Weekend:**
Fee 18 Holes: Weekday: $40   **Weekend:** $45
Twilight Rates: After 4pm   **Discounts:** Sr. & Jr., residents only
Cart Rental: $12.50pp/18, $8.50pp/9   **Driving Range:** No
Lessons: (203) 324-6507   **Schools:** No   **Junior Golf:** Yes
Membership: Yes   **Architect/Yr:** McCarthy, Gerrish/1925, Mungeum/1998
Other: Snack Bar / Restaurant / Bar-Lounge / Showers

The greens are usually in excellent condition. Course is a bit hilly. Open year round. Resident discounts and resident weekend lottery.

	1	2	3	4	5	6	7	8	9
PAR	4	4	3	5	4	5	4	4	3
YARDS	364	385	147	418	366	486	373	367	105
	10	11	12	13	14	15	16	17	18
PAR	4	4	4	3	4	3	4	5	4
YARDS	301	323	341	225	385	177	278	454	319

Directions: I-95 to Exit 7(Atlantic Street). Go straight. Right onto Washington Boulevard Left onto Broad Street. Go to Stillwater Road. Course is on Right.

**SW
CT**

East Mountain Golf Course

East Mountain Road
Waterbury, CT (203) 753-1425

Tees	Holes	Yards	Par	USGA	Slope
BACK	18	5817	67	68.0	114
MIDDLE	18	5591	68	66.9	112
FRONT	18	5211	67	70.7	119

Club Pro: Dave Giacondino
Payment: Most Major Credit Cards
Tee Times: Weekends, 3 days adv.
Fee 9 Holes: Weekday: $19
Fee 18 Holes: Weekday: $29
Twilight Rates: After 6pm
Cart Rental: $13.50pp/18, $8.50pp/9
Lessons: Yes **Schools:** No
Membership: Yes
Other: Bar-Lounge

Weekend: $20
Weekend: $31
Discounts: Senior & Junior
Driving Range: Yes
Junior Golf: Yes
Architect/Yr Open: Wayne Stiles/1932
GPS:

Landscaping improved throughout course. Special rate Tuesday-Thursday from 7-11am includes cart with 2 paid greens. Remodeled and renovated pro shop. Resident fees.

	1	2	3	4	5	6	7	8	9
PAR	4	4	4	3	4	5	4	3	4
YARDS	387	387	394	184	292	503	320	136	353
	10	11	12	13	14	15	16	17	18
PAR	4	3	4	4	3	4	4	3	4
YARDS	348	221	398	355	163	356	375	183	346

Directions: I-84 to Hamilton Avenue (Exit 23). Follow Route 69 West. Right onto East Mountain at Church.

Eastwood Country Club

1301 Torringford Street
Torrington, CT (860) 489-2630
www.playeastwood.com

Tees	Holes	Yards	Par	USGA	Slope
BACK	9	2933	36	67.8	113
MIDDLE	9	2791	36	66.5	111
FRONT	9	2359	36		

Club Pro: Greg Miller, PGA
Payment: Visa, MC, Amex
Tee Times: None
Fee 9 Holes: Weekday: $18
Fee 18 Holes: Weekday: $28
Twilight Rates: No
Cart Rental: $14pp/18, $8pp/9
Lessons: Yes **Schools:** No
Membership: Yes
Other: Restaurant / Clubhouse / Bar-Lounge

Weekend: $20
Weekend: $30
Discounts: Seniors & Juniors, weekdays
Driving Range: No
Junior Golf: Yes
Architect/Yr Open: 1963
GPS:

Open April - January. Greens in the best shape ever. "Course is in great condition and much improved." –SR Bunker renovation and new golf cart fleet. Course is in great shape and is much fun to play.

	1	2	3	4	5	6	7	8	9
PAR	4	4	4	5	4	3	4	3	5
YARDS	363	309	348	411	275	131	286	137	531
	10	11	12	13	14	15	16	17	18
PAR									
YARDS									

Directions: Route 8 to Exit 45. Go right off exit to Kennedy Drive. After 1 mile up hill to 4-way intersection. Left onto Torringford West Street. Course is 1 mile on left.

Fairchild Wheeler GC (Black)   ✪◑

2390 Eastern Turnpike
Fairfield, CT (203) 373-5911

Tees	Holes	Yards	Par	USGA	Slope
BACK	18	6559	71	72	128
MIDDLE	18	6322	71	71.0	119
FRONT	18	5234	72	70.0	119

Club Pro:
Payment: Visa, MC, Amex
Tee Times: 7 days adv.
Fee 9 Holes: Weekday: $18, $30 w/cart   **Weekend:** $24, $36 w/cart
Fee 18 Holes: Weekday: $28, $43 w/cart   **Weekend:** $35, $50 w/cart
Twilight Rates: After 5:30pm   **Discounts:** Residents
Cart Rental: $15pp/18, $12pp/9   **Driving Range:** Yes
Lessons: Yes, inquire **Schools:** No   **Junior Golf:** Yes
Membership: Yes   **Architect/Yr Open:** Robert White/1932
Other: Clubhouse / Snack Bar / Restaurant / Bar-Lounge / Lockers / Showers

Player Comments: "Solid course at relative bargain fees." "Remarkable improvements." Challenging course with some of the toughest par-4s around. Residents discount. Open year round.

	1	2	3	4	5	6	7	8	9
PAR	4	4	3	4	4	4	3	5	5
YARDS	405	377	128	367	321	432	212	431	500
	10	11	12	13	14	15	16	17	18
PAR	4	3	4	4	4	4	5	3	4
YARDS	417	153	407	421	314	418	512	191	396

Directions: Take Merritt Parkway (Route 15) Exit 46 to Route 59 South (Easton Turnpike). 1/2 mile on left.

Fairchild Wheeler GC (Red)   ✪✪½

2390 Eastern Turnpike
Fairfield, CT (203) 373-5911

Tees	Holes	Yards	Par	USGA	Slope
BACK	18	6568	72	72	125
MIDDLE	18	6126	72	71.3	124
FRONT	18	5330	72	68.7	117

Club Pro:
Payment: Visa, MC, Cash
Tee Times: Yes
Fee 9 Holes: Weekday: $18   **Weekend:** $24
Fee 18 Holes: Weekday: $28   **Weekend:** $34
Twilight Rates: After 5:30pm   **Discounts:** Senior & Junior
Cart Rental: $15pp/18, $12pp/9   **Driving Range:** Yes
Lessons: Inquire* **Schools:** No   **Junior Golf:** No
Membership: Yes   **Architect/Yr Open:** Robert White/1932
Other: Clubhouse / Snack Bar / Restaurant / Bar-Lounge / Lockers / Showers

Flat open course, good for beginners and seniors. Reduced rates for residents and other CT public course passholders. Open all year. Links-style course. *Lessons available from First Tee Corp.

	1	2	3	4	5	6	7	8	9
PAR	4	4	5	3	4	4	4	3	4
YARDS	440	402	480	127	308	412	337	190	387
	10	11	12	13	14	15	16	17	18
PAR	5	4	3	4	4	3	4	5	5
YARDS	504	419	106	422	304	202	340	501	472

Directions: Take Merritt Parkway (Route 15) Exit 46 to Route 59 South (Easton Turnpike). 1/2 mile on left.

Farmingbury Hills Country Club NR

141 East Street, Wolcott, CT
(203) 879-8038

Club Pro: Craig Kealey, PGA
Payment: Cash, Visa, MC
Tee Times: Weekends, 7 days adv.
Fee 9 Holes: Weekday: $19
Fee 18 Holes: Weekday: $28
Twilight Rates:
Cart Rental: $19pp/18, $10pp/9
Lessons: $30/half hour **Schools:** No
Membership: No
Other: Bar-Lounge / Restaurant

Tees	Holes	Yards	Par	USGA	Slope
BACK					
MIDDLE	9	2996	35	68.7	117
FRONT	9	2678	36	71.0	120

Weekend: $21
Weekend: $30
Discounts: Senior & Junior
Driving Range: Yes
Junior Golf: Yes
Architect/Yr Open:
GPS:

9-hole special: 7-8am, 12-1:30pm weekdays; 1-5:30pm weekends. Course is in great shape!

	1	2	3	4	5	6	7	8	9
PAR	4	4	4	4	4	3	4	3	5
YARDS	340	419	310	373	321	102	401	190	510
PAR									
YARDS									

Directions: I-84 to Cheshire Exit 28. Route 322 West, left up Southington Mountain. Right at top of hill, blinking light (East Street). Course is 1 mile on right.

Fox Hopyard Country Club ✪✪✪✪ 12

1 Hopyard Road
East Haddam, CT (860) 434-6644
www.golfthefox.com

Club Pro: Ron Beck, PGA
Payment: Visa, MC, Amex, Disc, Checks, Cash
Tee Times: 6 days adv.
Fee 9 Holes: Weekday: $45
Fee 18 Holes: Weekday: $89
Twilight Rates: Yes
Cart Rental: $21pp/18, $12pp/9
Lessons: $50/half hour **Schools:** Yes
Membership: Yes
Other: Restaurant / Bar-Lounge / Clubhouse / Showers / Lockers

Tees	Holes	Yards	Par	USGA	Slope
BACK	18	6512	71	72.6	131
MIDDLE	18	6109	71	70.7	124
FRONT	18	5111	71	70.7	123

Weekend: $50
Weekend: $99
Discounts: Junior
Driving Range: Yes
Junior Golf: Yes
Architect/Yr Open: Roger Rulewich, 2001

COUPON

Player Comments: " Great layout in unspoiled surroundings. Many memorable holes." "Sister course to Crumpin-Fox in MA. Wide fairways. Shots to the greens are high on risk and reward." –RW

	1	2	3	4	5	6	7	8	9
PAR	4	4	5	3	5	4	4	3	4
YARDS	356	358	457	172	464	320	366	160	350
	10	11	12	13	14	15	16	17	18
PAR	4	3	4	4	3	5	3	4	5
YARDS	382	153	372	408	188	508	189	399	507

Directions: From I-95 North, take Exit 70 (Old Lyme). Go left onto Route 156 for 9 miles. Right onto Route 82 and take first left onto Hopyard. Accessible from I-91 to Route 2 to Route 11. Call for directions from I-95 South and Route 9.

Gainfield Farms Golf Course

NR 13

255 Old Field Road
Southbury, CT (203) 262-1100

Tees	Holes	Yards	Par	USGA	Slope
BACK					
MIDDLE	9	1384	28		
FRONT	9	1203	27		

Club Pro: Bert Boyce, PGA
Payment: Cash, Check, Credit
Tee Times: Yes
Fee 9 Holes: Weekday: $16
Fee 18 Holes: Weekday: $26
Twilight Rates: No
Cart Rental: $28pp/18, $14pp/9
Lessons: Yes **Schools:** No
Membership:
Other: Snacks

Weekend: $17
Weekend: $28
Discounts: Senior, Junior, Ladies
Driving Range: Mat and net
Junior Golf: Yes
Architect/Yr Open: Al Zikorus/1993
GPS:

Executive style, resident discounts.

	1	2	3	4	5	6	7	8	9
PAR	3	4	3	3	3	3	3	3	3
YARDS	155	261	188	123	113	94	195	127	128
PAR									
YARDS									

Directions: I-84 to Exit 15, follow signs.

Grassy Hill Country Club

NR 14

441 Clark Lane
Orange, CT (203) 795-1422
www.grassyhillgolf.com

Tees	Holes	Yards	Par	USGA	Slope
BACK	18	6118	70	70.5	122
MIDDLE	18	5849	70	69.4	119
FRONT	18	5209	71	71.1	118

Club Pro: Brian Fitzgibbons, PGA
Payment: Visa, MC
Tee Times: 7 wkdys, 3 wknds
Fee 9 Holes: Weekday: $21
Fee 18 Holes: Weekday: $36
Twilight Rates: No
Cart Rental:
Lessons: $65/45 minutes **Schools:**
Membership: Men/Women Association
Other: Full Restaurant / Clubhouse / Bar-Lounge / Lockers / Showers

Weekend: $25
Weekend: $45
Discounts: Senior (M-F)
Driving Range: $5/lg
Junior Golf: Yes
Architect/Yr Open: 1927

Working to restore excellent conditions of fairways and greens.

	1	2	3	4	5	6	7	8	9
PAR	4	4	3	4	5	3	4	4	5
YARDS	385	410	158	301	563	145	363	360	432
	10	11	12	13	14	15	16	17	18
PAR	3	4	4	3	4	4	5	3	4
YARDS	109	384	277	175	319	421	496	165	326

Directions: I-95 to exit 39A. Turn right, pass Howard Johnson's. At second dual traffic light, turn right. 2-1/2 miles to Clark Lane. Turn right to Grassy Hill.

SW
CT

Great River Golf Club ✪✪✪✪ 15 ▶

130 Coram Lane
Milford, CT (203) 876-8051
www.greatrivergolfclub.com

Tees	Holes	Yards	Par	USGA	Slope
BACK	18	6901	72	73.8	149
MIDDLE	18	6475	72	71.6	137
FRONT	18	5865	72	69.4	124

Club Pro: Tom Rosati, PGA
Payment: Most Major
Tee Times: 5 days adv.
Fee 9 Holes: Weekday: $50 after 5pm **Weekend:**
Fee 18 Holes: Weekday: $110 M-TH **Weekend:** $130 F/S/S
Twilight Rates: Yes **Discounts:** None
Cart Rental: Included **Driving Range:** Yes
Lessons: $90-$120/45 min **Schools:** Yes **Junior Golf:** Yes
Membership: Yes **Architect/Yr Open:** Tommy Fazio/2000
Other: Restaurant / Outdoor Dining / Beverage Cart/ Snak Bar/ Clubhouse / Lockers / Showers /
Bar-Lounge / Indoor Learning Center / Conference Room, Banquet Facility 150+

Player Comments: "Excellent player's course." "2 times on vacations, everything was perfect." "Best public course I've played in CT." Semi-private. Golf Academy open all year.

	1	2	3	4	5	6	7	8	9
PAR	3	4	4	5	4	3	4	5	4
YARDS	166	394	404	513	379	144	391	520	358
	10	11	12	13	14	15	16	17	18
PAR	3	4	4	5	4	3	4	5	4
YARDS	337	187	501	388	359	484	405	181	364

Directions: I-95 to Exit 38 bearing right, go to Wheeler Farms Road, turn left. Turn left at Herbert Street. Turn left on Coram Lane, course is at end of lane. Call for directions from Hartford or NY via Wilbur Cross / Merritt Parkway and from 95 North.

Griffith E. Harris Golf Course ✪✪   16 ▶

1300 King Street
Greenwich, CT, (203) 531-7261
www.greenwichct.org

Tees	Holes	Yards	Par	USGA	Slope
BACK	18	6512	71	71.0	125
MIDDLE	18	6093	71	69.0	122
FRONT	18	5671	73	67.1	114

Club Pro: Joe Felder, PGA
Payment: Visa, MC, Checks
Tee Times: Same day for non-members
Fee 9 Holes: Weekday: $50 **Weekend:** $50
Fee 18 Holes: Weekday: $50 **Weekend:** $50
Twilight Rates: After 5pm **Discounts:** Senior & Junior
Cart Rental: $14pp/18, $9.50pp/9 **Driving Range:** $10/lg., $5/sm.
Lessons: Yes **Schools:** Yes **Junior Golf:** Yes
Membership: Town residents **Architect/Yr Open:** Robert Trent Jones/1965
Other: Full Restaurant / Clubhouse / Bar / Lockers / Showers

Restaurant renovated. Open to residents of town who are members and guests only. Front side fairly open and flat. Back side narrow and hilly. Open April 1 - December 1. Resident fee offered. New irrigation system.

	1	2	3	4	5	6	7	8	9
PAR	4	4	5	4	3	4	3	5	4
YARDS	407	365	503	378	169	437	138	519	323
	10	11	12	13	14	15	16	17	18
PAR	4	3	4	4	5	3	4	4	4
YARDS	291	198	310	380	448	140	251	426	310

Directions: Merritt Parkway South to King Street. Right turn approximately 3 miles to golf course on right. Any questions, call (203) 531-7200.

Guilford Lakes Golf Course ○○½

200 North Madison Road
Guilford, CT (203) 453-8214
www.guilfordlakesgc.com

Club Pro: Bill Fitzhenry
Payment: Visa, MC, Disc
Tee Times: 3 days adv.
Fee 9 Holes: Weekday: $14
Fee 18 Holes: Weekday: $28
Twilight Rates: No
Cart Rental: $2.75/pull
Lessons: Yes **Schools:** No
Membership: Yes
Other: Snacks / New Clubhouse Now Open

Tees	Holes	Yards	Par	USGA	Slope
BACK	9	1319	27		
MIDDLE	9	1165	27		
FRONT	9	739	27		

Weekend: $16
Weekend: $32
Discounts: Senior & Junior
Driving Range: No
Junior Golf: Park and Rec.
Architect/Yr Open: Al Zikorus/1999
GPS:

Player Comments: "Polished and professionally designed." –RW Reduced resident fees. Heavily tree-lined, gentle and hilly. Challenging for both beginner and intermediate.

	1	2	3	4	5	6	7	8	9
PAR	3	3	3	3	3	3	3	3	3
YARDS	135	111	130	122	105	180	155	79	148
PAR									
YARDS									

Directions: I-95, Exit 58 onto Route 77. North on Route 77, turn right onto Stepstone Hill Road. Straight to North Madison Road. Course is on the left.

H. Smith Richardson GC ○○○

2425 Morehouse Highway
Fairfield, CT (203) 255-7300
www.hsrgolf.com

Club Pro: Jim Alexander, PGA
Payment: Most Major Credit Cards
Tee Times: Weekends, 3 days adv.
Fee 9 Holes: Weekday: $26
Fee 18 Holes: Weekday: $38
Twilight Rates: No
Cart Rental: $26pp/18, $17pp/9
Lessons: Schools: No
Membership: Yes
Other: Lockers / Showers / Restaurant / Bar-Lounge

Tees	Holes	Yards	Par	USGA	Slope
BACK	18	6676	72	71.0	127
MIDDLE	18	6323	72	70.2	124
FRONT	18	5764	73	73.9	127

Weekend: $26
Weekend: $50
Discounts: Senior & Junior
Driving Range: Yes
Junior Golf: Yes
Architect/Yr Open: Hal Purdy/1972

This scenic, hilly course has a majestic view of Long Island Sound. Slopes on greens make putting challenging. Closed March. Discounted rates for shared carts.

	1	2	3	4	5	6	7	8	9
PAR	4	4	3	4	4	5	4	3	5
YARDS	375	310	160	339	397	503	383	180	486
	10	**11**	**12**	**13**	**14**	**15**	**16**	**17**	**18**
PAR	4	4	3	5	4	4	3	4	5
YARDS	373	351	176	502	405	350	140	373	520

Directions: From North: Merritt Parkway to Exit 44 to Black Rock Turnpike, take right on Congress Road, second left onto Morehouse. Course is half mile.
From South: Merritt Parkway to Exit 46, take left onto Congress Road, right on Morehouse Road.

Hawk's Landing Country Club ✪✪ 19

201 Pattonwood Drive
Southington, CT (860) 793-6000
www.hawkslandingcc.com

Club Pro: John Vitale
Payment: Visa, MC, Check
Tee Times: Weekends, 7 days adv.

Tees	Holes	Yards	Par	USGA	Slope
BACK	18	5825	70	68.6	124
MIDDLE	18	5365	70	66.4	119
FRONT	18	4015	71	63.9	106

Fee 9 Holes: Weekday: $18.50
Fee 18 Holes: Weekday: $32
Twilight Rates: After 6pm wkdys, 4pm wknds
Cart Rental: $28pp/18, $16pp/9
Lessons: Yes **Schools:** Yes
Membership: Yes
Other: Clubhouse / Bar-Lounge / Restaurant / Snack Bar

Weekend: $22
Weekend: $36
Discounts: Senior & Junior
Driving Range: Yes, grass tee
Junior Golf: Yes
Architect/Yr Open: Cornish/1967

COUPON

A full-service restaurant, a chipping and putting practice area, and a pavillion area perfect for meetings and weddings.

	1	2	3	4	5	6	7	8	9
PAR	4	3	5	4	4	4	3	4	3
YARDS	265	170	420	290	340	280	220	325	175
	10	11	12	13	14	15	16	17	18
PAR	4	4	3	5	4	5	3	5	3
YARDS	385	275	150	450	385	450	160	450	165

Directions: I-84 to Exit 32. Turn South onto Queen Street (Route 10), quick left onto Laning. Left onto Flanders and first left onto Pattonwood Drive.

Highland Greens Golf Course NR 20

122 Cooke Road
Prospect, CT (203) 758-4022
www.highlandgreens.com

Club Pro: No
Payment: Cash, Visa, MC
Tee Times: Same day

Tees	Holes	Yards	Par	USGA	Slope
BACK					
MIDDLE	9	1398	27		
FRONT	9	1322	27		

Fee 9 Holes: Weekday: $13
Fee 18 Holes: Weekday: $21
Twilight Rates: After 6:30pm
Cart Rental: $3/pull
Lessons: Yes **Schools:** No
Membership: Yes
Other: Snack Bar / Restaurant / Pub

Weekend: $14
Weekend: $22
Discounts: Senior
Driving Range: No
Junior Golf: Yes
Architect/Yr Open: Al Zikorus/1967
GPS:

Completely lighted for night play. Nightly rate after 6:30pm $15 for 9 holes. Slightly hilly. A lot of improvement made to the grounds. A challenging par 3, open April - first frost.

	1	2	3	4	5	6	7	8	9
PAR	3	3	3	3	3	3	3	3	3
YARDS	132	192	115	135	188	185	157	128	166
	10	11	12	13	14	15	16	17	18
PAR									
YARDS									

Directions: Take I-84 to Exit 26 to Route 70 East to Route 68 West. At top of hill, left onto Cooke Road. Course is 1.6 miles on right.

Hillside Links LLC

97 Lords Lane
Deep River, CT (860) 526-8893

Club Pro: Mark Erwin, Pro
Payment: Cash Only
Tee Times: Weekends/holidays
Fee 9 Holes: Weekday: $10
Fee 18 Holes: Weekday: $16
Twilight Rates:
Cart Rental: $2/pull
Lessons: Group & private **Schools:** No
Membership: Multi-Play Pass
Other: Golf Balls / Hats / Soda

Tees	Holes	Yards	Par	USGA	Slope
BACK					
MIDDLE	9	932	27		
FRONT					

Weekend: $11
Weekend: $17
Discounts: Senior 7 days $1 off
Driving Range:
Junior Golf: No
Architect/Yr Open: Don Carlson/1994
GPS:

COUPON

A challenging Par 3 walking course with sand and water. The feel of a full-size course on a small scale. Good for family fun. Spectators not allowed.

	1	2	3	4	5	6	7	8	9
PAR	3	3	3	3	3	3	3	3	3
YARDS	73	82	97	115	96	131	164	71	103
PAR									
YARDS									

Directions: Route 9 to Route 80 East and turn onto Hillside Terrace. Follow road to end.

Hop Brook Country Club

615 North Church Street
Naugatuck, CT (203) 729-8013

Club Pro: No
Payment: Cash, Check, Credit Card
Tee Times: Weekends, 2 days adv.
Fee 9 Holes: Weekday: $18
Fee 18 Holes: Weekday: $26
Twilight Rates: No
Cart Rental: $15pp/18, $10pp/9
Lessons: No **Schools:** No
Membership: Yes
Other: Clubhouse / Restaurant

Tees	Holes	Yards	Par	USGA	Slope
BACK	9	3047	36	68.2	116
MIDDLE	9	2862	36	66.6	112
FRONT	9	2413	36	67.0	114

Weekend: $23
Weekend: $31
Discounts: Sr. & Jr. weekdays
Driving Range: No
Junior Golf: Yes
Architect/Yr Open: 1927
GPS:

The course is short and turns hilly near the end. Substantial discounts for residents. Open March - December. Senior tees now on every hole. Female Senior Tees on 4 holes (Blue and White).

	1	2	3	4	5	6	7	8	9
PAR	5	4	4	4	3	5	3	4	4
YARDS	452	325	320	304	135	476	170	382	298
	10	11	12	13	14	15	16	17	18
PAR									
YARDS									

Directions: I-84 to Exit 17 to Route 63. Course is 3 miles down on left.

Hunter Golf Club

●●● 23

685 Westfield Road
Meriden, CT (203) 634-3366
www.huntergolfshop.com

Tees	Holes	Yards	Par	USGA	Slope
BACK	18	6604	71	71.9	124
MIDDLE	18	6198	71	70.2	121
FRONT	18	5569	72	72.7	131

Club Pro: Tex Kane, PGA
Payment: Cash, Credit
Tee Times: Yes
Fee 9 Holes: Weekday: $20　**Weekend:** $21
Fee 18 Holes: Weekday: $35　**Weekend:** $38
Twilight Rates: 90 minutes before dusk　**Discounts:** Sr. & Jr. weekdays
Cart Rental: $15pp/18, $9pp/9　**Driving Range:** Irons only
Lessons: Yes **Schools:** No　**Junior Golf:** Yes
Membership: Season Pass　**Architect/Yr Open:** Robert Pryde
Other: Clubhouse / Lockers / Showers / Snack Bar / Restaurant / Bar-Lounge

Open year round, weather permitting. Resident rates. "Greens and bunkers in great shape. If you haven't been here in awhile, it's worth a revisit." -DA

	1	2	3	4	5	6	7	8	9
PAR	4	3	4	4	5	3	4	4	4
YARDS	352	183	395	326	497	147	415	400	353

	10	11	12	13	14	15	16	17	18
PAR	5	3	4	4	4	4	4	3	5
YARDS	516	163	357	336	364	374	361	172	487

Directions: From I-91 South: Exit 19. Right off ramp to first stop sign. Right on Bee Street, course 1/2 mile on left. From I-91 North or Merritt Parkway North: Take East Main Street exit. Go straight through light onto Bee Street. Course 2 miles on left.

Indian Springs Golf Course

NR 24

132 Mack Road
Middlefield, CT (860) 349-8109
www.indiansprings-golf.com

Tees	Holes	Yards	Par	USGA	Slope
BACK					
MIDDLE	9	3000	36	68.9	116
FRONT	9	2616	36	73.0	127

Club Pro:
Payment: Cash, Credit Cards
Tee Times: Weekends only
Fee 9 Holes: Weekday: $16　**Weekend:** $18
Fee 18 Holes: Weekday: $29　**Weekend:** $33
Twilight Rates: No　**Discounts:** Senior & Junior
Cart Rental: $14pp/18, $7pp/9　**Driving Range:** $9/lg, $5/sm
Lessons: Variable **Schools:** Yes　**Junior Golf:** Yes
Membership: Yes　**Architect/Yr Open:** 1964
Other: Snack Bar / Bar-Lounge / Restaurant　**GPS:**

COUPON

Family-run golf course where you'll feel welcome. Jane's perennial flower gardens are a must-see, as well. Great for beginners and intermediates.

	1	2	3	4	5	6	7	8	9
PAR	4	5	3	4	5	4	3	4	4
YARDS	345	455	130	370	560	300	170	355	315

	10	11	12	13	14	15	16	17	18
PAR									
YARDS									

Directions: I-91 North to Exit 18 (Route 66) toward Middletown. At light, take a right onto Route 147. Take 1st left onto Way Road. Follow signs to course. Take I-91 South to Exit 19, left at stop sign. Take a right at light onto Route 147. Go 2 miles onto Way Road. Follow signs to course.

Laurel View Country Club   ✪✪   25 ▶

West Shepard Avenue
Hamden, CT (203) 287-2656
www.laurelviewcc.com

Club Pro: Edward Grant, PGA
Payment: Visa, MC
Tee Times: Weekends, 3 days adv.

Tees	Holes	Yards	Par	USGA	Slope
BACK	18	6899	72	74.3	135
MIDDLE	18	6372	72	72.1	131
FRONT	18	5558	73	71.8	130

Fee 9 Holes: Weekday: $20   **Weekend:** $22
Fee 18 Holes: Weekday: $31   **Weekend:** $35
Twilight Rates: No   **Discounts:** Senior & Junior
Cart Rental: $15pp/18, $9pp/9   **Driving Range:** $5/lg
Lessons: $40/half hour **Schools:** No   **Junior Golf:** Yes
Membership: Yes, residents   **Architect/Yr Open:** Cornish & Robinson/1969
Other: Clubhouse / Lockers / Showers / Snack Bar / Restaurant / Bar-Lounge

This Cornish course requires smart course managaement; hilly terrain provides interesting challenge. Open April 1 - December 1. Many favorable comments. Greatly improved fairways, greens, bunkers and tees.

	1	2	3	4	5	6	7	8	9
PAR	4	3	4	5	4	4	3	5	4
YARDS	330	132	390	505	435	310	230	510	420
	10	11	12	13	14	15	16	17	18
PAR	4	5	3	4	5	4	4	3	4
YARDS	320	560	155	280	470	380	390	160	395

Directions: I-91 to Exit 10, take left at the end of the ramp. At first light take left, right at next light (Dixwell Avenue). Through center of town, pass Town Hall on the right. 3/4 mile, take right (Shephard Avenue). Through 5 lights, take left (W. Shephard). Course 3/4 mile on left.

Longshore Park   NR   26 ▶

South Compo Road
Westport, CT (203) 341-1833

Club Pro: John Cooper, PGA
Payment: Visa, MC, Cash, Check
Tee Times: 3 days adv.

Tees	Holes	Yards	Par	USGA	Slope
BACK	18	5845	69	67.4	115
MIDDLE	18	5676	69	66.7	113
FRONT	18	5227	73	69.9	119

Fee 9 Holes: Weekday: $32 M-Th   **Weekend:** $37 F/S/S/H
Fee 18 Holes: Weekday: $44 M-Th   **Weekend:** $50 F/S/S/H
Twilight Rates: No   **Discounts:** None
Cart Rental: $15pp/18, $7.50pp/9   **Driving Range:** Yes
Lessons: Yes **Schools:** No   **Junior Golf:** Yes
Membership: No   **Architect/Yr Open:** Orrin E. Smith
Other: Snack Bar / Restaurant / Bar-Lounge   **GPS:**

Good course for beginners and intermediates. Course has been completely renovated.

	1	2	3	4	5	6	7	8	9
PAR	4	3	4	4	4	4	5	3	4
YARDS	341	146	390	287	296	413	520	127	346
	10	11	12	13	14	15	16	17	18
PAR	5	3	4	3	4	3	4	4	4
YARDS	459	192	289	189	401	100	383	344	397

**SW
CT**

Directions: I-95 to Exit 18 to U.S. Route 1, left at 2nd light, Green Farms Road. Follow to next light, take left onto Compo. Course is on right.

Lyman Orchards GC (Player)

Route 157
Middlefield, CT (860) 349-1793
www.lymanorchards.com

Tees	Holes	Yards	Par	USGA	Slope
BACK	18	6725	71	73.1	134
MIDDLE	18	6325	71	71.3	131
FRONT	18	5763	71	68.1	129

Club Pro: Jason Beffert
Payment: Visa, MC, Amex, Disc
Tee Times: 7 days adv. (888) 99Lyman
Fee 9 Holes: Weekday: $29 w/cart
Fee 18 Holes: Weekday: $49 w/cart
Twilight Rates: After 1:30pm
Cart Rental: Included
Lessons: $75/45 min. **Schools:** Yes
Membership: Yes
Other: Clubhouse / Lockers / Showers / Snack Bar / Restaurant / Bar-Lounge

Weekend: $31 w/cart
Weekend: $60 w/cart F, $65 w/cart S/S/H
Discounts: Senior & Junior M-Th
Driving Range: $7/lg., $4/md.
Junior Golf: Yes
Architect/Yr Open: Gary Player/1994

Player Comments: "Beautiful layout, stresses good shot making." "Great variety. Demands that you maintain focus for all 18 holes." –JD
Designed by Gary Player. Play all 36—make a day of it. M-Th Early Bird before 8am. Open March - November.

	1	2	3	4	5	6	7	8	9
PAR	4	4	4	3	4	4	3	5	4
YARDS	400	367	374	173	386	342	191	578	381
	10	11	12	13	14	15	16	17	18
PAR	4	3	4	3	5	4	3	5	5
YARDS	348	211	427	181	473	306	165	520	502

Directions: I-91 to Exit 15 (Route 68 East). Left onto Route 157. Course is 1 mile on the right.

Lyman Orchards GC (Jones)

Route 157
Middlefield, CT (860) 349-1793
www.lymanorchards.com

Tees	Holes	Yards	Par	USGA	Slope
BACK	18	7011	72	73.3	132
MIDDLE	18	6614	72	69.6	128
FRONT	18	6200	72	72.0	124

Club Pro: Jason Beffert
Payment: Visa, MC, Amex, Disc
Tee Times: 7 days adv. (888) 99Lyman
Fee 9 Holes: Weekday: $29 w/cart
Fee 18 Holes: Weekday: $49 w/cart
Twilight Rates: After 1:30pm
Cart Rental: Included
Lessons: $75/45 min. **Schools:** Yes
Membership: Yes
Other: Clubhouse / Lockers / Showers / Snack Bar / Restaurant / Bar-Lounge

Weekend: $31 w/cart
Weekend: $60 w/cart F, $65 w/cart S/S/H
Discounts: Senior & Junior M-Th
Driving Range: $7/lg., $4/md.
Junior Golf: Yes
Architect/Yr Open: Robert Trent Jones Jr./1967

Each hole designed by Robert Trent Jones Jr. to be a demanding par or a comfortable bogey. Bent grass fairways and Penn Cross tees and greens. M-Th Early Bird before 7:30am.

	1	2	3	4	5	6	7	8	9
PAR	4	3	4	5	4	4	3	4	5
YARDS	416	175	374	552	390	350	175	373	548
	10	11	12	13	14	15	16	17	18
PAR	4	3	5	4	4	4	4	3	5
YARDS	399	152	490	370	388	382	403	162	515

Directions: I-91 to Exit 15 (Route 68 East). Left onto Route 157. Course is 1 mile on the right.

Miner Hills Family Golf ✪✪

29

80 Miner Hills Drive
Middletown, CT (860) 635-0051

Tees	Holes	Yards	Par	USGA	Slope
BACK					
MIDDLE	9	1769	30	59.1	97
FRONT	9	1292	30	59.5	80

Club Pro: George Claffey
Payment: Cash, Check
Tee Times: Available
Fee 9 Holes: Weekday: $12   **Weekend:** $14
Fee 18 Holes: Weekday: $18   **Weekend:** $20 Sat, $25 Sun
Twilight Rates: Yes   **Discounts:** Senior & Junior
Cart Rental: $24pp/18, $12pp/9   **Driving Range:** Yes
Lessons: Yes **Schools:** 3 per year   **Junior Golf:** No
Membership: Season Passes   **Architect/Yr Open:** John S. Oot/1993
Other: Clubhouse / Snack Bar / Tournament & Banquet Facilities

COUPON

"A delightful surprise with several interesting holes. A great executive layout and well-maintained" –AP
Open March 25 until weather permits. Middletown, CT's only golf course! 30 minutes from downtown
Hartford and New Haven, CT.

	1	2	3	4	5	6	7	8	9
PAR	3	3	4	4	3	3	4	3	3
YARDS	160	150	298	253	173	210	260	120	145
PAR									
YARDS									

Directions: I-91 to Exit 20. Westfield district of Middletown, CT.

Oak Hills Park Golf Course   NR   **30**

165 Fillow Street
Norwalk, CT (203) 853-8400
www.oakhillsgc.com

Tees	Holes	Yards	Par	USGA	Slope
BACK	18	6307	71	70.5	126
MIDDLE	18	5920	71	68.5	123
FRONT	18	5221	72	70.7	124

Club Pro: Vincent Grillo, PGA
Payment: Cash, Visa, MC, Amex
Tee Times: Yes
Fee 9 Holes: Weekday: $30   **Weekend:** $30
Fee 18 Holes: Weekday: $46   **Weekend:** $50
Twilight Rates: After 4pm   **Discounts:** Sr. & Jr. residents M-F
Cart Rental: $15pp/18   **Driving Range:** No
Lessons: Yes **Schools:** Yes   **Junior Golf:** No
Membership: For residents   **Architect/Yr Open:** Alfred Tull/1969
Other: Snack Bar / Restaurant   **GPS:**

New clubhouse opened in May 2005.

	1	2	3	4	5	6	7	8	9
PAR	4	4	3	4	3	4	4	5	4
YARDS	374	295	109	307	174	284	336	484	440
	10	11	12	13	14	15	16	17	18
PAR	5	4	5	3	4	3	4	4	4
YARDS	528	365	501	154	386	205	342	336	300

SW
CT

Directions: I-95, Exit 13. Right turn onto Route 1. Left onto Richards Avenue; right turn onto Fillow
to Oak Hills Park.

Orange Hills Country Club ✪✪½ ▶ 31

389 Racebrook Road
Orange, CT (203) 795-4161
www.orangehillscountryclub.com

Club Pro: Kevin Mahaffy
Payment: Visa, MC
Tee Times: M-F 7 days, S/S 3 days
Fee 9 Holes: Weekday: $22
Fee 18 Holes: Weekday: $38
Twilight Rates: No
Cart Rental: $15pp/18, $8pp/9
Lessons: Yes **Schools:** No
Membership: No

Tees	Holes	Yards	Par	USGA	Slope
BACK	18	6519	71	72.3	126
MIDDLE	18	6111	71	70.6	119
FRONT	18	5616	74	71.5	120

Weekend: $26
Weekend: $48
Discounts: None
Driving Range: No
Junior Golf: Yes
Architect/Yr Open: Cornish/1961

Other: Clubhouse / Snack Bar / Bar-Lounge / Restaurant

Course is hilly with a tight back 9. Call for directions from Hartford. Collared shirts and soft spikes required. No denim allowed. Newly lengthened 16th tee.

	1	2	3	4	5	6	7	8	9
PAR	4	5	3	4	4	4	4	4	3
YARDS	390	481	148	435	349	365	399	300	134
	10	11	12	13	14	15	16	17	18
PAR	3	5	4	3	4	4	4	4	5
YARDS	207	466	365	153	377	339	331	413	459

Directions: Merritt Parkway: Exit 57, 2 lights to Route 114, right onto Route 114, 1.75 miles on left. From NYC: I-95 North, Exit 41, left off ramp. 4 lights to U.S. 1. Right onto U.S. 1, 1 block to Racebrook Road. Left onto Racebrook Road. 1/4 mile on right.

Oxford Greens, The Golf Club at ✪✪✪½ ▶ 32

99 Country Club Drive
Oxford, CT (203) 888-1600
www.oxfordgreens.com

Club Pro: Matt Burgess, PGA, Steve Keating, GM
Payment: Most Major Credit Cards
Tee Times: 7 days
Fee 9 Holes: Weekday:
Fee 18 Holes: Weekday: $65 M-Th
Twilight Rates: After 2pm
Cart Rental:
Lessons: $50/half hour **Schools:** Yes
Membership: Yes
Other: Restaurant

Tees	Holes	Yards	Par	USGA	Slope
BACK	18	6665	72	72.3	133
MIDDLE	18	6324	72	70.5	131
FRONT	18	5188	72	69.9	122

Weekend:
Weekend: $95 Th-Sun
Discounts: Local residents
Driving Range: Yes
Junior Golf:
Architect/Yr Open: Mark Mungeam/2005
GPS:

Also Black tees at 7186 yards, 75.4/135. #3 is the longest hole in CT: 630 yards. Carved through 600 acres of stunning countryside. "Fast greens. Maturing nicely--definitely worth a visit." –JD

	1	2	3	4	5	6	7	8	9
PAR	4	3	5	4	4	4	4	5	3
YARDS	345	165	535	405	370	300	365	510	175
	10	11	12	13	14	15	16	17	18
PAR	5	4	4	3	4	4	3	5	4
YARDS	517	330	370	147	405	363	132	485	405

Directions: I-84 to Exit 15 Southbury/Seymour. Follow Route 67 South for 6 miles to Riggs Street in Oxford. Left onto Riggs. Follow for approximately 2 miles to The Golf Club at Oxford Greens on right. The Golf Course is located at 99 Country Club Drive.

Pequabuck Golf Course  33

56 School Street
Pequabuck, CT (860) 583-7307
www.pequabuckgolf.com

Club Pro: Richard Toner, PGA
Payment: Visa, MC, Disc
Tee Times: Yes
Fee 9 Holes: Weekday: $21
Fee 18 Holes: Weekday: $42
Twilight Rates: No
Cart Rental: $14pp/18, $8pp/9
Lessons: Call for rates **Schools:** No
Membership: Yes

Tees	Holes	Yards	Par	USGA	Slope
BACK	18	6015	69	70.2	118
MIDDLE	18	5692	69	68.7	115
FRONT	18	5388	72	70.3	118

Weekend: $21
Weekend: $42
Discounts: None
Driving Range: Yes
Junior Golf: Yes
Architect/Yr Open: 1902

Other: Restaurant / Clubhouse / Bar-Lounge / Snack Bar

Front 9 open, back 9 tree-lined with difficult greens. Known for fairways and greens. Groups up to 16 guests. Dress code.

	1	2	3	4	5	6	7	8	9
PAR	4	4	5	3	4	3	5	3	4
YARDS	286	424	470	169	322	155	465	174	371
	10	11	12	13	14	15	16	17	18
PAR	3	4	4	4	4	4	3	4	4
YARDS	190	406	377	329	401	337	155	328	333

Directions: I-84 to Route Exit 72. Follow Route 72 into Terryville. Go under railroad bridge. Take right onto School Street. Follow to club.

Pine Valley Golf Course ✪✪½ 34

300 Welch Road
Southington, CT (860) 628-0879
www.pinevalleygolfct.com

Club Pro: Jack McConachie, PGA
Payment: Cash, Visa, MC
Tee Times: M-F 7 days, S/S 4 days
Fee 9 Holes: Weekday: $19.50
Fee 18 Holes: Weekday: $35
Twilight Rates: No
Cart Rental: $30/18, $15/9 per cart
Lessons: $50/half hour **Schools:** No
Membership: No

Tees	Holes	Yards	Par	USGA	Slope
BACK	18	6325	71	70.6	123
MIDDLE	18	6043	71	70.1	117
FRONT	18	5482	73	72.0	122

Weekend: $21.50
Weekend: $40
Discounts: None
Driving Range: No
Junior Golf: Yes
Architect/Yr Open: Al Zikorus, Orrin Smith/1960

Other: Clubhouse / Lockers / Showers / Snack Bar / Restaurant / Bar-Lounge / Practice Sand Trap
GPS: Yes

Hilly front 9, while the back 9 are more level with water holes and very tight greens. Accuracy is essential. Dress code. New tees.

	1	2	3	4	5	6	7	8	9
PAR	5	4	3	4	4	4	5	3	4
YARDS	497	404	125	345	345	291	505	141	405
	10	11	12	13	14	15	16	17	18
PAR	3	4	5	4	4	3	5	4	3
YARDS	170	366	510	420	353	160	476	340	180

Directions: I-84 to Exit 31 North on Route 229 1.5 miles. Left onto Welch Road. Course is 1/2 miles on left.

SW
CT

Pomperaug Golf Club

522 Heritage Road
Southbury, CT (203) 264-9484
www.heritagesouthbury.com

Club Pro: Dave Cook
Payment: Yes
Tee Times: 3 days adv.
Fee 9 Holes: Weekday: $25
Fee 18 Holes: Weekday: $37
Twilight Rates: No
Cart Rental: $14pp/18, $10pp/9
Lessons: $45/half hour **Schools:**
Membership: Yes

Tees	Holes	Yards	Par	USGA	Slope
BACK	9	2879	35	70	115
MIDDLE	9	2782	35	68.7	111
FRONT	9	2234	36	70.0	113

Weekend: $27
Weekend: $40
Discounts: None
Driving Range: Practice green
Junior Golf: No
Architect/Yr Open:

COUPON

Other: Hotel / Cooler / Beverage Cart / Stay & Play Packages

Semi-private course. Heritage International Hotel on premises. Dress code. Fun and challenging 9-hole course with water on every hole.

	1	2	3	4	5	6	7	8	9
PAR	4	4	4	5	3	4	4	3	4
YARDS	330	356	263	457	174	316	415	166	305
PAR									
YARDS									

Directions: I-84 to Route 67, Southbury, Exit 15. At 2nd light, take left onto Heritage Road. Course is 1 mile ahead on right.

Portland Golf Club

✪✪✪½ 36

169 Bartlett Street
Portland, CT (860) 342-6107
portlandgolfcourse.com

Club Pro: Mark Sloan, PGA
Payment: Cash/Visa
Tee Times: 7 days adv.
Fee 9 Holes: Weekday: $19
Fee 18 Holes: Weekday: $38
Twilight Rates: After 2pm
Cart Rental: $16pp/18, $9pp/9
Lessons: $40/half hour **Schools:** No
Membership: No

Tees	Holes	Yards	Par	USGA	Slope
BACK	18	6213	71	70.5	127
MIDDLE	18	5802	71	68.7	123
FRONT	18	5039	71	68.6	118

Weekend: $22
Weekend: $42
Discounts: Senior & Junior
Driving Range: Yes
Junior Golf: Yes
Architect/Yr Open: Cornish & Robinson/1974

Other: Clubhouse / Lockers / Showers / Snack Bar / Restaurant / Bar-Lounge

Player Comments: "Lots of doglegs." "Excellent conditions." "Worth playing, I'll be back." "Hilly." Open March 15th - January 1st.

	1	2	3	4	5	6	7	8	9
PAR	4	5	4	3	4	4	4	3	4
YARDS	365	485	350	166	270	287	351	140	301
	10	11	12	13	14	15	16	17	18
PAR	4	4	5	4	3	4	5	3	4
YARDS	303	373	489	377	177	360	471	165	372

Directions: Route 2 to 17 South (left at exit); 9.5 miles down take left on Bartlett; course is less than 1 mile. Call for directions from Route 9.

Portland West Golf Club ✪✪✪ ▶ 37

105 Gospel Lane
Portland, CT (860) 342-6111

Tees	Holes	Yards	Par	USGA	Slope
BACK	18	4012	60	60.5	102
MIDDLE	18	3620	60	59.3	100
FRONT	18	3154	60	58.4	87

Club Pro: Gerald J. D'Amora, PGA
Payment: Cash, Visa, MC
Tee Times: 7 days adv.
Fee 9 Holes: Weekday: $14   **Weekend:** $16.50
Fee 18 Holes: Weekday: $27   **Weekend:** $30
Twilight Rates: After 6pm $10, M-F 11-3pm $20pp/18, $10pp/9
Discounts: Senior & Junior
Cart Rental: $26pp/18, $16pp/9
Lessons: $45/half hour **Schools:** No   **Driving Range:** Yes
Membership: No   **Junior Golf:** Yes
Other: Restaurant / Bar-Lounge / Snack Bar   **Architect/Yr Open:** 1985
GPS:

Player Comments: "Excellent greens and fairways." "The 18th hole proves to be a difficult finish."
"A challenging executive par 60 course." "Nice scenery and fair prices. "

	1	2	3	4	5	6	7	8	9
PAR	3	3	3	4	3	4	3	3	4
YARDS	148	130	145	264	140	339	113	137	351
	10	11	12	13	14	15	16	17	18
PAR	4	3	3	3	3	3	4	4	3
YARDS	341	135	161	114	185	122	319	293	183

Directions: I-91 to Route 9 to Route 66; left onto Route 17 (Gospel Lane); course is 1/2 mile on right.

Quarry Ridge Golf Course ✪✪✪½ ▶ 38

9C Rose Hill Road
Portland, CT (860) 342-6113
www.quarryridge.com

Tees	Holes	Yards	Par	USGA	Slope
BACK	18	6389	72	70.9	124
MIDDLE	18	6049	72	69.5	119
FRONT	18	4852	72	68.7	117

Club Pro: John Lucas Jr.
Payment: Cash, Check, Visa, MC, AMEX
Tee Times: 1 week adv.
Fee 9 Holes: Weekday: $27   **Weekend:** $29
Fee 18 Holes: Weekday: $50   **Weekend:** $55
Twilight Rates: After 1pm wkdys only   **Discounts:** Senior & Junior
Cart Rental: Included   **Driving Range:** No
Lessons: $45/half hour **Schools:** No   **Junior Golf:** No
Membership: No   **Architect/Yr Open:** Al Zikorus/1993
Other: Restaurant / Clubhouse / Bar-Lounge   **GPS:**

Player Comments: "Challenging, with tight fairways and small greens. Scenic views of Connecticut River Valley." "Difficult, but popular. Well maintained." "Great layout." Faster greens, 10-minute tee times, faster play. Great restaurant open Fri, Sat, Sun night.

	1	2	3	4	5	6	7	8	9
PAR	4	3	4	5	4	5	4	4	3
YARDS	350	155	383	463	337	448	346	392	178
	10	11	12	13	14	15	16	17	18
PAR	4	5	4	4	3	4	3	5	4
YARDS	326	447	442	293	154	337	144	459	395

Directions: From Hartford: Route 2 to Route 17 (left Exit 7). Go 9 miles; take left onto Bartlett Street, go to end. Cross road to driveway of golf course.

**SW
CT**

Richter Park Golf Course ✪✪✪✪

39

100 Aunt Hack Road
Danbury, CT (203) 792-2550
www.richterpark.com

Club Pro: Ralph Salito Jr., PGA
Payment: MC, Visa, Cash
Tee Times: 3 days adv. (203) 748-5743
Fee 9 Holes: Weekday: No
Fee 18 Holes: Weekday: $59
Twilight Rates: After 4pm
Cart Rental: $26/18
Lessons: $60/45 min. **Schools:** Yes
Membership: Yes

Tees	Holes	Yards	Par	USGA	Slope
BACK	18	6744	72	73.3	134
MIDDLE	18	6304	72	71.6	128
FRONT	18	5114	72	69.8	126

Weekend: No
Weekend: $64
Discounts: Senior & Junior
Driving Range: No
Junior Golf: Yes
Architect/Yr Open: Ed Ryder/1971

Other: Clubhouse / Lockers / Showers / Snack Bar / Restaurant / Bar-Lounge

Player Comments: "Very challenging and difficult." Course keeps a reputation for making even the most skillful golfers work hard: narrow fairways, approach shots require precision; water on 14 fairways.

	1	2	3	4	5	6	7	8	9
PAR	4	5	3	4	3	4	5	4	4
YARDS	372	491	150	389	170	388	507	335	314
	10	11	12	13	14	15	16	17	18
PAR	4	4	5	3	4	4	5	3	4
YARDS	345	360	495	142	395	324	570	152	426

Directions: I-84 West to Exit 2B or I-84 East to Exit 2. Take right off ramp (Mill Plain Road); take second left onto Aunt Hack Road to course.

Ridgefield Golf Club ✪✪½

40

545 Ridgebury Road
Ridgefield, CT (203) 748-7008
www.rgconline.org

Club Pro: Frank Sergiovanni, PGA
Payment: Cash, Check, Visa, MC
Tee Times: Yes
Fee 9 Holes: Weekday:
Fee 18 Holes: Weekday: $45
Twilight Rates: After 4pm
Cart Rental: $14pp/18, $7pp/9
Lessons: Yes **Schools:** No
Membership:
Other: Snack Bar / Bar-Lounge

Tees	Holes	Yards	Par	USGA	Slope
BACK	18	6444	71	71.8	129
MIDDLE	18	6019	71	69.7	127
FRONT	18	5124	74	69.1	116

Weekend:
Weekend: $50
Discounts: Sr. & Jr. weekdays
Driving Range: $10/lg., $7/med., $4/sm.
Junior Golf: Yes
Architect/Yr Open: Tom & George Fazio/1975
GPS:

Excellent condition.

	1	2	3	4	5	6	7	8	9
PAR	4	4	3	4	3	5	4	4	4
YARDS	391	367	150	320	139	518	345	381	371
	10	11	12	13	14	15	16	17	18
PAR	5	4	3	4	5	4	4	3	4
YARDS	533	311	147	351	469	402	311	127	386

Directions: I-84 to Exit 1; Saw Mill Road to Old Ridgebury Road. Course is on Old Ridgebury.

Short Beach Par 3 GC

NR 41

1 Dorne Drive
Stratford, CT (203) 381-2070
golf@townofstafford.com

Club Pro: Michael Gaffney
Payment: Cash, Visa, MC
Tee Times: 6 days adv. wknds
Fee 9 Holes: Weekday: $12.25
Fee 18 Holes: Weekday: $24.50
Twilight Rates: No
Cart Rental: $7pp/9
Lessons: Yes **Schools:** No
Membership:
Other: Snack Bar/ Mini Golf course

Tees	Holes	Yards	Par	USGA	Slope
BACK	9	1369	27		
MIDDLE	9	1270	27		
FRONT	9	1162	27		

Weekend: $14.25
Weekend: $28.50
Discounts: Senior & Junior
Driving Range: No
Junior Golf: Yes
Architect/Yr Open: Goeffrey Cornish
GPS:

Par 3, 9 holes on beachfront. Proper attire required. Resident discounts. Open March - January.

	1	2	3	4	5	6	7	8	9
PAR	3	3	3	3	3	3	3	3	3
YARDS	125	154	98	170	88	130	218	162	125
PAR									
YARDS									

Directions: Call for directions.

Sleeping Giant Golf Course

NR 43

3931 Whitney Avenue
Hamden, CT (203) 281-9456

Club Pro: Carl Swanson, PGA
Payment: Cash Only
Tee Times: No
Fee 9 Holes: Weekday: $16
Fee 18 Holes: Weekday: $28
Twilight Rates: No
Cart Rental: $20pp/18, $12pp/9
Lessons: $30/half hour, $50/hour **Schools:** No
Membership: No
Other: Restaurant nearby

Tees	Holes	Yards	Par	USGA	Slope
BACK	9	2671	35	65.4	99
MIDDLE	9	2572	35	63.4	96
FRONT	9	2216	37	64.6	106

Weekend: $18
Weekend: $32
Discounts: Senior
Driving Range: Yes
Junior Golf: No
Architect/Yr Open: Ralph Barton
GPS:

"A nice little well-maintained course that is pure fun. The views of Sleeping Giant Mountain enhance the aesthetics. #3 is a nice par 3 to a punchbowl green" –AP Open year round, weather permitting.

	1	2	3	4	5	6	7	8	9
PAR	3	4	3	4	5	4	4	4	4
YARDS	125	399	170	355	440	331	199	217	336
PAR									
YARDS									

Directions: I-91 to Exit 10. Right onto Whitney Avenue. Course is 3 miles on the right.

**SW
CT**

South Pine Creek Par 3 Golf Course NR

43

Old Dam Rd.
Fairfield, CT (203) 256-3173
www.fairfieldct.org

Club Pro: Sean Garrity, PGA
Payment: Cash only
Tee Times: 5 days adv.
Fee 9 Holes: Weekday: $14
Fee 18 Holes: Weekday:
Twilight Rates: No
Cart Rental: $4/pull
Lessons: No **Schools:** No
Membership: No
Other:

Tees	Holes	Yards	Par	USGA	Slope
BACK					
MIDDLE	9	1242	27		
FRONT	9	1073	27		

Weekend: $18
Weekend:
Discounts: Senior & Junior
Driving Range:
Junior Golf: No
Architect/Yr Open:
GPS:

Residents half price. Great place to learn the game. H. Richardson affilate course.

	1	2	3	4	5	6	7	8	9
PAR	3	3	3	3	3	3	3	3	3
YARDS	143	145	120	166	153	117	121	187	90
PAR									
YARDS									

Directions: I-95 to Exit 21, Mill Plain Road. Turn left onto Post Road. At first set of lights take left. Course is 1/2 mile on left.

Southington Country Club NR

44

Savage Street
Southington, CT (860) 628-7032
www.southingtoncountryclub.com

Club Pro: Paul Brown, PGA
Payment: Visa, MC
Tee Times: Sat/Sun am
Fee 9 Holes: Weekday: $18.50
Fee 18 Holes: Weekday: $33
Twilight Rates: After 5pm
Cart Rental: $15pp/18, $8pp/9
Lessons: No **Schools:** No
Membership: Yes
Other: Snack Bar / Bar-Lounge

Tees	Holes	Yards	Par	USGA	Slope
BACK	18	5904	71	67.8	122
MIDDLE	18	5417	71	66.8	121
FRONT	18	5037	71	64.5	111

Weekend: $21.50
Weekend: $37
Discounts: Senior & Junior
Driving Range: No
Junior Golf: No
Architect/Yr Open: 1922
GPS:

Front 9 very hilly. Back 9 is level and easy for walkers. Under new management. Expanded bar and kitchen offerings. Putting and pitching greens.

	1	2	3	4	5	6	7	8	9
PAR	4	4	3	5	4	5	3	4	4
YARDS	377	306	144	481	387	508	192	338	324
	10	**11**	**12**	**13**	**14**	**15**	**16**	**17**	**18**
PAR	4	4	3	4	5	3	4	3	5
YARDS	297	310	93	238	442	196	248	152	384

Directions: I-84 to Exit 28. Take right onto Route 322. Travel about 3 miles. Take a left onto South End Road. Take first right onto Savage Street.

Sterling Farms Golf Course ✪✪✪½

 45

1349 Newfield Road
Newfield Avenue
Stamford, CT (203) 461-9090
www.sterlingfarmsgc.com

Tees	Holes	Yards	Par	USGA	Slope
BACK	18	6310	72	70.7	127
MIDDLE	18	6082	72	69.7	123
FRONT	18	5500	73	71.7	125

Club Pro: Angela Aulenti, PGA
Payment: Cash Only
Tee Times: 1 week adv.
Fee 9 Holes: Weekday: $30 (6-7:30am)   **Weekend:** $30 (6-7:30am)
Fee 18 Holes: Weekday: $50   **Weekend:** $50
Twilight Rates: After 4pm   **Discounts:** Sr. & Jr. weekdays
Cart Rental: $25pp/18, $15pp/9   **Driving Range:** Yes
Lessons: Call (203) 329-7888 **Schools:** Yes   **Junior Golf:** Yes
Membership: No   **Architect/Yr Open:** Geoffrey Cornish/1969
Other: Restaurant   **GPS:**

Course has hilly front 9; more level back 9. 2 of the course's five lakes come into play on the 14th hole. Resident rates.

	1	2	3	4	5	6	7	8	9
PAR	4	5	4	4	3	5	4	3	4
YARDS	331	489	316	350	191	465	382	179	326
	10	11	12	13	14	15	16	17	18
PAR	4	4	4	5	4	3	4	3	5
YARDS	397	307	341	477	393	147	301	215	475

Directions: Merritt Parkway South to Exit 35. Right onto High Ridge Road. Left onto Vine (5 lights). Left at end to Newfield Avenue. Club is 1/4 miles on right.

Stonybrook Golf Course

NR 46

263 Milton Road
Litchfield, CT (860) 567-9977
www.fairviewfarmgolfcourse.com/
stonybrook.htm

Tees	Holes	Yards	Par	USGA	Slope
BACK	9	2986	35	70.4	115
MIDDLE	9	2878	35	69.0	111
FRONT	9	2669	36	71.6	123

Club Pro: Rich Bredice, pro
Payment: Visa, MC
Tee Times: Weekends
Fee 9 Holes: Weekday: $18   **Weekend:** $20
Fee 18 Holes: Weekday: $34   **Weekend:** $38
Twilight Rates: No   **Discounts:** Junior
Cart Rental: $18pp/18, $9pp/9   **Driving Range:** No
Lessons: Available **Schools:** No   **Junior Golf:** Yes
Membership: Yes   **Architect/Yr Open:** Al Zikorus/1965
Other: Clubhouse / Snack Bar / Bar-Lounge / Lockers

Terrain is rolling; greens contoured (medium/fast).

	1	2	3	4	5	6	7	8	9
PAR	5	4	3	4	4	4	4	4	3
YARDS	530	374	150	366	325	300	375	295	163
PAR									
YARDS									

Directions: Route 8 to Exit 42; Route 118 West to 202 West to Milton Road.

**SW
CT**

Sunset Hill GC

NR ▶ 47

18 Sunset Hill Road
Brookfield, CT (203) 740-7800
www.sunsethillgolfclub.com

Club Pro: Gary Cilfone, PGA
Payment: Cash, Check
Tee Times: No
Fee 9 Holes: Weekday: $19
Fee 18 Holes: Weekday: $25
Twilight Rates: After 4pm
Cart Rental: $18pp/18, $9pp/9
Lessons: Yes **Schools:** Yes, inquire
Membership: Yes
Other: Clubhouse / Snack Bar / Bar-Lounge

Tees	Holes	Yards	Par	USGA	Slope
BACK					
MIDDLE	9	2394	35	62.6	100
FRONT	9	2346	35	66.3	100

Weekend: $23
Weekend: $29
Discounts: Senior & Junior
Driving Range: No
Junior Golf: Yes
Architect/Yr Open: 1897
GPS:

COUPON

Ongoing improvements. New tee on hole #3. Sister golf course is Eastwood CC. Open April - November.

	1	2	3	4	5	6	7	8	9
PAR	5	3	3	4	4	4	5	4	3
YARDS	452	145	116	278	304	270	426	278	125
PAR									
YARDS									

Directions: I-84 to Exit 9; follow Route 25 North 3 miles; take left onto Sunset Hill Road to course.

Tashua Knolls Country Club

✪✪✪ ▶ 48

40 Tashua Knolls Lane
Trumbull, CT (203) 452-5171
www.tashuaknolls.com

Club Pro: Jon Janik, PGA
Payment: Cash, Check, Credit
Tee Times: 7 days adv.
Fee 9 Holes: Weekday: $23
Fee 18 Holes: Weekday: $40
Twilight Rates: No
Cart Rental: $16pp/18, $11pp/9
Lessons: $60/40 min. **Schools:** No
Membership: No
Other: Snack Bar / Restaurant / Bar-Lounge / Lockers / Showers

Tees	Holes	Yards	Par	USGA	Slope
BACK	18	6540	72	71.9	125
MIDDLE	18	6119	72	70.0	121
FRONT	18	5454	72	71.7	124

Weekend: $27
Weekend: $45
Discounts: Sr. & Jr. residents M-F
Driving Range: $5/bucket
Junior Golf: Yes
Architect/Yr Open: Al Zikorus, 1976

"Second 9 holes opened 2005, less daunting than the first 9." –RV

	1	2	3	4	5	6	7	8	9
PAR	5	4	3	4	4	3	5	4	4
YARDS	532	317	151	342	353	192	480	354	356
	10	**11**	**12**	**13**	**14**	**15**	**16**	**17**	**18**
PAR	4	4	3	4	5	4	5	3	4
YARDS	349	367	154	262	495	373	506	145	391

Directions: Take Merritt Parkway (Route 15) to Exit 49 (Route 25); go straight, take left onto Tashua Knolls Lane. Course at top of hill.

The Orchards Golf Course　　　NR　49

137 Kozlowski Road
Milford, CT 203-877-8200

Tees	Holes	Yards	Par	USGA	Slope
BACK					
MIDDLE	9	1625	32		
FRONT	9	1433	32		

Club Pro:
Payment: Cash only
Tee Times: 6 days adv.
Fee 9 Holes: Weekday: $14.30　　**Weekend:** $15.40
Fee 18 Holes: Weekday: $27.60　　**Weekend:** $29.80
Twilight Rates: No　　**Discounts:** Senior & Junior
Cart Rental: $3.25/pull　　**Driving Range:** Putting Green
Lessons: No　**Schools:** No　　**Junior Golf:** No
Membership: No　　**Architect/Yr Open:**
Other: Snacks　　**GPS:**

Resident discounts. New groundskeeper.

	1	2	3	4	5	6	7	8	9
PAR	4	3	4	4	4	3	3	3	4
YARDS	242	93	222	207	217	120	167	91	266
PAR									
YARDS									

Directions: I-95 to Exit 39. Go South on Route 1 to Route 121 North (North Street). Turn right onto Kozlowski Road.

Tradition GC at Wallingford, The ✪✪✪　50

36 Harrison Road
Wallingford, CT (203) 269-6023
www.wallingfordtradition.com

Tees	Holes	Yards	Par	USGA	Slope
BACK	18	5772	70	68.8	121
MIDDLE	18	5398	70	66.9	119
FRONT	18	4458	70	68.0	121

Club Pro: Nick Lykowski, dir. of golf
Payment: Most Major Credit Cards
Tee Times: 7 days adv.
Fee 9 Holes: Weekday: $25 w/cart　　**Weekend:** $25 w/cart
Fee 18 Holes: Weekday: $47 w/cart　　**Weekend:** $57 w/cart
Twilight Rates: After 2pm　　**Discounts:** Senior & Junior
Cart Rental: $8pp/9　　**Driving Range:** Yes
Lessons: Yes　**Schools:** Yes　　**Junior Golf:** Yes
Membership: Yes　　**Architect/Yr Open:** Alfred Tull/1972
Other: Bar-Lounge / Snack Bar / Banquet Facility　**GPS:**

Player Comments: "Well-manicured greens. Great staff. Fairly priced." Dress code. Variety of special rates. Renovated club house.

	1	2	3	4	5	6	7	8	9
PAR	4	4	3	4	4	5	4	3	4
YARDS	347	320	106	370	342	518	281	152	389
	10	11	12	13	14	15	16	17	18
PAR	4	5	3	4	5	3	4	4	3
YARDS	256	447	131	431	409	139	380	275	105

Directions: I-91 to Exit 14. Take right onto Route 150 toward Wallingford. Take right onto Harrison Road.

Twin Lakes Golf Course

241 Twin Lakes Road
North Branford, CT
(203) 481-3776

Club Pro: Edward Grant, PGA
Anthony Celone, manager
Payment: Cash Only
Tee Times:
Fee 9 Holes: Weekday: $8
Fee 18 Holes: Weekday: $13
Twilight Rates: No
Cart Rental: Yes
Lessons: Yes **Schools:** Yes
Membership: No
Other: Snack Bar

Weekend: $10
Weekend: $16
Discounts: Junior 1st tee
Driving Range: No
Junior Golf: Yes
Architect/Yr Open:
GPS:

Tees	Holes	Yards	Par	USGA	Slope
BACK					
MIDDLE	9	1047	27		
FRONT					

Open March 15- October 15. This is a very short, 9-hole, par 3 course good for family fun. Season passes for unlimited play.

	1	2	3	4	5	6	7	8	9
PAR	3	3	3	3	3	3	3	3	3
YARDS	130	123	95	92	116	92	138	141	120
PAR									
YARDS									

Directions: I-95 to Exit 55 on left. Take a left at first light. Follow 2 miles, Twin Lakes Road on left.

Western Hills Golf Course

600 Park Road
Waterbury, CT (203) 756-1211
www.westernhillsgolfcourse.com

Club Pro: Tom Bracken, PGA
Payment: Visa, MC
Tee Times: 3 days adv.
Fee 9 Holes: Weekday: $19
Fee 18 Holes: Weekday: $29
Twilight Rates: After 6pm M-F, after noon S/S
Cart Rental: $27/18, $17/9 per cart
Lessons: Yes **Schools:** No
Membership: Yes
Other: Clubhouse / Snack Bar / Restaurant / Bar-Lounge / Banquet / Lockers / Showers

Weekend: $20
Weekend: $31
Discounts: Senior & Junior
Driving Range: No
Junior Golf: Yes
Architect/Yr: Wiliam & David Gordon/1962

Tees	Holes	Yards	Par	USGA	Slope
BACK	18	6356	72	69.5	120
MIDDLE	18	6136	72	68.5	118
FRONT	18	5237	72	69.5	127

COUPON

Scenic New England golf course with a variety of terrain and vistas. A good test of golf. The course is in the best shape ever! Rating is too low!

	1	2	3	4	5	6	7	8	9
PAR	4	5	4	4	3	4	5	4	3
YARDS	354	458	356	340	162	374	527	387	145
	10	11	12	13	14	15	16	17	18
PAR	4	3	4	5	4	5	3	4	4
YARDS	363	138	305	495	391	480	153	381	327

Directions: I-84 to Exit 17. Follow Route 63 North to Park Road. Right on Park Road to stop sign. Left at stop sign to clubhouse.

Whitney Farms Golf Course

NR 53 ▶

175 Shelton Road (Route 110)
Monroe, CT (203) 268-0707
www.whitneyfarmsgc.com

Tees	Holes	Yards	Par	USGA	Slope
BACK	18	6628	72	72.4	134
MIDDLE	18	6262	72	70.9	129
FRONT	18	5832	73	72.9	135

Club Pro: Paul McGuire, PGA
Payment: Visa, MC, Amex
Tee Times: Yes
Fee 9 Holes: Weekday: $30   **Weekend:** $37
Fee 18 Holes: Weekday: $55   **Weekend:** $69
Twilight Rates: After 4pm   **Discounts:** Srs. rate: $45 crt+green, M-Th
Cart Rental: Included   **Driving Range:** $6
Lessons: $50/half hour **Schools:** No   **Junior Golf:** No
Membership: No   **Architect/Yr Open:** Hal Purdy/1982
Other: Clubhouse / Lockers / Showers / Snack Bar / Restaurant / Bar-Lounge

All bunkers recently redone with new sand and new cart paths.

	1	2	3	4	5	6	7	8	9
PAR	4	4	5	3	4	5	3	5	3
YARDS	399	381	508	161	324	533	210	469	168
	10	11	12	13	14	15	16	17	18
PAR	4	5	3	4	4	3	5	4	4
YARDS	341	522	132	329	324	164	547	335	415

Directions: Merritt Parkway Exit 49 North to Route 25. Take right on Route 111 and follow for 4 miles. Take right at intersection of Route 110. Course is 1 mile on left.

Woodhaven Country Club

NR 54 ▶

275 Miller Road
Bethany, CT (203) 393-3230
www.woodhavengolf.com

Tees	Holes	Yards	Par	USGA	Slope
BACK	9	6774	72	72.7	128
MIDDLE	9	6294	72	70.6	123
FRONT	9	5370	72	72.0	125

Club Pro: Dale Humphrey, PGA
Payment: Cash, Check, MC, Visa
Tee Times: 7 days adv.
Fee 9 Holes: Weekday: $20   **Weekend:** $23
Fee 18 Holes: Weekday: $31   **Weekend:** $39
Twilight Rates: No   **Discounts:** Sr. & Jr. wkdys before 2pm
Cart Rental: $15pp/18, $8pp/9   **Driving Range:** Yes
Lessons: Yes **Schools:** No   **Junior Golf:** Yes
Membership: No   **Architect/Yr Open:** Al Zikorus/1968
Other: Snack Bar / Restaurant   **GPS:**

COUPON

Rebuilt traps and added new tee on hole #4. The course is scenic, challenging and easy walking; A family-owned "labor of love." Noted for tough greens.

	1	2	3	4	5	6	7	8	9
PAR	5	3	4	4	4	5	4	3	4
YARDS	517	156	331	375	342	542	350	152	382
	10	11	12	13	14	15	16	17	18
PAR	5	3	4	4	4	5	4	3	4
YARDS	530	168	374	435	360	570	370	152	400

Directions: Route 8 to Exit 22. East on Route 67. Left on Bear Hill Road. Bear left onto Miller Road.

SW CT

My Rounds in 2009

Date: _____ Course: _____

Slope/Rating: _____ Score: _____

Notes: _____

Date: _____ Course: _____

Slope/Rating: _____ Score: _____

Notes: _____

Date: _____ Course: _____

Slope/Rating: _____ Score: _____

Notes: _____

Date: _____ Course: _____

Slope/Rating: _____ Score: _____

Notes: _____

Date: _____ Course: _____

Slope/Rating: _____ Score: _____

Notes: _____

Date: _____ Course: _____

Slope/Rating: _____ Score: _____

Notes: _____

Date: _____ Course: _____

Slope/Rating: _____ Score: _____

Notes: _____

My Rounds in 2009

Date: _____ Course: _____

Slope/Rating: _____ Score: _____

Notes: _____

Date: _____ Course: _____

Slope/Rating: _____ Score: _____

Notes: _____

Date: _____ Course: _____

Slope/Rating: _____ Score: _____

Notes: _____

Date: _____ Course: _____

Slope/Rating: _____ Score: _____

Notes: _____

Date: _____ Course: _____

Slope/Rating: _____ Score: _____

Notes: _____

Date: _____ Course: _____

Slope/Rating: _____ Score: _____

Notes: _____

Date: _____ Course: _____

Slope/Rating: _____ Score: _____

Notes: _____

My Rounds in 2009

Date: _____ Course: _____

Slope/Rating: _____ Score: _____

Notes: _____

Date: _____ Course: _____

Slope/Rating: _____ Score: _____

Notes: _____

Date: _____ Course: _____

Slope/Rating: _____ Score: _____

Notes: _____

Date: _____ Course: _____

Slope/Rating: _____ Score: _____

Notes: _____

Date: _____ Course: _____

Slope/Rating: _____ Score: _____

Notes: _____

Date: _____ Course: _____

Slope/Rating: _____ Score: _____

Notes: _____

Date: _____ Course: _____

Slope/Rating: _____ Score: _____

Notes: _____

Directory of Coupons

Green Mountain in Killington, Vermont.

NEW ENGLAND
GOLFGUIDE®

Give the New England GolfGuide 2009 Edition

It's the perfect gift for golfers of all ages and abilities. One size fits all. The book is packed with data, scorecards, fees, and directions for all 650 New England public, semi-private and resort courses. With discount coupons for green fees worth THOUSANDS of dollars, plus coupons for driving ranges, the book pays for itself and is a gift that keeps on giving.

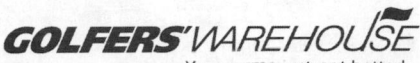

Baker's Golf Center

- **Type of Discount:**
  Frequent Golf Card available for large baskets. Buy 9 & the 10th is free.
- **Days of the Week:**
  7 days a week
- **Hours of the Day:**

858 South Main Street
Lanesborough, MA
413-443-6102
www.hometown.aol.com/ dstorie4

Pro: Dennis Perrone, PGA

Coupon expires 12/09. Cannot be combined with any other offer.

Bill Pappas Indoor Golf & Batting Cages

- **Type of Discount:**
  Free half hour practice with paid half hour.
- **Days of the Week:**
  7 days a week
- **Hours of the Day:**

75 Princeton Street
North Chelmsford, MA
(978) 251-3933
www.egolfschool.net

Pro: Bill Pappas, PGA

Clinics: Yes

Coupon expires 12/09. Cannot be combined with any other offer.

Brown's Driving Range

- **Type of Discount:**
  $1 off a medium or large bucket
- **Days of the Week:**
  7 days a week
- **Hours of the Day:**
  All day

60 Rainbow Road
Windsor, CT
860-688-1745

Pro: Dick Frechette

Coupon expires 12/09. Cannot be combined with any other offer.

Callahan's Sportech Golf @ The Mammoth Green Family Golf Center

- **Type of Discount:**
  $10 of one hour lesson
- **Days of the Week:**
  7 days a week
- **Hours of the Day:**

135 Nashua Road, Route 102
Londonderry, NH
(603) 432-4653

Pro: Jim Callahan, PGA

Clinics: Yes

Coupon expires 12/09. Cannot be combined with any other offer.

Driving Range Coupons

NEW ENGLAND
GOLFGUIDE

2 0 0 9

NEW ENGLAND
GOLFGUIDE

2 0 0 9

NEW ENGLAND
GOLFGUIDE

2 0 0 9

NEW ENGLAND
GOLFGUIDE

2 0 0 9

Callahan's Sportech Golf Indoor Lessons

- **Type of Discount:**
  $10 off one hour lesson
- **Days of the Week:**
  7 days a week
- **Hours of the Day:**
  Any time

1 Bittersweet Road
Nashua, NH
(603) 888-1976

Pro: Jim Callahan, PGA
Clinics: Yes

Coupon expires 12/09.
Cannot be combined
with any other offer.

FORE-U-GOLF Center

- **Type of Discount:**
  2 medium buckets
  for the price of 1
- **Days of the Week:**
  7 days a week
- **Hours of the Day:**
  All day.

298 Plainfield Road
West Lebanon, NH
(603) 298-9702

Pro: Cory Phillips, PGA
Clinics: Junior & Adult

Coupon expires 12/09.
Cannot be combined
with any other offer.

Golf Country @ Easton

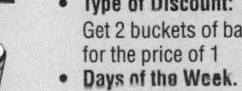

- **Type of Discount:**
  Get 2 buckets of balls
  for the price of 1
- **Days of the Week.**
  7 days a week
- **Hours of the Day:**

530 Turnpike Street
Easton, MA
(508) 238-6007
golfcountry.biz

Pro: Mike Lynott
Clinics: No

Coupon expires 12/09.
Cannot be combined
with any other offer.

Golf Country at Richardson's

- **Type of Discount:**
  Buy 1 large bucket,
  get 1 free
- **Days of the Week:**
  7 days a week
- **Hours of the Day:**
  All day

160 South Main Street
Middleton, MA
(978) 774-4476
www.golfcountry114.com

Pro: Chuck Frithsen, PGA
Clinics: No

Coupon expires 12/09.
Cannot be combined
with any other offer.

Driving Range Coupons

NEW ENGLAND
GOLFGUIDE

2 0 0 9

NEW ENGLAND
GOLFGUIDE

2 0 0 9

NEW ENGLAND
GOLFGUIDE

2 0 0 9

NEW ENGLAND
GOLFGUIDE

2 0 0 9

Lakeview Driving Range, Mini Golf, & Batting Range

- **Type of Discount:**
  Get 2 buckets of balls for the price of 1
- **Days of the Week:**
  7 days a week
- **Hours of the Day:**

1 Whalom Road
Lunenburg, MA
(978) 345-7070

Pro: John Ross, USGTA
Clinics: Yes

Coupon expires 12/09.
Cannot be combined
with any other offer.

Lancaster Golf Center Driving Range and Par 3

- **Type of Discount:**
  $1 off any size bucket
- **Days of the Week:**
  7 days a week
- **Hours of the Day:**
  All day

438 Old Union Turnpike Road
Exit 34 on Route 2
Lancaster, MA
(978) 537-8922
www.lancastergolfcenter.com

Pro: J. Gordon, PGA,
D. Lanciani
Clinics: Junior & Adult

Coupon expires 12/09.
Cannot be combined
with any other offer.

Lancaster Golf Center Par 3

- **Type of Discount:**
  1 round at 1/2 price on The Links Par 3 Course (9 holes 62-114 yards)
- **Days of the Week:**
  Weekdays only (except holidays)
- **Hours of the Day:**

438 Old Union Turnpike Road
Exit 34 on Route 2
Lancaster, MA
(978) 537-8922

Pro: Greg McFee, PGA,
John Gordon, PGA
Clinics: Junior & Adult

Coupon expires 12/09.
Cannot be combined
with any other offer.

Legends Golf & Family Recreation

- **Type of Discount:**
  Buy 1 large bucket, get 1 small bucket of balls free
- **Days of the Week:**
  7 days a week
- **Hours of the Day:**
  All Day

18 Legends Drive
Hooksett, NH
(603) 627-0099
www.legendsgolfnh.com

Pro: Bob Bean, PGA
Clinics: Junior & Adult

Coupon expires 12/09.
Cannot be combined
with any other offer.

Driving Range Coupons

NEW ENGLAND GOLFGUIDE

2 0 0 9

✂ -

NEW ENGLAND GOLFGUIDE

2 0 0 9

✂ -

NEW ENGLAND GOLFGUIDE

2 0 0 9

✂ -

NEW ENGLAND GOLFGUIDE

2 0 0 9

Prospect Golf
Driving Range

- **Type of Discount:**
  Buy 1 large bucket, get second for 1/2 price
- **Days of the Week:**
  Weekdays only (except holidays)
- **Hours of the Day:**
  9 am- 10 pm

Coupon expires 12/09.
Cannot be combined
with any other offer.

144 Waterbury Prospect Road
Prospect, CT
(203) 758-4121

Pro: Jeffrey DelRosso, PGA
Clinics: Junior & Adult

Sarkisian Farms
Driving Range

- **Type of Discount:**
  $1 off any size bucket
- **Days of the Week:**
  7 days a week
- **Hours of the Day:**
  All day

Coupon expires 12/09.
Cannot be combined
with any other offer.

159 Chandler Road
Andover, MA
(978) 688-5522

Pro: Mark Fedorehuk, PGA
Clinics: Junior & Adult

Sonny's Driving Range
& Training

- **Type of Discount:**
  1 small bucket of balls free
- **Days of the Week:**
  Tuesday-Sunday
- **Hours of the Day:**
  Closed Mondays

Coupon expires 12/09.
Cannot be combined
with any other offer.

108 Cove Road
Winterport, ME
(207) 223-5242
www.sonnysrange.com

Pro: Sonny Reynolds, USGTF

Star Land Sports
& Fun Park

- **Type of Discount:**
  Get 2 buckets of balls for the price of 1
- **Days of the Week:**
  7 days a week
- **Hours of the Day:**
  All day

Coupon expires 12/09.
Cannot be combined
with any other offer.

645 Washington Street, Rt. 53
Hanover, MA
(781) 826-3083
www.starland.us

Pro: No
Clinics: No

NEW ENGLAND GOLFGUIDE

2 0 0 9

NEW ENGLAND GOLFGUIDE

2 0 0 9

NEW ENGLAND GOLFGUIDE

2 0 0 9

NEW ENGLAND GOLFGUIDE

2 0 0 9

Stone Meadow Golf

- **Typo of Discount:**
  1 medium bucket of balls free
- **Days of the Week:**
  Weekdays only (except holidays)
- **Hours of the Day:**

675 Waltham Street
Lexington, MA
(781) 863-0445
www.stonemeadowgolf.com

Pros: George Liss,
Joe McKinney, PGA

Clinics: Junior & Adult

Coupon expires 12/09.
Cannot be combined
with any other offer.

Taber's Lakeside Stand

- **Type of Discount:**
  Get 2 buckets of balls for the price of 1
- **Days of the Week:**
  7 days a week
- **Hours of the Day:**

473 Lake Shore Drive
Auburn, ME
(207) 784-2521

Clinics: No

Coupon expires 12/09.
Cannot be combined
with any other offer.

The Only Game In Town

- **Type of Discount:**
  1 small bucket of balls free
- **Days of the Week:**
  7 days a week
- **Hours of the Day:**

275 Valley Service Road
North Haven, CT
(203) 234-7166
www.onlygameintown.com

Pro: Daniel Kirby

Clinics: No

Coupon expires 12/09.
Cannot be combined
with any other offer.

Whirlaway Golf Center & Driving Range

- **Type of Discount:**
  Buy 1 large bucket, get 1 small bucket free
  $10 off $50 purchase of golf merch., excl. balls
- **Days of the Week:**
  Mats only
- **Hours of the Day:**
  All day. Open all year.

500 Merrimack Street
Methuen, MA
(978) 688-8356
www.whirlawaygolf.com

Pro: Bill Lodge, PGA

Clinics: Yes

Coupon expires 12/09.
Cannot be combined
with any other offer.

Driving Range Coupons

NEW ENGLAND GOLFGUIDE

2 0 0 9

NEW ENGLAND GOLFGUIDE

2 0 0 9

NEW ENGLAND GOLFGUIDE

2 0 0 9

NEW ENGLAND GOLFGUIDE

2 0 0 9

Airways Golf Course
West Suffield, CT (860) 668-4973

- **Type of Discount**
  18 holes of golf, cart, sleeve of golf balls,
  and $4 lunch for $25 per person
- **Days of the Week**
  Weekdays only (except holidays)
- **Hours of the Day**
  All day

Coupon expires 12/31/09. Cannot be combined with any other offer.

Banner Country Club
Moodus, CT (860) 873-9075

- **Type of Discount**
  2 players for the price of 1
- **Days of the Week**
  Weekdays only (except holidays)
- **Hours of the Day**
  All day

Coupon expires 12/31/09. Cannot be combined with any other offer.

Blackledge Country Club - Anderson's Glen
180 West Street, Hebron, CT (860) 228-0250

- **Type of Discount**
  Free golf cart with 2 paid green fees
- **Days of the Week**
  Monday through Thursday (except holidays)
- **Hours of the Day**

Coupon expires 12/31/09. Cannot be combined with any other offer.

Blackledge Country Club - Gilead Highlands
Hebron, CT (860) 228-0250

- **Type of Discount**
  Free golf cart with 2 paid green fees
- **Days of the Week**
  Monday through Thursday (except holidays)
- **Hours of the Day**

Coupon expires 12/31/09. Cannot be combined with any other offer.

NEW ENGLAND GOLFGUIDE

2 0 0 9

NEW ENGLAND GOLFGUIDE

2 0 0 9

NEW ENGLAND GOLFGUIDE

2 0 0 9

NEW ENGLAND GOLFGUIDE

2 0 0 9

Blue Fox Run
Nod Road, Avon, CT (860) 678-1679

- **Type of Discount**
  Free golf cart with 2 paid green fees
  (rates may change without notice)

- **Days of the Week**
  M-Th except holidays

- **Hours of the Day**
  7 AM - 10 AM

Coupon expires 12/31/09. Cannot be combined with any other offer.

East Hartford Golf Course
East Hartford, CT (860) 528-5082

- **Type of Discount**
  2 players for the price of 1 with rental
  of power cart

- **Days of the Week**
  Weekdays only (except holidays). From 10/1
  to end of season.

- **Hours of the Day**
  All day

Coupon expires 12/31/09. Cannot be combined with any other offer.

Eastwood Country Club
Torrington, CT (860) 489-2630

- **Type of Discount**
  2 players for the price of 1

- **Days of the Week**
  Weekdays only (except holidays)

- **Hours of the Day**
  All day

Coupon expires 12/31/09. Cannot be combined with any other offer.

Fox Hopyard Country Club
East Haddam, CT (860) 434-6644

- **Type of Discount**
  $25 off green fee, 1 per coupon holder

- **Days of the Week**
  Monday through Thursday (except holidays)

- **Hours of the Day**
  All day, based on full rack rate

Coupon expires 12/31/09. Cannot be combined with any other offer.

Golf Course Coupons

NEW ENGLAND GOLFGUIDE

2 0 0 9

NEW ENGLAND GOLFGUIDE

2 0 0 9

NEW ENGLAND GOLFGUIDE

2 0 0 9

NEW ENGLAND GOLFGUIDE

2 0 0 9

Gainfield Farms Golf Course
Southbury, CT (203) 262-1100

- **Type of Discount**
  $2 off 9 holes with coupon
- **Days of the Week**
  7 days a week
- **Hours of the Day**
  All day

Coupon expires 12/31/09. Cannot be combined with any other offer.

Goodwin Golf Course
Hartford, CT (860) 956-3601

- **Type of Discount**
  2 players for the price of 1 (power cart rental required)
- **Days of the Week**
  Weekdays only (except holidays)
- **Hours of the Day**
  All day

Coupon expires 12/31/09. Cannot be combined with any other offer.

Harrisville Golf Course
Woodstock, CT (860) 928-6098

- **Type of Discount**
  $3 off green fees for up to 2 players
- **Days of the Week**
  Weekdays only (except holidays)
- **Hours of the Day**
  All day

Coupon expires 12/31/09. Cannot be combined with any other offer.

Hawk's Landing CC
Southington, CT (860) 793-6000

- **Type of Discount**
  $2 off a round or golf cart
- **Days of the Week**
  7 days a week
- **Hours of the Day**
  All day, Saturday and Sunday only after 1pm

Coupon expires 12/31/09. Cannot be combined with any other offer.

Golf Course Coupons

NEW ENGLAND
GOLFGUIDE

2 0 0 9

NEW ENGLAND
GOLFGUIDE

2 0 0 9

NEW ENGLAND
GOLFGUIDE

2 0 0 9

NEW ENGLAND
GOLFGUIDE

2 0 0 9

Hillside Links LLC
Deep River, CT (860) 526-8893

- **Type of Discount**
  $2 off green fees
- **Days of the Week**
  7 days a week
- **Hours of the Day**
  All day

Coupon expires 12/31/09. Cannot be combined with any other offer.

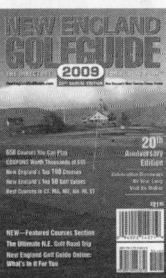

Hotchkiss School Golf Club
Lakeville, CT (860) 435-4400

- **Type of Discount**
  2 players for the price of 1 green fees.
  Cart rental required.
- **Days of the Week**
  Weekdays only (except holidays)
- **Hours of the Day**
  All day

Coupon expires 12/31/09. Cannot be combined with any other offer.

Indian Springs GC
Middlefield, CT (860) 349-8109

- **Type of Discount**
  Free golf cart with 2 paid green fees
- **Days of the Week**
  Weekdays before 3pm
- **Hours of the Day**

Coupon expires 12/31/09. Cannot be combined with any other offer.

Keney Golf Club
Hartford, CT (860) 525-3656

- **Type of Discount**
  2 players for the price of 1
- **Days of the Week**
  Weekdays only (except holidays)
- **Hours of the Day**
  All day. Cart rental required.

Coupon expires 12/31/09. Cannot be combined with any other offer.

NEW ENGLAND GOLFGUIDE

2 0 0 9

NEW ENGLAND GOLFGUIDE

2 0 0 9

NEW ENGLAND GOLFGUIDE

2 0 0 9

NEW ENGLAND GOLFGUIDE

2 0 0 9

Miner Hills Family Golf
Middletown, CT (860) 635-0051

- **Type of Discount**
  2 with motor cart: $12 each for 9 holes
- **Days of the Week**
  Weekdays only
- **Hours of the Day**
  Before 1 pm

Coupon expires 12/31/09. Cannot be combined with any other offer.

Pequot Golf Club
Wheeler Road, Stonington, CT (860) 535-1898

- **Type of Discount**
  $5 off green fees for up to 2 players
- **Days of the Week**
  Monday through Thursday
- **Hours of the Day**
  All day

Coupon expires 12/31/09. Cannot be combined with any other offer.

Pomperaug Golf Club
Southbury, CT (203) 264-9484

- **Type of Discount**
  Free golf cart with 2 paid green fees
- **Days of the Week**
  Weekdays only (except holidays)
- **Hours of the Day**
  All day

Coupon expires 12/31/09. Cannot be combined with any other offer.

Putnam Country Club at Chase Farm
Putnam, CT (860) 928-7748

- **Type of Discount**
  2 players for the price of 1
- **Days of the Week**
  Monday through Thursday (except holidays)
- **Hours of the Day**
  7am - 2pm. Cart rental required.

Coupon expires 12/31/09. Cannot be combined with any other offer.

NEW ENGLAND GOLFGUIDE

2 0 0 9

NEW ENGLAND GOLFGUIDE

2 0 0 9

NEW ENGLAND GOLFGUIDE

2 0 0 9

NEW ENGLAND GOLFGUIDE

2 0 0 9

Shennecosset Golf Club
Groton, CT (860) 445-0262

- **Type of Discount**
  Free golf cart with 2 paid green fees
- **Days of the Week**
  Weekdays only (except holidays)
- **Hours of the Day**
  All day

Coupon expires 12/31/09. Cannot be combined with any other offer.

Skungamaug River Golf Club
Coventry, CT (860) 742-9348

- **Type of Discount**
  Free golf cart with 2 paid green fees
- **Days of the Week**

- **Hours of the Day**

Coupon expires 12/31/09. Cannot be combined with any other offer.

Southington Country Club
Southington, CT (860) 628-7032

- **Type of Discount**
  2 players for the price of 1
- **Days of the Week**
  Weekdays only (except holidays)
- **Hours of the Day**
  Before Noon, golf carts not included

Coupon expires 12/31/09. Cannot be combined with any other offer.

Sunset Hill Golf Club
Brookfield, CT (203) 740-7800

- **Type of Discount**
  2 players for the price of 1 (cart rental required)
- **Days of the Week**
  Mon-Thurs except holidays
- **Hours of the Day**
  All day

Coupon expires 12/31/09. Cannot be combined with any other offer.

NEW ENGLAND GOLFGUIDE

2 0 0 9

NEW ENGLAND GOLFGUIDE

2 0 0 9

NEW ENGLAND GOLFGUIDE

2 0 0 9

NEW ENGLAND GOLFGUIDE

2 0 0 9

Timberlin Golf Club
Berlin, CT (860) 828-3228

- **Type of Discount**
  2 players for the price of 1, paid cart required
- **Days of the Week**
  Weekdays only (except holidays)
- **Hours of the Day**
  All day. Cart rental required.

Coupon expires 12/31/09. Cannot be combined with any other offer.

Tower Ridge
Simsbury, CT

- **Type of Discount**
  Buy 3 get 1 free
- **Days of the Week**
  7 days a week
- **Hours of the Day**

Coupon expires 12/31/09. Cannot be combined with any other offer.

Vineyard Valley Golf Club
Pomfret Center, CT (860) 974-2100

- **Type of Discount**
  2 players for the price of 1
- **Days of the Week**
  Weekdays only (except holidays)
- **Hours of the Day**
  All day

Coupon expires 12/31/09. Cannot be combined with any other offer.

Western Hills Golf Course
Waterbury, CT (203) 756-1211

- **Type of Discount**
  2 players for the price of 1
- **Days of the Week**
  Weekdays only (except holidays)
- **Hours of the Day**
  Before Noon green fees only, must pay for
  full cart

Coupon expires 12/31/09. Cannot be combined with any other offer.

Golf Course Coupons

NEW ENGLAND GOLFGUIDE

2 0 0 9

NEW ENGLAND GOLFGUIDE

2 0 0 9

NEW ENGLAND GOLFGUIDE

2 0 0 9

NEW ENGLAND GOLFGUIDE

2 0 0 9

Wintonbury Hills Golf Course
Bloomfield, CT (860) 242-1401

- **Type of Discount**
  25% discount for 2-4 players
- **Days of the Week**
  Weekdays only (except holidays)
- **Hours of the Day**
  6am - 4:50pm

Coupon expires 12/31/09. Cannot be combined with any other offer.

Woodhaven Country Club
Bethany, CT (203) 393-3230

- **Type of Discount**
  25% discount for 4 players
- **Days of the Week**
  Weekdays only (except holidays)
- **Hours of the Day**
  11am - 3pm

Coupon expires 12/31/09. Cannot be combined with any other offer.

Woodstock Golf Course
Roseland Golf Course, South Woodstock, CT
(860) 928-4130

- **Type of Discount**
  25% discount for 4 players
- **Days of the Week**
  Weekdays only (except holidays)
- **Hours of the Day**
  11am- 3pm

Coupon expires 12/31/09. Cannot be combined with any other offer.

Aroostook Valley Country Club
Fort Fairfield, ME (207) 476-8083

- **Type of Discount**
  2 players for the price of 1
- **Days of the Week**
  7 days a week
- **Hours of the Day**
  All day

Coupon expires 12/31/09. Cannot be combined with any other offer.

Golf Course Coupons

NEW ENGLAND GOLFGUIDE

2 0 0 9

NEW ENGLAND GOLFGUIDE

2 0 0 9

NEW ENGLAND GOLFGUIDE

2 0 0 9

NEW ENGLAND GOLFGUIDE

2 0 0 9

Bar Harbor Golf Course
Route 204, Tronton, ME (207) 667-7505

- **Type of Discount**
  Free golf cart with 2 paid green fees

- **Days of the Week**
  Weekdays only (except holidays)

- **Hours of the Day**
  All day

Coupon expires 12/31/09. Cannot be combined with any other offer.

Bath Country Club
Bath, ME (207) 442-8411

- **Type of Discount**
  $5 off green fees for up to 2 players

- **Days of the Week**
  7 days a week

- **Hours of the Day**
  After 12pm

Coupon expires 12/31/09. Cannot be combined with any other offer.

Bethel Inn Resort
Bethel, ME (207) 824-6276

- **Type of Discount**
  2nd green fees at 50% off

- **Days of the Week**
  Weekdays only (except holidays)

- **Hours of the Day**
  All day. Must make tee time no more than
  48 hours in advance.

Coupon expires 12/31/09. Cannot be combined with any other offer.

Bridgton Highlands Country Club
Bridgton, ME (207) 647-3491

- **Type of Discount**
  25% discount for 2-4 players

- **Days of the Week**
  7 days a week

- **Hours of the Day**
  After 1pm

Coupon expires 12/31/09. Cannot be combined with any other offer.

Golf Course Coupons

NEW ENGLAND GOLFGUIDE

2 0 0 9

NEW ENGLAND GOLFGUIDE

2 0 0 9

NEW ENGLAND GOLFGUIDE

2 0 0 9

NEW ENGLAND GOLFGUIDE

2 0 0 9

Brunswick Golf Club
River Road, Brunswick, ME (207) 725-8224

- **Type of Discount**
  Bring 3, 4th player plays free
- **Days of the Week**
  7 days a week
- **Hours of the Day**
  All day

Coupon expires 12/31/09. Cannot be combined with any other offer.

Bucksport Golf Club
Route 46, Bucksport, ME (207) 469-7612

- **Type of Discount**
  4 players for the price of 3
- **Days of the Week**
  7 days a week, not valid in July and August
- **Hours of the Day**
  All day

Coupon expires 12/31/09. Cannot be combined with any other offer.

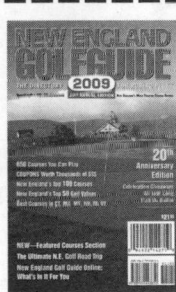

Cape Neddick Country Club
Ogunquit, ME (207) 361-2011

- **Type of Discount**
  $10 off each green fees for up to 4 players
- **Days of the Week**
  Weekdays only (except holidays)
- **Hours of the Day**
  All day. Valid April through November.

Coupon expires 12/31/09. Cannot be combined with any other offer.

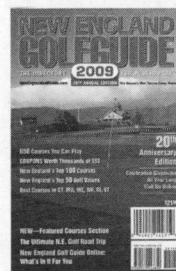

Caribou Country Club
Caribou, ME (207) 493-3933

- **Type of Discount**
  Free golf cart with 2 paid green fees
- **Days of the Week**
  7 days a week
- **Hours of the Day**
  All day

Coupon expires 12/31/09. Cannot be combined with any other offer.

Golf Course Coupons

NEW ENGLAND GOLFGUIDE

2 0 0 9

NEW ENGLAND GOLFGUIDE

2 0 0 9

NEW ENGLAND GOLFGUIDE

2 0 0 9

NEW ENGLAND GOLFGUIDE

2 0 0 9

Cobbossee Colony Golf Course
Monmouth, ME (207) 268-4182

- **Type of Discount**
  $5 off green fees for up to 2 players

- **Days of the Week**
  Weekdays only (except holidays)

- **Hours of the Day**
  All day

Coupon expires 12/31/09. Cannot be combined with any other offer.

Country View Golf Course
Route 7, Brooks, ME (207) 722-3161

- **Type of Discount**
  1/2 price Golf Cart with 2 paid green fees

- **Days of the Week**
  7 days a week

- **Hours of the Day**
  All day

Coupon expires 12/31/09. Cannot be combined with any other offer.

Deep Brook Golf Course
Saco, ME (207) 283-3500

- **Type of Discount**
  4 players for the price of 3

- **Days of the Week**
  Weekdays only (except holidays)

- **Hours of the Day**
  All day

Coupon expires 12/31/09. Cannot be combined with any other offer.

Dutch Elm Golf Course
Arundel, ME (207) 282-9850

- **Type of Discount**
  $5 off green fees for up to 2 players

- **Days of the Week**
  Weekdays only (except holidays)

- **Hours of the Day**
  After 11am only. Golf cart rental required.

Coupon expires 12/31/09. Cannot be combined with any other offer.

Golf Course Coupons

NEW ENGLAND GOLFGUIDE

2 0 0 9

NEW ENGLAND GOLFGUIDE

2 0 0 9

NEW ENGLAND GOLFGUIDE

2 0 0 9

NEW ENGLAND GOLFGUIDE

2 0 0 9

Fort Kent Golf Course
Fort Kent, ME (207) 834-3149

- **Type of Discount**
  1 player at 9 hole price for 18 holes
- **Days of the Week**
  7 days a week
- **Hours of the Day**
  All day. Valid 4/1/09 to 10/20/09

Coupon expires 12/31/09. Cannot be combined with any other offer.

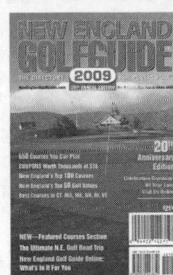

Fox Ridge Golf Club
Auburn, ME (207) 777-GOLF(4653)

- **Type of Discount**
  2 players for the price of 1
- **Days of the Week**
  Weekdays only (except holidays)
- **Hours of the Day**
  All day

Coupon expires 12/31/09. Cannot be combined with any other offer.

Frye Island Golf Course
Raymond, ME (207) 655-3551

- **Type of Discount**
  $5 off green fees for up to 2 players
- **Days of the Week**
  Weekdays only (except holidays)
- **Hours of the Day**
  All day. Valid May-June and September-October.

Coupon expires 12/31/09. Cannot be combined with any other offer.

Goose River Golf Club
Rockport, ME (207) 236-8488

- **Type of Discount**
  $5 off per person up to 4 people
- **Days of the Week**
  Weekdays only (except holidays)
- **Hours of the Day**
  All day except Tues & Weds (7am-3pm) only

Coupon expires 12/31/09. Cannot be combined with any other offer.

NEW ENGLAND
GOLFGUIDE

2 0 0 9

NEW ENGLAND
GOLFGUIDE

2 0 0 9

NEW ENGLAND
GOLFGUIDE

2 0 0 9

NEW ENGLAND
GOLFGUIDE

2 0 0 9

Green Valley Golf Club
Lincoln, ME (207) 732-3006

- **Type of Discount**
  Free Golf Cart with 2 regular paid green fees
- **Days of the Week**
  7 days a week
- **Hours of the Day**
  All day

Coupon expires 12/31/09. Cannot be combined with any other offer.

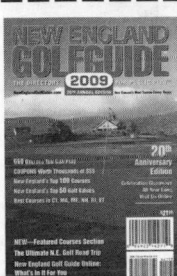

Hermon Meadow Golf Club
Bangor, ME (207) 848-3741

- **Type of Discount**
  Free Golf Cart with 2 regular 18 hole green fees
- **Days of the Week**
  Weekdays only (except holidays)
- **Hours of the Day**
  All day

Coupon expires 12/31/09. Cannot be combined with any other offer.

Highland Green Golf Club
Topsham, ME (207) 725-6318

- **Type of Discount**
  $5 off green fees for up to 2 players
- **Days of the Week**
  Weekdays only (except holidays)
- **Hours of the Day**
  All day

Coupon expires 12/31/09. Cannot be combined with any other offer.

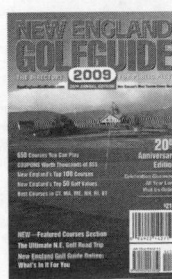

Houlton Community Golf Course
Houlton, ME (207) 532-2662

- **Type of Discount**
  Free 9 Hole Replay after 3pm (after 18-hole paid round)
- **Days of the Week**
  7 days a week
- **Hours of the Day**
  All day. Call for tee times.

Coupon expires 12/31/09. Cannot be combined with any other offer.

Golf Course Coupons

NEW ENGLAND GOLFGUIDE

2 0 0 9

NEW ENGLAND GOLFGUIDE

2 0 0 9

NEW ENGLAND GOLFGUIDE

2 0 0 9

NEW ENGLAND GOLFGUIDE

2 0 0 9

Island Green Golf Course
Holden, ME (207) 989-9909

- **Type of Discount**
  Free bucket of range balls
- **Days of the Week**

- **Hours of the Day**

Coupon expires 12/31/09. Cannot be combined with any other offer.

Jato Highlands Golf Course
Lincoln, ME (207) 794-2433

- **Type of Discount**
  Free golf cart with 2 paid green fees
- **Days of the Week**
  Weekdays only (except holidays)
- **Hours of the Day**
  All day

Coupon expires 12/31/09. Cannot be combined with any other offer.

Johnson W. Parks Golf Course
Pittsfield, ME (207) 487-5545

- **Type of Discount**
  2 players for the price of 1 with cart
- **Days of the Week**
  7 days a week
- **Hours of the Day**
  All weekdays, weekends and holidays after 1pm

Coupon expires 12/31/09. Cannot be combined with any other offer.

Kebo Valley Golf Club
Bar Harbor, ME (207) 288-3000

- **Type of Discount**
  15% off green fees
- **Days of the Week**
  7 days a week
- **Hours of the Day**
  Not valid for afternoon or twilight rates

Coupon expires 12/31/09. Cannot be combined with any other offer.

Golf Course Coupons

NEW ENGLAND GOLFGUIDE

2 0 0 9

NEW ENGLAND GOLFGUIDE

2 0 0 9

NEW ENGLAND GOLFGUIDE

2 0 0 9

NEW ENGLAND GOLFGUIDE

2 0 0 9

Kenduskeag Valley Golf Course
Kenduskeag, ME (207) 884-7330

- **Type of Discount**
  Free golf cart with 2 paid green fees
- **Days of the Week**
  Weekdays only (except holidays)
- **Hours of the Day**
  All day

Coupon expires 12/31/09. Cannot be combined with any other offer.

Lakeview Golf Club
Burnham, ME (207) 948-5414

- **Type of Discount**
  4 green fees for the price of 3
- **Days of the Week**
  Mondays through Thursday (except holidays)
- **Hours of the Day**

Coupon expires 12/31/09. Cannot be combined with any other offer.

Ledges Golf Club, the
York, ME (207) 351-3000

- **Type of Discount**
  Free golf cart with 2 paid green fees
- **Days of the Week**
  7 days a week
- **Hours of the Day**
  Weekends after 1pm. Must make tee time.

Coupon expires 12/31/09. Cannot be combined with any other offer.

Limestone Country Club
Limestone, ME (207) 328-7277

- **Type of Discount**
  $5 off green fees. Cart rental required.
- **Days of the Week**
  Weekdays only (except holidays)
- **Hours of the Day**
  All day

Coupon expires 12/31/09. Cannot be combined with any other offer.

NEW ENGLAND GOLFGUIDE

2 0 0 9

NEW ENGLAND GOLFGUIDE

2 0 0 9

NEW ENGLAND GOLFGUIDE

2 0 0 9

NEW ENGLAND GOLFGUIDE

2 0 0 9

Links at Outlook, The
South Derwick, ME (207) 384-4653

- **Type of Discount**
  Free golf cart with 2 paid green fees

- **Days of the Week**
  7 days a week (except holidays)

- **Hours of the Day**
  All day (except holidays.)

Coupon expires 12/31/09. Cannot be combined with any other offer.

Long Lake Country Club
Madawaska, ME (207) 895-6957

- **Type of Discount**
  Half price powercart with 2 paid green fees

- **Days of the Week**
  7 days a week

- **Hours of the Day**
  All day. Valid May 15 through October 15.

Coupon expires 12/31/09. Cannot be combined with any other offer.

Lucerne-in-Maine Golf Course
Dedham, ME (207) 843-6282

- **Type of Discount**
  Free golf cart with 2 paid green fees

- **Days of the Week**
  7 days a week

- **Hours of the Day**
  All day. Valid May 26 to September 6.

Coupon expires 12/31/09. Cannot be combined with any other offer.

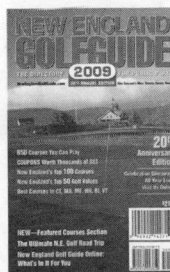

Maple Lane Inn and Golf Club
Livermore, ME (207) 897-3770

- **Type of Discount**
  18 holes of golf, golf cart & lunch for $30

- **Days of the Week**
  Weekdays only (except holidays)

- **Hours of the Day**
  All day

Coupon expires 12/31/09. Cannot be combined with any other offer.

NEW ENGLAND GOLFGUIDE

2 0 0 9

NEW ENGLAND GOLFGUIDE

2 0 0 9

NEW ENGLAND GOLFGUIDE

2 0 0 9

NEW ENGLAND GOLFGUIDE

2 0 0 9

Mars Hill Country Club
Mars Hill, ME (207) 425-4802

- **Type of Discount**
  20% off Green fees

- **Days of the Week**
  Weekdays only (except holidays)

- **Hours of the Day**
  All day

Coupon expires 12/31/09. Cannot be combined with any other offer.

Merriland Farm Par 3 Golf
Wells, ME (207) 646-0508

- **Type of Discount**
  2 players for the price of 1

- **Days of the Week**
  Weekdays only (except holidays)

- **Hours of the Day**
  All day. Valid April, May, June, Sept, & October.

Coupon expires 12/31/09. Cannot be combined with any other offer.

Naples Golf and Country Club
Route 114, Naples, ME (207) 693-6424

- **Type of Discount**
  25% discount for 2-4 players

- **Days of the Week**
  Weekdays only (except holidays)

- **Hours of the Day**
  After 1pm

Coupon expires 12/31/09. Cannot be combined with any other offer.

Nonesuch River Golf Club
Scarborough, ME (888) 256-2717

- **Type of Discount**
  Free small bucket of range balls with every
  18 holes of golf and power cart paid for

- **Days of the Week**
  7 days a week

- **Hours of the Day**
  All day

Coupon expires 12/31/09. Cannot be combined with any other offer.

Golf Course Coupons

NEW ENGLAND GOLFGUIDE

2 0 0 9

✂ -

NEW ENGLAND GOLFGUIDE

2 0 0 9

✂ -

NEW ENGLAND GOLFGUIDE

2 0 0 9

✂ -

NEW ENGLAND GOLFGUIDE

2 0 0 9

Northport Golf Club
Belfast, ME (207) 338-2270

- **Type of Discount**
  4 players for the price of 3
- **Days of the Week**
  Weekdays only (except holidays)
- **Hours of the Day**

Coupon expires 12/31/09. Cannot be combined with any other offer.

Oakdale Country Club
Mexico, ME (207) 364-3951

- **Type of Discount**
  $25 per person 18 holes with cart
- **Days of the Week**
  7 days a week
- **Hours of the Day**
  All day

Coupon expires 12/31/09. Cannot be combined with any other offer.

Palmyra Golf Course
Palmyra, ME (207) 938-4947

- **Type of Discount**
  Free golf cart with 2 paid green fees
- **Days of the Week**
  7 days a week
- **Hours of the Day**
  All day

Coupon expires 12/31/09. Cannot be combined with any other offer.

Paris Hill Country Club
Paris Hill Road, Paris, ME (207) 743-2371

- **Type of Discount**
  Walk 18 holes for $16, ride 18 holes for $26pp.
  Coupon must be presented.
- **Days of the Week**
  7 days a week
- **Hours of the Day**
  All day

Coupon expires 12/31/09. Cannot be combined with any other offer.

Golf Course Coupons

NEW ENGLAND GOLFGUIDE

2 0 0 9

NEW ENGLAND GOLFGUIDE

2 0 0 9

NEW ENGLAND GOLFGUIDE

2 0 0 9

NEW ENGLAND GOLFGUIDE

2 0 0 9

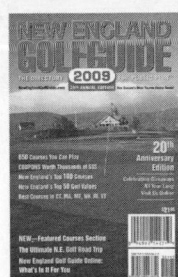

Point Sebago Golf Club
Casco, ME (207) 655-2747

- **Type of Discount**
  $5 off green fees for up to 2 players
- **Days of the Week**
  Weekdays only (except holidays)
- **Hours of the Day**
  After 1pm

Coupon expires 12/31/09. Cannot be combined with any other offer.

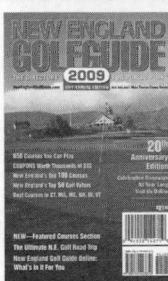

Poland Spring Country Club
Route 26, Poland Spring, ME (207) 998-6002

- **Type of Discount**
  2 players for the price of 1
- **Days of the Week**
  Mon-Thurs
- **Hours of the Day**
  After 1pm. Valid May 1 - June 15 and
  September 6 - October 30. Tee times required.

Coupon expires 12/31/09. Cannot be combined with any other offer.

Portage Hill Country Club
Route 11, Portage, ME (207) 435-8221

- **Type of Discount**
  2 players for the price of 1
- **Days of the Week**
  7 days a week
- **Hours of the Day**
  All day

Coupon expires 12/31/09. Cannot be combined with any other offer.

Presque Isle Country Club
Presque Isle, ME (207) 764-0430

- **Type of Discount**
  Play 18 holes for the 9 hole green fee
- **Days of the Week**
  7 days a week, May 1 - October 31, 2009
- **Hours of the Day**
  All day power cart required at regular rate

Coupon expires 12/31/09. Cannot be combined with any other offer.

NEW ENGLAND GOLFGUIDE

2 0 0 9

NEW ENGLAND GOLFGUIDE

2 0 0 9

NEW ENGLAND GOLFGUIDE

2 0 0 9

NEW ENGLAND GOLFGUIDE

2 0 0 9

Province Lake Golf Club
Route 153, Parsonfield, ME
(800) 325-4434

- **Type of Discount**
  25% discount for 2-4 players
- **Days of the Week**
  7 days a week
- **Hours of the Day**
  After 1pm

Coupon expires 12/31/09. Cannot be combined with any other offer.

River Meadow Golf Club
Westbrook, ME (207) 854-1625

- **Type of Discount**
  Free golf cart with 2 paid green fees
- **Days of the Week**
  Weekdays only (except holidays)
- **Hours of the Day**
  All day. Tee times recommended.

Coupon expires 12/31/09. Cannot be combined with any other offer.

Rockland Golf Club
Rockland, ME (207) 594-9322

- **Type of Discount**
  $10 off each green fees for up to 4 players
- **Days of the Week**
  7 days a week
- **Hours of the Day**
  After 12pm

Coupon expires 12/31/09. Cannot be combined with any other offer.

Sable Oaks Golf Club
South Portland, ME (207) 775-6257

- **Type of Discount**
  $10 off 18-hole green fees
- **Days of the Week**
  Monday-Thursday, except holidays
- **Hours of the Day**
  All day

Coupon expires 12/31/09. Cannot be combined with any other offer.

Golf Course Coupons

NEW ENGLAND GOLFGUIDE

2 0 0 9

NEW ENGLAND GOLFGUIDE

2 0 0 9

NEW ENGLAND GOLFGUIDE

2 0 0 9

NEW ENGLAND GOLFGUIDE

2 0 0 9

Salmon Falls Golf Course
Hollis, ME (207) 929-5233 or (800) 734-1616

- **Type of Discount**
  $60 for 2 players and golfcart for 18 holes
- **Days of the Week**
  7 days a week
- **Hours of the Day**
  All day

Coupon expires 12/31/09. Cannot be combined with any other offer.

Sanford Country Club
Route 4, Sanford, ME (207) 324-5462

- **Type of Discount**
  2 players for the price of 1
- **Days of the Week**
  Tuesdays only
- **Hours of the Day**

Coupon expires 12/31/09. Cannot be combined with any other offer.

Searsport Pines Golf Course
Searsport, ME (207) 548-2854

- **Type of Discount**
  $5 off green fees for up to 2 players
- **Days of the Week**
  7 days a week
- **Hours of the Day**
  All day. Cart rental required.

Coupon expires 12/31/09. Cannot be combined with any other offer.

Spring Meadows Golf Course
Gray, ME (207) 657-2586

- **Type of Discount**
  $5 off green fees for up to 2 players
- **Days of the Week**
  7 days a week
- **Hours of the Day**
  All day; not during July and August

Coupon expires 12/31/09. Cannot be combined with any other offer.

Golf Course Coupons

NEW ENGLAND GOLFGUIDE

2 0 0 9

NEW ENGLAND GOLFGUIDE

2 0 0 9

NEW ENGLAND GOLFGUIDE

2 0 0 9

NEW ENGLAND GOLFGUIDE

2 0 0 9

Sugarloaf Golf Club
Carrabassett Valley, ME (207) 237-2000

- **Type of Discount**
  Free golf cart with 2 paid green fees

- **Days of the Week**
  Weekdays only (except holidays)

- **Hours of the Day**
  All day

Coupon expires 12/31/09. Cannot be combined with any other offer.

Toddy Brook Golf Course
North Yarmouth, ME (207) 829-5100

- **Type of Discount**
  Free golf cart with 2 paid green fees

- **Days of the Week**
  Weekdays only (except holidays)

- **Hours of the Day**
  All day

Coupon expires 12/31/09. Cannot be combined with any other offer.

Turner Highland Golf Course
Turner, ME (207) 224-7060

- **Type of Discount**
  $35 with a cart

- **Days of the Week**
  7 days a week

- **Hours of the Day**
  All day

Coupon expires 12/31/09. Cannot be combined with any other offer.

Va-Jo-Wa Golf Club
Walker Settlement Road
Island Falls, ME (207) 463-2128

- **Type of Discount**
  2 players for the price of 1

- **Days of the Week**
  Weekdays only (except holidays)

- **Hours of the Day**
  All day

Coupon expires 12/31/09. Cannot be combined with any other offer.

Golf Course Coupons

NEW ENGLAND GOLFGUIDE

2 0 0 9

NEW ENGLAND GOLFGUIDE

2 0 0 9

NEW ENGLAND GOLFGUIDE

2 0 0 9

NEW ENGLAND GOLFGUIDE

2 0 0 9

Wawenock Country Club
Walpole, ME (207) 563-3938

- **Type of Discount**
  $30 per player for 18 holes with cart
- **Days of the Week**
  7 days a week
- **Hours of the Day**
  All day. Please call ahead for tee time.

Coupon expires 12/31/09. Cannot be combined with any other offer.

White Tail Golf Course
Charleston, ME (207) 285-7730

- **Type of Discount**
  10% off green fees and cart rentals
- **Days of the Week**
  Weekdays only (except holidays)
- **Hours of the Day**
  All day

Coupon expires 12/31/09. Cannot be combined with any other offer.

Acushnet River Valley Golf Course
Acushnet, MA (508) 998-7777

- **Type of Discount**
  Free golf cart with 2 paid green fees. Free 9 hole replay after 1pm (after 18-hole paid round). Wknd Special: Buy 9 holes after 3pm, get 9 free.
- **Days of the Week**
  Weekdays only (except holidays)
- **Hours of the Day**
  All day

Coupon expires 12/31/09. Cannot be combined with any other offer.

Amherst Golf Club
Amherst, MA (413) 256-6894

- **Type of Discount**
  1 player at 1/2 price
- **Days of the Week**
  Weekdays only (except holidays)
- **Hours of the Day**

Coupon expires 12/31/09. Cannot be combined with any other offer.

Golf Course Coupons

NEW ENGLAND
GOLFGUIDE

2 0 0 9

NEW ENGLAND
GOLFGUIDE

2 0 0 9

NEW ENGLAND
GOLFGUIDE

2 0 0 9

NEW ENGLAND
GOLFGUIDE

2 0 0 9

Ashfield Community Golf Club
Ashfield, MA (413) 628-4413

- **Type of Discount**
  $5 off green fees

- **Days of the Week**
  Weekends and holidays only

- **Hours of the Day**
  All day

Coupon expires 12/31/09. Cannot be combined with any other offer.

Atlantic Country Club
Plymouth, MA (508) 759-6644

- **Type of Discount**
  $5 off green fees

- **Days of the Week**
  Monday through Thursday

- **Hours of the Day**
  All day (excludes twilight hours)

Coupon expires 12/31/09. Cannot be combined with any other offer.

Back Nine Club, The
Lakeville, MA (508) 947-9991

- **Type of Discount**
  Free golf cart with 2 paid green fees

- **Days of the Week**
  Weekdays only (except holidays)

- **Hours of the Day**
  11am - 3pm

Coupon expires 12/31/09. Cannot be combined with any other offer.

Bas Ridge Golf Course
Plunkett Street, Hinsdale, MA (413) 655-2605

- **Type of Discount**
  2 green fees for the price of 1. Cart required.

- **Days of the Week**
  Weekdays only (except holidays)

- **Hours of the Day**
  8am - 3pm; not valid July & August

Coupon expires 12/31/09. Cannot be combined with any other offer.

NEW ENGLAND GOLFGUIDE

2 0 0 9

NEW ENGLAND GOLFGUIDE

2 0 0 9

NEW ENGLAND GOLFGUIDE

2 0 0 9

NEW ENGLAND GOLFGUIDE

2 0 0 9

Bay Pointo Country Club
Onset, MA (508) 759-8802, 1-800-24T-TIME

- **Type of Discount**
  18 holes and riding cart - $34 per person
  up to 4 players
- **Days of the Week**
  Monday-Friday, year-round
- **Hours of the Day**
  All day

Coupon expires 12/31/09. Cannot be combined with any other offer.

Beaver Brook Country Club
Main Street, Haydenville, MA (413) 268-7229

- **Type of Discount**
  2 players for the price of 1. Cart rental required.
- **Days of the Week**
  7 days a week
- **Hours of the Day**
  All day

Coupon expires 12/31/09. Cannot be combined with any other offer.

Bedrock Golf Club
Rutland, MA (508) 886-0202

- **Type of Discount**
  4 players for the price of 3
- **Days of the Week**
  7 days a week
- **Hours of the Day**
  All day

Coupon expires 12/31/09. Cannot be combined with any other offer.

Blissful Meadows Golf Club
Uxbridge, MA (508) 278-6113

- **Type of Discount**
  4 green fees for the price of 3
- **Days of the Week**
  Mon -Thursday only (except holidays)
- **Hours of the Day**
  All day

Coupon expires 12/31/00. Cannot be combined with any other offer.

NEW ENGLAND GOLFGUIDE

2 0 0 9

NEW ENGLAND GOLFGUIDE

2 0 0 9

NEW ENGLAND GOLFGUIDE

2 0 0 9

NEW ENGLAND GOLFGUIDE

2 0 0 9

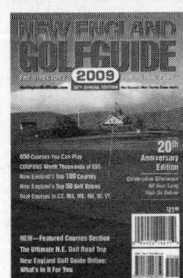

Bradford Country Club
Bradford, MA (978) 372-8587

- **Type of Discount**
  2 players, $80 for 18 holes with cart

- **Days of the Week**
  Weekdays only (except holidays)

- **Hours of the Day**
  All day. Must bring coupon.

Coupon expires 12/31/09. Cannot be combined with any other offer.

Bungay Brook Golf Club
Bellingham, MA (508) 883-1600

- **Type of Discount**
  Free golf cart with 2 paid green fees. Free small
  pail range balls with paid green fees.

- **Days of the Week**
  7 days a week

- **Hours of the Day**
  All day

Coupon expires 12/31/09. Cannot be combined with any other offer.

Butter Brook Golf Club
Westford, MA (978) 692-6560

- **Type of Discount**
  4 players for the price of 3

- **Days of the Week**
  Monday through Thursday

- **Hours of the Day**
  All day. Cart rental required.

Coupon expires 12/31/09. Cannot be combined with any other offer.

Captains Golf Course, The (Port)
Brewster, MA (508) 896-1716

- **Type of Discount**
  $5 off green fees for up to 2 players

- **Days of the Week**
  7 days a week

- **Hours of the Day**
  All day. Not valid for reservations made more
  than 5 days in advance.

Coupon expires 12/31/09. Cannot be combined with any other offer

NEW ENGLAND GOLFGUIDE

2 0 0 9

NEW ENGLAND GOLFGUIDE

2 0 0 9

NEW ENGLAND GOLFGUIDE

2 0 0 9

NEW ENGLAND GOLFGUIDE

2 0 0 9

Captains Golf Course, The (Starboard)
Brewster, MA (508) 896-1716

- **Type of Discount**
  $5 off green fees for up to 2 players

- **Days of the Week**
  7 days a week

- **Hours of the Day**
  All day. Not valid for reservations made
  more than 5 days in advance.

Coupon expires 12/31/09. Cannot be combined with any other offer.

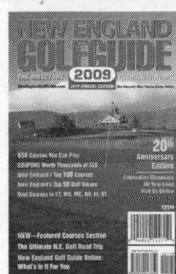

Carriage Pines Golf Club
Rowley, MA (978) 948-2731

- **Type of Discount**
  Earlybird & Twilight rates: $12 before 8am and
  after 6pm. Lunch special: 2 players w/cart $44
  M-Th 11:30-2:30.

- **Days of the Week**
  Weekdays only (except holidays)

- **Hours of the Day**
  All day

Coupon expires 12/31/09. Cannot be combined with any other offer.

Chelmsford Country Club
Chelmsford, MA (978) 256-1818

- **Type of Discount**
  Free golf cart with 2 paid green fees

- **Days of the Week**
  7 days a week

- **Hours of the Day**
  All day

Coupon expires 12/31/09. Cannot be combined with any other offer.

Cherry Hill Golf Course
Amherst, MA (413) 256-4071

- **Type of Discount**
  4 players for the price of 3

- **Days of the Week**
  7 days a week

- **Hours of the Day**
  Cart required

Coupon expires 12/31/09. Cannot be combined with any other offer.

NEW ENGLAND GOLFGUIDE

2 0 0 9

NEW ENGLAND GOLFGUIDE

2 0 0 9

NEW ENGLAND GOLFGUIDE

2 0 0 9

NEW ENGLAND GOLFGUIDE

2 0 0 9

Country Club of Billerica
Billerica, MA (978) 667-9121 ext. 22

- **Type of Discount**
  4 players for the price of 3
- **Days of the Week**
  Weekdays only (except holidays)
- **Hours of the Day**
  9am-2pm. Riding carts not included.

Coupon expires 12/31/09. Cannot be combined with any other offer.

Country Club of Greenfield
Country Club Rd., Greenfield, MA (413) 773-7530

- **Type of Discount**
  $140 foursome w/carts
- **Days of the Week**
  7 days a week
- **Hours of the Day**
  Please call ahead

Coupon expires 12/31/09. Cannot be combined with any other offer.

Crosswinds Golf Club
Plymouth, MA (508) 830-1199

- **Type of Discount**
  4 players for the price of 3
- **Days of the Week**
  Mon-Thurs (except holidays)
- **Hours of the Day**
  After 1pm. Rates subject to change.

Coupon expires 12/31/09. Cannot be combined with any other offer.

Crumpin-Fox Club
Bernardston, MA (413) 648-9101

- **Type of Discount**
  $25 off per guide holder or coupon holder.
- **Days of the Week**
  Weekdays only (except holidays)
- **Hours of the Day**
  All day. Valid from opening until May 15 and
  October 15th until closing.

Coupon expires 12/31/09. Cannot be combined with any other offer.

NEW ENGLAND GOLFGUIDE

2 0 0 9

NEW ENGLAND GOLFGUIDE

2 0 0 9

NEW ENGLAND GOLFGUIDE

2 0 0 9

NEW ENGLAND GOLFGUIDE

2 0 0 9

Cyprian Keyes Golf Club
Boylston, MA (508) 869-9900

- **Type of Discount**
  $25 off a Callaway Performance Center clubfitting
- **Days of the Week**
  7 days a week
- **Hours of the Day**
  Please call to reserve a time

Coupon expires 12/31/09. Cannot be combined with any other offer.

Dennis Highlands Golf Course
Dennis, MA (508) 385-8347

- **Type of Discount**
  2 players for the price of 1
- **Days of the Week**
  Monday through Thursday
- **Hours of the Day**
  All day. Cart is mandatory; not valid for
  advanced prepaid tee times.

Coupon expires 12/31/09. Cannot be combined with any other offer.

Dennis Pines Golf Course
South Dennis, MA (508) 385-8347

- **Type of Discount**
  2 players for the price of 1
- **Days of the Week**
  Monday through Thursday
- **Hours of the Day**
  All day. Cart is mandatory. Not valid for advanced
  prepaid tee times. Rates subject to change.

Coupon expires 12/31/09. Cannot be combined with any other offer.

D.W. Fields Golf Course
Brockton, MA (508) 580-7855

- **Type of Discount**
  $30 with cart
- **Days of the Week**
  M-F after Noon; Saturday/Sunday after 1
- **Hours of the Day**

Coupon expires 12/31/09. Cannot be combined with any other offer.

NEW ENGLAND GOLFGUIDE

2 0 0 9

NEW ENGLAND GOLFGUIDE

2 0 0 9

NEW ENGLAND GOLFGUIDE

2 0 0 9

NEW ENGLAND GOLFGUIDE

2 0 0 9

Edge Hill Golf Club
Ashfield, MA (413) 625-6018

- **Type of Discount**
  2 players for the price of 1

- **Days of the Week**
  Weekdays only (except holidays)

- **Hours of the Day**
  All day

Coupon expires 12/31/09. Cannot be combined with any other offer.

Egremont Country Club
Great Barrington, MA (413) 528-4222

- **Type of Discount**
  2 green fees for the price of 1

- **Days of the Week**
  Weekdays only (except holidays)

- **Hours of the Day**
  Tee off by 2pm. Cart mandatory.

Coupon expires 12/31/09. Cannot be combined with any other offer.

Ellinwood Country Club
Athol, MA (978) 249-7460

- **Type of Discount**
  2 players for the price of 1; cart rental required

- **Days of the Week**
  Weekdays only (except holidays)

- **Hours of the Day**
  All day

Coupon expires 12/31/09. Cannot be combined with any other offer.

Falmouth Country Club
Falmouth, MA (508) 548-3211

- **Type of Discount**
  $10 off each player, up to 4 players (resident prices)

- **Days of the Week**
  Monday through Thursday (except holidays)

- **Hours of the Day**
  Before 2pm must have coupon

Coupon expires 12/31/09. Cannot be combined with any other offer.

Golf Course Coupons

NEW ENGLAND GOLFGUIDE

2 0 0 9

NEW ENGLAND GOLFGUIDE

2 0 0 9

NEW ENGLAND GOLFGUIDE

2 0 0 9

NEW ENGLAND GOLFGUIDE

2 0 0 9

Fire Fly Country Club
Seekonk, MA (508) 336-6622

- **Type of Discount**
  4 players for the price of 3
- **Days of the Week**
  7 days a week
- **Hours of the Day**
  All day

Coupon expires 12/31/09. Cannot be combined with any other offer.

Fore Kicks Golf Course & Sports Complex
Norfolk, MA (508) 384-4433

- **Type of Discount**
  1 player at 1/2 price
- **Days of the Week**
  7 days a week
- **Hours of the Day**
  All day

Coupon expires 12/31/09. Cannot be combined with any other offer.

Forest Park Country Club
Adams, MA (413) 743-3311

- **Type of Discount**
  2 players for the price of 1
- **Days of the Week**
  7 days a week
- **Hours of the Day**
  Please call ahead on weekends for availability

Coupon expires 12/31/09. Cannot be combined with any other offer.

Garrison Golf Center
Haverhill, MA (978) 374-9380

- **Type of Discount**
  $2 off 9 holes when accompanied by 1 full-paying customer
- **Days of the Week**
  Weekdays only (except holidays)
- **Hours of the Day**
  All day

Coupon expires 12/31/09. Cannot be combined with any other offer.

Golf Course Coupons

NEW ENGLAND GOLFGUIDE

2 0 0 9

NEW ENGLAND GOLFGUIDE

2 0 0 9

NEW ENGLAND GOLFGUIDE

2 0 0 9

NEW ENGLAND GOLFGUIDE

2 0 0 9

Glen Ellen Country Club
Route 115, Millis, MA (508) 376-2775

- **Type of Discount**
  Free golf cart with 2 paid green fees
- **Days of the Week**
  Monday through Thursday (except holidays)
- **Hours of the Day**
  Call ahead for tee times. Range offer, M-F, all day.

Coupon expires 12/31/09. Cannot be combined with any other offer.

Groton Country Club
Groton, MA (978) 448-2564

- **Type of Discount**
  2 players for the price of 1
- **Days of the Week**
  Monday through Saturday
- **Hours of the Day**
  Call ahead for tee times; cart rental required

Coupon expires 12/31/09. Cannot be combined with any other offer.

Heritage Country Club
Charlton, MA (508) 248-5111

- **Type of Discount**
  25% discount for 2-4 players
- **Days of the Week**
  Monday-Friday
- **Hours of the Day**
  11am - 3pm. No holidays. No tournaments.

Coupon expires 12/31/09. Cannot be combined with any other offer.

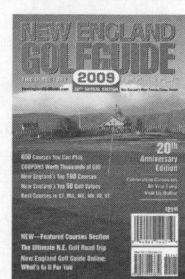

Hickory Ridge Country Club
South Amherst, MA (413) 253-9320

- **Type of Discount**
  2 players for the price of 1
- **Days of the Week**
  Weekdays only (except holidays)
- **Hours of the Day**
  All day

Coupon expires 12/31/09. Cannot be combined with any other offer.

Golf Course C

NEW ENGLAND GOLFGUIDE

2 0 0 9

NEW ENGLAND GOLFGUIDE

2 0 0 9

NEW ENGLAND GOLFGUIDE

2 0 0 9

NEW ENGLAND GOLFGUIDE

2 0 0 9

Highfields Golf & Country Club
Grafton, MA (508) 839-1945

- **Type of Discount**
  4 players for the price of 3

- **Days of the Week**
  Weekdays only (except holidays)

- **Hours of the Day**
  All day

Coupon expires 12/31/09. Cannot be combined with any other offer.

Hillcrest Country Club
Leicester, MA (508) 892-0963

- **Type of Discount**
  2 players for the price of 1 (must rent cart)

- **Days of the Week**
  Monday, Tuesday, Thursday, & Friday

- **Hours of the Day**
  All day

Coupon expires 12/31/09. Cannot be combined with any other offer.

Holly Ridge Golf Club
South Sandwich, MA (508) 428-5577

- **Type of Discount**
  $5 off green fees for up to 2 players

- **Days of the Week**
  7 days a week

- **Hours of the Day**
  7am to 3:30pm

Coupon expires 12/31/09. Cannot be combined with any other offer.

Hyannis Golf Club
Hyannis, MA (508) 362-2606

- **Type of Discount**
  $10 off green fees for up to 2 players

- **Days of the Week**
  Weekdays only (except holidays)

- **Hours of the Day**
  All day

Coupon expires 12/31/09. Cannot be combined with any other offer.

NEW ENGLAND GOLFGUIDE

2 0 0 9

NEW ENGLAND GOLFGUIDE

2 0 0 9

NEW ENGLAND GOLFGUIDE

2 0 0 9

NEW ENGLAND GOLFGUIDE

2 0 0 9

Lakeview Golf Club
Wenham, MA (978) 468-6676

- **Type of Discount**
  2 players for the price of 1
- **Days of the Week**
  Weekdays only (except holidays)
- **Hours of the Day**
  Before Noon

Coupon expires 12/31/09. Cannot be combined with any other offer.

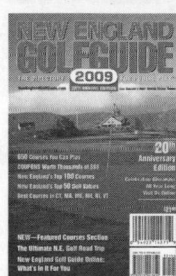

Ledges Golf Club
South Hadley, MA (413) 532-2307

- **Type of Discount**
  Free golf cart with 2 paid green fees
- **Days of the Week**
  7 days, must make tee time
- **Hours of the Day**
  All day M-F, after 1pm Saturday/Sunday

Coupon expires 12/31/09. Cannot be combined with any other offer.

Leicester Country Club
Leicester, MA (508) 892-1390 Ext. 12

- **Type of Discount**
  Free golf cart with 2 paid green fees
- **Days of the Week**
  Weekdays only (except holidays)
- **Hours of the Day**
  7am until 1pm depending on tee time
  availability. Must call for tee times.

Coupon expires 12/31/09. Cannot be combined with any other offer.

Links at Lancaster Golf, The
Lancaster, MA (978) 537-8922

- **Type of Discount**
  2 players for the price of 1
- **Days of the Week**
  7 days a week
- **Hours of the Day**
  All day

Coupon expires 12/31/09. Cannot be combined with any other offer.

NEW ENGLAND GOLFGUIDE

2 0 0 9

NEW ENGLAND GOLFGUIDE

2 0 0 9

NEW ENGLAND GOLFGUIDE

2 0 0 9

NEW ENGLAND GOLFGUIDE

2 0 0 9

Little Harbor Country Club
Wareham, MA (508) 295-2617

- **Type of Discount**
  $4 off regular green fees

- **Days of the Week**
  Weekdays only (except holidays and
  Wednesdays)

- **Hours of the Day**
  Before 3pm

Coupon expires 12/31/09. Cannot be combined with any other offer.

Lost Brook Golf Club
Westwood, MA (781) 769-2550

- **Type of Discount**
  $5 off each green fees for up to 2 players
  for 18 holes

- **Days of the Week**
  Weekdays only (except holidays)

- **Hours of the Day**
  All day

Coupon expires 12/31/09. Cannot be combined with any other offer.

Maplegate Country Club
Bellingham, MA (508) 966-4040

- **Type of Discount**
  4 players for the price of 3

- **Days of the Week**
  Before noon M-Th (excuding holidays)

- **Hours of the Day**
  Before Noon, must have coupon.
  Valid April - October 29, 2009.

Coupon expires 12/31/09. Cannot be combined with any other offer.

Marion Golf Course
Marion, MA (508) 748-0199

- **Type of Discount**
  2 players for the price of 1

- **Days of the Week**
  Weekdays only (except holidays)

- **Hours of the Day**
  With coupon only

Coupon expires 12/31/09. Cannot be combined with any other offer

NEW ENGLAND GOLFGUIDE

2 0 0 9

NEW ENGLAND GOLFGUIDE

2 0 0 9

NEW ENGLAND GOLFGUIDE

2 0 0 9

NEW ENGLAND GOLFGUIDE

2 0 0 9

Meadow Creek Golf Club
Dracut, MA (978 459-5129

- **Type of Discount**
  4 players for the price of 3
- **Days of the Week**
  7 days a week
- **Hours of the Day**
  Weekdays all day; weekends after 1pm

Coupon expires 12/31/09. Cannot be combined with any other offer.

Middleton Golf Course
Middleton, MA (978) 774-4075

- **Type of Discount**
  $5 off each green fees for up to 4 players
- **Days of the Week**
  Weekdays only (except holidays)
- **Hours of the Day**
  All day

Coupon expires 12/31/09. Cannot be combined with any other offer.

New England Country Club
Bellingham, MA (508) 883-2300

- **Type of Discount**
  $10 off green fee with cart rate.
- **Days of the Week**
  Monday - Thursday (except holidays)
- **Hours of the Day**
  Before 12pm

Coupon expires 12/31/09. Cannot be combined with any other offer.

New Meadows Golf Club
Topsfield, MA (978) 887-9307

- **Type of Discount**
  $5 off green fees for up to 4 players
- **Days of the Week**
  Monday - Thursday (except holidays)
- **Hours of the Day**
  All day. Not to be used during league or
  tournament play.

Coupon expires 12/31/09. Cannot be combined with any other offer.

Golf Course Coupons

NEW ENGLAND
GOLFGUIDE

2 0 0 9

NEW ENGLAND
GOLFGUIDE

2 0 0 9

NEW ENGLAND
GOLFGUIDE

2 0 0 9

NEW ENGLAND
GOLFGUIDE

2 0 0 9

Newton Commonwealth Golf Course
Newton, MA (617) 630-1971

- **Type of Discount**
  Free golf cart with 2 paid green fees
- **Days of the Week**
  Monday - Thursday, Friday before 10am
- **Hours of the Day**

Coupon expires 12/31/09. Cannot be combined with any other offer.

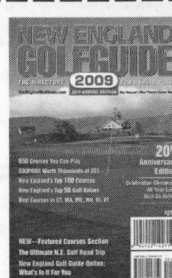

North Adams Country Club
Clarksburg, MA (413) 664-7149

- **Type of Discount**
  2 players for the price of 1
- **Days of the Week**
  Weekdays only (except holidays)
- **Hours of the Day**
  All day. Golf carts mandatory.

Coupon expires 12/31/09. Cannot be combined with any other offer.

Norton Country Club
Norton, MA (508) 285-2400

- **Type of Discount**
  $49.95 Lunch Special
- **Days of the Week**
  Monday through Thursday
- **Hours of the Day**
  All day

Coupon expires 12/31/09. Cannot be combined with any other offer.

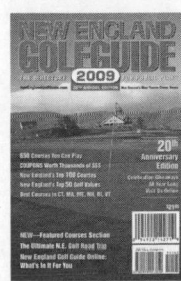

Norwood Country Club
Norwood, MA (781) 769-5880

- **Type of Discount**
  2 players for the price of 1
- **Days of the Week**
  Weekdays only (except holidays)
- **Hours of the Day**
  Before 2pm. 18 hole cart rental at regular
  weekday prices is required.

Coupon expires 12/31/09. Cannot be combined with any other offer.

Golf Course Coupons

NEW ENGLAND GOLFGUIDE

2 0 0 9

NEW ENGLAND GOLFGUIDE

2 0 0 9

NEW ENGLAND GOLFGUIDE

2 0 0 9

NEW ENGLAND GOLFGUIDE

2 0 0 9

Olde Barnstable Fairgrounds Golf Course
Marstons Mills, MA (508) 420-1141

- **Type of Discount**
  Free golf cart with 2 paid green fees
- **Days of the Week**
  M-Th September 15 - May 15, 2009
- **Hours of the Day**
  All day. Excludes holidays.

Coupon expires 12/31/09. Cannot be combined with any other offer.

Olde Scotland Links
Bridgewater, MA (508) 279-3344

- **Type of Discount**
  Free golf cart with 2 paid green fees
- **Days of the Week**
  Monday through Thursday (Except holidays)
- **Hours of the Day**
  All day. Not to be used during league, group
  or tournament play.

Coupon expires 12/31/09. Cannot be combined with any other offer.

Paul Harney Golf Club
East Falmouth, MA (508) 563-3454

- **Type of Discount**
  $5 off green fees for up to 2 players
- **Days of the Week**
  Weekdays only (except holidays)
- **Hours of the Day**
  Until 2pm

Coupon expires 12/31/09. Cannot be combined with any other offer.

Pembroke Country Club
Pembroke, MA (781) 826-5191

- **Type of Discount**
  4 players for the price of 3
- **Days of the Week**
  Weekdays only (except holidays)
- **Hours of the Day**
  All day. Cannot be combined with other offers.

Coupon expires 12/31/09. Cannot be combined with any other offer

NEW ENGLAND GOLFGUIDE

2 0 0 9

NEW ENGLAND GOLFGUIDE

2 0 0 9

NEW ENGLAND GOLFGUIDE

2 0 0 9

NEW ENGLAND GOLFGUIDE

2 0 0 9

Petersham Country Club
Petersham, MA (978) 724-3388

- **Type of Discount**
  Free golf cart with 2 paid green fees
- **Days of the Week**
  Weekdays only (except holidays)
- **Hours of the Day**
  All day. After Labor Day only.

Coupon expires 12/31/09. Cannot be combined with any other offer.

Pinecrest Golf Club
Holliston, MA (413) 525-4444

- **Type of Discount**
  Free golf cart with 2 paid green fees
- **Days of the Week**
  Weekdays only (except holidays)
- **Hours of the Day**
  All day.

Coupon expires 12/31/09. Cannot be combined with any other offer.

Pine Knoll Par 3 Golf Course
East Longmeadow, MA (413) 525-4444

- **Type of Discount**
  2 players for the price of 1
- **Days of the Week**
  Weekdays only (except holidays)
- **Hours of the Day**
  All day. Maximum 1 free per coupon.

Coupon expires 12/31/09. Cannot be combined with any other offer.

Pine Oaks Golf Course
South Easton, MA (508) 238-2320

- **Type of Discount**
  Free golf cart with 2 paid green fees
- **Days of the Week**
  Weekdays only (except holidays)
- **Hours of the Day**
  Before 3pm

Coupon expires 12/31/09. Cannot be combined with any other offer.

Golf Course Coupons

NEW ENGLAND GOLFGUIDE

2 0 0 9

NEW ENGLAND GOLFGUIDE

2 0 0 9

NEW ENGLAND GOLFGUIDE

2 0 0 9

NEW ENGLAND GOLFGUIDE

2 0 0 9

Pine Ridge Country Club
North Oxford, MA (508) 892-9188

- **Type of Discount**
  4 players for the price of 3

- **Days of the Week**
  7 days a week

- **Hours of the Day**
  All day

Coupon expires 12/31/09. Cannot be combined with any other offer.

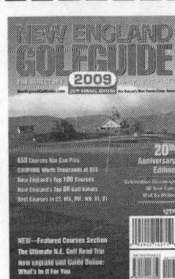

Pinecrest Golf Club
Holliston, MA (508) 429-9871

- **Type of Discount**
  Free golf cart with 2 paid green fees

- **Days of the Week**
  Weekdays only (except holidays)

- **Hours of the Day**
  All day

Coupon expires 12/31/09. Cannot be combined with any other offer.

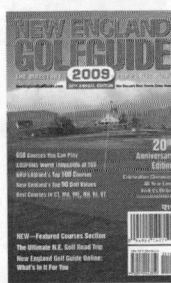

Pontoosuc Lake Country Club
Pittsfield, MA (413) 445-4217

- **Type of Discount**
  Buy 1 green fees, get second green fees
  at one-half off with cart rental

- **Days of the Week**
  Weekdays only (except holidays)

- **Hours of the Day**
  All day

Coupon expires 12/31/09. Cannot be combined with any other offer.

Poquoy Brook Golf Course
Lakeville, MA (508) 947-5261

- **Type of Discount**
  20% off non-sale golf apparel

- **Days of the Week**
  7 days a week

- **Hours of the Day**
  All day

Coupon expires 12/31/09. Cannot be combined with any other offer.

NEW ENGLAND GOLFGUIDE

2 0 0 9

NEW ENGLAND GOLFGUIDE

2 0 0 9

NEW ENGLAND GOLFGUIDE

2 0 0 9

NEW ENGLAND GOLFGUIDE

2 0 0 9

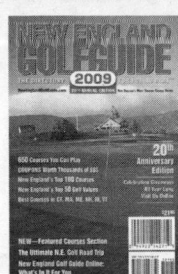

Quahoag Country Club
Monson, MA (413) 267-5294

- **Type of Discount**
  Free golf cart with 2 paid green fees

- **Days of the Week**
  Weekdays only (except holidays)

- **Hours of the Day**
  All day

Coupon expires 12/31/09. Cannot be combined with any other offer.

Quail Hollow Golf & Country Club
Old Turnpike Road, Oakham, MA (508) 882-5516

- **Type of Discount**
  1 green fees free with 1 paid

- **Days of the Week**
  Weekdays only (except holidays)

- **Hours of the Day**
  Valid May 1 to October 31, 2009

Coupon expires 12/31/09. Cannot be combined with any other offer.

Quashnet Valley Country Club
Mashpee, MA (508) 477-4112

- **Type of Discount**
  $5 off green fees for up to 4 players

- **Days of the Week**
  Monday through Thursday (except holidays)

- **Hours of the Day**
  All day. Not valid on discount rates/specials.

Coupon expires 12/31/09. Cannot be combined with any other offer.

Ranch Golf Club, The
Southwick, MA (413) 797-6741

- **Type of Discount**
  4 players for the price of 3

- **Days of the Week**
  Sunday through Thursday

- **Hours of the Day**
  7:30am - 1:30pm. Valid May - October 4, 2009.

Coupon expires 12/31/09. Cannot be combined with any other offer.

Golf Course Coupons

NEW ENGLAND GOLFGUIDE

2 0 0 9

NEW ENGLAND GOLFGUIDE

2 0 0 9

NEW ENGLAND GOLFGUIDE

2 0 0 9

NEW ENGLAND GOLFGUIDE

2 0 0 9

Rehoboth Country Club
Rehoboth, MA (508) 252-6259

- **Type of Discount**
  4 green fees for the price of 3
- **Days of the Week**
  Mon-Thurs only (except holidays)
- **Hours of the Day**
  7am - 11am

Coupon expires 12/31/09. Cannot be combined with any other offer.

Sagamore Spring Golf Club
Lynnfield, MA (781) 334-3151

- **Type of Discount**
  $5 off green fees for up to 4 players
- **Days of the Week**
  Weekdays only (except holidays)
- **Hours of the Day**
  10am-2pm M-F with coupon only

Coupon expires 12/31/09. Cannot be combined with any other offer.

Sandwich Hollows Golf Club
East Sandwich, MA (508) 888 3384x0

- **Type of Discount**
  Green fee for 18 holes $29.95 after 2pm
- **Days of the Week**
  7 days a week
- **Hours of the Day**

Coupon expires 12/31/09. Cannot be combined with any other offer.

Sassamon Trace Golf Course
Natick, MA (508) 655-1330

- **Type of Discount**
  $5 off green fees for up to 2 players
- **Days of the Week**
  Weekdays only (except holidays)
- **Hours of the Day**
  Before 2pm. Not valid on Junior & Senior rates.

Coupon expires 12/31/09. Cannot be combined with any other offer.

Golf Course Coupons

NEW ENGLAND GOLFGUIDE

2 0 0 9

NEW ENGLAND GOLFGUIDE

2 0 0 9

NEW ENGLAND GOLFGUIDE

2 0 0 9

NEW ENGLAND GOLFGUIDE

2 0 0 9

Scottish Meadow Golf Club
Warren, MA (413) 436-5108

- **Type of Discount**
  2 players for the price of 1
- **Days of the Week**
  Monday through Thursday only
- **Hours of the Day**
  8am to 12pm. Must take a cart.

Coupon expires 12/31/09. Cannot be combined with any other offer.

Shadow Brook Golf Course
South Attleboro, MA (508) 399-8918

- **Type of Discount**
  25% discount for 2-4 players
- **Days of the Week**
  7 days a week
- **Hours of the Day**
  All day

Coupon expires 12/31/09. Cannot be combined with any other offer.

Shaker Farms Country Club
Westfield, MA (413) 562-2770

- **Type of Discount**
  2 players for the price of 1 (cart not included)
- **Days of the Week**
  Weekdays only (except holidays)
- **Hours of the Day**
  All day

Coupon expires 12/31/09. Cannot be combined with any other offer.

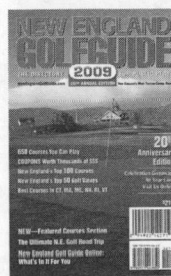

Shaker Hills Golf Club
Harvard, MA (978) 772-2227

- **Type of Discount**
  4 players for the price of 3
- **Days of the Week**
  Monday - Thursday only (except holidays)
- **Hours of the Day**
  All day

Coupon expires 12/31/09. Cannot be combined with any other offer.

NEW ENGLAND GOLFGUIDE

2 0 0 9

NEW ENGLAND GOLFGUIDE

2 0 0 9

NEW ENGLAND GOLFGUIDE

2 0 0 9

NEW ENGLAND GOLFGUIDE

2 0 0 9

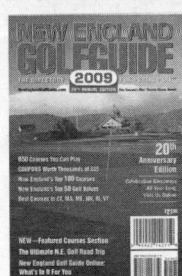

Skyline Country Club
Route 7, Lanesborough, MA (413) 445-5584

- **Type of Discount**
  2 players for the price of 1

- **Days of the Week**
  Weekdays only (except holidays)

- **Hours of the Day**
  All day

Coupon expires 12/31/09. Cannot be combined with any other offer.

Southers Marsh Golf Club
Plymouth, MA (508) 830-3535

- **Type of Discount**
  Free golf cart with 2 paid green fees

- **Days of the Week**
  7 days a week

- **Hours of the Day**
  All day

Coupon expires 12/31/09. Cannot be combined with any other offer.

Southwick Country Club
Southwick, MA (413) 569-0136

- **Type of Discount**
  1 player with cart $29, Senior with cart $25

- **Days of the Week**
  Weekdays only (except holidays)

- **Hours of the Day**
  All day

Coupon expires 12/31/09. Cannot be combined with any other offer.

Sun Valley Golf Course
Rehoboth, MA (508) 336-8686

- **Type of Discount**
  $2 off 1 round of golf ($1 seniors)

- **Days of the Week**
  Weekdays only (except holidays)

- **Hours of the Day**
  7am to 1pm

Coupon expires 12/31/09. Cannot be combined with any other offer.

Golf Course Coupons

NEW ENGLAND
GOLFGUIDE

2 0 0 9

NEW ENGLAND
GOLFGUIDE

2 0 0 9

NEW ENGLAND
GOLFGUIDE

2 0 0 9

NEW ENGLAND
GOLFGUIDE

2 0 0 9

Swansea Country Club
Swansea, MA (508) 379-9886

- **Type of Discount**
  Lunch Special $42 per person
- **Days of the Week**
  Weekdays only (except holidays)
- **Hours of the Day**
  11am - 1pm

Coupon expires 12/31/09. Cannot be combined with any other offer.

Tekoa Country Club
Westfield, MA (413) 568-1064

- **Type of Discount**
  Buy 1 green fees - get 1 free with 2 people purchasing a cart
- **Days of the Week**
  Weekdays only
- **Hours of the Day**
  Before 1pm

Coupon expires 12/31/09. Cannot be combined with any other offer.

Templewood Golf Course
Templeton, MA (978) 939-5031

- **Type of Discount**
  Free golf cart with 2 paid green fees
- **Days of the Week**
  Weekdays only (except holidays)
- **Hours of the Day**
  All day. Please call for availability.

Coupon expires 12/31/09. Cannot be combined with any other offer.

Townsend Ridge Country Club
Townsend, MA (978) 597-8400

- **Type of Discount**
  2 players for the price of 1. Must use golf cart.
- **Days of the Week**
  Weekdays only (except holidays)
- **Hours of the Day**
  All day

Coupon expires 12/31/09. Cannot be combined with any other offer.

Golf Course Coupons

NEW ENGLAND GOLFGUIDE

2 0 0 9

NEW ENGLAND GOLFGUIDE

2 0 0 9

NEW ENGLAND GOLFGUIDE

2 0 0 9

NEW ENGLAND GOLFGUIDE

2 0 0 9

Twin Brooks Golf Course
Hyannis, MA (508) 862-6980

- **Type of Discount**
  2 players for the price of 1
- **Days of the Week**
  7 days a week
- **Hours of the Day**
  All day. Not valid holidays.

Coupon expires 12/31/09. Cannot be combined with any other offer.

Twin Springs Golf Club
Bolton, MA (978) 779-5020

- **Type of Discount**
  2 players for the price of 1
- **Days of the Week**
  Monday - Thursday (except holidays)
- **Hours of the Day**
  6:30am to 3pm

Coupon expires 12/31/09. Cannot be combined with any other offer.

Wampanoag Golf Club
North Swansea, MA (508) 379-9832

- **Type of Discount**
  $31 per person for 10 holes w/cart
- **Days of the Week**
  7 days a week (except holidays)
- **Hours of the Day**
  7am-1pm weekdays/after Noon weekends.
  Valid through September 2009.

Coupon expires 12/31/09. Cannot be combined with any other offer.

Waubeeka Golf Links
So. Williamstown, MA (413) 458-8355

- **Type of Discount**
  4 players for the price of 3
- **Days of the Week**
  Weekdays only (except holidays)
- **Hours of the Day**
  After 11am

Coupon expires 12/31/09. Cannot be combined with any other offer.

NEW ENGLAND GOLFGUIDE

2 0 0 9

NEW ENGLAND GOLFGUIDE

2 0 0 9

NEW ENGLAND GOLFGUIDE

2 0 0 9

NEW ENGLAND GOLFGUIDE

2 0 0 9

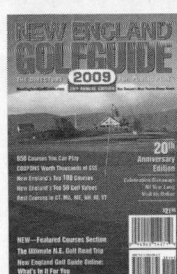

Waverly Oaks - Challenger 9
Plymouth, MA (508) 224-6016

- **Type of Discount**
  $5 off green fees for up to 2 players
- **Days of the Week**
  7 days a week
- **Hours of the Day**
  All day

Coupon expires 12/31/09. Cannot be combined with any other offer.

Waverly Oaks Golf Club
Plymouth, MA (508) 224-6016

- **Type of Discount**
  $5 off green fees for up to 2 players
- **Days of the Week**
  7 days a week
- **Hours of the Day**
  All day

Coupon expires 12/31/09. Cannot be combined with any other offer.

Wenham Country Club
Wenham, MA (978) 468-4714

- **Type of Discount**
  $5 off green fees for up to 4 players
- **Days of the Week**
  Weekdays only (except holidays)
- **Hours of the Day**
  All day

Coupon expires 12/31/09. Cannot be combined with any other offer.

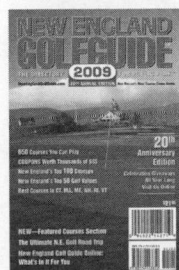

Wentworth Hills Golf Club
Plainville, MA (508) 699-9406

- **Type of Discount**
  $5 off green fees for up to 4 players
- **Days of the Week**
  Weekdays only (except holidays)
- **Hours of the Day**
  All day. Must present coupon to qualify.

Coupon expires 12/31/09. Cannot be combined with any other offer.

NEW ENGLAND GOLFGUIDE

2 0 0 9

NEW ENGLAND GOLFGUIDE

2 0 0 9

NEW ENGLAND GOLFGUIDE

2 0 0 9

NEW ENGLAND GOLFGUIDE

2 0 0 9

Westminster Country Club
Westminster, MA (978) 874-5938

- **Type of Discount**
  1 free green fees + cart with 3 paid
- **Days of the Week**
  Weekend after 2pm
- **Hours of the Day**

Coupon expires 12/31/09. Cannot be combined with any other offer.

Widow's Walk Golf Course
Scituate, MA (781) 544-0032

- **Type of Discount**
  4 play, 3 pay
- **Days of the Week**
  7 days a week
- **Hours of the Day**
  All day on weekdays. After 12 noon
  on weekends & holidays.

Coupon expires 12/31/09. Cannot be combined with any other offer.

Winchendon School Country Club
Winchendon, MA (978) 297-9897

- **Type of Discount**
  $5 off green fees for up to 2 players
- **Days of the Week**
  7 days a week
- **Hours of the Day**
  Call for tee times

Coupon expires 12/31/09. Cannot be combined with any other offer.

Woods of Westminster CC
Westminster, MA (978) 874-0500

- **Type of Discount**
  $36 for 18 holes, cart, and lunch
- **Days of the Week**
  Weekdays only (except holidays)
- **Hours of the Day**
  Monday-Friday before 12 noon, no holidays,
  no other offers combined with leagues.

Coupon expires 12/31/09. Cannot be combined with any other offer.

NEW ENGLAND GOLFGUIDE

2 0 0 9

NEW ENGLAND GOLFGUIDE

2 0 0 9

NEW ENGLAND GOLFGUIDE

2 0 0 9

NEW ENGLAND GOLFGUIDE

2 0 0 9

Worthington Golf Course
Worthington, MA (413) 238-4464

- **Type of Discount**
  $25 for 18 holes with cart
- **Days of the Week**
  Weekdays only (except holidays)
- **Hours of the Day**
  All day

Coupon expires 12/31/09. Cannot be combined with any other offer.

Androscoggin Valley Country Club
Route 2, Gorham, NH (603) 466-9468

- **Type of Discount**
  $80 for 2 players (includes cart)
- **Days of the Week**
  7 days a week
- **Hours of the Day**
  All day with tee times only. Must bring
  in coupon in NEGolfGuide.

Coupon expires 12/31/09. Cannot be combined with any other offer.

Apple Hill Golf Club
E. Kingston, NH (603) 642-4414

- **Type of Discount**
  $5 off green fees for up to 2 players
- **Days of the Week**
  Weekdays only (except holidays)
- **Hours of the Day**
  All day

Coupon expires 12/31/09. Cannot be combined with any other offer.

Applewood Golf Links
Windham, NH (603) 898-6793

- **Type of Discount**
  2 players for the price of 1
- **Days of the Week**
  Weekdays only (except holidays)
- **Hours of the Day**
  Before 4pm

Coupon expires 12/31/09. Cannot be combined with any other offer.

Golf Course Coupons

NEW ENGLAND
GOLFGUIDE

2 0 0 9

NEW ENGLAND
GOLFGUIDE

2 0 0 9

NEW ENGLAND
GOLFGUIDE

2 0 0 9

NEW ENGLAND
GOLFGUIDE

2 0 0 9

Atkinson Resort Golf Club
Atkinson, NH (603) 362-8700

- **Type of Discount**
  Free medium bucket of range balls with paid green fee
- **Days of the Week**
  7 days a week
- **Hours of the Day**
  All day

Coupon expires 12/31/09. Cannot be combined with any other offer.

Balsams Panorama Golf Club, The
Dixville Notch, NH (603) 255-4961

- **Type of Discount**
  $55 includes cart per person
- **Days of the Week**
  7 days a week
- **Hours of the Day**
  After 11am

Coupon expires 12/31/09. Cannot be combined with any other offer.

Balsams-Coashaukee Golf Course
Dixville Notch, NH (603) 255-4961

- **Type of Discount**
  25% discount for 2-4 players
- **Days of the Week**
  7 days a week
- **Hours of the Day**
  After 11:30am

Coupon expires 12/31/09. Cannot be combined with any other offer.

Beaver Meadow Golf Club
Concord, NH (603) 228-8954

- **Type of Discount**
  2 green fees and cart for $80
- **Days of the Week**
  Monday-Wednesday (except holidays)
- **Hours of the Day**
  After 12pm

Coupon expires 12/31/09. Cannot be combined with any other offer.

Golf Course Coupons

NEW ENGLAND GOLFGUIDE

2 0 0 9

NEW ENGLAND GOLFGUIDE

2 0 0 9

NEW ENGLAND GOLFGUIDE

2 0 0 9

NEW ENGLAND GOLFGUIDE

2 0 0 9

Bethlehem Country Club
Bethlehem, NH (603) 869-5745

- **Type of Discount**
  $25 w/cart weekdays
  $30 on weekends

- **Days of the Week**
  Weekdays only (except holidays)

- **Hours of the Day**
  All day. Not valid holidays.

Coupon expires 12/31/09. Cannot be combined with any other offer.

Blackmount Country Club
North Haverhill, NH (603) 787-6564

- **Type of Discount**
  $3 off power cart rental with paid green fees

- **Days of the Week**
  Weekdays only (except holidays)

- **Hours of the Day**
  All day

Coupon expires 12/31/09. Cannot be combined with any other offer.

Bramber Valley Golf Course
Greenland, NH (603) 436-4288

- **Type of Discount**
  $2 off 18 holes

- **Days of the Week**
  7 days a week

- **Hours of the Day**
  All day. Valid through November 1, 2009.

Coupon expires 12/31/09. Cannot be combined with any other offer.

Breakfast Hill Golf Club
Greenland, NH (603) 436-5001

- **Type of Discount**
  $5 off green fees for up to 2 players

- **Days of the Week**
  Weekdays only (except holidays)

- **Hours of the Day**
  Before 4pm

Coupon expires 12/31/09. Cannot be combined with any other offer.

NEW ENGLAND GOLFGUIDE

2 0 0 9

NEW ENGLAND GOLFGUIDE

2 0 0 9

NEW ENGLAND GOLFGUIDE

2 0 0 9

NEW ENGLAND GOLFGUIDE

2 0 0 9

Campbell's Scottish Highlands
Brady Avenue, Salem, NH (603) 894-4653

- **Type of Discount**
  18 holes, cart, & bag lunch for 2 golfers - $88
- **Days of the Week**
  Monday through Thursday (except holidays)
- **Hours of the Day**
  All day. Valid only March 30 - May 21 and
  October 13 - November 19.

Coupon expires 12/31/09. Cannot be combined with any other offer.

Canterbury Woods Country Club
Canterbury, NH (603) 783-9400

- **Type of Discount**
  2 players for the price of 1
- **Days of the Week**
  Weekdays only (except holidays)
- **Hours of the Day**
  All day. Cart rental required.

Coupon expires 12/31/09. Cannot be combined with any other offer.

Colebrook Country Club
Colebrook, NH (603) 237-5566

- **Type of Discount**
  2 players for the price of 1, cart rental required
- **Days of the Week**
  Weekdays only (except holidays)
- **Hours of the Day**
  All day. 18-hole power cart required.

Coupon expires 12/31/09. Cannot be combined with any other offer.

Country Club of New Hampshire
North Sutton, NH (603) 927-4246

- **Type of Discount**
  $5 off 18 hole green fees
- **Days of the Week**
  Monday-Thursday (except holidays)
- **Hours of the Day**
  All day. Power cart required.

Coupon expires 12/31/09. Cannot be combined with any other offer.

Golf Course Coupons

NEW ENGLAND GOLFGUIDE

2 0 0 9

NEW ENGLAND GOLFGUIDE

2 0 0 9

NEW ENGLAND GOLFGUIDE

2 0 0 9

NEW ENGLAND GOLFGUIDE

2 0 0 9

Crotched Mountain Golf Course
Route 47, Francestown, NH (603) 588-2923

- **Type of Discount**
  2 players for the price of 1
- **Days of the Week**
  Monday-Thursday
- **Hours of the Day**
  All day. Cart not included.

Coupon expires 12/31/09. Cannot be combined with any other offer.

Den Brae Golf Course
Sanbornton, NH (603) 934-9818

- **Type of Discount**
  25% discount for 2-4 players
- **Days of the Week**
  Weekdays only (except holidays)
- **Hours of the Day**
  All day

Coupon expires 12/31/09. Cannot be combined with any other offer.

Duston Country Club
Hopkinton, NH (603) 746-4234

- **Type of Discount**
  Free sandwich after round (up to $5 value)
- **Days of the Week**
  Weekdays only (except holidays)
- **Hours of the Day**

Coupon expires 12/31/09. Cannot be combined with any other offer.

Eagle Mountain House
Jackson, NH (603) 383-9090

- **Type of Discount**
  Free golf cart with 2 paid green fees
- **Days of the Week**
  Weekdays only (except holidays)
- **Hours of the Day**
  All day

Coupon expires 12/31/09. Cannot be combined with any other offer.

Golf Course Coupons

NEW ENGLAND GOLFGUIDE

2 0 0 9

NEW ENGLAND GOLFGUIDE

2 0 0 9

NEW ENGLAND GOLFGUIDE

2 0 0 9

NEW ENGLAND GOLFGUIDE

2 0 0 9

Eastman Golf Links
Grantham, NH (603) 863-4500

- **Type of Discount**
  4 players at $45 per person including cart

- **Days of the Week**
  7 days a week

- **Hours of the Day**
  M-Th all day; Fri/Sat/Sun after 12pm.
  Call up to 5 days ahead. Coupon required.

Coupon expires 12/31/09. Cannot be combined with any other offer.

Exeter Country Club
Exeter, NH (603) 772-4752

- **Type of Discount**
  2 players for the price of 1

- **Days of the Week**
  Weekdays only (except holidays)

- **Hours of the Day**
  All day

Coupon expires 12/31/09. Cannot be combined with any other offer.

Granite Fields Golf Club
Route 125, Kingston, NH (603) 642-9977

- **Type of Discount**
  Free golf cart with 2 paid green fees

- **Days of the Week**
  Weekdays only (except holidays)

- **Hours of the Day**
  Before 12pm. Valid between April 25 and
  October 1, 2009 only.

Coupon expires 12/31/09. Cannot be combined with any other offer.

Hales Location Golf Course
West Side Road, North Conway, NH (603) 356-2140

- **Type of Discount**
  $5 off green fees for up to 2 players

- **Days of the Week**
  Weekdays only (except holidays)

- **Hours of the Day**
  All day

Coupon expires 12/31/09. Cannot be combined with any other offer.

Golf Course Coupons

NEW ENGLAND GOLFGUIDE

2 0 0 9

NEW ENGLAND GOLFGUIDE

2 0 0 9

NEW ENGLAND GOLFGUIDE

2 0 0 9

NEW ENGLAND GOLFGUIDE

2 0 0 9

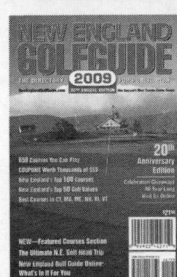

Hanover Country Club
Hanover, NH (603) 646-2000

- **Type of Discount**
  Free golf cart with 2 paid green fees

- **Days of the Week**
  Weekdays only (except holidays)

- **Hours of the Day**
  All day

Coupon expires 12/31/09. Cannot be combined with any other offer.

Hidden Valley Golf Course
Derry, NH (603) 887-7888

- **Type of Discount**
  2 players for the price of 1

- **Days of the Week**
  Weekdays only (except holidays)

- **Hours of the Day**
  All day. Carts extra.

Coupon expires 12/31/09. Cannot be combined with any other offer.

Highlands Links Golf Club
Plymouth, NH (603) 536-3452

- **Type of Discount**
  2 players for the price of 1 (at regular adult fee)

- **Days of the Week**
  7 days a week

- **Hours of the Day**
  All day

Coupon expires 12/31/09. Cannot be combined with any other offer.

Indian Mound Golf Club
Center Ossippee, NH (603) 539-7733

- **Type of Discount**
  50% off for second player (green fees only)

- **Days of the Week**
  7 days a week

- **Hours of the Day**
  All day. Call for availability.

Coupon expires 12/31/09. Cannot be combined with any other offer.

NEW ENGLAND GOLFGUIDE

2 0 0 9

NEW ENGLAND GOLFGUIDE

2 0 0 9

NEW ENGLAND GOLFGUIDE

2 0 0 9

NEW ENGLAND GOLFGUIDE

2 0 0 9

Intervale Country Club
Manchester, NH (603) 647-6811

- **Type of Discount**
  4 for the price of 3, 18 holes
- **Days of the Week**
  7 days a week
- **Hours of the Day**
  All day. Call for availability.

Coupon expires 12/31/09. Cannot be combined with any other offer.

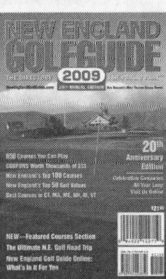

Jack O'Lantern Resort
Woodstock, NH (603) 745-3636

- **Type of Discount**
  Free sandwich after round (up to $8 value).
  Limit one, and 15% off golf merchandise.
- **Days of the Week**
  7 days a week
- **Hours of the Day**
  All day. Not valid holidays.

Coupon expires 12/31/09. Cannot be combined with any other offer.

Kingswood Golf Course
Wolfeboro, NH (603) 569-3569

- **Typo of Discount**
  2 players for the price of 1. Cart rental required.
  Free 9-hole replay after 3pm (after 18-hole paid
  round).
- **Days of the Week**
  7 days a week
- **Hours of the Day**
  Weekends after 1pm

Coupon expires 12/31/09. Cannot be combined with any other offer.

Lisbon Village Country Club
Bishop Road, Lisbon, NH (603) 838-6004

- **Type of Discount**
  Free golf cart with 2 paid green fees
- **Days of the Week**
  Weekdays only (except holidays)
- **Hours of the Day**

Coupon expires 12/31/09. Cannot be combined with any other offer.

Golf Course Coupons

NEW ENGLAND GOLFGUIDE

2 0 0 9

NEW ENGLAND GOLFGUIDE

2 0 0 9

NEW ENGLAND GOLFGUIDE

2 0 0 9

NEW ENGLAND GOLFGUIDE

2 0 0 9

Lochmere Golf & Country Club
Route 3, Tilton, NH (603) 528-4653

- **Type of Discount**
  18 holes, 2 players w/power cart, $88, with reserved tee time and this coupon
- **Days of the Week**
  Monday through Thursday (except holidays)
- **Hours of the Day**

Coupon expires 12/31/09. Cannot be combined with any other offer.

Maplewood Golf Club
Bethlehem, NH (603) 869-3335

- **Type of Discount**
  $5 off green fees
- **Days of the Week**
  Weekdays only (except holidays)
- **Hours of the Day**
  7am-6pm. 18 holes only, cart rental required.

Coupon expires 12/31/09. Cannot be combined with any other offer.

Mojalaki Golf Club & Academy
Franklin, NH (603) 934-3033

- **Type of Discount**
  $5 off green fees for up to 2 players for 18 holes
- **Days of the Week**
  Weekdays only (except holidays)
- **Hours of the Day**
  Before 2pm

Coupon expires 12/31/09. Cannot be combined with any other offer.

Mountain View Grand Resort & Spa
Whitefield, NH (866) 484-3843

- **Type of Discount**
  Free golf cart with 2 paid green fees
- **Days of the Week**
  Mid-week, except holidays
- **Hours of the Day**
  Coupon must be presented at time of play. Advance tee times recommended.

Coupon expires 12/31/09. Cannot be combined with any other offer.

**NEW ENGLAND
GOLFGUIDE**

2 0 0 9

**NEW ENGLAND
GOLFGUIDE**

2 0 0 9

**NEW ENGLAND
GOLFGUIDE**

2 0 0 9

**NEW ENGLAND
GOLFGUIDE**

2 0 0 9

Newport Golf Club
Newport, NH (603) 863-7787

- **Type of Discount**
  $5 off green fees for up to 2 players

- **Days of the Week**
  Weekdays only (except holidays)

- **Hours of the Day**
  All day, call for tee times. Not valid on outing days.

Coupon expires 12/31/09. Cannot be combined with any other offer.

Nippo Lake Golf Club
Barrington, NH (603) 664-7616

- **Type of Discount**
  $5 off green fees for up to 2 players

- **Days of the Week**
  7 days a week

- **Hours of the Day**
  After 11am

Coupon expires 12/31/09. Cannot be combined with any other offer.

Oak Hill Golf Course
Meredith, NH (603) 279-4438

- **Type of Discount**
  $5 off 18 hole green fees for up to 2 players

- **Days of the Week**
  7 days a week (except holiday weekends)

- **Hours of the Day**
  All day

Coupon expires 12/31/09. Cannot be combined with any other offer.

Owl's Nest Golf Club
Campton, NH (603) 726-3076

- **Type of Discount**
  2 players for the price of 1

- **Days of the Week**
  Monday-Thursday (except holidays)

- **Hours of the Day**
  After 11am

Coupon expires 12/31/09. Cannot be combined with any other offer.

Golf Course Coupons

NEW ENGLAND
GOLFGUIDE

2 0 0 9

NEW ENGLAND
GOLFGUIDE

2 0 0 9

NEW ENGLAND
GOLFGUIDE

2 0 0 9

NEW ENGLAND
GOLFGUIDE

2 0 0 9

Pease Golf Course
Portsmouth, NH (603) 433-1331

- **Type of Discount**
  Free golf cart with 2 paid green fees

- **Days of the Week**
  7 days a week

- **Hours of the Day**
  All day weekdays, after 1pm weekends and holidays

Coupon expires 12/31/09. Cannot be combined with any other offer.

Pheasant Ridge Country Club
Gilford, NH (603) 524-7808

- **Type of Discount**
  $5 off 18-hole green fee, power cart required

- **Days of the Week**
  Tuesday - Friday (except holidays)

- **Hours of the Day**
  All day. Power cart required.

Coupon expires 12/31/09. Cannot be combined with any other offer.

Pine Grove Springs Country Club
Route 9A, Spofford, NH (603) 363-4433

- **Type of Discount**
  2 players for the price of 1

- **Days of the Week**
  7 days a week (except Sunday am/tournaments)

- **Hours of the Day**
  All day

Coupon expires 12/31/09. Cannot be combined with any other offer.

Portsmouth Country Club
Greenland, NH (603) 436-9719

- **Type of Discount**
  25% discount for 2-4 players

- **Days of the Week**
  Monday through Thursday

- **Hours of the Day**
  All day. Valid before Memorial Day, after Labor Day only.

Coupon expires 12/31/09. Cannot be combined with any other offer.

NEW ENGLAND
GOLFGUIDE

2 0 0 9

NEW ENGLAND
GOLFGUIDE

2 0 0 9

NEW ENGLAND
GOLFGUIDE

2 0 0 9

NEW ENGLAND
GOLFGUIDE

2 0 0 9

Sagamore-Hampton Golf Club
North Hampton, NH (603) 964-5341

- **Type of Discount**
  25% discount for 2-4 players
- **Days of the Week**
  Weekdays only (except holidays)
- **Hours of the Day**
  All day. Golf cart not included, 18 holes only.

Coupon expires 12/31/09. Cannot be combined with any other offer.

Shattuck Golf Course, The
Jaffrey, NH (603) 532-4300

- **Type of Discount**
  Free golf cart with 2 paid green fees
- **Days of the Week**
  7 days a week
- **Hours of the Day**
  All day

Coupon expires 12/31/09. Cannot be combined with any other offer.

Souhegan Woods Golf Club
Amherst, NH (603) 673-0200

- **Type of Discount**
  $5 off 18-hole green fees
- **Days of the Week**
  Monday-Thursday only (except holidays)
- **Hours of the Day**
  All day. Power cart required.

Coupon expires 12/31/09. Cannot be combined with any other offer.

Stonebridge Country Club
Goffstown, NH (603) 497-8633

- **Type of Discount**
  $10 off a twosome with a riding cart
- **Days of the Week**
  Monday through Thursday
- **Hours of the Day**
  All day

Coupon expires 12/31/09. Cannot be combined with any other offer.

NEW ENGLAND GOLFGUIDE

2 0 0 9

NEW ENGLAND GOLFGUIDE

2 0 0 9

NEW ENGLAND GOLFGUIDE

2 0 0 9

NEW ENGLAND GOLFGUIDE

2 0 0 9

Sunset Hill Golf Course
Sugar Hill, NH (603) 823-7244

- **Type of Discount**
  Free golf cart with 2 paid green fees
- **Days of the Week**
  7 days a week
- **Hours of the Day**
  All day

Coupon expires 12/31/09. Cannot be combined with any other offer.

Waukewan Golf Club
Center Harbor, NH (603) 279-6661

- **Type of Discount**
  4 players for the price of 3. 18-hole greens fee only.
- **Days of the Week**
  7 days a week
- **Hours of the Day**
  All day

Coupon expires 12/31/09. Cannot be combined with any other offer.

Waumbek Country Club, The
Jefferson, NH (603) 586-7777

- **Type of Discount**
  $10 off 2 players with cart
- **Days of the Week**
  Monday-Friday (except holidays)
- **Hours of the Day**
  All day. Power cart rental required.

Coupon expires 12/31/09. Cannot be combined with any other offer.

Wentworth Resort Golf Club
Rt. 16, Jackson, NH (603) 383-9641

- **Type of Discount**
  $5 off each green fees for up to 2 players
- **Days of the Week**
  Monday-Thursday
- **Hours of the Day**
  After 1pm. Must call ahead. Must notify of coupon when making tee time.

Coupon expires 12/31/09. Cannot be combined with any other offer.

Golf Course Coupons

NEW ENGLAND GOLFGUIDE

2 0 0 9

NEW ENGLAND GOLFGUIDE

2 0 0 9

NEW ENGLAND GOLFGUIDE

2 0 0 9

NEW ENGLAND GOLFGUIDE

2 0 0 9

Whip-Poor-Will Golf Club
Hudson, NH (603) 889-9706

- **Type of Discount**
  $5 off 18-hole green fees
- **Days of the Week**
  Monday-Thursday (except holidays)
- **Hours of the Day**
  All day. Power cart required.

Coupon expires 12/31/09. Cannot be combined with any other offer.

White Mountain Country Club
North Ashland Road, Ashland, NH
(603) 536-2227

- **Type of Discount**
  $5 off 18-hole green fees
- **Days of the Week**
  Monday-Thursday (except holidays)
- **Hours of the Day**
  All day. Power cart required.

Coupon expires 12/31/09. Cannot be combined with any other offer.

Windham Country Club
Windham, NH (603) 434-2093

- **Type of Discount**
  Free bucket of balls per player
- **Days of the Week**
  Weekdays only (except holidays)
- **Hours of the Day**
  All day

Coupon expires 12/31/09. Cannot be combined with any other offer.

Woodbound Inn GC
Jaffrey, NH (603) 532-8341

- **Type of Discount**
  2 players for the price of 1
- **Days of the Week**
  Weekdays only (except holidays)
- **Hours of the Day**
  All day

Coupon expires 12/31/09. Cannot be combined with any other offer.

Golf Course Coupons

NEW ENGLAND GOLFGUIDE

2 0 0 9

NEW ENGLAND GOLFGUIDE

2 0 0 9

NEW ENGLAND GOLFGUIDE

2 0 0 9

NEW ENGLAND GOLFGUIDE

2 0 0 9

Beaver River Golf Club
Richmond, RI (401) 539-2100

- **Type of Discount**
  $43 with cart
- **Days of the Week**
  Monday-Thursday
- **Hours of the Day**
  8am-1pm

Coupon expires 12/31/09. Cannot be combined with any other offer.

Country View Golf Club
Harrisville, RI (401) 568-7157

- **Type of Discount**
  2 players for the price of 1 with the purchase of cart fees
- **Days of the Week**
  Monday-Thursday (except holidays)
- **Hours of the Day**
  AM only

Coupon expires 12/31/09. Cannot be combined with any other offer.

Fairlawn Golf Course
Lincoln, RI (401) 334-3937

- **Type of Discount**
  2 players for the price of 1
- **Days of the Week**
  7 days a week
- **Hours of the Day**

Coupon expires 12/31/09. Cannot be combined with any other offer.

Laurel Lane Country Club
West Kingston, RI (401) 783-3844

- **Type of Discount**
  4 players for the price of 3
- **Days of the Week**
  Monday-Thursday only
- **Hours of the Day**
  All day

Coupon expires 12/31/09. Cannot be combined with any other offer.

Golf Course Coupons

NEW ENGLAND GOLFGUIDE

2 0 0 9

NEW ENGLAND GOLFGUIDE

2 0 0 9

NEW ENGLAND GOLFGUIDE

2 0 0 9

NEW ENGLAND GOLFGUIDE

2 0 0 9

Midville Country Club
West Warwick, RI (401) 828-9215

- **Type of Discount**
  Free golf cart with 2 paid green fees
- **Days of the Week**
  Weekdays only (except holidays)
- **Hours of the Day**
  All day.

Coupon expires 12/31/09. Cannot be combined with any other offer.

North Kingstown Muni. Golf Course
North Kingstown, RI (401) 294-0684

- **Type of Discount**
  Foursome special if you have 4 players, $37 per player
- **Days of the Week**
  M-Th; April, May, September, October
- **Hours of the Day**
  Up until 12pm

Coupon expires 12/31/09. Cannot be combined with any other offer.

Pinecrest Golf Course
Carolina, RI (401) 364-8600

- **Type of Discount**
  $5 off green fees for up to 2 players
- **Days of the Week**
  Weekdays only (except holidays)
- **Hours of the Day**
  Tee Times 10am - 2pm

Coupon expires 12/31/09. Cannot be combined with any other offer.

Richmond Country Club
Richmond, RI (401) 364-9200

- **Type of Discount**
  $5 off green fees for up to 2 players
- **Days of the Week**
  Weekdays only (except holidays)
- **Hours of the Day**
  After 12pm only

Coupon expires 12/31/09. Cannot be combined with any other offer.

Golf Course Coupons

NEW ENGLAND GOLFGUIDE

2 0 0 9

NEW ENGLAND GOLFGUIDE

2 0 0 9

NEW ENGLAND GOLFGUIDE

2 0 0 9

NEW ENGLAND GOLFGUIDE

2 0 0 9

Rose Hill Golf Club
Wakefield, RI (401) 788-1088

- **Type of Discount**
  4 green fees for the price of 3
- **Days of the Week**
  Weekdays only (except holidays)
- **Hours of the Day**
  7am-2pm

Coupon expires 12/31/09. Cannot be combined with any other offer.

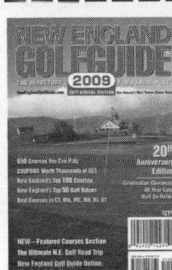

Washington Village Golf Course
Coventry, RI (401) 823-0010

- **Type of Discount**
  2 golfers with power cart: $35/9, $17.50 each
- **Days of the Week**
  7 days a week
- **Hours of the Day**
  All day

Coupon expires 12/31/09. Cannot be combined with any other offer.

Wood River Golf
Hope Valley, RI (401) 364-0700

- **Type of Discount**
  Free golf cart with 2 paid green fees
- **Days of the Week**
  Weekdays only (except holidays)
- **Hours of the Day**
  All day

Coupon expires 12/31/09. Cannot be combined with any other offer.

Barton Golf Club
Barton, VT (802) 525-1126

- **Type of Discount**
  2 green fees for the price of 1, cart rental required
- **Days of the Week**
  7 days a week
- **Hours of the Day**
  All day

Coupon expires 12/31/09. Cannot be combined with any other offer.

Golf Course Coupons

NEW ENGLAND GOLFGUIDE

2 0 0 9

NEW ENGLAND GOLFGUIDE

2 0 0 9

NEW ENGLAND GOLFGUIDE

2 0 0 9

NEW ENGLAND GOLFGUIDE

2 0 0 9

Bellows Falls Country Club
Route 103, Rockingham, VT (802) 463-9809

- **Type of Discount**
  2 players for the price of 1
- **Days of the Week**
  Weekdays only (except holidays)
- **Hours of the Day**
  All day

Coupon expires 12/31/09. Cannot be combined with any other offer.

Blush Hill Country Club
Waterbury, VT (802) 244-8974

- **Type of Discount**
  2 players for the price of 1
- **Days of the Week**
  7 days a week
- **Hours of the Day**
  All day. Cart rental required.

Coupon expires 12/31/09. Cannot be combined with any other offer.

Country Club of Barre
Plainsfield Road, Barre, VT (802) 476-7658

- **Type of Discount**
  2 players for the price of 1
- **Days of the Week**
  Mon, Tues, Wed, Fri, all day; Sat/Sun after 12pm
- **Hours of the Day**
  Not valid holidays

Coupon expires 12/31/09. Cannot be combined with any other offer.

Crown Point Country Club
Springfield, VT (802) 885-1010

- **Type of Discount**
  2 players for the price of 1
- **Days of the Week**
  Weekdays only (except holidays)
- **Hours of the Day**
  All day

Coupon expires 12/31/09. Cannot be combined with any other offer.

Golf Course Coupons

NEW ENGLAND
GOLFGUIDE

2 0 0 9

NEW ENGLAND
GOLFGUIDE

2 0 0 9

NEW ENGLAND
GOLFGUIDE

2 0 0 9

NEW ENGLAND
GOLFGUIDE

2 0 0 9

Farm Resort & Golf Course
Route 100, Morrisville, VT (802) 888-3525

- **Type of Discount**
  25% discount for 2-4 players

- **Days of the Week**
  7 days a week

- **Hours of the Day**
  After 1pm. Call for tee times. Cart rental
  required. www.farmresortgolf.com

Coupon expires 12/31/09. Cannot be combined with any other offer.

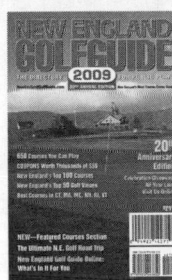

Haystack Golf Club
Mann Rd., Wilmington, VT (802) 464-8301

- **Type of Discount**
  Free range balls for each player when
  a foursome

- **Days of the Week**
  7 days a week

- **Hours of the Day**
  All day

Coupon expires 12/31/09. Cannot be combined with any other offer.

Jay Peak Resort Golf Course
Jay, VT (802) 988-2611

- **Type of Discount**
  Free golf cart with 2 paid green fees

- **Days of the Week**
  7 days a week

- **Hours of the Day**
  All day

Coupon expires 10/15/09. Cannot be combined with any other offer.

Killington Golf Resort
Killington, VT (802) 422-6700

- **Type of Discount**
  $49+tax per person, 18 holes w/cart

- **Days of the Week**
  Weekdays only (except holidays)

- **Hours of the Day**
  All day. Offer expires October 15, 2009.

Coupon expires 12/31/09. Cannot be combined with any other offer.

NEW ENGLAND GOLFGUIDE

2 0 0 9

NEW ENGLAND GOLFGUIDE

2 0 0 9

NEW ENGLAND GOLFGUIDE

2 0 0 9

NEW ENGLAND GOLFGUIDE

2 0 0 9

Lake Morey Country Club
Fairlee, VT (802) 333-4800

- **Type of Discount**
  $5 off green fees for up to 2 players
- **Days of the Week**
  7 days a week. Valid April 1 to June 1 and September 15 to October 31.
- **Hours of the Day**
  All day.

Coupon expires 12/31/09. Cannot be combined with any other offer.

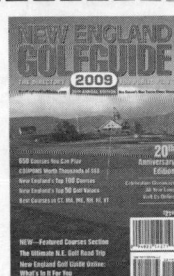

Neshobe Golf Club
Brandon, VT (802) 247-3611

- **Type of Discount**
  $5 off green fees for up to 2 players
- **Days of the Week**
  Weekdays only (except holidays)
- **Hours of the Day**
  All day. Course may close for special events.

Coupon expires 12/31/09. Cannot be combined with any other offer.

Newport Country Club
Newport, VT (802) 334-2391

- **Type of Discount**
  2 players for the price of 1, cart required
- **Days of the Week**
  Weekdays only (except holidays)
- **Hours of the Day**
  After 11am. Cart rental required. Valid April/ May/June/September/October.

Coupon expires 12/31/09. Cannot be combined with any other offer.

Okemo Valley Golf Club
Ludlow,VT (802) 228-1396

- **Type of Discount**
  2 green fees for the price of 1
- **Days of the Week**
  Monday through Thursday only
- **Hours of the Day**
  After 1pm. Valid May-October.

Coupon expires 12/31/09. Cannot be combined with any other offer.

Golf Course Coupons

NEW ENGLAND GOLFGUIDE

2 0 0 9

NEW ENGLAND GOLFGUIDE

2 0 0 9

NEW ENGLAND GOLFGUIDE

2 0 0 9

NEW ENGLAND GOLFGUIDE

2 0 0 9

Orleans Country Club
Orleans, VT (802) 754-2333

- **Type of Discount**
  2 players for the price of 1. Requires full cart rental.

- **Days of the Week**
  Weekdays only (except holidays)

- **Hours of the Day**
  After noon. No holidays or tournament days.

Coupon expires 12/31/09. Cannot be combined with any other offer.

Proctor Pittsford Country Club
Pittsford, VT (802) 483-9379

- **Type of Discount**
  $5 off full price green fees

- **Days of the Week**
  Weekdays only (except holidays)

- **Hours of the Day**
  All day

Coupon expires 12/31/09. Cannot be combined with any other offer.

Ralph Myhre Golf Course
Middlebury, VT (802) 443-5125

- **Type of Discount**
  Free golf cart with 2 paid green fees

- **Days of the Week**
  7 days a week

- **Hours of the Day**
  All day

Coupon expires 12/31/09. Cannot be combined with any other offer.

Rocky Ridge Golf Club
Rt. 116, St. George, VT (802) 482-2191

- **Type of Discount**
  Free golf cart with 2 paid green fees; based on weekend rate

- **Days of the Week**
  7 days a week

- **Hours of the Day**
  After Noon

Coupon expires 12/31/09. Cannot be combined with any other offer.

Golf Course Coupons

NEW ENGLAND GOLFGUIDE

2 0 0 9

NEW ENGLAND GOLFGUIDE

2 0 0 9

NEW ENGLAND GOLFGUIDE

2 0 0 9

NEW ENGLAND GOLFGUIDE

2 0 0 9

St. Johnsbury Country Club
Route 5, St. Johnsbury, VT (802) 748-9894

- **Type of Discount**
  2 green fees for the price of 1, cart rental req'd.
- **Days of the Week**
  Weekdays (except holidays). Must present coupon.
- **Hours of the Day**
  After 12 Noon - call for times

Coupon expires 12/31/09. Cannot be combined with any other offer.

Stratton Mountain Golf Club
Stratton Mountain, VT (802) 297-4114

- **Type of Discount**
  2 players for the price of 1
- **Days of the Week**
  Weekdays only (except holidays)
- **Hours of the Day**
  After 1pm

Coupon expires 12/31/09. Cannot be combined with any other offer.

Sugarbush Golf Club
Warren, VT (802) 583-6725

- **Type of Discount**
  Free golf cart with 2 paid green fees
- **Days of the Week**
  Weekdays only (except holidays)
- **Hours of the Day**
  All day

Coupon expires 12/31/09. Cannot be combined with any other offer.

White River Golf Club
Rt. 100, Rochester, VT (802) 767-4653

- **Type of Discount**
  Free golf cart with 2 paid green fees
- **Days of the Week**
  Weekdays only (except holidays)
- **Hours of the Day**
  All day. Tee times required.

Coupon expires 12/31/09. Cannot be combined with any other offer.

NEW ENGLAND
GOLFGUIDE

2 0 0 9

NEW ENGLAND
GOLFGUIDE

2 0 0 9

NEW ENGLAND
GOLFGUIDE

2 0 0 9

NEW ENGLAND
GOLFGUIDE

2 0 0 9

Wilcox Cove Golf Course
Highway 314, Grand Isle, VT (802) 372-8343

- **Type of Discount**
  2 players for the price of 1
- **Days of the Week**
  Weekdays only (except holidays)
- **Hours of the Day**
  All day. Not available July 1 through Labor Day.

Coupon expires 12/31/09. Cannot be combined with any other offer.

Williston Golf Club
Williston, VT (802) 878-3747

- **Type of Discount**
  Free golf cart with 2 paid green fees
- **Days of the Week**
  7 days a week
- **Hours of the Day**
  All day

Coupon expires 12/31/09. Cannot be combined with any other offer.

Woodbury Golf Course
South Woodbury, VT (802) 456-7421

- **Type of Discount**
  2 players for the price of 1
- **Days of the Week**
  7 days a week
- **Hours of the Day**
  All day

Coupon expires 12/31/09. Cannot be combined with any other offer.

Woodstock Inn & Resort Golf Club
Route 106 South, Woodstock, VT
(802) 457-6674

- **Type of Discount**
  2 players for the price of 1
- **Days of the Week**
  Weekdays only (except holidays)
- **Hours of the Day**
  All day

Coupon expires 12/31/09. Cannot be combined with any other offer.

Golf Course Coupons

NEW ENGLAND GOLFGUIDE

2 0 0 9

NEW ENGLAND GOLFGUIDE

2 0 0 9

NEW ENGLAND GOLFGUIDE

2 0 0 9

NEW ENGLAND GOLFGUIDE

2 0 0 9

NEGG 2009 Reader Questionnaire

Send this in and be automatically entered to win in our e-newsletter giveaways, approximately once a month through the year. You'll also save on the 2010 Edition.

Name: _____

Email: _____

Phone Number: _____ State: _____ Gender: ❏ M ❏ F

New England GolfGuide will never sell, rent, or give away your personal information.

Please tell us your favorite courses:

1. _____ 6. _____
2. _____ 7. _____
3. _____ 8. _____
4. _____ 9. _____
5. _____ 10. _____

What is your handicap today?

❏ 0-5   ❏ 5.1-10   ❏ 10.1- 15   ❏ 15.1- 18   ❏ 18.1-24   ❏ 24.1+

How many rounds do you play every year? _____

How many of those in New England? _____

In what other states/countries do you play? _____

How do you choose courses to play? (Check all that apply)

❏ Price   ❏ Location   ❏ Rating   ❏ Style (I.E. links, flat, resort, etc)
❏ Friend's recommendation   ❏ Newness   ❏ Saw a story

(For questions below, if you have more than one, answer for your current favorite)

What brand are your irons? _____

What brand is your driver? _____

What brand is your putter? _____

How many wedges do you have? _____

    Please specify brands and degrees _____

Do you own a hybrid? Please specify brand and degree _____

What's your favorite ball? _____

How often do you go to the practice range every year? _____

On the range what precentage do you practice:

      Driver: _____ Long irons/fairway woods: _____

      Mid-irons: _____ Short irons/wedges: _____

      Chipping: _____ Putting: _____ Trouble shots: _____

What is your favorite shot? _____

With what shot do you struggle most? _____

What is your favorite type of hole? (I.E. Short, long, dogleg right, short par 4, water carry, etc): _____

What is your least favorite type of hole? _____

What is the biggest cause of slow play? _____

How many lessons did you take in 2008? _____

Do you plan to take lessons in 2009? ❑ Yes ❑ No ❑ Maybe

Have you ever attended a golf school? _____ What year(s)? _____

Do you plan to attend golf school in 2009 or 2010? ❑ Yes ❑ No ❑ Maybe

Are you a member of a golf club?

      ❑ Private ❑ Semi-Private ❑ Public ❑ Travelling Tournament Club

Do you enjoy tournament play? ❑ Yes ❑ No ❑ Don't know

Where did you buy your *New England GolfGuide*? _____

I use the Golf Guide for the: ❑ Course Info ❑ Coupons ❑ Both

Fell free to add as much to this as you like on separate pages.

Thanks so much. Feel free to email or write us anytime.

Please mail this to:

Editor, New England Golf Guide, 464 Common Street, Suite 358, Belmont, MA 02478

So You Want to be an NEGG Course Rater?

We're often asked how one becomes a course rater. Here's what we seek.

....

■ A USGA handicap of 22 or better. We select some at the lower level and some at the higher level. The people we pick each year will represent a spectrum of abilities, just like our readers.

■ The ability to write articulately about your golfing experiences. We have a form that needs to be filled out for every course.

■ You must demonstrate some knowledge of course architecture, to the degree that you can distinguish a good design from a mediocre one.

■ You must demonstrate that you have played more than 50 courses in various locations.

■ You must be able to complete at least 15 ratings between April and August 20.

■ You must expect to pay for each round. Some courses will comp you but often you'll be playing without the course knowing you are conducting a rating.

■ You must have access to email.

■ We look for a diversity of rater hometowns. We will definitely need people all across the north country in 2009.

■ You will undergo a phone or in-person interview.

■ You must be at least 28 years old.

If you meet these criteria, write us a note (please do not call) telling us why you'd make a great rater. We will answer every single query.

....

Send your note to:
Raters, New England Golf Guide
464 Common Street, Suite 358, Belmont, MA 02478

GOLFERS'WAREHOUSE
Your game just got better!

We're on a mission.

For golfers.

Golfers' Warehouse, New England's own golf superstore, offers golfers every type of golf product imaginable from golf clubs and training aids to golf apparel, shoes, gifts and accessories.

However, the mission of Golfers' Warehouse is not just to sell products, but also to transform customers into better golfers. *Here's how we can help your game.*

Golfers' Warehouse Store Locations

Hartford, CT
75 Brainard Road
(860) 522-6829

Cranston, RI
60 Freeway Drive
(401) 4a67-8740

Braintree, MA
2 Campanelli Dr
(781) 848-9777

Burlington, MA
43 Middlesex Turn.
(781) 270-4653

Danvers, MA
10 Newbury Street
Danvers Crossing
(978) 777-4653

Natick, MA
321-D Speen St.
(508) 651-2582

PGA Golf Instruction
Several stores have PGA golf professionals on staff offering video golf lessons to players of all abilities. Special clinics and individual instruction are available for junior golfers to prepare them for school golf teams and summer golf. Visit golferswarehouse.com for a list of instructors, a calendar of events, and to book a lesson.

Computerized Club Fitting
Golfers' Warehouse invested in new technology powered by Swing Labs Technologies in each store to help golfers pinpoint the perfect golf clubs for their game. The player is able to see how each club performs and the software along with an experienced Golfers' Warehouse clubfitter will recommend the best brand, head design, loft, shaft, and golf ball type.

Multiple Hitting Bays and Putting Green
Golfers' Warehouse offers hundreds of demos for customers to try before they buy. Customers can hit them in one of the multiple hitting bays in each store or take them out on the course.

Golf Club Repair and Customization
Golfers' Warehouse has a full service golf club repair shop in each store. Trained club technicians can repair or customize clubs with different shafts, grips, lie angles and finishes.

Golf Tournament Program
Golfers' Warehouse offers tournaments free tees and scratch tickets for every player, hole-in-one contests, and volume discounts.

GHIN Handicaps
Players can join the Golfers' Warehouse club and establish a GHIN handicap through the Golfers' Warehouse website, golferswarehouse.com.

Blog
Golfers' Warehouse offers a club environment where customers can post comments to the Golfers' Warehouse Blog at http://golferswarehouse.blogspot.com.

golferswarehouse.com

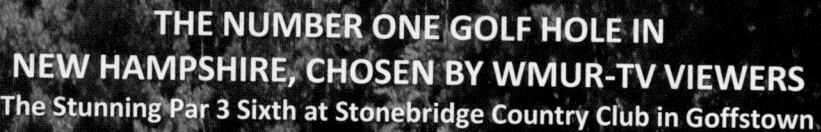

Lochmere Country Club | Tilton, MA

Lochmere is a fine golf course situated in the beautiful New Hampshire Lakes region. Designed by well-known architects Philip Wogan and George Sargent, each challenging hole has a personality of its own.

The club is owned and operated by the Chaille family. A semi-private course that is one of the most scenic and challenging courses in the Northeast, its reputation is growing of late. Even though the course opened in 1992 (with 10 holes) and added the remaining 8 in 1997, in the past couple of years it has emerged from the shadows of "hidden gem," to become a regional favorite. Accessible by Routes I-93 and 3, Lochmere in Tilton is an easy reach from most of central and northern New England.

The course has a driving range, a practice green, and a function hall with a bar. Memberships are available but the public is welcome seven days a week. This 18-hole championship golf course has lush fairways and large well-manicured greens that are consistently in great shape. The course measures 6,697 yards from the championship blue tees and provides every level of golfer with a challenge with its strategically placed tees, water hazards, and bunkers.

The course will test your shot-making ability to the limit.

We do one thing well.
We just happen to do it four ways.

Dreams take shape in many ways. Gut-wrenching power cat-like response and next generation technology comes standard in all of them. From the pure top-down roadster experience to the sports-car agility of the Cayenne. Every Porsche is engineered with a no-compromise approach to performance.
Visit us today at Rietzl Porsche, offering personalized sales and service excellence since 1970.

Cayenne, Cayman, Boxster, 911 Carrera

Rietzl Porsche
781-261-5000
59 Pond Street
Norwell, MA 02061
rietzl.porschedealer.com

PORSCHE